ORACLE®   *Oracle Press*™

Oracle Discoverer 10g Handbook

Michael Armstrong-Smith
Darlene Armstrong-Smith

McGraw-Hill

New York   Chicago   San Francisco
Lisbon   London   Madrid   Mexico City   Milan
New Delhi   San Juan   Seoul   Singapore   Sydney   Toronto

The McGraw·Hill Companies

The McGraw-Hill Companies
160 Spear Street, Suite 700
San Francisco, California 94105
U.S.A.

To arrange bulk purchase discounts for sales promotions, premiums, or fund-raisers, please contact **McGraw-Hill** at the above address.

Oracle Discoverer 10g Handbook

1234567890 DOC DOC 019876

ISBN 0-07-226214-1

Acquisitions Editor	**Proofreaders**
Lisa McClain	Claire Splan
Project Editor	Susie Elkind
Carolyn Welch	**Indexer**
Contributing Authors	Claire Splan
Chris DeYoung	**Composition**
Mark Rittman	Apollo Publishing Services
Acquisitions Coordinator	**Illustration**
Alex McDonald	Apollo Publishing Services
Technical Editor	**Series Design**
Abhinav Agarwal	Peter F. Hancik, Lyssa Wald
Copy Editor	**Cover Series Design**
Bob Campbell	Damore Johann Design, Inc.

This book was composed with Adobe® InDesign®

We would like to dedicate
this book to our mothers
Teresa Armstrong-Smith
and Teri Hans.
Our mothers are our
number one fans and we are theirs.
How does anyone get anywhere
in this world without a good mom?

About the Authors

Michael Armstrong-Smith is the Principal Consultant for Armstrong-Smith Consulting, specializing in Oracle Discoverer training and implementation. A fellow of the Institute of Analysts and Programmers and a member of Oracle's customer advisory board on business intelligence, he has over 24 years of systems development experience. Michael is a leader in the field of business intelligence, with specialist knowledge of data warehouses and, of course, Oracle Discoverer. He is also a conference speaker and has spoken on Discoverer at conferences throughout the U.S. and Canada. Armstrong-Smith Consulting has a weblog and forum on all things Discoverer at http://learndiscoverer.com.

Darlene Armstrong-Smith is President and Senior Curriculum Developer for Armstrong-Smith Consulting. Darlene is also an instructional designer and a professional trainer. She has 13 years' experience designing and implementing system conversion training, and has served as a training consultant to government agencies, financial institutions, and major health care organizations. She has written and delivered manuals and policies and procedures for various organizations ranging from training in highly technical software to "soft skills" such as team building, employee motivation, and public speaking.

About the Contributing Authors

Mark Rittman is Director of Consulting at SolStonePlus, an Oracle Partner based in the UK, who specializes in business intelligence and data warehousing. Mark is the Chair of the UKOUG Business Intelligence & Reporting Tools SIG, writes a weblog at http://www.rittman.net, and speaks on Oracle Discoverer at events in the UK, Europe, and the USA.

Chris DeYoung has spent six years teaching Discoverer and the Oracle Application Server for Oracle University. He has served as lead instructor for the Discoverer product and has seen the product mature from version 3 all the way through the current version 10g. He has a masters degree in Instructional technologies and is a certified Oracle Developer. After working with literally hundreds of different Discoverer customers, he has a very rich perspective on how Discoverer can be used to its fullest potential.

Contents

PART I
Getting Started with Discoverer

PART II

Editing the Query

PART III

Advanced Discoverer Techniques

PART IV

Using the Discoverer Administration Edition

PART V

Appendixes

Acknowledgments

hen you write a book, you develop a "love-hate" relationship with just about everyone working on the project. A husband and wife team working on a book together could cause all kinds of problems, but we are crazy in love enough to get through it without coming to blows. Everyone in our family will be so happy when we can stop saying, "I can't, I have to work on the book." We want to acknowledge our children for their sensitivity and patience. We also want to acknowledge each other for demonstrating genuine kindness under difficult conditions.

We received some special help writing this edition of the Discoverer Handbook. We felt it was very important to add information on the Administration tool in the second edition. However, we knew that additional expertise was critical in getting it right. The chapter on Discoverer configuration and the appendix on functions could not have been written without the help of our good friend and colleague Chris DeYoung. Chris brought a special enthusiasm for details, which has really enhanced the book.

Another addition to the Handbook was the chapter on OLAP. OLAP was brand new to Discoverer in 2005, so trying to come up to speed with it while discovering all of the other new features was impossible. We called upon another colleague (and Michael's fellow Brit) Mark Rittman to give us all an introduction to this new feature of Discoverer. Mark is a real Discoverer master and helped us to deliver a chapter that has wetted all of our appetites for Discoverer OLAP.

So far, it sounds like a whole lot of love. Where is the hate? The real "love-hate" relationships are between the authors and their editors. In retrospect, we could easily say that we loved our editor, Lisa McClain, throughout the entire project, but that would be a lie, and you know where liars go! Some mornings opening our e-mail was the hardest thing to do because we knew that we were going to be hounded for delinquent chapters or missing screen shots. But the end result is a book we are proud of and that was not drastically overdue. Lisa was truly good to us and treated us with respect and sensitivity. We appreciate her hard work more than we can say.

We would also like to acknowledge our copy editor Bob Campbell, without whom we would sound like idiots. Michael uses too many words, which Bob gently removed without hurting his feelings. Darlene, on the other hand, does not use enough words, and Bob was diplomatic in stating that something could use a better explanation.

Our final acknowledgement is to our technical editor from Oracle Abhinav Agarwal. His passion for Discoverer was evident as he helped us to make sense of all the new features. Because of Abhinav, this book is accurate technically and conceptually.

Introduction

T he first step in writing the second edition of the *Oracle Discoverer Handbook* was to determine who our audience was. In the first edition, we limited the content to the end-user edition of Discoverer, with the focus primarily on Desktop. In this edition, we have changed our target audience to cover not only end-users but administrators as well. The focus for end-users has switched to Discoverer Plus. However, Desktop is still covered, and we have also included information on both Viewer and Portal. We felt we would be doing our readers a disservice if we did not include the Administration Edition in this book; we have, therefore, added a complete new section dedicated to administrators.

Our second challenge was deciding which release of Discoverer to include. At first we thought we could cover multiple releases, but were soon overwhelmed with the effort and potential page count involved. The decision was made to focus our attention on 10.1.2.

We also knew that users of Discoverer at all levels were in need of a tutorial on this powerful and very complex piece of software. We made the decision to reach out to all users—from the novice end-user to the true power user.

We believe there is something in this book for every Discoverer end-user and administrator. The novice will be taken from the very first step of each task through to its successful completion. The power user will find information he or she may have otherwise needed to look for elsewhere. We have organized the steps for every task into useful and easy-to-follow workflows, and have tried to provide as much detail as possible. The administrator will find help and support to release the power of Discoverer to their end-users. We have shared with you skills and methods that have taken us years to develop.

When we took on the challenge of writing this tutorial, our desire was to bring all of Discoverer's powerful features into one source. You will find many hitherto undocumented Discoverer features in this book as well as dozens of tips and tricks.

How This Book Is Organized

This book is divided into four sections and four appendixes:

- **Part I, Getting Started with Discoverer:** Part I covers the basic history and philosophy of Discoverer. It also contains an extensive description of the types of databases with which Discoverer can interface. Following this introductory material, we deal with the login sequence and all steps of the Discoverer Workbook Wizard.

■ **Part II, Editing the Query:** Part II focuses on turning a basic Discoverer query into much more. We begin with formatting issues, such as font, colors, headings, and numbers. We then move on to graphing in Discoverer and turning a query into a well-formatted and ready-to-deliver report. Chapter 9 is all about analyzing data. This is a powerful tutorial on the elements of analysis as well as how to use Discoverer's various tools to analyze your data. Chapter 10 covers using Discoverer Viewer. We felt there was enough power in this great new release of Viewer that it deserved its own chapter. Don't overlook the advantages of using this tool in your organization.

■ **Part III, Advanced Discoverer Techniques:** The first three chapters of Part III take all of the Discoverer tools and give detailed instructions on how to use them effectively, including refining items, drilling, and building effective conditions, along with refining parameters, calculations, sorting, and percentages. The next two chapters of Part III deal with query management, user preferences, the toolbar, and how to interact with the Discoverer administrator. With the inclusion of OLAP in Discoverer, we felt the need to offer an introduction to the OLAP tool; therefore, the final chapter of this section is dedicated to the power and features of Discoverer OLAP.

■ **Part IV, Using the Discoverer Administration Edition:** In this section, we have attempted to pass on as much of our knowledge and experience in building and managing great business areas as we could in the pages allowed. We could have easily written a one-thousand page book on the Administration Edition alone, but we surely would have killed each other had we tried. Chapter 20 covers configuration. This highly technical chapter is a must-read for anyone wanting to know how to manage Discoverer on an Application Server.

■ **Part V, Appendixes:** There are four appendixes in this book. Appendix A is "Michael's Gold Mine of Questions and Answers." As you can imagine, questions come in to us at what is sometimes an alarming rate, but Michael tries to answer them all. We have attempted to include as many of the questions he has answered over the years as possible. Appendix B contains a detailed list of all of Discoverer's functions, including syntax, descriptions, and examples. It also contains a detailed list of format masks and a simple introduction to the use of analytic functions. Appendix C contains a description of the various types of databases you can use with Discoverer. This appendix also covers views and in particular Noetix Views. Appendix D gives a description of the tutorial database we used throughout this book.

PART

I

Getting Started with Discoverer

CHAPTER
1

An Overview of Discoverer

his chapter will introduce you to Oracle Business Intelligence Discoverer 10*g* (10.1.2), henceforth referred to as Discoverer, the award-winning reporting and analysis tool from Oracle Corporation. We will discuss business intelligence and see how Discoverer is perfectly suited to be your company's tool of choice. We will discuss some of the recent business intelligence trends and how Discoverer fits in with these trends.

The 10.1.2 release of Discoverer, which came out at the end of December 2004, is very exciting and places Oracle firmly at the helm of the information revolution. This new release is more powerful than ever before and has given a whole new look and feel to the two web-based products, Oracle Business Intelligence Discoverer Plus and Oracle Business Intelligence Discoverer Viewer, henceforth referred to as Plus and Viewer. Perhaps the single biggest innovation, though, is the capability for Plus and Viewer to access OLAP (Online Application Processing) data. We will discuss this in more detail later in the book.

We continue the overview by discussing the benefits of using the standard Windows GUI, and how adoption of point-and-click technology is essential in the modern world. We follow with a discussion of some of the more general aspects of query writing by showing you the differences between ad hoc and predefined queries. The final section in this overview tells you how to use various sources of help to find out more about Oracle Discoverer.

Business Intelligence and Your Organization

When we wrote the first edition of *The Discoverer Handbook* four years ago, it was obvious that we were sold on Discoverer back then. We are even more "bullish" on it today. Using it in connection with an Oracle database, the world's finest and most commonly used database system, you have tremendous reporting power at your disposal. It is our pleasure to report that Oracle has indeed improved and enhanced Discoverer's capabilities over the years, and even more so with the latest 10.1.2 release. With this release, Oracle has firmly moved itself into the forefront of business intelligence and has added the tag line "The Information Company" to its name.

As one of the leading providers of both traditional and web-based business intelligence, Oracle Corporation has gone to great lengths to try to understand the links and interactions between databases (and database technologies) and delivery of information. Anyone interested in delivering information within his or her business should look to Oracle. The terms "information delivery," "business intelligence," and "decision support" are all included under the same umbrella. In fact, these terms are often used interchangeably. While the definitions remain vague, an organization's need is clear. Companies are investing billions of dollars, pounds, euros, yen, and so forth into information technology. The goal for all of these companies is to gather data and make use of it, enabling faster and better-informed business decisions.

Companies can no longer be satisfied with knowing how many sales were made today. They want to know how many sales were made last week, last month, last year. They want to know if their company's bottom line is improving and be able to forecast trends with better accuracy. As a company executive once said to one of the authors, "Tell me something about my company that I don't already know." By harnessing the power of Discoverer, users can gain insights into their businesses that would be simply difficult or even impossible without writing hundreds of sophisticated SQL queries. Put Discoverer in the hands of an expert data analyst, and you will surprise even the most seasoned users of other products. Another executive recently said "Show me those things that are within my area of control that are not within normal limits or … appear to be heading away from normal … you know, those things that I should be aware of."

If you don't already have Discoverer and you have an Oracle database, the time has come to get it. In 22 years in the business of delivering information we have not seen another product surface with such ease of use and robustness. A very pleasant surprise is that Discoverer will link to just about any Open Database Connectivity (ODBC)–compliant database. So, if you have not yet made the switch to using Oracle databases, you can still benefit from the power and ease of use built into the Discoverer product. Add to this the fact that Discoverer can now produce reports using OLAP data in addition to relational data, even drilling from OLAP into relational, and you will understand why we are so excited about this release.

Organizations today are generating unprecedented amounts of data to support their day-to-day functions—but collecting and collating data is no longer enough. An organization must have a means of turning that data into that most precious of business commodities, information. Anyone with decision-making power needs the ability to view and manipulate company data. Oracle Discoverer does just that. It can unleash your data, turning it into a true asset for your business.

Business Intelligence and Trends

You have seen us use the term *business intelligence* several times so far in this book. But what is business intelligence? According to the Data Warehousing Institute, www.dw-institute.com, the definition of business intelligence is:

> the processes, technologies, and tools needed to turn data into information, information into knowledge, and knowledge into plans that drive profitable business action. Business intelligence encompasses data warehousing, business analytic tools, and content / knowledge management.

The term *business intelligence* has been around for some time and was first used in a Gartner Group report back in 1996, but the principles have been around a lot longer than that. In their time, these principles have been called management information systems (MIS), business support systems (BSS), and now BI. Whatever the name, the principles remain the same. However, recently there have been some exciting new trends, trends that Discoverer is ideally placed to help you with.

Recent Business Intelligence Trends and Discoverer

We have noticed that there is a trend to shift away from departmental to enterprise-wide reporting systems. When you add to this the fact that IT management is being pressured to make more and more data available in near real time, you can see that the need for data is increasing. As the need for data increases, the need for better reporting tools also increases. Oracle Business Intelligence Discoverer 10g (10.1.2) is ideally placed to help you.

A recent trend that we are seeing more and more is data mining. Oracle's own version of this, called Oracle Data Mining, has been available since 2004. According to Oracle, "Data analysts can find patterns and insights hidden in their data. Application developers can quickly automate the extraction and distribution of new business intelligence—predictions, patterns, and discoveries—throughout the organization." The end result of a data mining algorithm is data in a table. If you use Discoverer Administrator to build a business area on this data, you can then use one of the Discoverer end-user tools to query the data mining results.

Before we get into discussing analytic applications, there are a couple of other trends that we would like to mention. The first is Oracle Self-Service BI, which Oracle says "gets the right information to the right person at the right time." Using the HR Self-Service application, Discoverer users can access their own personal information. Another trend is what is called the democratization of data. Put in its simplest form, this means making data available to the masses. The Internet is perhaps the greatest expression of this trend, where one can find information on just about any subject in the world, and all without leaving home. According to a report published by professors Hal Varian and Peter Lyman of the School of Information Management and Systems, "A century ago, the average person could only create and access a small amount of information. Now, ordinary people not only have access to huge amounts of data, but are also able to create gigabytes of data themselves and, potentially, publish it to the world via the Internet."

A major trend that we are seeing is the use of analytic applications. According to TDWI, www.tdwi.org, the business intelligence market can be broken down into the following two types of analytic application:

- Packaged
- Custom

Packaged Analytic Applications

This is generally referred to as the "buy" option. You buy a vendor-supplied package that provides out-of-the-box analytics. According to TDWI, this type of package "contains an integrated set of analytic tools, data models, ETL mappings, business metrics, predefined reports, and 'best practice' processes that accelerate the deployment of an analytic application in a given domain."

Oracle's newest offerings in this market are Daily Business Intelligence (DBI) and Enterprise Planning and Budgeting (EPB), both of which rely heavily on Discoverer, and BI Beans, which are the building blocks of almost every Oracle business intelligence application. Although packaged applications are in their infancy, we expect to see a large uptake in this technology in the future as vendors make them customizable.

Daily Business Intelligence　If you are using Oracle Applications, this product is the replacement for BIS (Business Intelligence System). BIS is currently in maintenance mode, and the last enhancements were shipped with Apps 11.5.8. From 11.5.9 onward you will be using DBI. This product makes heavy use of materialized views and uses the same security model as Apps. The base product, which uses the same HTML server as Performance Analyzer, Balanced Scorecard, and EPB, is not customizable at this time. However, it does use a special database schema, called FEM, on top of which you can create a Discoverer EUL. If you want to customize DBI, you will have to use Discoverer, which enables you to customize its EUL by adding new items and so on.

Enterprise Planning and Budgeting　Once again, this product is only available if you are using Oracle Applications. It uses the same BI Beans that are used in Plus and the Spreadsheet Add-In so that what you see is very much like Discoverer. However, because EPB uses OLAP technology, you could very easily use Discoverer Plus for OLAP to query that data if you choose to. EPB is a controlled release, since Oracle wants to make sure you get it right.

Custom Analytic Applications

This is generally referred to as the "build" option. You build your own analytics using tools provided by a vendor. According to TDWI, this solution "is primarily built using tools, code, or customizable templates to provide the exact look-and-feel functionality desired by an organization for its analytic environment."

Because packaged applications generally do not cover everything that an organization wants, many IT managers are wary of using them. Customizing a packaged application can be expensive and subsequently difficult to upgrade. We have seen a large uptake in custom applications where organizations build their own data warehouse. Using Oracle Warehouse Builder and Discoverer, you can create such an environment. To date, we have not seen any significant movement away from the custom to the packaged approach, and we believe there is still significant demand for the "build" approach.

Custom applications can themselves be further broken down into two categories:

- Shrink-wrapped products, like Discoverer and Cognos, which come with prebuilt embedded functionality

- Building-block products, like BI Beans, that actually allow you to create your own BI applications and products

As you can see, whichever method you choose for obtaining your information, Discoverer is ideally placed to help you with your data reporting. We hope the preceding discussion on the trends of business intelligence helps you to understand that Discoverer is a key component in Oracle's BI offerings.

Discoverer's Role in Business Intelligence

As stated earlier, Oracle has firmly positioned Discoverer right at the heart of its business intelligence strategy. But Discoverer is more than just a component of a suite of tools (albeit an extremely powerful suite). It has the ability to stand on its own two feet, to make a place for itself within your company, and to be your analysis tool of choice. This book, therefore, will now concentrate on Discoverer itself. So just where does this tool come from, and how can it fit in with your company's business intelligence strategy?

Oracle Introduces Discoverer

With the introduction of the Windows version of Discoverer (now called Oracle Business Intelligence Discoverer Desktop) in the late 1990s, Oracle gave anyone working in business intelligence an award-winning, easy-to-use ad hoc query and analysis tool. It was developed as a means to view data stored in Oracle databases, and to analyze and create reports based upon that data. Discoverer is a tool that places power in the hands of the user—power that until Discoverer came along was the domain of developers. It empowered users to gain immediate access to information stored in OLTP systems, data warehouses, and even the Oracle E-Business Suite, otherwise referred to as Oracle Applications, or just Apps.

Subsequent improvements have moved Discoverer out into a league of its own. Its simple-to-use graphical user interface (GUI) makes navigation easy. It is highly intuitive, and its end-user workbook and administration Load Wizards guide you through all the steps you need in order to either create a query or manage the End User Layer. The seasoned computer user will adapt to its point-and-click features quickly and easily. The novice will be guided by wizards to create what may be their first database queries and reports.

If your background is PC-based, you will be familiar with tools such as Microsoft Excel. Discoverer has a similar look and feel and is extremely easy on the eyes. There are no cumbersome screens or navigation paths, there are shortcuts to most of the functionality, and (just as in many Windows products) there are usually two or even three ways to do the same thing. Many of these shortcuts are undocumented and only surface when you say to yourself something like, "I wonder if Discoverer can do this?"—and then click your mouse or press the appropriate shortcut keys. More often than not, the authors have been pleasantly surprised to find that Discoverer can.

Discoverer on the Web

With the Windows version so popular and easy to use, a fully working Web version (as opposed to a Web viewer) was released in the spring of 2000. Much of the functionality of the Windows version was missing from the first offerings, but with the 4i release Oracle began to fill in the gaps. The release of 9i (9.0.2) in 2002, followed by the 10g release 1 (9.0.4) in 2004, brought about significant enhancements to the functionality of the web components. With each additional release, Oracle did two things. First, the company made Plus (as the web edition was now called) act more and more like Desktop (as the Windows edition had now become known), and second, it continued adding new functionality.

In December 2004, Oracle released the second edition of 10g (10.1.2). With this release come many more features and, for the first time, an updated Plus interface. So far as the authors can tell, the Plus edition now has only two Desktop features missing from its arsenal. These are the ability to save workbooks to the file system and the ability to create worksheets that use subqueries. In our opinion, we feel that the great strides made by Oracle and the improvements that have been made to the Plus edition no longer make sitting on the fence a viable option. Now is the time to jump in with both feet and use Plus. If you have not as yet seen a demonstration of the new Discoverer 10.1.2 (called Drake during beta testing), hold on to your hat. You are in for a very pleasant surprise. This book will focus exclusively on this release.

Oracle is rightly promoting its web solutions as being an integral part of its suite of business intelligence tools. These tools—Discoverer, BI Beans, Reports, Oracle Data Miner, Oracle Personalization, Oracle Warehouse Builder, the Spreadsheet Add-In, and of course, the Database—are the key components of Oracle's complete business intelligence solution. Together, these tools provide superior ease of use and exceptional performance, enabling companies to make better, quicker, and more informed decisions.

The Eight Parts of Discoverer

Discoverer consists of eight separate components:

- Oracle Business Intelligence Discoverer Plus

- Oracle Business Intelligence Discoverer Viewer

- Oracle Business Intelligence Discoverer Desktop

- Oracle Business Intelligence Discoverer Administrator

- EUL Command Line utility for Java

- Oracle Discoverer Portlet Provider

- Oracle Enterprise Manager Application Server Control

- Oracle BI Spreadsheet Add-In

Oracle Business Intelligence Discoverer Plus

This version, one of the two web-based end-user query tools, uses a downloadable Java applet to enable the user to interact with the database. This applet uses BI Beans, a set of reusable Java components that are the building blocks for many of Oracle's new web-based tools. Born out of Desktop in the late 1990s, it has been progressively improved over the years such that now it has almost all of the Desktop features, plus additional features that are not available in Desktop. Although there are too many additional features to be described here, the ability of Plus to access both OLAP and relational data deserves special mention. This capability alone places Discoverer at the forefront of business intelligence. We will address all of the additional features in subsequent chapters. Plus can be used both stand-alone and as part of a full-blown application server environment. Licensing is also different depending upon whether you are using Plus in stand-alone mode or as part of an application server. When used stand-alone, it is cheaper than when used as part of an application server, which is good news if all you want to do is use Plus and Viewer. As already mentioned, the new Plus has a completely new look and feel when compared to what existing users of Discoverer 4*i*, Discoverer 9*i*AS, or Discoverer 10*g* Release 1 have been used to. Starting with a brand-new login screen, Plus looks new, feels new, and is new. It has better algorithms than its predecessors, which means that it can interact more efficiently with the database.

Oracle Business Intelligence Discoverer Viewer

This version, utilizing HTML (Hypertext Markup Language) technology, is the product of choice for executing and running workbooks. It is the second of the web-based end-user tools and allows the user to view and execute an existing query. While you cannot create new workbooks in Viewer, if you have been granted the appropriate privileges by your Discoverer manager, you can, for the first time, save changes. The changes that you can save are those made by drilling, pivoting, changing page items, and changing graph types and sizes. Formatting or stoplight format changes are *not* saved. Viewer is licensed in exactly the same way as Plus, and the two come bundled together for the purchase of one license. You cannot purchase just Plus or just Viewer though; they come hand in hand. You can think of them as being two peas in a pod. If you have one product, you have both. Of course, it is your choice whether you actually use them both or restrict your users to one or the other. Many organizations today are making use of Viewer as their tool of choice for delivering end-user reports, and if you have not used it, we strongly recommend you take a look. Like Plus, Viewer also has a new interface, which makes for easier navigation.

Oracle Business Intelligence Discoverer Desktop

This version is the end-user query tool that you would use if you are not using the Web. It is Oracle Discoverer's original flagship product and as such is very stable. We have used this tool for many years, and it is an excellent product. As mentioned earlier, there are some features of Desktop that are not available in any of the other end-user components. In addition to being able to save to the file system and create workbooks that use subqueries, Desktop also has 3-D graph rotation and the ability to embed images into titles and into the background of your report. Desktop is licensed separately from the web components and will usually be the first tool employed by your organization. It is cheaper and easier to install and therefore lends itself ideally for evaluation. Unfortunately, Oracle has not continued development of Desktop as it has for Plus. What this means is that there are several pieces of added functionality that you will find in Plus but not in Desktop. We suspect that Oracle's intention is to drop Desktop in the future. However, do not fear, because Oracle will continue to support Desktop and provide run-time compatibility between all components of Discoverer and Desktop for as long as Desktop ships. For now it remains a core component of the Oracle Business Intelligence family of products.

Oracle Business Intelligence Discoverer Administrator

This version, available on Windows only, is client based and allows you to create and maintain the relational End User Layer. All of the background work that is needed to prepare relational data for the end user is done here. In the original handbook, we did not cover Discoverer Administrator at all; however, there was such an outcry that we decided it could not be left out of the second edition. We will, therefore, cover Discoverer Administrator in quite some detail in this second edition. For those of you who are employed as Discoverer managers, there is no change to the tried and tested interface that you have come to love. Apart from a few additional features, the new Discoverer Administrator tool has a very similar look and feel to the 3.1, 4.1, and 9.0.2 versions. Of all the metadata preparation tools on the market, we believe that Discoverer Administrator, while being extremely powerful, is also the easiest of all to use. Normally, more power means more complexity and hence less ease of use, but not in this case. Discoverer Administrator can make data available to end users in a fraction of the time that it would take in other relational metadata preparation tools. Add to this the fact that Discoverer Administrator works with and understands Oracle Applications better than any other metadata tool, bar none, and you have a win-win situation.

NOTE
OLAP data cannot be managed using Discoverer Administrator. This data is managed using Analytic Workspace Manager or Oracle Warehouse Builder.

EUL Command Line Utility for Java

This, the new incarnation for the EUL Command Line utility, is another of the OracleBI Discoverer web-based tools. It is not an end-user tool, but a utility that allows Discoverer managers to perform relational, End User Layer maintenance tasks, tasks that hitherto have been the domain of Discoverer Administrator. There are still some tasks, like adding new folders or editing custom folder properties, that cannot be done using the Java command-line utility. We were, however, pleasantly surprised at the utility's ease of use in managing those tasks that it can maintain. If you can master this interface, you can avoid ever having to log into Discoverer Administrator at all. We say "perhaps" because, in our opinion, there are just too many occasions when it is more cost-effective to use Discoverer Administrator to warrant not using it. We are in no doubt that Oracle will continue developing the EUL Command Line utility for Java, and we believe that it will not be very long before you will be able to maintain the entire relational End User Layer using this tool.

Oracle Discoverer Portlet Provider

This version is web based and is only available if you are using the Oracle Application Server Portal. Discoverer portlets are thus a component of Oracle Application Server Portal. Using a portal, your organization can create a front end or dashboard for its business intelligence needs. For executives and senior management, these dashboards will be your interface of choice. Placing Discoverer portlets onto a dashboard enables you to make worksheet data available without the need for the executive to have to log in to Plus or Viewer. For more detailed data analysis, your executives can drill through from a Discoverer portlet back into Viewer. There are three types of Discoverer portlet: a list of workbooks portlet, a worksheet portlet, and a gauges portlet, all of which will be described later in the book. We will guide you through all of the steps that you as a Discoverer manager need to follow in order to use the Discoverer Portlet Provider to set up Discoverer portlets for use within your Oracle Application Server Portal.

Oracle Enterprise Manager Application Server Control

This version is also web based but is definitely not an end-user tool! Using OEM (Oracle Enterprise Manager), the Discoverer manager maintains settings that control how Plus, Viewer, and the Discoverer Portlet Provider function. OEM is also the tool that is used to make OLAP data available for querying inside Discoverer. Should you want to hook up the stand-alone versions of Discoverer Plus and Viewer to an infrastructure database to take advantage of Identity Management (IM) or Metadata Repository (MR) control, the OEM interface is where this is done also. As you will see later in the book, even though OEM sounds complicated, it really is not but is a joy to use.

Oracle BI Spreadsheet Add-In

This is a client-based tool that adds Discoverer BI functionality to Microsoft Excel. Like Plus, this tool is built using BI Beans. So what does this mean for you? What this means is that when you use the Add-In to access data inside a spreadsheet, the wizard screens that you see are identical to the screens that you would see when using Discoverer Plus for OLAP. As you may have guessed, the Spreadsheet Add-In is only available for accessing OLAP data. It cannot be used to access relational data that has been made available via an End User Layer. We will discuss the Spreadsheet Add-In later in the book when we discuss OLAP. The Add-In can be found on the same CD that you used to install Desktop and Discoverer Administrator.

How to Use This Book

This book focuses on the Oracle Business Intelligence 10*g* (10.1.2) release of Discoverer. The first part of the book is primarily aimed at end users and will be invaluable to the beginner as well as to experienced report writers. The second part of the book is for administrators and as such will concentrate on the more technical aspects of the product. We hope that this book will therefore become known as your one-stop shopping place for everything to do with Discoverer. In the end-user part of this book reference will be made to many administrative functions that, when utilized, will improve the user's awareness of what features are available within the product. This will enable end users to know what their administrators can do for them.

Discoverer managers will find much useful information for optimizing the product for maximum performance. By seeing and understanding how end users will use the tool, they will also learn how to provide a better service. Working together as a team, the Discoverer manager, report writers, and end users will thus be able to use this product to its maximum effectiveness. In the part of this book on administration, we will show you how to take requests from end users, analyze those requests, and then use one of the administrative tools to improve the effectiveness of the End User Layer. We firmly believe that Discoverer administration is an art, not a science, something to be enjoyed and not seen as a chore.

You may have already purchased Discoverer and be wondering what it can do for your company. You have probably heard about its easy-to-use interface and its ability to link to just about any database you can name, or maybe you're just caught up in the business intelligence revolution that is shaping our modern world. Whatever your reason for purchasing this book, and whatever your level of expertise with Discoverer, the authors feel that there is something here for everyone.

Example Database

Throughout this book we have used an Oracle 10*g* database and created sales records for a fictitious company called Global Widgets. This database has been used to demonstrate the creation of useful and meaningful business areas and queries. We have also added a mix of examples, showing both Discoverer Desktop and Discoverer Plus functionality. When there is a functional difference between the two end-user products, we will show both together. When the difference is cosmetic only, we will give the description but not necessarily add a figure or illustration.

In the example database, our fictional company, Global Widgets, uses a fiscal year that begins on the Saturday following the last Friday in September. Thus Q1 (quarter one) runs from October to December, Q2 from January to March, and so on. We have done this to demonstrate Discoverer's ability to deal with fiscal years, because we are aware that not all companies base their fiscal year on the calendar year. Global Widgets used to deal exclusively with orders received and processed using traditional channels, but during 1999 they started using e-commerce. We have done this so that we can show you examples of queries where we analyze sales performance of the two channels.

You will also be shown how to analyze data from various sales districts and regions as a means of demonstrating Discoverer's drilling and filtering capabilities. The fiscal date hierarchy also allows us to demonstrate drilling, but this time from year to quarter to month to day. As a Discoverer manager, you will see how to create these hierarchies.

Appendix D provides an entity-relationship diagram (ERD) of the example database and a list of tables and indexes. The database is also available for download on both the Oracle Press and Learn Discoverer web sites.

A New Direction in Reporting

In the past, it was the job of the developer to take the requirements of the business unit and turn them into queries and reports. Often, this was accomplished with the use of a middle layer of people: the analyst and the database administrator (DBA).

The business unit representative explained to the analyst what information was needed in the report. The analyst, in conjunction with the DBA, looked at the information available in the database and determined the best way to extract it and how it should be presented. This information was conveyed to the developer, who wrote the programming code for the report.

The developer passed the programming code on to the DBA, who implemented the new programming into the system.

The final step gave the report to the business unit, who would usually say it was all wrong—and the process would begin again.

This example may seem a bit extreme, but the truth is that this type of organizational setup can sometimes resemble the children's game "telephone." Of course, there are many companies with excellent communications in the links between the users, analysts, developers, and DBAs. However, even under the best of circumstances this can be a time-consuming and labor-intensive way for queries and reports to be created.

No one knows better what information is needed and how it should be organized than the person who will be using it. With Discoverer, the end user is now able to do the following:

- Create queries
- Analyze data in seconds rather than days or weeks
- Create his or her own custom reports

The Discoverer GUI

Oracle has developed a graphical user interface (GUI) in Oracle Discoverer that is a natural to use for those well acquainted with standard spreadsheets, databases, web browsers, and Microsoft Windows. The authors commend Oracle for embracing the traditional Windows environment

FIGURE 1-1   *The Discoverer Desktop startup screen*

and creating a user interface that will be comfortable and familiar to most end users. Many of the readers will remember, and may still be using, mainframe, UNIX, VMS, and DOS-based legacy systems. You have probably been hoping for a better interface. With Oracle Discoverer, you now have one.

Figures 1-1 and 1-2 show the GUI startup screens for Discoverer Desktop and Plus.

FIGURE 1-2   *The Discoverer Plus startup screen*

The Benefits of a GUI

Back in the 1950s and 1960s, the standard interface available in computing was poor. The user was usually faced with a black screen with green letters on a mainframe terminal. Users were forced to memorize commands and screens, and there were no such things as icons, dialog boxes, or windows. During the mid-1960s, research was taking place to allow the direct manipulation of graphical objects. By 1975, when David Canfield Smith coined the term "icon" in a Stanford Ph.D. thesis, the computing world was gearing up for a revolution. This revolution culminated in the first real GUI interface on the Apple Macintosh in 1984. The following are some of the benefits of a GUI:

- You can have your database on a non-PC platform, and enjoy the features of the PC on your desk.

- Use your mouse to point and click, drag and drop, use shortcuts, and bring up context-sensitive (bubble) help.

- Print to local or network printers.

- Attach reports to your e-mail system.

- Enjoy WYSIWYG—what you see is what you get—presentation.

Ad Hoc Queries vs. Predefined Queries

Predefined reports and queries are at the heart of most information systems. Companies invest millions in development. Most database systems come with a myriad of predefined reports. You either use the same reports everyone else uses, or spend a great deal of money and time having them modified to meet your company's needs.

Ad hoc queries are a relatively new concept, one that can be difficult to come to terms with. Given they have had some education in how it is done, users can build queries. With a good foundation in the principles of query writing, the end user can produce queries and reports almost instantly. However, a person without an understanding of these principles may spend hours on a query and end up with data that is completely useless. You will begin learning to create queries and reports that will give you the information you need in Chapter 4. You will also learn how to avoid writing "the query from the Twilight Zone." Later, in Chapter 8, you will be shown how to turn a Discoverer query into a report.

Nonpredictability vs. Predictability

Prewritten reports and queries are predictable—predictable in their output, predictable in their formatting, and predictable in their internal processing. Every time you run them, they will give you the same data, same formatting, same font, and the same sort order. Predictability is fine to a point, but in the twenty-first century more and more companies are realizing that they need to think outside of the box to compete in today's market. You probably need to know something today that you did not need to know yesterday. To wait two or three weeks for a programmer to define a new report might be too late, and the opportunity will be lost.

Ad hoc reports, by their very nature, are unpredictable. The same data can be output and formatted in a seemingly endless variety of ways. When you, as a report writer, start the Query Wizard and begin to select the bits of information you think you need, you don't know what the return will be. When the query has been run, the real fun begins.

As the Discoverer manager, it is your job to ensure that the data is made available to your report writers in a way that makes their job as easy as possible. You will use the Administrator tool to give the data meaningful business names, preformatted and aggregated to enable users to use your definitions without the need of extensive data dictionaries.

Easy to Change vs. Fixed Queries

In an *ad hoc* query, the data can be rearranged, unneeded information removed or masked, cross tabs created, and drill-downs formed to dig deeper and deeper. Oracle Discoverer performs these tasks with one click of the mouse.

A *fixed* query is virtually impossible for a user to change. Most users can see a better way to do it but don't have the power to make the change. It would be great if the Management Information Systems (MIS) department could have programmers poised in the aisles waiting for a user to raise his or her hand. They could then rush to the user's side, find out what was needed, and make the programming change before lunch. This is of course impossible, unless you use Armstrong-Smith Consulting, so ad hoc queries are the answer.

Until the most recent release of Discoverer, end users using Discoverer Viewer could, to all intents and purposes, work with only fixed queries. This is because they were unable to save any changes that they had made. Providing the user has the correct privileges, as granted by the Discoverer manager, the new Viewer interface now allows a user to save a query that he or she has just modified.

The Benefits of Both Types of Queries

It may sound as though there is no place in the modern organization for a fixed query or report. This is not the reality. In many cases, the report is so complex and the amount of knowledge required about the database structure is so vast that there is no choice but to have a fixed report that has been created by a skilled programmer or report writer. Another benefit to the fixed report is that some reports will never change. A Total Quantity Shipped report will be the same quarter after quarter, year after year.

Some benefits of the ad hoc query and report are as follows:

- Instantaneously accessing data
- Creating crosstabs (pivot tables)
- Drilling (slicing and dicing)
- Sorting
- Adding calculations and percentages

Some of these terms may be familiar to you, some not. We will cover these various concepts and more as we teach you to use this powerful tool.

NOTE
There needs to be a balance between the fixed report and the ad hoc report. It is impractical for an organization to rely solely on one type or the other. Some companies may see the use of Oracle Discoverer as a means of downsizing their business intelligence departments with a "users can do it all" mentality. This would be folly, and the authors are not suggesting it. Discoverer should be seen as a complement to the fixed report and a means of seeing "what you don't already know." Indeed, in the right hands, Discoverer can be used to create both report types.

Oracle Applications Standard Reports vs. Discoverer Reports

Now that you are familiar with the generic terms of fixed and ad hoc queries and reports, let's be specific. Oracle Applications is probably being used by most of the readers of this book. You might be using Discoverer already, or you may be considering whether or not to add it to your list of tools. This section may help you in your decision and should help you to correctly position Discoverer in your suite of reporting tools.

If you have implemented all of the modules of Oracle Applications, you may be aware that Oracle provides more than 700 prewritten standard reports. Getting to know these reports is a mammoth undertaking and not to be underestimated. These reports are an excellent resource to your organization, and it is to your benefit to take full advantage of them. It is a sad waste of time and effort to use Discoverer to create reports that already exist in Oracle Apps. In other words, *don't reinvent the wheel.*

A consulting company with expertise in Oracle Apps can help you sift through the standard reports and find the ones that are best suited to your needs. Some companies have a great enough demand for reporting that a full-time reports analyst should be employed. This analyst is responsible for taking the users' requirements and finding the reports that fill them. They can then make recommendations to either use a standard report "as is," rework an existing report, or say that no standard report fulfills the requirements.

This is where Discoverer comes into the picture. Discoverer should not be seen as the replacement for Oracle standard reports. It is an enhancement to give you greater power to access your data—and wow, what power!!

Library Reports vs. Requirements

Having decided that you have no other choice but to use Discoverer, you should take a look at your organization's Discoverer library documentation. Perhaps you will find that a Discoverer report already exists that covers your requirements. Wouldn't that be nice? Perhaps you will find a report that is so close to meeting your requirements that a small tweak would solve your problem too. Should you find that either of these scenarios exist, you should approach your library manager to see if access to the report can be granted or if the report can be modified.

If all else has now failed, you have no choice but to build the report yourself or, if you are lucky enough to have report writers, request that the report be built for you. You will find that Discoverer is a joy to work with, so dive right in, the water is warm and there are no undercurrents to sweep you out to sea. Should you find yourself getting out of your depth, there are plenty of places to go to get help.

Getting Help with Discoverer

Oracle and the Oracle community have provided comprehensive resources for getting help about Discoverer.

The very first place to look for help is within the product itself by selecting Help from the menu bar. For those readers familiar with standard Windows applications, this will be second nature.

To access the Help menu, click Help on the Menu bar.

From the Help menu you can select the following:

- **Help Topics** An Oracle-provided index of help topics (see Figure 1-3)

- **Using Help**   Instructions from Microsoft on how to use the Windows help features

- **Quick Tour**   A brief overview of the main features of the Discoverer End-User Edition

- **Cue Cards**   A set of crib sheets to step you through some common topics

- **Manual**   This feature takes you to the online end-user manual provided by Oracle

Figure 1-3 shows the Discoverer Desktop Help window.

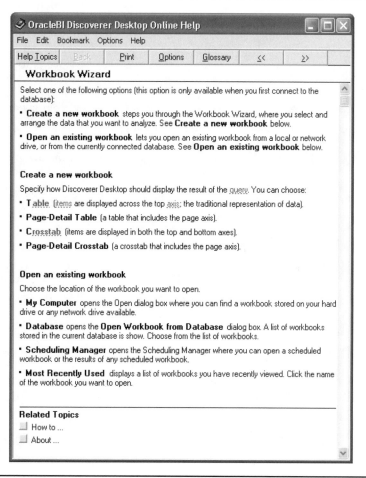

FIGURE 1-3   *The Discoverer Desktop Help window*

Other sources of help can be found on the Web. Some of the most useful help sites are listed here:

Source of Help	Web Site	Contents and Features
Oracle's web site	http://www.oracle.com/technology/products/discoverer/index.html	Here you will find white papers, FAQs, Quick Tours, demos, etc.
Oracle's MetaLink site	http://metalink.oracle.com	This site is available to companies who have purchased support from Oracle. You will be required to register. In order to register, you will need to know your company's customer support identifier (CSI) number. The site contains technical libraries, a Discoverer forum, and even a means of creating service requests (SRs), formerly known as technical service requests or TARs, online.
Oracle's Discoverer Forum	http://forums.oracle.com/forums/forum.jsp?forum=56	This site, the second of the Oracle Discoverer forums, is also dedicated to providing help on Discoverer. Unlike when using MetaLink, you do not need a CSI number to use the forum, although you will need to register if you want to place new forum messages or provide answers to help other users.
Oracle University's Online Library	http://www.oracle.com/education/oln/ou_online_home.html	This site is available to companies or individuals who have purchased an online learning agreement. The library that you will find in here contains over 20 self-paced courses for Discoverer. An annual subscription is required to access this library. If you attend an Oracle University training course on Discoverer, you may well find that a one-year subscription is included in the price.
ODTUG web site	www.odtug.com/	This is a members-only site for the Oracle Development Tools User Group. You can join by completing the online registration form. The site contains case studies, feature articles, links to related material in the ODTUG *Technical Journal*, and a technical journal online.

Source of Help	Web Site	Contents and Features
OAUG web site	www.oaug.org/	This site belongs to the Oracle Applications User Group. It contains information on upcoming conferences and meetings. There are even special interest groups (SIGs) that have been set up. The Business Intelligence / Data Warehouse SIG is the group for Discoverer.
IOUG web site	http://www.ioug.org/	This site belongs to the International Oracle Users Group. It contains technical information on discussion forums and even has a technical repository. It is not the place to go if you are an end user, but if you are a Discoverer administrator, you will find plenty of interesting, technical subjects to use as bedtime reading.
Learn Discoverer web site	http://learndiscoverer.com	This site belongs to the authors. It contains information about training courses and consulting services, as well as general information concerning Discoverer. You will also find white papers and presentations available for download free of charge.

Summary

Oracle Business Intelligence Discoverer 10g (10.1.2) is slick, easy to use, and intuitive. From the introduction of the Desktop (aka Windows) version in the 1990s, through to the latest 2006 Plus and Viewer (Web) releases, Discoverer has played an ever-increasing role in business intelligence. With the release of Discoverer Plus, the product has brought a full release of the Desktop Edition to the Internet.

You have learned that this book is aimed at both the end user and the Discoverer manager. Throughout the book you will be shown examples of queries and reports taken from a fictitious company database. We are sure that the examples accurately reflect "real-world" situations that will be useful in teaching you good query design using Discoverer.

In the section entitled "A New Direction in Reporting," we have described how things used to be in many companies and how Discoverer can overcome many obstacles in reporting. The Discoverer GUI makes Discoverer intuitive and user friendly. You have also learned how ad hoc queries differ from predefined queries and the benefits of both.

Finally, we have given you a table showing the variety of help resources available to the end user and Discoverer administrator alike.

CHAPTER
2

Users and Databases

verybody is familiar with the terms "hardware" and "software." When something goes wrong with a system, it is to these that people usually look when seeking out the reason why. Because of this, not all companies invest as much as they should into the other, and probably more important, resource: the user. That said, users can do a lot to help themselves when they are required to start working with Discoverer.

This chapter will deal with the general responsibilities of the end user and then go on to discuss the concept of setting up, using, and managing Discoverer libraries. We will introduce you to the Discoverer manager, the library manager, Discoverer report writers (formerly known as superusers), and report viewers. Throughout this chapter we will make reference to other staff members, such as DBAs and Discoverer administrators, but we will leave discussion of these people for the next chapter.

What Starts Right Stays Right

Managing Discoverer is an art—not a science—and is not something you can just throw a resource at and expect to see a successful, efficient, smooth-running environment. Without adequate training and guidance, you will not get the most out of Discoverer.

A colleague of ours coined the saying "what starts right stays right." This advice, while applicable to all computer-based systems, is of paramount importance when used in the context of business intelligence. Let's say you want to get from A to B but don't have a road map or plan that tells you how to get to B from A. In this situation you could start out by taking a first step in any number of directions. No matter which direction you start, so long as you take the correct turns and twists along the way, you might eventually end up at B. It is these twists and turns that cost your company time and money, valuable resources that you cannot afford to waste.

The benefit of doing it correctly—the first time—is peace of mind and credibility with your customers, whoever they may be. Success in many respects has more to do with delivering reliably on organizational expectations than with simply installing the technical software environment. Quite possibly, the risk and political exposure on your project may be such that it should warrant investment in the development and implementation of a formal plan—addressing critical aspects of structure, process, and discipline. Time and time again we see companies that have not gone all the way and subsequently complain that they are not getting the most out of their investment in business intelligence. In order to successfully set up a Discoverer environment, you need to invest time, money, and the right resources.

So wouldn't it be nice if someone were to lay out a road map in front of you and tell you which direction to start out in? In this and the next chapter we will do just that. We will lay out the basic concepts and direction that you need to take in order to get going so that you can get to a fully working, well-managed Discoverer environment in the shortest possible time. If you do not set up the basics, you face a major chance of failure or costly rework. Our experience with similar projects indicates that what starts right stays right.

The Responsibility of the End User

If you don't understand your responsibilities as a Discoverer end user, you are lost. Queries cannot be defined if you are not aware of the data available to you, if you don't know which folders contain the data, and if you are unclear on what end result you are after. Therefore, before you begin to explore the power of Discoverer, you will need to understand the following:

- Your business

- Your reporting requirements

- Your database

Your Business

The most important question you can ask yourself is "What is my business?" Are you the CEO of your own small company? Perhaps you are an analyst in the accounting department of a large manufacturing firm. Whatever your business, the first step in viewing company data is to understand what it is you need to know about your business, and then to try to get a feeling for what it is that you don't already know.

If you don't know about your company—what it does and how you fit into the scheme of things—how can you begin to create reports that can have a meaningful impact upon your business? You need to at least understand your company's objectives and then get someone to explain how your role fits in to the overall plan. Once you have ascertained exactly how important you are to your company, you can begin to make some headway into the area of query creation for your department. But where do you start?

The best way to begin is by looking at any predefined queries and reports that already exist. These may arrive on your desk in the form of a weekly or monthly report. Perhaps a clever programmer developed this report to meet some long-forgotten request. That request may have come from your department, perhaps even from your predecessor. It may also have come from another department; perhaps someone in your unit felt it would be useful.

If that report was designed and created more than a year ago, chances are that no one remembers why it was built in the first place. You may be lucky and find that someone actually documented the report and what it does. More likely, you will have nothing other than the query itself, a query that probably means very little to you today.

Each time the report is found in your inbox, you read it with some frustration because it does not really answer the questions you have. Sure, it answers questions A, B, and C, but what you really need to know is D and what you want to know is E. Because you know your business, you know the answers that are missing from your existing reports. More important, you know the questions to pose in order to get the answers you need.

Your Reporting Requirements

Now that you know how to look for what is missing, it is time to brainstorm. Write down everything you want to know about your business. Be as detailed as you can, but bear in mind that you will not likely get everything you want. It is something like a Christmas wish list. Don't just write down what you need to know, but also what you would like to know. The following story illustrates how understanding what you want to know leads to more questions.

A successful commercial real estate firm realized the need to automate and centralize information, and it had a database built. The database contained the names of building owners, building information, building tenants and all of their lease information, maintenance companies, and other information. Not understanding the kinds of questions to ask, users approached the database timidly at first. The DBA was asked questions like, "Can you tell me which tenants' leases expire in the next six months?" Then she was asked, "Which tenants have an increase in their rent in the next three months?" Soon, the users asked more and more questions, and the DBA responded by creating more queries and more reports.

The people in this company had come to realize the power of the information in the database and were asking the right questions. It is your responsibility to do the same. Once you have ascertained what is missing, you need to formulate a plan to aid you in getting what you need.

Determining End-User Requirements

Your best resource for defining end-user requirements is your current pool of end users, your business unit managers, and your database administrators. These people can be a great source of help and inspiration when all seems lost. Remember to find out if anyone else is using Discoverer, and see whether they know how to get the data that you need for your report. Your Discoverer manager and library manager (the concept of the library will be explained later in this chapter) are also great sources of help, and they should be used as well.

Employ an Incremental Approach

Don't try to answer every question by using one query, and don't try to answer all your questions in one session. Take your time, and remember that whatever fit the bill perfectly last year may not do so now. Requirements change, business direction changes, and people change. Try to remember this when you are analyzing requirements.

Flexibility is a great asset to have, and using a "develop, demonstrate, and revise" approach will work wonders. Develop a report that will handle the current needs, demonstrate that it works and satisfies requirements, and then be prepared to revise it when the time arises. Discoverer is a powerful tool and will allow you to change your query at any time. When your manager realizes that you have that power under control, he or she will naturally see other ways to harness your Discoverer talents.

Documenting Your Requirements

Perhaps one of the hardest and most unenvied of all tasks is documentation. We all try to avoid doing this as if it were some terminal disease from which there was no hope of recovery. Yet, when the chips are down, the first thing we all go looking for is the selfsame documentation, and how pleased we are when we find that we did in fact write down why management wanted our query to pull in data from only four of the five sales regions.

So, what should you document? Well, you at least need to identify who told you that something had to be done this way rather than that. You need to give examples of report layouts and specify any special requirements (which will later become conditions) that need to be applied in order to make the query do what you want.

This may all seem to be overkill, and in some cases this may be so. But we can tell you that not documenting is usually far worse than overdocumenting. Remembering that requirements change is itself a reason to write down why you have done something. Having documented what your query is supposed to do, you need to be aware of the data that is available to you and where you can go to find help about that data.

Your Database

Perhaps the most daunting responsibility anyone tasked with creating queries can have is to understand the database they are working with. You cannot know what questions to ask of the database if you don't know what data is available to you. It is in this step that you must become a partner with your Discoverer administrator. The Discoverer administrator can familiarize you with the database structure you are using and the data that is available to you.

NOTE
It is important to remember that just because there is data in the database, that does not mean it will be available to you. Security issues and "need to know" are important parts of access. If there is some part of the database that you have not been granted access to and want, you will need to make a case for why you should be granted access.

It is also important for you to know what type of database system you are using. Is it a live production system, a copy of production, or a data warehouse? Each system has different characteristics and parameters that you need to familiarize yourself with if you are to become an expert in Discoverer.

OLTP Systems

The "live" databases, otherwise known as online transaction processing (OLTP) systems, are where the work is being done. Invoices are being entered, orders taken, payments recorded, inventory counted, and other tasks are being performed. It is in "production" that the data is the freshest because it is all happening now. So the question might be asked, "Why don't we just do all of our querying and reporting from the production database and forget about those other systems?" The answer is simple.

An OLTP system has been designed and built for entering and storing transactions quickly. It is not built for querying or reporting. You may ask, "What is the difference?" There are several reasons that the transaction systems and reporting systems are different:

- The database structures are different.

- Reporting from an OLTP system is slow.

- The data is volatile.

- OLTP table names are not easy to understand.

- OLTP systems are frequently purged of their data.

By their very nature, OLTP systems need to be tuned in order to perform well. This tuning ensures that transactions can be entered and stored efficiently. Running large reporting queries will slow the transactions down. This is not acceptable to users of the OLTP system.

NOTE
The comment about table names being not easy to understand is a moot point if your Discoverer manager renames the folders. If your system does not have user-friendly table names, you should speak with your Discoverer manager and ask him or her if it is possible to change them.

The Database Structures Are Different   If you are familiar with database design, you will have heard of *normalization*. This technique uses many tables and never repeats an item of data. It uses small indexed tables to hold everything. On your transaction tables, an OLTP system stores ID numbers or codes as cross-references (foreign keys or lookups) to other tables. For example, in the OLTP system, the city San Francisco is only listed in the City lookup table with a code of 430. Every customer in San Francisco is listed in the Customer table with the code 430.

In a data warehouse we generally use denormalized table structures. Continuing the present example, where the code 430 is used to reference San Francisco, we will replace the code with the name. This means that the word San Francisco will be repeated many times. Using this technique speeds up reporting, but you can see how it would slow down a transactional system. To create a report that displays descriptions instead of key values (e.g., San Francisco instead of the value 430), the SQL behind the report has to join multiple tables to get the results.

Reporting from an OLTP System Is Slowwwww   Because an OLTP system is optimized for entering transactions, it is not optimized for reporting. The database that can do both quickly and efficiently has not yet been invented. However, Oracle is making great strides in this direction. One day this will no doubt be possible. Until then, the reality is that when you use your OLTP system for reporting, it can be deadly slow.

You might find yourself beginning to run your query, go get a cup of coffee, visit a friend, call to make a vet appointment for Muffy to get her teeth cleaned, and then come back to find that your query has timed out. To make matters worse, you will have impacted your online colleagues, who will already have been complaining that the database is running slow. You may even find that the DBA terminated your query because it was drawing too many system resources. How wonderful it would be if the company built a database just for you!

The Data Is Volatile   In an OLTP system, the data is changing constantly. If you run a report at 9:00 A.M. and your coworker runs the same report at 11:00 A.M., and you both bring the report to the 3:00 P.M. staff meeting, the reports will be different. In the two hours between the reports, new orders will have been placed, invoices paid, shipments made, and so on.

To further compound the problem, your supervisor will see the difference in your reports and may decide to check the figures for herself at 3:30 P.M. Guess what—her answers will be completely different, so maybe she decides you are both incompetent and the two of you get the sack! Of course, this is an extreme example, but it does illustrate one problem with using an OLTP system for reporting.

OLTP Table Names Are Not Easy to Understand   When you are selecting the criteria for your query, you need to know where the data comes from. In an OLTP system, the table names are not obvious. You might think that the City table would be called "City". You will probably be wrong. It might have a simple, but still difficult to decipher, name like "location_names_all", or it might be called "table_19975". Just imagine the nightmare in trying to report using these names. This may sound far-fetched, but the truth of the matter is that system designers frequently don't take the needs of end users into account when designing databases.

If you have Oracle Applications and want to build a report showing all shipments and returns, did you know that the tables you need are so_headers_all, so_lines_all, so_line_details, so_picking_lines_all, mtl_so_rma_receipts, mtl_so_rma_interface, and ra_addresses_all? Not only do you need to know the names of all these tables, you need to know how to link them together, and also which schema owns them. Here, the four tables that begin with the characters "so" are owned by the OE user, the two "mtl" tables are owned by the INV user, while the table that begins with "ra" is owned by the AR user. Confusing, isn't it? The typical end user would have no idea where to begin because the system was built for storing transactions—not reporting.

If your company has decided not to invest in another alternative, you have no choice but to report from the OLTP system. Perhaps your company is small and has only one person in MIS, or perhaps it simply cannot afford one of the alternative systems. Whatever the reason, you should work with your Discoverer manager, who is able to at least change the names of the tables to something more meaningful. He or she may even be able to build some views of the database for you, bringing together common tables for your reporting needs. A view, by the way, is a means of hiding the logic that goes into joining tables together. Not only do they look like tables, but you can query from them as if they were tables.

If you are using Oracle Applications, your company may have purchased a product called NoetixViews or BIS from Oracle. These companies have analyzed common end-user requirements and have put together a complete set of views for all of the modules. Both BIS views and NoetixViews will be explained in greater detail in Appendix C.

OLTP Systems Are Frequently Purged of Their Data Most OLTP systems do not store large amounts of history. Since these systems are designed for immediate response, their data is often purged within a few months of capture. Therefore, you cannot get any significant historical information from an OLTP system.

Snapshot Databases

These are copies of your data. They can be one of the following two types:

- A complete copy of your OLTP system

- A partial copy of the database saved to a local server

Complete Copy of the OLTP System The preceding section outlined the drawbacks of reporting from an OLTP system. Many companies minimize these drawbacks by making a complete copy of their OLTP database for use in reporting. The benefits of a complete copy are as follows:

- The data is constant. If you run your report at 9:00 A.M. and your colleague runs the same report at 11:00 A.M., you will both have the same information for your 3:00 P.M. meeting—and hopefully keep your jobs.

- There is no impact on the OLTP system. You will not have unhappy coworkers complaining about your query mucking up the system.

Some companies take a full copy of their OLTP system every night following the close of the working day, placing that copy on a different machine from the OLTP system.

The disadvantages to the complete copy are as follows:

- You could still have the problems over database structure and table names (see the accompanying note).

- It is still inherently an OLTP system, and so it is not designed for reporting.

- The data is not up to date—in some cases, it may be 24 hours or more old. This may not be seen as a disadvantage, depending on what you will use the data for. If you want to analyze shipments made yesterday, the snapshot is to your advantage. If you want to analyze today's shipments, you must wait until the next refresh cycle.

- Because it is a copy of the OLTP system, you cannot do historical reporting.

NOTE
One of the reasons for having a database administrator is to present the data to you in a meaningful way. This includes simplifying the view of the database, although this should be transparent to the end user.

Complete snapshot copies are becoming increasingly popular. They overcome some of the disadvantages of reporting from an OLTP system, as long as you are aware of your company's refresh cycle.

A Partial Copy of the Database Saved to a Local Server   If your company uses a centralized database, it could be located many thousand of miles or kilometers from your office. In order to improve performance, you can make local copies of some of the tables you need for your reports. Snapshots can be used to copy all or part of a table. If your database is in Paris and your office is in Denver and you are interested in reporting only on North American data, your DBA can arrange to copy only the data you need.

The simplest forms of partial copy take the tables in their entirety, rather than the more complex forms, which use queries to extract just the portions you need. The advantages of this approach are as follows:

- The data is constant.

- There is no impact on the OLTP system.

- The performance in relation to speed is increased.

- The DBA can define some indexes specifically designed for your reporting needs.

The disadvantages are as follows:

- You still have the problems over database structure and table names.

- It is still inherently an OLTP system, and so it is not designed for reporting.

- The data is not up to date—in some cases, it may be 24 hours or more old.

- If you have copied only parts of the database and you now need to report on something outside of the copied data, you cannot.

- Because it is a copy of the OLTP system, you cannot do historical reporting.

Data Mart or Data Warehouse

Data marts and data warehouses are commonly discussed together, and some industry experts will tell you that the two cannot exist side by side. We will not involve ourselves in that debate. We will simply tell you what they are.

Data Warehouses   According to Bill Inmon, commonly regarded as the father of data warehousing, a data warehouse is a "subject-oriented, integrated, non-volatile, time-variant collection of data used in support of management decisions." What the heck does that mean?

Quite simply, this means that a data warehouse is a business-relevant (subject-oriented) collection of data from various sources. The data can come from the OLTP system, from spreadsheets, from word processor documents, even from your customers. In essence, the data warehouse will contain all of the items needed to satisfy the reporting requirements for your business area.

Because the data can come from various sources, it has to be manipulated into a common format (integrated). For example, your customers may all provide you with information about their sales of your products, but they probably will send you that data using their own in-house codes and ID numbers. It is necessary to convert these numbers into your codes. This is accomplished by the integration process.

Once the data has been collected into the data warehouse, it will not change and cannot be deleted (being nonvolatile), implying that you will have historical data. As a data warehouse is a read-only database, users cannot change it. The only way the data can change is during the refresh cycle when new data is added.

Because the data is collected periodically, you will be able to report trends over time according to the refresh cycle. What this means is that if you collect your data every day, you can analyze your daily sales. If you refresh your data only weekly, you can analyze weekly sales, and so forth (time-variant). You need to specify what your requirements are so that the data warehouse is built accordingly. If you are working from an existing data warehouse, you might not have the necessary clout to change the refresh cycle, but you certainly need to know what it is.

The advantages of a data warehouse are as follows:

- It is optimized for reporting.

- It contains historical data.

- It does not impact the OLTP system.

- It has meaningful table names.

- It is not subject to change.

- You can perform data mining ("tell me something I don't already know").

- It contains data from multiple sources, not just your OLTP system.

The disadvantages of a data warehouse are as follows:

- It can be extremely expensive to build and maintain. You may need to have buy-in from senior management to get approval for a data warehouse.

- You need large amounts of storage space, potentially one terabyte or more.

- Because there is a huge amount of data, it is possible to write queries that seem to run forever and never come back with an answer (the query from the Twilight Zone).

- The data is not up to date—in some cases, it may be 24 hours or more old.

- Data warehouses are not easily changed. If you spot an error in the data warehouse, you will have to correct it in the source system. If that system cannot be changed, the data warehouse cannot be changed and you will have to live with incorrect data. For example, company "ABC Widgets" could be stored in the database as "A.B.C. Widgets", "AB and C Widgets", or "AB&C". Unless you know about these possible irregularities, you will get incomplete results. You may have a difficult time persuading your company to change their procedures to satisfy the data warehouse.

NOTE
The data cleansing procedures available in ETL (extract transform load) tools do address the issue of inconsistent naming to some extent.

■ Because the data is coming from different sources, you may not be able to get the same answer from your OLTP system as you do from the data warehouse. It will be difficult, if not impossible, to identify if any OLTP transactions are missing from the data warehouse.

You may find it interesting that some very large companies like Amazon, Best Buy, and France Telecom have data warehouses with fact tables containing hundreds of millions of records, some even running into the billions.

Data Mart   A *data mart* is a table or set of tables that has been created for a specific reporting requirement. They provide a subject-oriented view of the data in your system and contain significantly smaller amounts of data than in your OLTP or data warehouse systems. Where they exist, they will be the prime focus of the online analytical processing (OLAP) by the end users. The table structure(s) will be simple, the table names will correspond to folders within business areas, and the data items should have user friendly, meaningful names.

NOTE
The names of the data items should not be an issue if your DBA has created user friendly, meaningful names. In the vast majority of cases, this will be true; however, sometimes you may need to speak with the DBA and request that the names be changed.

Data marts are like snapshots in that they are refreshed periodically. In fact, most data marts are actually refreshed from a data warehouse if you have one, making your data marts a subset of your data warehouse. When you don't have a data warehouse, they are refreshed from the OLTP system. Unlike snapshots—but like data warehouses—they have been optimized for reporting purposes. In fact, their sole purpose in life is reporting.

Typically, one data mart contains all of the data you need to satisfy the reporting requirements for a single business area. Using the Oracle example highlighted in the previous section, where you had to pull from at least seven tables to obtain a complete shipping report, all of this data is now found in a single shipping table. It also has been given the delightful name Shipping.

The advantages of a data mart are as follows:

■ It is a single source of data for a business area.

■ It has no impact on the OLTP system.

■ It is optimized for reporting.

■ It is fast, because it has special indexes created to enable you to extract the data quickly.

■ When sourced directly from an OLTP system, it can be quick to build and less expensive than a data warehouse. It could even be used as a prototype for a future data warehouse.

As with all things, there are disadvantages, namely:

■ It usually contains data to satisfy predefined reports. If you suddenly decide you need more data in a report, you can't have it easily. You will need to submit a request to your administrator to have the data mart structure, and possibly the data warehouse, changed. This can be a difficult and time-consuming process.

■ Data marts are not typically built to cross-link one business area to another. This is not a Discoverer limitation, but a business rule implementation. For example, your company may have sales regions across the world and have built a data mart for each region. If your company has decided to prevent users in one region querying the sales data from another, your Discoverer administrator will not be prevented from cross-linking the data marts.

■ If they are pulling from an OLTP system, they are not historical.

■ Because the data is usually a subset of another system, you may not be able to get the same answer from your OLTP system as you do from the data mart. In fact, if your data mart is sourced from a data warehouse, you are two steps away from the source.

For a more detailed explanation of data warehouses and data marts, we recommend you read *Oracle8 Data Warehousing: A Practical Guide to Successful Data Warehouse Analysis, Build, and Roll-Out,* by Michael J. Corey, Michael Abbey, Ian Abramson, and Ben Taub (Oracle Press, 1998). A more up-to-date warehousing reference book is *Oracle 10g Data Warehousing,* by Lilian Hobbs, Susan Hillson, Shilpa Lawande, and Pete Smith (Digital Press, 2004).

The Discoverer Library Concept

The concept of a Discoverer library is relatively new and was developed by us as a way to help our clients save money, time, and resources. Although it is not an integral part of Discoverer, we got the idea from the libraries in Oracle Applications and expanded on that concept. We have gone into companies where we have seen multiple report writers creating views, materialized views, End User Layers, business areas, workbooks, and worksheets that are virtually identical. Imagine the number of wasted man-hours and the assault on your bottom line when the left hand does not know what the right hand is doing. The end result is that the wheel is reinvented over and over again and chaos reigns. To rub salt into the wounds, now imagine what happens when the original developer leaves the company. Implementation of Discoverer libraries in your company will end the chaos.

The Definition of a Library

So what is a Discoverer library? In its most simple form a Discoverer library is

■ A collection of reports based upon a common theme or a collection of reports for a single business segment

■ A collection of reports that have been validated for accuracy and adherence to corporate standards, and are guaranteed to work

■ Controlled by a library manager

A well-defined Discoverer library will contain reports that are documented, with that documentation available to all users. This documentation will allow users to read a description of the report as well as to see where the data comes from, what algorithms are being used, and perhaps even a screenshot or two. Such a practice will help to alleviate bottlenecks in your system by eliminating the need for users to run or create reports unnecessarily. It also allows users to see reports that have already been created but have not yet been added to their personal report list. Users can then submit a request to the library manager for access. The users should feel confident that, after reviewing the documentation, they are opening or requesting access to reports that will satisfy their needs. They will also know that the reports have been validated and that the information will be correct and up to date.

The Definition of a Library Manager

A library manager is defined as being a responsible person who

- Is a subject matter expert with knowledge of the business segment for which he or she is responsible

- Has a separate username and password for managing the library

- Has the power to accept or deny changes from report writers

- Has the power to accept or deny requests for access to reports in their library

- Ensures that corporate standards are being adhered to

- Could be given some Discoverer admin rights in order to undertake some tasks normally performed by the Discoverer manager

Only the library manager should have the power to add, update, or delete reports from the library. End users should have the ability to use a library report, but they should not be able to change it. The library manager should also have a very good working knowledge of the end-user versions of Discoverer.

The Report Writer Concept

The concept of a report writer (formerly known as a superuser) has been around for some time, and so the principles proposed here will probably not come as a surprise to you. On the other hand, you may find them to be a new idea.

The Definition of a Report Writer

A report writer is defined as being a subject matter expert with

- An expert knowledge of the functionality of Discoverer

- A sense of business acumen—basically a pretty good idea of what his or her part of the business does

- A good grounding in needed formulas, definitions, and so forth

- A sense of the business unit's strategic goals and objectives

- A temperament suited to helping others

- A very good understanding of the database(s) used by the business unit

Most companies have one or two Discoverer users who stand out from the rest because they possess these qualities. Pooling these staff persons as an additional resource can have great benefits for a company, as we will show. Some companies choose to increase their IT department by employing Discoverer experts as report writers.

The Benefits of Having Report Writers

There are a number of reasons for having report writers in your organization. The following list is not exhaustive but is given as a means to show how beneficial it might be to designate report writers within your company:

- They are a first line of support for Discoverer-related issues to other end users.

- They will have additional know-how to go about solving problems with queries and reports.

- They will be able to give at least some introductory Discoverer training to other end users.

- They will be responsible for producing your company's standard reports.

- They have an excellent working relationship with both the library manager and the Discoverer manager.

In smaller companies, report writers can also be the library managers.

The Benefits of Being a Report Writer

It may seem at first that becoming a report writer would simply mean more work. There are, however, a number of benefits:

- You would receive additional Discoverer training, thus becoming an expert in this growing field (not a bad addition to your résumé, but don't tell that to your boss when you ask for additional training).

- You will have a direct line to the library and Discoverer managers for help and guidance in solving problems.

- You will have greater database access rights than a normal end user.

- You should be included in strategic planning for your business unit when Discoverer issues are discussed.

- You will have the ability to help other end users by being their first line of support for Discoverer-related issues.

Choosing Your Report Writers

You may not be in a position to become a report writer, but you might be the person who will choose your company's or department's report writers. When first choosing a report writer, there are a number of questions you should ask yourself about the person under consideration:

- Is the person a subject matter expert in the business area that he or she will be serving?

- Does the person have an expert knowledge of Discoverer or the ability to become an expert?

- Does the person have the respect of his or her fellow users?

- Does the person have the ability to act as a first line of support to other end users?

You may find that some managers resist the idea of designating report writers, because they fear the IT department will see them as a pretext for reducing its level of support. After all, IT members are supposed to be the experts in everything to do with computers, aren't they? Well, this used to be true in the days of mainframe computers, when the IT staff were locked away behind glass walls. But ask most modern users about computers and they nearly all have one at home. They know how to use the Internet, they know how to use spreadsheets and word processors, and they no longer need to have their hands held by the IT department.

Companies are looking to employ computer-literate staff, the same staff who will soon become experts in Discoverer. Whether or not your company chooses to embrace this pool of knowledge at this time is an internal matter. What we can say is that Discoverer is a powerful tool, it has been designated by Oracle as being a key component of its business intelligence strategy, and the ability to master this product will be a much sought-after commodity. The IT department, not being fully aware of business issues, will not be in a position to fill this role.

Summary

In this chapter, we have discussed in detail the roles and responsibilities of the end user in connection with Discoverer. It is important for you to understand your business, your reporting needs, and how your data is stored. Once you understand these things, you are ready to determine exactly what your reporting requirements are.

You have also learned how things change in business and how your reporting needs will change with those things. An incremental approach will lead to a need for documentation as you build queries and reports.

How your data is stored and the differences between OLTP systems, snapshots, data warehouses, and data marts were discussed in detail. You have learned the benefits and drawbacks of each type of system and how you will need to interact with them.

Next, we discussed the library concept and how to implement this in your company. You learned the definitions of both libraries and library managers. Finally, we discussed the report writer concept and how to implement this in your company. You learned the benefits of having report writers, what it is to be a report writer, and the attributes of a good report writer. We also discussed why the IT department is not always a good replacement for report writers.

CHAPTER
3

Getting Started in Discoverer

n this chapter, you will learn about the importance of some key members of your Discoverer team. Depending upon the complexity of your environment, you will have one or more of the following: a Discoverer manager, a library manager, a DBA, an Apps administrator, and a report writer. Developing good relationships with these key personnel can be very beneficial in your successful use of Discoverer.

We will introduce you to some important terms that will be useful to your success in using Discoverer, and we will also extend the concept of the Discoverer library. You will also learn how Discoverer manages SQL queries and their interaction with your source database. You will come to understand the process that must be followed prior to gaining access to the system, and gain some insight into what happens behind the scenes.

We will introduce you to Discoverer's "memory," referred to by Oracle as its "Sticky Feature." Just before we show you how to launch Discoverer, we give you a list of cool things it can do. Then, at last, you will be launching and logging in to Discoverer.

Key Personnel

In all companies, no matter what you call them, there are a number of key personnel with whom you should become familiar. If the size of your organization gets in the way of knowing these people personally, you should at least have a basic understanding of their job function. The key personnel with whom you need to form a relationship are as follows:

- Your Discoverer manager

- Your library manager

- Your database administrator

- Your Apps administrator (Apps mode only)

- Your report writer(s)

In some smaller organizations, or where Discoverer has not yet gained significant inroads into your company, you may not have separate roles for these job functions. In this case you may well find that the roles are handled by just one or two people. For the purposes of clarity, we will describe the basic functions of each role separately.

Discoverer Manager

The Discoverer manager is probably the most important member of the support staff with whom you need to maintain contact. The Discoverer manager is responsible for the following:

- Maintaining the End User Layer (EUL)

- Maintaining user access to the EUL

- Defining Discoverer strategy and monitoring Discoverer performance

- Setting the default item names and table characteristics (essential for Plus)

- Being a source of help for all Discoverer-related matters

The Discoverer manager works with the individual business unit and library managers to identify the data required for each business area (sometimes called business functions). Oracle has provided two separate tools, one called Discoverer Administrator, and the other, the Discoverer EUL Command Line for Java. The Discoverer manager works with these tools to create the seamless interface that you will encounter. These tools provide a highly secure, centralized link to the EUL.

NOTE
The EUL is the interface between you and the database. What you see when you log in to Discoverer is the EUL. It maintains all of the links between you and the underlying database. Whenever you create a Discoverer query, it is converted into a Structured Query Language (SQL) statement by the EUL. When you submit your query, Discoverer converts it into efficient SQL code and sends it to the database, keeping you from needing to know (1) the underlying database and (2) SQL. In other words, thank goodness for the EUL!

For more information about the roles and responsibilities of the Discoverer manager, including what he or she can do for you, please refer to Chapter 19.

Library Manager

The library manager is another very important member of the support staff with whom you need to maintain contact. The library manager is responsible for the following:

- Maintaining the approved list of reports within the library

- Accepting or denying requests for new reports

- Accepting or denying requests for access to reports

- Being a source of help to management for report availability

NOTE
Library manager is a term that we have introduced; it is not a tool or component in the Discoverer product family.

The library manager works closely with the Discoverer manager and the report writers within his business unit to identify the reports that are required. Having identified that a new report is required, the library manager then works with one of his department's report writers to create the report. Once a report has been written and has passed acceptance testing by the users, the manager should take an objective look at the report to make sure that corporate standards have been adhered to and that the report documentation effectively describes what information the report does and how it should be used. Assuming that all standards and documentation are correct, the library manager should take control of the report and make it available within the library. An extended definition of a library is given later in this chapter.

NOTE
The library manager does not write the reports. He or she is working on a higher plane and has more responsibility for report availability and accuracy than for the inner workings of the report.

Database Administrator

Besides being the person we all love to hate, the DBA is a crucial piece of the Discoverer jigsaw puzzle. Without these warm and charming people, the databases would cease to function. Their main responsibilities are as follows:

- Maintaining the databases

- Maintaining user access to the databases

- Defining database strategy and monitoring database performance

- Being yet another source of help

DBAs are a much-maligned group of people and are misunderstood by many. They have an unenviable role in the organization and bear the brunt of everyone's frustrations whenever the system goes down. The fact of the matter is that systems go down by their very complex nature, and it is the DBA for the most part that gets the system going again.

We are so used to having our systems up and running for 100 percent of the time that even a break in service of 15 minutes seems like a lifetime. The DBA has to find where in this complex system the breakdown is and repair it. Most of the time you don't even know that a problem existed, because they monitor the system constantly and correct many problems before they even affect the uptime. So, next time your system goes down and you feel like venting at your DBA, just get them a pack of cookies from the vending machine instead and go answer some e-mails.

Oracle Applications (Apps) Administrator

If your company is using Discoverer in Apps mode, this person is key to your successful interaction with the applications. The main responsibilities of the Apps administrator, as they relate to Discoverer, are as follows:

- Maintain user access to the applications.

- Maintain the Oracle Apps responsibilities.

- Maintain the Apps flex field definitions (user-defined data fields available within Oracle Apps that organizations can use as required in order to add new data to the system).

Like our beloved DBAs, the Apps administrators are also much maligned and overworked. As a senior manager once quipped to one of the authors, "If all the Apps administrators in all the world were laid end to end, they would still not reach a conclusion." We think the poor, unfortunate administrators he was describing simply had far too much on their plate. So before you go bending the ear of your administrator, ask yourself whether your request is urgent or whether perhaps it could wait until tomorrow. We are sure you will get a better response, and if this does not work, bribery works too!

Report Writers

Within your company, you may be lucky to find that your department or business unit has designated report writers. It is your responsibility to locate and pick the brains of these "superusers." Report writers are users just like you, but they have been given added responsibilities and extra training. Their responsibilities may include the following:

■ Being your primary source of help for all Discoverer workbook- and worksheet-related issues

■ Being a subject matter expert in Discoverer

■ Knowing your business unit's goals and objectives

■ Being the link between the user community and both the Discoverer and library managers

■ Being able to submit reports for inclusion in the library

For more information about the roles and responsibilities of report writers, please refer back to Chapter 2.

Having learned about the key personnel within your organization, you are now ready to turn to Discoverer itself, but first you will need to have everything set up.

Gaining Access to Discoverer

Before you can even begin to think about logging in to Discoverer, the following steps will need to have been completed:

NOTE
This section assumes that Discoverer is part of a corporate installation. You may want to install Discoverer for testing or trial purposes. This can be done by downloading Discoverer for free from OTN under a developer's license. Discoverer is now easy enough to install that release 10.1.2 can be up and running in as little as twenty minutes.

1. If your company is installing Discoverer directly on to your PC, a request will have to be submitted for this to be done. Perhaps your company has decided not to install Discoverer this way, and to use a terminal server instead (see the following note explaining terminal servers). In this case, a request will have to be made for that software to be installed. If your access to Discoverer is to be via the Web, your IT department should ensure that you have your company's standard browser correctly installed and configured. Whichever method your company uses to provide access to Discoverer, we would hope that you will be provided with an icon on your desktop that can be double-clicked to launch the login sequence. This step may sound elementary, but it is amazing how many times these basic requirements are overlooked.

2. You or your manager will need to request that access to Discoverer be made available to you. In the request, you will need to specify which database you need and to which business areas you should be granted access. The request should also contain your telephone number, your position, and whether you need to have full Discoverer access (report writer) or just the ability to run prewritten queries (report viewer).

   If you are new to the company, your manager should complete this on your behalf and send it to your library manager, or to your Discoverer manager if libraries are not in use.

Perhaps your manager can name another person within your department who has the same access you need and ask for that access to be duplicated. The more information you can give to your Discoverer or library manager, the easier will be the setup.

3. Your library manager will take your request and coordinate it with the DBA, Apps administrator, and Discoverer manager. If your company is using Discoverer in standard mode, the DBA will create a database account for you, assigning a username and password as determined by your company's standards. However, if your company is using Discoverer in Apps mode, your Apps system administrator will create an account for you, assigning a username, a password, and one or more responsibilities as determined by your company's standards.

4. After your DBA or Apps administrator has created the user account, your Discoverer manager will complete his or her tasks by granting you access to the required business areas or responsibilities and possibly arranging for you to attend a training course. This course could either be an official Oracle-given course at one of their many training centers, or it could be given internally if your company has a training department. You might even be in training right now using this book as your text!

5. After your Discoverer manager has completed his or her tasks, he will pass the request back to the library manager for completion. The library manager will ensure that all relevant reports to which you need access have been shared with you.

6. Finally, when all of the preceding steps have been completed, you will receive notification from your library manager, or your Discoverer administrator if you do not have a library manager, that your account has been set up and has been activated. In this notification, you will be informed of any usernames, passwords, and database connect strings that you may need to use. We say "may" because Discoverer Plus has what are known as public connections. These connections hide the complexity of the login requirements from you. Depending upon the setup within your organization, you may or may not have public connections. If these are in use, the security requirements that are in force within your organization may require you to enter a password. In addition, if you are using Oracle Applications your Apps responsibility will be made known to you. You will also be informed what user level you have been assigned (report writer or report viewer) as well as having any appropriate reports shared with you. If you are going to be connecting to Discoverer via the Web, you will also be given the appropriate URL.

NOTE
If your main database is not located at your work site, your company may well have decided to use one or more terminal servers. These powerful PCs (usually Windows NT or 2003 servers) are used as a link between you and the database and have a full working copy of Discoverer 10g Desktop on them. They are usually installed in your data center with a direct connection to the database. You connect to a terminal server from your PC using your network, and then you can use it just as if it were your own PC. The benefits of this approach are reduced network traffic and improved performance. Anyone who has tried running Discoverer from their own PC connected to a database more than 1,000 miles away will know what we mean.

Having had the correct setups completed, you are now ready to use Discoverer.

Key Definitions

Before we get into the Discoverer login sequence, we will explain four key definitions that you need to know.

Workbooks and Worksheets

Discoverer uses workbooks. Anyone familiar with spreadsheets should understand the concept of workbooks. A *workbook* is a group of worksheets. Each workbook can be thought of as being like an Excel document. Every *worksheet* in a workbook is a single query (a SQL statement that returns data from the database—see the next section). You can think of worksheets as being like individual Excel spreadsheets. Every worksheet in a workbook will usually be related in some way to the other worksheets, but it does not need to be. We recommend, however, that you not keep unrelated worksheets in the same workbook. This makes for sloppy design and difficulties in both maintenance and security.

For example, you may have a workbook that pulls in the data for the sales in your eastern region. One worksheet may have sales broken down by salesperson, another may have sales sorted showing highest sales to lowest by customer, and yet another may show the regional sales compared to last year. The worksheets are related, but each one puts a different spin on the data and answers a different business question. Let's say you now add a worksheet that shows fixed assets. Any subsequent requests for access to your sales reports cannot be done without also granting access to the fixed asset report. Believe us when we say that this causes problems. We have been there and done that, and it does not work well.

NOTE
Multiple worksheets should be used cautiously at first, and perhaps you should not use them at all in your first few workbooks. The idea behind Discoverer is its ease of use. Getting bogged down in worksheet maintenance is not always to your advantage. Also, having too many worksheets can cause issues with performance and memory, so please do not get carried away. Each worksheet in a workbook is related to its own query.

Queries

We have already used the term "query" a number of times in this book. However, you may not know what a query is. A *query* is simply a question that is posed of the database. When you tell Discoverer to run a worksheet, it generates a SQL query and sends the code to the database. Hopefully, the answer you expect comes back. An example of a query is "how many blue widgets did we sell in the southwest region last week?" If the query was created correctly, the answer will come back to you in a matter of seconds. Some queries will take a long time, though, especially if you are not careful with your worksheet design. In Chapter 4 we introduce you to the query from the Twilight Zone, the query that seems to run forever, and show you how to construct Discoverer worksheets that avoid this issue.

Reports

As with queries, we have already used the term "report" several times, and we feel it is important that you understand what we mean by a report as opposed to a query, worksheet, or workbook. A *report* is a worksheet that has been formatted to a level acceptable for delivery to a department, companywide, or even to external customers. Reports use headers and footers, company logos, company colors, fonts, and layout characteristics that adhere to your corporate standards. Finally, we recommend that reports be centrally maintained and administered as a library.

Libraries

A Discoverer *library* is a collection of reports based around a common theme or business unit. The reports in a library differ from the normal workbooks and reports that are owned by individual report writers. Library reports are

- **Owned by a library manager** The manager will not normally be a real user but a role or responsibility that can be granted to a user. Adopting this method of working ensures the continued existence of the library following the departure of the manager either from the company or from that position. By default, the Discoverer manager also has the library manager role for all libraries.

- **Guaranteed to be accurate and perform efficiently** Candidate reports will have stringent user testing to confirm that they do what they are supposed to do. Before being put forward as candidates for the library, new reports will require user signoff and documentation.

- **Guaranteed to adhere to corporate standards** These standards will dictate the layout, style, and naming conventions that are to be used. There should be an agreed list of abbreviations to which all library reports will conform. Standard headers and footers will be employed, and the data will be displayed in your corporate colors. A confidentiality statement will be used where necessary. The adoption of these standards ensures that your reports display a corporate image. The library manager is responsible for checking that the standards are being correctly used. Reports that do not conform will be rejected and sent back to the report writer.

- **Centrally documented** Library documents will have meaningful descriptions for the report requirements, column names, and function definitions. Any special requirements such as parameter usage will be explained in detail. There should also be a set of example screenshots from the report. Users will be able to use this documentation to understand what the report does and thus make a decision as to whether it satisfies the need that they have.

- **Secure with access being strictly controlled** Access to a library report will require a request from either an end user or the end user's manager. No user will be allowed to change a library report. Following the approval of a request the library manager will liaise with the Discoverer manager to ensure that the user has access to the relevant business area. When this confirmation has been received, the library manager will share the report with the user. Finally, the user will be informed that his or her request has been accepted and that the report is now available to him or her.

- **Maintained centrally** Following a request for a change to a library document, the library manager will consult with the requesting end user or department head and that department's report writer. The end result of this consultation will be either acceptance or rejection of the request. When a change request is accepted, the library manager will release the workbook containing the report and assign it to a report writer. Following a change, the report will need user testing, signoff, and updated documentation prior to acceptance back into the library.

Sticky Features

Discoverer has a memory. From time to time, Discoverer will make a note of "last used" options. The next time you are given a choice for one of these options, Discoverer will remember what you last did and default to that setting. The authors call this Discoverer's Sticky Feature.

Main Features of Discoverer

We have told you how great Discoverer is and how easy it is to use. According to *PC Week,* "Oracle's Discoverer breaks new ground with its high-performance mix of dynamic and precomputed queries, while its usable interface ensures its power can be put to immediate use."

We have not told you all of the terrific things Discoverer does. It might be in your mind that all you can do is view data and create queries. This is far from the truth. If you are used to working with spreadsheets or even DOS-based systems, you may not be aware of some of the features that Discoverer has available. The following table shows a list, though not exhaustive, of some of these features.

Folders based on tables and views	Items based on columns
Descriptions of folders and items	Lists of values
Joins based on primary- and foreign-key definitions	Default date hierarchies (year-quarter-month)
Drills to related items, other workbooks, or even hyperlinks	Complex objects (pivots, filters, calculations, functions)
Complex joins (folders joined to other folders)	Derived items (items based on other items)
Graphing	Percentages
Exceptions	Exporting to other applications
Sorting (simple, group sorting, sort within sort)	Totaling (grand totals and subtotals)
Formatting (fonts, colors, justification, italics, bold, numeric)	Adding bitmaps to reports (Desktop only)
Applying titles	Adding page breaks and pagination
Queries based upon other queries (subqueries, but only in Desktop)	Printing and print preview
Scheduling	Sharing queries with other users
Shortcuts	Right mouse button support (context menus)
Templates for complex calculations	Report parameters

The list above by no means includes all of the features of Discoverer but is meant to give you a flavor of what to expect in the coming chapters. Okay, now the bit you have been waiting for. In the next section, you will learn to log in and get started in Discoverer.

Discoverer Login Sequence

From this point forward in the book, we will be describing step-by-step instructions for using Discoverer. We suggest you perform these steps for yourself as a way of reinforcing the skills you are learning. Imagine you are in a classroom and the book is your instructor. We will first of all show you how to connect using Discoverer Desktop, and then we will show you how to connect using 10.1.2 Plus and Viewer.

Connecting Using Discoverer Desktop

You launch Discoverer Desktop using the same process you use for all of your Windows applications. You can either use the Start menu or double-click an icon on your desktop.

If your company uses a terminal server for the connection to Discoverer, you should first connect to the terminal server and then launch Discoverer from the Start menu of that machine. Whichever approach your company has adopted, follow the procedures that are the standard in your company. If you are not sure how to log in, you should contact your library manager, report writer, or Discoverer manager.

Having successfully launched Discoverer Desktop, you will be presented with the following login screen.

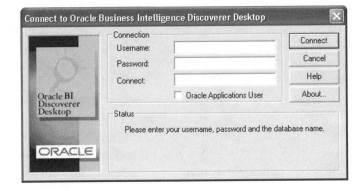

Enter your username and password in the appropriate fields in the startup screen. You will also need to know and enter the name of the database you want to access. This takes us back to the earlier part of this chapter, on your Discoverer manager and the DBA. Since each company will address these issues uniquely, we can give you only generic instructions.

When you have entered your username, password, and database, click Connect. You will be allowed three attempts to get this right before Discoverer terminates your connection. However, don't worry, because Discoverer does not lock you out; it only closes and makes you start again.

If you are using Discoverer in Apps mode, you can either type a colon following your username or check the box labeled Oracle Applications User. If you successfully connect, you will next be presented with the Choose A Responsibility dialog box. In here you should select the Oracle responsibility that you wish to connect using and then click OK.

NOTE
Entering a colon after your username is a trick that tells Discoverer that you want to connect using Apps mode. If you know your Apps responsibility, you can type it following the colon.

Launching 10.1.2 Discoverer Plus or Viewer

Logging in to Discoverer Plus or Viewer is done via your web browser. Your Discoverer manager will give you a Uniform Resource Locater (URL) for the application as it is stored on your company's web server. This may sound complicated, but it really isn't. Just remember to ask for the instructions for launching, and then follow those instructions.

TIP
Don't forget to add the URL to your bookmarks or Web favorites.

Unlike in previous versions of Discoverer Plus where to launch Discoverer you needed to click the large Start button, when you first launch the URL to start Discoverer 10.1.2 Plus, the URL that you use will take you straight to the connection screen. The same is true for the 10.1.2 Discoverer Viewer. The items presented to you on the connection screen differ depending whether your organization is using Discoverer stand-alone or as part of an application server.

Connecting to a Stand-Alone Instance

When you connect to a stand-alone instance of Discoverer Plus or Viewer, you will see a screen entitled Connect To Oracle BI Discoverer, with a subheading of Connect Directly.

Connect Directly
Enter your connection details below to connect directly to OracleBI Discoverer.
* Indicates required field.

Connect To	OracleBI Discoverer ⌄
* User Name	
* Password	
* Database	
End User Layer	
Locale	Locale retrieved from browser ⌄
	Go

✔ TIP End User Layer names are case-sensitive.

In this illustration you will see that Discoverer offers you a set of connection boxes. Depending upon the type of connection you choose, you will be offered either five or six of the following boxes:

- **Connect To**   This is a mandatory drop-down box. Use this box to select the type of connection that you want to make. You have three choices. These are

    - **Oracle BI Discoverer**   Use this option to connect to standard End User Layers.

    - **Oracle Applications**   Use this option to connect to Oracle Apps End User Layers.

    - **Oracle BI Discoverer for OLAP**   Use this option to connect to OLAP cubes.

- **User Name**   This is a mandatory box; you must enter your username.

- **Password**   This is a mandatory box; you must enter your password.

- **Database**   This is also a mandatory box, and you must enter the database that you wish to connect to. If you are unsure as to what you should enter here, you should contact your Discoverer manager.

NOTE
The connection information is different when you are connecting to a relational or Apps data source and when you are connecting to an OLAP data source. The OLAP connection is discussed in Chapter 16.

■ **End User Layer** This is an optional box and will be displayed only if you are connecting to a standard or Apps EUL. If you find that you cannot connect, try entering the name in uppercase.

■ **Locale or Responsibility** This box changes its context depending upon the connection that you are trying to make. When you are connecting to a standard EUL or to an OLAP database, this box will allow you to set your language locale. Change this to the language you desire to work in. When you are connecting to an Apps-mode EUL, this box will allow you to type your Oracle responsibility.

After you have entered or selected the information, click Go. Provided that you entered the correct information, Discoverer will open up a connection to the selected database. If Discoverer fails to make the connection, you should look at whatever error message is displayed and then take corrective action. In our experience the most usual connection errors are either that you entered an incorrect username/password combination or that you failed to type the EUL name in uppercase.

Connecting to an Application Server Instance
When your system is part of an application server, you will not only be presented with the Connect Directly set of connection information as shown in the illustration in the preceding section, but you will also be presented with the Choose Connection dialog.

There are two types of connection, Public and Private. These are described as follows:

- **Public Connection**   This type of connection uses a set of predefined connection criteria that have been provided for you by your Discoverer manager. All you need to do is click the connection that you want to use. Depending on whether the Discoverer manager has previously set the password for the connection, when you click the connection you will either be connected directly into Plus or Viewer or be prompted for the password. Not all organizations use public connections, and if you have the correct privileges, you may need to create your own private connection. The information about public connections is stored in the infrastructure database of the application server.

- **Private Connection**   This type of connection is predefined by you, or at least by someone who had access to your computer. As the information about private connections is stored as cookies within the computer, you should use private connections only when you are confident that you will be the only person using the computer. If you are not the only person having access to the computer and you still want to use a private connection, we recommend that you create it minus the password. This way, anyone using your computer, including yourself, will always be prompted for the password.

NOTE
Private connections in a stand-alone Discoverer environment use cookies to store details about the connection you create. Therefore, these private connections are available to someone who uses your computer, logs in as you, and uses the same browser; e.g., if you create the connection using Internet Explorer and someone else uses Firefox, that user will not see the private connection that you created. However, if your company is using Single Sign-on (SSO), where Discoverer is attached to an Infrastructure database, your private connection will be stored within the database and thus be available to you no matter which machine you use.

Public and private connections display identically to one another on screen. To identify what type of connection is in use, click the Show button alongside the connection name. Clicking Show displays the following additional detailed information about the connection.

Choose Connection

Create Connection

Details	Connection ▽	Description	Update	Delete
▷Show DISCO			🖉	🗑
▼Hide METADRAKE			🖉	🗑

Connect To OracleBI Discoverer		**Connection Key** cf_a104	
User Name DRAKE		**Connection Type** Public	
Database meta1		**End User Layer** DRAKE	
Locale English			

As you can see, clicking the Show button displays information about the connection type and the user being used for the login, as well as the database and EUL that are being used in the connection.

As previously stated, public connections are created and maintained by your Discoverer manager. You therefore cannot change these types of connection. However, providing that you have the necessary privileges, you are able to create and work with your own private connections.

NOTE
If your organization is using Single Sign-on (SSO), you will see an SSO login screen before the Discoverer connection screen. You can see this login screen in the following illustration. You must enter your SSO username and password. This extra level of security is used to authenticate valid users of the system.

Sign In

Enter your Single Sign-On user name and password to login

User Name ☐
Password ☐

[Login] [Cancel]

Creating a Private Connection   If you can see a button called Create Connection, you have the privilege to create your own private connection. If the "create private connection" privilege has not been switched on, then the button is still visible on the Discoverer Plus/Viewer connections page but is grayed out, so that it cannot be clicked.

To create your own private connection, follow this workflow:

1. Click the button called Create Connection to open the Create Connection dialog box.

Create Connection

Use this page to enter the details of the connection that you wish to create. Choose a name that is easy to remember, followed by an optional description and locale. Enter the account details for this connection before proceeding.

[Cancel] [Apply] [Apply and Connect]

Connection Details
* Indicates required field.

Connect To | OracleBI Discoverer ▾ |

* Name | New Connection |

Description | This is a test for a new connection |

Locale | Locale retrieved from browser ▾ |

Account Details

* User Name | drake |

* Password | ••••• |

* Database | meta |

☑ **TIP** You will be prompted to select an End User Layer and/or an Applications Responsibility if more than one exists.

2. In the Create Connection dialog box you will notice two sections, a section called Connection Details and a section called Account Details.

3. In the Connection Details section, enter the following:

    a. In Connect To, supply the connection type using the drop-down box provided.

    b. In Name, enter a meaningful name for the connection. It is possible to create a private connection using the same name that exists for a public connection, because connections are stored and identified by their connection ID; however, we do not recommend it. We suggest you always use unique names for your connections.

    c. In Description, enter an optional description for this connection. While this step is optional, should you decide to create a private connection using the same name as already exists for a public connection, we recommend using the description to differentiate your connection from the public one.

    d. In Locale, set the default language for this connection.

4. In the Account Details section, enter the following:

    a. In User Name, enter the name of the user to connect by.

    b. In Password, enter the password for the user. If you leave this blank, you will be prompted for the password when you run the connection.

    c. In Database, enter the name of the database you want to use for this connection. The name provided here must equate with a name that exists within the TNSNAMES. ORA file on the server. If you do not know the name of the database, you should ask your Discoverer manager.

5. After you have provided all of the preceding information, click either Apply or Apply And Connect. Discoverer will attempt to connect to the database using the criteria that you provided. If you provided valid criteria, the connection will be created, and if you clicked Apply and Connect, the connection will be executed and you will be connected to the database. However, if you entered any invalid criteria, the connection creation will fail, with a message displayed at the top-left corner of the screen.

NOTE
There are two common reasons for a failed connection. These are an invalid username/password combination and an invalid database name. An invalid username/password combination will result in a "ORA-01017: Invalid username/password; logon denied" message, whereas an invalid database name will result in a "ORA-02154: TNS could not resolve the connect identifier specified" message.

6. If the connection criteria that you provided were correct, you may see a further End User Layer dialog box. This box is displayed when there is more than one EUL available to the user in the database specified. A list of the available EULs will be given. You should select one of them from the drop-down list provided and then click Continue.

NOTE
If you see a message saying "You must upgrade your EUL tables to use this software release," this means that you are attempting to connect to a non-10.1.2 EUL. This is not allowed.

Editing a Private Connection   If you have previously created a private connection, you have the ability to change its definition. To edit an existing private connection, follow this workflow:

1. Locate the private connection that you wish to edit.

2. Click the Update Connection button alongside the connection (it looks like a pencil). This opens up a new screen entitled Update Connection. This screen has three components. These are

   a. The current Connection Details.

   b. The current Account Details.

   c. A Change Password button.

3. Make the required changes to the Connection and Account Details.

4. In addition to the changes that you can make to the Connection and Account Details, you will notice that there is an additional, optional button called Change Password. Click this if you want to change the account password. You will need to know the old password to make this change. Having entered a new password, click Apply; you will be returned to the Update Connection screen.

5. Having made all of the updates, click OK.

6. Once again the connection criteria will be validated. If they are valid, the connection information will be changed. If not, you will need to rework the criteria until you have a valid connection.

Deleting a Private Connection   If you have previously created a private connection, you have the ability to delete it. To delete an existing private connection, follow this workflow:

1. Locate the private connection that you wish to delete.

2. Click the Delete Connection button alongside the connection (it looks like a trash can). This opens up a new screen entitled Warning. This screen has three components. These are

   a. The connection information

   b. The message "You have selected the following connection for deletion. Do you wish to continue?"

   c. Two buttons named No and Yes

3. To delete the connection, click Yes; otherwise, click No or use the back button in your browser to return to the previous screen.

TIP
Unlike Discoverer Desktop, Discoverer Plus is not sticky when it comes to logging you in. If you close your browser, it will not remember who you are or where you were last connected. You will have to type these again. This is part of Oracle's security guidelines for the present, but the authors hope this will be fixed in a future release.

Starting a Workbook

Assuming you have successfully logged in to either Discoverer Desktop or Plus, you are now in the first screen of the Discoverer Workbook Wizard. In Discoverer Desktop, this wizard has the following six workflow steps:

1. Choose whether to open an existing workbook or to create a new one. If you elect to create a new workbook, you will also be prompted to choose the display type. If you open an existing workbook, the workbook opens and the wizard will close.

2. Select items for your worksheet.

3. Define the screen layout.

4. Define any conditions.

5. Define any sort criteria.

6. Define any calculations.

However, in Plus, Oracle has reduced the number of steps in the wizard to five. These are:

1. Choose the worksheet type.

2. Choose items and define conditions and calculations.

3. Define the initial layout.

4. Define an initial sort order.

5. Define parameters.

The steps that you will find in the Plus edition are far more logical than in any of the prior versions of Discoverer. To be honest with you, we never could see the reason for defining the screen layout before defining calculations. This is because you would have to adjust the screen layout again following the addition of any calculations. The new logical ordering of the steps is a big improvement and one that you will surely find easy to work with.

By following the instructions step-by-step, you can quickly be creating queries.

NOTE
It may seem simple enough to use the Workbook Wizard, and you might be asking yourself, "Why do I need this book?" The answer is that using the wizard is easy, but creating an effective query is not. Chapters 10, 11, and 12 will focus on advanced query techniques to help you to create better and more complex queries.

Summary

You have learned the importance of your Discoverer team: the Discoverer manager, the library manager, the DBA, the Apps administrator, and the report writer. Forging a good relationship with each of these important contacts will be of benefit as you become an expert in Discoverer.

We have introduced you to some important terms and features of Discoverer, including managing your workbooks with libraries. You have also learned about SQL queries and how Discoverer manages them. We have explained about Discoverer's Sticky Feature. In addition, we have given you a step-by-step procedure for gaining access to the system. Finally, we showed you how to launch Desktop and Plus in preparation to begin using the Workbook Wizard.

In the next chapter, the fun begins! You will be taken through the first steps of the Workbook Wizard to create what might be your first Discoverer query. In Chapter 5, the remaining steps of the Workbook Wizard will be covered, showing how more complex criteria can be added to your queries using the wizard.

CHAPTER

4

The Workbook Wizard: The Essential Steps

n Chapter 3, you were shown how to launch Discoverer and log in to your database. In this chapter you will learn about the Workbook Wizard and how to go about creating your first query. We call the first four steps the essential steps, in that these are the basic steps that you need to use in order to produce a working query.

We will teach you a simple workflow that you should follow to build your queries. If you follow this workflow, you will find that this is the quickest way to get a new query up and running. We will also teach you how to use constraints in order to avoid creating "The Query from the Twilight Zone," the dreaded query that seems to run forever.

Finally, we show you how to make Discoverer run your query and then teach you how to save it using a meaningful name. We know you will enjoy coming to grips with this brilliant tool, so let's begin.

The Workbook Wizard

As discussed in Chapter 3, the Discoverer Desktop Workbook Wizard has six steps, while Discoverer Plus has only five steps, but all of the functionality. However, the quickest way to build a new query is to use only four of the steps. These steps form a simple workflow and will be covered in this chapter.

The Workbook Wizard Steps

As previously stated, depending upon which version of Discoverer you are using, the number of steps in the wizard will change. In the following sections, we tell you the ordering of the steps in both versions. We also tell you at a glance which of the steps are essential and which are optional.

Desktop Steps

In Discoverer Desktop, there are six steps to the Workbook Wizard. These are

- Choose worksheet type—essential

- Choose items—essential

- Define the initial layout—essential

- Define conditions—essential

- Define an initial sort order—optional

- Define calculations—optional

Plus Steps

In Discoverer Plus, there are five steps to the workbook wizard. These are

- Choose worksheet type—essential

- Choose items, define conditions and calculations—first two essential, calculations are optional

- Define the initial layout—essential

- Define an initial sort order—optional

- Define parameters—optional

As you can see, the overall number of steps in Plus has been reduced. The sequencing of the steps has also been changed, which, in our opinion, is a great step forward. We never could understand why you would ever want to define the initial layout before having created calculations. This is because as soon as you create a calculation, you would need to revisit the layout to determine where to place that calculation.

A Simple Workflow

In this chapter, we will take you through the essential steps by applying the following workflow:

1. Choose a worksheet type.
2. Choose the items.
3. Arrange the layout of the data.
4. Define conditions to avoid the "Query from the Twilight Zone."
5. Finish.

If you follow the preceding workflow, omitting the optional steps of the Workbook Wizard, you can quickly generate a new query.

The Workbook Wizard Options

When you first open the Desktop Workbook Wizard, as seen in Figure 4-1, or the Plus Wizard, as shown in Figure 4-2, you are prompted whether to create a new workbook or open an existing workbook. As you can see, Discoverer displays a graphic on the left-hand side. As you move through the steps of the Workbook Wizard, the graphic changes to represent the step that you are currently working in. In Discoverer Plus you will see some cool new features in the background. Just ignore them for now (if you can).

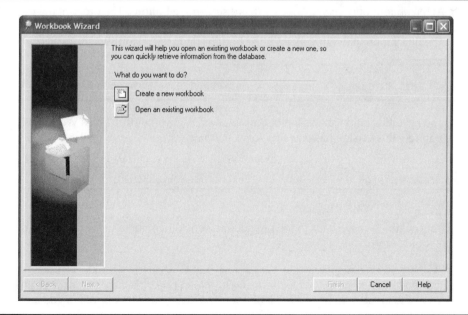

FIGURE 4-1 *The Desktop Workbook Wizard, screen one*

FIGURE 4-2 *The 10.1.2 Plus Workbook Wizard, screen one*

At the bottom of each Workbook Wizard screen are buttons. The order of the buttons varies, but the functionality is the same.

The illustration that follows shows the buttons on the Desktop Workbook Wizard:

The next illustration shows the buttons on the Discoverer 10.1.2 Plus Workbook Wizard. As you can see, this version has one additional button.

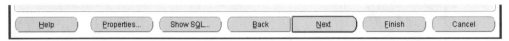

Back
Use this button to move back to the previous screen. When you are on screen one of the Workbook Wizard, this button is inactive (gray).

Next
Use this button to move to the next screen. On screen one, this button is inactive until you tell Discoverer to create a new workbook or open an existing workbook. When you are on the final screen of the Workbook Wizard, this button is inactive (because there is no next!).

Options/Properties

In Desktop this button is called Options, while in Plus the button has been renamed to Properties. Whatever name you see, use this button to set up defaults for query formats and display settings. These will be covered in detail in Chapter 14. When you are on screen one of the Workbook Wizard, this button is grayed out until you get to screen two. Should you wish to set any of these attributes, you should do so when you get to screen two.

Finish

Use this button to tell Discoverer that you have finished creating the query. This is not available on the first screen unless you have moved to screen two and then come back. It is possible to create a query that does not select anything from the database. This is not a bug, and there may be good reasons to do just this. For example, you could create a query that returns the current fiscal month, using functions only. This query could be saved as a template for future queries that may need to use the fiscal month.

> **NOTE**
> *You can click Finish at any time; however, choosing Finish too soon can result in "The Query from the Twilight Zone" (this will be covered later in this chapter).*

Cancel

Use this button to tell Discoverer that you don't want to continue with the current query.

Help

In Desktop, this button opens a standard Windows help file on using the Workbook Wizard. In Plus, it opens a second browser and displays the Discoverer Plus online help (in HTML format). The help that has been provided by Oracle is excellent and is highly recommended. It is very detailed and informative and will help you through most workbook creation issues.

Show SQL (Discoverer Plus only)

This button opens the SQL Inspector dialog box, which allows you to view and copy the SQL for the items you select for the query. The dialog box also has a tab called Plan that allows you to look at the explain plan for the SQL that Discoverer is generating. Please be aware that the explain plan you see here is not necessarily the explain plan for the final query that will be submitted to the database. This is because the Oracle database has a feature called optimization. This feature grants the database permission to look at any query that gets submitted to it and adjust the SQL to the form that is the most efficient. The dialog box will remain empty, and the button grayed out, until you select at least one item.

NOTE
If you are familiar with other Windows applications, you might be in the habit of using keyboard hot keys or shortcut keys instead of your mouse. Both versions of Discoverer make these keys available throughout, although there are some minor differences between the versions. If you have not used hot keys or shortcut keys before, they are a combination of either the ALT or CTRL keys with another key. For example, on screen one of the Workbook Wizard, ALT-N selects Next. You can tell which key to press by looking for the letter that has the underscore.

Workbook Wizard Step 1: Create a New Workbook or Open an Existing Workbook

Upon successfully getting past the login screen, you will be taken to the first screen of the Workbook Wizard. This window has buttons to Create a new workbook or Open an existing workbook. You have the option to make additional choices at this point in Discoverer Plus. For now we will not select them, but how to use them will become apparent as we go on. We will begin by creating a new workbook.

Create a New Workbook

While both versions intrinsically do the same thing, the mode of operation is sufficiently different to warrant separate explanations for Plus and Desktop.

Desktop   From the initial screen of the Workbook Wizard, select Create a new workbook. This brings up the second part of the initial screen of the Workbook Wizard. In Desktop, Discoverer now asks you "How do you want to display the results" and then displays four buttons for Table, Page-Detail Table, Crosstab, and Page-Detail Crosstab, as shown in Figure 4-3.

Discoverer Plus   Screen one of the Discoverer Plus Workbook Wizard contains all of the choices that are available on the first two screens of the Desktop Workbook Wizard. However, your options are now displayed as check boxes and radio buttons instead of buttons, but their functionality is the same. You will also note that on this page you can add a graph, add a title, and add a text area to your workbook. As these are not essential to building a query, we will not show these features in this chapter, but we will show them to you in subsequent chapters.

   These are the check boxes and radio buttons for the various objects that can be displayed in your worksheet:

■   **Title**   Check this box if you want to display a title for your worksheet. As this is not essential to building a query, we recommend you uncheck this at this time. You can enable it later, when you have finished creating your query and are getting ready to turn it into a report. Please see Chapter 6 for more information.

- **Page Items**   Uncheck this box if you do not want to create a worksheet with page items. By default this is enabled.

- **Crosstab/Table**   Use these radio buttons to tell Discoverer that you want to create a crosstab (pivot table) or table. The default is Table.

- **Graph**   Uncheck this box if you do not want to create and display a graph during worksheet creation. Unless you are an expert worksheet creator, and as this is not essential to creating a query, we do not recommend creating graphs at this time. The time to add a graph is after you have converted your query into a report. Chapter 7 discusses graphing in detail. If you decide that you do want to create your graph now, check the box and then use the Placement drop-down to tell Discoverer where to place the graph. By default, graphing is enabled and the placement will be below the crosstab or table.

- **Text Area**   Check this box to enable a text area that will display at the bottom of the worksheet. In this text area you will place additional information, hints, and suggestions that will help the user execute your worksheet. Once again, as this is not essential to creating a query, we recommend you uncheck this box at this time. The use of the text area is discussed in Chapter 5.

FIGURE 4-3   *Workbook Wizard, Step 1, with display type buttons*

NOTE
You can change the default settings for the Title and Text Area using Tools | Options. Please refer to Plus Options in the Sheet Format section of Chapter 15 for more information. Unfortunately, the defaults for Page Items, Crosstab, Table, and Graph are not under your control.

Select the objects to display in the worksheet

☐ Title

☑ Page Items

○ Crosstab ● Table

☑ Graph

Placement: Graph below Table

☐ Text Area

Example:

There are four display choices for a query:

- Table

- Crosstab

- Page-Detail Table

- Page-Detail Crosstab

NOTE
Discoverer Desktop remembers the type of display you used last and offers it as the default for your next worksheet.

Table

For anyone experienced with spreadsheets, the table is a familiar sight. In the table, data is organized in rows (across) and columns (down). By default, Discoverer numbers the output rows down the left-hand side and assigns names to the column headings as defined by your Discoverer Manager. Typically these names come from the source database. Tables are essentially data organized in a list. In Discoverer, you can rename the column headings to make them more meaningful. You can even turn off the row numbers. This will be covered later in the chapter.

Crosstab (Pivot Table)

The Crosstab option, short for cross-tabulation, will be less familiar to some end users than the standard table. In a crosstab, the interrelationship of two or more sets of data is viewed. This multidimensional view of data is one of the most exciting features of Discoverer. Crosstabs can look at data from various sources and allow the user to view the interrelationships of the data "on the fly." For those familiar with the Excel pivot table, the functionality is similar. However, the Discoverer crosstab is far easier to use and the data much easier to access.

NOTE
You might hear the output of a crosstab referred to as multidimensional. That is because a crosstab is made up of at least two dimensions of data: one item for the column edge (at the right) and one for the data points or row edge (the data you actually see in the table). You can also add a row edge axis (at the top) and a page axis (in the Page Items area); these are nice to have but are not essential. In Discoverer, you can have multiple items in the top and side axes, giving you greater power in your analysis of the data. We will look more closely at multidimensional data in Chapter 9, when we discuss analysis.

In Figure 4-4, the data from the Products folder is shown as a table.

In the standard table, you see the data as a list of related items. This is fine for most types of output, but where more analysis is needed, or where the list is pages long, the crosstab can be a better choice. In Figure 4-5, the same data is shown as a crosstab.

Page-Detail Tables and Page-Detail Crosstabs

A page detail is used when there is a large amount of data to display. In this type of worksheet, an element or elements of the data are moved to the page axis. Page items are ideal when you want to view your data one slice at a time.

NOTE
Page detail refers to the overall concept of opening up the page axis, and is the final result that you see in your query. The page axis is the space at the top of the worksheet labeled Page Items. It is into this area that you place data items from the table or crosstab.

Oracle Business Intelligence Discoverer Desktop - [First Workbook.DIS]					

File Edit View Sheet Format Tools Graph Window Help

Double-click here to edit this title.

	Prodid	▸ Product Name	Product Size	Unit Cost SUM	Unit Price SUM	▸ Line Name
▸ 1	11	DS-1200	MINI	3.85	5.35	MINI-WIDGET
▸ 2	12	MS-1200	MINI	3.95	5.55	MINI-WIDGET
▸ 3	13	MS-1300	MINI	4.10	6.00	MINI-WIDGET
▸ 4	14	DS-1300	MINI	4.02	5.95	MINI-WIDGET
▸ 5	21	AB-2000	SMALL	7.22	13.50	WONDER-WIDGET
▸ 6	22	AB-2500	SMALL	5.99	12.75	MEGA-WIDGET
▸ 7	23	AB-3000	SMALL	9.88	21.25	SUPER-WIDGET
▸ 8	41	QB-5000	MEDIUM	8.33	17.66	WONDER-WIDGET
▸ 9	42	QB-5500	MEDIUM	8.33	17.66	WONDER-WIDGET
▸ 10	43	QB-6000	MEDIUM	8.33	17.66	WONDER-WIDGET
▸ 11	44	CD-100	MEDIUM	6.21	15.25	MEGA-WIDGET
▸ 12	45	CD-200	MEDIUM	6.21	15.25	MEGA-WIDGET
▸ 13	46	AVR-500	MEDIUM	11.48	26.95	SUPER-WIDGET
▸ 14	47	AVR-550	MEDIUM	11.48	26.95	SUPER-WIDGET
▸ 15	61	QB-1000	LARGE	12.42	23.45	WONDER-WIDGET
▸ 16	62	QB-2000	LARGE	12.42	23.45	WONDER-WIDGET
▸ 17	63	QB-3000	LARGE	12.42	23.45	WONDER-WIDGET
▸ 18	64	CD-500	LARGE	10.62	22.18	MEGA-WIDGET
▸ 19	65	CD-550	LARGE	10.62	22.18	MEGA-WIDGET
▸ 20	66	CD-625	LARGE	10.62	22.18	MEGA-WIDGET
▸ 21	67	AVR-800	LARGE	15.94	34.65	SUPER-WIDGET
▸ 22	68	AVR-900	LARGE	15.94	34.65	SUPER-WIDGET

Sheet 1 / Sheet 2 \ Sheet 3 \ Sheet

FIGURE 4-4 *A Standard Discoverer table*

There are two reasons for using page detail:

■ When you have a large amount of data to display and you want to use drop-down lists. This will, in essence, give you multiple sheets, one behind the other.

NOTE
Page detail worksheets should be used sparingly, as they consume a lot of memory. The most efficient type of worksheet is the table.

■ When you have a unique constraint (applied as a condition). For example, take a look at Figure 4-5. If we had opted to place a condition on the product size so that only medium sizes were selected, we would be wasting a column by leaving the size item in the main body of the table. We should move the product size to the page axis.

Figure 4-4 shows all sizes of widgets and widget model numbers. In a real business database there might be thousands of part numbers or even millions. By moving one or more items from the body of the table to the page axis, you can choose to see only one part of the table at a time. In Figures 4-6 and 4-7, you can see that we have moved the product size to the page axis. Size becomes a drop-down list, and you can view each size individually.

FIGURE 4-5   *Products folder shown as a crosstab*

FIGURE 4-6   *The Products folder shown as a table with page detail*

FIGURE 4-7 *The Products folder shown as a crosstab with page detail*

TIP
After you have selected your data and run the query, look to see if you have a single item being selected in a column. If you have, turn on the page-detail feature and move the item to the top of the page. To turn on page items, from the menu bar, select View | Page Items.

Open an Existing Workbook

Whenever you open an existing workbook, Discoverer does one of three things, depending upon your preferred options. The three alternatives are as follows:

- Ask for confirmation (the default).

- Run the query automatically.

- Don't run the query and leave the sheet empty.

The mechanism for setting these options is explained in Chapter 14.

NOTE
If your preference is to be prompted, and you have multiple worksheets, then one of Discoverer's Sticky Features remembers which worksheet you had open last. Discoverer calls this the active worksheet. This is the one that is prompted. As you navigate into each of the other worksheets, Discoverer will prompt you again. However, if your preference is for the worksheets to run automatically, and you have multiple worksheets, Discoverer runs the last one you had open. As you navigate to the other worksheets, Discoverer runs them automatically.

Workbook Wizard Step 2: Selecting the Data

The next step in creating a query is to select the data you want. After selecting the display type, click Next. This brings up the second step of the Workbook Wizard, shown in Figures 4-8 and 4-9.

The Desktop Window

The Desktop window, as shown in Figure 4-8, has the following three areas:

- A folders, items, and business area selection box with the heading Available

- A box with the heading Selected where you place your choices

- A Find button, with the icon of a flashlight. Clicking this button opens the Find dialog box.

The Find dialog boxes are described later in this chapter.

FIGURE 4-8 *The Desktop Workbook Wizard Step 2*

FIGURE 4-9 *The Plus Workbook Wizard Step 2*

The Plus Step 2 Window

The Plus window, as shown in Figure 4-9, has the following five areas:

■ A selection box, with the heading Available, that has three tabs: an Items tab, a Conditions tab, and a Calculations tab. Inside the Items tab you will see the business areas, folders, and items that are available for selection within the worksheet. Items that are being used within the worksheet have a tick mark alongside them. This will help you easily identify what is in use and what is not. If you see an unchecked item and decide that you would like to use it, right-click the item and from the pop-up menu, select Add to Worksheet. Similarly, you can remove an existing item from the worksheet by selecting Remove from Worksheet from the same menu.

■ A box with the heading Selected where you place your choices.

■ A Views drop-down, located immediately above the Selected box. This drop-down allows you to alter the display in the Selected box. By default, the folder names are hidden. Clicking Views pops up a box from where you can choose to either Show Folders or Hide Folders.

■ A set of four additional buttons:

■ **New** Use this button to create new conditions, calculations, percentages, and totals.

- **Edit** Use this button to edit existing conditions, calculations, percentages, and totals.

- **Show** Use this button to show the details about predefined conditions. You will not be allowed to edit the condition, but you will be able to see the criteria that your Discoverer manager used to create it.

- **Delete** Use this button to delete a user-defined condition, calculation, percentage, or total.

■ A Find button, with the icon of a flashlight. Clicking this button opens the Find dialog box. The Find dialog boxes are described later in this chapter.

You can select from a business area to which you have access. Each business area contains folders, and within the folders are the items you will select to create your query.

NOTE
You will notice that there are two additional tabs available in the Plus Workbook Wizard Step 2. These tabs, titled Conditions and Calculations, allow you to create and apply conditions and calculations. You can add conditions at this point, or you can come back to it before running the query. Remember, we always recommend adding conditions before running a new query. We do not suggest you add calculations at this point. We will show you how to do this later.

Choosing a Business Area

The first thing you must do is choose the business area you want to work with from the Available drop-down list. If the one you want is not shown, press the down arrow and select the business area from the list, as shown here.

NOTE
Discoverer Desktop remembers the name of the business area you were last working with. When you come back to create another workbook, Discoverer inserts as the default that business area. In the current release, Plus does not do this. It is hoped that this feature will be incorporated into a future release of Plus.

Choosing a Folder

Once you have selected the business area you want, Discoverer displays a list of all the folders that are available to you from that business area, as shown in Figure 4-10. Open a folder you want to use by clicking the plus sign to the left of the folder. Each folder contains a list of items. These items form the basis of your query.

Choosing an Item

Having chosen a folder to work with, you are ready to select the item(s) from that folder. There are three ways to do this:

■ **Point and click** Point to the item you want, click it to highlight it, and then click the selection arrow as shown here.

■ **Drag and drop** Click the item you want and drag it over into the Selected box.

FIGURE 4-10 *Folders open, showing the items*

■ **Add to worksheet** In Plus only, right-click the item you want and from the pop-up box select Add to Worksheet.

TIP

If you have decided to include more than one item from the same folder, you can select multiple items by holding down the control (CTRL) key and clicking each of the items you want to select. As you click them, they will be highlighted. When you have them all selected, click the selection arrow, or click one of the highlighted items and drag it (and the others) into the Selected box, as shown in Figure 4-11.

When an item is selected, the selection arrow becomes active. When there are one or more items in the Selected box and you highlight one of them, the de-selection arrow is activated. Use the de-selection arrow to remove unwanted items from the selected box.

FIGURE 4-11 *Items selected for the query*

In Discoverer Plus you can view the selected items with the folders shown or hidden.

Finding an Item in Desktop

When using Discoverer Desktop, if you are not sure whether or not an item exists within the business area that you have selected, use the Find dialog box. This dialog box allows you to search for items in the business area, producing a list of all items that match the search criteria.

To use the Find dialog box to locate an item, follow this workflow:

1. Click the Find button. Discoverer opens the Find dialog box shown here:

NOTE
The Find button is located to the right of the Discoverer business area drop-down list. This button has the icon of a flashlight on it.

2. Type the name or partial name of the item that you want to search for into the Find What box.

3. In the Look In box, select the business area you want Discoverer to use for the search. Click the arrow to obtain a drop-down list of your available business areas. To tell Discoverer to search all business areas, select the item called All Business Areas.

4. Check Match Whole Word Only if you want Discoverer to find an exact match.

5. Check Match Case if you want Discoverer to match the case.

6. Click Find. Discoverer searches the business area and displays a list of all items matching the criteria you entered. In the following illustration, we asked Discoverer to search for items containing the word "cost." As you can see, Discoverer located an item called "Cost Price" in the sales folder, and a second item called "Unit Cost" in the products folder.

7. From the list of items, highlight the one that you want to use.

8. Click Go To. Discoverer closes the Find dialog box and returns you to the Workbook Wizard Step 2. The folder containing the item is automatically opened; the item that you found will be highlighted and available for selection.

9. If Discoverer could not find an item matching the search criteria, this dialog box is displayed. As you can see, Discoverer informs you that the search has failed and prompts you to try again. To abandon the search at this point, click Cancel.

In our opinion, this ability of Discoverer to locate items in business areas is excellent. We recommend that you use the preceding workflow frequently, especially when you are not sure whether or not the item exists.

Finding an Item in Plus

Just as you did for Desktop, when using Discoverer Plus, you can use a Find button to search for items in the business area, producing a list of all items that match the search criteria.

To use the Find dialog box in Plus to locate an item, follow this workflow:

1. Click the Find button. Discoverer opens the Find dialog box shown here:

NOTE
*As in Desktop, the Find button is located to the right of the Discoverer
business area drop-down list. This button has the icon of a flashlight
on it.*

2. Use the Search In box to select the business area you want Discoverer to use for the
   search. Click the arrow to obtain a drop-down list of your available business areas. To
   tell Discoverer to search all business areas, select the item called All Business Areas.

3. Use the Search By box to tell Discoverer what search action to take. The available search
   actions are

   ■ Contains

   ■ Starts with

   ■ Ends with

   ■ Exactly matches

4. In the Search For box, you should type the name or partial name of the item that you
   want to search for.

5. Check the Case-sensitive button if you want Discoverer to match the case.

6. Click Go. Discoverer searches the business area and displays a list of all items matching
   the criteria you entered. In the following illustration, we asked Discoverer to search for
   items containing the word "cost." As you can see, Discoverer located an item called "Cost
   Price" in the sales folder, and a second item called "Unit Cost" in the products folder.

7. From the list of items, highlight the one that you want to use.

8. Click OK. Discoverer closes the Find dialog box and returns you to the Workbook Wizard Step 2. The folder containing the item is automatically opened; the item that you found will be highlighted and available for selection.

9. If Discoverer could not find an item matching the search criteria, the following message is displayed: "No values were found matching your request. Try typing a different word or phrase, or selecting a different option from the dropdown list in the search area above." As you can see, Discoverer informs you that the search has failed and prompts you to try again. To abandon the search at this point, click Cancel.

Item Types

Discoverer uses icons to represent different types of data and the options you have to choose from when making your selections. These types of data and options are as follows:

- Strings and dates

- Numbers

- Predefined conditions

Strings and Dates   The icon to the left is the one you will see most often. It represents either strings (names, cities, customers, etc.) or dates. If the item has a plus sign to the left of it, you have some options for placing constraints on the data. This is called a list of values (LOV).

Plus sign indicating ——————— a list of values

For example, if the Customer folder contains an item called postcode and this item has a plus sign, clicking the plus sign gives you a list of customer postcodes. If you are interested only in seeing the data for selected postcodes, you can choose only those postcodes you want to see, thus applying a constraint.

NOTE
If you cannot see a plus sign next to a data item, and you believe that a list of values would help you create your queries more efficiently, you should speak with your Discoverer manager. He or she has the ability to create these lists for you.

Numbers   The data represented by this icon (it is supposed to look like a numeric keypad) is numeric, like selling and cost prices. When you click the plus sign next to an item with this icon, you have at least six subitems to choose from. If you don't choose, the choice is made for you and defaults to whatever the Discoverer manager has set up. Most often this will be SUM (the default will be in boldface, as shown in Figure 4-12).

The following is the list of available choices and their definitions. You will not always see all of these options, as the type of data and how your Discoverer manager has set it up determines what is available. It is also possible to have an LOV with numeric items. When such a list exists, it will appear before the other available functions.

■ **SUM**   Returns a sum of all the values.

■ **COUNT**   Returns the number of values in the query where the expression is not null.

■ **MAX**   Finds the maximum value of the expression.

■ **MIN**   Finds the minimum value of the expression.

■ **AVG**   Computes the mathematical average.

■ **Detail**   This does not apply any aggregation. For example, if you have a line-detail table that is showing shipments for the same line over several days, select Detail if you want to see one row per shipment. If you select SUM, you will see a single row with all of the shipment details totaled (including the line number!).

NOTE
If you forget what each of the items does, simply click the item and the Workbook Wizard status bar gives the description.

Predefined Conditions   If you are familiar with Microsoft Excel and Access, you will recognize this as the Filter by Item icon. In Discoverer, it serves a similar function. Your Discoverer manager can set predefined conditions and add them to the business area.

For example, assume you don't give credit to some of your customers. You need a report showing which of your customers have a credit limit and what the amounts are. It makes sense to ask your Discoverer manager to create a predefined condition on the item Credit Limit, which will include only customers with a credit limit greater than zero. The condition appears in the folder like any of the other items and can be identified by the Predefined Condition icon (the filter). You can select the condition for your query, but if you don't want to use it, you don't have to.

FIGURE 4-12   *Numeric item with default in bold*

By selecting a predefined condition, you won't need to create one of your own when setting up your queries. Predefined conditions can be applied or deactivated at any time by right-clicking the condition and from the drop-down list select Remove From Worksheet (see Figure 4-13). You will be shown in Chapter 13 how to use predefined conditions and apply other conditions to your queries.

> **NOTE**
> *Predefined conditions can be optional or mandatory. Mandatory conditions are always applied, and not visible to the end user.*

> **NOTE**
> *Predefined conditions are created by the Discoverer manager. They cannot be modified except by the Discoverer manager. However, the end user can combine two or more conditions defined by the manager to create a complex condition. If the condition you want is not covered by any predefined condition or combination of conditions, you will need to create one of your own. Complex conditions are explained in Chapter 12.*

Selecting Items for Your Query

The order in which the chosen items are displayed in the Selected box is governed by the following:

- The folder in which the item resides.

- The ordering of the items in that folder. If your Discoverer manager listed the folders alphabetically, then the order of the folders in the Selected box will be alphabetical—no matter in what order you made your selections.

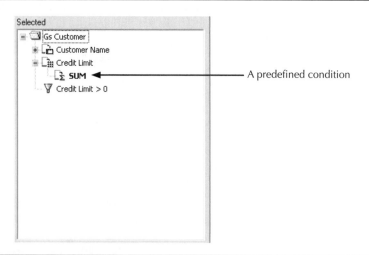

FIGURE 4-13   *Query using a predefined condition*

NOTE

This note is for managers who may be reading this section. If you arrange the ordering of the folders in the order in which your users will most likely need them, this will speed up the selection process. Similarly, you might order the items within a folder by placing the most commonly used items near the top of the list. Both of these tips will help your users make their selections quicker.

A very useful feature of the product is that when an item has been selected, only the folders that have links to the chosen item remain active. This helps you to know where the links are, and what data is available to use in the query. When folders are not available to you for selection, they will be grayed out. However, you can still see the items inside the folder by clicking the plus key.

NOTE

Your Discoverer manager can set the ordering of the folders and items in the most logical order for you to select. If you believe that the ordering is not correct, you can ask him or her to change it.

Discoverer knows about the links between the folders, and you should make a point to read your company's documentation in order to know which folders link together. You will have to select from the folders in a logical sequence.

NOTE

If you are using Noetix Views, we recommend that you have the Noetix Views Help file open when you are making your selections. The help provided by Noetix is probably one of the best online help manuals around. Not only does the help file describe the folders and the items in them, but it also tells you which folders can be joined to the current folder. For more details on using Noetix Views, refer to Appendix C.

Workbook Wizard Step 3: Arranging the Order of the Output

The next step in creating a query is to arrange the order of the output. After selecting the data you want to view, click Next.

NOTE

Don't worry about conditions just yet; we will get to these in the next section.

This brings up the third screen of the Workbook Wizard, in which you arrange the order you want the data displayed. No matter which order you selected the items, Discoverer will always display them in the order of their listing within the business area. The Wizard Step 3 screen, shown in Figure 4-14, is the place where Discoverer gives you a chance to change that order and make two other choices.

FIGURE 4-14 *Workbook Wizard Step 3: Arranging the order of the output*

You can choose to:

■ Show Page Items

■ Hide Duplicate Rows

Show Page Items

Check this box if you want to turn the table or crosstab into a page-detail table or crosstab (we will show more examples of page-detail tables and crosstabs in Chapter 9).

NOTE
If you did not select page items in Workbook Wizard Step 1, you can choose it now. This will cause Discoverer to open a new box called Page Items. This new box will be located above the column headings.

Hide Duplicate Rows

Depending upon the data you have selected, you may find that your query has two or more identical rows. If you want to see only one of these you should check this box.

In the following example, Global Widgets sells products to 39 customers in 17 countries. We want a report that shows only a distinct listing of the countries that Global Widgets has customers in. The GS_Customer folder has information about customers. In this table there are items called City Name and Country Code. Building a worksheet that selects only the Country Code from the GS_Customers folder, without checking the Hide Duplicate Rows box, will produce a list with 39 country codes, some of which are duplicates.

In Figure 4-15, you will notice that the US and GB are listed several times, while BR, MX, and PT are listed twice. For the sake of the preceding example, we want to see each country listed only once.

With the Hide Duplicate Rows box checked, the list now contains only the 17 countries in which we have customers. Looking at the list in Figure 4-16, you will see that BR, GB, MX, PT, and US are listed only once. This satisfies the requirement to see what countries have customers.

NOTE
You won't always want to hide duplicate rows; in fact, your report might be inaccurate if you do. You can use duplicate rows for a more complex view of the data.

	Country Code
12	BR
13	GB
14	GB
15	FR
16	IT
17	ES
18	US
19	US
20	US
21	US
22	CA
23	MX
24	MX
25	BR
26	JP
27	HK
28	KR
29	CH
30	US
31	US
32	US
33	US
34	PE
35	PL
36	US
37	US
38	CL
39	US

FIGURE 4-15 *Country code from GS Customers with duplicates*

	Country Code
1	BR
2	CA
3	CH
4	CL
5	ES
6	FR
7	GB
8	HK
9	IT
10	JP
11	KR
12	MX
13	PE
14	PH
15	PL
16	PT
17	US

FIGURE 4-16   *Country code from GS Customers without duplicates*

Arranging the Order of the Columns

To change the order of the columns, simply click the column you want to move and drag it to the desired location. If you have selected a large number of items for the query, you may not be able to see them all onscreen. You should start by locating the item you want to display in column 1 and move it first, following with each of the other items in turn.

TIP
If you cannot see column 1 onscreen and you need to move the current column to that position, you should click the column you want to move, hold down the mouse button, and drag the item off the active screen (which will reset). Now move the item to the desired position and then release the mouse button. This now works in Plus as well as in Desktop. In previous versions of Plus you had to move the item over as far as you can, and then scroll over and move it again.

Workbook Wizard Step 4: Setting User-Defined Conditions

The next step in creating a query is to set the conditions. After arranging the table layout in Desktop, click Next. In Discoverer Plus, conditions are set on the previous screen, so you need to click the Back button to return to Step 2, and then select the Conditions tab.

What Are Conditions?

Conditions are constraints, criteria, or filters that you apply to your query. All of these terms can be used interchangeably. If you have used other products such as Microsoft Access, you are used to the terms *criteria* and *filters* in query writing. In terms of SQL, a condition is a "where" clause.

A condition is a set of criteria that filters data in a worksheet. You use a condition when you want to limit the amount of data or refine the level of detail in the sheet. You are essentially eliminating data that you do not want to view or analyze.

The following three examples illustrate the concept of conditions in queries:

■ You know that fiscal quarter 2 is always the best for sales and you want to analyze sales data from that quarter in order to produce a presentation for your shareholders. You can set a condition that will return only the numbers for quarter 2 and filter out everything else. The condition quarter=Q2 will satisfy this example.

■ Your company has one salesperson per district and rewards them by giving a vacation to all who have generated sales in excess of ten million. By setting a condition that reports district sales revenue in excess of ten million, you can tell at a glance who gets the all-expense-paid trip to the Bahamas for two. The condition Revenue>10000000 will meet the requirement for this query.

■ You have decided to create a report analyzing the margin between sales and costs. In order to do this correctly, you need to exclude zero-cost items from the query. Setting a condition Cost<>0 will give you the numbers you need.

You are not restricted in the number of conditions you may create. However, there is a trade-off between applying conditions and query performance. Ideally, you should attempt to apply your conditions to items that are indexed. If you do this, you will improve the performance of the query. Applying conditions to nonindexed items could have a negative impact on performance. The more nonindexed conditions you apply, the longer your query could take to run. Check with your Discoverer manager or system documentation to see which database items are indexed.

NOTE
If you have NoetixViews, you should look inside the Noetix Views Help file. Open the folder containing the item you want to apply the condition to and look to see if the item name begins with A$. Noetix uses this prefix to indicate which items are indexed. It is strongly recommended to always apply conditions to these items, if at all possible. For more information concerning NoetixViews, see Appendix C.

Creating Conditions in Desktop

Having clicked Next on the previous screen, you will now be in the fourth screen of the Workbook Wizard, as shown in Figure 4-17. This window contains three boxes:

■ **View Conditions for**   A drop-down box where you can choose to view conditions for all items, the active items, or a specific item only

■ **Conditions**   A list box showing all of the conditions based upon the selection made in the View Conditions for drop-down box

■ **Description**   A box showing the description of the condition highlighted in the conditions box

FIGURE 4-17 *Desktop Worbook Wizard Step 4: setting up User-defined conditions*

The screen also contains three new buttons:

- **New** This button is used to create a new condition.

- **Edit/Show** This button toggles between Edit, for conditions that you can edit, and Show, for predefined conditions that you cannot edit but can view in the Show Conditions window.

- **Delete** Be careful using this one. It does just what it says and without prompting! You can use the Undo feature to undo the delete operation, but it is best not to delete the condition in the first place.

View Conditions for Drop-down Box You will need to select one of the items from the "View Conditions for" drop-down box. The choices are described here:

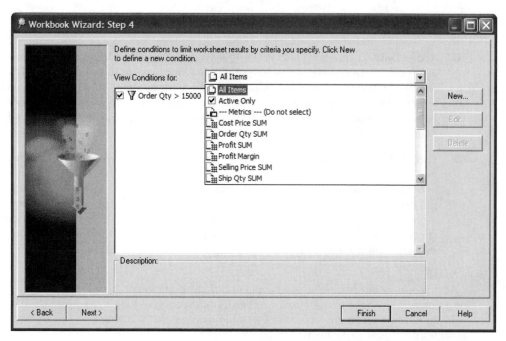

- **All Items** This is the default and will show all conditions used within the entire workbook. If you have more than one worksheet in the workbook, viewing conditions for all items will list those conditions from the other worksheets as well as the one you are working on. This could be confusing, and you might delete a condition by accident because you believed you did not need it. You might have a workbook with worksheets from different business areas. If you try to select a condition that applies to an item that is not used in the current worksheet's business area, you will get the following error message in Desktop:

This issue does not arise in Plus because Plus will not allow you to select incompatible conditions or items.

- **Active Only** This option allows you to view only those conditions that are being used in the current worksheet. If you have multiple worksheets in the workbook and they use completely different sets of items, perhaps even from different business areas, you may want to select this option. It will, in some situations, help reduce confusion to use the Active Only option; however, *use this option with care.* You might already have the exact condition created, but you will not know it if you select Active Only.

- **Specific Items** Discoverer maintains a list of all the items in your query, whether or not they have conditions. Clicking the down arrow not only lists the options already referred to but also includes all the items in the query. You may choose to view the conditions for just one of these items. If you have multiple conditions on the same item and your query is producing unexpected results, you will probably find that you have a wrongly defined condition. Selecting to view the conditions for just the item concerned will allow you to ascertain where the error lies.

NOTE
After you have finished debugging your conditions, don't forget to switch the view back to All Items or Active Only. If you save the query and exit, when you come back into the worksheet Discoverer will reset the view to All Items.

Conditions The large box in the middle of the window shown in Figure 4-18 contains the conditions (predefined and user defined) available for use in this workbook. When you have more than one condition, Discoverer will highlight by default the first condition in the box.

FIGURE 4-18 *Workbook Wizard Step 4*

NOTE
There is a Sticky Feature that will remember the last condition you selected and that will be the one highlighted when you come back to the conditions step of the Workbook Wizard.

Description   The gray box below the list of conditions contains a description of the selected condition in the box shown earlier in Figure 4-18.

Condition description

In this box, Discoverer will display a description of the highlighted condition. You may use this "at a glance" feature to get help on the condition. Many conditions are short and sweet, and you can view the entire condition without even looking in the Description box. However, some conditions are complex, and the Description box can display the user- or manager-defined description of the condition. If no description has been provided, Discoverer will display the condition itself.

The New, Edit, and Show Buttons   These buttons open three windows that appear to be identical but function in slightly different ways. The only evidence you have of which window you are in is the title bar.

- **New**   Use this button to open the New Condition dialog box, shown in Figure 4-19, to create a condition to use in your query.

- **Edit**   Use this button to open the Edit Condition dialog box. This button is visible only when you have selected a condition that you can edit. An example of an editable condition is one you or another user has defined or a constraint you applied in Step 2 of the Workbook Wizard.

- **Show**   Use this button to open the Show Conditions dialog box. This button is visible only when you have selected a condition that cannot be edited. Predefined conditions cannot be edited, but you can view how the condition was created.

FIGURE 4-19 *The Desktop New Condition dialog box*

These dialog boxes will be shown in greater detail in Chapter 7, along with how to create useful and meaningful conditions.

Creating Conditions in Plus

Having clicked the Back button on the previous screen, you will now be returned to the second screen of the Workbook Wizard. As already mentioned earlier, this screen has three tabs. To get to the section of the screen that handles conditions, click the Conditions tab as shown in Figure 4-20. This window contains five areas:

■ A selection box, with the heading Available, that has three tabs: an Items tab, a Conditions tab, and a Calculations tab. Inside the Conditions tab you will see the predefined and user-defined conditions that are available for selection within the worksheet. Conditions that are being used within the worksheet have a tick mark alongside them. This will help you easily identify what is in use and what is not. If you see an unchecked condition and decide that you would like to use it, right-click the condition and, from the pop-up menu, select Add to Worksheet. Similarly, you can unhook an existing condition from the worksheet by selecting Remove from Worksheet. This does not delete the condition but simply disconnects it from use.

■ A box with the heading Selected where you place your choices. You will already see the items that you selected in Step 2.

■ A Views button, located immediately above the Selected box. This button allows you to alter the display in the Selected box. By default, the folder names are hidden. Clicking

FIGURE 4-20   *Plus Workbook Methodology Step 4: Setting up user-defined conditions*

the Views button pops up a box from which you can choose to either Show Folders or Hide Folders.

- A set of four additional buttons:

    - **New**   Use this button to create a new condition.

    - **Edit**   Use this button to edit an existing condition.

    - **Show**   Use this button to show the details about a predefined condition. You will not be allowed to edit the condition, but you will be able to see the criteria that your Discoverer manager used to create it.

    - **Delete**   Use this button to delete a user-defined condition. Once again, use this button with caution, because you will not be warned that you are deleting a condition.

- Just as in Desktop, there is a box at the bottom of the screen that displays a description of the condition. Unlike in Desktop, this box is unnamed. However, because it is the only unnamed box on the screen, it is easily recognizable.

Creating a new condition in Plus is very easy because you simply click the New button and, from the pop-up menu, select New Condition. This opens the Plus New Condition dialog box as shown here.

This dialog box is very similar to the Desktop dialog box seen earlier in this chapter and works in exactly the same way. Here is a simple workflow for creating a condition using this box:

1. Choose whether to give the condition a name by checking/unchecking the button called Generate name automatically. If you uncheck this box, you must give the condition a name.

2. While the box for the description is optional, we recommend using it. In here you should place a meaningful description for your condition, in language that your most novice users would understand. This is a useful aide to documentation.

3. In the Formula area create the condition itself. Please refer to Chapter 14 to gain a full understanding of creating effective conditions.

4. Click OK. You will now see the condition displayed in both the Available and Selected boxes. Note the tick mark alongside the condition in the Available box. As mentioned earlier, this is a really cool way of knowing which conditions are in use and which are not.

The Query from the Twilight Zone and How to Avoid It

The term "The Query from the Twilight Zone" was first introduced to one of the authors by an Oracle trainer during a course on data warehousing several years ago. Since then it has become an intrinsic part of the Armstrong-Smith methodology because it describes perfectly the type of query that users should avoid writing.

So what is it? Well, to put it simply, it is a query that never—or seemingly never—returns any information. Once submitted, the query just appears to run forever; apparently having been submitted to that "big database in the sky" from whence nothing ever returns. Somewhere out there in the bowels of data land are millions of queries still searching for their elusive data, and hopefully the users are not still sitting at their desks waiting for the results!

Having all the data from your company available to you, coupled with the newly unleashed power of Discoverer, makes for a tempting dabble into querying everything. Look at the following example:

Let's say you work for a company that produces widgets and you currently have 10,000 finished products. Your bill of materials defines what components make up those widgets and the current monthly cost of each of those components. So let's say each of your widgets has 50 components and that you are a fairly large company with 20 manufacturing plants worldwide. We are sure this sounds familiar to many of you. At this point, you therefore have to maintain monthly costs for 10 million (10,000 × 50 × 20) different components.

If you were trying to build a query to analyze your current costs, you would not want to let your first attempt run against all of those records, would you? To further compound the issue, imagine trying to compare the current month's costs against those during the past year. This query would compare the current 10 million with the 110 million from the previous 11 months. This example may seem somewhat extreme, but it isn't. There are thousands of companies like this, many of which are actually bigger and more complex.

The query just described that analyzes 10 million records may, depending upon what kind of hardware your company has, actually produce a result inside four or five hours. Realistically, though, your Discoverer manager will probably have set a limit for the maximum length of time he or she will allow you to run your query, and your query will have timed out. We therefore have to explore ways of reducing the length of time required to build your query.

There are many ways to reduce the length of time when building a query. Six of these are as follows:

- Using data marts and summary tables

- Applying constraints to avoid creating long-running queries

- Applying Discoverer query governors to reduce the time allowed or the maximum number of rows of data returned

- Applying a sort order after the query results have been ascertained

- Creating totals and subtotals on a subset of the data

- Applying calculations after the query has run

 NOTE
These are Discoverer-specific methods, not to be confused with database optimizations, which are a whole different ball game.

The first three will be covered in this chapter, and the last three will be covered in Chapter 5.

 NOTE
You may want to look at the preceding list as a workflow. By applying the steps listed, you should be able to effectively manage large data selections without creating "The Query from the Twilight Zone."

Using Data Marts and Summary Tables

Data marts and summary tables can greatly reduce the time taken to produce reports that require large amounts of data. Therefore, whenever you have to create a query that needs to report a large amount of data, you should consult with your Discoverer manager and inquire whether or not there are any data marts in existence. As described earlier, a data mart is basically a table that has been specially created for reporting and has indexes specially built for reporting. Summary tables can be created by your Discoverer manager. Where these exist, Discoverer will analyze your query and, if all the items you want can be found within a summary table, redirect your query to use that table. In an Oracle database, these tables are called materialized views. The great advantage of these is that these can be preaggregated and have indexes defined on the items that you choose to place conditions on.

While you yourself cannot point your query to a summary table, discussing your requirements with your Discoverer manager may well reveal that such a table exists. Where these do exist, you may want to consider amending your requirements so that you include only those items that are contained within the summary table. If this is not possible, your Discoverer manager may well be the friendly sort of person who would not mind either changing the existing summary or creating a new one for you.

If there are no data marts or summary tables in existence, you may want to discuss your requirements with your report writer or Discoverer manager. These people may be able to help you start the process for having one of these objects created for you. Do not feel that you need to give up on any queries that you want to create. There is always something you can do, and there is always something that can be done for you. You should therefore stay close to and make use of the resources available.

Applying Constraints to Avoid Creating Long-Running Queries

The first thing every good query writer learns is how to apply constraints. Discoverer calls these conditions. You need to work with your Discoverer manager and possibly your DBA to find out as much as you can about the nature of the data that you will be working with.

You need to know which tables contain large numbers of items and what the values are within your main indexes so that you can define suitable conditions. Very large tables need to be constrained on their index items. If you attempt to create your conditions on nonindexed items, then this will hardly make any impression on the time taken to run your query because the system will still have to search all of the items in order to decide whether each of those items meets your condition.

In the example query we are using, where we have 10 million current cost records, you would need to find out what code your system uses to define the current month's costs (Oracle Applications calls the current cost the *frozen cost*, and usually it has the code value 1). This will at least reduce the number of items being searched to those 10 million records.

Applying Temporary Constraints to Quickly View Preliminary Output   If you get to work closely with your Discoverer manager and spend some time learning about the data in your system, you will soon become aware that querying from some tables will take a very long time. This experience, coupled with some common sense, will tell you to look for ways to minimize the time it takes to at least get some preliminary output. You don't want to wait several hours to see the column ordering, nor wait that long only to discover you left something out or included something you didn't need.

NOTE
Setting temporary constraints in order to get preliminary output is an essential tool in your armory and will result in a rapid building process.

Returning to our example query, we have already ascertained what the code value is for the current month, but this would still result in a query of 10 million records. While the end result may be that we do in fact want to produce a report of that magnitude, during the construction of the query we do not want to be running against that volume of data. We would therefore look to reduce the number of items being queried. This is done by 1) limiting the query to search only one manufacturing facility (reducing the query down to 500,000 items) and 2) limiting it further by restricting the query to, say, only ten finished products (reducing it down to a manageable 500 items). This query will run very quickly, and you can now concentrate on defining your sort criteria, totals, and subtotals, along with the final data formatting characteristics.

Using Discoverer's Query Governor

Discoverer has a rather clever way to artificially cut down the length of time that it takes to run a query. This is called the query governor. No matter which version of Discoverer you are using, the way you access the query governor is via the toolbar. From the toolbar, select Tools | Options and select the Query Governor tab. This opens the Query Governor dialog box shown here.

The Query Governor dialog box has two important settings that you can apply:

- Prevent queries from running longer than

- Limit data retrieved to

The usage of both of these is detailed next.

NOTE
The use of the query governor itself can slow things down a little because when it is switched on, Discoverer needs to gather statistics.

Prevent Queries from Running Longer Than   Use this setting to set a time limit for how long you are prepared to wait for your results. We recommend you initially set this really low, to something like 1:00 minute. You will then get some idea as to how much data is returned in that time.

Limit Data Retrieved To   Use this setting to set a row limit for how many rows of data you are prepared to work with in your initial query. We recommend you initially set this low to something like 50. Again, you will get a great idea as to how long it will take to pull back that much data.

NOTE
Your Discoverer manager will have set maximums for these settings. As an end user you have the ability to reduce those settings at will, but you cannot set them higher than the preset maximum.

Viewing the Results

Although there are more steps to the Workbook Wizard, we feel the best way to proceed is to leave the wizard now and run the query. Don't worry—the remaining steps of the wizard will still be available to you after running the query. There is a good reason for this. We feel that people new to creating queries should keep them simple to begin with and build them up by steps. If you continue through the remainder of the wizard, you could find that after all of your work, you have created a query that will return no data, or so much data that you are timed out of the system before it can finish running. Build the foundation of the query and see the basic data, and then go on from there.

To view the results of the query, click Finish. Discoverer closes the Workbook Wizard, runs the query, and displays the results. Figure 4-21 shows the results from a typical Desktop query.

In Figure 4-22 you can see the same results displayed in Discoverer Plus. The Available Items pane and the Selected Items pane are available to the left of the query. We think these are very useful features, and we will show you how to use these in a subsequent chapter.

Interrogating the Results of a Query

When viewing the results of a query that has been run in Discoverer, you may want to check if a certain piece of data has been retrieved. The long, laborious way of doing this is to use the mouse to page through the results until you find the item that you want. In Discoverer, the quickest way to check whether an item has been retrieved is to use the Find Results dialog box.

NOTE
The Find feature looks only within the current page item combination.

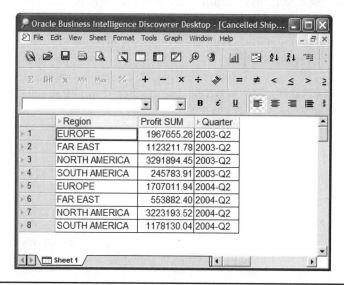

FIGURE 4-21 *A basic query in Desktop*

FIGURE 4-22 *The Discoverer Plus default view*

Interrogating the Results in Desktop To check if an item has been returned among the results of a Desktop query, use the following workflow:

1. With the results of the query visible onscreen, from the menu bar, select Edit | Find, or from the keyboard, press CTRL-F. Either way, Discoverer opens the Find dialog box shown in Figure 4-23.

2. In the box entitled Find Text That, use the drop-down list to select the type of search that you want to do. The options are

   ■ Contains

   ■ Exactly Matches

   ■ Begins With

   ■ Ends With

   ■ Is NULL

3. In the box entitled Look In, use the drop-down list to indicate whether you want Discoverer to search in the Data and Headings or Data Only. When working with a table, you have the option of searching in Data Only. It is only when you are in a crosstab that you can look at the Data and Headings also.

4. In the Search Text box, type the item that you want Discoverer to search for.

5. Check the Match Case box if you want Discoverer to search for results that match exactly the case of the item that you entered in Step 4.

NOTE
If you are certain that the item can only be in the case that you have specified, checking Match Case will increase the efficiency of the find and perform the search faster.

6. Click Find Next. Discoverer will now search for the item that you entered.

7. If the item is found, Discoverer displays, in the background, the first row containing that item. In this illustration, you can see that Discoverer has located the value 1690 in our results.

8. Repeat Steps 6 and 7 as many times as required, viewing all rows that contain a match of the search criteria.

9. If the item you are looking for is not located within the results, or there are no more items matching the search criteria, Discoverer will display an error message.

FIGURE 4-23 *Desktop Find dialog box*

Interrogating the Results in Plus   To check if an item has been returned among the results of a Plus query, use the following workflow:

1. With the results of the query visible onscreen, from the menu bar, select Edit | Find, or from the keyboard, press CTRL-F. Either way, Discoverer opens the Find dialog box shown in Figure 4-24.

2. Use the box entitled Search In to tell Discoverer whether to search in Data only, or Both Data and Headings. The option to search by both data and headings is available only in crosstab queries and will be grayed out in a table. When that option is available, click the down arrow to obtain a drop-down list of the available options.

3. Use the box entitled Search By to tell Discoverer what search action to take. The available search actions are

    ■ Contains

    ■ Starts with

    ■ Ends with

    ■ Exactly matches

    ■ Is Null

FIGURE 4-24 *Plus Find dialog box*

4. In the Search For box, type the name or partial name of the item that you want to find.

5. Check the Case-sensitive button if you want Discoverer to match the case.

6. Click Find Next or Find Previous. Discoverer searches the results and highlights, in the background, the next or previous item that matches the criteria you entered.

NOTE
Discoverer will search from whichever cell currently contains the focus. If your active cell is near the end of the results, Discoverer may not find anything between there and the end of the data. What happens now is that Discoverer begins searching from the top of the data.

7. In the following illustration, we asked Discoverer to search for something containing the word "small." As you can see, Discoverer located an item called "SMALL" in the column called Product Size.

	▶ Profit SUM	▶ Ship Qty SUM	▶ Product Name	▶ Product Size
1	11440746.92	881911	CD-100	MEDIUM
2	10383271.72	775574	CD-200	MEDIUM
3	6490671.82	468575	CD-500	LARGE
4	5121106.13	332898	CD-550	LARGE
5	19945287.32	1750997	CD-625	LARGE
6	5842488.74	798849	AB-2000	SMALL
7	5907659.67	702475	AB-2500	SMALL
8	9981105.10	783452	AB-3000	SMALL
9	20288355.43	1258289	AVR-500	MEDIUM
10	12324147.95	729518	AVR-550	MEDIUM
11	5778221.91	313635	AVR-800	LARGE
12	10693809.69	542121	AVR-900	LARGE
13	739513.00	480295	DS-1200	MINI
14	973487.40	456926	DS-1300	MINI
15	1241306.60	668871	MS-1200	MINI
16	612993.20	298853	MS-1300	MINI
17	4523599.57	376108	QB-1000	LARGE
18	5284350.01	442918	QB-2000	LARGE
19	5853476.20	497296	QB-3000	LARGE
20	9570416.13	829052	QB-5000	MEDIUM
21	9039564.02	826217	QB-5500	MEDIUM
22	9828919.51	819342	QB-6000	MEDIUM

Find dialog box:
Search in: Data only
Search by: Contains
Search for: small
☐ Case-sensitive
Find Previous   Find Next
Help   Close

8. When you have completed your search, click Close.

9. If the item you are looking for is not located within the results, Discoverer displays this error message.

No match found

Cannot find any data containing "extra large" in the worksheet.

OK

Saving the Query

Computers never crash, do they? One of the quirky things about computers is that they sometimes appear to have minds of their own. They know when you're busy, they know when you've got an important document or query onscreen that you haven't yet saved, and they know that you're taking a risk by not saving your work! Of course, if you save your work regularly, guess what? The system never crashes—but hold off on saving and you know what will happen. Yes, the evil elf inside the system decides to teach you a lesson and crashes your computer, so you lose everything. The authors don't know which chip on the motherboard has been programmed to do this, but if we did, we wouldn't need to write this section because we would be rich and famous.

The truth of the matter is that computer systems do crash, network connections fail at the most awkward of times, and laptops run out of battery power. What we are trying to instill into you is the discipline to save your work regularly.

Therefore, before doing anything else, save the query, and do it now. Don't take a coffee break, don't admire the output of your first query, and don't tempt fate! There is nothing more frustrating than creating the best query anyone has ever built and then to lose it before you get a chance to save it or show it to your boss. And how is it that the second attempt never produces the same result? We don't know, but with the foundation of your query built and saved, you can refine it by formatting it, applying sort orders, calculations, totals, and so on, or you can use it as the basis for creating more complex queries.

NOTE
Discoverer saves your query, the items, the layout, and the formatting characteristics, along with any calculations or conditions you may have applied. It does not save the output of your query. This subject will be dealt with in Chapter 8.

There are five ways to make Discoverer save a new query:

- Press CTRL-S.

- Click the Save icon on the toolbar.

- Click File | Save.

- Click File | Save As.

- Click File | Close.

- Click File | Exit.

When you take the last option, Discoverer asks if you would like to Save Changes to Workbook1, as shown here.

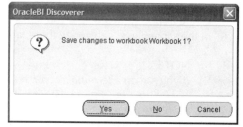

- **Yes**   Displays the Save Workbook dialog box (see Figure 4-25).

- **No**   Closes the workbook without saving.

- **Cancel**   Exits the Close dialog box and keeps the workbook open without saving it.

Whichever way you decide to save your query, Discoverer displays the Save Workbook dialog box shown in Figure 4-25.

NOTE
If you are working in Plus, Discoverer cannot save to My Computer. Therefore, you will not be prompted to choose where to save the workbook. Discoverer Plus takes you straight to the Save Workbook to Database dialog box (see Figure 4-28).

FIGURE 4-25 *Save Workbook dialog box*

Discoverer prompts you with "Where Do You Want to Save This Workbook?" and gives you the following two options:

- **My Computer** This allows you to save your workbook on your computer, to a floppy drive, or to a network account on your server. When you first create a new query, we recommend that you take this option, unless you are working in Plus, in which you have no choice and will be saving to the database server.

- **Database** This allows you to save your workbook to your database server. When you are working in Desktop, you should save only fully completed and working queries to the database, saving test and uncompleted work to the file system.

My Computer

Choosing this option will allow you to save your worksheet to either your hard disk, a floppy disk, or your network account, and by default will give it the extension DIS. If you are going to save your workbooks on either your hard disk or a network account, we recommend that you create a special area where you can safely save them. This way, you can store all your queries in the same place, categorize them, and organize them into folders.

NOTE
If you are on a terminal server, remember that the hard disk you see is not on your PC, but on the terminal server itself. Your company will probably have defined a folder or folders on the server for your use. Make sure that you always save your files into your assigned area. If you want to see your work after logging off the terminal server, copy it back to your PC hard disk or network account before you exit.

Having opted to save your workbook, click Save.
Discoverer now opens up the Save As dialog box shown in Figure 4-26. This box has four main areas:

- Save in

- Available Workbooks

FIGURE 4-26 *The Save As dialog box*

- File name
- Save as type

Save In   This area displays the current folder into which your worksheet will be saved. If you do not want to save your worksheet in this folder, you should switch to another folder or create a new folder by pressing the New Folder icon.

Available Workbooks   This area lists all of the workbooks that you currently have saved in the folder highlighted.

File Name   This area enables you to type in a meaningful name for your workbook. By default, Discoverer will name your query Worksheet1.DIS.

NOTE
We don't recommend saving workbooks using the default name; instead, you should give your query a meaningful name (see the following section).

Save as Type   This area allows you to change the file format you can save your query in. By default, Discoverer will give your workbook the extension .DIS and save it as an Oracle Discoverer workbook. If you do not want to save your query using this extension, you can click the down arrow and select All Files (*.*) You can now save your query using any extension of your choosing. However, the file type is still an Oracle Discoverer workbook and can only be used as such.

NOTE
We don't recommend saving workbooks using any extension other than the default. If you do decide to save your workbooks using different extensions, you will make it more difficult for yourself to later locate and maintain your workbooks.

Having given your query a name and chosen where to save it, click Save. Your query is now safe, and if your system decides to crash, it will make no difference.

Database

Choosing this option will save your workbook to your Discoverer account on the database server. Workbooks typically do not take up a lot of space—on average less than 100KB for a moderately complex workbook. The other advantage of saving it to the database is that it is secure, is available from anywhere you can access the database, and gets backed up along with the rest of the data in your database.

Having opted to save your workbook to the database, click Save. Discoverer now opens up the Save Workbook to Database dialog box, as shown in Figure 4-27.

Saving to the Database from Within Desktop   Once you have clicked Save to save to the database from within Desktop, Discoverer displays the dialog box shown in Figure 4-27. This box has five areas:

- Available workbooks

- Name

- Save

- Cancel

- Help

Available Workbooks   This area lists all of the workbooks that you currently have saved under your account in the database.

Name (New Name in Plus)   This area enables you to type in a meaningful name for your workbook.

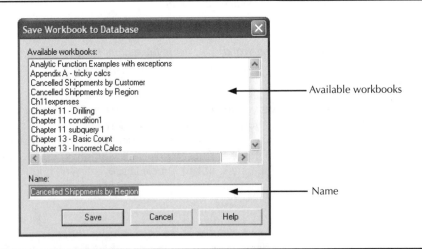

FIGURE 4-27   *The Desktop Save Workbook to Database dialog box*

Save   Clicking Save saves the workbook. If you choose to save using the same name as an existing workbook, Discoverer warns you that a workbook already exists by that name and asks if you would like to overwrite it, as shown here.

You have the following three options:

- **Yes**   This will overwrite the file.

- **No**   This exits the Warning dialog box and allows you to type in a new name for the workbook.

- **Cancel**   This also exits the Warning dialog box and allows you to type in a new name for the workbook.

Cancel   Clicking this cancels the Save and returns you to your results.

Help   Clicking this calls up the Discoverer Help screen.

NOTE
In Discoverer Desktop, if you do not see the option to save to the database, this is because your Discoverer manager has disabled this option. You may need to speak with him or her if you think you should be able to do this.

Saving to the Database from Within Plus   Once you have clicked Save to save to the database from within Plus, Discoverer displays the dialog box shown in Figure 4-28. This box has nine areas:

- View
- View Style
- Name Contains
- Clear
- Workbooks
- New Name
- Help
- Save
- Cancel

View   Clicking this allows you to select all workbooks that you have access to or just the workbooks that you own.

FIGURE 4-28 *The Plus Save Workbook to Database dialog box*

View As This button, alongside the words Name Contains, allows you to choose a style for displaying the workbooks that you have access to. When you click it, you are offered the following three choices:

- **Workbook Tree** Displays in alphabetical order.

- **User Tree** Displays in alphabetic order of owner and then in alphabetic order of the workbooks.

- **Table** This option also displays in alphabetical order, and except for the absence of the lines to the left of the workbook names, it is exactly the same as the Workbook Tree.

Name Contains If you have a lot of workbooks that you have access to, use this box to filter the workbook list. As you begin typing characters into this box, Discoverer automatically filters by those characters. The authors like this feature and would like to see it used in other Discoverer filter boxes.

Clear If you have already begun typing something into the Name Contains box, clicking this button instantly clears the box and stops filtering the workbook list.

Workbooks   This box displays the workbooks you have access to after applying the style and filters. The workbooks are displayed by Name, Owner, and Date Modified. You can sort on each of these by clicking the appropriate heading. Clicking a heading once will sort the list in ascending order, while clicking the same heading a second time will sort the list in descending order.

New Name   As you click an existing workbook in the Workbooks box, the name of the workbook will be displayed here. You can either save over and replace an existing workbook that you own or type in your own name for the new workbook.

Help   Click this button to get context-sensitive help about saving workbooks.

Save   Click this button to save the workbook. If there is already a workbook saved by the name that you are trying to use, you will be warned and asked if you want to overwrite the existing workbook. Your options are Yes, No, and Cancel. Clicking No or Cancel returns you to the dialog box without saving the workbook.

Cancel   Click this button if you want to cancel saving the workbook.

NOTE
If your Discoverer manager has disabled the option to save to the database, you are up the river without a paddle! Obviously, if you cannot save to My Computer and you are barred from saving to the Database, you have nowhere to save your query. Run, do not walk, to your Discoverer manager and ask him or her to enable saving to the Database. But seriously, there may be good reason why some users are barred from saving queries to the database. Perhaps they are novices to Discoverer, or perhaps your company restricts creation of queries to staff working in-house. If this applies to your company, you will only be able to run queries, not create them.

If you are working in Discoverer Plus and have created a new query, but your Discoverer manager has barred you from saving to the database, the accompanying note has explained that you will not be able to save the query at all. Any attempt to leave the query will receive a warning that you have insufficient privileges.

Giving the Query a Meaningful Name

As with all files that you save to your computer, especially to a networked computer, you should get into the good habit of giving your Discoverer workbooks and worksheets meaningful names. There can be nothing more frustrating than having a database full of workbooks with meaningless names when you are looking for the one that will give your manager your end-of-year results.

Avoid naming your queries names like Bob's first query, Bob's test query, or My query. This will only end up frustrating you and your colleagues. Describe what the query is referencing, such as "Q2 sales by region 2005" or "Gross Margin by Product Feb 2005." These names tell you exactly what the query is about and will not leave you guessing. They will also keep you from saving queries that you don't use (because the name does not tell you what it is for, but you are afraid to delete it) and will prevent you and your colleagues from reinventing the wheel. The authors have seen the same queries duplicated many times simply because they were not given meaningful names and were therefore not reused but re-created.

The age of the eight-character DOS naming convention is long gone. Let it die and give your files meaningful names!

Summary

In this chapter, you have learned a simple workflow for creating new queries. We explained that in Discoverer Desktop, there are six steps to the Workbook Wizard, while in Discoverer Plus, there are five steps with more functionality included in each step.

By following the first four steps of the Workbook Wizard, you learned to create a working query and to avoid "The Query from the Twilight Zone." Feels good, doesn't it? You also learned to view the results and save your work. As a novice in Discoverer, this is a good approach, and should be used until you have become more experienced in creating queries. In fact, even seasoned Discoverer users adopt this approach, and they rarely use the remaining steps of the wizard before viewing the initial output.

However, it would be remiss of us to not explain the remaining steps of the Workbook Wizard. These will be covered in the next chapter.

CHAPTER
5

The Workbook Wizard:
The Optional Steps

n Chapter 4, you were shown the essential steps in using the Workbook Wizard to create a working query. In this chapter, you will learn the remaining steps of the Workbook Wizard: sorting, calculations, percentages, totals, and parameters. We say that these steps are optional because they can be added after you have a functional query.

Because the steps of the Workbook Wizard covered in this chapter are optional, it is necessary that you learn how to reopen the Workbook Wizard to add them to your query. In the second part of this chapter, you will learn how to add a text area to add help to your worksheets. You will also learn to open the Edit Sheet dialog box in Desktop and the Edit Worksheet dialog box in Plus to edit an existing query. Even though they are named differently, they are essentially the same box. This form contains all of the steps of the Workbook Wizard in a multitabbed configuration, thus making Discoverer's functionality easy to access. We will also introduce you to the Available Items pane and the Selected Items pane in Plus. These are new features that make Discoverer even easier to use.

The Text Area in Plus

Before moving into the optional steps of the Workbook Wizard, we want to introduce you to a new feature of Plus called the *text area*. We like this feature very much because it can be a great help to end users. When you create a workbook to be used by others, this text area will help your users understand how to use the worksheets. You can add helpful hints about the conditions, calculations, parameters, etc., in use in the worksheet. This illustration shows the text area in use in a query.

Use and formatting of the text area will be described in detail in Chapter 14.

The Optional Steps of the Workbook Wizard

The following steps occur in both the Plus and Desktop Workbook Wizards. Although they are not accessed the same way, they are functionally the same:

- Creating a sort order

- Creating user-defined calculations

- Creating user-defined percentages

- Creating user-defined totals

- Creating user-defined parameters

NOTE
Throughout the final steps of the Workbook Wizard, you may decide to run your query at any time by clicking Finish. You can even skip a step if you wish, simply by clicking Next. As long as you stay in the Workbook Wizard, you can return to a previous step by clicking Back.

Workbook Wizard Step 5: Creating a Sort Order (Tables Only)

Let us assume that you have not run and saved your query. For a table query, the next step after creating user-defined conditions is creating a sort order. For crosstab queries, this step is omitted and you should continue with the setting of calculations. While it is possible to add sort criteria to crosstab queries, the Workbook Wizard does not allow you to do this. If you are using a crosstab, you need to complete your query, display the results onscreen, and then apply or refine your sort.

This section therefore applies only to table queries. From here until the end of this section on sorting, we will assume that you are working with a table query. After applying conditions, in Desktop click Next. In Plus you need to navigate to Step 4 of the wizard.

This brings up the sort screen of the Workbook Wizard. The Desktop screen is shown in Figure 5-1, while the Plus screen is shown in Figure 5-2. These screens consist of the following features:

- **Sorting box**   This box will be empty until you add a sort order. As you apply sorts to your items, Discoverer will display them in here in the order in which you defined the sort.

- **Add**   Click this to add an item to sort.

- **Delete**   Click this to delete a sort.

- **Move Up**   Click this to promote a sort.

- **Move Down**   Click this to demote a sort.

- **Format (Plus Only)**   Click this to apply formats to your data and to control how page breaks are controlled. As you can see in Figure 5-2, this button is only available in Plus.

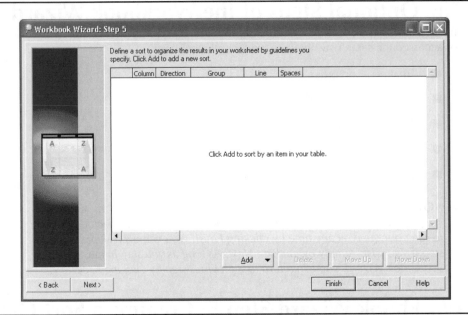

FIGURE 5-1 *The Desktop Sort screen*

FIGURE 5-2 *The Plus Sort screen*

Sorting: What Is It?

Sorting arranges text in alphabetical order or numbers in numerical order in either Low to High (ascending, a–z, 1–10) or High to Low (descending, z–a, 10–1) order. This creates an orderly means of viewing data, such as employees alphabetically or customer sales from highest to lowest. Anyone familiar with Excel has used sorting before and will probably be looking for a Sort button. Discoverer has these also, but not in the Workbook Wizard. In here, you need to take a more complicated approach. This is one of the reasons we suggest not defining your sort orders in the Workbook Wizard. Figure 5-3 shows an example of a numeric sort in Low to High order.

NOTE
There is one important problem with sorting that you must watch out for. When sorting in a crosstab, you cannot sort on calculated items. You can only sort on items that came directly from the data source. It is necessary to duplicate the crosstab as a table, where you can sort on calculated items. We think that this is a bug and hope it will be fixed soon.

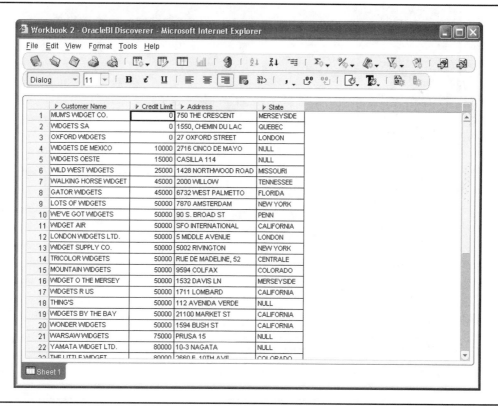

FIGURE 5-3 *Simple Low to High sort (Credit Limit sorted, unsorted Customer Name)*

Discoverer also allows for group sorting. If you are not familiar with group sorting, think of a group sort as a more specialized form of Low to High or High to Low sort. When you select this type of sort, Discoverer leaves blank all repeating items, thus making your reports much easier to read and more aesthetically pleasing.

Figure 5-4 shows the same data used in Figure 5-3, sorted as a group sort.

Creating a New Sort

When creating a new sort, you should use the following workflow:

1. Open the Edit Sheet/Worksheet dialog box.

2. Select the Sort tab.

3. Click Add.

4. Select the item you want to sort on. In Plus, Discoverer automatically selects the first named column, in alphabetical order, and creates a normal, Low to High sort. In Desktop, you will be offered a drop-down of all available items.

5. Define the sort parameters.

6. Click OK to finish.

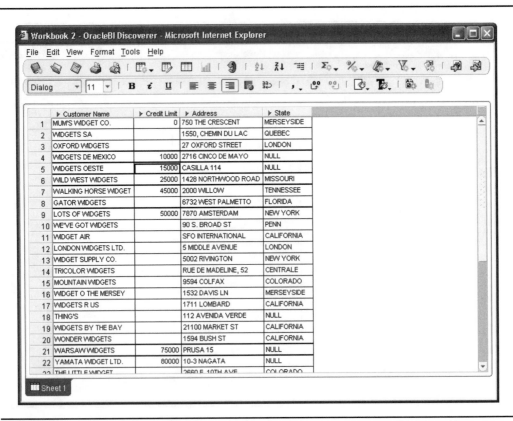

FIGURE 5-4 *Simple Low to High group sort (Credit Limit as a group sort, Customer Name unsorted)*

When you first enter Step 5 of the wizard, the main box in the center of the screen will be empty (see Figures 5-1 and 5-2). You need to think about what item or items you want to apply a sort on. Unfortunately, unlike conditions, there are no administrator-created sorts, so it is all up to you.

Because you can create multiple sorts in your query, you should try to create them in a logical sequence, defining the primary sort first. If you cannot define the logical sequence at this time, do not worry, because you can change the sequence later. The important thing is to get the items sorted. There is no limit on the number of sorts you can define, other than the number of items in your query, but we recommend you restrict your choices to a maximum of two or three within the Workbook Wizard. Creating complex sort sequences greater than this is very difficult to visualize, and we strongly advise you to create these later.

NOTE
Adding complex sorts on numerous columns, while possible and tempting to do, should be used with caution. Every sort you ask Discoverer to do will cause your query to take longer and consume more memory. We recommend you apply sorts only when necessary, using the minimum number of sort sequences to produce the desired result.

When you have decided what column(s) needs to be sorted, click Add.

Sorting in Desktop
As mentioned earlier, after you click Add, Desktop displays a drop-down list of all the items in your query.

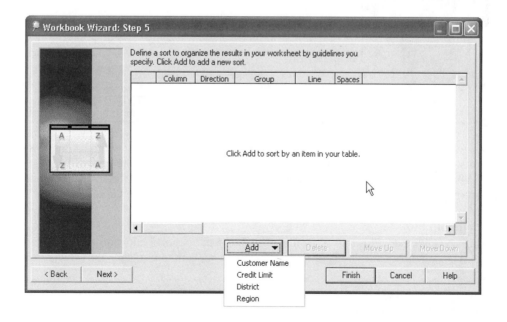

From the list, pick the item that you have decided to use for the primary sort item. Discoverer will create your first sort and add its definition to the box. You now have the following additional choices:

■ **Column** Displays the name of the item you chose for your sort.

■ **Direction** Click this to set the sort order (defaults Low to High) for the item. The available options are Low To High and High To Low.

■ **Group** Click this for a drop-down list of group sort options. The available options are None, Group Sort, Page Break, and Hidden.

■ **Line** Click this if you want to change the width of the line between group-sorted items.

■ **Spaces** Click this if you want to add extra line spacing between group-sorted items.

The Desktop sort criteria are shown in the following illustration.

At this point, you will notice that the Delete button is activated. If you have made a mistake and selected the wrong item for your sort, click Delete and it will be removed.

Assuming you have chosen the correct item, Discoverer defaults the sort into ascending order; it is not a group sort (as indicated by the word None under the Group heading).

Sorting in Plus

After you click Add, Plus inserts the first available item, in alphabetical order, into the sorted items box automatically. If this is not the item that you want to use, click the down arrow alongside the item and from the drop-down list select the item you want. You will also notice that the Delete button is now active, and that you have the following additional choices:

- ■ **Column**   Displays the name of the item you chose for your sort.

- ■ **Direction**   Click this to set the sort order for the item. The available options are Low To High, and High To Low.

- ■ **Sort Type**   Click this for a drop-down list of the two available sort types, Normal and Group Sort. Discoverer defaults to Normal.

- ■ **Hidden**   Check this check box if you want the sorted column to be hidden.

The Plus sort criteria are shown in the following illustration.

We showed you how to add lines, blank spaces, and page breaks in group sorts in Desktop. These can also be added in Plus using the Format Data dialog box, which is a multitabbed form that is used for formatting the data in a worksheet. You will learn about this dialog box in detail in Chapter 6. However, we feel that this is the right place to show you the Breaks tab of this dialog box.

Quick Sorting

Sometimes sorting is a simple matter of adding one group sort and perhaps one additional sort ascending. These can be accomplished using drop-down menus or toolbar buttons. Also, sorts that you create using any method can be deleted using a drop-down list that appears with a right click.

Adding a Quick Sort from a Drop-Down List

To add a quick sort, use the following workflow:

1. Right-click in the column upon which you want to base your sort.

2. From the drop-down, select Group Sort, Sort Low To High, or Sort High To Low.

Adding a Quick Sort from the Toolbar

To add a quick sort from the toolbar use the following workflow:

1. Click in the column upon which you want to base your sort.

2. On the toolbar click the button for Group Sort, Sort Low To High, or Sort High To Low.

To Quickly Remove a Normal Sort Using a Drop-Down

A normal sort, no matter how it was created, can be deleted by right-clicking and using a drop-down list or by using the toolbar. To remove a normal sort using a drop-down, use the following workflow:

1. Right-click in the column with the sort you want to remove.

2. From the drop-down select Sort Low To High, or Sort High To Low. This will remove the check mark and delete the sort.

NOTE
*Clicking group sort on a previously unsorted item will sort it
ascending and also place a group sort.*

To Quickly Remove a Group Sort Using a Drop-Down

A group sort, no matter how it was created, can be deleted by right-clicking and using a drop-down list. To remove a normal sort using a drop-down, use the following workflow:

1.   Right-click in the column with the group sort you want to remove.

2.   From the drop-down select Group Sort. This will remove the group sort and change it to a Low to High or High to Low sort, depending on how you had the original group sort defined.

3.   Right-click again and select Sort Low To High or High To Low. The sort has now been completely deleted.

To Quickly Remove a Normal Sort Using the Toolbar

To remove a normal sort from the toolbar, use the following workflow:

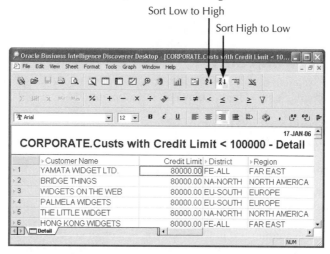

1.   Click in the column with the sort you want to remove.

2.   From the toolbar deselect Sort Low To High, or Sort High To Low. This will change the button from indented to normal and delete the sort.

To Quickly Remove a Group Sort Using the Toolbar (Desktop Only)

To remove a group sort in Desktop from the toolbar, use the following workflow:

1.   Right-click in the column with the group sort you want to remove.

2.   From the toolbar click the Group Sort button. This will change it from indented to normal and will remove the group sort and change it to a Low to High or High to Low sort, depending on how you had the original group sort defined.

3.   From the toolbar click Sort Low To High or Sort High To Low. This will change it from indented to normal and the sort will be completely deleted.

Refining a Sort

Having created your first sort, you may find that it needs refining. Perhaps you want to have the data sorted High to Low, or to change the sort type in order to apply a group sort.

Refining a Sort in Desktop

These are the methods for changing the sort order or sort type in Desktop:

- To toggle between Low to High and High to Low, click the up or down arrow beneath the heading Direction. You will see the direction indicator change accordingly.

- To change the sort type, click the down arrow beneath the heading Group, and from the drop-down list select Group Sort, Page Break, or Hidden.

Refining a Sort in Plus

These are the methods for changing the sort order or sort type in Plus:

- To switch between Low to High and High to Low, click the down arrow alongside the current setting and select the new option from the drop-down list.

- To change the sort type, click the down arrow beneath the heading Sort Type, and from the drop-down list select Group Sort.

Building a Group Sort

We will now explain in detail how you can add and refine your own group sort. Because the method used is sufficiently different between Desktop and Plus, we will describe each separately.

Building a Group Sort in Desktop

To build a group sort in Desktop, follow this workflow:

1. Determine what type of group sort to employ.

2. Define the line width.

3. Define the line spacing.

When building a group sort in Desktop, you first of all need to decide what type of sort to use. Click the down arrow beneath the heading Group. Discoverer produces a drop-down list of the available group sort types:

- **None**   Select this option if you do not want to use a group sort.

- **Group Sort**   Select this option to convert your existing sort into a group sort. This automatically opens up the Line and Spaces options, both of which are explained under the headings that follow.

- **Page Break**   Select this option if you want Discoverer to insert a page break into the final output every time the group sort encounters a new value. In the final display onscreen, Discoverer indicates that there is a page break by inserting a broken line between the groups of sorted items. Whenever you print a report containing a page break, Discoverer will begin each group on a new page.

■   **Hidden**   Select this option if you do not wish to display any of the data values for that item onscreen. You should apply this type of sort with great care, because it may not be obvious to someone looking at your report that the query is applying a sort on a hidden item.

NOTE
The Hidden option can be very powerful, and the following are good examples of its usage. First, suppose HR wants to produce a report, by department, of the employees based on their salaries but does not want to print out the actual salary amounts. Applying a sort on the salary figures and then hiding those items from the report will print out the employees in order of salary. Second, suppose you want a report showing your best-performing departments in terms of sales, without printing the actual sales figures. You would simply create a sort on the sales figures and hide them.

Having selected the type of group sort to use, you now have two final options that you can set.

Line Width   By default, Discoverer sets this to 1. If you want to change the width of the line separator, click the down arrow alongside the number 1 under the heading Line. This displays the following drop-down list.

As you can see, you can choose to use no lines or you can choose a line width of between 1 and 10.

Line Spacing   By default, Discoverer sets this to 0. If you want to change the spacing between the groups of sorted items, click the down arrow alongside the number 0 under the heading Space.

Use the up and down arrows to set the number of spaces you want to appear between each group of sorted items.

Building a Group Sort in Plus

To build a group sort in Plus, use this workflow:

1. Define the sort type.

2. Determine whether the sort item should be hidden.

3. Apply the remaining sort options.

To change the sort type, click the down arrow beneath the heading Sort Type. Discoverer produces a drop-down list of the available sort types. These are

■ **Normal**   Select this option if you do not want to use a group sort.

■ **Group Sort**   Select this option to convert your existing sort into a group sort.

If you do not wish to display any of the data values for the item that is being used for the sort, you can hide it from the final display. As with Desktop, you should apply this option with great care, because it may not be obvious to someone looking at your report that the query is applying a sort on a hidden item. Having determined that you want to hide the item, check the box entitled Hidden.

You can now set additional options to further refine the group sort. These options are available from the Breaks tab of the Format Data dialog box, as shown in the following illustration.

To open the Format Data dialog box, click the Format button. It is located to the right of the sort that you just created. The available options on the Breaks tab are available only when you are formatting a group-sorted item. All of these options are grayed out for items that are not part of a group sort. The options that you can set are

- **Line**   Check this box if you want to insert a solid line between the groups of sorted items. By default this box is checked.

- **Line Width**   Until Line is checked, this box is grayed out. By default, the line width is set to 1. Use the drop-down list to change the width to anything from 1 to 10.

- **Line Color**   Until Line is checked, this box is grayed out. By default, the line color is set to black. Click the button to pop up a palette of available colors. If you do not see the color that you want to use, on the palette click Edit. This opens up the Color Palette Editor. In Plus, you can even create your own custom colors.

- **Blank Row**   Check this box if you want to insert blank rows between the groups of sorted items. By default, this box is unchecked.

- **Number of Blank Rows**   Until Blank Row is checked, this box is grayed out. By default, the number of blank rows is set to 1. Use the up and down arrows to increase or decrease the number of blank rows that you want Discoverer to insert.

- **Page Break**   Check this box if you want Discoverer to insert a page break into the final output between the groups of sorted items. By default, this box is unchecked. When it is selected, in the final display onscreen, Discoverer indicates that there is a page break by inserting a broken line between the groups of sorted items. Whenever you print a report containing a page break, Discoverer will begin each group of sorted items on a new page.

Adding Another Sort

Having created one sort, you may decide to add a second, third, and so on. This will cause items to sort within other items.

For example, in our original sort shown in Figure 5-4, we have a group sort by credit limit. However, the customers are not sorted. It would be a better report to have the customers also sorted alphabetically. We therefore need to add a second sort to our query. To do this, click Add. You will once again go through the steps outlined earlier in this chapter in the section entitled "Creating a New Sort."

NOTE
Any item that has already been selected for sorting will not appear in the drop-down list again. You can apply only one sort to an item. When there are no more items available for sorting, the Add button is deactivated.

Figure 5-5 shows a Discoverer Plus example of a multiple-sort sequence. We have taken the previously group-sorted list (see Figure 5-4) and applied a second sort on the Customer column.

FIGURE 5-5   *Credit Limit/Customer group sorted by Credit Limit and Customer ascending*

Rearranging the Sort Order

Whenever you have two or more sorts in use, you should look carefully at the relationship between the items and determine if the sort sequence is correct. Earlier, we suggested that you should try to create your sorts in the order that you want to see them in the final report. However, with even the best design or analysis, sometimes you may have created them in the wrong order.

If you decide you have a sort in the wrong place, you can use the Move Up and Move Down buttons to promote or demote items. These buttons become active only when you have created two or more sorts. You can also use your mouse to click and drag the items to change their position within the sort sequence. To drag, click on the drag zone provided next to each sort.

For example, suppose we had created a query with the items' ship date, product number, and quantity shipped. We want to have our final display in date order with the products in alphabetical order by date. However, by mistake we created the sort on the products before we created the sort on the dates. The result will appear as in Figure 5-6. By promoting the ship date above the product, our display will be correct as shown in Figure 5-7.

FIGURE 5-6 *Ship date, product and ship quantity, sorted by product then date*

Why Not Sort in the Wizard?

When you are working with queries that need to pull a large amount of data, we recommend that you not attempt to create your sort sequences inside the Workbook Wizard. We recommend against this because sorting increases the amount of time it takes to run a query and consumes memory. If you have defined complicated sorts, you will add an unnecessary overhead to your query. This overhead could actually cause your query to exceed the maximum query time set by your Discoverer manager, and your query could time out.

When you have a working copy of your query, you can concentrate on the sort criteria. You should look at the data that your query has brought in and try to define the best way to display that data. Presenting your data using appropriate and meaningful sort criteria should be done only after you have some data onscreen as a result of a reduced set of constraints.

In Chapter 9, you will learn how the different types of sort affect your report and how to create a useful sort order. Even though there is no step in the Crosstab Wizard for sorting, you can do this, but only after you have created the initial query. We will show you how to add sorts to Crosstab worksheets in Chapter 9 also.

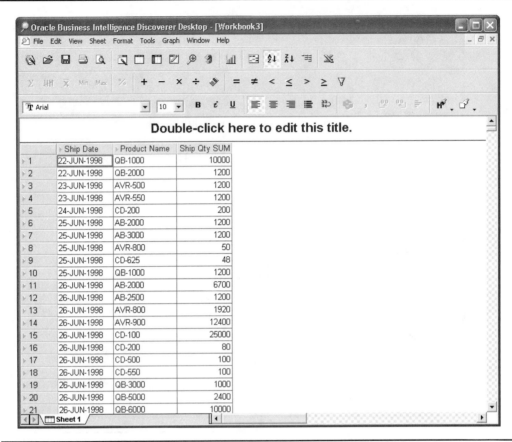

FIGURE 5-7 *Ship date, product and ship quantity, sorted by date then product*

After applying crosstab conditions or adding sort orders to a table, in Desktop click Next. This brings up the sixth screen of the Workbook Wizard. In Plus, we recommend you click the Back button twice to return to the second screen of the Workbook Wizard, and then click the Calculations tab.

NOTE
The hierarchy of sorts can affect the appearance of your data in ways that may not be obvious at first. For example: if you have a group-sorted item and you then add a sort on another item, the new sort applies only at the group level.

Workbook Wizard Step 6: Creating User-Defined Calculations

The ability to add your own calculations is, along with conditions and parameters, one of the features that set Discoverer apart from other query tools. Master calculations, and you are on your way to mastering Discoverer. Because Desktop and Plus are sufficiently different, we will describe the Wizard screens separately.

Desktop Calculations Screen

As shown in Figure 5-8, the Desktop Workbook Wizard Step 6 contains three boxes and three buttons:

- **View Calculations For box** This is a drop-down box where you can choose to view calculations for all items or a specific item only. In Discoverer Desktop, you also get an option to view active-only calculations.

- **Available Calculations box** This box will be empty until you add a calculation. As you add calculations to your query, Discoverer will display them here in the order in which you create them.

- **Description box** This box shows the description of the calculation highlighted in the Calculations box.

- **New button** Click this to add a new calculation.

- **Edit button** When it is active, click this to edit an existing calculation.

- **Delete button** Click this to delete a calculation. As with conditions, be careful using this one because it does just what it says and without prompting!

FIGURE 5-8 *Desktop Workbook Wizard Step 6*

Plus Calculations Tab

As shown in Figure 5-9, the Plus Calculations tab has the standard buttons available throughout the wizard, with three additional default settings. These are

- **My Calculations** Displays a list of the calculations you have defined.

- **My Percentages** Displays a list of the percentages you have defined.

- **My Totals** Displays a list of the totals that you have defined.

Calculations: What Are They?

The word "calculate" means to compute mathematically, to ascertain by computation, to reckon, to estimate, or to plan. Calculations have been with us almost from the dawn of time, and throughout the ages man has been trying to devise new and quicker ways to perform them. The computer you are working on right now has the capability to perform millions of calculations per second (MIPS). In a business environment, you will most likely want to use calculations to aid you in estimating, trending, and forecasting.

Calculations give you more power in ad hoc reporting. When no underlying item in the database contains the data you want, Discoverer allows you to create new items. The formulas used to create these items can be very simple, or they can be complex mathematical or statistical expressions.

FIGURE 5-9 *The Plus Calculations tab*

When using calculations, you can use existing items from the database, the operators multiply (*), divide (/), add (+), and subtract (-), literals such as 1, 100, and 65.5, and functions. You can also use calculations that have been created for you by your Discoverer manager.

It is possible to see profits, costs, and margins calculated and grouped in a matter of minutes. Using mathematical formulas, calculations enable you to produce more complex queries. They usually apply some sort of algorithm or equation to the query results. A simple example of a calculation in a query is subtracting a product's cost price from its selling price to see the profit. A more complex calculation would be to see the profit margin, which is the sum of the profit (itself a calculation) divided by the sum of the selling price.

Figure 5-10 shows a simple calculation used in a query. You can see that the selling price minus the cost price is shown as the profit Calculation0.

NOTE
Discoverer makes available calculations grouped by categories such as 'Analytical', 'Conversion', 'Date', 'Group', 'Numeric', 'String', and 'Others'.

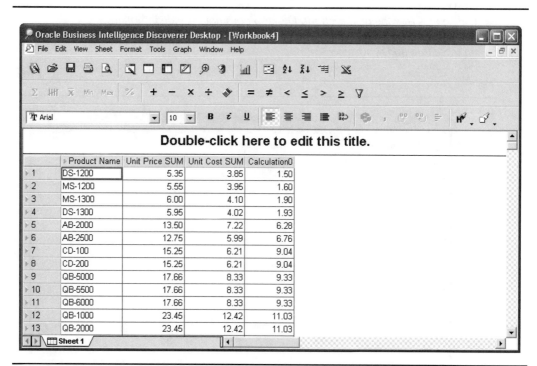

FIGURE 5-10 *A simple calculation in Desktop*

Creating a Calculation in Desktop

When creating a new calculation in Desktop, use the following workflow:

1. Click New. This opens the Edit Calculation dialog box (see Figure 5-11).

2. Give a meaningful name for your calculation. This name will appear as the column heading. By default, Discoverer inserts the word "calculation" followed by an integer.

3. Alongside the heading Show are two radio buttons. These are

   - **Items** These are items that exist within folders that are linked to your query, whether in use or not.

   - **Functions** These are predefined functions that exist within the database. Please refer to Appendix B for a full list of available functions. This appendix describes the syntax for every function and also gives meaningful examples of their use.

4. Build your calculation using a combination of expressions and operators.

5. Click OK to finish.

NOTE
Unlike Plus (see the next section), Desktop does not provide templates for creating analytic functions. You need to create calculations based on these functions yourself.

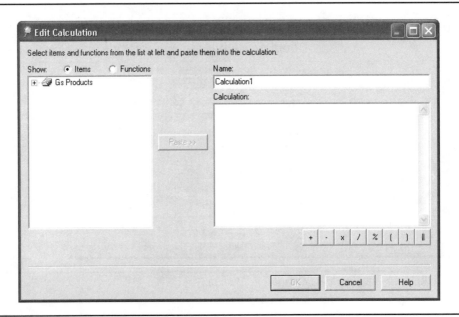

FIGURE 5-11 *Desktop Edit Calculation dialog box*

Creating a Calculation in Plus

When creating a new calculation in Plus, use the following workflow:

1. Launch the New Calculation dialog box (see Figure 5-12).

NOTE
There are two ways to launch the New Calculation dialog box. The first way is to click New and then from the drop-down box select New Calculation. The second way is to right-click My Calculations and from the pop-up box select New Calculation.

2. Give a meaningful name for your calculation. This name will appear as the column heading. By default, Discoverer inserts the word "calculation" followed by an integer.

3. Click Show to see a list of available expressions. These are

   - **Functions** These are predefined functions that exist within the database. Please refer to Appendix B for a full list of available functions. This appendix describes the syntax for every function and also gives meaningful examples of their use.

   - **Selected Items** These are the items that are in use in your query.

   - **Available Items** These are items that exist within folders that are linked to your query but are not yet in use.

   - **Calculations** These are calculations that you have previously created. Yes, you can create calculations based on other calculations! Discoverer is the only business intelligence tool on the market that allows you to use nested analytical functions, up to any level.

   - **Parameters** These are parameters that you have previously created. Obviously, at this point we have not created any parameters, so for now ignore this option.

4. Build your calculation using a combination of expressions and operators.

5. To use an analytic function, click the Insert Formula from Template button. Discoverer now displays a list of the available analytic functions. We will describe how to access and use these functions in Appendix B.

6. Click OK to finish.

FIGURE 5-12 *Plus New Calculation dialog box*

Understanding Calculations

When you first enter Step 6 of the Desktop Wizard (see Figure 5-8) or first enter the Calculations tab in Plus (see Figure 5-9), the main box in the center of the screen will be empty. You need to think about what item or items you want to use in your calculations. Like conditions, there are administrator-created calculations for you to choose from. You select these predefined calculations in exactly the same way as you select the items in your query. In Chapter 4, you were shown the different icons for the types of items you could select. Simple predefined calculations appear as a numeric item, and aggregate calculations appear as a calculator.

In the example that follows, the Discoverer manager has created simple calculations for standard margin, markup, and profit. There is also an administrator-defined aggregate calculation called "profit margin." The first three appear as normal items, and you can use the usual mathematical functions of SUM, AVG, and so forth on these. The item called profit margin, however, is an aggregate item. These are items that have been created by either dividing the SUM of one item into another or preapplying SUM to a calculation. This type of aggregated calculation stands alone in that it cannot have any other function applied to it, hence the absence of any (+) character.

Because you can create multiple calculations in your query, you should try to create them in a logical sequence, defining simple calculations first. There is no limit on the number of calculations you can define. Creating complex calculations requires a great deal of preplanning, perhaps working out your calculations on paper before you begin to define them in the Workbook Wizard. One of the most common mistakes made by end users is defining or attempting to define extremely complex calculations in the Workbook Wizard.

NOTE
It is always worthwhile to try out complex calculations on small data sets, where it is easy to verify the results before trying them on large data sets. Calculations will run faster on small data sets than large ones.

When you have decided what columns you need for a calculation, click New.

Previous Figure 5-11 shows the Edit Calculation dialog box used in Discoverer Desktop, and Figure 5-12 shows the New Calculation dialog box used in Discoverer Plus. These dialog boxes consist of the following sections:

- **Name**   The name given here will appear as the column heading.

- **Calculation box**   Type or paste the components for your calculation here.

- **Available box** This box displays a list of the items that are available for selection within the calculation.

- **Paste** Click this button to add an item, function, parameter, or other calculation to the Calculation box.

- **Operators** A set of buttons for standard mathematical operators. Clicking one of these pastes the operator into the calculation.

- **Description** Displays a description of an item, calculation, or function.

- **Show drop-down box** This is a drop-down list of the items, functions, parameters, or other calculations available to use in this calculation. This box is available only in Plus.

- **Items** Click this radio button to display a list of the items available to create your calculation. This button is available in only Desktop.

- **Functions** Click this radio button to display a list of functions available to create your calculation. This button is available only in Desktop.

- **Insert Formula from Template** Click this button to see a list of the analytic functions that are available for use within the calculation. This button is available in Plus. When a function is selected for use, a template dialog box opens up. In this dialog box, Discoverer preselects the most suitable options. A full description of this dialog box can be found in Appendix B.

When you have created a calculation, click OK. This causes Discoverer to test the mathematical properties of your calculation. If you have defined an incorrect calculation, Discoverer will warn you and you will have to correct your formula before continuing. Discoverer also tests out the syntax of the calculation to ensure that basic errors in your calculation are caught at the first step itself.

Assuming you have created a valid calculation, Discoverer inserts it into the box for calculations and ticks the check box automatically. Also at this point, you will notice that the Edit and Delete buttons that were inactive are now activated, and in Desktop Discoverer has inserted the formula into the Description box. For some reason, our version of Plus shows 'No description available', which we can only assume is a bug. If you have made an error in your formula, use the Edit button to reopen the Calculation dialog box and change it. If you decide you no longer need this calculation, click Delete and it will be removed. In Plus you can also right-click the calculation. When you do this, a drop-down box is displayed, from which you can select Edit or Delete. You can also opt to remove a calculation from the worksheet. This does not delete the calculation but merely deactivates it.

Discoverer adds the calculations into the box in the order you create them. You can use your calculations or the administrator-predefined calculations to create more complex algorithms.

NOTE
Be very careful creating calculations that employ division. You need to ensure that the divisor column does not contain any zero values; otherwise, you will encounter the dreaded divide-by-zero error, which will cause your query to fail. You will have to either apply a condition on the column that is being used as the divisor (Column<>0), or create your calculation using a DECODE function to tell Discoverer what to do when it encounters this situation. A DECODE calculation can be thought of as an IF . . . THEN clause. This will be explained fully in Chapter 13. If you are debugging a query that contains division, the first step is to check for the required nonzero condition and implement one of the two solutions outlined here. This is probably the single most common reason why calculations fail.

Why Not Calculate in the Wizard?

Applying calculations is one of the most challenging and complicated aspects of query design. It is recommended that you not attempt to create calculations using the Workbook Wizard until you have become proficient in the use of Discoverer. The authors have spoken with numerous expert Discoverer users, and none of them said they attempt to add calculations in the wizard. They wait until they have a working query with the data needed and then begin to create their calculations.

As with all querying tools, the more complicated the query, the higher the risk becomes that you will make an error—usually with no data being returned. This becomes even riskier when adding calculations, especially calculations using division. One expression in the wrong place and you could wait several minutes for a query to run, only to come back with a message that no data was found. The best way around this type of frustration is to build yourself a basic working query and then add your calculations.

NOTE
If your Discoverer manager has predefined calculations for your use, you will probably be safe adding these by using the Workbook Wizard.

If you are working in Desktop, you have now completed all the steps of the Workbook Wizard and you should click Finish. In Plus, there are three more steps.

Discoverer Plus Workbook Wizard Remaining Steps

This section of the Workbook Wizard is only applicable to Discoverer Plus. If you are using Desktop and have no interest in Plus, you may want to skip this section. However, most companies are moving toward Web-based analysis, and we would recommend that you continue reading.

Having completed calculations, the Discoverer Plus Workbook Wizard additionally allows you to create

- User-defined percentages

- User-defined totals

- User-defined parameters

All of these options are available in Desktop, but not as part of the Workbook Wizard. We will show you later in the chapter how to access these in Desktop.

Creating User-Defined Percentages in the Plus Workbook Wizard

As shown earlier in Figure 5-9, the Plus Calculations tab has the standard buttons available throughout the wizard, with three additional default settings. These are

- **My Calculations** Displays a list of the calculations you have defined.

- **My Percentages** Displays a list of the percentages you have defined.

- **My Totals** Displays a list of the totals that you have defined.

Thus, because we just completed adding our first calculations, there is no need to navigate away from the Calculations tab. In fact we stay right here throughout both of the next two steps as we create percentages and totals.

Percentages: What Are They?

The word "percent" comes from the Latin words "per" (meaning by) and "centum" (meaning hundred). A percentage is quite simply the rate of an item per hundred, or in accounting terms, a commission, duty, or interest based on one hundred. Most countries in the world use a currency based on one hundred parts: one hundred cents in a dollar, one hundred centimes in a franc, one hundred pennies in a pound. These allow for very simple percentage calculations, but it wasn't always this way. As recently as 1970, England had 240 pennies in one pound, but to make it worse they had 12 pennies in a shilling and 20 shillings in a pound (incidentally, the guinea that is still used in race horse trades is 21 shillings).

Calculating percentages of numbers with the answer being part of one hundred is a typical data analysis task. Discoverer allows you to choose the data to use both for the percentage calculation itself and for the value used to represent the percentage (grand total, subtotal, etc.). Don't worry about the terms used at this stage, as these will all be fully covered.

NOTE
As percentages are just a specialized form of calculation, many of the comments that were given in the preceding section on calculations are valid for percentages as well.

Percentages are mathematical formulas that enable you to analyze your data more effectively. They apply standard mathematical algorithms to the item you have chosen. A simple example of a percentage in a query is "Show me the percentage of my sales by channel for the month of January 2000." A more complex percentage would be to see the same query extended for the whole of fiscal quarter Q2, with the percentages being applied over the whole quarter's profit margin—which is the sum of the profit (itself a percentage) divided by the sum of the selling price.

Figure 5-13 shows a simple percentage being applied in a query. You can see that the selling price has been totaled by channel and that the percentage of sales is shown by channel and by total. Because the month is only used to define a condition, it has been moved to the Page Items box.

NOTE

Because of rounding in percentages, don't expect your percentage totals to always add to up 100 percent. This is a common phenomenon, and anyone familiar with spreadsheet programs such as Excel has encountered this situation.

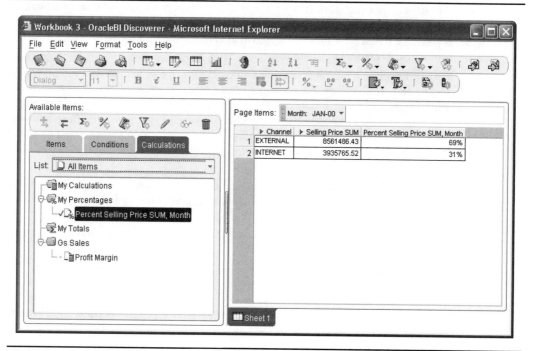

FIGURE 5-13   *Selling price as percentage by channel for January 2000*

Creating a New Percentage

When creating a new percentage you should use the following workflow:

1. Launch the New Percentage dialog box (see Figure 5-14).

NOTE
There are two ways to launch the New Percentage dialog box. The first way is to click New and then from the drop-down box select New Percentage. The second way is to right-click My Percentages and from the pop-up box select New Percentage.

2. Uncheck the box called "Generate name automatically" and give a meaningful name to your percentage. This name will appear as the column heading. If you leave this blank, the percentage column will have no label. By default, Discoverer prefixes the column heading with the word Percent. This is not good practice; Discoverer only does this to help you out just in case you forget to name the percentage yourself.

3. Click the Data Point drop-down box to see the list of available data points, and select the data item you want to apply the percentage on from the list. If you have only one item that can be used, Discoverer inserts that item by default and disables the drop-down.

4. Choose whether you want your percentage to be based on a grand total of all values or on a subtotal, and then check the appropriate radio button. If you opt to create a percentage based on a subtotal, you will also need to tell Discoverer which item it should use to create the subtotal.

5. Next you need to determine whether you want Discoverer to calculate the percentages according to only values in the current page or values across all pages. If you are not using Page Items or have only one Page Item, then the choice makes no difference. The only time you really need to make a decision is when Page Items are in use and you have multiple pages. We advise you to be careful when calculating percentages across multiple pages because it may not be evident to the casual observer that this is what you have done.

6. Choose whether to include totals in your percentages. If you do so, you may also give a label for the percentage. This is not mandatory, and you may leave it either with the default or nothing at all.

7. If you wish to use a different color of font for your percentage, click the Format Data button.

8. Click OK to finish.

You need to think about what item or items you want to use in your percentages. Unlike calculations, there are no administrator-created percentages for you to choose from. However, you can have calculations that give the answer as a percentage, but these cannot be edited as percentages.

Because percentages usually stand alone as data items, it doesn't really matter in what order you create them. Although you probably wouldn't have more than one or two in your query, there is no limit on the number of percentages you can define. Creating valid and meaningful percentages can be somewhat taxing at first, but don't worry, because most of the fun of working with Discoverer lies in examining and trying things out for yourself.

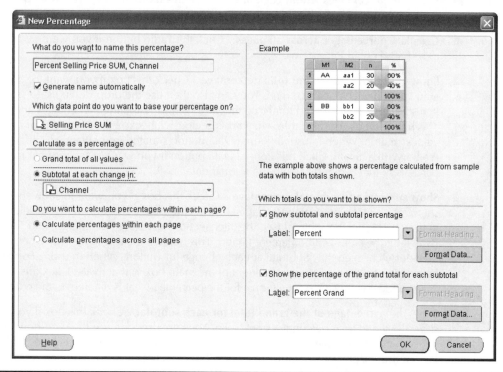

FIGURE 5-14 *New Percentage dialog box*

When you have decided what data item you need for a percentage, launch the New Percentage dialog box. This dialog box contains the following sections:

- **What do you want to name this percentage?** The name given here will appear as the column heading. Discoverer will create a name for you if you don't specify one. Figure 5-14 shows Discoverer inserting default names. We recommend you review Discoverer's names and change them to something more meaningful.

- **Generate name automatically** Check this box if you want Discoverer to name percentages for you (not a good idea).

- **Which data point do you want to base your percentage on?** This is a drop-down list of the data points that you can use to base percentages on. If there is only one data point, the drop-down will be inactive.

- **Grand total of all values** Click this radio button if you want your percentages to be based on the grand total of all values.

- **Subtotal at each change in** Click this radio button if you want your percentages to be based on a subtotal. Having clicked this button, select the item on which you want to create the subtotal from the drop-down list.

- **Calculate percentages within each page** Click this radio button if you want percentages to be based only on the items displayed onscreen.

- **Calculate percentages across all pages** Click this radio button if you want percentages to be based on all Page Items.

- **Show grand total and grand total percentage** Check this box if you want to show the grand total percentages onscreen. You can also then use the drop-down list to select items for labeling the grand total (see the later section "Labeling Percentages and Totals"). This box will only be available when you previously checked the "Grand total of all values" button. When in use, a Format Data button situated immediately to the right of the box will activate. Click this Format Data button if you want to set a format for the percentage that is different from the normal data.

- **Show subtotal and subtotal percentage** Check this box if you want to show the subtotals and their percentages on screen. You can use the drop-down list to select items for labeling the subtotal (see the later section "Labeling Percentages and Totals"). By default the label will be Percent Grand. This box will be available only when you previously checked the "Subtotal at each change in" button. When in use, a Format Data button situated immediately to the right of the main box will activate. Click this Format Data button if you want to set a format for the percentage that is different to the normal data.

- **Show the percentage of the grand total for each subtotal** Check this box if you want to show the grand total percentages onscreen. You can also then use the drop-down list to select items for labeling the grand total (see the section "Labeling Percentages and Totals" later in this chapter). By default the label will be Percent. This box will be available only when you previously checked the "Subtotal at each change in" button. When in use, a Format Data button situated immediately to the right of the box will activate. Click this Format Data button if you want to set a format for the percentage that is different to the normal data.

When you have created a percentage, click OK. Unlike calculations, where Discoverer has to test the mathematical properties of the calculation, percentages always work. There is no such thing as having defined an incorrect percentage, although the results you see onscreen may not be that obvious at first—as we shall show you in a moment.

Assuming you have created a valid percentage, Discoverer inserts it into the box under the My Percentages subheading and places a tick mark alongside. Percentages are added into the box in the order you create them.

Also at this point, you will notice that the Edit and Delete buttons are activated and Discoverer has inserted the formula into the Description box. If you have made an error in your formula, open the Edit Percentage dialog box and correct it. To open the Edit Percentage dialog box, click the Edit button (looks like a pencil) or right-click the percentage and select Edit from the drop-down list. If you decide you no longer need this percentage, click Delete or right-click the percentage and from the drop-down list select Delete. The percentage will be removed.

NOTE
You will not be warned when deleting percentages, so take care.

When you have completed adding percentages to your query, you can either click Finish, which causes Discoverer to run the query, or move to Step 8 of the Workbook Wizard by clicking Next.

Examples of Percentages

Because there are many options available to you within the Workbook Wizard, we will show you examples of each type. For the purpose of these examples, we have specified a query that pulls in the selling price SUM, the sales channel, the fiscal year (with a condition to constrain to just FY 1999), and the fiscal quarter. The fiscal year has been moved to the Page Item box. We will start by using a very simple percentage calculation and progress through all of the options so that you can see at a glance what each option does. In all of these examples, the only data point open to us is the selling price SUM.

Example 1: A Simple Percentage

In this example, we will apply the following options:

- Calculate as a percentage of the grand total

- Calculate percentages for current Page Items only

- Do not show any totals

This is by far the easiest type of percentage to create and apply within your query, and probably the easiest for anyone viewing your output to understand. When you set the options and then click OK, Discoverer will create the percentage calculation. As you can see, Discoverer has sorted the query by channel and quarter. You can see at a glance that Global Widgets' best quarter was Q1, 1999, with 46 percent of sales for the year. You may also spot that there were no sales from the Internet in that quarter; this is because they didn't start their e-business until the beginning of Q2.

Example 2: Showing the Grand Total

In the next example, we have edited the previous percentage and redefined it as follows:

- Calculate as a percentage of the grand total

- Calculate percentages for current Page Items only

- Show grand total and grand total percentage, and use the label "Percent"

When you set these options, Discoverer will refine the percentage calculation. As you can see, Discoverer shows grand totals for both the Selling Price SUM and the Percentage columns. You can also see that Discoverer has inserted the default name "Percent Selling Price SUM." Again, we recommend that you review these default names and change them to something more meaningful. We have not done so here in order to highlight how Discoverer inserts default names.

Example 3: Showing Subtotals

In the next example, we have further edited the percentage and redefined it as follows:

- Calculate as a percentage of the subtotal based on the channel.

- Calculate percentages for current Page Items only.

- Show subtotals and subtotal percentages, using the label "Percent."

When you set these options, Discoverer will refine the percentage calculation. As you can see, Discoverer is showing subtotals by channel for both the Selling Price SUM and Percentage columns. We can see at a glance that the best quarter for Global Widgets via their external channel was Q1, which accounted for 51 percent of that channel's annual sales. Their best quarter from the Internet came in Q3, with 44 percent of annual sales.

NOTE
In order to correctly apply a percentage using subtotals, you need to define sorts on the items you want to subtotal. Using the preceding example, we have created a group sort on the channel and applied a normal ascending order sort on the fiscal month.

Example 4: Showing Subtotals and a Grand Total

In the next example, we have further edited the percentage and redefined it as follows:

- Calculate as a percentage of the subtotal based on the channel.

- Calculate percentages for current Page Items only.

- Show subtotals and subtotal percentages, using the label "Percent."

- Show grand totals and grand total percentages, using the label "Percent Grand."

By setting these options, Discoverer will refine the percentage calculation. As you can see, Discoverer is now showing not only the subtotals by channel for both the Selling Price SUM and Percentage columns, but also the percentage of each as compared to the grand total. We can now see that the external channel accounted for 90 percent of all sales for FY 1999, with the Internet accounting for just 10 percent.

Example 5: Showing Subtotals and a Grand Total Using Page Items

In the next example, we have further edited the percentage and redefined it as follows:

■ Calculate as a percentage of the subtotal based on the channel.

■ Calculate percentages for all Page Items.

■ Show subtotals and subtotal percentages, using the label "Percent."

■ Show grand totals and grand total percentages, using the label "Percent Grand."

In order to create this percentage example, we have edited our condition on the fiscal year, bringing in data for 1998 as well. We therefore have a two-year reporting period for this query. When we set these options, Discoverer will refine the percentage calculation to be as shown next.

As you can see, Discoverer is still showing subtotals by channel and a grand total. At first glance, the results may appear to be incorrect; however, they are not. If you look closely at the percentage totals for the external channel, you will see that Discoverer has inserted values of 45 percent for the subtotal and 42 percent for the grand total. What this means is that in FY 1999, Global Widgets had external sales that accounted for 45 percent of all of the external sales in the two-year period, and that this amount equated to 42 percent of *all* sales in the same period. Looking at the Internet channel, you can see that *all* of their Internet sales came in 1999, and that this accounted for just 5 percent of the total sales in the same period.

NOTE
Oracle added the capability to create percentages based on page items when they introduced their Web version of Discoverer. The preceding example can therefore only be created in Plus.

Why Not Perform Percentages in the Wizard?

As the preceding examples have shown, applying percentages and understanding what the various Discoverer options mean can be quite daunting, even to a seasoned query writer. Percentages can also take some time to compute, and it may not be the best use of your time to worry about percentages until after you have a working version of your query. For this reason, we again recommend that you not attempt to create percentages using the Workbook Wizard until you have become proficient in the use of Discoverer.

You have now completed Step 7 of the Desktop Workbook Wizard. Click Next to move to Step 8.

Creating User-Defined Totals in the Plus Workbook Wizard

As shown earlier in Figure 5-9, the Plus Calculations tab has the standard buttons available throughout the wizard, with three additional default settings. These are

- **My Calculations** Displays a list of the calculations you have defined.

- **My Percentages** Displays a list of the percentages you have defined.

- **My Totals** Displays a list of the totals that you have defined.

Thus, because we just completed adding our first calculations and percentages, there is no need to navigate away from the Calculations tab. We stay right here while we create totals.

Totals: What Are They?

Discoverer Desktop defines a total as "The result of a calculation that summarizes data in a sheet. Examples of totals are minimum, maximum, average, and sum." The definition within Plus states, "When working with numeric information, you often need to see various summations of the data. Totals can sum rows and columns of numbers, find averages and standard deviation, compute subtotals and grand totals, and so on. When you add a total to a worksheet, Discoverer automatically adds a column or row to the worksheet for the totals data."

If you read both definitions closely, there is a clue in the Plus definition that Oracle has enhanced the totaling capabilities of Discoverer in their Web version. This is absolutely true, and Plus has more options for totaling than are available in the Windows version.

Calculating totals of numbers is again a typical data analysis task. Discoverer allows you to choose the data to use both for the total itself and for the value used to represent the total (grand total, subtotal, etc.). Don't worry about the terms used at this stage, as these will all be fully covered.

NOTE
If in the previous step you created a percentage based on either a grand total or a subtotal, you would not want to create it again here. If you have decided not to create totals based on percentages, you now have the option of creating them in this step of the Workbook Wizard.

Like percentages, totals are mathematical formulas that enable you to analyze your data more effectively. They apply standard mathematical algorithms to the item you have chosen. A simple example of a total in a query is "Show me the grand total of product ordered for the month of January 2000." A more complex total would be to see the same query extended to include subtotals for each change of product.

Figure 5-15 shows a simple total being applied in a query. You can see the total amount of product sold. Again, because the month is only used to define a condition, it has been moved to the Page Item.

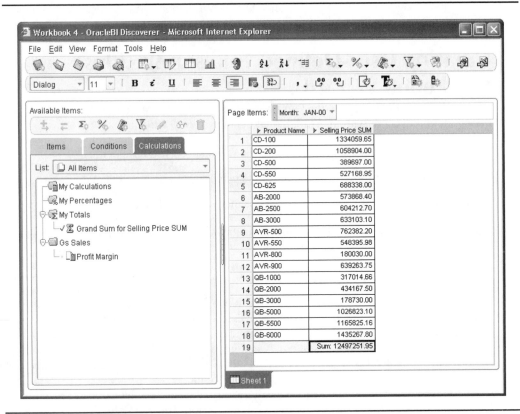

FIGURE 5-15 *Grand total of products for January 2000*

Creating a New Total

Before you launch the New Total dialog box, you need to think about what item or items you want to use in your totals. Unlike calculations, there are no administrator-created totals for you to choose from. However, you can have totals that are based on percentages, but these cannot be edited as totals.

Because totals usually stand alone as data items, it doesn't really matter in which order you create them. Although you probably wouldn't have more than one or two in your query, there is no limit on the number of totals you can define.

When creating a new total, you should use the following workflow:

1. Launch the New Total dialog box (see Figure 5-16).

NOTE
There are two ways to launch the New Total dialog box. The first way is to click New and then from the drop-down box select New Total. The second way is to right-click My Totals on the Calculations tab and from the pop-up box select New Total.

2. The first thing to do is to choose which data point or points you want the total to be on. Click the drop-down button and from the list pick the item that you want to use. You have the option to select a single item or all items. Unfortunately, there is no option to select combinations of items for totaling. To make Discoverer add a total for all items, from the drop-down box select the item called All Data Points.

3. Choose the type of total you want to apply by clicking the drop-down button and selecting the total from the list. After you have selected the total, Discoverer inserts a brief description, in your language, of what that total will produce.

4. Choose whether you want to see a grand total of all values or subtotals, and then check the appropriate radio button. If you opt to create subtotals, you will also need to tell Discoverer which item it should use to create the subtotal. Discoverer will automatically create a Group Sort in Low to High order for the item that is being subtotaled.

NOTE

if you start out with a subtotal and then change your mind and alter it to being a grand total, whatever group sort was created for handling the subtotal will remain in place. If you do not want the group sort, you will need to navigate to the Sort window of the wizard to remove it.

5. Choose whether to display totals for a single row or not. This is a very useful check box and one that we make extensive use of. We recommend you do likewise.

6. Next you need to determine whether you want Discoverer to calculate the totals only according to the values in the current page or across all pages. If you are not using Page Items or have only one Page Item, then the choice makes no difference. The only time you really need to make a decision is when Page Items are in use and you have multiple pages. We advise you to be careful when creating totals across multiple pages because it may not be evident to the casual observer that this is what you have done.

7. You next need to decide what label you want Discoverer to use for the total. You can allow Discoverer to insert a label automatically, by checking the box called "Generate label automatically". Should you choose not to allow Discoverer to do this, uncheck this box and add your own label. You can either type the label yourself or select one of the predefined labels from the drop-down list provided (see the section "Labeling Percentages and Totals," later in this chapter). You can even use labels that combine your own label with a predefined label from the drop-down list.

8. Finally, click the Format Data button to set a format that is different to the normal data. We recommend that you adopt the habit of applying different colors to totals because this draws the recipient's eyes to the subtotal or total.

9. Click OK to finish.

Unlike calculations, where Discoverer has to test the mathematical properties of the calculation, totals always work. There is no such thing as having defined an incorrect total, although the results you see onscreen may not be that obvious at first, especially if your totals are being computed across multiple pages! Assuming you have created a valid total, Discoverer inserts it under the heading called My Totals. It also places a tick mark alongside the total to indicate that it is in use within the query. Totals are added and displayed in the order you create them.

FIGURE 5-16   *The New Total dialog box*

Also at this point, you will notice that the Edit and Delete buttons are activated and Discoverer has inserted the formula for the total into the Description box. If you have made an error in your total, use the Edit button to reopen the Total dialog box and change it. If you decide you no longer need this total, click Delete and it will be removed.

When you have completed adding totals to your query, you can either click Finish, which causes Discoverer to execute the query, or you can move to on the final step of the Workbook Wizard, parameters, by clicking Next three times.

Labeling Percentages and Totals

In the preceding two sections of this chapter, for percentages and totals, we told you that Discoverer has a set of predefined label options that you can use to help you create your own labels. The three predefined labels that are available to you are

- **Insert Item Name**   When you select this option, Discoverer inserts the name of the item on which you are subtotaling. If you are subtotaling by Sales Channel, for example, and the heading for the data item is Channel, then Discoverer will insert the word Channel into the label. However, if you select this label option when the item only has a grand total, Discoverer inserts the label All Items.

- **Insert Data Point Name**   When you select this option, Discoverer inserts the column name of the sorted item into the label. If you are sorting on the Selling Price, for example, and the heading for the data item is Price, then Discoverer will insert the word Price into the label.

■ **Insert Value**   When you select this option, Discoverer inserts the actual value for the item on which you are subtotaling. If you are subtotaling by Sales Channel, for example, and you have two channels, EXTERNAL and INTERNAL, then Discoverer will insert the channel names into the appropriate subtotal. However, if you select this label option when the item has only a grand total, Discoverer inserts the label All Values.

NOTE
The three words &Item, &Date, and &Value, corresponding to the labels in the preceding list, are codes that tell Discoverer to insert the item name, data point name, or value respectively. These codes can either be selected from the drop-down list or be typed in. The format used always begins with the & character followed by a word, with the first letter of that word in uppercase.

Creating User-Defined Parameters in the Plus Workbook Wizard

Figure 5-17 shows the final step of the Discoverer Plus Workbook Wizard. This step in the Workbook Wizard has a dialog box containing the following two boxes and five buttons:

■ **Available Parameters box**   This box will be empty until you add a parameter. As you add parameters to your query, Discoverer will display them here in the order in which you create them.

■ **Description box**   This box shows the description of the parameter highlighted in the Available Parameters box.

■ **New button**   Click this to add a new parameter.

■ **Edit button**   When active, click this to edit an existing parameter.

■ **Delete button**   Click this to delete a parameter. As with conditions, again, be careful because it does just what it says and without prompting!

■ **Move Up button**   If you have multiple parameters, click this to promote the highlighted parameter. The order controls the sequence in which the parameters are prompted when the query is run.

■ **Move Down button**   If you have multiple parameters, click this to demote the highlighted parameter.

Parameters: What Are They?

Parameters offer choices each time the query runs. They are placeholders that accept dynamic input values either from the keyboard or from another workbook. Parameters are typically used in two situations:

■ To provide input to a condition

■ To provide input to calculations

FIGURE 5-17 *Parameters step of the Plus Workbook Wizard*

Parameter Input to a Condition

This is the most usual usage for a parameter. In this usage, Discoverer will associate a parameter with a condition and then, when executed, pass the received dynamic value to the condition for filtering. Whenever you create a parameter that is to be associated with a condition and no such condition yet exists, Discoverer will also create the condition.

Parameter Input to a Calculation

This is the more complex, yet probably the cleverer, usage for parameters. In this usage, Discoverer will not associate the parameter with a condition but will make the input that it receives available for use in calculations. For example, we could accept from the user an upper number and a lower number for use in a statistical calculation. We will cover this method of parameterization in Chapter 13 when we discuss advanced handling of parameters.

For the remainder of this section, we will be working with parameters that are associated with conditions.

As previously stated, whenever you create a parameter where no condition currently exists, Discoverer will create a condition and will link the parameter to that condition. Parameters are unlike regular conditions in that they allow you to use different criteria each time the query is run. For example, say you have created a query that shows total sales for the past seven years with a condition Year>=1993. Every time you run this query, you see all of the sales from 1993 until today. If you want to run the query for just the last five years, you would need to edit the condition and save the query. If you add a parameter to the condition, Year>=[Year Entered], you will be prompted before the query runs to add the value for the earliest year you want to see. This avoids the need to edit and resave the query.

Figure 5-18 shows the prompt you will see before the query runs.

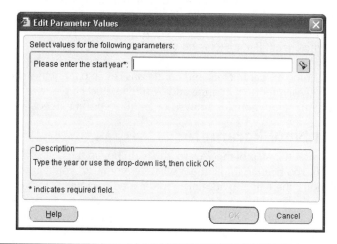

FIGURE 5-18   *Edit Parameter Values dialog box*

As you can see, Discoverer displays a dialog box allowing you to enter the exact filter you want to apply to your query in terms of a certain condition. This capability allows the same query to be used by many people with different reporting needs.

Differences Between Conditions and Parameters

One of the things that new Discoverer users find difficult to understand is the difference between a condition and a parameter, and when to apply them. Both are filters, and both are used to constrain your query.

Conditions are fixed filters, and you will see exactly the same results every time you run the query. The only way to change the output is to edit the query and change the condition. However, some users don't have the ability to edit queries because a constraint has been applied to their profiles by the Discoverer manager. This constraint is primarily used for new Discoverer end users who haven't yet taken training and learned how to edit correctly. Another reason all end users don't have editing rights is system integrity. You would not want to have a query you spent many hours creating edited by a novice end user, and find that it no longer works.

Parameters are variable filters, so you don't see exactly the same results every time you run the query. A well-written parameterized query can satisfy dozens of different user requests without the need to edit the query or jeopardize its integrity. This is an excellent reason for having report writers. It allows queries to be built by them on behalf of your department. Other end users and report viewers can then be granted access rights to run the query. They would simply fill in the parameters that fit their needs without having to rebuild or create a new query. In other words, there is no need to "reinvent the wheel." We have heard of Discoverer users that have, in extreme cases, used only 10–15 worksheets to satisfy requirements that at one point required more than a hundred different worksheets, all by using effective parameters.

Another difference between conditions and parameters is that parameters help you to open a workbook quickly to see only the data you need. Your day-to-day mission-critical queries need to be parameterized, allowing them to be used by many people time and time again. Conditions, being designed more for ad hoc analysis, are aimed at helping you find very specific data. For example, suppose you are puzzled because the sales from Europe for a particular product are lower than expected. You could not have anticipated this, and therefore you will not have a prewritten query. You will need to create an ad hoc query using conditions to isolate by both Europe and the product in question. This query will probably be used only once and will never need to be parameterized. Parameters and conditions can be mixed for creating more sophisticated filtering procedures.

The rule of thumb on parameters and conditions is that parameters should always be utilized in queries that are used more than once and by multiple users, whereas conditions should be created in queries that are more for analysis or ad hoc reporting needs.

Creating a New Parameter

When you first enter this step of the wizard, the main box in the center of the screen will be empty (see Figure 5-19). You need to think about what item or items you want to use in your parameters. Unlike calculations, there are no administrator-created parameters for you to choose from.

It does not make any difference to Discoverer what order you create your parameters. In fact, in most cases, it makes no difference in what order they are run. However, you will probably want to present them to the user in a logical sequence. This sequence could simply be alphabetical, or you may want to offer the parameters in their sort order. Whatever method you choose, you should always do it the same way—thus creating query standardization.

NOTE
If you are using cascading parameters, where the input from one parameter is used to filter the available items in subsequent parameters, the order is important. We discuss cascading parameters in Chapter 13.

If your company already has reporting standards, you should follow them. For example, if your company always prompts for a date before a customer, so should you. Similarly, if your company has standards for naming prompts, you should use these—thus making your queries look professional. The last thing you want to do is create a wonderful query that does not adhere to your company standards.

When creating a new parameter, you should use the following workflow:

1. Click New. This opens the New Parameter dialog box, as shown in Figure 5-19.

2. Give a name for your parameter. This is only an internal name used by the system; however, you should still give it a short, meaningful name. If you leave this blank, Discoverer will insert a name for you.

3. Click the Item drop-down box to see the list of available items, and select the data item you want to apply the parameter on from the list.

4. Determine whether you want this new parameter to be associated with a condition. If you do decide that this is what you want, Discoverer will create the condition for you at the same time that it creates the parameter.

5. If the parameter is being used in a condition, click the Operator drop-down box to see a list of the available operators. From this list you need to select one operator. You will notice that the Condition box has been updated to give you a visual interpretation of the condition that Discoverer will now create.

6. Enter the text you want to prompt the user with. For example, **Enter the year**. Leaving this blank causes Discoverer to generate a prompt for you.

7. Enter a description of the parameter that is easy to understand. Discoverer will display this to the user as context-sensitive help. Unlike in the previous steps, if you leave this blank, Discoverer will not create a description for you. The user will therefore get no context-sensitive help.

8. Next you need to determine whether you want Discoverer to use the same parameter value for all worksheets in the workbook, or whether to allow users to key in a different parameter value for each worksheet. We like the idea of restricting parameter values to all worksheets. This way, when a user navigates from worksheet to worksheet, Discoverer will automatically use the same parameter value, thus ensuring that the data is consistent.

9. Determine whether the parameter is mandatory or not. If you determine that the parameter is mandatory, at run time Discoverer will display an asterisk alongside the parameter prompt, even in Desktop. This indicates to the user that a value is required. If you determine that the parameter is optional, at run time no asterisk will be displayed, and the user can elect to run the query without any input. Should the user provide no input whatsoever, Discoverer will assume that the user wants to query ALL values.

10. Determine whether users can select multiple values or not. For example, if you check this box and the prompt was for a product, the user would be given a list of all products and allowed to check the ones they want. We think this is a really clever feature, as you will see later. Leaving this box unchecked allows users to only enter single values when prompted.

11. Choose whether to allow users to select either indexes or values. This box will only be active if the database has an index on the table and the Discoverer manager has created a cross-reference to that index in the properties of the item. This feature is new in 10.1.2, and we think it is extremely useful for improving system performance.

12. Provide a default value for the parameter or, if a list of values or indexes exist for the item against which you are creating the parameter, choose from the drop-down list of values. Discoverer does not require a default value to be entered.

13. Choose whether you want to employ cascading parameters. A cascading parameter is where the value from one parameter is taken to filter the list on subsequent parameters. For example, let's say we have two parameters, one each for Region and District. If the user selects a Region, we can use the Region as a filter to the District. This restricts the District list of values to only those districts within the selected region. We will cover this usage of parameters in Chapter 13.

14. Click OK to finish.

Unlike calculations, where Discoverer has to test the mathematical properties of the calculation, parameters always work. There is no such thing as having defined an incorrect parameter, although the results you see onscreen may not be that obvious at first.

Assuming you have created a valid parameter, Discoverer inserts it into the box for parameters. If you checked the box to create a condition, Discoverer will insert a number alongside the parameter. Parameters are initially added into the box in the order you create them. If you go back to the second step of the wizard and click the Conditions tab, you will see that Discoverer has created a new condition. If the name that Discoverer has given this condition does not follow your naming convention, change it now.

Back in Step 5 of the wizard, you will notice that the Edit and Delete buttons are activated, and Discoverer has inserted the description you created into the Description box. If you have

FIGURE 5-19 *New Parameter dialog box*

made an error, use the Edit button to reopen the Parameter dialog box and change it. At this stage, you will no longer be allowed to change the operator being used for the condition. If you need to change this, you will have to edit the condition itself. If you did not create a condition, editing the parameter will not allow you to do this either. The only way to do this now is to create a new condition by going back to Step 2 of the Workbook Wizard. If you decide you no longer need this parameter, click Delete and it will be removed.

Rearranging the Parameter Order

Whenever you have two or more active parameters, you should look carefully at the list and determine if the parameter sequence is logical. If you decide you have a parameter in the wrong place, you can use the Move Up and Move Down buttons to promote or demote items. These buttons become active only when you have created two or more active parameters. The sequence determines the order in which parameters are offered to the end user. If you are using cascading parameters, make sure you offer the unconstrained parameters first before you invite input to the filtered parameters. If you attempt to move the dependent parameter above the primary parameter, Discoverer will prompt you with a warning. However, it does not allow you to cancel the action, but we will tell you how to handle this warning in Chapter 13.

NOTE
An active parameter is a parameter that has either been associated with a condition or is being used as input to a calculation. Only these parameters will be used as prompts.

Why Not Create Parameters in the Wizard?

Although parameters do not add an overhead to your query in the same way that calculations, sorting, totaling, and percentages do, we still recommend that, when working with new queries, you do not create them inside the Workbook Wizard. We do strongly recommend that you create conditions, and these should suffice for getting the query up and running.

When you have a working copy of your query, you should concentrate on the conditions and look to see which ones can be parameterized. You are also in a better position to ascertain whether you need any new conditions and have the choice whether to do this as a parameter or not. Finally, taking the time in the Workbook Wizard to create parameters, when your query may not even work, can be very frustrating and time-consuming.

When you have completed adding parameters to your query, you have finished with the Workbook Wizard. You can either click Finish, which causes Discoverer to run the query, or you can click Back to go back to validate previous steps.

Editing the Sheet After the Query Has Run

Because we recommend that you only use the Workbook Wizard for the first four steps of a query, we need to show you how to reopen the Workbook Wizard after you have a working query.

In Desktop, from the menu, select Sheet | Edit Sheet or click the Edit Sheet icon on the toolbar. This opens a multitabbed form with one step of the Workbook Wizard per tab. In Plus, the form has a slightly different layout. The Plus form is shown in Figure 5-20.

NOTE
Throughout the rest of the book we will refer often to the Edit Sheet dialog box in Desktop and the Edit Worksheet dialog box in Plus. These two dialog boxes function in almost identical ways. For the sake of simplicity, when we refer to these two dialog boxes, we will call them the Edit Sheet/Worksheet dialog box.

The forms in both Desktop and Plus function in the exact manner of their respective Workbook Wizards, but you do not have the Back and Next buttons. You can click randomly from tab to tab, adding the criteria you want to your query. When you are done adding criteria, click OK and your query will run with the changes you have made.

In addition to the Edit Sheet/Worksheet dialog box, each of the forms from the Workbook Wizard can be accessed directly from the menu bar. In both versions of Discoverer, the Tools menu option gives you a drop-down list of available forms. In addition, Desktop offers an analysis bar, while Plus has an analysis area on the toolbar containing buttons to access the tools. For more detail on the analysis bar and the analysis area, see Chapter 9. For more instruction on using all of the tools offered in the Workbook Wizard, see Chapters 10, 11, and 12.

FIGURE 5-20 *The Plus Edit Worksheet dialog box*

In Plus you have more options for making changes after the query has run. You can reopen the wizard using the menu bar Edit menu. Here you can choose which of the tabs on the wizard to open. After it is open, you can make changes to any of the tabs. You can also open the Edit Worksheet dialog box by clicking the Edit Worksheet button on the toolbar. The Edit Worksheet dialog box functions just like the wizard. You can also edit the query directly from the Plus window. The panes to the left allow you to add or delete items on the fly or modify calculations and conditions.

The Available Items Pane

The top pane is called the Available Items pane. It contains many features of the Workbook Wizard. At the top is a toolbar with tools to help you edit your query. Next is a list box with business areas available to you as well as the search button. The box at the bottom of the Available Items pane contains the actual folders from the Business area you selected. There are also two other tabs for Conditions and Calculations. All of these items are used in exactly the same way as in the Workbook Wizard. In this illustration you can see the features of the Available Items pane:

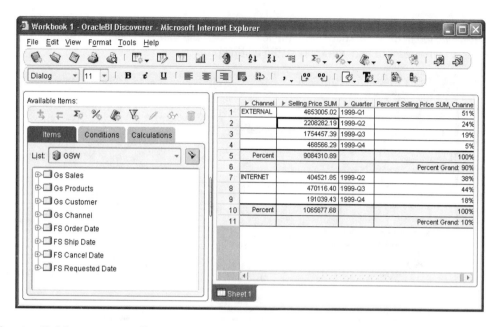

The Available Items Toolbar

The toolbar contains the following buttons:

- **Add to Worksheet**   Use this button to move a selected item to the worksheet.

- **Remove from Worksheet**   Use this button to remove a selected item from the worksheet.

- **New Total**   Use this button to open the New Total dialog box.

- **New Percentage**   Use this button to open the New Percentage dialog box.

- **New Calculation**   Use this button to open the New Calculation dialog box.

- **New Condition**   Use this button to open the New Condition dialog box.

NOTE
You can use the Add to Worksheet and Remove from Worksheet buttons to move items in and out of your query, or you can simply drag and drop.

The Selected Items Pane

The bottom pane is called the Selected Items pane. It contains the items you selected for use in your query.

As we refer to the Edit Worksheet dialog box, you will see that the Available Items pane and the Selected Items pane share the same features. Use the panes as often as possible to save time. It is an effective tool and will simplify the editing process.

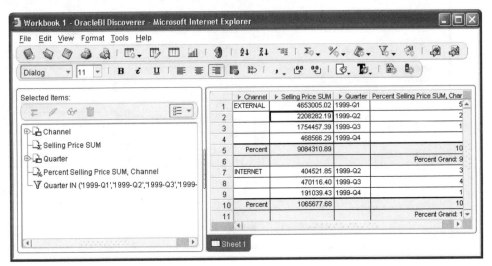

Summary

In this chapter, you have learned the optional steps of the Workbook Wizard as well as how to reopen the Workbook Wizard with the Edit Sheet and Edit Worksheet forms. We have given the definitions of sorts, calculations, percentages, totals, and parameters, and how they can be used in a query. You have also been shown the steps used to add these functions to a query.

In each section we have explained why it is recommended to complete the first four essential steps and run your query prior to adding sorts, calculations, percentages, totals, and parameters.

These topics and those in Chapter 4 have given definitions of the Workbook Wizard steps and an overview of each function. This will get you started creating simple queries. More in-depth examples will be given and skills taught in Chapters 11 and 12.

PART
II

Editing the Query

CHAPTER

6

Formatting the Output in Discoverer Desktop and Plus

s we have already explained, Discoverer can be used to produce both ad hoc queries, which answer a specific one-off question, and queries that will be used by multiple users. Both can remain as queries, but as soon as you decide that the output needs to be viewed by somebody else, it becomes a report. This is especially true if you are planning on giving the results to senior management.

When you have a fully working query of this type, it needs to be formatted. Put in its simplest form, formatting is the shape, size, typeface, and general appearance of a document. Formatting is an important step in turning your query into an easy-to-read, attractive, and well-organized report. This is true whether or not you intend the output to be viewed onscreen, printed, or exported. The latter two possibilities will be dealt with in Chapter 8.

In this chapter, you will learn how to rename and reposition column headings in order to fit your needs. You will be shown how to rearrange the order and position of the output.

Another way to use formatting to improve a query is to change fonts and font sizes, font and background colors, and text justification. This chapter will show you in detail how to perform these functions. You will also be taught how to format numbers as currency, with commas, and with the correct number of decimal places.

You will be taught to add titles to your query, and how to format them with font, sizes, and colors, as well as how to add bitmaps to the title. Finally, you will be shown how to add graphics to the background of a query to add interest and flair.

NOTE
If you use an older release of Plus, you might be frustrated with the limitations in formatting. These limitations were nearly all eliminated with release 9.0.4 (10g release 1,) and with 10.1.2 the formatting issues are gone. Now that the 10.1.2 release uses the table/crosstab BI Beans, it is possible to do in-context formatting. Discoverer Plus OLAP goes one step further and allows users to also perform individual cell–level formatting.

Giving Your Headings Meaningful Names (Desktop and Plus)

As was discussed in Chapter 2, your Discoverer administrator can give items in business areas meaningful names. However, one business area could be used by a variety of departments, and what is meaningful to one department might not be to you.

Throughout the book, whenever you have had an opportunity to create new items, such as calculations, percentages, parameters, and totals, we have recommended giving these meaningful names as well. Even though in many cases Discoverer will insert a name for you, this is not a good habit to get into. What is meaningful and obvious to Discoverer, and even to you at the time, may not be so obvious to you later. Therefore, as soon as you have a working query, the first thing you should do is look at the column names and decide if they are meaningful. If they are not, you need to change them.

Discoverer adds the word SUM, AVG, or the like to each numeric heading. While this may be okay for an ad hoc query, you should change this on your report by removing it from each heading. You must change each heading individually.

As you change column names, Discoverer resizes the width of the column to match the name, even if that means you won't be able to see all of your data. If Discoverer has resized the column to be too small, see the section on resizing later in this chapter to correct it.

NOTE
You cannot rename columns in Viewer.

How to Rename Columns in Desktop

To change the name of a column, use the following workflow:

1. Place your cursor on the column heading.

2. Right-click. This displays the following pop-up list of options:

3. Select Item Properties. This displays the following Item Properties dialog box:

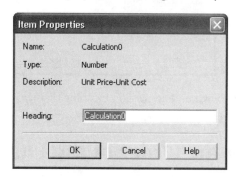

4. Change the heading name in the Item Properties dialog box.

5. Click OK or press ENTER to finish.

How to Rename Columns in Plus

To change the name of a column, use the following workflow:

1. Place your cursor on the column heading.

2. Right-click. This displays the following pop-up list of options:

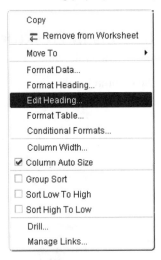

3. Select Edit Heading. This displays the following dialog box:

4. Change the heading name in the Edit Heading dialog box.

5. Click OK or press ENTER to finish.

Rearranging the Order of the Output

After you have renamed your columns, the next step is to make sure that the columns are really in the order you want them. When you were in the Workbook Wizard, you arranged the order of the columns. After running the query, you may find that the order just does not look right, and you can see how rearranging them will make your report easier to read.

How to Rearrange Columns

There are two ways to rearrange columns in Desktop and three ways in Plus. You can rearrange them in the worksheet or in the Edit Sheet/Worksheet dialog box. We will give you all methods, but we always suggest you use the simplest. For rearranging single columns, we recommended using the worksheet. When rearranging multiple columns, you can use either method. If you are certain of the order you desire, do it in the worksheet. If you are not sure how you want the columns arranged, use the Edit Sheet/Worksheet dialog box. This option allows you to "try out" an arrangement; however, you can click Cancel if you want the order returned to its original configuration.

Moving a Single Column in Desktop and Plus Using Drag and Drop

To move a single column using drag and drop, use the following workflow:

1. Click and hold on the column heading you want to move.

2. Drag the column heading to the desired location and then release the mouse button.

Figure 6-1 shows a column being moved to the left. In Desktop the mouse pointer changes to a double-headed arrow. In Plus the mouse pointer changes to a hand.

FIGURE 6-1 *Moving a column using drag and drop*

Moving a Single Column in Plus from a Drop-Down List

To move a single column in Plus from a drop-down list, use the following workflow:

1. Click the column heading you want to move.

2. Right-click and from the following drop-down list select Move To.

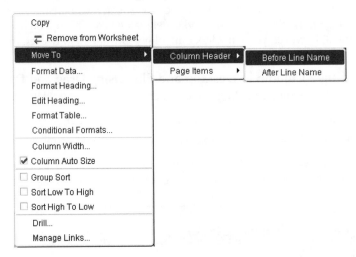

3. Select Column Header to move the column before or after another column, or Page Items to move the column to the page items.

Moving Multiple Columns

To move multiple columns, or to "try out" a configuration, use the following workflow:

1. From the menu bar, in Desktop select Sheet | Edit Sheet, or in Plus select Edit | Worksheet, or from the toolbar click the Edit Sheet/Worksheet icon—either of these methods displays the Edit Sheet/Worksheet dialog box (Figure 5-20 in the preceding chapter).

2. Click the Table/Crosstab Layout tab. Drag and drop the columns into their desired locations, as seen on the next page.

3. Click OK or press ENTER to finish.

NOTE
If you have started to reorder the columns and wish to abort the changes you have made, do not click OK or press ENTER. Click Cancel to have Discoverer abandon all column moves and reinstate the ordering as it was before you started.

We don't recommend using this method for moving a single column because it involves unnecessary keystrokes.

Formatting Data

After you have changed your column names, you should look at the data items in each column and decide whether they need formatting. Discoverer recognizes three different types of data—text, dates, and numbers—and each can be formatted in a variety of ways.

Formatting Tools

Discoverer provides tools on the toolbar for formatting data. These buttons perform many of the standard formatting functions. We will explain what each button does later in the appropriate section of this chapter.

NOTE
*If you cannot see the formatting bar in Desktop, click View |
Formatting Bar to make it appear. In Plus, click View | Toolbars,
then click Fromatting Bar.*

Format Data Dialog Box

Discoverer provides a Format Data dialog box in Desktop that has three tabs: one each for formatting fonts, setting the alignment, and changing the background color. In Plus the tabs for formatting font alignment and background color have been consolidated into one tab called

Format. There is one additional tab that changes depending on the type of data in the column. For example, a column for text will have a tab named Text, while a column for numbers will have a tab named Number, and so on.

NOTE
In Plus, there is one additional tab, called Breaks. This tab is for formatting the breaks in a group sort and was described in Chapter 5 in the section "Creating a New Sort."

Many of the functions that are available within the Format Data dialog box are also available on the formatting bar. There are two ways to access the Format Data dialog box:

- From a pop-up list
- From the menu bar

From a Pop-Up List

To access the Format Data dialog box from a pop-up list, use the following workflow:

1. Right-click anywhere in the column you want to format. This displays a pop-up list of options.

2. Select Format Data. This displays the dialog box.

NOTE
To apply the same format to multiple columns, hold down the CTRL key and select the columns you require. If you select columns of different types, only the Font, Alignment, and Background Color tabs will be available. Selecting multiple columns of the same data type with the same formatting characteristics causes all tabs to be active.

From the Menu Bar

To access the Format Data dialog box from the menu bar, use the following workflow:

1. Click anywhere in the column you want to format.

2. From the menu bar, select Format | Data, as shown in this illustration.

3. Discoverer opens the Format Data dialog box.

The Format Data Dialog Box

As you can see in the next illustration, there are four tabs to the Desktop dialog box. These are:

- **Font** Select this tab to change the font, style, size, color, and effect.

- **Alignment** Select this tab to change the horizontal and vertical alignment.

- **Background Color**   Select this tab to change the background color of your data.

- **Date, Text, or Number**   Select this tab to set specific formatting requirements for the data type of the column. The heading will change according to the data type.

In Plus the first three tabs have been consolidated into the Format tab seen here.

The Font Tab (Part of the Format Tab in Plus)

Clicking the Font tab displays the Font dialog box, as shown here.

- ■ **Font** Select the font you require from the list provided.

- ■ **Style** Select Regular, Bold, Italic, or Bold Italic.

- ■ **Size** Select the font size you require.

- ■ **Color** Select the foreground color for the data.

- ■ **Effects** Select Strikeout or Underline.

- ■ **Sample** This shows you how your selections will look. As you move from tab to tab, this will show whatever effect you have applied so far.

If you have no more formatting to do, click OK. This will apply your changes to the data and close the dialog box. If you have more formatting to do, click one of the other tab headings and proceed.

Apart from the strikeout effect, all of the preceding font characteristics can also be applied directly from the formatting bar.

The formatting bar has several buttons that provide shortcuts to the most popular formatting functions, as shown here:

- **Font** Select the font you require from the list provided.

- **Font Size** Select the font size you require.

- **Bold** Click this button to display your data in bold.

- **Italic** Click this button to display your data in italics.

- **Underline** Click this button to display your data underlined.

- **Foreground Color** Click this button to change the foreground color.

- **Background Color** Click this button to change the background color.

The Alignment Tab (Part of the Format Tab in Plus)

Clicking the Alignment tab displays the Alignment dialog box:

- **Horizontal** Select Left, Center, or Right alignment, and also choose whether to allow your data to wrap within the column.

- **Vertical** Select whether to display the data in the Top, Center, or Bottom of the cell.

- **Sample** This shows you how your selections will look.

Only the following horizontal alignment characteristics can be applied directly from the formatting bar:

- **Align Left** Click this button to align the data to the left.

- **Align Center** Click this button to align the data to the center.

- **Align Right** Click this button to align the data to the right.

- **Wrap Text** Click this button to wrap the text in the column. You cannot wrap text in the headings, and text will only wrap when there is a space in the data.

The Background Color Tab

Clicking the Background tab displays the Background Color dialog box:

- **Background Color** Select the color you wish for the background. Check No Fill to display no background color.

- **Sample** This shows you how your selections will look.

The Date, Number, or Text Tab

We often use dates in reports, and there are a multitude of ways to format them. Clicking the Date tab displays the Format Date dialog box:

The Date tab gives you five controls to choose from.

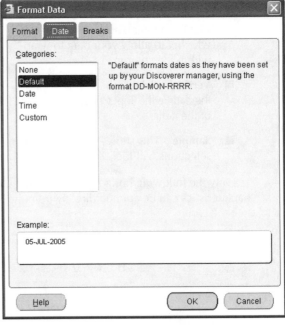

- **Categories** Select from None, Default, Date, Time, and Custom.

- **Type** This selection list appears if you have selected a category other than None or Default. It is a list of all types available. If you are working with the category Custom, an edit box will open allowing you to create custom types.

- **Add** This button is displayed when you select the category Custom. If you have created a custom type, click this button to add it to the list.

- **Delete** This button will remove a custom type.

- **Sample** This shows you how your selection or custom type will look.

None This displays the date in the format exactly as it is stored in the database. If you are unsure what the format is for your database, click Custom. The top item on the custom list is the date format used on your database.

Default This is the default selection and displays dates using the format mask set up by your Discoverer administrator. The most common format mask in use within Oracle is DD-MON-YYYY, which would display March 4, 1996, as 04-MAR-1996. If you are unsure what format has been set by your Discoverer administrator, click Custom. The second item on the custom list is the date format specified by your Discoverer administrator and is labeled Default.

Date/Time/Custom   The Date selection gives you a list of the most common date formats available. Discoverer displays the list using the actual format as it would appear in your query.

The Time selection gives you a list of the most common time formats available. Discoverer displays the list using the actual format as it would appear in your query.

The Custom selection gives you an opportunity to create a customized date and/or time. Discoverer gives you a list of the most common types, this time using standard masks. For example, instead of showing a format of 04-Mar-1996, the mask would display as DD-Mon-YYYY.

When you view the custom list, the top two items on the list are given the names None and Default. *None* means that no special date format was set by your Discoverer administrator and that the format used by the database is being applied. *Default* means that a special date format was set by your Discoverer administrator.

The following table displays the relationships between the formatted dates and times and their format masks:

Date	Time	Custom Mask
03/04		MM/DD
03/04/96		MM/DD/YY
03/04/1996		MM/DD/YYYY
03-04		MM-DD
03-04-96		MM-DD-YY
03-04-1996		MM-DD-YYYY
04-Mar		DD-Mon
04-Mar-96		DD-Mon-YY
04-Mar-1996		DD-Mon-YYYY
04 March 1996		DD fmMonth YYYY
March 4, 1996		fmMonth DD, YYYY
Monday, March 04, 1996		fmDay, fmMonth DD, YYYY
04-Mar-96 12:15 PM	04-Mar-96 12:15 PM	DD-Mon-YY HH:MI AM
04-Mar-96 12:15:30	04-Mar-96 12:15:30	DD-Mon-YY HH24:MI:SS
	12:15	HH:MM
	12:15 PM	HH:MM AM
	12:15:30	HH:MM:SS
	12:15:30 PM	HH:MM:SS AM
	12:15	HH24:MM
	12:15:30	HH24:MM:SS

In this list, you see various format masks. By combining uppercase and lowercase characters, you can create additional masks.

For example, the list includes a mask for DD-Mon-YYYY that would display October 14, 1958, as 14-Oct-1958. If you wished to display this date as 14-OCT-1958, you would simply create a new type using the mask DD-MON-YYYY.

For a full list of all date and time format masks, please see Appendix B.

NOTE
If you are not sure about the relationship between dates, times, and their format masks, select a date or time from the date or time list. You can see its mask by clicking Custom. This can be very helpful when creating complex calculations that use date functions.

NOTE
There are no date formatting features available from the formatting bar.

Adding a New Date or Time Mask   To add a new date or time format to the list available, you must follow this workflow:

1. Open or create a query containing a date.

2. Place your cursor in any column containing a date.

3. Right-click. This displays a pop-up list of options.

4. Select Format Data. This opens the Format Data dialog box.

5. Select the Date tab.

6. Select the Custom category.

7. In the box titled Type, enter the mask for the format you require. As you type, Discoverer will convert that mask into a date or time and display this in the Sample box. See Appendix A for a list of available masks.

8. When you have entered the new type, click Add. The new type will be added to the bottom of the list.

9. If you want the new format to be applied to the column, click OK or Apply. If you only want to create the new format but do not wish to use it, click Cancel.

The Number Tab

By default, Discoverer formats numbers with no decimal places, no comma separator, and negative numbers displayed using a minus sign in front of the number—for example, –1234.

The Number tab is quite a busy little box and changes depending upon the category you choose. It has three areas that are common to all of the number categories: a list of categories, a check box for showing graphic bars, and a Sample window.

■ **Categories**   Always present. Select from None, Default, Number, Currency, Percent, Scientific, and Custom.

■ **Show Graphic Bars**   In Desktop, check this to add a graphic bar indicating the size of your numbers in relation to each other. This is not available in Plus.

■ **Example**   Always present. This shows you how your selection or custom type will look.

■ **Description**   Only displayed for None and Default. This area displays a brief description of the current setting.

The categories Number, Percent, and Scientific, in addition to the areas we've just detailed, contain three additional areas:

■ **Decimal Places**   Increase or decrease the number of decimal places to display.

■ **Use 1000 Separator**   Check this to display a comma separator in large numbers. Not available for percentages or scientific.

■ **Negative Numbers**   Choose from the list how you want Discoverer to display negative numbers. Not available for scientific numbers.

As shown next, the Currency category has a drop-down for determining whether or not to use a currency symbol. Use the Display Symbol drop-down to select from a list of available currencies.

The final number category is for adding custom number formats, as shown here:

- ■ **Type** This selection list appears if you have selected the category of Custom. It is a list of all types available. An edit box will allow you to create custom types.

- ■ **Add** This button is displayed when you select the category Custom. If you have created a custom type, click this button to add it to the list.

- ■ **Delete** This button will remove a custom type.

The following table displays the standard number formats and how they will appear onscreen:

Format Mask	Will Display 1234 As
999999990	1234
999999990D99	1234.00
999990D99	1234.00
999G990	1,234
999G990PR	1,234
999G9990D99	1,234.00
9990V99	123400
9.99EEEE	1.23E+03
HH:MI:SS	20:34 (20 minutes 34 seconds)
0HH:MI:SS	00:20:34
9EEEE	1E+03
9D99EEEE	1.23E+03
99G999G990D99	1,234.00
99999999990	1234
99G999G999G990	1,234

For a full list of all number format masks, please see Appendix B.

The following illustration shows the numeric buttons of the Desktop formatting bar:

- **Currency Format**   Click this to apply standard currency formatting that places a dollar sign, two decimal places, and comma separators.

- **Number Format**   Click this to apply standard number formatting, that is, two decimal places and no comma separators. In Plus, the currency Format and Number Format options appear together on a drop-down list.

- **Increase Decimal**   Click this to add one decimal place to your number.

- **Decrease Decimal**   Click this to remove one decimal place from your number.

- **Graphic Format**   Not available in Plus; in Desktop, click this to display a graphic bar.

Adding a New Number Mask   To add a new number format to the list available, you must follow this workflow:

1. Open or create a query containing a number.
2. Place your cursor in any column containing a number.
3. Right-click. This displays a pop-up list of options.
4. Select Format Data. This opens the Format Data dialog box.
5. Select the Number tab.
6. Select the Custom category.
7. In the box titled Type, enter the mask for the format you require. See Appendix A for a list of available masks.
8. When you have entered the new type, click Add. The new type will be added to the bottom of the list and an example displayed in the Sample box.
9. If you want the new format to be applied to the column, click OK or Apply. If you only want to create the new format but do not wish to use it, click Cancel.

The Text Tab
Clicking the Text tab opens the Text dialog box, as shown here:

- **Categories**   Select from None, Default, or Text.

- **Type**   When you select the category Text, you can choose from None, Default, Uppercase, Lowercase, or Capitalized.

- **Sample**   This shows you how your selection or custom type will look.

None of these features are available from the formatting bar.

NOTE
Throughout the preceding section, whenever we have referred to a category of None, this means that the data will be displayed in the format as defined on the database. Whenever we refer to the Default category, the data will be displayed as formatted by the Discoverer administrator.

Formatting Columns

After you have formatted your data, you should look at the columns and decide if any formatting is required. This includes formatting column headings, deleting columns, and resizing columns.

Formatting Column Headings

As when you are formatting data, Discoverer provides a Format Heading dialog box. There are two ways to access the Format Heading dialog box:

- From a pop-up list
- From the menu bar

From a Pop-Up List

To access the Format Heading dialog box from a pop-up list, use the following workflow:

1. Click the heading you want to format.

2. Right-click the heading. This displays a pop-up list of options.

3. Select Format Heading. This displays the following dialog box in Desktop.

This box has the same functionality as the Format Data dialog box that was explained in the section titled "Formatting Data." The only difference is that the Format Heading dialog box has only the first three tabs, for font, alignment, and background color. In Plus the tabs are consolidated into one tab called Format.

NOTE
To apply the same format to multiple headings, hold down the CTRL
key and select the columns you require.

From the Menu Bar
To access the Format Heading dialog box from the menu bar, use the following workflow:

1. Click the heading you want to format.

2. From the menu bar, select Format | Headings. This displays the dialog box.

Formatting Multiple Headings and Columns in Plus
In Plus there is a way to do all of your heading and column formats in one place. To format multiple headings and columns, use the following workflow:

1. From the menu bar click Format | Item Formats. This opens the Format dialog box with a list of all of the items in the worksheet, as shown here:

2. Select the item you want to format. You can format the data and the heading, as well as edit the heading name. These dialog boxes should be familiar to you, as their functionality has been described to you earlier in this chapter.

3. When you have completed all of the formatting you require, click OK.

Deleting Columns from a Worksheet
While you were rearranging and formatting the column headings, you may have spotted a column that is unnecessary. You may have included something that has no bearing on the desired final result. For example, Global Widgets always ships what is ordered. Including Order Qty and Ship Qty in the same query would be redundant, and you could remove one of them.

Another reason for removing a column is when the sole purpose for including it was to enable the column to be used in a calculation or condition. Now is the time to get rid of these columns. Do not worry about your calculations or conditions, as Discoverer will remember which columns were used and will continue using them after you have deleted them from the output. This holds true even when the item being deleted was the only item being selected from a folder. We think this is a really clever feature. This will be explained in detail in Chapter 12.

How to Delete a Column

There are three ways to delete a column from the output of your query:

- From the keyboard
- From a pop-up list
- From the Edit Sheet/Worksheet dialog box
- And one additional way in Plus: drag and drop

Always use the simplest method, which in this case is by using the keyboard.

From the Keyboard

To delete a column using the keyboard, use the following workflow:

1. Click the column heading for the column you want to delete.
2. Press the DELETE key.

From a Pop-Up List

To delete a column from a pop-up list, use the following workflow:

1. Right-click the heading of the column you want to delete. This displays a pop-up list of options.
2. In Desktop, select Delete. In Plus, Select Remove from Worksheet.

NOTE
For both of the preceding workflows, you can delete multiple columns by holding down the CTRL *key as you make your selections.*

From the Edit Sheet/Worksheet Dialog Box

If you are not sure which columns you want to delete and simply want to see how the worksheet will look without some of the columns, you should use this method.

To delete columns from the Edit Sheet/Worksheet dialog box, use the following workflow:

1. From the menu bar, select Sheet | Edit Sheet/Worksheet, or from the Toolbar click the Edit Sheet/Worksheet icon. Either of these displays the Edit Sheet/Worksheet dialog box (see Figure 5-20 in the preceding chapter).

2.   Click the Table Layout tab.

3.   Highlight the column you want to delete.

4.   Press the DELETE key on your keyboard.

5.   Click OK or press ENTER to finish.

NOTE
If you have deleted the wrong column, do not click OK or press ENTER.
Clicking Cancel causes Discoverer to abandon the delete
and reinstate the column.

Drag and Drop in Plus
To delete a column by drag and drop, use the following workflow:

1.   Click the column heading of the column you want to remove from the worksheet.

2.   Drag it to the Available Items pane and release your mouse.

Resizing Columns
There are four ways to resize columns in Discoverer. Some of these are very precise, while others
are free-format and simply resize to whatever manual width setting you apply to the column.
    The four ways you can resize a column are as follows:

■   Drag the column edge to the required width.

■   Double-click a column edge (precise).

■   Manually resize a single column using the Format menu.

■   Auto-size using the Format menu (precise).

NOTE
To view the current width of a column in Desktop, place the cursor
on the right-hand edge of the column, and then click and hold the left
mouse button. This causes Discoverer to embolden all of the column's
right-hand edge and to display the current width at the bottom of the
screen (see Figure 6-2).

Resizing by Dragging the Column Edge to a Required Width
Resizing a column using this method is quick but imprecise, and comes down to user preference.
This method is sufficient for working on the screen, but not usually accurate enough for printing
or creating a report. Discoverer will resize a column to any width you choose, even if that means
being unable to see all of the data. There are valid occasions when you may want to do this. For
example, a company using long product names may decide that the first 20 characters in the
name are sufficient for the purpose of displaying on reports.

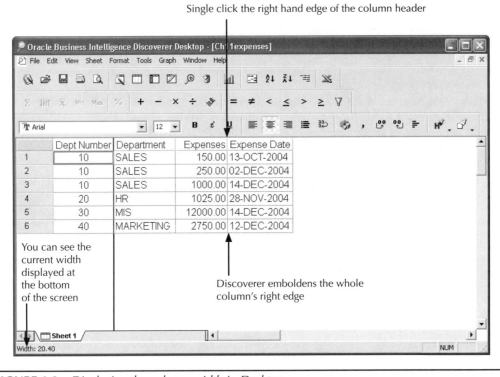

Single click the right hand edge of the column header

FIGURE 6-2   *Displaying the column width in Desktop*

NOTE
*We don't understand why Oracle has done this, but the only way
to resize a column in a Plus crosstab is by using this dragging
method. This is a real problem when the columns going down the
left side of the crosstab have more than about forty characters. We
recently encountered this issue in a crosstab we were designing. The
second left-side column of our crosstab was a varchar with over 100
characters. Because the column went beyond the width of the screen,
we could not scroll to get to the edge of the column to resize it, but
no other method of resizing is available. In the end we had to go into
the admin edition and restrict the number of characters allowed in the
field. According to Oracle this has been fixed, and the fix will become
available in a patch.*

To resize a column by dragging its edge, follow this workflow:

1. Place the mouse pointer on the right-hand edge of the column header you want to resize.
    This causes the pointer to change to the resize pointer.
2. Hold down the left mouse button and drag the pointer to the left or right. As you do this,
    the column width will increase or decrease.
3. When the column is the width you require, release the mouse button.

Resizing by Double-Clicking a Column's Edge

Resizing a column using this method is very precise and causes Discoverer to auto-size the width of the column. Auto-sizing means that Discoverer automatically works out the width of the column from the width of the header and the width of the longest data item in the column. It will resize the column to make it one character bigger than either the width of the header or the width of the longest data item.

To auto-size a column by double-clicking its edge, follow this workflow:

1. Place the mouse pointer on the right-hand edge of the column you want to resize. This causes the pointer to change to the resize cursor.

2. Double-click the left mouse button. This causes the column width to auto-size.

Manually Resizing a Single Column Using the Format Menu

This method of resizing a column is again imprecise and somewhat hit-and-miss. You will probably repeat the resizing several times before you get the column to the width that appears correct. If you want to resize a number of columns, you will have to repeat the method for each column.

NOTE
This method is not available in crosstabs.

To manually resize a single column using the Format menu, follow this workflow:

1. Click anywhere in the column you want to resize. This causes Discoverer to highlight the column.

2. From the menu, select Format | Columns | Width. This displays the following Column Width dialog box:

3. Enter a number for the width of the column. The number you enter is the number of characters that will display, based on an 8-point font. You can enter decimal places if you wish.

4. Click OK.

Auto-Sizing Using the Format Menu

This method of resizing columns is very precise and should be used when creating a report or printing, or when you want to resize multiple columns. There is nothing hit-and-miss about this method because the columns are auto-sized.

NOTE
This method is not available in crosstabs.

To auto-size a column or columns using the Format menu, follow this workflow:

1. Highlight the column or columns to be auto-sized. You do this by clicking in a column, holding down the CTRL key, and then clicking any other desired columns. To select all columns, click the blank item immediately to the left of the first data item. The following illustration shows where to click:

2. When you have selected a column or columns, from the menu select Format | Columns | Auto Size. This causes Discoverer to automatically resize all of the highlighted columns.

Formatting Totals

If you have added totals to your query, you can format them. Discoverer uses the Format Data dialog box to let you format totals. You can also use some of the toolbar buttons when working with totals.

Formatting Totals Using the Format Data Dialog Box

The Format Data dialog box is accessible in two ways:

■ From the menu bar

■ From the Total pop-up list

From the Menu Bar

To access the Format Data dialog box from the menu bar, use the following workflow:

1. From the menu bar, select Tools | Totals.
2. Highlight the total you want to format.
3. Click the Edit button. This opens the Edit Total dialog box.
4. Click the Format Data button. This opens the Format Data dialog box.

From the Total Pop-Up List

To access the Format Data dialog box from the Total pop-up list, use the following workflow:

1. Right-click the row containing the total.
2. From the pop-up menu, select Edit Total. This opens the Edit Total dialog box.
3. Click the Format Data button. This opens the Format Data dialog box.

If you have only one total in your worksheet, clicking any cell in the row containing the total displays the Edit box for that total. When you apply the format to a single total, Discoverer applies the format to the complete row. If you have multiple totals in your worksheet, clicking the cell containing a total displays the Edit box for that total. Clicking any other cell in the Totals row displays the Edit Totals dialog box, from which you will have to select the total you want to format.

NOTE
There is no way to format all totals at once. When you have multiple totals in your worksheet, you can only apply a format to those cells that are totals.

Formatting Totals from the Formatting Bar

After you have created a total or totals in your worksheet, rather than calling up a dialog box, Discoverer allows you to format totals directly from the formatting bar.

To format from the formatting bar, you should do the following:

1. Click the row containing the total. Discoverer then activates some of the formatting buttons on the formatting bar.
2. Click any of the buttons: Font, Font Size, Bold, Italic, Underline, Wrap Text, Foreground, and/or Background Colors. This applies that format setting to the total.

If you have only one total in your worksheet, clicking any cell in the row containing the total activates the formatting bar. When you click one of the formatting buttons, Discoverer applies that format to the whole row. If you have multiple totals in your worksheet, the formatting bar is activated only when you click one of the cells containing a total. In this situation, Discoverer applies the format only to that total. Clicking any cell that does not contain a total disables the formatting bar.

Formatting Exceptions

One of the analysis features of Discoverer is the ability to format data exceptions. We will explain how to create and format these in Chapter 8 when we discuss using Discoverer to analyze data.

Adding a Title to Your Query

Discoverer handles titles by offering the Edit Title dialog box. The box has two tabs in Desktop, one for formatting the text and one for adding bitmaps to the title. The Bitmaps tab also serves the purpose of allowing you to preview the title. In Plus there is only one tab, for formatting. A bitmap cannot be added to a workbook in Plus; however, using the OEM of Discoverer, a logo can be added to the top of the browser environment. This will be shown to you in Chapter 20. You can also insert text codes into the title, such as workbook name or any conditions present in the query.

NOTE
You can give an individual name to each worksheet in a workbook.

Editing the Title

To edit the title of a query, use one of the following three methods:

- Double-click the title bar. The title bar is directly above the column headings and page details.

- Right-click the title bar, and from the drop-down menu select Edit Title.

NOTE
If you cannot see the title bar, you can activate it from the Tools | Options menu. Click the Crosstab or Table tab and check the box Title. In Plus, use View | Title.

- From the Plus menu bar, use Edit | Title. From Desktop, use Sheet | Edit Title.

If you haven't created a default title, Discoverer will display "Double-click here to edit this title" as the title. This doubles for the instructions, so don't be confused when the Edit Title dialog box opens and still seems to be giving instructions to double-click.

NOTE
You can create your own default title from the Crosstab or Table tab on the Options menu. This default is created in exactly the same way as you create a normal title, so all that you read in this section equally applies to creating a default title. This illustration shows the Table Options tab in Desktop.

Whichever method you chose to edit the title, Discoverer now displays the Edit Title dialog box. This box has two tabs in Desktop, a Text tab and a Bitmap tab. In Plus there is no tab.

The Edit Title/Text Tab

Using the Text tab, you can change the font, font size, font properties, and alignment, as well as foreground and background color. You are also given a drop-down list of special text codes that you can add to the title, as shown here:

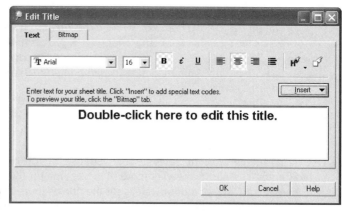

- ■ **Formatting toolbar**
  These buttons work in the same way as on the main Discoverer formatting bar.

- ■ **Insert**   Select from a list of special text codes. See the following table.

- ■ **Title box**   As you select options for your title, Discoverer inserts the options here. You can also type text into the box.

The following table explains the special text codes available:

Text Code Name	Description
Workbook Name	The name of your workbook.
Sheet Name	The name of the current sheet.
Date	The date the query is run.
Time	The time the query is run.
Page Number	The current page number.
Total Pages	A count of all pages in the worksheet.
Conditions	The name of each condition in the worksheet is displayed, separated by a comma.
Data Points	The column name for each data point (mathematical expression) in the worksheet is displayed, separated by a comma.
Axis Items	The column name for all items in the worksheet is displayed, separated by a comma.
Page Items	The column name for every Page Item in the worksheet is displayed, separated by a comma. You can edit the list and remove any that you don't want to display.
Conditional Formats	The description for every exception in the worksheet is displayed, separated by a comma. In Desktop, the code is called Exceptions.

NOTE
The preceding text codes display on the Text tab with an ampersand (&) as the first character. This character is programming code and will not display as part of the title. You can force Discoverer to show an individual page item by typing its name into the Title box preceded by an ampersand.

To create a new title; select the text "Double-click here to edit this title" and type in your new workbook title. You might want to make the worksheet name the title, in which case select Worksheet from the Insert drop-down list.

With the text of the new title selected, use the formatting tools at the top of the dialog box to format the text. If you want more than one line for the title, press ENTER to go to the next line. There are no tabs or multiple areas for the title as there are in the header and footer, so creating a complex and well-formatted title is not easy. The authors recommend that you use the Header and Footer options of Page Setup to create a better title and stick to a simple one- or two-line title with a graphic here.

NOTE
Headers and footers will be covered in detail in Chapter 8.

The Bitmap Tab (Desktop Only)

Using the Bitmap tab, you can insert bitmaps into the background of your title. For example, perhaps you want to insert your company's logo.

The Bitmap tab consists of the following three sections:

- ■ **File Name box** Use the Browse button to locate a bitmap, and the Clear button to delete it. When a bitmap is selected, Discoverer displays the path and name of the file.

- ■ **Display Bitmap As box** Check the radio buttons to center the bitmap in the background, to tile the bitmap in the background, or to display the bitmap aligned with the text. You can align a bitmap above, below, to the left of, or to the right of the text.

- ■ **Preview box** Discoverer displays how the bitmap will look when combined with the options selected from the Text tab.

NOTE
You can create a bitmap of your company's logo by scanning it from a piece of stationery. Let us give you a word of warning about scanned images. These images are rarely as good as original artwork and certainly not good enough for printing onto reports that will be sent externally. It is likely that your company has standard artwork, and you should speak with your Discoverer administrator to find out where the images are stored.

To add a bitmap to a title, use the following workflow:

1. Click the Bitmap tab on the Edit Title dialog box.

2. Click the Browse button. This causes Discoverer to display the Open dialog box:

3. Find the bitmap you want to insert.

4. Click Open. Discoverer displays the full path and name of the bitmap, and also shows you how the bitmap will look.

5. Select an option for displaying the bitmap. You can choose from Centered Background, Tiled Background, or Aligned With Text. If you choose Aligned With Text, you will need to select how it will be aligned. You can choose from Left Of Text, Right Of Text, Above Text, or Below Text.

6. When you are satisfied that you have the correct bitmap, and that it is displayed correctly, click OK. This will display the title in your query.

7. The following example shows a title with a bitmap aligned to the left:

NOTE
If you do not want to use the selected bitmap, you can remove it and start again by clicking Clear.

TIP
Discoverer remembers the way you last displayed a bitmap and offers this as the default the next time you insert a bitmap.

Suppressing a Title from Displaying

To suppress a title from displaying in Plus, use View | Title. To suppress a title in Desktop, use the following workflow:

1. From the menu bar, select Tools | Options.
2. Select the Crosstab or Table tab.
3. Uncheck the Title check box.

NOTE
Suppressing a title from displaying does not delete the title. It still exists and can be reactivated by rechecking the Title check box.

Adding a Background Bitmap (Desktop Only)

This final section on formatting shows you how to add a bitmap as a background to your whole worksheet. Again, as we explained in the section dealing with bitmaps in titles, you should try to use existing artwork rather than scanning in your own image.

Try to use bitmaps that have light colors and do not distract the eye away from the report itself. We therefore recommend using caution when using bitmaps as a background.

NOTE
When using any form of bitmap, you should ensure that you are not infringing on any copyright or proprietary rights. If you are not sure whether you can use a bitmap or not, you should consult your company's legal department for advice. The best advice we can give you is, if in doubt, don't use it. You don't want to invoke a lawsuit on your company just because you infringed on a copyrighted image.

Setting a Background

There are two ways to set a background:

- From a pop-up list
- From the menu bar

From a Pop-Up List

To set a background from a pop-up list, use the following workflow:

1. Right-click anywhere on the worksheet that you want to add a background to. This displays a pop-up list of options.
2. Select Set Background. This causes Discoverer to display the Open dialog box.
3. Find the bitmap you want to insert.
4. Click Open. Discoverer displays the bitmap tiled in the background.

From the Menu Bar

To set a background from the menu bar, use the following workflow:

1. From the menu bar, select Format | Sheet | Set Background. This displays the Open dialog box.
2. Find the bitmap you want to insert.
3. Click Open. Discoverer displays the bitmap tiled in the background.

Clearing a Background

If you already have an existing background and now wish to remove it, you must use the Clear Background command. There are two ways to clear a background:

■ From a pop-up list

■ From the menu bar

From a Pop-Up List

To clear a background from a pop-up list, use the following workflow:

1. Right-click anywhere on the worksheet that you want to clear a background from. This displays a pop-up list of options.
2. Select Clear Background.

From the Menu Bar

To clear a background from the menu bar, use the following workflow:

■ From the menu bar, select Format | Sheet | Clear Background.

Summary

In this chapter, you have learned the need to give meaningful names to query column headings and any item that might become a heading. You have been shown how to rearrange the order of the columns and rename the headings.

You have been shown how formatting can improve a query by changing fonts and font sizes, font and background colors, and text justification.

This chapter has shown you how to format numbers as currency, with commas and with the correct number of decimal places.

Finally, you have been taught to format totals and add titles to your query. You have also learned how to add graphics to a query by placing bitmaps into the title as well as adding graphics to the background.

By adding formatting to a query, you will add interest and make the query easier to read and more pleasing to view. Formatting the query gives you an excellent beginning in turning a query into a report. In Chapter 8, you will learn more about reporting in Discoverer.

CHAPTER
7

Using Graphs
to Present Data

n important feature of good reporting is the use of graphs. Graphs are a powerful, visual representation of the data from your database. Discoverer uses a Graph Wizard to take you through the steps of creating a graph. Since the first edition of this book, Oracle has brought graphing forward dramatically in Discoverer. Graphing has been available in both Desktop and Plus since release 4, and it is featured prominently in Plus today.

NOTE
Any graph created in Desktop cannot be displayed in Plus or Viewer. Equally, you cannot display a graph created in Plus in Desktop; however, if you create a graph in Plus, it will display in Viewer.

You can use both tables and crosstabs to create a graph, but you cannot select certain parts of the data to use in the graph. Discoverer uses all of the data points to create the graph and decides for you what it is you want. You are left with only the power to format it.

If you want to use only some of the data points of a table or crosstab, Discoverer will allow you to move those unwanted data points to the page items. However, you should be wary of doing this, as unexpected results could arise.

If you want to use only some data points of a table or crosstab, it is necessary to turn on the page-item feature and move the data points you don't want included in the graph to the page axis. Later, when you have finished graphing, you will need to return the columns to the body of the worksheet.

If you want only data that meet certain conditions, you will have to create those conditions. This will be a big change for those used to creating graphs in Excel, where you can select only the data you want to use in the graph from your table. The upside is that once the graph has been created, it is easy to tweak until you get it right. If you make a change to the worksheet, the changes are made to the graph instantly with no intervention from the user. The graph will also be automatically updated each time the query is run.

NOTE
Because Discoverer will only create graphs based on data points, you need to create calculations that change the desired items into data points. This is the trick to getting graphs on non–data point items.

There are enough different types of graph styles to choose from, including 3-D models, that you should be able to find a format that meets your needs. There are also bountiful formatting options, including a nifty little paint can to pour your color selection in place. There are now more than 55 graph types and subtypes available. You can also unlink the layout from the graph, which gives you some amount of freedom over your display. There is also a trend line plotting capability exposed in Plus in 10.1.2 that you can apply to your graphs.

Discoverer allows graphing options that even Excel does not provide, such as split dual Y graphs. Even dual Y and combination graphs require an incredible amount of manual work to get working in Excel.

In this chapter, you will learn to create, modify, and format graphs. You will be shown how to begin with the Graph Wizard and then use the graph toolbar as well as the Modify Graph dialog box to make changes to the graph. You will learn about the various types of graphs available and how to create titles and add legends.

The Available Graph Styles

There are 14 different graph types available, and each graph type has one or more subtypes available. In this section, we will show you the same query as each type of graph.

The query used to show the graphs is a comparison of sales for Global Widget's four regions in Q2 of 2003 and 2004.

	Region	Profit SUM	Quarter
1	EUROPE	1967655.26	2003-Q2
2	FAR EAST	1123211.78	2003-Q2
3	NORTH AMERICA	3291894.45	2003-Q2
4	SOUTH AMERICA	245783.91	2003-Q2
5	EUROPE	1707011.94	2004-Q2
6	FAR EAST	553882.40	2004-Q2
7	NORTH AMERICA	3223193.52	2004-Q2
8	SOUTH AMERICA	1178130.04	2004-Q2

Area (Desktop and Plus)

The area graph shows trends in values across categories.

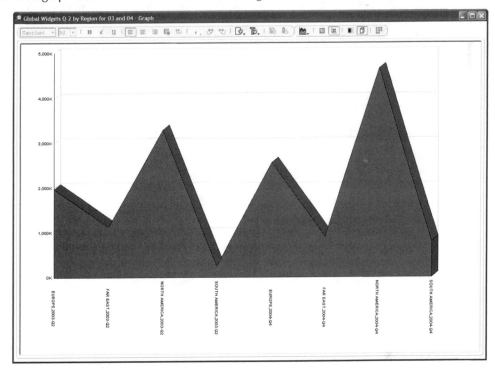

Bar (Desktop and Plus)

The bar graph shows values in comparison to beginning and ending values. This is useful in graphing financial data and stock prices. The Y axis shows the values, and the X axis shows the categories.

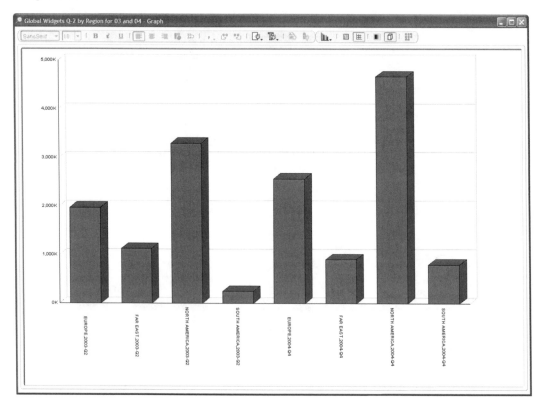

Combination (Plus Only)

The Combination graph shows bars and lines, bars and areas, lines and areas, or all three if you choose. We found this type of graph so complicated that it was hard to make sense of. If you are an experienced grapher, try it out, but it is not for the faint of heart. For this example, we needed more data to compare, so we added the quantity shipped to the worksheet.

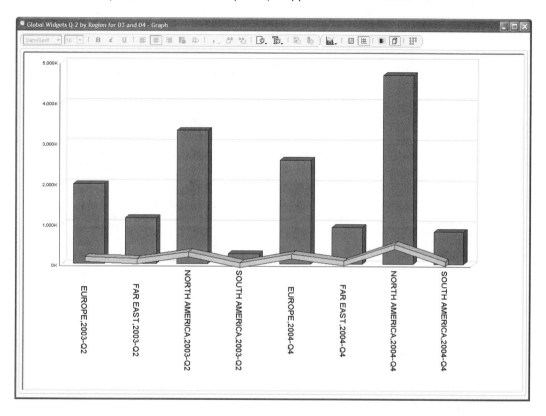

Cube (Grouped with 3-D Options in Plus)

The cube graph shows trends in values across categories, separated by category. The top of the cube represents the value. The Y axis shows the values, and the X axis shows the categories.

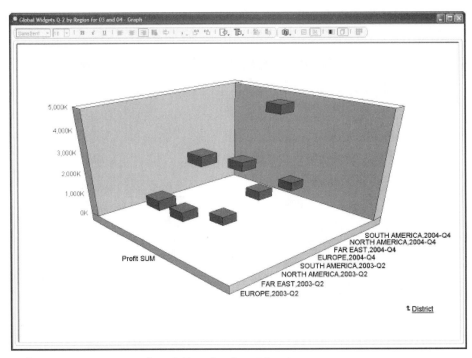

Doughnut (Grouped with Pie in Plus)

The doughnut graph shows values across categories. Each value is shown as a portion of the whole.

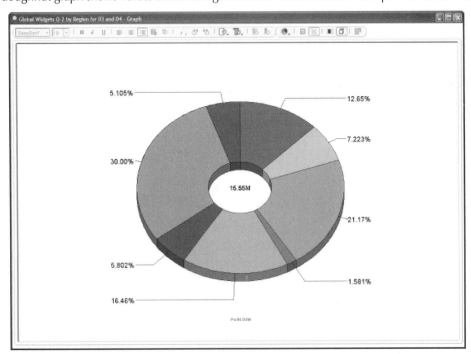

Fit to Curve (Desktop Only)

The fit-to-curve graph shows trends in values across categories. The points represent values separated by category. The line is used to demonstrate the trend in the value changes. There is one curve graph in Plus, grouped with the 3-D graphs; otherwise, this type is available only in Desktop.

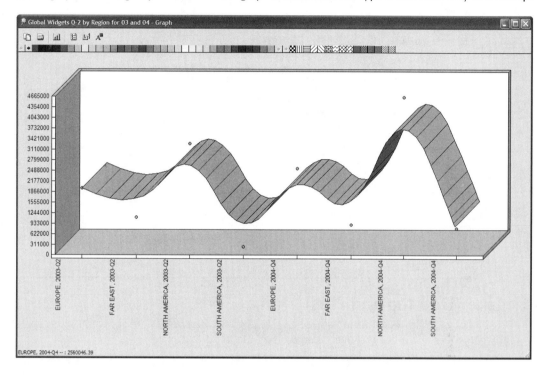

Hi-Low-Close (Desktop,) Stock (Plus)

The hi-low-close graph is identical to the bar graph on page 4 in our example. This type of graph is more useful for stock market data to show the relationship of the high, low, and closing prices of a particular stock or the market itself.

Horizontal Bar (Desktop and Plus)

The horizontal bar graph shows trends in values across categories. It is a regular bar graph turned on its side.

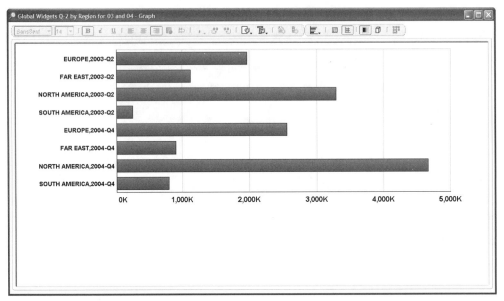

Line (Desktop and Plus)

The line graph shows trends in values across categories. The values are shown as dots separated by categories and a line is drawn to emphasize the trend.

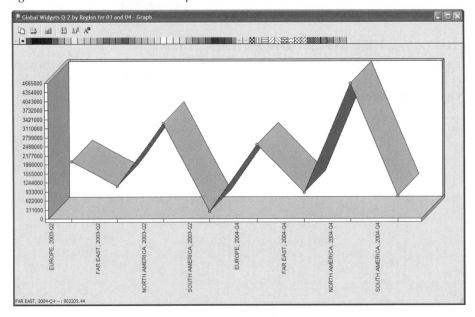

Pareto (Desktop and Plus)

The pareto graph shows trends in categories across categories. A line is drawn above to show the trend associated with each change.

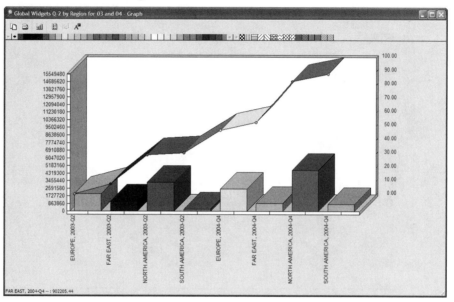

Pie (Desktop and Plus)

The pie graph shows values across categories. Each value is shown as a portion of the whole pie.

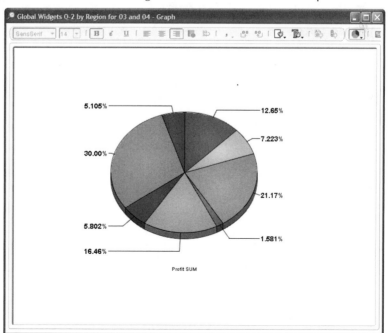

Point (Desktop Only)

The point graph shows trends in values across categories. The points show data separated by values and categories.

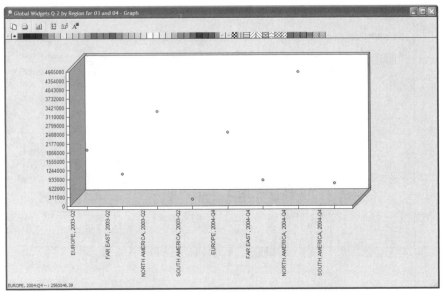

Polar (Desktop and Plus)

The polar type of graph plots data as angle-length points.

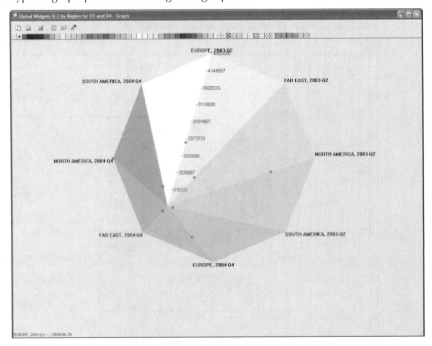

Scatter (Desktop), Scatter/Bubble (Plus)

The scatter graph shows changes in values in comparison to other values. Each axis must represent a number. Using our example query, the results are the same as the point graph.

Surface (Grouped with 3-D in Plus)

This graph shows values across categories; however, with the example query, there was no data shown on the graph.

The Discoverer Desktop Graph Window

Discoverer displays graphs in the Graph window. The first time you open the window, you will be taken through the Graph Wizard to assist you in creating the graph. After you have created a graph in Discoverer, it becomes a permanent part of the worksheet that it is based on.

NOTE
In Plus, a graph is always part of any worksheet you create; the only option you have is whether to display it or not. Also, the first time you choose to display the graph, you are taken through the wizard.

Figure 7-1 shows a simple query, and Figure 7-2 shows the graph based upon the query.

The Features of the Discoverer Desktop Graph Window

Unlike Excel, Discoverer does not embed the graph into the worksheet. Instead, the graph is created in its own sheet that can be opened for viewing as the associated worksheet is changed or updated. This is a nice feature, and we especially like the way the graph automatically refreshes itself with the changing data.

FIGURE 7-1 *A simple query*

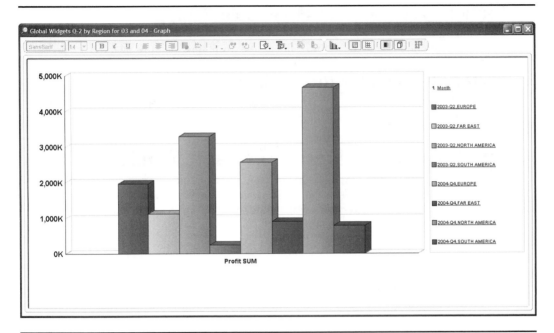

FIGURE 7-2 *A graph based on a simple query*

Figure 7-3 shows the features of the Discoverer Graph window.

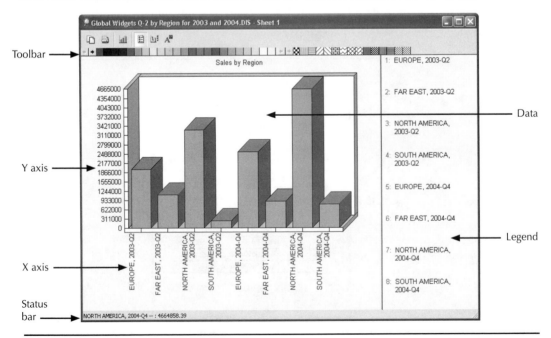

FIGURE 7-3 *The Discoverer Graph window*

Toolbar

The Discoverer Graph window has a toolbar used to work with the graph details, as shown here:

Print—prints graph

Type—opens a dialog box to change the graph type

Snapshot—places a snapshot (a copy) of the graph into the Windows Clipboard to paste into other applications

Show/Hide X Labels—toggles between showing and hiding the X labels

Show/Hide Legends—toggles between showing and hiding the legend

Graph Titles—opens a dialog box to change or add graph titles

Y Axis

Discoverer creates a scale appropriate to the data of the original worksheet. This is shown in the Y axis (along the left side of the graph). For example, if the worksheet is based on sales for the first quarter of Q1 by region, and the highest sales were $534,109, Discoverer would create a scale in increments from $0 to $535,000. You can format the scale yourself as well as add decimal points.

Scroll Bar

Some types of graphs, such as bar charts, contain a large number of bars. You might need to use the scroll bar to see all of the data items of the graph.

NOTE
You can also use the Auto-Fit option to make sure that the entire graph fits within the confines of the Graph window.

Status Bar

As you point to various data items on the graph, Discoverer will display the associated data in the status bar.

Legend

The legend shows the color and the label used to display the corresponding worksheet data.

Horizontal and Vertical Gridlines

The gridlines are vertical and horizontal lines that can be turned on or off. You can choose to use vertical, horizontal, or both. This can be helpful in reading the graph details.

Data

The data is simply the bars of the bar chart, or the slices of the pie chart. It is a graphical representation of the data in your worksheet.

X Axis

The X axis shows the labels used to identify the data. When your data has long names, they will be replaced by numbers. If you have short names, they will be shown below the associated data and will eliminate the need to show the legend.

NOTE
New since the release of 9.0.4 is the concept of reference lines; you can add up to three reference lines per Y axis. This is available under the Plot Area tab of the Graph Wizard.

Creating a Graph in Desktop

To create a graph, you can use the Graph button on the main Discoverer toolbar or use the menu bar.

To begin using the Discoverer graphing tool, select Graph | Edit Graph from the menu bar or click the Graph button on the toolbar.

The Desktop Graph Wizard

Following one of the two methods previously described will open the Graph Wizard. There are four steps to the Graph Wizard that take you step-by-step through the process of building your graph. The four steps are as follows:

- Selecting the graph type

- Formatting the graph type

■ Titles and legends

■ Adding special graph options

Don't worry if you are not sure how your graph will turn out. If you are not satisfied with the results, it is easy to edit the graph until you are. You can also click Back at any time to return to the previous step(s).

Graph Wizard Step 1: Selecting the Graph Type

The first step in creating your graph is to select the graph type. The features of the Graph Wizard Step 1 are as follows:

■ **Graph types**   Select the type of graph you want to use to best represent your data.

■ **Graph example**   See an example of the graph type.

■ **Description box**   See a description of the graph type. If the description is too long for all of it to be seen, click the Description box and the box will expand to show the complete description.

Figure 7-4 shows the first step of the Discoverer Desktop Graph Wizard.
To select the graph type, use the following workflow:

1. Click the graph type you want to use.

NOTE
If you change your mind about what type of graph you want, you can change it later.

2. Click Next.

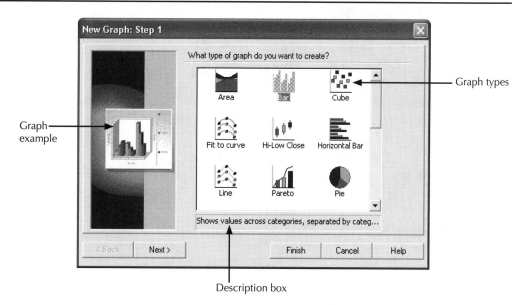

FIGURE 7-4   *Graph Wizard Step 1*

Graph Wizard Step 2: Selecting the Graph Format

After selecting the graph type, Discoverer will advance you to Step 2 of the Graph Wizard—selecting the graph format. Discoverer gives you, in most cases, several format choices for the graph type you have selected. The features of the Graph Wizard Step 2 are as follows:

- **Graph format style**   Select the type of graph you want to use to best represent your data.

- **Graph format style example**   See an example of the graph with the format selected.

- **Description box**   See a description of the graph format style. If the description is too long for all of it to be seen, click the Description box and the box will expand to show the complete description.

Figure 7-5 shows the second step of the Discoverer Desktop Graph Wizard. To select the graph type, use the following workflow:

1. Click the graph format style you want to use.

2. Click Next.

Graph Wizard Step 3: Titles and Legends

The next step is to add titles to your graph. You can have titles on the top, the bottom, and both sides. You can also format the font type, style, size, and color, as well as use underline or

FIGURE 7-5   *Graph Wizard Step 2*

strikeout effects. Step 3 also gives you an opportunity to show the graph legend and to format it, and format the fonts for the X and Y axes. The features of the Graph Wizard Step 3 are as follows:

- **Titles**   Add titles for top, left, bottom, and right of the graph.

- **Legend**   Select to show and format the font of the legend.

- **Axis**   Format the fonts of the X and Y axes.

Figure 7-6 shows the third step of the Discoverer Desktop Graph Wizard.

To add titles, add a legend, and format the font of the X and Y axes of your graph, use the following workflow:

1. Decide where you want to add titles to your graph.

2. Click in the field for the title you want to add and format.

3. Type in the title.

4. Click the Font button to the right of the title.

5. Select the font type, style, size, color, and effect.

6. Click OK.

7. Decide whether or not you want to show the graph legend.

8. Format the legend using the same method described in Steps 5 and 6.

9. Format the X and Y axes.

10. Click Next.

FIGURE 7-6   *Graph Wizard Step 3*

Graph Wizard Step 4: Adding Special Graph Options

Step 4 of the Graph Wizard allows you to change some options of the graph. This is where you can either accept the default scale Discoverer chooses or create your own. You can also add decimal places to the scale. The features of the Graph Wizard Step 3 are as follows:

- **Y axis scale**   Use the scale created by Discoverer, or type in the scale of your choice.

- **Decimals**   Use this to determine how many decimal places will be displayed.

- **Show gridlines**   Click to show horizontal or vertical gridlines.

- **Graph series by**   Select to use the data in the columns or rows of the workbook to be the X axis for the graph.

Figure 7-7 shows the fourth step of the Discoverer Desktop Graph Wizard. To format the options of your graph, use the following workflow:

1. Decide if you want to create your own scale or use the default set by Discoverer.

2. If you choose to change the scale, click in the Maximum field and type the highest number you want to use for the scale.

3. Click in the Minimum field and type the lowest number you want to use for the scale.

4. To add decimal places to the scale, click in the Decimal field and type the number of decimal places you want to use for the scale.

5. Decide if you want to add gridlines to your graph and click the check box for the gridlines you want to use—vertical, horizontal, or both.

FIGURE 7-7   *Graph Wizard Step 4*

6.   Decide whether you want to use the data from the worksheet's rows or columns for the X axis and select the corresponding radio button. If you are not sure which series you want to use, a hint is displayed below the radio buttons.

7.   Click Finish.

You have completed creating your graph, and Discoverer will close the Graph Wizard and open the Graph window (shown earlier in Figure 7-3).

Graphing in Discoverer Plus

Graphing in Plus has some of the same basic limitations of Desktop and has fewer available graph types. However, there is definitely some new power in formatting graph information on the X and Y axes. The graphs in Plus are not as flexible as in Desktop, and all of the 3-D options are grouped together instead of being with their graph type.

You also approach graphing differently in Plus. You are presented with graphing options in Step 1 of the Workbook Wizard. If you choose not to add a graph at the beginning, don't worry; you can add one later. There is no Graph Wizard in Plus. Instead it uses a multitabbed Edit Graph dialog box.

NOTE
*Graphing in Plus is a Sticky Feature. Discoverer will remember the
graph type that you chose and will default to it the next time you
create one.*

Creating a Graph in the Plus Workbook Wizard

To create a graph in conjunction with a new query in the Plus Workbook Wizard Step 1, use the following workflow:

1.   From the menu bar select File | New.

2.   Click the Graph box shown here:

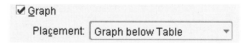

3.   Select the location of the graph from the Placement drop-down list. The options for graph placement are

   ■   Graph right of Table

   ■   Graph left of Table above

   ■   Graph above Table

   ■   Graph below Table (the default)

   ■   Graph in separate window

You will want to try different locations on the screen for your graph. We recommend that if you have a small amount of data—for example, sales by quarter in a single year—showing the graph in the same window is fine, as seen here:

If you have a large amount of data, such as sales by customer, the graph might be too small to display correctly in the same screen. For this example, try putting the graph in a separate window, as shown here:

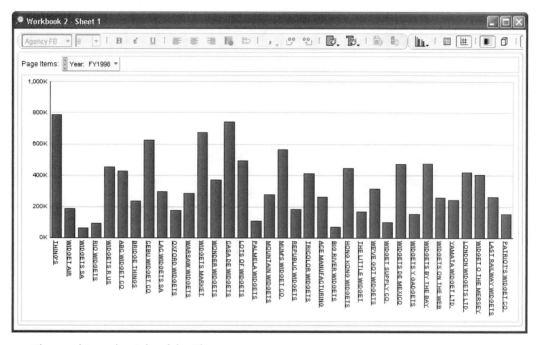

The graphic to the right of the Placement drop-down list shows you how the graph will appear in your query. Complete the steps of the Workbook Wizard. Your graph will be generated when the query runs.

Example:

Creating a Graph in Plus after a Query Has Been Generated

If you decide to add a graph to an existing query, select Edit | Graph or click the graph button on the toolbar shown here. The Edit Graph dialog box will open.

Edit Graph Dialog Box – Type Tab

The first step in creating your graph is to select the graph type. The features of the Edit Graph Wizard Type tab are as follows:

- **Graph types** Select the type of graph you want to use to best represent your data.

- **Graph Subtype** Shows an example of the graph type.

- **Description box** Description of the graph type. Figure 7-8 shows the first step of the Discoverer Plus Edit Graph dialog box.

FIGURE 7-8 *Choosing a graph type*

To select the graph type, use the following workflow:

1. Click the graph type you want to use.

NOTE
If you change your mind about the type of graph you want, you can change it later.

2. Click OK.

Edit Graph Dialog Box – Style Tab

This is a very cool feature of Discoverer graphing in Plus—one whose value will immediately be apparent to most users. No longer do you have to muck around to get that "nice and correct" look and feel for your graphs: fonts, foreground color, background color, text size, series color, etc. Discoverer does all that for you!

After selecting the graph type, you will move on to the Style tab. Discoverer gives you, in most cases, several style choices for the graph type you have selected. The features of the Edit Graph Style tab are as follows:

- **Style**   Oracle has preset a variety of color options.

- **Sample**   Shows an example of the graph with the style options selected.

- **Gradient Effect**   Click here to show gradients in your colors or deselect if you want the colors to be flat.

- **3-D Effect**   Click here to turn on or off 3-D effects.

Figure 7-9 shows the Style tab of the Discoverer Plus Edit Graph dialog box. To select the graph style, use the following workflow:

1. Click the graph style you want to use.

2. Select or deselect Gradient Effects.

3. Select or deselect 3-D Effects.

Edit Graph Dialog Box – Titles, Totals, and Series Tab

The next step is to add titles to your graph. In Plus you can have titles only on the top of the graph. You can also format the font type, style, size, and color, as well as alignment. The Titles,

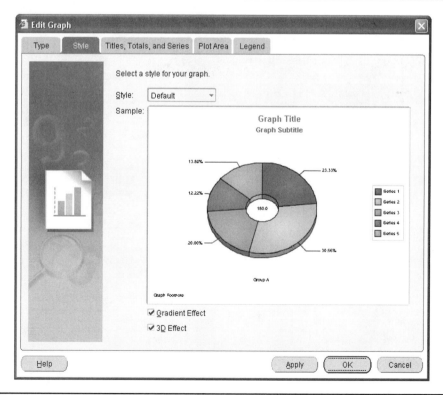

FIGURE 7-9   *Choosing a graph style*

Totals, and Series tab also gives you an opportunity to decide what you want to display in the graph. The features of the Edit Graph dialog box Titles, Totals, and Series tab are as follows:

- **Show Title**   Add a title to the graph.

- **What would you like to display in your graph?**   Decide whether to show totals only, data only, or both totals and data in the graph.

- **Show null values as zero**   Click this box to show null values as zero.

- **Graph Series By**   Here you choose to graph by columns or by rows.

- **Pie chart options**   Click this button to show additional options for Pie charts.

Figure 7-10 shows the Titles, Totals, and Series tab of the Edit Graph dialog box.
To add titles, totals, and series to your graph, use the following workflow:

1. Type in the title of your graph, or click the Insert button and select from the drop-down list if you want to use any of the predefined title elements. You can choose any combination of the following with text of your own:

   - Sheet Name

   - Workbook Name

FIGURE 7-10   *Entering a title; choosing totals and series*

- Date
- Time
- Page Items
- Axis Items
- Data Points

2. Click the Title Font button to the right of the title.   [Title Font...]
3. Select the font type, style, size, color, and alignment.
4. Click OK.
5. Decide whether or not you want to show the graph legend.
6. Format the legend using the same method as in Steps 2–4.
7. Format the X and Y axes.
8. Click OK.
9. Select the type of data you want to display in your graph. The option will be grayed out if it is unavailable in the query.
10. Choose whether to graph by column or by row.
11. For pie charts, click the Pie Chart Options button to open the Pie Chart Options dialog box.

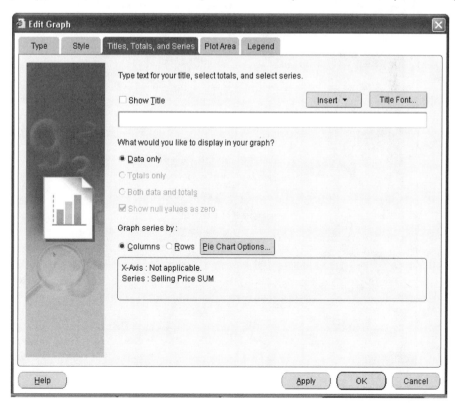

12. Select the column or row on which you want to graph your pie chart.

13. Click OK.

Edit Graph Dialog Box – X-Axis Tab

The Edit Graph dialog box – X-Axis tab seen in Figure 7-11 allows you to format how the X axis of your graph will look.

The X axis is the axis going across the bottom of the graph and has the following features:

■ **X-Axis title** Add a title that will go across the bottom of the graph. After you have created a title, you can deselect the box and the title will not show.

■ **Insert** Use this button in the same way that you added a title to the graph.

■ **X-Axis Title Font** Opens the Format Font dialog box to format the X axis title.

■ **Line Thickness** Use this drop-down list to select the weight of the line of the X axis.

■ **Line Color** Use this drop-down to change the color of the X axis line.

■ **Show Labels for all Tick Marks on the Axis** Check this radio button to show all tick marks along the X axis (every data item).

FIGURE 7-11 *X-Axis tab of the Edit Graph dialog box*

■ **Show Labels for Some Tick Marks on the Axis**   Check this box to show only some of the tick marks on the axis. When you select this radio button, you will be give three more options:

■ **Automatically Skip Labels to Fit**   Check this radio button if you want Discoverer to determine what X axis labels to show.

■ **Start with Tick Mark**   This allows you to choose which tick mark to start with. It seems to us that the first tick mark is the place to start with as a benchmark. This option is good to use if don't need to see each data item but want to show the data incrementally.

■ **Tick Marks to Skip between Labels**   If you have thirty data items and don't need to see each individual one, skipping every three would leave you with fewer labels on the axis and give you a cleaner graph. However, don't use this option when you need to see everything, such as customer names or quarters in years.

■ **X-Axis Label Font**   Use this button to open the X-Axis Label Font dialog box shown in the following illustration. This button works like the other Format Font dialog boxes with one exception: you can change the orientation of the text. This is helpful if labels are long, such as city names or customer names. You can choose

■ **Automatic**   This is the default and will display the labels in normal left-to-right text orientation.

■ **0**   This also displays the text in normal orientation.

■ **90**   This will put the text in bottom-to-top orientation.

■ **270**   This will put the text in top-to-bottom orientation.

To format the X axis of your graph, use the following workflow:

1. Add a title for the X axis and format the font.
2. Modify the line color and thickness if desired.
3. Make changes to the frequency of tick marks.
4. Format the X-axis label font.

Edit Graph Dialog Box – Y-Axis Tab

The next step is to format the option for the Y axis (the data shown on the left side of the graph). Click the Edit Graph dialog box – Y-Axis tab as seen in Figure 7-12.

The Edit Graph dialog box – Y-Axis tab has the following features:

- **Y-Axis title**   Add a title that will go across the bottom of the graph. After you have created a title, you can deselect the box and the title will not show.

- **Insert**   Use this button in the same way that you added a title to the graph.

- **Y-Axis Title Font**   Opens the Format Font dialog box to format the Y axis title. You can also set the Y axis title orientation to 90 or 270.

- **Line Thickness**   Use this drop-down list to select the weight of the line of the Y axis.

- **Line Color**   Use this drop-down to change the color of the Y axis line.

- **Set the scale you would like to use on this axis**   Use this area to set the scale of the graph. This section has the following options:

FIGURE 7-12   *Y-Axis tab of the Edit Graph dialog box*

- **Minimum**   Use this field to change the lower axis range from the default to a custom scale. Choose Set automatically if you want Plus to select the range for the graph.

- **Maximum**   Use this field to change the higher axis range default. Select the Set automatically check box if you want Discoverer to select the best range for you.

- **Increment**   Use this field to change the default incremental axis range. Select the Set automatically check box for Plus to set the best range for the graph.

- **Base line value**   Use this field to specify a starting value for the Y axis.

- **Logarithmic Scale**   Use this to set the logarithmic scale you want to use. The options are: Base 10, Base 2, and Base e (exponential).

- **Reference Lines**   Use this button to open the Reference Lines dialog box shown here. Reference lines are a good way to see at a glance certain benchmarks. For example, you require customers to exceed sales orders of $25,000 per quarter to receive a 10 percent discount, and $50,000 to receive a 15 percent discount. Your graph can have reference lines set at $25,000 and $50,000 to see which customers fall in the required sales to keep their discounts. Reference lines are not available in pie or 3-D graphs.

To format the Y axis of your graph, use the following workflow:

1. Add a title for the Y axis and format the font.
2. Modify the line color and thickness if desired.
3. Format the Y axis label font.
4. Decide if you want to create your own scale or use the default set by Discoverer.
5. If you choose to change the scale, click in the Maximum field and type the highest number you want to use for the scale.
6. Click in the Minimum field and type the lowest number you want to use for the scale.
7. Decide if you want to use an alternate logarithm and base to your scale.
8. If reference lines are available, set them using the Reference Lines dialog box.
9. Format the Y axis label font.

Edit Graph Dialog Box – Y1-Axis and Y2-Axis Tabs

When using a pareto graph, you will have 2 Y axes, Y1 and Y2. The tabs are identical, and instead of setting up scales, you set up the increments in which you want to see the data displayed. You can also set up reference lines.

Edit Graph Dialog Plot Area Tab

The Edit Graph dialog Plot Area tab, shown in Figure 7-13, is used to add color and character to the graph. You can add

- **Background Color**   Use this color palette to select the background color of the graph.

- **Border Color**   Use this color palette to place a colored frame around the plot area.

- **Show Horizontal Gridlines**   Check this box if you want horizontal gridlines to show on the plot area of the graph. This option is not available in all graph types.

- **Show Vertical Gridlines**   Check this box if you want vertical gridlines to show on the plot area of the graph. This option is not available in all graph types.

- **Show data labels for . . .**   This option is available for each different type of graph and is designed for that graph specifically. We will not explain every nuance of the data label, but we recommend that you take a look at the options you have for labeling.

- **Show Data Tips when Mouse is over . . .**   Check this box for mouse tips when your mouse hovers over the graph. Click the button to the right to view your different options.

- **Select options for the series displayed in your graph**   Use this area to change the colors of the data points in the graph.

Edit Graph Dialog Legend Tab

The Edit Graph dialog Legend tab, shown in Figure 7-14, is used to add a legend to your graph, select the colors and fonts, and determine its location.

Modifying a Graph in Plus

Because you are not using a wizard in Plus, it is very easy to modify your graph. Simply reopen the graph using the Graph button, or from the menu bar select Edit | Graph. Select the tab and make your modification.

Modifying a Graph in Desktop

After the graph has been created, it is easily modified. The Modify Graph dialog box is viewed in one of two ways. If you open it from the worksheet, it is displayed in exactly the same format as the Graph Wizard. If, however, you open it from the graph itself, it opens as a four-tab form with the same steps as the Graph Wizard. Each of the tabbed dialog boxes is used in exactly the same way as the four steps of the wizard.

NOTE
Remember that you do not need to do anything for the data to be updated with changes to the query. Discoverer does this for you automatically.

FIGURE 7-13   *The Edit Graph Plot Area tab*

To Modify the Graph from the Worksheet

When the graph is closed, you can either use the Graph button on the toolbar or use the menu bar. If you use the menu bar, you will notice that only two options are available to you in Desktop: Graph | Show and Graph | Edit Graph. The rest of the items are available only when the graph is open and the Graph window is maximized. After you modify the graph, the Graph window will open.

To open the Modify Graph dialog box from the worksheet, use the following workflow:

1. Select Graph | Edit Graph.

2. Follow the instructions in the "The Desktop Graph Wizard" section earlier in this chapter.

3. After making the desired modifications, click OK.

FIGURE 7-14 *The Edit Graph Legend tab*

To Modify the Graph from the Graph Window

It is easier to modify the graph with the Graph window open because you have the toolbar available. Many of the changes you will want to make can be made from the toolbar. With the Graph window open, you can also access all of the options on the Graph drop-down list on the menu bar. Unless the Graph window is maximized, it seems as though the menu bar is not available to you, but it is. Click the menu bar of the worksheet and it will become active, leaving the Graph window open in the front in an inactive state.

You can also access all of the same options by right-clicking in the Graph window. This opens a pop-up list of options for working with the graph.

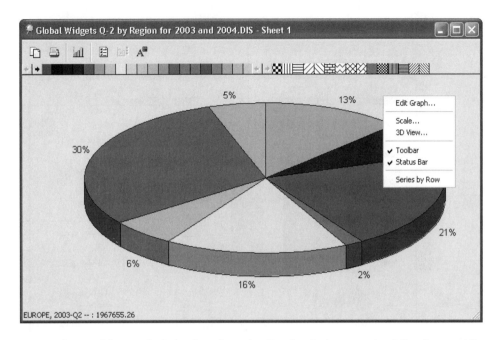

To open the Modify Graph dialog box from the Graph window, use the following workflow:

1. From the menu bar select Graph | Edit Graph or right-click in the Graph window and select Edit Graph.
2. Select the tab you want to use.
3. Follow the instructions in the "The Desktop Graph Wizard" section earlier in the chapter.
4. After making the desired modifications, click OK.

Resizing the Graph

You will, in most cases, need to resize the graph or some of its components. Most of the graph elements can be resized. Figure 7-15 shows the resizable elements of a graph.

To resize a graph element, use the following workflow:

1. Click the resizable element until the mouse pointer changes to a double-headed arrow.
2. Drag until the desired size is obtained.

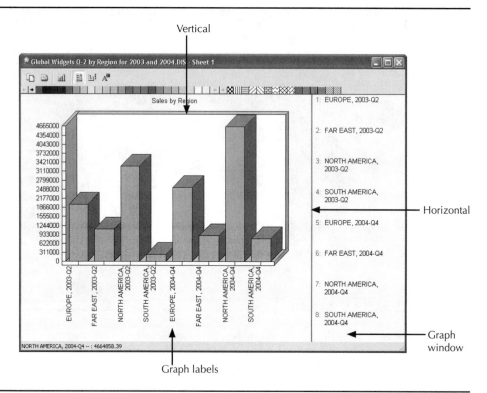

FIGURE 7-15 *The resizable elements of a graph*

Modifying the Scale

Although you set the scale in the Modify Graph dialog box, there is a separate dialog box that allows for the setting of more options. Along with minimum and maximum, you can also set the scale unit. For example, if you are analyzing sales in terms of units sold and you want a graph that shows sales in thousands of units, you should set the scale unit to one thousand. This is equally effective for showing dollar values in the millions. Simply set the scale unit to one million, and you will reduce the size of the numbers on the Y axis, while still showing the relationship of the data. The number on the scale is shown in the upper-left corner of the Graph window as a fraction, such as 1/1000 for setting the scale unit to one per thousand.

Discoverer sets the increments between the numbers on the Y axis in terms of the lowest and highest number being analyzed. The increments are divided equally and will change automatically when the query updates. By choosing Fixed instead and selecting a number, you can create smaller or larger increments. Be careful when choosing, however; if you choose too large a number, the gaps between increments may be so small you might not be able to see them all. If you make the increment too small, it may be difficult to effectively analyze the data.

One other thing you can do in the Scale and Numbers dialog box is to change the scale from linear to logarithmic. We recommend leaving the setting at linear unless you are analyzing scientific or complex mathematical formulas.

To open the Scale and Numbers dialog box from the Graph window, use the following workflow:

1. From the menu bar, select Graph | Scale or right-click in the Graph window and select Scale.

2. Make the modifications desired.

3. Click OK.

Changing Colors

After the graph is created, use the color and pattern section of the toolbar to change colors. Discoverer uses a drag-and-drop system for changing colors and patterns.

To change a color or pattern on the graph, use the following workflow:

1. Click the color or pattern you want to use.

2. Hold down the mouse button until the mouse pointer changes to a paint can.

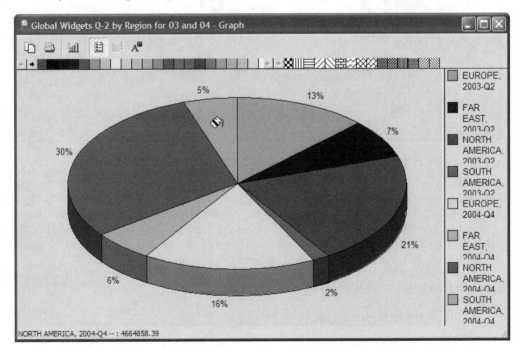

3. Drag the paint can (mouse pointer) to the data on the graph you want to change.

4. Release the mouse button.

Using Pull-Outs

When using a pie or doughnut type of graph, you can "pull out" one or more sections of the graph. Do this to emphasize certain data, such as the highest and lowest sales regions or Q1 for the past three years.

To pull out an element on a pie or doughnut graph, use the following workflow:

1. Click the data section of the pie you want to pull out.

2. Drag it away from the center of the graph.

3. Continue the preceding steps until you have pulled out all of the data you want to emphasize. This is shown in the following illustration.

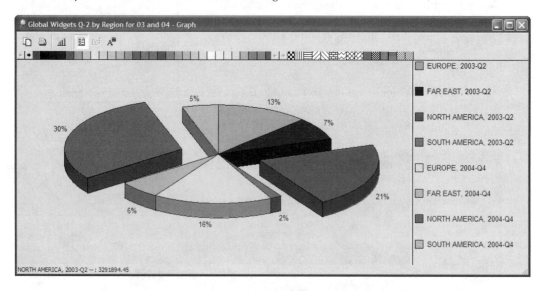

Modifying 3-D Effects

When you select the type and format for the graph in the wizard, you have limited control over the formatting. Some of the graph types have one or more 3-D formatting options. Using 3-D formatting can add interest and character to a graph, and most graph types default to a 3-D format. If you choose to use a 3-D format, you can modify it after you have finished creating the graph with the 3D View Properties dialog box. The options available include changing the angle of the graph, applying a full 3-D view, and making the graph deeper or more shallow.

To open the 3D View Properties dialog box, select Graph | 3D View or right-click the graph and select 3D View. The box contains the following features:

- **3D check box**   Applies standard 3-D effects.

- **Full 3D view check box**   Adds full 3-D effects.

- **Shadow check box**   Adds or removes shadows in the graph.

- **X Angle box**   Changes the X axis angle.

- **Y Angle box**   Changes the Y axis angle.

- **Depth sliding scale**   Slide this scale to increase and decrease the depth of the 3-D effects.

- **X and Y axes diagram**   Drag the dots to change the angle of the X and Y axes.

Figure 7-16 shows the 3D View Properties dialog box.

Oracle makes an excellent recommendation when working with the 3D View Properties dialog box. Write down all of the settings before you begin to modify the 3-D effect so that you can return them to the defaults if you wish. Then you are free to experiment with different rotations and angles.

To change the 3-D effects of a graph, use the following workflow:

1. Check the Full 3D View check box.

2. Click and drag the dots on the X and Y axes diagram; the numbers in the X and Y Angle boxes will change as you do this.

3. Move the depth sliding scale to increase or decrease the depth of the graph.

4. Click Apply to view the changes to the graph.

5. When done with the modifications, click OK.

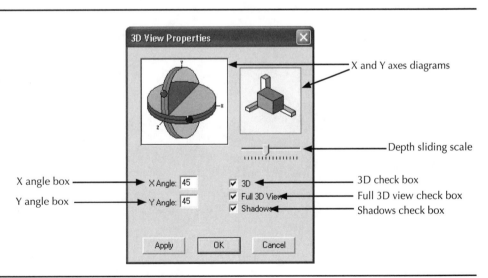

FIGURE 7-16   *3D View Properties dialog box*

Summary

In this chapter, you have learned how to use the Graph Wizard to create graphs in Desktop or the Edit Graph dialog box in Plus based on your queries. You have learned to add interest and detail by adding titles, changing fonts, and adding legends and labels. You have been shown how to modify your graphs in a variety of ways, including using pull-outs, adding 3-D effects, and changing the scale of the Y axis.

Graphs are an excellent way to represent your data visually. By using the Discoverer graph tool, you will add a new dimension to your queries.

CHAPTER
8

Turning a Discoverer
Query into a Report

t may seem premature at this point to show you how to create a report. However, we feel that once you have a working query, you should know how to turn it into a report. In the coming chapters, you will learn more advanced Discoverer techniques on building bigger and better queries. As you do, the lessons you learn here will enable you to create reports based upon those queries.

A Discoverer report is simply a well-formatted query. There is no wizard to guide you, or button to click, that will magically turn your query into a stunning printable report. You have a bit of work to do, but we think it is fun to format reports!

Report aesthetics are all-important. If you present your report in a logical order, using meaningful, business-friendly column names and fonts that are pleasing to the eye, you are well on the way toward having your report accepted by those who will read it. Sloppy reports with bad formatting, misspelled column names, and illogical ordering invite criticism such as "If he or she can't even give me a report with a good layout, maybe I should get someone to double-check the figures." A well-written report induces confidence in the creator.

Many companies have a standard for reporting. If your company is one of those that do have a standard, it is important to learn it and use it in your reports. It is possible, however, that there is no established standard. If this is the case, you may be the one that introduces such a standard to your company.

Avoid using frilly or unusual fonts. Times New Roman and Arial are normal default fonts for a reason. They are easy to read and pleasing to the eye. Also, adding too much detail to headers and footers, or using too many different colors, can distract from the data. The old adage "keep it simple, stupid" is a good one to adopt in reporting. Another reason to stick with normal fonts is how they will appear on the Web. You can't assume that everyone has the same font sets as you do. Even though virtual font mapping takes place, mapping Java fonts to the physical fonts installed on a user's computer, one cannot always be guaranteed of the results when using esoteric fonts.

We have already covered the steps for creating and formatting titles, column headings, widths, and colors, and changing fonts in the data, so we will not repeat them here. These formatting steps have been added to the workflow to give you an idea of where to do them if they were not done as the query was created. Many queries are around for a long time just waiting to become a report, and so have a good deal of the formatting already done. We call these "wish queries" because they are queries that wish they were reports, or more likely, there is someone who is saying, "I wish I had a report that did this or answered that" when there is already a query that does. It simply needs to be turned into a printable report.

In this chapter, you will learn a workflow that will prepare your queries to be turned into reports. You will learn how to format the report for printing, including how to format the sheet, headers, footers, and margins; how to format the table options to determine if the printable report will have gridlines or not; and how to insert page breaks. We will show you how to use the Page Setup feature to give you greater flexibility in how your pages will print. We will also teach you to use the Print Preview feature of Discoverer as a tool for fine-tuning the report.

Discoverer has the ability to export reports into other applications. You will be shown the steps to follow for exporting your reports as spreadsheets, HTML, and text files.

A Workflow for Building Reports

Although you have already been taught the basic concepts included in the report workflow, we offer them here to help you save time and unneeded effort in report building. The workflow ensures that you perform your formatting in the right order, so you don't need to do the same thing twice. For example, if you format the width of your columns and then rename them, the column might not be wide enough to accommodate the new name and you will need to format the width again. This is a waste of time. Thus, by following the workflow, you can avoid duplication of effort.

Included in the workflow are reminders on when to save your query. It may seem elementary, but we feel that there are good times to save in terms of changes you have made to your report. It might also be a good idea for you to save your query by some other name as a backup in case you get carried away and want to begin again from the base query.

Report Workflow

Use the following workflow to begin turning a query into a report:

1. Create a working query that avoids the Twilight Zone.

2. Rearrange the columns in the query and move to the Page Items those columns that have the same data repeated in every row.

3. Decide whether any columns could be better displayed on their own sheet and move these also to the Page Items (using Page Items will be discussed in more detail when we explain analysis in Chapter 9).

4. Rename any item that does not have a meaningful name.

5. Adjust column widths.

6. Save the query.

7. Refine temporary conditions and create new ones to select only the data from the database that you want to use in the final report—if you make a mistake, you can always reload from the saved copy. Conditions should be refined, honed, and so forth as many times as needed. This step is also included in the analysis workflow that will be covered in detail in the next chapter.

8. Create any calculations that you need. This step adds or replaces data items that cannot be pulled in directly from the database. You may want to concatenate some items, create new items based on values in other columns, or even replace difficult-to-understand codes with more meaningful values. This step is also included in the analysis workflow that will be covered in detail in the next chapter.

9. Save the query again.

NOTE
When working with Plus, it is even more advisable to save often, as network connections can be unreliable—it is better to save and undo your steps if needed than not to save and lose a lot of work.

10. Upon completion of your calculations, you should review the final arrangement of the columns. Even though you may have done an initial column order during Step 2, now that you have added calculations, you should make sure that these new items are also in the right place. In particular, you should place all items that will be sorted in the first columns, with the primary sort item in column 1 and so on.

11. Delete unwanted columns. Yes, you can delete columns that have been used in calculations and in conditions, and the calculation or condition will still work. This step will be covered in Chapter 11, when we cover advanced queries.

12. Apply any sorting that you need. By this stage, your query should contain all of the database and calculated items that will be used to produce the final result, with all items in their correct order. You should now apply all of the sort criteria that will be used to make an understandable and presentable report.

13. Save the unfinished report.

14. Create subtotals and totals that you need. Having created a sort order, you should decide whether or not you need to include any subtotals and totals. These are an essential element if your report will be used for analysis. This step is also included in the analysis workflow that will be covered in detail in the next chapter.

15. Save the report.

16. Create and format a report title.

17. Format headings.

18. Format data.

If you have followed the preceding workflow, you are ready to do the following:

1. Format the report for printing.

2. Format the sheet, headers, footers, and margins.

3. Format the table options to determine if the printable report will have gridlines or not.

Formatting the Report for Printing

It may seem premature to begin with print setup, but we have a good reason to start here. There is not a place in the Page Setup dialog box to format the paper size, so it must be done in the Print Setup dialog box. Since you will be using Print Preview as a tool for fine-tuning the report before printing, it is essential that the paper size be set before moving on. We have also discovered that in the Print Setup dialog box, there are some performance issues in Desktop that need to be covered to save you some frustration.

NOTE
Print Setup and Page Setup are sufficiently different in Desktop and Plus to describe them separately.

Print Setup in Desktop

To prepare your report for printing in Desktop, use the following workflow:

1. Select File | Print, and the Windows Print dialog box will open. Here, you have a standard print setup.

NOTE
When you click the Print button in Desktop, be prepared for your
report to print, because you will not be prompted in any way.

2. Select the printer that will be used to print the report. It is important to use the correct printer because they all print differently.

3. Set the print range.

4. Select the number of copies.

5. Click the Properties button. This opens the Printer Setup window. Depending upon the printer you have, you will have different setup options. There are usually several tabs. The ones that we are concerned with here are the orientation and paper size.

6. Set the paper size that you feel will best display your report.

7. Set the orientation that will best suit the layout of your report.

8. Click OK, and the Properties dialog box closes, taking you back to the Print dialog box.

9. This is where it becomes a little tricky. You have set up your paper size and orientation, but you are not ready to print your report. If you are like us, you will expect as we did, when we clicked OK, that your property selections have been saved. This is not the case. If you click Cancel at this point, the paper size and orientation, as well as any other changes you made, will return to what they were before you started. You must click OK from the Print dialog box as well as the Properties box to save your print setup, thus causing your print job to run.

10. Your report is not ready to print, so you might want to do what we did, and turn off the printer if possible. If your computer is slow enough, you might be able to hit the Cancel button in time. Or if your printer is slow, you can open the Print Queue window and cancel it there. Of course, another possibility is to simply let it print and see what your preliminary output is.

11. Click OK.

Print Setup in Plus

Previous releases of the web version were so bad at printing that we were relieved to see the printing features improved in this release; however, Print setup in Plus still gives us a little bit of heartburn. Each time you open the Print Setup dialog box, it is set to the default settings. That is fine if the default is what you want but not fine if you want to deviate from it. If you are going to use the report workflow we gave you at the beginning of this chapter, you will need to reset Print Setup every time you want to use Print Preview. It is not as bad as it sounds, because in Plus you have a Print Preview button in Print Setup. This is a definite improvement. To prepare your report for printing in Plus, use the following workflow:

1. Select File | Print, and the Print dialog box will open.

2. Choose to print the Entire Workbook or the Current Worksheet.
3. Select the view to print. By selecting the check boxes, you can print the table or crosstab only, you can print the graph only, or you can print both.
4. Select how to print the Page Items. You can print only the selected Page Item that is currently showing, or All Combinations. All Combinations will print all of the items in the page details.
5. Select the number of copies.
6. Click OK. This will open the standard Windows Print dialog box.

7. Click Properties and go through the tabs for your printer to set up the paper size and orientation. You can also set the orientation in the Page Setup dialog box, which we will show you later in the chapter.

8. Set the paper size that you feel will best display your report.

9. Set the orientation that will best suit the layout of your report.

10. Click OK, and the Properties dialog box closes, taking you back to the Print dialog box.

11. As with Desktop, this is where it becomes a little tricky. You have set up your paper size and orientation but are not ready to print your report. If you are like us, you expected, when you clicked OK, that your property selections had been saved. This is not the case. If you click Cancel at this point, the paper size and orientation, as well as any other changes you made, will return to what they were before you started. You must click on OK from the Print dialog box as well as the Properties box to save your print setup, thus causing your print job to run.

12. Your report is not ready to print, so you might want to do what we did, and turn off the printer if possible. If your computer is slow enough, you might be able to hit the Cancel button in time. Or if your printer is slow, you can open the Print Queue window and cancel it there. Of course, another possibility is to simply let it print and see what your preliminary output is.

13. Click OK.

Page Setup

When creating a report in Discoverer, you have many of the same page setup options as when working in some familiar word processors and spreadsheets. You can set page margins, add headers and footers, change the orientation from portrait to landscape, as well as set up print features.

NOTE
None of the functions of the Page Setup dialog box are available on the formatting bar.

To open the Page Setup dialog box, click File | Page Setup.

The Sheet Tab in Desktop

The Sheet tab is divided into four sections:

■   **Print What**   In this area, you can select whether to print only the Selected Sheet (the sheet you are working on), All Sheets in the workbook, and any Graphs you have included in the workbook.

There is also a selection box you can check to show All Page Detail/Combinations. If your worksheet includes page detail, selecting this will print all combinations available. For example, say the page detail is Year with 1998, 1999, and 2000 in the drop-down list, but only 1999 is showing in the worksheet. If you check this box, all three years will print.

■   **Page Order**   This area allows you to determine the order the pages will print when the data on the worksheet is too large to print on one page. For example, if the worksheet is twelve columns wide but only eight columns will fit on a page, using the default, Down,

Then Across, will print all pages with the first eight columns first and then the pages with the remaining four columns.

The second option is Across, Then Down. We prefer this option, because it prints each page with the first eight columns followed immediately by a page with the remaining four columns, thus keeping all of the items together.

■ **Orientation**   Here, you will select whether to print in Portrait or Landscape orientation (select the same orientation used in the Print setup).

■ **Scale**   In this area, you can select to scale the report so that it will fit better on a page. This feature is available only if you are using a PostScript printer.

The Worksheet Tab in Plus

The Worksheet tab is divided into five areas:

■ **Paper Size**   This area shows the paper size you chose in the Print Setup dialog box. You cannot change it here. It is just a display.

■ **Orientation**   This area shows the page orientation you chose in the Print Setup dialog box. You can change it here if you wish.

■ **Title**   Choose whether to print the title on only the first page of the report or on all pages.

■ **Text Area**   If you have chosen to put a text area in your report, you can choose whether to print the text area on only the last page of the report or on all pages.

■ **Page Items**   Choose to print only the Page Items showing or all combinations of Page Items.

The Table/Crosstab Tab in Plus

In Plus you have a Table or Crosstab tab, depending on which type of layout you have chosen.

- **Table/Crosstab Page Order**   This area allows you to determine the order the pages will print when the data on the worksheet is too large to print on one page. For example, if the worksheet is twelve columns wide but only eight columns will fit on a page, using the default, Down, Then Across, will print all pages with the first eight columns first and then the pages with the remaining four columns.

  The second option is Across, Then Down. We prefer this option, because it prints each page with the first eight columns followed immediately by a page with the remaining four columns, thus keeping all of the items together.

- **Repeat**   Check this box if you want row, column, and Page Item headers on every page.

- **Table/Crosstab Scaling**   In this area, you can choose to scale the report so that it will fit better on to a page. This feature is available only if you are using a PostScript printer.

Header and Footers

Headers and footers are a great way to add to a report detail that will repeat on each page, such as page numbers, or the date the report was printed, or even the name of the report's author. In Desktop, the Header and Footer tabs of the Page Setup dialog box function in exactly the same way. In Plus, the Header and Footer tabs have been combined into one. We will demonstrate the steps for creating a header and a footer at the same time.

The first time you use these screens, the Available Headers or Available Footers list will show "none." As you create headers and footers, you can add them to the list of available headers and footers. Thus you can use the same ones each time to create continuity and consistency in your report writing.

There is also an Insert button. Use this button to insert codes for items such as date, time, filename, and location. It is a good idea to place these codes in the same locations each time you use them. Those who read your reports will appreciate the continuity and find your reports easier to navigate than if you use a variety of formats. You can also add a line between your header and the body of the report. The Line button allows you to select from predefined line widths. Play with these options, look at other reports that you find attractive and easy to read, and then adapt them to your own reports. Headers and footers are an excellent way to add distinction to your reporting.

The Header and Footer tabs contain

- **Available Headers** or **Footers**   A drop-down list of available headers or footers. There are no available headers and footers in Plus.

- **Add & Remove**   Two buttons used to add and remove headers or footers. This button does not exist in Plus.

- **Line Width**   A drop-down box to set the line width that separates the header or footer from the body of the report.

- **Insert**   A drop-down button used to insert predefined codes.

- **Font**   Opens the Fonts dialog box to allow formatting of the header or footer.

■ **Left Section**, **Center Section**, **Right Section**   Sections where you create the header or footer.

■ **Preview**   A button to see a print preview of the report.

The next illustration shows the Header tab of the Page Setup dialog box. Remember that the Header and Footer tabs are identical in appearance and functionality in Desktop and combined into one in Plus.

To create a header or footer, use the following workflow:

1. Click the Header or Footer tab.

2. Select an available header or footer in Desktop or create your own in Desktop or Plus.

3. To create your own header or footer, click in the Left, Center, or Right section.

4. Type in the text you want, or use the Insert drop-down button as seen in the illustration that follows to select from predefined codes. These codes can insert

   ■ Workbook Name

   ■ Sheet Name

   ■ Date

   ■ Time

   ■ Page Number

   ■ Conditions

   ■ Data Points

   ■ Axis Items

   ■ Page Items

You can even add Parameter names and values. We demonstrate how this is done in Chapter 13, in the section called "Using Parameters in the Title, Header or Footer."

5. Format the font type, size, and color.

6. Select a line width, if desired.

7. Click Preview to see the report as it will print.

8. Make any adjustments to the header or footer.

9. When you are satisfied with the header or footer, click OK.

Margins

Adjusting margins is a good way to gain added control over how your report will print. The default margins are 1 inch for the top and bottom margins and 0.75 inch for the side margins. This might work for you if you have a small report, but for larger reports, some fudging may be in order. There are times the data is just a wee bit too much for a good page layout, and by adjusting the margins you can get it all on one page—or at least get the data to break better.

Use some caution when adjusting margins. It is possible to make them so small that data will actually print over the header or footer. Most printers also have a printable area, and you could lose some data from the printout where the printer could not print.

Another formatting option you have in the Margins tab is whether or not to center the report on the page. You can select horizontally or vertically or both. You will probably always want to center the report horizontally. This will give a nice look to the report; however, vertical centering should be used sparingly. Sometimes the report is small, and vertical centering will bring the report too far down the page.

The Margins tab has the following sections:

- **Units**   This option is available in Plus only. Select from Inches, Pixels, or Centimeters.

- **Margins**   Four up/down boxes used to adjust the margins.

- **From Edge**   Two up/down boxes used to adjust how far from the edge of the page the header or footer will print.

- **Center on Page**   This option is available in Desktop only. Two check boxes are used to center the report on the page horizontally or vertically.

- **Preview**   A button to see a print preview of the report.

To set the margins, use the following workflow:

1. From the Page Setup dialog box, click the Margins tab.
2. In Plus only, select the Units of measure you want to use.
3. Use the up/down buttons in the Margins section to set the margins, or type in the margin you want.
4. Use the up/down buttons in the From Edge section to determine how far from the edge of the paper you want the margins to print. Be careful to not set these larger or the same as the margins, and do not set them outside your printer's printable area.
5. In Desktop only, center the report on the page horizontally, vertically, or both.
6. Click Preview to see the report as it will print.
7. Make any adjustments to the margins.
8. When you are satisfied with the margins, click OK.

Before moving on to the next section, you might want to revisit column widths at this time. It is possible that by slightly widening or narrowing the column widths, your report will fit better on the page. By going back and forth between column widths and margin sizes, you can fine-tune the report layout. You might even want to take another look at font sizes to see if your report will fit better on the page. Use Print Preview often as you prepare your report to print.

Table and Crosstab Gridlines

Remember that Discoverer is WYSIWYG—you will need to format the table itself if you don't want to see gridlines printed in your report. This is done through the Options dialog box. In Desktop the Options dialog box defaults to the Table or Crosstab tab, depending upon the type of query you are working with. In Plus you will need to select the Sheet tab.

We are disappointed that the gridlines cannot be turned off for printing only, as you can turn them off in Excel. Most of us like to work on a table with the gridlines showing but turned off for a final report. It is a nuisance to have to change back and forth. We hope this functionality will be incorporated into a future release of Discoverer.

If you chose to leave the gridlines on for your report, you might want to change the gridline color. Be careful with this type of formatting and be sure that it is not just pretty but actually helps display the data in a meaningful way.

Table Gridlines

The following illustration shows the Table tab of the Options dialog box in Desktop.

The next illustration shows the Sheet tab of the Options dialog box in Plus.

To change the gridline properties of a table, use the following workflow:

1. From the menu bar, select Tools | Options. In Plus you will need to select the Sheet tab.
2. Deselect the Horizontal and Vertical gridlines as desired.
3. If leaving the gridlines on but changing the gridline color, click the box to the right of Gridline Color.
4. Select a new color from the color selection box.
5. Click OK.

Crosstab Gridlines

Crosstabs have two more choices associated with the crosstab. You can also choose whether or not to show the axis item labels and whether to show axis gridlines in 3-D. Additionally, you can choose the style of your crosstab here. You can choose to show crosstab labels inline (labels stacked on top of each other) or in an outline format (staggered labels and data items). The latter of the two requires more space, so if the size of the report is a concern, you might try inline. Work with it until you have it in a format that is easy to read and aesthetically pleasing. The illustrations that follow show an inline crosstab and an outline one.

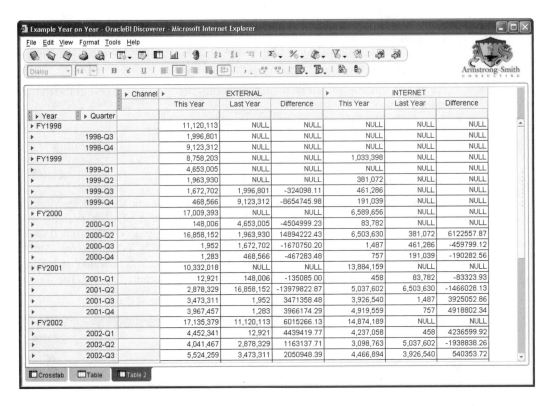

	Channel ▶		EXTERNAL			▶	INTERNET		
			This Year	Last Year	Difference		This Year	Last Year	Difference
▶ Year	▶ Quarter								
▶ FY1998			11,120,113	NULL	NULL		NULL	NULL	NULL
▶	1998-Q3		1,996,801	NULL	NULL		NULL	NULL	NULL
▶	1998-Q4		9,123,312	NULL	NULL		NULL	NULL	NULL
▶ FY1999			8,758,203	NULL	NULL		1,033,398	NULL	NULL
▶	1999-Q1		4,653,005	NULL	NULL		NULL	NULL	NULL
▶	1999-Q2		1,963,930	NULL	NULL		381,072	NULL	NULL
▶	1999-Q3		1,672,702	1,996,801	-324098.11		461,286	NULL	NULL
▶	1999-Q4		468,566	9,123,312	-8654745.98		191,039	NULL	NULL
▶ FY2000			17,009,393	NULL	NULL		6,589,656	NULL	NULL
▶	2000-Q1		148,006	4,653,005	-4504999.23		83,782	NULL	NULL
▶	2000-Q2		16,858,152	1,963,930	14894222.43		6,503,630	381,072	6122557.87
▶	2000-Q3		1,952	1,672,702	-1670750.20		1,487	461,286	-459799.12
▶	2000-Q4		1,283	468,566	-467283.48		757	191,039	-190282.56
▶ FY2001			10,332,018	NULL	NULL		13,884,159	NULL	NULL
▶	2001-Q1		12,921	148,006	-135085.00		458	83,782	-83323.93
▶	2001-Q2		2,878,329	16,858,152	-13979822.87		5,037,602	6,503,630	-1466028.13
▶	2001-Q3		3,473,311	1,952	3471358.48		3,926,540	1,487	3925052.86
▶	2001-Q4		3,967,457	1,283	3966174.29		4,919,559	757	4918802.34
▶ FY2002			17,135,379	11,120,113	6015266.13		14,874,189	NULL	NULL
▶	2002-Q1		4,452,341	12,921	4439419.77		4,237,058	458	4236599.92
▶	2002-Q2		4,041,467	2,878,329	1163137.71		3,098,763	5,037,602	-1938838.26
▶	2002-Q3		5,524,259	3,473,311	2050948.39		4,466,894	3,926,540	540353.72

The following illustration shows the Crosstab tab of the Options dialog box in Desktop.

To change the gridline properties of a crosstab, use the following workflow:

1. From the menu bar, select Tools | Options.
2. Deselect the Horizontal and Vertical gridlines as desired.
3. If leaving the gridlines on but changing the gridline color, click the box to the right of Gridline Color.
4. Select a new color from the color selection box.
5. Check the Axis Labels box if you want the names of the axis items to appear in your report.
6. Check Axis Gridlines if you want gridlines to appear around the axis items in Desktop.
7. Select the Crosstab Style.
8. Click OK.

Inserting Page Breaks in Tables (Sorry, No Page Breaks in Crosstabs)

Page breaks are useful when you want to add logical breaks between data items. For example, your reports show the sales for all of your regions. You want a page break between each of the regions. By group-sorting by region in your report, you can also add a page break between them. When you add a page break to items that cover more than one page, the column headings repeat as well as the item name at the top of each column.

To create a page break, follow this workflow:

1. Click Tools | Sort.
2. Click the item you want to group sort and create a page break on.
3. From the Group drop-down list, select Page Break.
4. Click OK.

Exporting Your Report to Another Application

Once you have a great report formatted and ready for printing, you might also want to send the file to someone who does not have Discoverer. Discoverer files can be exported in many different formats, the most common being Excel, HTML, Comma Separator Delimited (CSV), and Tab Delimited (Text). In addition to these, there is also PDF in Plus and Viewer.

Excel is an excellent spreadsheet program, and many companies use it. However, with some experimentation, we have discovered that exporting to Excel can be extremely time-consuming. It is recommended that instead of exporting into an Excel format, you use CSV, which Excel imports easily. This method will save you time and frustration.

HTML is also a popular format and creates files that anyone with a browser can view. The downside, of course, is that the data can only be viewed in HTML and not worked with. Discoverer Viewer result sets are displayed as HTML and allow users to open predefined queries and perform some limited analysis, such as drilling down a hierarchy. HTML data can, however, be copied and pasted into a spreadsheet or word processor. The data will have to be reformatted, but it can be worked with.

To export a Discoverer report to another application, use the following workflow:

1. Click File | Export. This opens the Export dialog box shown here:

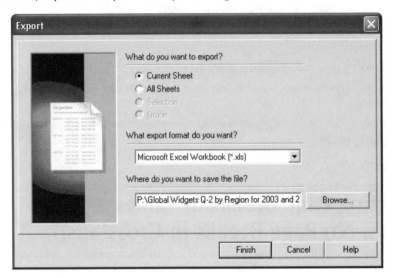

2. Select the part of the workbook you want to export. If you want to export a graph, the graph needs to be the active window and will export as a wmf file.

3. From the drop-down list, select the format you want to export the file in.

4. Give the location you want to save the file to.

5. Click Finish. The file is now ready to be used in another application.

Summary

In this chapter, you have learned a workflow to use in preparing your queries to be turned into reports. You have been shown how to format the report for printing and how to format the sheet, headers, footers, and margins. We have also shown you how to format the table options to determine if the printable report will have gridlines or not, and how to insert page breaks.

We have shown you how to use the Page Setup feature to give you greater flexibility in how your pages will print, as well as how to use the Print Preview feature of Discoverer as a tool for fine-tuning the report. You have also learned how to export reports into other applications such as spreadsheets, as HTML, and as text files.

CHAPTER
9

Using Discoverer to Analyze Data

here is an almost endless variety of possible combinations of facts in table and crosstab design, and it would be impossible for us to describe them all to you in this book. In fact, as we have explored the various permutations that Discoverer allows, we have come to the conclusion that we could almost write an entire book on just table layouts and their relationship with analysis.

Therefore, in this chapter, we will teach you how we go about analyzing data in Discoverer using basic and clear-cut methods. As you become more skilled in the use of the product, you should begin experimenting and see how it will work for you.

In this chapter, you will learn the meaning of analysis and the five basic types of analysis—statistical, classification, deviation, trend, and aging—that we will describe using Discoverer. You will learn how to perform these types of analysis, using both Desktop and Plus. We will introduce an analysis workflow that we hope will help you go about analyzing your data more effectively.

We will show you more ways to access the tools that were introduced to you in Chapters 4 and 5. You will be introduced to the tools available on the toolbars and be shown how to cut your analysis time by using the terrific features of Discoverer. Throughout the chapter, we will talk about analysis and statistics and describe some of the fundamentals and pitfalls involved.

What Is Analysis?

Analysis provides the capability to discover new and meaningful information by using existing data. Analysis techniques massage the data in some way, either by constraining the initial selection by restricting the data to just a subset of what is available, or by reducing the final output to make it more meaningful. Facts are taken and then dissected, compared, rearranged, put back together, and finally reported.

Having decided upon the data items you need for your query and having ordered those items into columns and rows and formatted them, you have completed the first part of your task. However, before you can turn your query into a report, you need to decide whether any analysis of the data is required.

Think about what it is that your analysis is trying to do. Throughout this chapter on analysis, you must stay focused and remember to always keep in mind what question it is that you are trying to answer. If you do this, you will be visualizing at least a part of the final display and already be anticipating what to do if the figures do not in fact produce the result you wanted.

Types of Analysis

The world of analysis is full of different methodologies and approaches. There are also many types of analysis techniques available to you, and we want to give you an understanding of five of them that can be used inside Discoverer. We hope you will find these useful. They are as follows:

- Statistical analysis

- Classification analysis

- Deviation analysis

- Trend analysis

- Aging analysis

We will also enclose some ideas and examples from our own database to show you the results that can be obtained from these different analysis techniques. Full details on how to build these examples can be found at the end of this chapter.

Statistical Analysis

The *statistical* approach uses rules or conditions and is based on data relationships. Usually what you will end up with are statistics, but how are statistics derived? Online analytical processing (OLAP) is an example of this statistically oriented approach and is one of the forms of analysis that Discoverer is particularly good at. An example of a statistical application may determine that all sales orders beginning with a 5 are regular sales orders, while orders beginning with a 7 are returns. By analyzing only the returns and determining that 18 percent of the sales orders begin with a 7, you can accurately state that 82 percent of sales orders are regular orders—without ever querying those orders that begin with 5. Of course, this statement is true only if all of the other sales orders begin with a 5. If you have another class of orders that begin with a different number, then the statement is untrue, so you need to be careful about making statements from statistics.

Common sense can really cloud statistical results. For instance, we heard about a technology firm who had determined that 40 percent of all sick days were taken on a Friday or a Monday. Armed with this information, and before they realized their mistake, they immediately began clamping down on their employees. You see, they had overlooked the fact that 40 percent represents two days out of a five-day working week and therefore what they were seeing was a perfectly normal spread, rather than a reflection of opportunist employees trying to extend their weekends.

There is a popular saying in England that "one can drive a bus through statistics." While this may sound somewhat exaggerated, in fact there is more than a grain of truth to this statement. One of the authors went to school with a professor of mathematics who in later life became a professional witness at trials. Depending on which side he was contracted to, he would find statistics to prove the case either for the prosecution or for the defense. We often wonder what would have happened if another professor of mathematics had been contracted for the other side! In a saying made popular by Mark Twain, "There are three kinds of lies: lies, damned lies, and statistics."

So now that we have shown you the pitfalls, let us talk about creating statistics. Many statistics are produced to satisfy corporate or personal objectives. Perhaps someone is looking for data to prove that a particular product has sold exceptionally well, accidentally or otherwise overlooking the fact that the product also had an exceptional number of returns. The end result of that analysis may have produced a set of statistics that do not tell the complete story.

For example, suppose you were asked to write a query that analyzed all of the sales for the past year, showing how each region had fared when compared to the other regions. It should be evident that your query needs to be constrained to just one year, and so, adding a condition on this item will be the first technique you apply. Having constrained or filtered your query to include only the year in question, you would run the query and take a look at the output to decide what other analysis tools need to be applied. These rules are the building blocks for further analysis.

Let us therefore build the preceding query using our database. As the specification states, we need to include the year, the region, and the sales amount (the selling price). If we build this as a crosstab, we can place the region on the side axis and the year in the page axis. Finally, adding a percentage on the selling price makes the query look like what is shown in Figure 9-1.

As you can see in the example, the percentage of sales for Europe was almost 28 percent, which means that the sales for all other regions must be just over 72 percent. There is no need to add them up because by deduction this statistic must be true.

		Selling Price SUM	Percent Selling Price SUM
▸ Region			
▸ EUROPE		18,299,570	27.96%
▸ FAR EAST		7,459,468	11.40%
▸ NORTH AMERICA		33,147,177	50.65%
▸ SOUTH AMERICA		6,540,476	9.99%
Percent		65,446,690	100.00%

Page Items: Year: FY2004 ▾

FIGURE 9-1 *Statistical example: sales for 2004 based on region*

We know this example is very simple, but it is given just to show you how you can take one figure that you do know to derive another statistic that you do not.

Discoverer provides many statistical functions that the typical business analyst understands. Among these are mean, median, variance, standard deviation, covariance, percentiles, and so on. Please take a look at Appendix B for a full listing of the functions available to you in Discoverer.

A Discussion about Averages

Many people think that the term "mean" means the same thing as "average." It doesn't. The term mean is a mathematical term, whereas the term average is often used loosely as a description for a person or a data item. In mathematics, average is "a number that typifies a set of numbers of which it is a function." In other words, average can stand for mean, median, or mode. So what is the difference between these three terms?

- **Median** This is the middle value in a distribution or set of numbers, above and below which lie an equal number of other values.

- **Mean** This is a number that typifies a set of numbers, such as a geometric or arithmetic mean; it is what most people think of as being the average value of a set of numbers.

- **Mode** This is the value or item that occurs most frequently in a set or series of statistical data.

Look at the following two sets of data:

Example set 1   15   16   17   17   17   18   19

Analyzing this first set of data, representing the ages of the seven students in a school who enjoy drama, we get:

- **Mean** 17
- **Median** 17
- **Mode** 17

Example set 2   15   17   17   17   21   29   52

Analyzing this second set of data, representing the ages of the seven night school students who enjoy drama, we get:

- **Mean** 24

- **Median** 17

- **Mode** 17

As you can see, the median age and the modal age for both sets of students are the same, whereas the mean age is completely different. Which "average" you choose will determine whether you consider the average age for students who enjoy drama to be the same for both normal schools and night schools. If statistics teach us nothing else, they show us that there is no such thing as an average.

We hope this discussion helps you understand why people have difficulty in interpreting statistical averages. Many people try to make their statistics fit the normal distribution, but there are *non-normal* distributions too. The statistics that are used for normal distributions are often inappropriate when the distribution is patently non-normal.

Classification Analysis

The *classification* approach groups data according to some similarity in the data or some derived commonality. Knowledge of your company—and more to the point, the database itself—can be an important string to your bow in this scenario. This background knowledge of how your data is being used can be a tremendous asset in helping you understand whether the classifications that you have determined are valid.

What we are implying is that you should use sorting and paging to manipulate your data. Moving the data around onscreen like this is another of the things that Discoverer does very well. Unless you change the selections or conditions, you can manipulate the data onscreen without any impact to the system. This is because once Discoverer has completed the base query, it stores all of the resulting data in memory, allowing you the pleasure of manipulating it to your heart's content.

If you use Discoverer Viewer, you will instantly recognize that this scenario is exactly what Viewer is designed to do. By allowing you to manipulate the data onscreen without changing the base query, Viewer is the perfect tool for undergoing classification analysis.

Let us show you what we mean by using Viewer. Figure 9-2 shows the cost price, selling price, and total amount of profit made in each quarter of 2004, by each product, with the query grouping the products by their respective product lines.

By moving some of the items around, we can display exactly the same data using a completely different classification. In Figure 9-3, the same query has been manipulated to show the profit only for all products in all product lines.

See the section entitled "How to Build the Example Queries" near the end of this chapter for full instructions on how to construct and manipulate this query.

NOTE
If you are unsure as to what we did, we moved the data points out into the page items so that each data point became a drop-down. This allows us to look at the data for cost price, selling price, and profit independently.

FIGURE 9-2 *Classification example: profit for 2004 by product*

Deviation Analysis

In its simplest form, *deviation* analysis uses percentages and exceptions to the rule to identify areas for improvement. A series of numbers such as sales figures, electrical consumption, and attendance records are excellent types of data for this kind of analysis. To perform this analysis, you would work out a percentage of each item when compared to the total. Then you would apply an exception to identify those items that are deviating too high or too low.

FIGURE 9-3 *Classification example: profit for 2004 for all product lines*

Having worked out the percentage deviations, you will want to highlight those items whose deviation is beyond what you consider to be the norm. The use of conditional and stoplight formatting comes into its own, bringing out the anomalies even more.

In Figure 9-4, we have analyzed the sales for all of Global Widgets products that begin with "QB" by status and channel. We wanted to know whether there was any difference between the channels. In particular, we wanted to analyze the percentage of orders shipped and cancelled, and to see if there was anything for us to report. For us, a percentage shipped of 90 percent or more is considered acceptable, while cancellations greater than 10 percent are considered unacceptable. We know from experience that products that begin with "QB" are the highest sellers.

In Figure 9-4, we have taken the percentage of the order quantity for each status, by product and channel. The results surprised us and only went to underline the benefit of doing this type of analysis. As you can see, only three of our "QB" products in the External channel—that is, our normal non-Internet channel—have a percentage shipped of 90 percent or higher. Looking at the Internet channel, we were amazed to see that only two products made the cut.

If you look at the report in more detail, you can see that we have a high percentage of open, non-shipped orders for product QB-2000 in the External channel, whereas the same product in the Internet channel has little in the way of backlog. Looking further, you can see that we also have a very high percentage of cancellations for QB-1000 (coincidentally for the External channel). These figures will make for an interesting discussion the next time we have a board meeting with the VP of External Sales!

See the section entitled "How to Build the Example Queries" near the end of this chapter for full instructions on how to construct and manipulate this query.

Trend Analysis

Trend analysis, as the name suggests, looks for trends and makes assumptions or forecasts based on those trends. Many people today, either through lack of understanding or lack of available time, focus their reporting mainly on showing status and identifying problems. An example of a status report could be a list of orders shipped yesterday or the number of employees who came into work on time, while a problem report could be the list of orders that did not ship or the employees that did not get in on time. These reports are based on facts and figures within the database and are obtained by constraining the data to look at a particular flag or status.

Page Items: Year: FY2005 ▾

Channel	Product Name	▸ Status	Percent Order Qty SUM			
			▸ CANCELLED	▸ HOLD	▸ OPEN	▸ SHIPPED
▸ EXTERNAL	▸ QB-1000		28.403%	3.408%	10.796%	57.392%
	▸ QB-2000		2.781%	0.290%	55.150%	41.780%
	▸ QB-3000		3.230%	3.876%	0.517%	92.377%
	▸ QB-5000		3.577%		10.612%	85.811%
	▸ QB-5500				4.815%	95.185%
	▸ QB-6000		5.923%		3.555%	90.523%
▸ INTERNET	▸ QB-1000		0.137%		5.220%	94.643%
	▸ QB-2000				1.228%	98.772%
	▸ QB-3000		11.344%		12.218%	76.438%
	▸ QB-5000		8.646%		6.145%	85.209%
	▸ QB-5500		12.443%		20.471%	67.086%
	▸ QB-6000		18.975%		11.814%	69.211%

FIGURE 9-4   *Deviation example: status percentage by product and channel*

An organization that concentrates on status or problem reports will typically be in "fire-fighting" mode, reacting after the event to something that has already happened. By its very nature, this reactive form of reporting does not offer much in the way of trending or performance reporting—the latter being required if the organization is to establish guidelines to determine whether performance expectations are being met.

Let's look at one of the preceding examples and see if we can use trending to give us a better type of report. We will take the example of the late employees. While it is important to know how many were late, wouldn't it also be useful to know who was habitually late or whether a particular day—perhaps the Monday following a holiday—was more likely to have a higher rate of latecomers or absenteeism? By knowing these figures, you could easily extrapolate—that is, you can infer or estimate other values by projecting outward from a known value or values.

If your company is in the business of selling products, one of the hardest things to do is to try to forecast how many of these products will be required each quarter. Traditionally, the company will turn to its sales force and ask each salesperson to submit a forecast, based on discussions with each person's customers. If you are in the manufacturing business with an army of salespeople, you know only too well what happens next: the predictions are too high. But just how do you reign in an overly enthusiastic salesperson who insists that the projections are correct?

The answer is, by looking back over time and comparing how products have actually sold, and then compare those actuals with the forecasts received from the sales force. Perhaps you can see a trend that will allow you to predict a better, more accurate forecast this time.

Now we'll build an example within Discoverer. Using a crosstab, we created a query to find total sales by region for each of our past years. We then added a percentage and obtained the results shown in Figure 9-5, shown graphically in Figure 9-6. As you can see, the trend shows that, on average, the North American region has about 50 percent of sales in any one year, whereas the Far East started out well in 1998 but then continually lost percentage points to the other regions until 2005, when it regained some of the lost ground of earlier years.

See the section entitled "How to Build the Example Queries" near the end of this chapter for full instructions on how to construct and manipulate this query.

Using this information, we will take whatever sales have been forecast for these districts and extrapolate total quantities required for our factory for the next quarter. Therefore, if the North American region sales force forecasts 58,400 for the next quarter, because they average 50 percent of all sales, we can estimate that we will need to have 116,800 products available altogether. Let's say that the South American region forecasts 10,000. Based on their 8.6 percent in 2005, this would produce a total demand of 116,280 units. Finally, if Europe forecasts 35,000, this equates to 116,665 units. You can see that these three forecasts validate each other, and we will probably be safe issuing an order for our factories to build 120,000 units.

| | | Percentage | | | | | | | |
	Year	FY1998	FY1999	FY2000	FY2001	FY2002	FY2003	FY2004	FY2005
Region									
EUROPE		32.6%	30.2%	32.5%	33.7%	32.4%	29.5%	27.4%	29.8%
FAR EAST		16.3%	12.1%	10.1%	11.6%	10.4%	11.9%	10.7%	12.4%
NORTH AMERICA		43.1%	50.0%	49.8%	48.4%	49.0%	52.5%	52.9%	49.2%
SOUTH AMERICA		8.0%	7.7%	7.6%	6.4%	8.2%	6.2%	9.0%	8.6%

FIGURE 9-5 *Trend example: yearly sales by region*

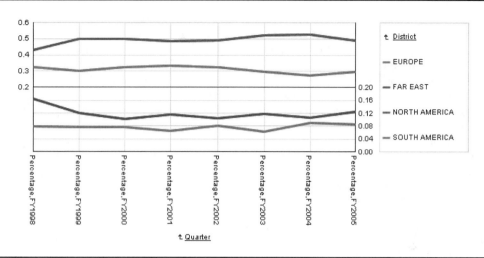

FIGURE 9-6 *Trend graph example: yearly sales by region*

Let's now assume that our Far East region comes in with a forecast of 115,000 units, a not unreasonable number, you might think. However, based on their average sales of 12.4 percent, this would require us to build a total of 927,420 units, an amount that is way out when compared to the other three regions. In this situation, we will ask our Far East sales department to recheck their forecast and come back with a reason why the sales should be that high. We would not just accept the forecast, because if we did, we would almost certainly end up with excess inventory at the end of the quarter.

NOTE
Perhaps someone transcribed the number for the Far East wrong, because if we compute 15,000 instead of 115,000, we end up with a total forecast of 120,000, much more in line with what we expect.

Aging Analysis

Aging analysis, as the name suggests, looks at data from the past and gives an analysis as to how well the company has performed over time. This is very similar to trending but not quite the same. For example, suppose you were a manufacturing company and you were keen to show how well you were making shipments to your customers. You, and your shareholders, might be interested in knowing how many sales orders you managed to deliver on time. As with all statistics, the key to making this work is to accurately determine your definitions. You need to carefully define what you mean by an on-time delivery.

However, before you can define and measure what makes an on-time delivery, you need to get down to basics and define what constitutes a delivery. Is this the date you shipped the item from your factory or the date that the item arrived at the customer? If you are building a ship, is it the date it slipped into the water, the date it was delivered to your customer, or the date it completed its sea trials? Statistics again, you see. We can drive a bus through them, depending which date you pick.

Having defined what constitutes the delivery date, you now need to determine what other date you will compare this date to in order to work out how long it took to ship the item. Are you going to take the customer's original request date, or are you going to take the date your system said that you would ship the item? After you have determined how many days, months, or years it took you to ship the item, you now need to determine what defines an on-time shipment.

For some companies, shipping to the customer later than two days after the customer wanted it might classify this shipment as being a late delivery. However, if you are in the business of constructing an oil tanker that takes years to build, you might consider delivering the ship within two months of the requested date as being on time.

In our fictional company, because it is a global company with shipments over long distances, we define an on-time shipment as being within three days. However, not only do we want to know how many orders ship on time, but we also want to know the percentage of our product that does not ship within the required three days. In our case we have decided that we want to create the following four aging buckets:

- Orders that ship within 3 days of their requested date: On Time

- Orders that ship within 7 days

- Orders that ship within 14 days

- Orders that take longer than 14 days

The final result is displayed in Figure 9-7.

As you can see, in 2003 three of our four regions managed to get an on-time delivery rate of 70 percent or more. We are not trying to say that this is good by any means. However, our VP insisted that these numbers were too low and asked us to recalculate, removing the second category (orders that ship within 7 days) and redefine on time as being up to 7 days. When we did that, we got the answer shown in Figure 9-8.

The answer we now get is amazing and shows that we have an on-time percentage of over 95 percent in all regions. This is what we will report to our shareholders. Remember how earlier we commented that you can drive a bus through statistics? We just did! We changed the formula to satisfy our internal politics. Of course, if someone asks how many shipped within three days, we will have to give the previous answer, but if we don't offer that information voluntarily, we haven't lied and we haven't done anything wrong, we simply altered our reporting criteria. The bottom line didn't change, and the amount of profit we made is unaffected.

Page Items: Year: FY2003 ▾

	On Time Percentage			
	▸ a. On Time	▸ b. Within 1 week	▸ c. Within 2 weeks	▸ d. Over 2 weeks
▸ EUROPE	68.3%	27.6%	3.3%	0.8%
▸ FAR EAST	76.1%	21.5%	2.0%	0.5%
▸ NORTH AMERICA	75.4%	22.8%	1.4%	0.4%
▸ SOUTH AMERICA	71.1%	25.8%	2.3%	0.8%

FIGURE 9-7 *Aging example: on-time deliveries by year*

Page Items: Year: FY2003 ▾

		On Time Percentage		
		▸ a. On Time	▸ b. Within 2 weeks	▸ c. Over 2 weeks
▸ EUROPE		95.9%	3.3%	0.8%
▸ FAR EAST		97.6%	2.0%	0.5%
▸ NORTH AMERICA		98.3%	1.4%	0.4%
▸ SOUTH AMERICA		96.9%	2.3%	0.8%

FIGURE 9-8   *Aging example: on-time redefined*

We hope that, having seen how powerful an aging report can be, you will take the time to learn how to create these for yourself. See the section entitled "How to Build the Example Queries" near the end of this chapter for full instructions on how to construct this query.

Fundamentals of Analysis

Here is another quote that we think captures the essence of business intelligence: "The greatest value lies in getting information out of the database, not so much putting it in." Unfortunately, we do not know where this comes from; otherwise, we would give the necessary credit.

Knowledge discovery is what most enterprises strive for, wish for, yet mostly dream about. In our opinion, not enough resources are being dedicated to finding out what information is available. Vast amounts of money are being spent on transactional systems, with super-fast servers and dedicated data lines, yet reporting databases are frequently relegated to secondary, and sometimes outdated, machines.

The amount of data being collected and stored in databases today far exceeds the capability of humans to reduce and analyze that data with any accuracy. What we need is some sort of methodology to overcome the difficulties involved in accurately transforming the raw data into knowledge. Therefore, getting the most from your stored data depends on the following:

- Your understanding of discovery techniques

- Your understanding of how to apply those techniques

- Your ability to use all of the features of Oracle Discoverer

Many OLTP business databases are growing at an unparalleled rate. Yet, it is the very fact that we have this large amount of data available to us that makes it possible to analyze with any accuracy in the first place. The irony of this situation is that the more data we have, the longer our queries take to run—yet the more accurate our analysis becomes.

Therefore, in order to effectively analyze data from large databases, you need to understand the following fundamentals:

- Good analysis is based on large amounts of data (a data warehouse, for example).

- Accuracy is essential (filtering out unwanted data).

- Some form of methodology or workflow is required.

■ A query tool is required (Discoverer, of course).

■ Analysis sometimes produces interesting or unexpected results.

■ The results should be presented in a manner that is understandable to humans.

This book has tried to address all of these fundamentals. We have used workflows wherever we can, and the preceding chapter explained how to turn your query into a report that is capable of being understood by human beings.

Uncontrolled queries can very quickly exceed the capacity of the system. Therefore, before you begin to analyze anything, some questions need to be asked:

■ Do you want to include detail or summary data?

■ Do you want to work from the top down or from the bottom up?

■ Do you want to focus on one piece of your organization or the complete entity?

■ Do you want to export the information to a spreadsheet tool to do more complex analysis?

■ Do you want your users to be able to slice the data? If so, use page items.

■ Do you want your users to be able to dice the data? If so, teach the users how to use pivoting.

Before you take any more steps in the analysis of your data, answer these questions. It will save you time and keep you from "spinning your wheels." After you have answered these questions, you are ready to proceed to the analysis workflow.

An Analysis Workflow

While this book is not designed to teach analysis, it would be deficient of us not to include some basic tips on how to go about analyzing data. We understand that you may already be an experienced analyst who does not need another lesson in analysis. On the other hand, you may have been employed as an analyst for the first time and be wondering how Discoverer can help you achieve your objectives.

Throughout an early career in the field of analysis, one of us was employed to analyze data for a large company that specialized in the leasing and management of vehicles to corporate clients. Being asked to analyze any form of data for the first time is a daunting task, but when the results of the analysis will be sent to customers who will then take actions based upon that report, the task can become frightening. So, just where does one start and how does one analyze something?

During those early days with the company just referred to, the author spent many hours with senior analysts defining and refining the best way to use the tools available. While the tools may have improved, the fundamental steps to analyze data have not. We would like to share with you those same steps, and we believe that, by following this workflow, you will quickly be able to achieve at least a rudimentary understanding of how to analyze data.

In the preceding chapter, we gave you a reporting workflow. Within that workflow were several analysis steps. These steps have been extracted to form the following analysis workflow:

1. Revisit any existing conditions and create new conditions to select only the data from the database that you want to use in the final report.

2. Create calculations.

3. Create percentages.

4. Create subtotals and totals.

5. Apply sorting.

6. Create conditional formats (formerly known as exceptions).

7. Use the information and produce a report.

Not all of these steps will be used in all cases. However, we recommend that as you analyze your data, you follow the preceding workflow; omitting unneeded steps will benefit you.

Core Examples Used in This Chapter

After many hours of experimentation, the authors have come to the conclusion that analyzing data in a crosstab is slicker and more user-friendly when compared to a standard table.

Using Plus against our database, we created two identical queries, a table and a crosstab. These queries will form the basis for most of the analysis examples in the rest of this chapter. Throughout this chapter we will show you examples of these queries being executed in Desktop and Plus. This first illustration is a table, while the second

Page Items:	Product Name: AB-2500 ▾		
	▸ Quarter	▸ Ship Qty SUM	▸ Selling Price SUM
1	2004-Q1	44578	568369.50
2	2004-Q2	40871	521105.25
3	2004-Q3	42519	542117.25
4	2004-Q4	45614	581578.50

is a crosstab. Both queries produced the same basic result by selecting the quantity shipped and the selling price for all products sold in financial year 2004. We have moved the product to the page axis and opted to view the results for just the product AB-2500.

Page Items:	Product Name: AB-2500 ▾	
	Ship Qty SUM	Selling Price SUM
▸ Quarter		
▸ 2004-Q1	44578	568369.50
▸ 2004-Q2	40871	521105.25
▸ 2004-Q3	42519	542117.25
▸ 2004-Q4	45614	581578.50

While most of the analysis techniques in this chapter can be demonstrated using these two queries, some cannot. Whenever we encounter a technique that cannot be shown with the preceding queries, we will include a more suitable example.

NOTE
Did you remember the two reasons for using page items (moving items to the page axis)? You place items there either when you want to see multiple pages of data or when you have items that would display the same data in every row. In the preceding two queries, you can see that we have moved the product to the page axis. This is because we didn't define any condition on the product and wanted to be able to see the quarterly results for other products by clicking on the drop-down arrow.

Description of the Analysis Tools Available

In Chapters 4 and 5, you were shown the Discoverer tools available to you as part of the Workbook Wizard. We also showed you how to access these tools through the Edit Sheet/ Worksheet dialog box. But you will recall that in Desktop, the Edit Sheet dialog box gives you access to only some of the tools and should be used only when you want to edit several worksheet definitions at once. All of the tools are available in the Edit Worksheet dialog box of Plus, so you can use it if you wish.

Anyone familiar with computer software knows that there are at least three ways to do anything! Discoverer is no exception. There are two more ways to access the Discoverer tools: from the menu bar and through smart menus. When you access the tools using these methods in Desktop, they open as stand-alone dialog boxes, and not as the multi-tabbed Edit Worksheet dialog box that you will see in Plus; therefore, you can edit only a particular tool. In Plus, when you select one tool you actually open the Edit Worksheet dialog box, and it dynamically places the focus into the tab for the tool that you want to work with. This is yet another of those wonderful new little features of Discoverer Plus.

The process you follow for using these tools is virtually identical in every case. You can decide to turn on a tool to analyze the data, turn off the tool to return the data to its previous state, edit the definition to change the analysis being performed, create additional definitions, and apply the analysis tool to one or more data items. All of these options are under your control (refer to Chapters 4 and 5 for instructions on using these tools and Chapters 11, 12, and 13 for advanced techniques).

There is one additional tool available, and that is the tool to find exceptions. Exceptions highlight data that falls outside of an established "norm." For example, maybe you want to highlight in red any product that has a markup of less than 33 percent. You can create an exception that will do just that. Exceptions, or to give them their correct Discoverer Plus name, conditional formats, are a terrific weapon in the analyst's armory. In previous versions of Discoverer you could add only a single exception or conditional format. Stoplighting, which is totally new to the 10.1.2 Plus version, is a new type of three-in-one conditional format that allows you to set upper and lower limits to a single definition. These will be covered later in the chapter.

Turning a Tool On and Off

In both versions of Discoverer, you can activate a tool from the menu bar. Clicking Tools displays a drop-down menu (this one is from Discoverer Plus).

You can see that this menu has several options. The Desktop version has only seven of these options: Conditions, Sort, Totals, Percentages, Calculations, Parameters, and Options. In this chapter, we are only concerned with:

- Conditions
- Sort
- Totals
- Percentages
- Calculations

Drill ...
Collapse
Manage Links ...
Sort...
Conditions...
Calculations...
Percentages...
Totals...
Parameters...
Parameter Values
Refresh Sheet
✔ Auto Refresh
Retrieve All Rows
Show SQL...
Manage Workbooks...
Manage Schedules...
Options...

We have excluded the Parameters option because these are a specialized form of condition that will be covered in Chapters 12 and 13. The final menu item, Options, also has nothing to do with analysis and so is not discussed here. This menu item is explained in detail in Chapter 15.

The final way to access the tools is through smart menus. After a tool has been used to create an analysis definition, right-clicking in the column where it has been used will give you a smart menu offering a selection to edit the item definition.

In Plus, you can also access Conditions, Calculations, Percentages, and Totals from within the Available Items pane. You locate the areas called My Conditions, My Calculations, My Percentages, and My Totals. Right-clicking these headings brings up a pop-up menu that allows you to create a new item of the type on which you clicked. Items that are in use are shown with a check mark in the Available Items pane. You can turn a definition on and off by right-clicking the definition and selecting either Add to Worksheet or Remove from Worksheet.

In Desktop, whichever method you choose to launch an analysis tool, a dialog box appears. This box shows any analysis definitions that you have already created and whether they are currently in use or not. In front of each definition is a check box. You can turn a definition on and off by checking and unchecking this box.

NOTE

After you have created analysis definitions, do not be too hasty to delete them. If you have decided that a definition is no longer required, in Desktop simply uncheck it for now, or in Plus right-click the definition and select Remove from Worksheet from the pop-up menu. This leaves the definition intact but does not apply that definition to the current query. Adopting this method of working will allow you to come back later and reuse the definition if required.

The Analysis Toolbar Buttons

Do you remember, in Chapters 4 and 5, that we recommended you not create calculations, percentages, or totals in the Workbook Wizard? In this section we will show you another good reason why. The real power of GUI applications is toolbar buttons, and Discoverer has many very useful ones. Learn the buttons and you are a mouse click away from opening another powerful tool. As you will see, these toolbar buttons provide shortcuts that allow you to create calculations, percentages, and totals by a single click of your mouse.

NOTE

If you cannot see the analysis bar on your Desktop screen, activate it from the menu bar by clicking View | Analysis Bar. In Plus it is part of the standard toolbar. Activate it by clicking View | Toolbars | Standard.

The Desktop analysis bar, shown here, has a number of buttons and is broken up into four main areas, each divided from the next by a line:

The Plus approach to these tools is slightly different. Instead of a large toolbar with lots of buttons, each main button when clicked opens the dialog box for that operation. Each main button has drop-downs containing buttons for the associated functions. This illustration shows the Totals button and its associated drop-down tools. Together, we call this the Totals area. There are similar "areas" for Percentages, Calculations (referred to as the Operator area in this list), Conditions, and Parameters.

- **Totals area**   This area contains five buttons, one each for the functions for sum, count, average, min, and max.

- **Percentage area**   In Desktop this area contains a single button. In Plus this area contains a New Percentage button with a drop-down alongside, although the drop-down has a single entry that performs exactly as if you had clicked the New Percentage button. After you have highlighted a column of data, click this button to create a percentage. In both Desktop and Plus, the percentage is automatically created for you. In most cases, because the default selected by Discoverer is not always quite right, you will usually end up having to edit the percentage that has just been created. We would have preferred to see the New Percentage dialog box open up first, thus allowing us to set up the percentage in advance of executing it.

- **Operator area**   This part of the bar contains buttons for the four basic mathematical operators (plus, minus, multiply, and subtract). Both versions have a New Calculation button to launch the New Calculations dialog box. Here is the Plus area.

- **Conditions area**   This area contains six buttons that allow you to create conditions based on testing if values are equal, non-equal, less than, less than or equal to, greater than, and greater than or equal to. There is also a New Condition button to launch the New Condition dialog box itself. Here is the Plus area.

- **Parameters area**   This area exists in Plus only and consists of a single New Parameter button that launches the New Parameter dialog box.

We will describe each area in turn and tell you what each button does. Many of the buttons on the toolbars are mathematical and will work only if you include numerical data in your query. Having created a query, you now simply highlight the column or columns containing the data you want to analyze, and click the button for the operation you want Discoverer to perform. It really is that easy!

NOTE
After you highlight a column, moving the cursor along the analysis bar causes Desktop to highlight, in a bigger font, those analysis features that are available to you. Any function that does not display in this bigger font cannot be applied to the data you have selected. In Plus, Discoverer places an outline around the active buttons as you move the cursor along the bars.

Totals Area

The first part of the analysis bar, which we call the totals area, provides five buttons, one each for the functions sum, count, average, min, and max. Unless you highlight a column of data (remember, to highlight a column of data, place your cursor on the column heading and click the mouse button), these buttons will be inactive.

You can also select a single cell and have a total created for that column or item. If you are using group-sorted items, Discoverer is smart enough to recognize this and will insert subtotals.

You cannot highlight multiple data points and expect Discoverer to insert totals for all of these columns. You may think that it should, and to be fair to you, so did we. In Plus, if you select multiple data points and create a total, in a table the total will be created on the first item that you selected, but in a crosstab the total will be created on the last item that you selected. In Desktop, when you select multiple data points, all of the buttons in the totals area will be inactive, thus preventing you from creating any erroneous totals.

NOTE
In Plus, if you select any nondata point in a crosstab and then click one of the drop-down buttons, Discoverer always launches the New Total dialog box. However, if you select a data point and repeat this exercise, Discoverer dynamically creates the total. In Desktop, Discoverer assumes you want to calculate the total on all data points and dynamically creates the total.

Tables Are Complicated to Analyze

Before we get too far into this section, we would like to remind you one more time that we strongly recommend you analyze using crosstabs whenever possible.

The following example may help convince you that analyzing in a table, especially from the totals area, can be unpredictable. First of all, we clicked the heading for the quarter. In Desktop, you can see here that Discoverer has highlighted all of the quarters and enabled only the Count, Minimum, and Maximum buttons in the totals area:

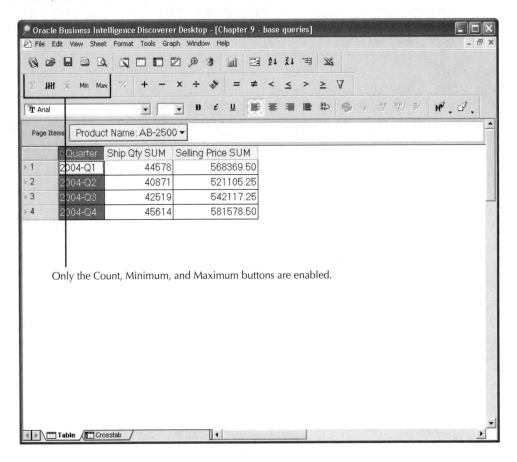

Let's repeat this in Plus. We again clicked the heading for the quarter. When we went to the totals area, because we saw that all of the drop-down buttons were still active we clicked on Sum. Rather than create a total, as is the normal behavior when we do this, Discoverer opened the following New Total dialog box:

As you can see, Discoverer has changed the total to being a Count. While the authors understand why this is happening, we are sure it could be confusing to the novice user. You therefore need to be careful when clicking the Totals buttons in the totals area when in Plus to make sure that you are on the correct column. As previously mentioned, in Desktop there is no such issue, because Desktop grays out the options that do not apply.

Crosstabs Are Great to Analyze

Before we get into explaining what the different buttons can do, we want to show you why analyzing a crosstab is simpler and easier to understand when compared to a table. The biggest advantage is that you can apply any of the functions in the totals area to all of the data points at the same time. You do this by clicking the heading for one of the side axis items, and then clicking one of the buttons in the totals area of the analysis bar.

For example, here we have highlighted the quarter heading. As expected, in Desktop all of the buttons in the totals area are now active.

The illustration that follows shows the result of applying the sum function. You can see that Discoverer inserted a grand total for all of the data points.

		Ship Qty SUM	Selling Price SUM

Page Items: Product Name: AB-2500 ▼

Quarter		Ship Qty SUM	Selling Price SUM
2004-Q1		44578	568369.50
2004-Q2		40871	521105.25
2004-Q3		42519	542117.25
2004-Q4		45614	581578.50
Sum		173582	2213170.50

Grand total for all of the data points

NOTE
The format applied to any of the functions in the totals area is the default format as specified on the Format tab of the Tools | Options dialog box. Also note that you can apply a total only to a numeric column of data.

Using Totals with Sorts

As we said earlier, Discoverer offers increased flexibility when you are using group sorts, especially in a crosstab. In the examples shown next, we have taken our base queries and moved the product out of the Page Items area, thereby allowing us to see all of the data for each product grouped together.

For the following table, the product has been placed in front of the quarter. We then defined a group sort on the product and placed a standard low-to-high sort on the quarter.

	▶ Product Name	▶ Quarter	▶ Ship Qty SUM	▶ Selling Price SUM
1	AB-2000	2004-Q1	35140	474390.00
2		2004-Q2	41640	562140.00
3		2004-Q3	57382	774657.00
4		2004-Q4	73340	990090.00
5	AB-2500	2004-Q1	44578	568369.50
6		2004-Q2	40871	521105.25
7		2004-Q3	42519	542117.25
8		2004-Q4	45614	581578.50
9	AB-3000	2004-Q1	63292	1344955.00
10		2004-Q2	39957	849086.25
11		2004-Q3	53714	1141422.50
12		2004-Q4	57290	1217412.50
13	AVR-500	2004-Q1	60627	1633897.65
14		2004-Q2	58210	1568759.50
15		2004-Q3	97466	2630751.20
16		2004-Q4	84705	2282799.75

For the crosstab shown here, the product and quarter have been moved to become side axis points. As you can see, Discoverer automatically created a group sort and, because our crosstab is defined as being Outline, also inserted a subtotal by product.

▶ ▶ Quarter	Ship Qty SUM	Selling Price SUM	
▶ AB-2000	207502	2801277.00	◀
▶ 2004-Q1	35140	474390.00	
▶ 2004-Q2	41640	562140.00	
▶ 2004-Q3	57382	774657.00	
▶ 2004-Q4	73340	990090.00	
▶ AB-2500	173582	2213170.50	◀ — Subtotal by product
▶ 2004-Q1	44578	568369.50	
▶ 2004-Q2	40871	521105.25	
▶ 2004-Q3	42519	542117.25	
▶ 2004-Q4	45614	581578.50	
▶ AB-3000	214253	4552876.25	◀
▶ 2004-Q1	63292	1344955.00	
▶ 2004-Q2	39957	849086.25	
▶ 2004-Q3	53714	1141422.50	
▶ 2004-Q4	57290	1217412.50	

No matter which of the two queries we now work on, clicking the heading for any of the data points, and then clicking on any of the buttons in the totals area, works the same as for a nonsorted query. Discoverer simply inserts a grand total on that item. However, clicking one of the sorted items causes Discoverer to insert a subtotal.

Sum Button

To show you how easy it is to create a sum using the analysis bar, we highlighted the Quantity Shipped column and clicked the Sum button. As you can see, Discoverer automatically inserted a grand total of the quantity shipped. Defining a total this way produces the same result as creating a total in the Totals dialog box, based on the sum function.

The illustration that follows shows a grand total applied to a table.

Page Items: Product Name: AB-2500 ▾

	▸ Quarter	▸ Ship Qty SUM	▸ Selling Price SUM
1	2004-Q1	44578	568369.50
2	2004-Q2	40871	521105.25
3	2004-Q3	42519	542117.25
4	2004-Q4	45614	581578.50
5		Sum: 173582	

Grand total applied to a table

The next illustration shows a grand total applied to a crosstab.

Page Items: Product Name: AB-2500 ▾

	Ship Qty SUM	Selling Price SUM
▸ Quarter		
▸ 2004-Q1	44578	568369.50
▸ 2004-Q2	40871	521105.25
▸ 2004-Q3	42519	542117.25
▸ 2004-Q4	45614	581578.50
Sum	173582	

Grand total applied to a crosstab

If you are working with a crosstab and you want to insert a grand total for all data points, there are three ways to correct the situation.

Edit the Existing Total Definition   To insert a grand total by editing the definition for the existing total, use the following workflow:

1. Right-click the axis label for the total. This displays a drop-down list of options.
2. Select Edit Total from the list. This opens the following Edit Total dialog box.

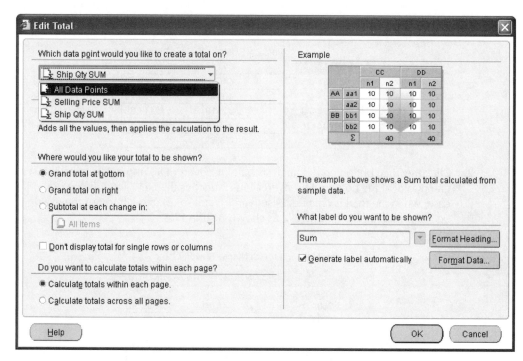

3. Click the down arrow beside the item currently being totaled, and change the drop-down selection to All Data Points.

4. Click OK. The results are shown next.

Page Items: Product Name: AB-2500 ▾

	Ship Qty SUM	Selling Price SUM
▸ Quarter		
▸ 2004-Q1	44578	568369.50
▸ 2004-Q2	40871	521105.25
▸ 2004-Q3	42519	542117.25
▸ 2004-Q4	45614	581578.50
Sum	173582	2213170.50

Subtotals on all data points

Create a Grand Total for All Data Points   To create a grand total for all data points, use the following workflow:

Page Items: Product Name: AB-2500 ▾

	Ship Qty SUM	Selling Price SUM
Quarter		
2004-Q1	44578	568369.50
2004-Q2	40871	521105.25
2004-Q3	42519	542117.25
2004-Q4	45614	581578.50
Sum	173582	

1. Click the axis label. In Desktop, this highlights all of the time periods in the axis. In Plus, as you can see, only the label itself is highlighted.

Page Items: Product Name: AB-2500 ▾

	Ship Qty SUM	Selling Price SUM
▶ Quarter		
▶ 2004-Q1	44578	568369.50
▶ 2004-Q2	40871	521105.25
▶ 2004-Q3	42519	542117.25
▶ 2004-Q4	45614	581578.50
Sum	173582	

2. Click the Total button on the analysis bar. Discoverer Desktop automatically inserts a grand total at the bottom. Discoverer Plus launches the New Total dialog box. In either case, when the total is created, Discoverer is not smart enough to use the existing definition but inserts a new row, as shown next in Plus.

Page Items: Product Name: AB-2500 ▾

	Ship Qty SUM	Selling Price SUM	
▶ Quarter			
▶ 2004-Q1	44578	568369.50	
▶ 2004-Q2	40871	521105.25	
▶ 2004-Q3	42519	542117.25	
▶ 2004-Q4	45614	581578.50	
Sum	173582		
Sum	173582	2213170.50	◀──── New row inserted

3. Click the axis label for the old total. This highlights the label.

4. In Desktop only, press the DELETE key on your keyboard. The row and the definition will be removed. The total will not be deleted, however, but only suppressed from being displayed in the report.

5. In Plus, right-click the total in the Available Items pane and from the pop-up menu select either Remove from Worksheet or Delete.

Create New Definitions for the Other Data Points The third way to correct the situation is to add individual totals to the data points that are currently not totaled. Highlight, in turn, each data point label you wish to be totaled, and click the Total button. When we did that in our example, Discoverer added the word "Sum" in front of each total, as shown next.

Page Items: Product Name: AB-2500 ▾

	Ship Qty SUM	Selling Price SUM
▶ Quarter		
▶ 2004-Q1	44578	568369.50
▶ 2004-Q2	40871	521105.25
▶ 2004-Q3	42519	542117.25
▶ 2004-Q4	45614	581578.50
	Sum: 173582	Sum: 2213170.50

NOTE

If you decide that you want to have the word "Sum" appear only once, you should create a new total using the axis label, as described in the preceding paragraph. However, in Desktop, when you now press the DELETE key, Discoverer does nothing. You will have to use the Totals dialog box if you want to disable or delete these two totals. In Plus, as before, right-click the total in the Available Items pane and from the pop-up menu select either Remove from Worksheet or Delete.

Count Button   Highlighting a column of data and clicking this button inserts a count of the number of rows in the query. Let us assume that we want to know how many sales orders shipped in January 2000. Using our example query, highlighting the Sales Order column and clicking on Count caused Discoverer to insert the count.

	▶ Month	▶ Order Number	▶ Ship Qty SUM
270	JAN-00	2562	20
271	JAN-00	2563	100
272	JAN-00	2564	100
273	JAN-00	2565	100
274	JAN-00	2568	7200
275	JAN-00	2569	4800
276	JAN-00	2570	4800
277	JAN-00	2571	1200
278	JAN-00	2572	1200
279	JAN-00	2573	2400
280	JAN-00	2574	2400
281	JAN-00	2575	24
282	JAN-00	2577	8
283		Count: 282	Sum: 418058

↑
Count

NOTE

You will notice that Discoverer has placed the count of sales orders on the same row as the total number of items shipped. Older versions of Discoverer do not do this but will display the two figures on separate rows.

Average Button   Highlighting a column of data and clicking this button inserts a calculation of the average of the data items in the row or rows highlighted. Let us assume that we want to know the average number of items shipped on each sales order. Using our example query again, highlighting the Shipped Quantity column and clicking Average caused Discoverer to insert the average of 1,482.

	▶ Month	▶ Order Number	▶ Ship Qty SUM
270	JAN-00	2562	20
271	JAN-00	2563	100
272	JAN-00	2564	100
273	JAN-00	2565	100
274	JAN-00	2568	7200
275	JAN-00	2569	4800
276	JAN-00	2570	4800
277	JAN-00	2571	1200
278	JAN-00	2572	1200
279	JAN-00	2573	2400
280	JAN-00	2574	2400
281	JAN-00	2575	24
282	JAN-00	2577	8
283		Count: 282	Sum: 418058
284			Average: 1482

Minimum Button   Highlighting a column or columns of data and clicking this button inserts a calculation of the lowest-valued item in the column(s). For example, assume we want to know the minimum number of items that we shipped on any one sales order. Using our query, highlighting the Shipped Quantity column and clicking Minimum caused Discoverer to insert the minimum value in the column.

	Month	Order Number	Ship Qty SUM
269	JAN-00	2561	20
270	JAN-00	2562	20
271	JAN-00	2563	100
272	JAN-00	2564	100
273	JAN-00	2565	100
274	JAN-00	2568	7200
275	JAN-00	2569	4800
276	JAN-00	2570	4800
277	JAN-00	2571	1200
278	JAN-00	2572	1200
279	JAN-00	2573	2400
280	JAN-00	2574	2400
281	JAN-00	2575	24
282	JAN-00	2577	8
283		Count: 282	Sum: 418058
284			Average: 1482
285			Minimum: 1	◄——— Minimum added

Maximum Button   Highlighting a column or columns of data and clicking this button inserts a calculation of the highest-valued item in the column(s). For example, assume we want to know the maximum number of items that we shipped on any one sales order. Using our query, highlighting the Shipped Quantity column and clicking Maximum causes Discoverer to insert the maximum value in the column.

	Month	Order Number	Ship Qty SUM
269	JAN-00	2561	20
270	JAN-00	2562	20
271	JAN-00	2563	100
272	JAN-00	2564	100
273	JAN-00	2565	100
274	JAN-00	2568	7200
275	JAN-00	2569	4800
276	JAN-00	2570	4800
277	JAN-00	2571	1200
278	JAN-00	2572	1200
279	JAN-00	2573	2400
280	JAN-00	2574	2400
281	JAN-00	2575	24
282	JAN-00	2577	8
283		Count: 282	Sum: 418058
284			Average: 1482
285			Minimum: 1
286			Maximum: 26400	◄——— Maximum added

NOTE
Min and max can be applied to dates and strings just as easily as to numbers. If we had highlighted the Date Shipped column and clicked first Minimum and then Maximum, Discoverer would have inserted the first and last dates in January that we shipped the displayed product.

Percentage Area

The second part of the analysis bar, which we call the percentage area, provides a single button for creating percentages. Highlighting any column of numeric data activates this button. When you create a percentage this way, Discoverer creates a new column displaying a percentage based on the grand total, for each row. It names the column by prefixing the word "Percent" in front of the source column name. For example, if the source column is named Selling Price, the new column will be called Percent Selling Price.

To change the percentage definition, use the following workflow:

1. Right-click the column heading and select Edit Percentage from the drop-down list, or from the menu bar select Tools | Percentages.

2. Change the percentage definition (refer to Chapter 5 for an explanation of percentage definitions and see Chapter 13 for more advanced techniques).

3. Click OK.

Operators Area

The third part of the analysis bar contains buttons for the four main mathematical operators Add (+), Subtract (-), Multiply (*), and Divide (/), along with a button to launch the Calculations dialog box.

Add (+), Subtract (-), Multiply (*), and Divide (/) Buttons

These four buttons work in exactly the same way and usually require you to highlight two columns of numeric data before you click one of the buttons. We say "usually" because Discoverer will allow you to highlight non-numerical columns before clicking the Add button. Doing this causes Discoverer to concatenate the two columns of data together.

Follow this simple workflow to create new calculations based on these four operators:

1. Highlight a column of data.

2. Hold down the CTRL key and highlight a second column of data.

3. Click one of the four operators.

In Desktop, Discoverer launches the appropriate dialog box. In Plus, Discoverer dynamically creates and executes the calculation, generating a default name of Calculation1. As all of the Desktop dialog boxes look the same, we will only describe the Subtract dialog box.

As you can see in the following bullet points, the Subtract dialog box contains the following six areas:

- **Name**   The name typed here will appear as the column heading for the calculation.

- **Defined as**   These two boxes contain the names of the two columns upon which the calculation is based.

- **Advanced**   Click this to launch an advanced dialog box for the appropriate calculation.

- **OK**   Clicking OK completes the calculation, closes the dialog box, and displays the results in a column named by whatever name you gave the calculation.

- **Cancel**   Clicking Cancel abandons the calculation and returns you to the original query.

- **Help**   Clicking Help launches the standard Discoverer help system.

When you use the add and multiply functions, it makes no difference which column you highlight first. However, when you use the subtract and divide functions, the order is vitally important. The data in the second column will be subtracted from or divided into the data in the first column.

If you are working in Plus and you have highlighted the columns in the wrong order, you will need to use the Edit Calculation dialog box to remedy the situation. The issue is easier to correct in Desktop because you can click the down arrow beside each of the columns in the dialog box to change the columns being used.

Calculation Button
Clicking this button launches the Edit Calculations dialog box. This button is always active.

Conditions Area
The final part of the analysis bar is the conditions area. This area contains seven buttons, one each that allow you to create conditions based on values being equal (=), non-equal (<>), less than (<), less than or equal to (<=), greater than (>), and greater than or equal to (>=), as well as a button to launch the New Condition dialog box itself. This final button is always active.

The first six buttons can save you time and effort in creating conditions based on the data that has been returned by your query. For example, assume that you have a query that has returned the total quantity sold by product. If you want to see the query conditioned to display only the quantity from product CD-100 and higher, use the following workflow:

1. Click in the cell containing the data item CD-100.

2. Click the >= button. This opens the New Condition dialog box, with the item, condition, and value prefilled.

3. Click OK. This completes and applies the condition to the query. Discoverer does not re-run the query because the condition specified constrains the data to a subset of the data that you originally selected.

NOTE
Just as with calculations, you can select a dimension and filter on it with a simple click. To do this, you click in the cell that you want to use for the filter and then click the appropriate condition button. Discoverer will dynamically create the condition for you and re-execute the query to apply the new filter.

Finding Exceptions Using Formatting
As we mentioned earlier in the chapter, exceptions highlight data that falls outside of an established norm. You can create many exceptions concerning the same data items. If you have overlapping exceptions, be careful not to turn both on at the same time. Let's say you have two exceptions for the Profit SUM, one for all values over 10,000 and the other for values

between 40,000 and 60,000. If you inadvertently select two or more conflicting exceptions, a message asks you to reselect the exception so that they don't conflict.

To use exceptions effectively, you need to bear in mind the following criteria:

■   Define the exception itself, such as "is greater than 10,000" or "is less than 25%" or "is between 10,000 and 50,000."

■   Define the format of the data that the exception will be applied to so that you can see it easily among the rest of the data.

Desktop and Plus handle exceptions in different ways. Desktop uses the term exception, whereas Plus calls it conditional formatting. Even though the differences are minimal, we will show you how to perform this operation by version.

Using Desktop to Highlight Exceptions

To create exceptions, use the following workflow:

1. Select Format | Exceptions from the toolbar, or right-click on a column of data and select Format Exception from the drop-down menu displayed. This opens the Exceptions dialog box shown next. The functionality of this dialog box is the same as the other tools.

2. Click New. This opens the Exception dialog box. We will not explain its use until further on in this section.

3. Define the exception.

4. Click OK. This will close the Exception dialog box.

5. Click OK in the Exceptions dialog box (yes, we know the names of the boxes are the same except for the "s" on the end).

It is quite easy and intuitive to create an exception in Discoverer.

Using Plus to Create Conditional Formatting

To create conditional formatting, use the following workflow:

1. Select Format | Conditional Formats from the toolbar, or right-click on a column of data and select Conditional Formats from the drop-down menu displayed. This opens the Conditional Formats dialog box shown next.

2. Click New Conditional Format. This opens the New Conditional Format dialog box. We will not explain its use until further on in this section.

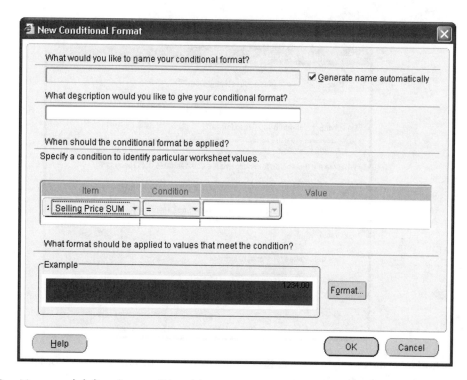

3. Name and define the conditional format. We generally allow Discoverer to auto-name the conditional formats because it uses the syntax of the conditional formatting and it is quite clear what it is.

4. Click OK. This will close the New Conditional Format dialog box.

5. Click OK in the Conditional Formats dialog box.

Using Plus to Create Stoplight Formatting

A new feature of Plus is Stoplight Formatting. Stoplighting takes conditional formatting to the next level. For example, you want to see at a glance the sales categories that each of your customers fall into. Customers with sales of less than $10,000 per year are unacceptable, while customers with sales over $60,000 are desirable. You can use stoplighting to highlight in red customers who fall into the unacceptable sales category, in green which customers are in the desired range, and in yellow everyone in between.

To create stoplight formatting, use the following workflow:

1. Select Format | Conditional Formats from the toolbar, or click on a column of data and select Conditional Formats from the drop-down menu displayed. This opens the Conditional Formats dialog.

2. Click New Stoplight Formatting. This opens the New Stoplight Formats dialog box.

3. Name the Stoplight Format. Remember to give it a meaningful name or let Discoverer name it automatically.

4. Select the data point upon which you want the stoplighting.

5. Enter your unacceptable and desirable thresholds. You do not select the middle range; it is quite simply everything that falls in between the other two.

6. Edit the colors of the stoplight by clicking the Edit Colors button; then use the drop-down to change the colors and click OK.

7. Select whether or not you want to show the actual data point values or just the stoplight colors in the cells.

8. Click OK. This will close the Stoplight Formats dialog box.

9. Click OK in the Conditional Formats dialog box.

Here is a sample stoplight:

Page Items: Product Name: AB-2500

	Ship Qty SUM	Selling Price SUM
▸ Quarter		
▸ 2004-Q1	44578	568369.50
▸ 2004-Q2	40871	521105.25
▸ 2004-Q3	42519	542117.25
▸ 2004-Q4	45614	581578.50

There is another extremely useful feature of stoplight formats that allows you to hide the data values for a column that has had stoplight formatting applied to it. If you look back to the last illustration, at the bottom left of the dialog box is a check box called "Hide data values for stoplight formats." If you check this, Discoverer will display the stoplight cell colors for the column but will suppress the data values.

NOTE
You can still see the values by clicking on the small cell underneath the column heading and the data itself. Discoverer will redisplay the values but in a very faint color. To rehide the values click anywhere inside the data that has been stoplight formatted.

How to Build the Example Queries

In the section of this chapter dealing with the different types of analysis, we showed you the results of queries to display examples of the five different types. This section shows you how we went about building those queries, and highlights which analysis tools were used.

Statistical Analysis

If you recall, this query was quite simple and was a crosstab built using the year, region, and selling price sum. The year was placed on the top axis because we didn't want to display the same data item in every row. The region was placed in the side axis, while the selling price sum was left on the top axis.

To complete the query, in Desktop we clicked the label entitled Selling Price SUM and then the Percentage button on the analysis bar. In Plus, we clicked the drop-down alongside the New Percentage button and selected % Percentage. In both cases we created the new percentage as shown next.

The completed query can be seen earlier in Figure 9-1.

Classification Analysis

This query is, once again, a crosstab. This one selects the cost price, selling price, profit, product name, product line, and quarter, with a condition that the quarters are all for 2004. We did not apply a condition on the product line, but we did move it to the page axis in order to be able to select one product line at a time. After moving the product name and quarter to the side axis, the resulting output is as in Figure 9-2.

So far, so good. But just how did we end up with the result shown in Figure 9-3? First of all, despite how it may look, we have to tell you that it really is the same query. We did not edit any of the selections, nor did we change any of the conditions. Moving the items between the various axes did everything.

If you remember, we told you that we would be showing you how to do all of this manipulation in Viewer. We will also show you how to do the same thing in both Desktop and Plus.

Manipulating in Viewer

In Viewer, before we can move the data points from their traditional axis to the page axis we need to move another item into the data point axis first. This is because the data point axis in a crosstab in Viewer must contain something.

The first thing we did was to expand the Layout link on the tools menu, which you will find just above the page items. Next we moved the Quarter to below the Cost Price using these settings:

Next we moved the Cost Price to the page items, using these settings:

▼ **Crosstab**
▼ Tools **Layout** Format Stoplight Rows and Columns
....
Move ✔   Measure (Cost Price,...) ✔   To Page Items ✔   Go

The intermediate result now looks like this:

To complete the pivoting, we moved the Line Name from the page item and placed it on the side axis immediately before the Product Name. Finally, we minimized the Tools menu so that the final result was what you saw previously, in Figure 9-3.

Manipulating in Desktop and Plus

Unlike in Viewer, in both Desktop and Plus you can move the items around without the need for something to be in the data points axis. Of course, as you will see, until you put something into the data points, you will not see results.

The first thing we did was to move the data point items from the top axis to the page axis. It doesn't matter which data point you pick because, if you select and move one, Discoverer actually moves them all. For the record, we clicked the cost price and dragged it to the page axis. When we released the mouse button, Discoverer moved all three items and built a drop-down box, as you can see next.

In order to make some costs display, we have to move something to the top axis. So, we dragged the quarter there, which immediately caused Discoverer to display the price for each quarter, as shown here.

Page Items:	Line Name: MEGA-WIDGET ▼	Data Point: Selling Price ▼		
▶ Qtr	▶ 2004-Q1	▶ 2004-Q2	▶ 2004-Q3	▶ 2004-Q4
▶ Product				
▶ AB-2500	568369.50	521105.25	542117.25	581578.50
▶ CD-100	637877.00	742141.25	972218.00	351055.00
▶ CD-200	1083344.75	512522.00	670573.00	662810.75
▶ CD-500	886334.98	578454.40	899620.80	688666.82
▶ CD-550	497719.20	596642.00	280798.80	368631.60
▶ CD-625	1743991.22	1565442.22	2644499.22	2078066.38

NOTE
There are no costs displayed in the main body of the uppermost report previously shown because there is no item in the top axis. This is one of the most common reasons why users complain that they can see no output from a query of this type. In any query, you must have at least one item in the top axis.

You can see from the preceding illustrations that the output has changed, yet we can assure you that Discoverer did not requery the database. This is one of the wonderful features of Discoverer that will be covered in more depth when we discuss advanced queries in a later chapter.

Having moved the quarter to the top axis, the next thing we did was to click the product line and move it to the side axis. The next illustration shows this step completed, with the product line having been placed before the product name. You can see that Discoverer automatically does a group sort in this situation.

Page Items: Data Point: Selling Price

	Qtr	2004-Q1	2004-Q2	2004-Q3	2004-Q4
Line Name / Product					
MEGA-WIDGET / AB-2500		568369.50	521105.25	542117.25	581578.50
CD-100		637877.00	742141.25	972218.00	351055.00
CD-200		1083344.75	512522.00	670573.00	662810.75
CD-500		886334.98	578454.40	899620.80	688666.82
CD-550		497719.20	596642.00	280798.80	368631.60
CD-625		1743991.22	1565442.22	2644499.22	2078066.38
MINI-WIDGET / DS-1200		101821.20	179551.35	61022.10	113896.15
DS-1300		226433.20	85085.00	182236.60	267226.40
MS-1200		452169.60	55416.75	519258.00	249505.80
MS-1300		246888.00	107280.00	226320.00	76866.00
SUPER-WIDGET / AB-3000		1344955.00	849086.25	1141422.50	1217412.50
AVR-500		1633897.65	1568759.50	2630751.20	2282799.75
AVR-550		816585.00	695849.00	1914635.80	1840577.20
AVR-800		399168.00	379001.70	733921.65	273735.00
AVR-900		473319.00	721066.50	1431772.65	946638.00
WONDER-WIDGET / AB-2000		474390.00	562140.00	774657.00	990090.00
QB-1000		208423.60	571734.45	409202.50	718531.45
QB-2000		1063692.00	528586.45	765877.00	520308.60
QB-3000		694612.45	454742.40	725074.00	568428.00
QB-5000		868872.00	410065.20	630497.32	862514.40
QB-5500		817658.00	532731.56	503610.22	732890.00
QB-6000		889534.20	466877.42	952050.60	627989.60

Automatic group sort

Finally, as you can see here, we clicked the drop-down arrow alongside the DataPoint.

From the drop-down list provided, we selected the profit, which resulted in the output you saw previously in Figure 9-3.

Page Items: Data Point: Profit

		Cost Price	2004-Q
Line Name		Selling Price	01347.
MEGA-WIDGET		• Profit	78125.
CD-100			
CD-200			642192.
CD-500			461949.

NOTE

By the way, if you are wondering how we got the side axis items to line up as they do, you can do this in Plus by right-clicking anywhere in the crosstab and from the pop-up menu selecting Format Crosstab. In the Format Crosstab dialog box we made sure the Crosstab style was set to Inline. In Desktop, you do this using Tools | Options off the menu bar. Select the Crosstab tab and then make sure that Axis Labels and Axis Gridlines are checked, with the Gridline Style set to 3D, and the Style set to Inline.

Deviation Analysis

This query is a little more complex than the other examples, but you should be able to easily follow how we did it. We used a crosstab, of course, because we couldn't have performed the manipulations that we wanted had we chosen a table.

The selections were very easy. We took the order quantity and the status from the sales folder, the product name from the product folder, and the channel. Before we left the Workbook Wizard, we moved the channel and product name to the side axis and then defined the following condition on the product name: "Product Name like 'QB%'." This condition will constrain our selection to just those products that begin with "QB." After running the query, the result is as shown next. Notice how Discoverer has automatically built a group sort on the channel.

| | | ▸ Status | | Order Qty SUM | | |
▸ Channel	▸ Product Name		▸ CANCELLED	▸ HOLD	▸ OPEN	▸ SHIPPED
▸ EXTERNAL	▸ QB-1000		32713	1202	6176	174015
	▸ QB-2000		7451	100	20304	124325
	▸ QB-3000		10220	1200	27935	232960
	▸ QB-5000		15540	600	53863	423039
	▸ QB-5500		4272	NULL	12012	415125
	▸ QB-6000		60181	400	17866	417681
▸ INTERNET	▸ QB-1000		16700	NULL	10434	202826
	▸ QB-2000		6932	172	22900	319353
	▸ QB-3000		31618	NULL	14501	264746
	▸ QB-5000		31972	1	51869	406433
	▸ QB-5500		74039	100	45389	411142
	▸ QB-6000		82860	1	68033	401730

The next part is straightforward, just requiring us to create percentages. We clicked the label for the top axis item called Order Qty SUM, and then we clicked the Percentage button. This simple task opened the following New Percentage dialog box.

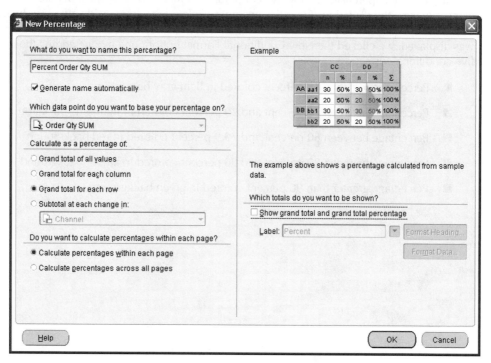

To set up the percentage as we want it, we changed the percentage to "Grand total for each row" and unchecked the box called "Show grand total and grand total percentage." After clicking OK to close the dialog box, we clicked in any of the percentage cells and increased the decimals to three places. Next, we opened up page items and added the Order year to the page items, displaying the data for 2005, our last complete year. To complete the setting up of the query, we clicked the heading called Order Qty SUM and removed it from the worksheet, leaving just the percentage as you can see here.

Page Items: Year: FY2005 ▾

			Percent Order Qty SUM			
		▶ Status	▶ CANCELLED	▶ HOLD	▶ OPEN	▶ SHIPPED
▶ Channel	▶ Product Name					
▶ EXTERNAL	▶ QB-1000		28.403%	3.408%	10.796%	57.392%
	▶ QB-2000		2.781%	0.290%	55.150%	41.780%
	▶ QB-3000		3.230%	3.876%	0.517%	92.377%
	▶ QB-5000		3.577%	NULL	10.612%	85.811%
	▶ QB-5500		NULL	NULL	4.815%	95.185%
	▶ QB-6000		5.923%	NULL	3.555%	90.523%
▶ INTERNET	▶ QB-1000		0.137%	NULL	5.220%	94.643%
	▶ QB-2000		NULL	NULL	1.228%	98.772%
	▶ QB-3000		11.344%	NULL	12.218%	76.438%
	▶ QB-5000		8.646%	NULL	6.145%	85.209%
	▶ QB-5500		12.443%	NULL	20.471%	67.086%
	▶ QB-6000		18.975%	NULL	11.814%	69.211%

Almost done, apart from adding five conditional formats based on the percentage so that we can easily view the deviation. To do this, we right-clicked anywhere inside our worksheet and from the pop-up menu selected Conditional Formats. In the Conditional Formats dialog box that was displayed, we clicked the New Conditional Format button, one by one adding the following five conditional formats:

- Percentage less than 10 percent colored in light gray background

- Percentage between 10 percent and 20 percent colored in light blue background

- Percentage between 60 percent and 79.9 percent colored in red background

- Percentage between 80 percent and 90 percent colored in amber background

- Percentage greater than 90 percent colored in green background

The final result with the NULL values displayed as blanks is illustrated in Figure 9-4.

Trend Analysis

Yet another crosstab. Now there's a trend for you!

If you recall, this query displays the percentage of sales for each region for all of the years that the company has been in operation. We started by selecting the ship quantity, the year, and the region. As in the example for statistical analysis, we need to use the region without displaying the customer or the city.

Having selected our data, we placed the region in the side axis, and the year in the top axis, moving the year below the ship quantity. The following illustration shows the query after we executed it with the items in their correct positions.

	Year	Ship Qty SUM							
Region		▸ FY1998	▸ FY1999	▸ FY2000	▸ FY2001	▸ FY2002	▸ FY2003	▸ FY2004	▸ FY2005
▸ EUROPE		166318	138447	534160	444769	563879	809976	966468	915916
▸ FAR EAST		83001	55344	166534	152658	181349	325124	377303	380876
▸ NORTH AMERICA		219608	229443	819279	639731	854399	1438680	1862310	1511826
▸ SOUTH AMERICA		40605	35303	125336	84260	142273	169008	317668	264726

To complete the query, we clicked the top axis label called Ship Qty SUM and then clicked the Percentage button on the analysis bar. We completed the New Percentage dialog box as follows.

As you can see, this time we named the percentage to be Percent, setting it to calculate on "Grand total for each column." We also unchecked the box called "Show grand total and grand total percentage." Next, just as we did with the deviation worksheet, we deleted the Ship Qty SUM column, leaving just the percentage itself. The final result is shown in Figure 9-5, with the corresponding line graph shown in Figure 9-6.

Aging Analysis

Guess what kind of worksheet we are going to build? Yes, once again, if you said crosstab, you are correct. This query displays the number of sales orders that shipped on time by region.

We started by selecting the COUNT of the order number, the ship date, the order date, and the region name. To make sure we really only count sales orders that have shipped, we created a condition on the Status, limiting it to 'SHIPPED' only. Having chosen our base items, we created a new calculation called Diff that simply subtracts the Order Date from the Ship Date. We cannot include any null dates in our query, because these will give a completely invalid answer. Therefore we have to place a condition on Diff such that this is not null. Because we only want to see the number of days that an item took to ship, we no longer need these two dates, so these need to be removed from the query. However, this cannot be done until after we have created the initial query; otherwise, we will end up summing the total number of days, which is not what we want to see.

To set up our initial worksheet, we place the Region and both dates on the side axis. The initial results looked like this:

	Region	Order Date	Ship Date	Diff
▶	▶ EUROPE	▶ 19-JUN-1998	▶ 26-JUN-1998	7.00
			▶ 24-JUL-1998	35.00
		▶ 22-JUN-1998	▶ 25-JUN-1998	3.00
			▶ 29-JUN-1998	7.00
		▶ 23-JUN-1998	▶ 23-JUN-1998	0.00
		▶ 24-JUN-1998	▶ 24-JUL-1998	30.00
		▶ 25-JUN-1998	▶ 26-JUN-1998	3.00
			▶ 23-JUL-1998	28.00
		▶ 29-JUN-1998	▶ 01-JUL-1998	2.00
		▶ 30-JUN-1998	▶ 22-JUL-1998	22.00
			▶ 24-JUL-1998	24.00
		▶ 06-JUL-1998	▶ 23-JUL-1998	17.00
			▶ 24-JUL-1998	18.00
		▶ 07-JUL-1998	▶ 24-JUL-1998	17.00
		▶ 10-JUL-1998	▶ 17-JUL-1998	7.00
		▶ 13-JUL-1998	▶ 29-JUL-1998	32.00
		▶ 15-JUL-1998	▶ 20-JUL-1998	15.00
		▶ 16-JUL-1998	▶ 23-JUL-1998	7.00
			▶ 24-JUL-1998	16.00
			▶ 10-AUG-1998	25.00
			▶ 21-AUG-1998	36.00

Next, we created another calculation called Order Count as the COUNT of the Order Number. We also removed both of the dates from the worksheet and then placed Diff on the side axis in front of the Region, so that the intermediate result now looks like this.

	Diff	Region	Order Count
▶	0.00	▶ EUROPE	296.00
		▶ FAR EAST	128.00
		▶ NORTH AMERICA	532.00
		▶ SOUTH AMERICA	71.00
▶	1.00	▶ EUROPE	799.00
		▶ FAR EAST	342.00
		▶ NORTH AMERICA	1318.00
		▶ SOUTH AMERICA	239.00
▶	2.00	▶ EUROPE	322.00
		▶ FAR EAST	131.00
		▶ NORTH AMERICA	567.00
		▶ SOUTH AMERICA	94.00
▶	3.00	▶ EUROPE	337.00
		▶ FAR EAST	121.00
		▶ NORTH AMERICA	554.00
		▶ SOUTH AMERICA	85.00

Next, we created a new calculation that works out the on-time category. We used the following CASE statement:

```
CASE WHEN Diff <= 3 THEN 'a. On Time' ELSE
CASE WHEN Diff <= 7 THEN 'b. Within 1 week' ELSE
CASE WHEN Diff <= 14 THEN 'c. Within 2 weeks' ELSE
'd. Over 2 weeks' END END END
```

NOTE
*The leading characters, such as 'a.' and 'b.' in the preceding calculation,
are needed to make sure that the categories display in the desired order.*

We then removed Diff from the worksheet and placed the new Category on the top axis. To make the query more meaningful, we added the Ship Year and placed it in the page items. We also started looking at year 2003, as you can see here.

Page Items: ⠿ Year: FY2003 ▼

	Order Count			
	▶ a. On Time	▶ b. Within 1 week	▶ c. Within 2 weeks	▶ d. Over 2 weeks
▶ EUROPE	329.00	133.00	16.00	4.00
▶ FAR EAST	156.00	44.00	4.00	1.00
▶ NORTH AMERICA	604.00	183.00	11.00	3.00
▶ SOUTH AMERICA	91.00	33.00	3.00	1.00

To complete the query, we clicked the top axis label called Order Count and then clicked the Percentage button on the analysis bar. We completed the New Percentage dialog box as follows.

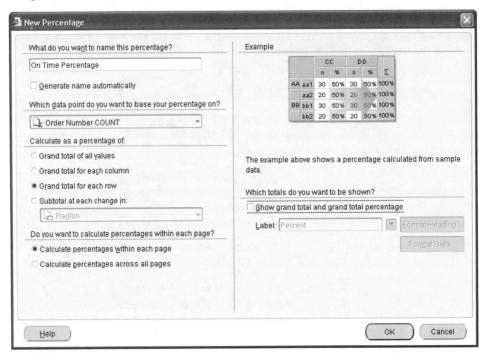

As you can see, this time we named the percentage to be On Time Percentage, setting it to calculate on "Grand total for each row." We also unchecked the box called "Show grand total and grand total percentage." Next, just as we did with the deviation worksheet, we deleted the Order Count column, leaving just the percentage itself. The final result is shown in Figure 9-7.

Overcoming the Manager Who Is Wary of Your Analysis

Do you have a manager who is wary of analysis? Whenever you present him or her with a page full of your analysis results, does that manager start asking questions? This is good. A good manager should not take your analysis results at face value but will need to have some further background information on hand before presenting the findings to the board.

Therefore, before you present that great analysis report to your manager, make sure you can answer the following questions:

- Where did the data come from?

- Who ran the survey?

- Is there an ulterior motive for having the results go one way?

- How was the data collected?

- What questions were asked, who asked them, and who was asked?

Your manager will be wary of comparisons. Remember that two events happening at the same time are not necessarily related, so be careful not to produce statistics to show that they are unless you have additional information to back you up.

Your manager will also be wary of numbers taken out of context. This technique, often referred to as "cherry picking," concentrates only on the data that supports your conclusion and ignores everything else.

Summary

Once we have a large amount of data, this should provide the basis and sufficient information to drive and push you to seek additional knowledge. Since large amounts of data are required, processing efficiency is essential—that is, we must have a means to effectively filter out unwanted data. A tool like Discoverer that provides these techniques at the click of a button is highly desirable. Accuracy is then required to ensure that whatever information is obtained, the knowledge gleaned from that information is valid. The results should be presented in a manner that is both understandable and interesting—that is, it must have potential value to the readers of the report.

In this chapter, you learned the meaning of analysis and the five basic types of analysis—statistical, classification, deviation, trend, and aging—which we described using Discoverer. You learned how to perform these types of analysis, using both Desktop and Plus. We introduced an analysis workflow that we hope will help you go about analyzing your data more effectively.

We also showed you more ways to access the tools that were introduced to you in Chapters 4 and 5. You were introduced to the tools available on the toolbars and shown how to cut your analysis time by using the terrific features of Discoverer. Throughout this chapter, we talked about analysis and statistics and described some of the fundamentals and pitfalls involved.

CHAPTER
10

Business Intelligence
Discoverer Viewer 10g
Release 2 (10.1.2)

n this chapter you will learn about Discoverer Viewer 10g Release 2 (10.1.2), another part of Oracle Business Intelligence. In the first edition of this book, we did not cover Viewer at all. There was good reason for that. Four years ago the tool did not offer much, and we were really not very impressed with it. We do, however, think that this release of Viewer is really terrific.

Viewer is a thin-client HTML-based version of Discoverer Plus. It is packaged with Plus, so if you are using Desktop only, you will not have access to Viewer. It allows you to view reports that were created in both Desktop and Plus, but there are limitations to Viewer's ability to see everything created in Desktop. In other words, it is fully integrated with Plus but not Desktop. This release has many cool features that make it much more than just a viewer. We think it should be called "Viewer on steroids."

Why Use Viewer?

You might be wondering why you should even consider using Viewer. You can't create new workbooks with it, but you can apply parameters and you can slice and dice data. You can use the advanced drilling features of Plus, including drilling in graphs. There are lots of formatting options available, including what we think are really important features, namely conditional formatting and stoplighting. We don't recommend using it for report formatting. Leave the big jobs to Plus and Desktop. They are your workhorses. If you are not a library manager or a report writer, Viewer might be the best tool for you.

If you have not yet considered using Viewer, read on. We went to one client to do some upgrade training to show them the new features of Discoverer 10.1.2. When we began to prepare the course, most of the decision makers told us not to bother demonstrating Viewer. We suggested that we add a half-hour segment to introduce Viewer, and they agreed. By the time we finished the class, those same decision makers exclaimed that 75 percent of their Discoverer users would be using Viewer exclusively. It really is that good, and since it is licensed with Plus, we think you should give it a closer look.

The Benefits of Viewer

The following are some of Viewer's top selling points:

- **A user-friendly browser interface with all the features you expect from a web-based application**   You can use your Back and Forward buttons, and bookmark your favorite reports. We like the look and feel of Viewer and think most end users will find it a comfortable and friendly environment for report viewing.

- **Consistency with Discoverer Desktop and Plus**   The EUL and business areas that have already been built are immediately accessible in Viewer, and all reports created in Desktop or Plus can be analyzed in Viewer.

- **Full customization**   You can make your Viewer look like a page from your company intranet by adding a company logo and company colors.

- **Database security**   Viewer uses the same security that is set up by the Discoverer manager for use in Desktop and Plus.

- **National language support**   Viewer supports many different languages, which you choose from the Connect or Options page.

- **The ability to publish to Oracle Portal**   Discoverer workbooks can be published quickly and easily to Portal.

- **Better integration with the Discoverer portlet provider**   This allows for a single-worksheet Viewer mode when analyzing Discoverer worksheets from Portal.

- **The ability to perform at the individual cell level**   This includes selections, formatting, and conditional formatting all within an individual cell, thanks to Discoverer's leveraging of the thin-client BI Beans in Viewer, and all within the confines of standard DHTML, CSS, and JavaScript—standard browser technologies.

- **An improved graph toolbar**   It allows changes to the graph type and subtype, size, 3-D effects, and gradient colors.

- **The ability to drill from graphs**   Drilling is an important feature of Discoverer, and you are able to leverage this feature directly within your graphs. When viewing a graph, you will see a small "drill" label. The label describes where the drill path will take you; for example, if the graph gives a representation of sales by quarter, the drill path will be to the next level up in the hierarchy, in most cases month.

- **An improved worksheet navigator**   It now allows you to select the worksheet to run, instead of previous releases, which would run the last saved/active worksheet in the workbook selected. Also, the ability to "zoom in" to a workbook means improved usability and improved performance, especially if you have a large number of workbooks in your catalog.

New or Improved Features

As we mentioned before, we have not been big advocates of the older versions of Viewer, but some of the older features have been vastly improved. The new features of Viewer are many, and some of them are so good, we are delighted to now endorse it as part of an enterprise-wide business intelligence plan. The new or improved features of Viewer are

- Support of the database OLAP option

- Single Sign-on support

- E-mail support

- Save to database capability

- Customization of Viewer's look and feel

- Drilling into related data, even in graphs

- Slicing and dicing for improved analysis

- Improved printing by converting worksheets to PDF format

- Export to Excel, Excel Web Query, and PDF

- Worksheet formatting, including conditional formatting and stoplight formatting

- Improved handling of parameters and selecting from list of values

- Improved graph handling

The Connect Page

It is necessary for you to gain specific instructions from your Discoverer administrator on how you will access and log in to Viewer. There is additional information on access procedures in Chapter 3, in the section called "Gaining Access to Discoverer." This is the Viewer Connect page.

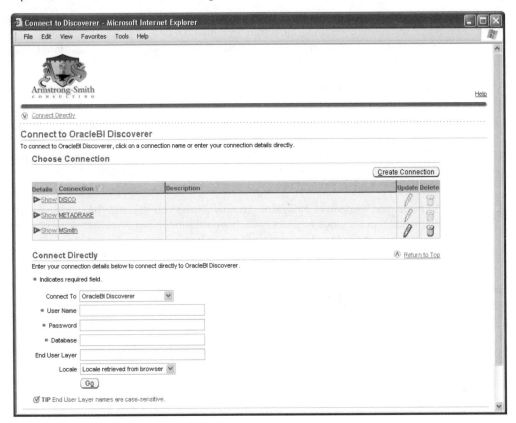

The Worksheet List

After logging in, the first Viewer page is the Worksheet List. In Viewer you select a single worksheet from a workbook. If you want to work with multiple worksheets within a workbook, Viewer makes it easy with links. Remember, this is HTML, and navigating from workbooks and worksheets is as easy as navigating any web site.

Figure 10-1 shows the Worksheet List in Viewer. As you can see, the layout is clean, simple to understand and use. The only limitations are how well the workbooks and worksheets have been named, if a library system is in place, and if meaningful descriptions have been added to the workbooks.

Starting at the top left of the screen, you can see how a corporate identity can be added to Viewer in the form of a company logo. The default is the Oracle logo, but this is easily changed by your Discoverer manager.

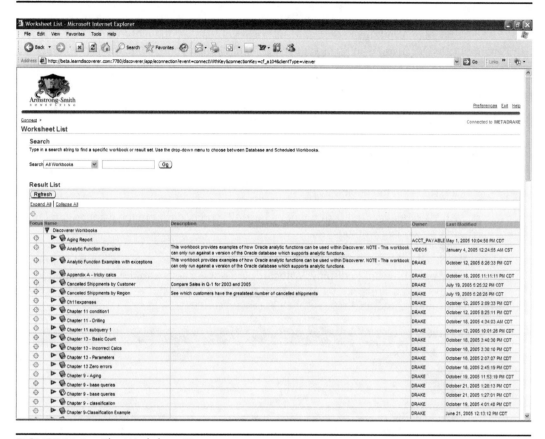

FIGURE 10-1 *The Worksheet List*

To the right of the logo are three helpful links:

- **Preferences** Set up your own performance preferences. This can be compared to the Tools | Options menu in Desktop and Plus. We will show you these choices later in the chapter, in the section called "Setting Up User Preferences in Viewer."

- **Exit** Use this link to log out. It is important to get into the habit of logging out this way because it is how you close your Discoverer connection. Just clicking the *X* in the upper-right corner of the browser only closes the browser and you are left with an open connection to the database, as well as an active session on your middle tier, which will continue to use up memory till the session is terminated after a period of inactivity.

- **Help** This takes you to the Oracle BI Discoverer Help System. It is context-sensitive and will take you to help depending on where you are when you click the link.

Below the top banner you see where you are. The path on the Worksheet List page is back to Connect. Click this link and you are back at the connection page. Below the path is the name of the page: Worksheet List. On the far right you can see the name of the EUL that you are connected to. If you want to change the EUL, click the connect link and you will be taken back to the connection page to make the change.

Searching for a Worksheet

The next area of the Worksheet List page is the Search area. You can search for a specific workbook or worksheet. You can choose from a search of

- **Database Workbooks** The query will run and display the most current data.

- **Scheduled Workbooks** The query has already run at a scheduled time and the results are stored in the database.

- **All Workbooks** The search will include all workbooks from the database and from the scheduled workbooks.

Using the Search Feature of the Worksheet List Page Simply type in all or part of the name of the workbook you want to display. Wildcards are not necessary. In the next illustration, we have used the search string "cust". As you can see, there is a mix of workbooks containing the word "Cust" and "Customer".

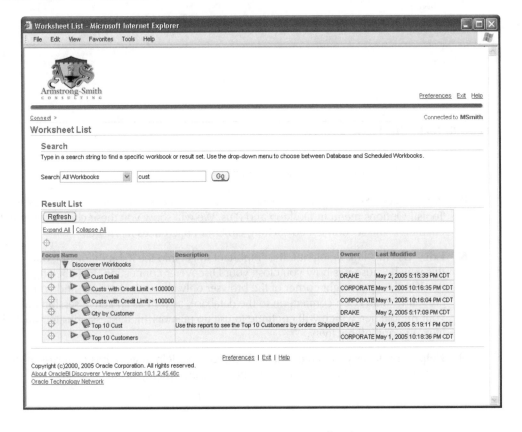

If you don't perform any type of search, the Result List will contain all workbooks that you have been granted permission to view. You could have dozens of workbooks available to you, so getting in the habit of using some simple searches to limit the list is a good idea.

Result List

The area called Result List is the list of available workbooks corresponding to your search. It has the following features, as shown in Figure 10-2:

- **Refresh**   Clicking the Refresh button will make sure that the list is up-to-date. This is important if new workbooks are being created and added to the library. If, for instance, you click the Back link from another worksheet and forget to click Refresh, this will keep you from seeing if a new workbook has been added to the database or if a scheduled workbook has run.

- **Expand all/Collapse all**   Clicking Expand all will expand the list of worksheets within the list of workbooks from the current search. Clicking Collapse all will close the list of worksheets and show only the workbook names.

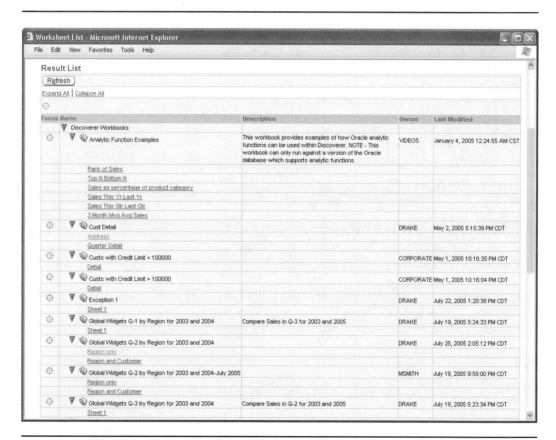

FIGURE 10-2   *The Result List*

- **Focus**   Clicking the focus icon next to a workbook name will limit the list to that workbook and the worksheets it contains.

- **Name**   In the name column you will see a small triangle. When the list is collapsed, the triangle displays a plus sign. Click the triangle and the list will expand to display the worksheet in the workbook and the icon will change to a minus sign.

- **Description**   If your report writers are in the habit of giving meaningful descriptions to their workbooks, you will see them in this column. Descriptions are a great way of reducing the time you spend opening the wrong worksheets. If your organization has not implemented a policy of adding meaningful descriptions, you might suggest that the time has come to begin the practice.

NOTE
Only workbook descriptions are available in Viewer. Worksheet descriptions that you may have added in Plus are not visible in Viewer.

- **Owner**   The Owner is the person who created the workbook and saved it to the database. If your organization is using a library, the owner is the library manager.

- **Last Modified**   This column shows the last date and time that the workbook was modified.

Opening a Worksheet from the Results List

To open a worksheet in Viewer, use the following workflow:

1. Expand the workbook from which you want to select a worksheet.
2. Click the name of the worksheet you want to open.
3. The query will run and open in the browser.

The Main Viewer Page

After selecting the worksheet to open, you will see the main Viewer page. Figure 10-3 shows a sample workbook opened in Viewer.

NOTE
The banner at the top of the screen has not changed. This is the banner you will see on all Viewer pages. Also, each page will display the connection you are using.

Beneath the banner you can see that the path has grown. As you can see in the next illustration, we now have links back to Connect and Workbooks.

FIGURE 10-3   *A sample workbook in Viewer*

Below the links are the workbook name and the current worksheet. The area directly below the names shows the last time this worksheet was run.

Last run **August 1, 2005**

Actions

The Actions area seen in this illustration gives you useful links to perform a variety of functions:

Actions

Rerun query
Save as
Revert to saved
Printable page
Export
Send as email
Worksheet options

- **Rerun query**   Use this link to rerun the query. This is useful when you are reporting against live data and need to check for updates.

- **Save as**   Yes, you heard right. You can now make changes to a worksheet in Viewer and save them to the database. This is a right that your Discoverer administrator can give or deny, so if the link is not there, it means you don't have that privilege.

- **Revert to saved**   If you make changes to the worksheet but want to see it in its original layout and formatting, click this link.

- **Printable page**   This link takes you to a setup page to prepare the worksheet to print to PDF format.

- **Export**   This link takes you to a page to select from a variety of export options, such as Excel, PDF, comma or tab delimited, and HTML.

- **Send as email**   This link takes you to a page where you choose the file type (these are the same as the Export options) to e-mail and then go on to an e-mail form. E-mailing must be set up by your Discoverer administrator, so if it does not work, you will need to check with her to see if it can be made available to you.

- **Worksheet options**   This takes you to a page where you can set up how to view the worksheet.

Printable Page   To set up the worksheet for printing, use the following workflow:

1. Click the Printable page link. This opens the Printable page screen Content tab seen in Figure 10-4.

2. Select from General Options to Show title:

   - On the first page, or

   - Never

3. Select from General Options to Show text area:

   - On the first page, or

   - Never

4. Select from General Options how to print the data:

   - Print all row and columns.

   - Print only the rows and columns that are displayed in the crosstab or table.

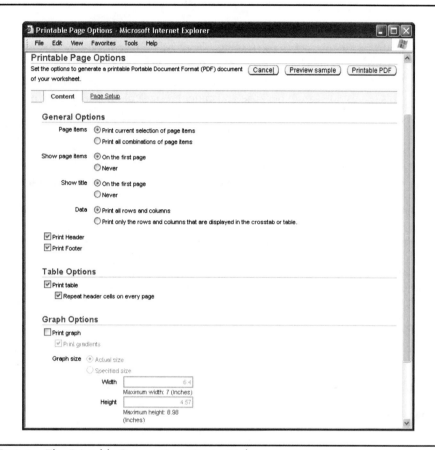

FIGURE 10-4   *The Printable Page options Content tab*

5. From General Options choose to print headers and footers by leaving the boxes checked, or uncheck them to suppress them from printing.

6. From Table Options use the check box to print the table or crosstab. Deselect the box if you do not want the table or crosstab to print. This option is useful if you only want to print the graph.

7. From Table Options use the check box Repeat header cells on every page. If you are printing a table or crosstab, you will want to keep this one checked. We can't think of an instance when you would not want to see header cells on each page.

8. From Graph Options use the check box to print the graph. Deselect the box if you do not want the graph to print.

9. From Graph Options use the check box Print gradients if you want the gradient colors shown on screen to print.

10. From Graph Options use the radio buttons to determine the size of the graph in the print out. You can select actual size or you can determine the exact size of the graph.

11. Click the Page Setup tab.

12. Select the Paper size, orientation, and margins.

13. Select whether or not to use scaling. This is useful when you have a large worksheet that is wider than one page and you want to try to get it all on one page.

14. From the Column Sizes section you can modify the width of the columns for printing. This is a useful feature because you cannot resize columns in Viewer but might want to change the widths for printing. Don't get too excited about this feature, though, as you will have to reset these options every time you open the worksheet for printing. Discoverer Viewer does not retain the settings.

15. Leave the Wrap text box checked or the data will be clipped off.

16. Click Printable PDF to print the PDF or Preview Sample to view a sample PDF.

NOTE
The difference between Printable PDF and Preview Sample is that the Preview Sample generates a PDF of the worksheet based on the first 50 (or maybe 100) rows of data and the graph. The thinking is that 50 rows should be sufficient for the user to get an idea as to how the printed worksheet will appear, while the preview generation process will not be too resource-intensive. PDF generation is a CPU- and memory-intensive operation on the middle tier.

17. When the PDF has been created, you will get a link to open the PDF. Click the link and determine if the PDF is as you like it and ready to print or if it needs more work.

Export   You can export your Discoverer Viewer worksheets to any of the following file types:

- CSV (comma delimited)

- DIF (data interchange format)

- Formatted Text (space delimited)

- GIF image

- HTML

- Microsoft Excel Workbook

- Oracle Reports XML

- PNG image

- PDF

- SYLK (symbolic link)

- Text (tab-delimited)

- Web Query for Microsoft Excel 2000+

- WKS (Lotus 1-2-3)

To set up the worksheet for export, use the following workflow:

1. From an open worksheet click the Export link.
2. From the Choose Export Type screen select the format you want to use from the drop-down list seen in the following illustration:

3. Click the Export button. The page will change and you now see Export Ready at the top of the page and the following message: "The export you requested is ready. Please click the button below to open the exported document to view or save it."
4. Click the button labeled Click to view or save. You will get this dialog box.
5. Click Open to view the file or Save to save it.
6. When you are finished with the export file, use the links at the top of the browser to get back to the worksheet or to open another worksheet.

Send as E-mail   Another very nice feature of Discoverer Viewer is the power to e-mail reports. The worksheet goes through the Export process to prepare it as an attachment first. Then you are presented with a simple e-mail utility to enter sender and recipient information, a subject line, and a message.

This is a feature that must be set up by your Discoverer administrator, so check to see if e-mailing is available to you.

To send a Discoverer Viewer report by e-mail, use the following workflow:

1. From an open worksheet, click the Send as email link.

2. From the Choose Attachment Type page select the Export type from the drop-down list.

3. Click Next. This opens the Send Email page seen here:

4. Fill out the e-mail form. You can review the file before sending by clicking the View Attachment button.

5. Click Finish.

6. When you are finished with the e-mail, use the links at the top of the browser to get back to the worksheet or to open another worksheet.

Worksheet Options   Use the Worksheet Options link to set up the item you want to display in the current worksheet. You can select from the following:

- **Title**   Select this check box to show the title.

- **Table/Crosstab**   Select this check box to show the table or crosstab.

- **Graph**   Select this check box to show the graph associated with the worksheet.

- **Both**   Select this radio button to display the graph and the table/crosstab data.

- **Text Area**   Select this check box to show the text area in the worksheet.

- **Show null values as**   If no data is returned for a field in a worksheet, you can determine how you want the null value to appear. If you want the word NULL to appear, leave the setting as it is. If you want 0 to appear, type **0**, and if you want the field to be blank, clear it.

- **Show values that cannot be aggregated as**   When a worksheet tries to aggregate an item that cannot be aggregated (for example Rank), you can define here how the data is displayed. For example, if you enter "N/A" in this field, worksheets will display the text "N/A" where the data cannot be aggregated.

Worksheets

The Worksheet area (below the Actions area) has links to all of the worksheets contained in the current workbook. Using these links is similar to using the tabs in Desktop or Plus. When you click a link to another worksheet in the workbook, the new query will run and display. Remember that this is HTML. You can use your browser buttons to go back and forth between the worksheets. The queries won't rerun; instead, the pages are cached. If you need to see up-to-the-minute data, you will need to use the Rerun Query link from the Actions area.

The Table or Crosstab Display Area

In this area the table or crosstab is displayed; however, there is the ever-present triangle to the left of the word "table" or "crosstab." When the table or crosstab is displayed, the triangle will have a minus sign on it. If you don't want to see the table or crosstab and want to see only the graph, for example, click the triangle and the table will close. The triangle icon will now show a plus sign, and to reopen the table/crosstab, click it again.

▽ Table

▷ **Tools** Layout Format Stoplight Sort Rows and Columns

	►Customer Name	►Credit Limit SUM	►Address	►State	►Postcode
1	ABC WIDGET CO	100000.00	123, YOCKSAM-DONG	KANGNAM-GU	135-080

NOTE
You are basically collapsing and expanding the table/crosstab using the triangle icon. When you want to expand it, the query does not rerun, but the cached data is displayed.

Tools

Five tools are available in Discoverer Viewer that you can use to slice and dice the data. You can reorder the columns, move columns into page items, add formatting (even conditional formatting and stoplighting), and sort. You can also decide how many rows and columns you want to display per page. You no longer have to worry about very wide crosstabs scrolling off to the right—you simply decide how many columns you want to view. You can view the fortieth column while still being able to view the edge axis labels and values.

In Figure 10-5 you can see a worksheet open in Viewer. The tools are listed below the table type. You can make the following format changes:

- **Layout**   Use this feature to change the arrangement of the columns.

- **Format**   Use this feature to change the font formatting as well as background and foreground colors. You can also use this feature to add conditional formatting.

- **Stoplight**   Use this feature to add exception formatting.

- **Sort**   Use this feature to sort the data.

- **Rows and Columns**   Use this feature to change the number of rows and columns to display per page of the browser.

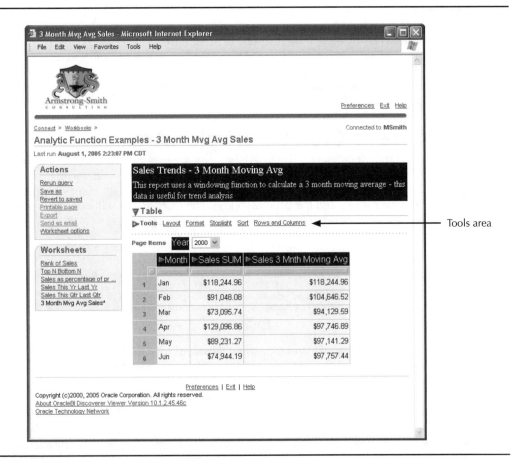

FIGURE 10-5   *A worksheet with Viewer tools*

Layout

You can completely change the layout of a table or crosstab in Viewer. You can move or swap columns, and you can move items into page items or out of page items. Any rearranging of rows and columns you can do in Desktop or Plus you can do in Viewer. It is not drag-and-drop, but it is still quite simple. If you get the layout completely messed up, don't worry, just click the Revert to saved link and start over.

There is no toolbar in Viewer, only the Tools menu seen in the following illustration.

Moving or Swapping Columns

To move or swap columns in a table or crosstab, use the following workflow:

1. Click Layout from the Tools menu.

2. Select Move or Swap from the drop-down list seen here:

3. Select the column you want to move from the drop-down seen here:

4. Select where you want to move it from the following drop-down:

5. Click Go.

Adding or Moving Page Items There is also a link called More. This takes you to a Table Layout page seen next that gives you more layout options, including adding and moving page items.

To add or move page items, use the following workflow:

1. Select the Show Page Items check box.

2. Next to each column name in the worksheet is an icon with an up arrow. Click this icon on the column or columns you want to add to page items.

3. The item or items have been added to the Page Items area and have an icon with a down arrow next to each page item name. To move them back out of page items, click the down arrow.

4. When you are done rearranging the columns, click Apply.

5. You are taken back to the table/crosstab page.

Format

We are really happy to have formatting available in this release of Discoverer Viewer. It makes the tool much more useful for end users who want to prepare a worksheet for printing. The only thing missing as far as formatting is concerned is the ability to format numbers. If, for example, dollar signs and decimal places were not formatted in the creation of the worksheet, you are stuck with the unformatted numbers.

When you click the Format tool, what looks like a toolbar appears below the Tools menu. Simply select the column you want formatted and then click the format button that you want to apply. You can

- Bold fonts

- Italicize fonts

- Underline fonts

- Change the background color

- Change the font color

There is also a link called More following the buttons. Clicking this link takes you to a page where you can perform all of the same functions. We think it is simpler to use the buttons.

Conditional Formatting The Format tool also has a link to create conditional formatting. Conditional formatting is used to color ranges of data within a column, for example, customers with sales over $20,000. When conditional formatting (called exception formatting in Desktop) has been added to a worksheet during its creation, you will see it in Discoverer Viewer. You can also create conditional formats in Viewer, but there are limitations that do not exist in Desktop and Plus. While you can apply conditional formats to any type of data in Desktop and Plus, such as Order Status or Region, in Viewer you are limited to numeric fields. We hope that Oracle can improve this feature in future releases.

To create conditional formatting, use the following workflow:

1. Click Format from the Tools menu, then click the Create Conditional Format link from the Format menu.

Create Conditional Format Link

2. This opens the Create Conditional Cell Format page.

3. Give your conditional format a meaningful name.

4. Select the numeric column to which you want to add the conditional format from the Item drop-down list.

5. Select the operator from the Operator drop-down list.

6. Enter the value in the Value field.

7. Select the formatting you wish to apply from the Format area.

8. Click Apply.

Conditional Formats   The final link in the Format menu is Conditional Formats. This link takes you to a page where you can manage all of your conditional formatting, stoplight formatting, and header (column name) formats. We will describe the use of this page at the end of the next section.

Stoplight

The next link in the Tools menu is Stoplight. Stoplight formatting is similar to conditional formatting. It formats data in a column using three ranges: Unacceptable, Acceptable, and Desirable. As with conditional formatting, if stoplight formatting is created in Plus (stoplighting is not available in Desktop), it will display in Discoverer Viewer. Because they use ranges, stoplight formats are always based on numeric fields, for example: all customers with sales under $10,000 in red, all customer with sales between $10,000 and $40,000 in yellow, and all customers with sales over $40,000 in green.

To apply stoplights, use the following workflow:

1. From the Tools menu select Stoplight. This opens the stoplight bar below the Tools menu.

2. Select the column upon which you want to base your stoplight from the Format drop-down list.

3. In the Unacceptable field type in the highest number of the low range.

4. In the Desirable field type in the lowest number of the high range. Notice how the Acceptable range is calculated for you using all values between the low and high ranges.

5. If you don't want to use the default colors, click the pallet icon to the right of each range and select a color from the color pallet.

6. Click Go. The stoplight format is applied as seen here.

The Conditional Formats Link

In both the Formats and Stoplight menus is a link called Conditional Formats. This link takes you to a page where you can manage the formats you have created in Discoverer Viewer. It does not, however, manage the conditional formats that were created using Desktop or Plus. Those are a fixed part of the worksheet, and you have no control over them in Viewer.

If you have created stoplights or conditional formatting in the current worksheet using Discoverer Viewer, you will see them here. You can also use this utility to create, edit, or delete new stoplights and conditional formatting. You cannot format column headers using the Format menu; instead, you must use this utility.

The Conditional Formats page is divided into three sections:

- **Stoplight Formats** Use this area to manage stoplights you have created in Discoverer Viewer.

- **Cell Formats** Use this area to manage conditional formats you have created in Discoverer Viewer.

- **Header Formats** Use this area to format the column headers.

If you want to deactivate the formatting, simply click the check box next to the format name to remove the check mark.

Sort

You can add both normal and group sorts in Discoverer Viewer. The Sort link on the Tools menu opens the sort menu.

To apply a normal sort in Discoverer Viewer, use the following workflow:

1. From the Sort menu select the column you want to sort from the Sort drop-down list.
2. Select A-Z or Z-A from the Order drop-down list.
3. Click Go.

To apply multiple and group sorts (up to three), use the following workflow:

1. Click More from the Sort menu. This opens the Multiple Sort page.
2. From the Column Header drop-down list select the column you want to sort.
3. From the Sort Order drop-down list select the order.
4. From the Sort Type drop-down list select Normal or Group.
5. If you want to sort on a column but do not want the column visible, click the Hide Column check box next to the sort.
6. Click Apply.

To remove a sort, use the following workflow:

1. Click More from the Sort menu. This opens the Multiple Sort page.
2. From the Sort Order drop-down list in the row you want to remove the sort from, select No Sort Order.

Rows and Columns

The final link on the Tools menu is Rows and Columns. Here you select how many rows and columns you want to appear on a page. You can limit the number so that you do not need to scroll down; instead, you will use the down link to go to the next page. You can also set up a default in your Preferences that will limit the number of rows and columns for all worksheets.

Hyper-Drilling

Hyper-drills that have been created using Plus are available for use in Discoverer Viewer. This is another great feature of this tool. Hyper-drilling allows you to go deeper into the data; for example, you are looking at sales for 2004 and see that sales were particularly high in June, so you want to examine the sales for June in more detail. When a hyper-drill is available, with a simple click of the mouse another worksheet, or even another workbook will open with the detailed information you seek. You can also drill to higher-level detail.

NOTE
For information on hyper-drilling and its uses please refer to Chapter 11.

You know when a hyper-drill is available by the small, triangle-shaped Drill to link icon to the left of the drill item. The illustration that follows shows a hyper-drill on District.

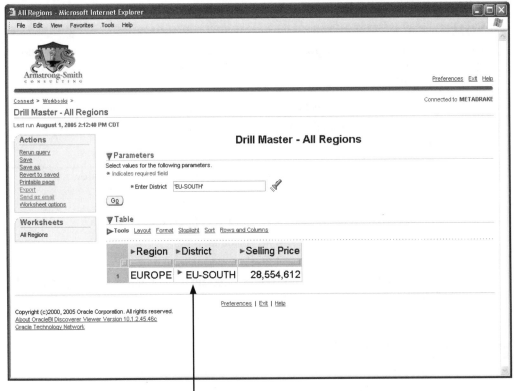

Hyper-drill icon

Clicking the icon gives you a pop-up list of available hyper-drills, as an item can have multiple drill links.

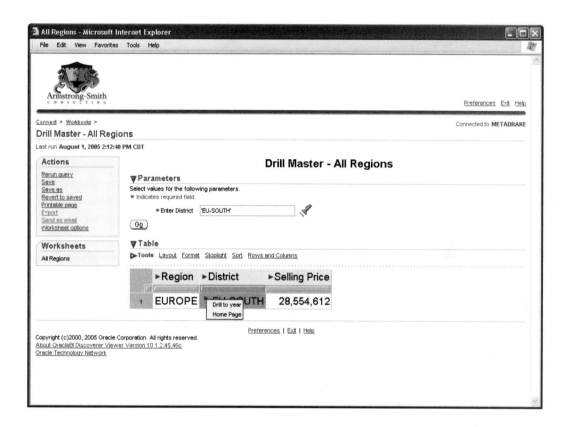

Click the link you want to follow, and the current worksheet will close and the hyper-link will open.

Graphs

When a graph has been created using Plus, you will be able to work with it in Discoverer Viewer. You even have tools that will allow you to change the graph type, the size of the graph, and the graph's 3-D and gradient effects.

NOTE
Graphs created in Desktop are not available in Discoverer Viewer.

To hide the graph, click the plus sign alongside the word "Graph" in the graph area of the worksheet.

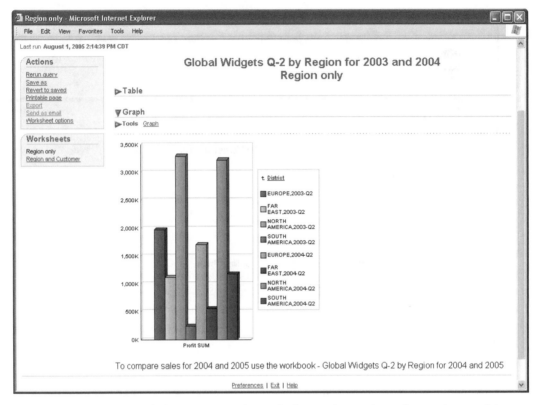

To open the graph, click the minus sign alongside the word "Graph" in the graph area of the worksheet.

To modify the graph, use the following workflow:

1. With the graph open, click the minus sign on the icon alongside the word "Tools" in the graph area of the worksheet. The graph tools will open.

2. Change the graph type by selecting from the two Type drop-down menus.

3. After you make your choice, click Go directly to the right of the type menus.

4. To change the size of the graph display, experiment typing in numbers between 300 and 800 in the width and height boxes. Keeping the number close will help to maintain good width-to-height ratios.

5. After typing in the width and height, click Go directly to the right of the boxes.

6. Use the check boxes to the right to turn on and off 3-D effects and color gradient effects.

Drilling in Graphs

Using graphs to drill in Discoverer Viewer is great way to use the tool for your data analysis. If a graph is based on an item that is part of a hierarchy, you can drill to another level in the graph. In the next illustration the graph is based on Regions. In the graph legend, there is an up arrow. This indicated a drill hierarchy exists. In this case the drill will go from Region to District.

NOTE
There is also a new option available only in Viewer that allows you to specify whether the graph should be for the entire worksheet or only for the subset of data that is currently displayed in the table/crosstab.

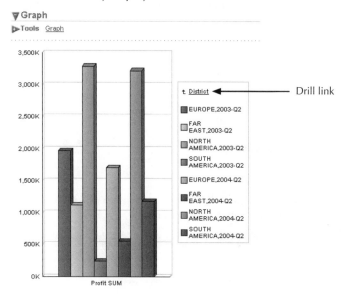

Clicking the up arrow will take you deeper into the data, now showing a new graph displaying the Districts. Also notice that the worksheet has changed to reflect the District, and looking at the graph legend, you see that there is a new drill available to City.

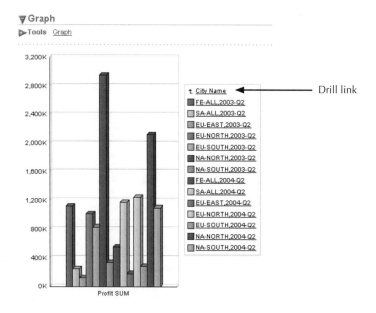

Setting Up User Preferences in Viewer

The Preferences link opens the Preferences page. Here you have an opportunity to make a few customizations to your personal Viewer environment. It is similar to the Tools | Options dialog box in Plus. Changing these options affects all worksheets, not just the current one. The page is divided into five sections:

- Query Governor

- Measure Unit

- Axis Label

- Summary Data

- Fan Trap Detection

Query Governor

Use the Query Governor to limit the amount of time and data retrieved when a worksheet runs. The Query Governor section is shown here.

NOTE
The Query Governor options are preset by your Discoverer administrator. You cannot change these options to allow for more than the administrator has given to you.

- **Warn me if the predicted time exceeds**   Check this box and enter a value in seconds.

- **Prevent queries from running longer than**   Check this box and enter a value in seconds.

- **Limit retrieved query data to**   Enter a row limit.

- **Retrieve data incrementally in groups of**   Enter the number of rows you want to be retrieved. If the database contains more rows than the number required for the query, Discoverer warns you that not all data was retrieved.

- **Cancel list of values retrieval after**   Enter in seconds the amount of time you will wait for a list of values.

Measure Units

Select from the drop-down list whether you want measures displayed in inches or centimeters.

Axis Labels

Choose when to show axis labels with the following three options:

- **Always**   Axis labels are always shown in crosstab worksheets after they are opened.

- **Never**   Axis labels are hidden in crosstab worksheets after they are opened.

- **Worksheet**   Axis labels are shown or hidden in crosstab worksheets depending on how they were last saved.

Summary Data

Using summary data means that the work you do most often can be done faster. When you run a query, Discoverer checks summary tables set up by the Discoverer administrator to see if saved data will satisfy your requirements. If the saved data will suffice, Discoverer loads the data quickly. If the summary tables' data does not meet your needs, Discoverer redirects the request to the rest of the database and sends the query to the database.

NOTE
The available preferences depend on whether your database supports materialized views or not.

For databases that support materialized views, the following options are available:

■ **Always, when available** Select this option if you don't need up-to-the-minute data for your analysis.

■ **Only when summary data is not out of date (stale)** Select this option if you need up-to-the-minute data.

■ **Never** Choose this option if you always want Discoverer Viewer to ignore the summary tables and use the latest data.

The following options are available for databases that don't support materialized views:

■ **Always, when available** Choose this if up-to-the-minute data is not important for data analysis.

■ **When summary data is more recent than nn days** Choose this option when time-sensitive data is necessary for worksheets. Specify the number of days from the last data update.

Summary

In this chapter you have learned the power of Discoverer Viewer. You have seen how it can be used in data analysis and how easily it slices and dices data. You have been shown how easy it is to format data and add special formatting such as stoplights and conditional formats.

We have shown you how to rearrange columns and rows and place page items. You have seen how Discoverer Viewer can be used to export and e-mail reports using a variety of common file types and how easy it is to set up a report for printing. Discoverer Viewer is also an excellent tool for viewing graphs, and graphs can be used for drilling into as well as out of hierarchical data.

Find a place for Discoverer Viewer in your organization. This powerful thin-client HTML tool will become the standard for data analysis among non–report writers.

PART
III

Advanced Discoverer
Techniques

CHAPTER
11

Refining Items, Drilling, and Hyper-Drilling

uring the first ten chapters of this book, we taught you how to create worksheets using the Workbook Wizard, how to analyze your data, and how to convert your queries into reports.

Most queries are not very efficient when first built. You run them to make sure that they at least work. Having avoided "The Query from the Twilight Zone" and decided that a query is worth keeping, you may have followed the steps in Chapter 9 and converted it into a report. Later, however, when working on a completely different problem, you may realize that a previous query satisfies most of the requirements. With a little tweaking and manipulation, you can modify or refine one query and turn it into another.

In this and the following two chapters, we will show you how to refine an existing query, how to fine-tune it, how to make it work more efficiently, or how to convert it into another query.

This chapter deals with refining the query items and drilling data. We will also show you the new and very powerful Plus feature called *hyper-drilling*. This allows you to either drill from one worksheet to another, going ever deeper into details, or to drill out to a URL. This feature alone is worth the upgrade to 10.1.2.

Refining Query Items

Perhaps the most frequent task you will perform in Discoverer is refining the items in a query. Refining can be as simple as adding or removing an item, but even this can have its pitfalls, as you will see in the next section. The real fun comes when you start pivoting and drilling. These techniques allow a much more sophisticated method of refining a query. It actually takes a little time to understand the full implications of what is involved, so let's begin with the simplest: adding and removing items.

Adding or Removing Items

By far the simplest and most common way of refining a query is to select a new item, or take an item away. Refining a query using these techniques sounds so easy—you take away an item, or add a new item, and that's it, you have a new query. If only it really were this simple!

Unfortunately, these techniques are also one of the easiest ways to run into problems. Later in this section, we will detail some of the most common errors that you may encounter.

Adding a New Item

This is the simplest way to refine a query, but it can still be somewhat tricky. We will introduce you to a workflow, plus give you an example of the most complicated way to add data by adding an item using an intermediate folder.

There are two ways to add new items to an existing worksheet. You can use the Edit Sheet dialog box, or in Plus only, you can use the Available Items pane. As with most things with Discoverer, there is usually an easy way and, shall we say, a not-so-easy way.

First, we will show you the easy way to add a new item using the Available Items pane. Then we will walk you through using the Edit Sheet dialog box, which, as you will see, is not quite as easy. If you are not yet using 10.1.2, adding a new item using the Edit Sheet dialog box is the only method available. Perhaps after reading this section, you will be upgrading!

To add a new item to an existing Plus worksheet using the Available Items pane, use the following workflow:

1. Decide what item needs to be added.

2. In the Available Items pane, locate the item that you want to add.

3. Use one of the following three ways to add the item:

   ■ Right-click the item and from the pop-up list select Add to Worksheet.

   ■ Drag the item from the Available Items pane to the Selected Items pane.

   ■ Drag the item directly from the Available Items pane to the table or crosstab. If you use this method, you can place the item exactly where you want it. This is our recommended way. Using the other methods, the item will be placed as the last item in the worksheet. You will then need to move it to the desired location.

To add a new item to an existing worksheet using the Edit Sheet dialog box, use the following workflow:

1. Decide what item needs to be added.

2. Open the Edit Sheet dialog box.

3. Examine Discoverer's open folders and see if the item you want is in a folder that you are already using. If the item you want is in one of the folders you are already using, proceed directly to Step 7 of this workflow.

4. If the item you want is not in one of the folders that are currently in use, is it in a folder that is available? By this, we mean, is the folder containing the item you want an active folder, or is it currently deactivated? If the item you want is in an active folder, proceed to Step 7 of this workflow.

NOTE
Remember, a folder that is active has its name highlighted, while a folder that is inactive has its name grayed out.

5. If the item you want is not in one of the active folders, can the folder be activated by applying a join or joins through one or more intermediate folders? If the folder you want to get to cannot be accessed this way, you will not be able to add the desired item to your current query. Unfortunately, you will have to build a new query. There are two reasons Discoverer prevents you from joining unrelated folders in queries. These are

   ■ To prevent you from creating meaningless queries, and

   ■ To avoid creating outer joins on two unrelated tables that could result in the "Query from the Twilight Zone"

NOTE
To determine if there is an intermediate folder, look in your system's help file. If you are using Noetix Views, look in the Noetix help file and examine the Z$ items. These are joins to other folders. Refer to Appendix C for a full explanation.

6. If the item that you want is in a folder that can be accessed by joining through an intermediate folder, you will need to open the intermediate folder and then select any item from it. This should now make available the folder that contains the item that you want to add.

NOTE
You can use multiple intermediate folders to get to the folder that contains the item you require. Repeat Step 6 as many times as required, until the item you need becomes available.

7. Open the folder containing the item that you want, and add the item to your query.

8. If you used any intermediate folders to join to the folder containing the item you just added, you should remove those folder items now. Don't worry about removing these items, because Discoverer will remember exactly how to join to the folder containing the item that you want.

9. Before you leave the Edit Worksheet dialog box, revise the table layout, conditions, sort order, and calculations. In the Plus Edit Worksheet, you can also revise the totals, parameters, and percentages.

10. Click OK. Discoverer now reruns the query and includes the item that you want.

11. Apply any formatting you require.

12. Save the query. Remember to save it under a new name if you want to also keep a copy of the original.

Adding an Item Using an Intermediate Folder

Let us start from the following completed query and walk through all of the steps in the workflow. As you can see next, this simple query displays the total quantity ordered and the cost price for all customers.

	Cust Name	Order Qty SUM	Cost Price SUM
1	ABC WIDGET CO	298160	2621529.97
2	ACE MANUFACTURING	354744	3430321.83
3	BIG RIVER WIDGETS	278457	2368120.27
4	BRIDGE THINGS	171041	1542731
5	CASA DE WIDGETS	744294	6694309.1
6	CEBU WIDGET CO	755633	6981829.49
7	GATOR WIDGETS	321616	2754201.28
8	HONG KONG WIDGETS	562448	4920948.71
9	LAC WIDGETS SA	498452	4649537.16
10	LAST RAILWAY WIDGETS	536368	4842040.18
11	LONDON WIDGETS LTD.	535016	4983079.95
12	LOTS OF WIDGETS	417979	3698212.85
13	MOUNTAIN WIDGETS	510652	4178928.58
14	MUM'S WIDGET CO.	665422	5960663.23
15	OXFORD WIDGETS	490931	4461223.22
16	PALMELA WIDGETS	95398	937186.55
17	PATRIOT'S WIDGET CO.	633317	5316409.02
18	REPUBLIC WIDGETS	373977	3443942.94

Let us assume that we have been asked to change this query—to now display the totals by product line as well as by customer. Step 1 is complete, and as Step 2 requires us to open the Edit Worksheet dialog box, we did just that. In Steps 3 and 4, we examined the currently used and active folders, and determined that the product line was not in any of those. As you can see here, the Product Line folder is inactive.

Product Line is grayed out ⟶

Step 5 of the workflow requires us to check whether any intermediate folder exists that can be joined to one of our in-use folders. After careful examination of our database (refer to Appendix D for a full data model of our database), we saw that there is indeed a join between the Products folder and the Product Line folder. Therefore, as required by Step 6, we opened the Products folder and selected the product name. As you can see, these actions activated the Product Line folder.

Adhering to Step 7 of the workflow, we now were able to open the Product Line folder and added the product line item to our query. Removing the Products folder from our list of completed items thereby completed Step 8. As you can see, even though we decided not to include anything from the Products folder, that folder enabled us to select the product line.

Finally, we completed the remaining steps of the workflow. We moved the product line alongside the customer name, applied a group sort on the customer, and a normal low-to-high sort on the product line.

	► Cust Name	► Prod Line	► Order Qty SUM	► Cost Price SUM
1	ABC WIDGET CO	MEGA-WIDGET	110167	1060335.42
2		MINI-WIDGET	38573	151925.85
3		SUPER-WIDGET	61087	601609.56
4		WONDER-WIDGET	88333	807659.14
5	ACE MANUFACTURING	MEGA-WIDGET	86193	806411.50
6		MINI-WIDGET	23939	95119.25
7		SUPER-WIDGET	131189	1439882.02
8		WONDER-WIDGET	113423	1088909.06
9	BIG RIVER WIDGETS	MEGA-WIDGET	113525	1040415.18
10		MINI-WIDGET	48820	154401.95
11		SUPER-WIDGET	47867	536271.34
12		WONDER-WIDGET	68245	637031.80
13	BRIDGE THINGS	MEGA-WIDGET	49260	502238.04
14		MINI-WIDGET	14754	58410.24
15		SUPER-WIDGET	52583	591311.54
16		WONDER-WIDGET	54444	390771.18
17	CASA DE WIDGETS	MEGA-WIDGET	210221	1701538.28
18		MINI-WIDGET	77494	303773.76
19		SUPER-WIDGET	249527	2788824.63
20		WONDER-WIDGET	207052	1900172.43

The final result, as just shown, has effectively demonstrated how to add an item to a query using an intermediate folder. By adhering to the workflow outlined, we completed adding the product line without any difficulty.

NOTE
You can also add new items to a worksheet by using Discoverer's drilling capabilities. These are explained in detail later in this chapter, in the section entitled "Drilling Into and Out of Data."

Removing an Item from Your Query

Removing a single item from a query is straightforward and easy to do. Of course, you can remove an item by launching the Edit Worksheet dialog box and removing the item from the selections, but did you know you could just highlight the item and delete it by pressing the DELETE key? Refer to Chapter 6 for more information on removing items from queries.

In Plus, there are two additional ways to remove an item from a query. First, you can right-click the item and from the pop-up list select Remove from Worksheet. You can also highlight the item in the Available Items pane and click the Remove from Worksheet button on the toolbar of the pane.

Common Problems Associated with Adding or Removing Items

The most common problems users encounter when attempting to add or remove items are

- Attempting to join multiple business areas

- Attempting to combine aggregate and detail data

- Attempting to join to the same child folder from multiple parent folders

- Multiple join methods from a child folder to a parent folder

- Missing joins

- Fan traps

- Lack of documentation

Attempting to Join Multiple Business Areas

Unless your Discoverer manager has made it possible for you to link business areas together, you will usually not be able to select items from multiple business areas at the same time.

In the following example, we already have a query that selects the order quantity and cost price by product. After editing the sheet, we tried to select from another business area.

As you can see in the following illustration, all of the folders in the other business area are deactivated:

Attempting to Combine Aggregate and Detail Data

Another common error users make when adding new items to an existing query is to fail to define the new item to be at the same level of aggregation as the existing items.

In the following example, we have an existing query that selects the total quantity ordered by sales channel for the fiscal month of February 2000. From the Available Items pane, we attempted to add the ordered quantity detail to the same query. As you can see, Discoverer gave us a warning.

While Discoverer will not prevent you from mixing aggregate and detail data in the same query, be warned—your results may be incorrect. We ignored the warning that Discoverer gave us and ran the query anyway. This produced a very interesting result. As you can see, we placed a group sort on the channel and then subtotaled by channel. You might expect the subtotal for order quantity sum and order quantity total to be the same, but they are not! The correct answer is the one for the subtotal based on the order quantity sum, but if you did not know this, you could easily quote the wrong total to your manager or, worse still, to a customer or your shareholders, and understate the quantity booked by almost 200,000 items!

▶ Channel	▶ Order Qty SUM	▶ Order Qty
	52000	13000
	28200	14100
	420000	15000
	31200	15600
	16000	16000
	18000	18000
	52800	26400
	30000	30000
	34800	34800
INTERNET	201	1
	46	2
	3	3
	72	4
	175	5
	24	6
	14	7
	360	8
	9	9
	690	10

Attempting to Join to the Same Child Folder from Multiple Parent Folders

Pay particular attention when combining aggregate data with detail data, because this can give you problems. Data warehouses, for example, are usually built around a star schema with one or more fact tables and multiple dimensions. When multiple fact tables are employed, one of them usually contains only aggregated data, while the other(s) contain varying amounts of detail. If you have a query that pulls data from the aggregated folder, and then refine that query to also pull from the detail folder, you will have problems. Not only will Discoverer try to mix this data in the same row, but Discoverer will not be able to correctly identify which fact folder to use when joining to the remaining dimension folders.

In Discoverer terms this is a fan trap. As you can see in this illustration, Discoverer states that it could not add the second detail item because it has detected a fan trap. To work around this issue, please look at the section dealing with fan traps later in this chapter.

NOTE
For an explanation of star schema terminology, please refer to Appendix C.

Multiple Join Methods from a Child Folder to a Parent Folder

Another easy-to-make mistake relates to incorrectly joining a child folder to a parent folder. The most common mistake that we have seen relates to users misunderstanding their company's use of foreign currencies and multiple currencies.

In the modern era, many companies use multiple currencies from around the world. Within the Sales Order folder, there could be amounts stored in the local, regional, and corporate currencies. A local currency is the currency of the transaction (USD, GBP, TWD, CHF, and so on). A regional currency is the currency in which a region aggregates its amounts (for example, the European region could decide to aggregate using the Euro). A corporate currency is the currency in which the company decides to report its quarterly and annual returns.

If you are using Oracle E-Business Suite, you will probably already be aware that this application supports only the local, or transactional currency, and the set of books currency. The set of books currency equates to the regional currency just outlined.

However, most systems will probably have only one currency folder, containing the currency code and currency description for all currencies in use, probably using the ISO (International Organization for Standardization) set of currency codes. When users attempt to add currency codes into a query that is using multiple currencies, they need to be very careful to choose the correct link; otherwise, they could display the EURO code alongside the local amounts.

NOTE
While Discoverer will prompt for which join to make, it is down to the user to make the correct choice. Making a wrong join at this stage could cause the query to produce the entirely wrong result. You will have no choice but to rebuild the query, because once you have chosen a join, there is no going back.

For example, using our currency code model outlined previously, suppose you have a query that reports by both regional and local currencies. Next, we want to add the currency code for the local currency. When you try to add this item, Discoverer recognizes that there is more than one way to join to this folder and opens the Join Folders dialog box.

As you can see here, Discoverer tells you that there is more than one way of joining the folders you have selected. You should select the join that you want to use and click OK.

NOTE
This is a perfect example of why you need to take time to understand your data model. It is the responsibility of your Discoverer manager to display this model in terms that are meaningful to your job. Discoverer prompts you with the names of the joins. It is a poor implementation if your Discoverer manager chooses to display the primary- and foreign-key names, names that will probably be meaningless to you. It is your responsibility to know which join you need. A description of each join is displayed when selected to give you more information. If you have any doubt as to which one you should select, contact your Discoverer manager.

A new feature of 10.1.2 is the ability for Plus users to see the joins between the folders. To enable the viewing of join information in Plus, use the following workflow:

1. Launch Discoverer Plus.

2. Navigate to the Tools | Properties dialog box.

3. Click the Advanced tab. Discoverer displays the advanced options as shown in Figure 11-1.

4. Check the box called Show Joins.

5. Click OK.

Having enabled the viewing of join information, Discoverer Plus, shown in this illustration, shows the joins in the Available Items pane.

To summarize this section, when adding or removing items from a query with multiple join capabilities between the folders, you need to take extra special care. You need to make sure that you are fully aware of what joins are already being employed within the query.

Missing Joins

When you are attempting to add an item to your query, you may find that there is no join to the folder containing the item that you want. With many databases, there is usually more than one way to join folders together. First, you should see if there is a way to open up the folder you want by linking via an intermediate folder. If you cannot find a way to join to the folder that you want, you need to talk to your Discoverer manager.

FIGURE 11-1 *Discoverer Plus Advanced tab of Options dialog box*

The two most common reasons that you cannot join folders together are as follows:

■ The Discoverer manager did not expect this type of query to be used, and has not made the join available to you.

■ The Discoverer manager purposely did not make the join available to you, because it would result in incorrect aggregation or expose sensitive data.

In either of these cases, you should discuss your requirements with your Discoverer manager. He or she may be able to define a new join that will allow you to select the items that you need.

Fan Traps

The fan trap problem has plagued administrators for a very long time, and until the launch of version 4.1 of Discoverer a few years ago, the fan trap was one of the most feared situations that could arise. Prior to that release, all Discoverer could do was detect that a fan trap had occurred and then prevent the query from running.

In order to protect against the fan trap occurring, Discoverer has, as the default, an option to prevent you from building a query that contains fan traps. On the Advanced tab of the Options dialog box, as shown in Figure 11-1, you can see in the center that Discoverer has an option to disable fan trap detection.

NOTE
Unless you are very proficient at writing queries and know how to control fan traps, we strongly advise you not to disable this protection.

Oracle states that "Discoverer is the only product on the market that detects a fan trap, rewrites the query, and executes the query on the server." But does Discoverer really do this? We are very pleased to answer in the affirmative and will show you some example SQL later in this discussion.

But what is a fan trap? Put very simply, a fan trap is a SQL query that generates unexpected results. The most common manifestation occurs when a master table is joined to two detail tables separately and results in incorrectly aggregated measures. To the end user the definition is meaningless, yet the consequences can be catastrophic.

In the past, with the fan trap scenario you also needed to be careful when creating totals because Discoverer would generate incorrect values. This has now been resolved, and Discoverer will not compute a total or subtotal when a fan trap situation exists. Throughout the following section we will demonstrate this by including subtotals in all our examples.

Let us give you an example of what we mean by a fan trap. We have created a new business area that contains three folders: a Department folder, a Budget folder, and an Expense folder. The following three illustrations show the contents of each of these folders.

	Dept Number	Department
1	10	SALES
2	20	HR
3	30	MIS
4	40	MARKETING
5	50	TRAINING

This illustration that follows shows all of the data in the Department folder. As you can see, there are just five departments. We want you to concentrate on department 10, the Sales department. We will show you how the fan trap will cause this department's amounts to be calculated incorrectly.

The following illustration shows the data in the Budget folder. For each department, there is an allotted budget for the categories Equipment and Travel, along with the date the budget was set. We again draw your attention to the rows for department 10, the Sales department. As you can see, this department's budget for Equipment is 5,000, while for Travel their budget is 40,000. You can also see that subtotals have been enabled and that the totals are correct.

	▸ Dept Number	▸ Budget Date	▸ Budget Reason	▸ Budget Amount
1	10	04-NOV-2004	EQUIPMENT	5000.00
2		05-NOV-2004	TRAVEL	40000.00
3				Sum: 45000.00
4	20	06-NOV-2004	EQUIPMENT	2000.00
5		06-NOV-2004	TRAVEL	200.00
6				Sum: 2200.00
7	30	01-DEC-2004	EQUIPMENT	25500.00
8		01-DEC-2004	TRAVEL	10000.00
9				Sum: 35500.00
10	40	12-OCT-2004	EQUIPMENT	4250.00
11		12-OCT-2004	TRAVEL	25000.00
12				Sum: 29250.00
13	50	12-OCT-2004	EQUIPMENT	2090.00
14		12-OCT-2004	TRAVEL	200.00
15				Sum: 2290.00

The next illustration shows the data in the Expense folder. For some departments, there have been some expenses recorded. As you can see, for the Sales department, number 10, we have recorded three expenses so far, and inserted subtotals, so that department 10 has incurred a total amount of 1,400. Please make a note that there are no expenses for department 50 and so no data is displayed.

	▸ Dept Number	▸ Expense Date	▸ Expense Amount
1	10	13-OCT-2004	150.00
2		02-DEC-2004	250.00
3		14-DEC-2004	1000.00
4			Sum: 1400.00
5	20	28-NOV-2004	1025.00
6			Sum: 1025.00
7	30	14-DEC-2004	12000.00
8			Sum: 12000.00
9	40	12-DEC-2004	2750.00
10			Sum: 2750.00

Our intention is to build a query by pulling data from all three folders, with the notion of showing the total amount of budget and expenses incurred to date. For our sales department, we know that the total budget is 45,000, and the total expenses so far are 1,400.

First of all, we attempted to build the query with Discoverer's fan trap detection in place. In the following illustration, you can see that we have almost completed building the query. We have already selected the detail items that we want from the Department and Expense folders, and also included the total Budget Amount from the Budget folder. So far, so good, and as you can see from the next illustration, Discoverer is not only happy with our selections but has executed the query correctly and inserted subtotals.

NOTE

With the fan trap protection enabled, Discoverer will allow you to include as many detail items as you want from one of the parent folders. It will also allow you to include the total amount from the other folder.

	▸ Dept Number	▸ Expense Date	▸	Expense Amount	▸ Budget Amount
1	10	13-OCT-2004		150.00	45000.00
2		02-DEC-2004		250.00	45000.00
3		14-DEC-2004		1000.00	45000.00
4	Total			1400.00	
5	20	28-NOV-2004		1025.00	2200.00
6	Total			1025.00	2200.00
7	30	14-DEC-2004		12000.00	35500.00
8	Total			12000.00	35500.00
9	40	12-DEC-2004		2750.00	29250.00
10	Total			2750.00	29250.00
11	50	NULL		NULL	2290.00
12	Total				2290.00

Before we continue, we would like to draw your attention to a number of items. First, you will notice that even though there are no expenses for division 50, Discoverer has now included that item in the result. Second, take a close look at the subtotals that have been produced. You will notice that no subtotal has been generated for expenses against department 50, and that no subtotal has been produced for the budget against department 10. Can you see why?

The answer as to why no subtotal has been created for the expenses against department 50 is straightforward because, as previously mentioned, there are no expenses for that department. But why no budget total for department 10? This is because Discoverer has repeated the value 45,000 three times, once against each expense. If we were to attempt to add these, we would get the wrong answer.

The solution is to create a group sort on the budget total and then to subtotal only on the expenses. As you can see in the following illustration, we now have the correct answer, with the budget being displayed only once for each set of expenses. There is no ambiguity and no need to total the budget.

	▸ Dept Number	▸ Budget Amount	▸ Expense Date	▸	Expense Amount
1	10	45000.00	13-OCT-2004		150.00
2			02-DEC-2004		250.00
3			14-DEC-2004		1000.00
4					Total: 1400.00
5	20	2200.00	28-NOV-2004		1025.00
6					Total: 1025.00
7	30	35500.00	14-DEC-2004		12000.00
8					Total: 12000.00
9	40	29250.00	12-DEC-2004		2750.00
10					Total: 2750.00
11	50	2290.00	NULL		NULL
12					Total: NULL

Are you interested in the SQL that Discoverer has generated for this query? Discoverer has rewritten the SQL to use two subqueries to generate the results. In the two illustrations that follow, the first shows the SQL that Discoverer has generated, and the second shows the Explain Plan.

NOTE

To see the SQL and Explain Plan windows, use Tools | Show SQL.

If we now attempt to add another item from the Budget folder, for example the Budget Date, we are no longer querying the total budget by expense detail. We are now attempting to query the budget detail along with the expense detail. This is the scenario that Oracle is trapping. As expected, Discoverer will not allow this but displays an error message.

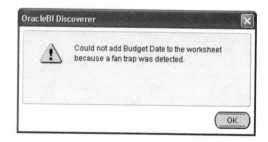

This error tells us that we are trying to create a query that pulls detail information from two parent folders at the same time. Oracle knows that this type of query usually generates incorrect results and so has inserted a trap for this.

In order to overcome this error, and to show you what happens when the fan trap is ignored, next we disabled the fan trap protection. We were able to build and run the query, but the results were totally incorrect. Look at this illustration closely.

	▸ Dept Number	▸ Budget Date	▸ Budget Reason	▸ Budget Amount	▸ Expense Date	▸ Expense Amount
1	10	04-NOV-2004	EQUIPMENT	5000.00	13-OCT-2004	150.00
2		04-NOV-2004	EQUIPMENT	5000.00	02-DEC-2004	250.00
3		04-NOV-2004	EQUIPMENT	5000.00	14-DEC-2004	1000.00
4		05-NOV-2004	TRAVEL	40000.00	13-OCT-2004	150.00
5		05-NOV-2004	TRAVEL	40000.00	02-DEC-2004	250.00
6		05-NOV-2004	TRAVEL	40000.00	14-DEC-2004	1000.00
7	Sum					
8	20	06-NOV-2004	EQUIPMENT	2000.00	28-NOV-2004	1025.00
9		06-NOV-2004	TRAVEL	200.00	28-NOV-2004	1025.00
10	Sum					
11	30	01-DEC-2004	EQUIPMENT	25500.00	14-DEC-2004	12000.00
12		01-DEC-2004	TRAVEL	10000.00	14-DEC-2004	12000.00
13	Sum					
14	40	12-OCT-2004	EQUIPMENT	4250.00	12-DEC-2004	2750.00
15		12-OCT-2004	TRAVEL	25000.00	12-DEC-2004	2750.00
16	Sum					

As you can see, we do indeed have all of the items in the query, but the answer we got for the Sales department is incorrect. If you add up the total amount budgeted for department 10, you will see that this comes to 135,000 (three times more than expected), while for expenses, the amount is 2,800 (twice more than expected). The reason that this has happened is that Discoverer has built a temporary table and made joins in the data for every occurrence of budget and expense (the master folders), by department (the detail folder). Budget is overstated threefold because there are three expense items. Expenses are doubled because there are two budget reasons. This query does not show us anything useful. We don't even get any subtotals being computed! So we abandoned this query and re-enabled the fan trap protection.

The final example of Oracle's fan trap resolution involves displaying the total budget by department alongside the total expenses. Even with the fan trap detection enabled, Discoverer is still able to generate this query. This is because once again Discoverer rewrote the SQL and used subqueries to generate the correct results. No alert was given during this process, and the illustration that follows shows the results of running the query. As you can see, the totals for both budget and expenses are correct.

	▸ Dept Number	▸ Budget Amount	▸ Expense Date	▸	Expense Amount	▸ Budget Date
1	10	5000.00	13-OCT-2004		150.00	04-NOV-2004
2			02-DEC-2004		250.00	04-NOV-2004
3			14-DEC-2004		1000.00	04-NOV-2004
4		40000.00	13-OCT-2004		150.00	05-NOV-2004
5			02-DEC-2004		250.00	05-NOV-2004
6			14-DEC-2004		1000.00	05-NOV-2004
7					Total:	
8	20	2200.00	28-NOV-2004		2050.00	06-NOV-2004
9					Total: 2050.00	
10	30	35500.00	14-DEC-2004		24000.00	01-DEC-2004
11					Total: 24000.00	
12	40	29250.00	12-DEC-2004		5500.00	12-OCT-2004
13					Total: 5500.00	

Lack of Documentation

Probably the one thing that will put you at the biggest disadvantage is a lack of adequate documentation. It is essential that you, and preferably your company, keep documentation about queries. It is very common to find users building queries, saving them, using them for a while, and then totally forgetting all about them.

At some point in the future there is a change requirement. Perhaps the person who created the query is no longer with the company, or you find a batch of queries sitting in a folder on your network and you have no idea who created them. So what do you do? What usually happens is that someone reinvents the wheel—sits down in his or her cubicle for several weeks and produces a complete new batch of queries.

Adequate documentation could have avoided some of this work. At least recording who did what and why, along with a specimen printout and a list of items and conditions, could have circumvented the need to draft a new batch of queries. If your company has not yet recognized the need for documenting Discoverer queries, that time will come.

When all is said and done, prevention is better than the cure. What a wonderful feeling you will have when you can sit back and relax while your coworkers document their queries, safe in the knowledge that your queries were all documented a long time ago.

Pivoting and Drilling

Pivoting and drilling are two of the really "nice to use" features of Discoverer. In an experienced user's hands, the tools can be made to manipulate data in ways that were undreamed of only a couple of years ago.

Pivoting Data

In Chapter 9, we showed you how to move items between the various axes. If you recall, there are three of these: the top axis, the side axis, and the page axis. Simple tables and crosstabs have both side and top axes, even if the side axis on a table is used only to display row numbers. Turning on Page Items opens up the third axis, the page axis.

NOTE
The Oracle development team refers to the top axis as the row-edge, and the side axis as the column-edge. We have included this comment just in case you may hear the axes being described this way in the future.

The term given to moving data between these axes is called *pivoting*. Using this technique, you can rearrange your data to reveal relationships that may not be apparent. To many people, pivoting is also known as "dicing."

If you are using Plus, you can perform what is called *interactive* pivoting. This type of pivot swaps items between axes.

In order to interactively pivot items in Plus, use the following workflow:

1. Decide on the two items that you wish to interactively pivot. For ease of explanation, we will call the first item the base item and the other item the target item.

2. Click one of the items and hold down the left mouse button.

3. Drag the base item on top of the target item.

4. Release the mouse button. You will see that Discoverer interactively pivots the two items.

Duplicating Tables and Crosstabs as New Worksheets

There are times when you will build a query that you think is just right and you don't want to touch it for fear of messing it up. However, you can see that with a few changes it will serve another purpose. You have two choices: you can save the workbook as a new file, leaving the original workbook intact, or you can duplicate the query within the workbook. It is a good idea to keep queries with a similar purpose together as a means of data management. Discoverer has made it very easy to duplicate queries as new worksheets within the same workbook.

You can duplicate either a crosstab or a table as a table. You do this through the Duplicate as Table dialog box. The Duplicate as Table dialog box is identical to the Edit Sheet Worksheet dialog box; however, when you finish making your refinements and click OK, you will have a new worksheet in your workbook.

Duplicating a Worksheet as a Table in Desktop

You have three methods of opening the Duplicate as Table dialog box in Desktop:

- From the menu bar by clicking on Sheet | Duplicate as Table.

- From the toolbar by clicking the Duplicate as Table button.

- From a pop-up list, which you access by right-clicking the Sheet tab at the lower-left corner of the worksheet and clicking Duplicate as Table.

Duplicating a Worksheet as a Table in Plus

You have two methods of opening the Duplicate as Table dialog box in Plus:

- From the menu bar, select Edit | Duplicate Worksheet, and then click Duplicate as Table.

- From the toolbar, click the drop-down alongside the New Worksheet button, and from the list select Duplicate as Table.

Duplicating a Worksheet as a Crosstab in Desktop

The method for duplicating a worksheet as a crosstab is virtually identical to that for a table. These are the only differences:

- From the menu bar, select Sheet | Duplicate as Crosstab.

- From the toolbar, click the Duplicate as Crosstab button shown here.

- From a pop-up list, which you access by right-clicking the Sheet tab at the lower-left corner of the worksheet and clicking Duplicate as Crosstab.

Duplicating a Worksheet as a Crosstab in Plus

The method for duplicating a worksheet as a Crosstab is virtually identical to that of a table. The only differences are

- From the menu bar, select Edit | Duplicate Worksheet, and then click Duplicate as Crosstab.

- From the toolbar, click the drop-down alongside the New Worksheet button, and from the list select Duplicate as Crosstab shown here.

Renaming Worksheets

If you are going to have multiple worksheets in a workbook, it is a good idea to give them meaningful names. Discoverer gives them the default names of Sheet 1, Sheet 2, and so on. It is a simple task to rename the sheets, and it will help to keep you organized within the workbook. We like meaningful names, and Discoverer will allow you to give the sheets very long names. However, just as with filenames, don't get carried away, because if you use too long a sheet name, you will not be able to see the tabs of the other sheets without using a set of navigation arrows in the lower left of the workbook.

Renaming Worksheets in Discoverer Desktop

You can access the Rename Sheet dialog box in the following three ways:

- From the menu bar, by clicking on Sheet | Rename Sheet.

- From a pop-up list, which you access by right-clicking the Sheet tab at the lower-left corner of the worksheet and clicking Rename Sheet.

- By double-clicking the Sheet tab at the lower-left corner of the worksheet.

To rename a worksheet, use the following workflow:

1. Use one of the preceding methods to open the Rename Sheet dialog box.

2. Type in the new worksheet name.

3. Click OK.

Renaming Worksheets in Discoverer Plus

The Rename Sheet dialog box that you have been used to working with in Desktop has been replaced with the much more comprehensive Worksheet Properties dialog box, which has three tabs. Here you can set sheet gridlines color, row numbers, inline-outline mode, and worksheet description, and you can also view the Worksheet identifier and a description. Using the Aggregation tab, you can change the way that Discoverer Plus computes totals. If you find that Discoverer fails to compute a total, you can use this tab to alter the way that the computations are calculated.

To rename a worksheet in Discoverer Plus, use the following workflow:

1. Double-click the Sheet tab at the lower-left corner of the worksheet. This opens the Worksheet Properties dialog box shown here:

2. Click the General tab.

3. Type in the new worksheet name.

4. Click OK.

Drilling Into and Out of Data

Drilling into and out of data is a technique that enables you to view more data about a related item. Drilling is also a shortcut for adding another item to your query. For example, suppose you have a query that shows all votes cast for each person in a presidential election and you want to see how those votes were cast in each state. Discoverer will allow you to view this data with a few clicks of the mouse, without having to rebuild the query. Drilling can be done from the Drill dialog box or directly from a drill icon located alongside the headings in your result set.

Compared to previous releases of Discoverer, drilling has been significantly enhanced in 10.1.2 Plus. You can now drill to any item in the same folder(s) even if those items are not available in the current hierarchy. This gives you yet another way of adding items to a worksheet, even from Viewer!

Drilling in Desktop

To drill within Desktop, use the following workflow:

1. Click in the cell, row, or column containing the data you want to drill from.

2. Right-click and select Drill from the drop-down list, or select Sheet | Drill from the menu bar. This opens the Desktop Drill dialog box, as seen in Figure 11-2.

3. Make the desired selections.

The Desktop Drill dialog box has the following features:

- **Drill Up/Down**   Click this radio button to drill to an item in the "Where do you want to drill to?" selection box. If there are no items available in the selection box, the OK button will be disabled. This option allows you to drill to items that belong to a predefined hierarchy, such as Customer Name to a Region to District. An exciting aspect of Discoverer's drilling capabilities is that you can drill to any level in the hierarchy, skipping the levels you don't need. You can even do filtered drills. This ability to drill up or down a hierarchy is available within the Plus Drill dialog box, and also directly from within the heading of any item that is part of a hierarchy.

- **Drill to a Related Item**   Click this radio button to drill up or down to an aggregate level to data that is related but is not part of a predefined hierarchy, such as Customer Name to Order Number or City Name to Address. Discoverer will restrict the list of drillable items to only those items that exist within the folders that form the basis of the original query. This ability to drill to a related item is available within the Plus Drill dialog box, and also directly from within the heading of any item in Plus.

- **Drill to Detail in another Sheet**   Click this radio button to drill to data in another worksheet. When you click OK, Discoverer opens a New Sheet dialog box that initially contains all of the items that come from the folders in the original query. Before completing the New Sheet dialog box, you should remove unwanted items and rearrange the order. This ability to drill to detail in another sheet is also available within the Plus Drill dialog box.

- **Where do you want to drill from?** The row or column that you were in when you opened the dialog box will appear as the default. To change the item to be drilled from, click the down arrow for a drop-down list of available items. Depending upon whether the item now selected is part of a predefined hierarchy, the content of some of the other boxes may change.

- **Where do you want to drill to?** This is a list of available drill items. The content of the list varies, depending upon other selections you make within the dialog box. For example, if you check the Drill Up/Down box and select to drill from an item that is part of a predefined hierarchy, this box will contain a list of the items in the hierarchy. Beside each item will be an arrow, indicating whether you can drill up or down to that item. If you opt to drill to a related item, this box will give you a list of the remaining items in the folders used in the current worksheet. Use this to add single items to your worksheet. If you opt to drill to detail in another sheet, this box displays "Show component rows of selected values" as the only option.

- **Options** Clicking this button opens the Desktop Drill Options dialog box, as seen in Figure 11-3.

NOTE
Discoverer remembers the settings you make in the Drill Options dialog box, and it uses these as the default each time you drill. Even if you don't open the Drill Options dialog box, these options will still be applied.

FIGURE 11-2   *The Desktop Drill dialog box*

FIGURE 11-3 *The Desktop Drill Options dialog box*

The Desktop Drill Options dialog box allows you to customize the drill results. As shown in Figure 11-3, the Desktop Drill Options dialog box consists of the following areas:

- **When drilling to a new item, current item is** This area allows you to either expand the query to include the new item or replace the current item with the new item.

- **Place drill results in** Here, you decide whether you want the drill results to be displayed in the current worksheet or in a new worksheet.

- **Display results as** If you want to display the results in a new worksheet, in this area
you can decide whether to display them as a table or a crosstab.

- **Before query is run** Tick this box if you want to modify the new worksheet before it runs. When you complete the drill by clicking OK in the Drill dialog box, Discoverer opens the New Sheet dialog box. This box is identical to the Edit Sheet dialog box and allows you to make any edits and modifications you want before the query runs.

Drilling in Plus
To drill within Plus, use the following workflow:

1. Click in the cell, row, or column containing the data you want to drill from.

2. Right-click and select Drill from the drop-down list, or select Tools | Drill from the menu bar. This opens the Plus Drill dialog box, as seen in Figure 11-4.

FIGURE 11-4   *The Plus Drill dialog box*

The Plus Drill dialog box has the following features:

■ **Where do you want to drill from?**   Use the drop-down list to select the item you want to drill from.

■ **Where do you want to drill to?**   This drop-down list has four options: Drill Up/Drill Down, Drill to a Related Item, Drill to Detail, and Drill to Link. The drill selection box, located immediately below the drop-down, changes depending upon the selection chosen from the list. Apart from the Drill to Link option, the other three options work the same way as the selections that you can make in the Desktop Drill dialog box described in the previous section. If drill links to other worksheets or to a URL have been enabled, when this option is selected you will be able to drill out using those links.

■ **Show Advanced**   Clicking this button opens the extended version of the Plus Drill dialog box, as shown in Figure 11-5.

The Plus extended Drill dialog box has the same functionality as the Desktop Drill Options dialog box but is much tidier and easier to work with. This extended box has the following features:

■ **Expand sheet to include new item**   Check this radio button if you want Discoverer to expand the sheet to include the new item. This is only available if you select Drill Up/ Drill Down or Drill to a Related Item.

■ **Replace current item**   Check this radio button if you want Discoverer to replace the existing item with the item being drilled to. This is only available if you select Drill Up/ Drill Down or Drill to a Related Item.

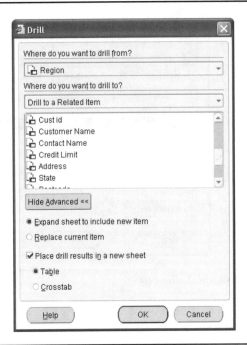

FIGURE 11-5 *The Plus extended Drill dialog box*

- **Place drill results in a new sheet**   Check this box if you want to place the drill results in a new sheet. Having checked this box, you then have to decide whether the new sheet should be a table or a crosstab. If you select Drill to Detail, this box will be checked by default. In addition, the new sheet type will default to the same worksheet you are drilling from. This option is available for all drill types except Drill to Link.

Plus has no equivalent of the Desktop "Let me modify query before proceeding" button. Therefore, if you opt to see the results of the drill in a new worksheet, after clicking OK, the new worksheet will be created immediately, the query executed and the results displayed. Further, if you chose Drill to Detail, every single item within the folders used in the current worksheet will now be included within a new worksheet. This can result in a very cumbersome and unwieldy report, especially if you elected to create a new crosstab. Unless your Discoverer administrator has paid dutiful attention when assigning the default positions of data items within the EUL, you may well find that you end up with dozens of items in the top axis of a crosstab, effectively creating an unusable worksheet. You therefore need to take great care when drilling to detail in a new worksheet.

Drilling from Within the Heading
Drilling directly from within the heading of an item can be done whenever you see the drill icon being displayed alongside the heading. The drill icon looks like a small triangle.

NOTE
In Desktop, the drill icon is only displayed whenever the item is part of a predefined drill hierarchy. In Plus, the drill icon is always available.

There are three types of drilling available from within the heading:

■   Drill using a predefined drill hierarchy

■   Drill to related

■   Drill by collapsing the data

Drill Using a Predefined Drill Hierarchy   If the item is part of an existing drill hierarchy, Discoverer will enable the drill icon. Clicking this item allows you to drill to another item within the hierarchy. When drilled, the new item will be included within the current worksheet.

Drill to Related   This type of drill, accessible from within Plus only, is available from within the heading of every item in the worksheet. When selected, Discoverer displays a pop-up list of all items that exist within the folders that form the basis of the original query. Clicking on an item causes Discoverer to include that item within the current worksheet. You cannot select multiple items for inclusion. If you want to include multiple items, you need to repeat the drill for each item.

NOTE
If you get into the habit of keeping the Available Items pane open, you will find that it is far easier to add items to your worksheet from this pane than by using the drill to related method.

Drill by Collapsing the Data   This type of drill, accessible from a Plus crosstab only, is available from within the group sorted items in the side axis. When the pop-up list of drill options is displayed, a new option, called Collapse, will be inserted into the list. If you choose this option, Discoverer will remove all of the remaining side items for the row you are in, effectively displaying a subtotal for the item you just collapsed.

Be careful using Collapse, because once collapsed the only way to get the worksheet back into its original state is to undo the drill by using Edit | Undo from the menu bar. If you execute multiple consecutive collapses, only the last collapse can be undone. To rectify this situation, you will have to edit the worksheet, remove all of the collapsed items, and then add them back in.

NOTE
Do not save worksheets that contain collapsed items. Because Discoverer handles the collapse by creating multiple SQL statements, if you save a worksheet that has collapsed items, the next time you open that worksheet, Discoverer will be forced to execute multiple SQL queries before it can display any results. This is a very common reason for extremely poor worksheet performance.

Drilling into Data from a Graph

Discoverer allows you to drill into data from a graph. This is a clever feature for those of us who are visual in the way that we work. Graph drilling is also available in both Plus and Viewer with 10.1.2. You can now single-click (or double-click, depending on where you are in the graph) and drill to a greater or lesser level of detail. Graph drilling follows a drill-and-replace model of drilling. You can choose to drill from the axis labels, from the legend, or even from the series bars (in the case of bar graphs).

To drill into data from a graph, use the following workflow:

1. From the graph that you have created, double-click the item that you want to drill from. This opens the Drill dialog box.

2. Determine the type of drill that you want to do.

3. Click the Options button in Desktop or the Show Advanced button in Plus to define whether you want to add items in a new sheet.

4. If you are going to use a new sheet, in the New Sheet dialog box, remove any items that are not required and define any other criteria that you want to use.

5. Click OK.

For example, we have a pie graph (see the following illustrations, which first of all show the results in Desktop and then in Plus) showing the status of all of our sales for Q3 of 2005.

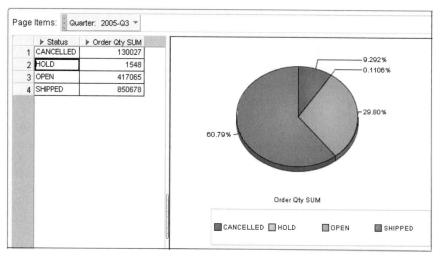

We can see instantly that the cancellations for that quarter are extremely high. When compared to the other totals, cancellations make up the third largest order quantity. Looking then at the third largest piece of the pie graph, it is evident that cancellations are making up over 9 percent of the total. We want to know why this is so, and we will use Discoverer's drill capability to find out. The process for doing this is simple. Because you are already familiar with the Drill dialog box, we will not explain it again here. However, we will show you the end result of drilling into data from a graph.

First, we double-clicked in the graph on the Cancellations wedge in the pie. This opened the Drill dialog box. Because we wanted to see more of the detail associated with the cancellations, we opted to display the results in a new sheet. As we believe that analysis is easier in a crosstab, this is the type of worksheet that we selected. Before we completed the drill, we edited the new worksheet and removed the items that did not appear to be of interest. The resulting crosstab is shown next.

Hyper-Drilling

Hyper-drilling allows a user to drill out from the current worksheet to either another worksheet or a URL. You can use the drill-to-worksheet feature to drill down from a high-level report to see a lower level of data, or from a lower-level report to roll up into a higher level of aggregation. The drill-to-URL feature allows a user to drill to an Internet page. Using this feature, you could, for example, decide to drill out to a customer's web site or to one of your own company intranet pages.

If you are using Discoverer Plus for OLAP, you can even drill into a relational worksheet, passing the context of the OLAP worksheet to the drilled worksheet using parameters. When drilling to other worksheets like this, you can choose to drill to either Plus or Viewer. For more detailed information regarding OLAP, please see Chapter 16.

The individual drill itself, as seen in Desktop, Plus, and Viewer, is called a *drill link*. Multiple drill links can exist at the same time, thus enabling you to drill out to several worksheets and, if you so wish, several URLs. You can follow only one drill path at a time and cannot simultaneously drill out in more than one direction at the same time.

NOTE
User-defined hyper-drills can be created only in Plus. Once they are created, though, you can use any of the end-user tools, Desktop, Plus, or Viewer, to execute that drill.

A third type of hyper-drill exists, but this one gets created for you by the Discoverer manager. This type of hyper-drill allows a user to drill out to a file. Using this type of drill, you could, for example, drill out to open the customer's contract (stored as a Microsoft Word file), to view the customer's latest credit report (stored as an Excel spreadsheet), or even to send an e-mail to your customer contact via your e-mail system. This section of the book will focus on the hyper-drills that an end user can create. We will cover Discoverer manager–created hyper-drills later in the book.

As previously mentioned, these are the hyper-drills a user can create:

- Drill out to another worksheet.

- Drill out to a URL.

Drilling Out to Another Worksheet

To effectively drill from one worksheet to another takes a little planning and forethought. We recommend that you take some time to think about what drills you intend to create. In other words, step back and try to see the big picture. You cannot create a hyper-drill if you have nowhere to drill to, so when creating a worksheet hyper-drill, you need to have created and saved the lower-level worksheet first. We know this sounds obvious, but you would be surprised how many people miss this step and jump right into creating the higher-level worksheet.

NOTE
The two worksheets can be in the same workbook or in different workbooks. While the choice is yours, we recommend that you think carefully before mixing worksheets with differing intents in the same workbook.

Having created the drill-to worksheet, you can now create the drill-from worksheet. First of all, we will show you what the hyper-drill looks like in use. In the following example, we created two workbooks, Drill Master and Drill Detail. The Drill Master, as you can see in the next illustration, shows the selling price by Region and District.

Drill Master - All Regions

	▸ Region	▸ District	▸ Selling Price
1	EUROPE	▸ EU-EAST	7,623,655
2	EUROPE	▸ EU-NORTH	47,977,651
3	EUROPE	▸ EU-SOUTH	28,554,612
4	FAR EAST	▸ FE-ALL	32,548,685
5	NORTH AMERICA	▸ NA-NORTH	95,115,056
6	NORTH AMERICA	▸ NA-SOUTH	40,278,515
7	SOUTH AMERICA	▸ SA-ALL	22,572,670

If you take a closer look at the cells in the District column, you will notice that there is a small upright triangle alongside the data in each cell. This is the hyperlink button. Clicking this pops up a list of the available hyperlinks. As you can see next, in our case we have only one link, a link that allows us to Drill to Year.

Drill Master - All Regions

	▸ Region	▸ District	▸ Selling Price
1	EUROPE	▸ EU-EAST	7,623,655
2	EUROPE	▸ EU-NORTH	47,977,651
3	EUROPE	▸ EU-SOUTH	28,554,612
4	FAR EAST	▸ FE-ALL	32,548,685
5	NORTH AMERICA	▸ NA-NORTH	95,115,056
6	NORTH AMERICA		278,515
7	SOUTH AMERICA	▸ ░ Drill to year	2,572,670

If this link is followed in Viewer or Desktop, a second worksheet is automatically opened, displaying the selling price by year for the District that was chosen in the higher-level worksheet. In Plus you will get a warning telling you that you are about to close the current worksheet and open another one. You will be prompted "Do you wish to continue?"

OracleBI Discoverer

⚠ This action will close the current workbook. The following workbook and worksheet will be opened:

Workbook: DRAKE.Drill Detail
Worksheet: Price by Year

Do you wish to continue?

Yes   No

If you click Yes, Discoverer will close the current worksheet and open the drilled-to worksheet. Discoverer will also pass on any parameter or cell values as necessary. Following the link through to the lower-level workbook, you can see that Discoverer displays the selling price by year for the district that we clicked in the higher-level worksheet.

Drill Detail - Price by Year

Page Items: Region: NORTH AMERICA ▾

	▸ District	▸ Year	▸ Selling Price
1	NA-SOUTH	FY1998	935,035
2	NA-SOUTH	FY1999	844,362
3	NA-SOUTH	FY2000	2,062,873
4	NA-SOUTH	FY2001	2,192,424
5	NA-SOUTH	FY2002	4,391,377
6	NA-SOUTH	FY2003	6,855,802
7	NA-SOUTH	FY2004	13,557,250
8	NA-SOUTH	FY2005	9,439,393
9			40,278,515

Building a Hyperlink to Another Worksheet

To build a hyperlink to another worksheet, follow this workflow:

1. Build the lower-level worksheet and note the parameters that you wish to pass.

2. Create and save a higher-level worksheet.

3. Execute the higher-level worksheet so that data is displayed on screen.

4. Locate the cell from where you wish your users to be able to drill.

5. Right-click the cell and, from the pop-up menu, select Manage Links. The Manage Links dialog box, as shown in Figure 11-6, will now open.

6. The Manage Links dialog box is the place where you create, edit, delete, or reorder the links in your worksheet. It has the following areas:

   ■ **Item**   This is the name of a worksheet item.

   ■ **New Link**   Click this button to create a new hyperlink.

   ■ **Edit Link**   Click this button to edit an existing hyperlink.

   ■ **Delete Link**   Click this button to delete an existing hyperlink.

   ■ **A set of move up / move down buttons**   If there are multiple links from the same items, these buttons allow you to order the list of links. You can move an item up or down one place, or you can move an item to the top or to the bottom of the list.

   ■ **OK**   Click this button to save the changes that you have made and return to Discoverer Plus.

7. Click the New Link button. This opens the New Link dialog box as shown in Figure 11-7.

8. The New Link dialog box is where you create a new hyperlink. It has the following areas:

   ■ **What would you like to name this link?**   Type a meaningful name into this area. The name that you type here is the name that will appear in the list of hyperlinks when the user clicks in the cell.

FIGURE 11-6   *Manage Links dialog box*

FIGURE 11-7   *The New Link dialog box for drilling to a worksheet*

- **Where do you want to link to?**   Your valid options are Worksheet and URL. Use the drop-down button to change the selection.

- **Destination**   This area will be displayed only when you are creating a URL link. Discoverer automatically inserts the characters "http://" and is waiting for you to type the remainder of the URL.

- **Destination Workbook**   This area will be displayed only when you are creating a worksheet link. Use the Browse button to select the workbook containing the worksheet that you wish to use.

- **Destination Worksheet**   This area will be displayed only when you are creating a worksheet link. It will be accessible only after you have selected the workbook that contains the worksheet you wish to use. Use the drop-down button to select the worksheet you will be using.

- **Parameters**   If the worksheet that you are drilling to has parameters, you can optionally choose what values Discoverer will pass to those parameters whenever the user drills through. You are not mandated to preassign any parameters. If you choose not to preassign the parameters, then the user who is following your link will be required to supply the parameters at run time. However, should you decide to preassign parameters, and we recommend that you do, click the Parameters button. Discoverer will display the Parameters dialog box shown next.

9. The Parameters dialog box enables you to preassign values to the parameters that exist in the lower-level worksheet. You assign one of the following values:

- The parameter that was accepted as input to the current worksheet, or

- The cell value from the current worksheet

10. To pick a value to pass to the next worksheet, click the drop-down button alongside the parameter. Discoverer will now display the valid values that can be passed. These will be displayed in the following order:

- Data points

- Cell values

- Parameter values

11. Continue assigning values to the parameters in the lower-level worksheet. When all parameters have been assigned a value, click OK to close the New Link dialog box. Then, click OK to close the Manage Links dialog box.

NOTE
The OK button will be grayed out until you have completed the New Link dialog box.

Drilling Out to a URL

Drilling out to a URL is very straightforward. If the worksheet that you are in contains a URL hyper-drill, you will know because Discoverer displays a different icon than for a worksheet hyper-drill. In this illustration you can see two hyper-drills, one for a worksheet and one for a URL:

Building a Hyperlink to a URL

To create a hyperlink to a URL, follow this workflow:

1. Build the lower-level worksheet and note the parameters that you wish to pass.

2. Create and save a higher-level worksheet.

3. Execute the higher-level worksheet so that data is displayed on screen.

4. Locate the cell from where you wish your users to be able to drill.

5. Right-click the cell and from the pop-up menu, select Manage Links. The Manage Links dialog box, as shown earlier in Figure 11-6, will now open.

6. Click the New Link button. This opens the New Link dialog box as shown in Figure 11-8.

Pass values from the worksheet to the URL

FIGURE 11-8   *New Link dialog box for drilling to a URL*

7. The New Link dialog box is where you create a new hyperlink. It has the following areas:

 ■ **What would you like to name this link?**   Type a meaningful name into this area. The name that you type here is the name that will appear in the list of hyperlinks when the user clicks in the cell.

 ■ **Where do you want to link to?**   Your valid options are Worksheet and URL. Use the drop-down button to change the selection to URL.

 ■ **Destination**   This area will be displayed only when you are creating a URL link. Discoverer automatically inserts the characters "http://" and is waiting for you to type the remainder of the URL.

8. Click OK to complete the New Link dialog box.

9. Click OK to close the Manage Links dialog box.

Drilling Out to an Application

If you are used to working with an Internet browser, you will know that a link such as "file:///C:/ Book/pfile.txt" will work. Unfortunately, Discoverer's end-user URL hyperlink functionality does not allow drilling to an application in this method. Do not despair, however, because your Discoverer manager can create hyper-drills to external applications. As mentioned earlier, we will not explain how to create these in this section, as this functionality will be explained later in the book.

So how can you tell if your Discoverer manager has created an application hyperlink for you? The answer to this depends upon whether you are using Desktop, Plus, or Viewer to execute the query.

Drilling to a File in Desktop

If you are using Desktop, Discoverer displays the name of the file that it will call and also inserts an icon alongside the item. If you are familiar with previous versions of Desktop, you will be disappointed to know that the application icons that used to be displayed no longer appear to be used. Now only one icon is shown for all file types, the same icon that is used for hyper-drilling to a worksheet.

Drilling to a File in Plus

In Plus, Discoverer displays the same icon as displayed in Desktop. However, Discoverer does not display the name of the file that will be called. If the worksheet is a table and you place your cursor over a cell that contains a hyperlink, Discoverer will show you the file that it will call. If the worksheet is a crosstab, you need to click the icon and then select Drill to Link from the pop-up box. Only then will Discoverer show you the name of the file that it will call.

Drilling to a File in Viewer

In Viewer, Discoverer displays only the same icon that is displayed in Desktop and Plus. When the icon is clicked, a very small blank box opens up beneath the icon. If you click this box, Discoverer will attempt to display the file that is listed.

NOTE
Neither Plus nor Viewer seem to be able to call the e-mail application. This seems to be the domain of Desktop, and this limitation is a great pity because the ability to e-mail from within Discoverer is one of Desktop's best, if little known, features.

Summary

In this chapter you have been shown how to further manipulate your queries to make them more powerful. You have been shown how to add and remove items from your queries and the most common problems associated with doing so. We have also shown you the fan trap and how to avoid it, as well as possible solutions to this problem.

You have been taught how pivoting data items between axes allows you to view the same data in different ways. You were also shown how sometimes when pivoting the data items there are no data points displayed at all. It happens to us all, so work with it and become more expert; then, your queries can become more meaningful.

We showed you how to duplicate tables and crosstabs. This is a simple process, and because so many queries can be created using almost the same data, you should give it a try. This will keep you from creating almost the same workbook over and over and help you to organize your work. Another method of organization is renaming workbooks within worksheets. You have been taught how a few simple steps will save you time and possible frustration in the future.

Finally, you were shown how to drill into data to "dig deeper" into a data item. Drilling is an excellent way to get a closer look at a particular piece of the data. You also learned how easy it is to drill from a graph. Using the visual approach can sometimes keep you from missing something that would not jump out at you if it were viewed only as numbers or text.

In the next chapter, you will learn the power of creating conditions, from the simple to the complex.

CHAPTER
12

Building Effective Conditions

fter refining the query items, and pivoting the data, perhaps the next most common way to refine a query is to refine the conditions. The ability to add, edit, or remove conditions is one of the things you need to master in order to become an expert in Discoverer.

In Chapter 4, we introduced you to the Workbook Wizard. One of the essential steps that you were shown was setting user-defined conditions. However, in that chapter, we advised you to only create enough conditions to avoid "The Query from the Twilight Zone." Those conditions were very simple. In this section, we will show you how to build effective conditions and explain all of the options that are available to you.

Adding Conditions

The most frequently used way of adding conditions is to use the Conditions dialog box, but as you will see in this section, this is not the only way.

There are, in fact, three ways to add conditions to a Discoverer query. These are as follows:

■ Using Show Values from a drop-down list

■ Using the conditions area buttons on the analysis bar

■ Clicking New in the Conditions dialog box

Using Show Values to Add a Condition in Desktop

This menu item is probably one of the least known yet, at the same time, one of the best features of Discoverer Desktop. It is also one of the easiest ways to create new conditions. While this feature has not yet been added to Plus, in Plus you have the Available Items and Selected Items panes that you do not have in Desktop.

NOTE
Conditions can be created, using Show Values, only for items that have a list of values. If you have a data item that does not have a list of values, you should ask your Discoverer administrator if it is possible to have such a list made available. Until a list of values exists, you will not see the Show Items menu option.

Whenever you add conditions using this method in Desktop, Discoverer opens the Values dialog box. As shown in Figure 12-1, this dialog box consists of the following features:

■ **Select values for** Discoverer displays the full list of values for the item concerned, along with a check box indicating whether the item is already being used in the query. If there is no active condition currently in use for the item concerned, Discoverer automatically checks all of the boxes. If there is a condition on the item, Discoverer checks only those items that are constrained by the current condition. Discoverer then allows you to manually check and uncheck items using the mouse.

■ **Select All** Check this box if you want Discoverer to include all values for the item in your query.

- **Select None**   Check this box if you want Discoverer to include no values at all for the item in your query. Doing this and clicking OK causes Discoverer to return nothing. This option should be used only as a means of clearing the current selections, before manually selecting the items that you want.

To use Show Values to add a new condition to a query, use the following workflow:

1. Right-click the heading for any axis item that has a list of values.
2. From the drop-down menu, select Show Values. This opens the Values dialog box as displayed in Figure 12-1.
3. Make the desired selections.
4. Click OK. Discoverer will now create a condition based upon your selections and then rerun the query.

Let's show you how quickly you can modify a query and add new conditions using Show Values. We have started out with a very simple query containing just the department name, department number, expense amount and expense date, and no conditions. This caused Discoverer to display a list of all expenses currently on file. There are only six of these, and you can see here that this is a very simple query:

	Dept Number	Department	Expenses	Expense Date
1	10	SALES	150.00	13-OCT-2004
2	10	SALES	250.00	02-DEC-2004
3	10	SALES	1000.00	14-DEC-2004
4	20	HR	1025.00	28-NOV-2004
5	30	MIS	12000.00	14-DEC-2004
6	40	MARKETING	2750.00	12-DEC-2004

To demonstrate how easy it is to add a condition using Show Values, we right-clicked the heading for the department name and selected Show Values from the drop-down list. This opened the Values dialog box. Examining the contents of the box, you can see (in Figure 12-1) that all of the departments, as we would expect, are checked.

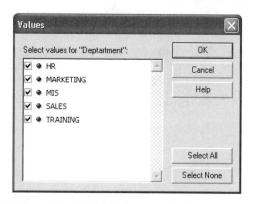

FIGURE 12-1   *Discoverer Desktop Values dialog box*

Next, we unchecked the box alongside the MIS department.

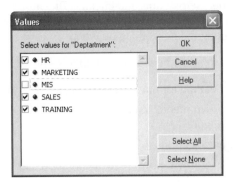

After we clicked OK, Discoverer reran the revised query, omitting the MIS department from the result. Opening the Conditions dialog box, you can see that Discoverer has indeed created a new condition for using the IN expression.

Let us now revise the query again, by once more opening the Values dialog box and changing the criteria for the department. This time we will check the MIS department but uncheck both Marketing and Training. Taking a close look at the Conditions dialog box that follows, you can see that Discoverer did not amend the original condition. Instead, Discoverer created a new condition and deactivated the original one.

To make the situation even more complicated, we reopened the Values dialog box and re-created the situation as it was a few steps ago. That is, we checked all departments except MIS. Looking at the following illustration, you can see that Discoverer has created a third condition and deactivated the second one.

This new condition has exactly the same constraint set as the first condition that we created, yet Discoverer did not recognize this. This fault of Discoverer—to not be able to detect that a condition already exists—is the only drawback that we can see to stop us recommending that you always create conditions using Show Values.

Be aware when using Show Values that these conditions are created when using the IN expression. When using IN, you are restricted to using 254 items. If you have more than 254 items, Discoverer will report an error. You will have to use a different construct, perhaps using a complex condition.

Adding Conditions Using the Toolbar

The analysis bar in Discoverer Desktop and the Conditions toolbar button in both Desktop and Plus offer you another way to create conditions.

As we explained in Chapter 9, the Desktop analysis bar has four areas. The fourth area, shown in Figure 12-2, is what we call the "conditions area." Chapter 9 introduced you to the analysis bar and gave a brief description of each of the four areas.

In Plus, there is no separate analysis bar; instead, there are four buttons on the toolbar, each with its own unique set of drop-downs. Each drop-down contains the buttons that are available on the Desktop analysis bar. We think this is a great idea, as it requires fewer toolbar buttons and allows for more viewable real estate space for building and executing your query. Figure 12-3 shows the Conditions button and its drop-down of condition types.

The conditions area of the toolbars have seven buttons, one each that allows you to create conditions based on whether terms are equal (=), nonequal (<>), less than (<), less than or equal

FIGURE 12-2 *Conditions area of the Desktop analysis toolbar*

FIGURE 12-3 *Conditions drop-down area of the Plus toolbar*

to (<=), greater than (>), or greater than or equal to (>=), plus a button to launch the Conditions dialog box itself. In Desktop, the first six buttons are active only when a column, row, or cell is highlighted. In Plus, these six buttons are always active. In both versions, however, the Conditions button is always active.

> **NOTE**
> *In Plus, if you click one of the six buttons without a column, row, or cell being highlighted, Discoverer opens the New Condition dialog box and waits for you to define the condition manually. This is another great feature and one we are sure you will love.*

Using the Buttons to Create a New Condition in Desktop

Clicking one of the first six condition buttons opens the New Condition dialog box, which is described later in the chapter. When you enter the box as a result of clicking one of the buttons, you will find that all three of the basic components of a condition (the item, the expression, and the value) have been completed for you. All that is required to complete the condition is to click OK.

As we explained, clicking in a data cell or a column or row heading activates the main Conditions buttons on the analysis bar. We gave you a simple example of its use in Chapter 9, but to save your having to go back to that section, we will give you that workflow once again.

To create a condition using the Desktop analysis bar, use the following workflow:

1. Click either a column or row heading, or in any cell.
2. Click the button for the condition you want to apply. Discoverer opens the New Condition dialog box and fills in as much information as it can.
3. Amend the condition if required.
4. Click OK. Discoverer now creates the condition and executes the query.

> **NOTE**
> *If you want to make other changes to the query, you must cancel the running of the query. To do this, click Cancel while the query is running. When prompted to return the query to its original state, click No.*

Let us give you an example. We built the following crosstab of total quantity ordered, by product by order status. As you can see, all of the buttons in the conditions area of the analysis bar, except the Conditions button itself, are inactive.

All six condition buttons are inactive.

Conditions button itself is active.

Let's assume that we wanted to print the order quantities for what is currently open. We need to have a condition where the status = OPEN. This is a very simple condition to build. Following our workflow outlined earlier,

1. We clicked on the cell containing the status OPEN. This caused Discoverer to activate the conditions buttons.

2. We next clicked on the = button. This opened the New Condition dialog box. As you can see here, Discoverer correctly populated the Item, Condition, and Value(s) boxes for us.

Item filled in correctly with Status

Condition filled in with =

Value automatically filled in with OPEN

3. There is nothing to amend, because Discoverer has created everything that we need.

4. To complete the condition, we clicked OK. As you can see, Discoverer adjusted the query for us and created a list of only the open order quantities. We could now send this list to our planning department, which would ensure that we had enough purchase orders to satisfy the demand.

	Status	Order Qty SUM OPEN
Product		
AB-2000		37257
AB-2500		45570
AB-3000		42290
AVR-500		114069
AVR-550		82009
AVR-800		28114
AVR-900		56843
CD-100		92580
CD-200		86372
CD-500		16196
CD-550		25104
CD-625		126417
DS-1200		7880
DS-1300		23280
MS-1200		46180
MS-1300		18988

NOTE
One word of caution when using the conditions buttons: As for Show Values, Discoverer is not smart enough to recognize that a condition already exists. If we repeat the preceding exercise, clicking Open, followed by the = symbol, Discoverer will create another condition identical to the first.

Using the Toolbar Buttons to Create a New Condition in Plus

Using the toolbar buttons to create new conditions in Plus is more intuitive and requires fewer steps than in Desktop. It is fully automated with the click of a button. This does not, however, mean that you cannot refine the condition later.

To create conditions with the Plus toolbar buttons, use the following workflow:

1. Click either a column or row heading, or in any cell.

2. Click the button for the condition you want to apply. The conditions will be applied automatically.

If you have the Available Items pane open, click the Conditions tab and look in the area called My Conditions. You will see that a condition has been created and that it has a check mark to the side of the condition name. This means that the condition is in use. If the condition needs refinement, you can open it for editing.

NOTE
If you have the Selected Items pane open, you will also see the condition get added to the list of selected items.

We will use the same example we gave in the preceding section on Desktop. We built the following crosstab of total quantity ordered, by product by order status.

	Status	Order Qty SUM			
		▶ CANCELLED	▶ HOLD	▶ OPEN	▶ SHIPPED
▶ Product Name					
▶ AB-2000		71214	2	37257	801835
▶ AB-2500		66459	0	45570	702499
▶ AB-3000		90184	5600	42290	783092
▶ AVR-500		159651	5075	114069	1259079
▶ AVR-550		58400	10	82009	731468
▶ AVR-800		41470	40	28114	311735
▶ AVR-900		51466	600	56843	543121
▶ CD-100		79670	3600	92580	882011
▶ CD-200		85287	15488	86372	776394
▶ CD-500		56100	7200	16196	468575
▶ CD-550		58410	3800	25104	332898
▶ CD-625		167503	4169	126417	1737998
▶ DS-1200		85160	0	7880	480315
▶ DS-1300		38869	200	23280	456926
▶ MS-1200		90872	0	46180	669671
▶ MS-1300		11220	0	18988	299855
▶ QB-1000		49413	1202	16610	376841
▶ QB-2000		14383	272	43204	443678
▶ QB-3000		41838	1200	42436	497706
▶ QB-5000		47512	601	105732	829472
▶ QB-5500		78311	100	57401	826267
▶ QB-6000		143041	401	85899	819411

Let's assume that we wanted to print the order quantities for what is currently open. We need to have a condition where the status = OPEN. This is a very simple condition to build. Following our workflow outlined earlier,

1. We clicked the cell containing the status OPEN.

2. We next clicked the drop-down arrow for the Conditions button and selected = Equals from the drop-down list. The query runs automatically and creates a list of only the open order quantities. We could now send this list to our planning department, which would ensure that we had enough purchase orders to satisfy the demand.

NOTE
As with Desktop, Discoverer Plus is not smart enough to recognize that a condition already exists. If we repeat the preceding exercise, Discoverer Plus will create another condition identical to the first.

Using the Conditions Dialog Box to Add a Condition in Desktop and Plus

The third way to add new conditions to your query is via the Conditions dialog box. In fact, if you want to use Advanced conditions, these can only be created using the Conditions dialog box. To open this box, use one of the following three methods:

■ Click the Conditions button from the analysis bar in Desktop, or click the Conditions toolbar button in Plus.

■ From the menu bar, select Tools | Conditions.

■ Use the Conditions tab on the Edit Sheet / Edit Worksheet dialog box.

In Plus only, there is a fourth way to add a new condition:

■ From the Available Items pane, click the Conditions tab and then from anywhere in the pane, right-click. From the pop-up you should select New Condition.

Creating a Condition Using the Conditions Dialog Box or Conditions Tab

When creating conditions using the Desktop Conditions dialog box or the Plus Conditions tab, you should use the following workflow:

1. If you are working in Plus, click the New Condition button on the toolbar. The New Condition dialog box will open, and you should proceed to Step 4.

2. If you are working in Desktop, click the Conditions button on the analysis bar. The Conditions dialog box will open. If you know the item on which you want to build the condition, from the View Conditions for drop-down list of the Conditions dialog box, select the item you want to apply the condition to. If you do not yet know the item, or you want to choose an item that is not being used within the worksheet, proceed to the next step.

3. In Desktop click New.

4. Discoverer will open the New Condition dialog box, as shown in Figures 12-4 and 12-5. In Desktop, Discoverer automatically inserts the item you selected in Step 2 into the Item field of the formula area. In Plus, Discoverer automatically inserts the item from the cell that you were in when you launched the New Condition dialog box.

5. If this is not the item that you want, or if there is no item shown, select one now from the drop-down list. A detailed explanation of the choices available to you at this point is given later in this chapter when we deal with the basic components of a condition.

6. From the Condition drop-down list, select the expression you want to apply to the item. By default, Discoverer inserts the expression =. The available expressions are explained later in this chapter when we deal with the basic components of a condition.

7. In the Values box, type in the value(s) you want Discoverer to constrain the item on, or from the drop-down list select one or more values. This drop-down list, in addition to a list of values, also contains options to select multiple values, create a calculation, select an item, create a new parameter, and create a new subquery. These options are explained in detail later in this chapter when we discuss the basic components of a condition.

NOTE
In Plus, Discoverer automatically inserts the item value from the cell that you were in when you launched the New Condition dialog.

8. Make sure the box entitled Match case in Desktop, or Case-sensitive in Plus, is checked. The reason for this is explained later in this chapter when we discuss the New Condition dialog box in detail.

9. If you want to define an advanced condition, click the Advanced button. Discoverer's advanced condition features are discussed later in this chapter.

10. If the name that Discoverer has generated for you is not to your liking, uncheck the box entitled Generate name automatically and type a suitable name for the condition into the Name box.

11. Enter a description, if desired. This is optional. Remember that if others will use this worksheet, giving a description to the condition will help them decide if they should use it or not. Adding a meaningful description will also help you in the future when you are asked to modify the worksheet.

NOTE
We advise you to listen to the voice of experience and add meaningful descriptions whenever you can. These are an invaluable part of your documentation. No matter how good your memory is, we guarantee that you will never be able to remember why you created all conditions. Anyway, you need to think of your successor and be as complete as you can with your documentation. After all, you don't want to be responsible for your organization's workbooks forever, do you?

12. Click OK to close the New Condition dialog box.

13. If you are using Desktop, you will be returned to the Conditions dialog box, where you will see your condition highlighted in the list of conditions. To execute the condition, you need to close the Conditions dialog box by clicking OK.

14. If you are using Plus, the condition will automatically be applied to the worksheet and you will see that the condition has been added to the list of conditions in the Conditions tab of both the Available and Selected Items panes.

FIGURE 12-4   *Discoverer Desktop New Condition dialog box*

FIGURE 12-5 *Discoverer Plus New Condition dialog box*

The New Condition Dialog Box

The New Condition dialog box is shown in Figures 12-4 and 12-5. This box consists of the following features:

- **Name** Discoverer automatically generates a name for your condition based on the criteria that you use to build the condition. Normally, the name given by Discoverer will suffice. However, Discoverer will allow you to create your own name, but only if you uncheck the box described next.

- **Generate name automatically** By default, Discoverer names conditions for you, and it does this very well. Uncheck this box only if you want to name the condition yourself; then go back to the Name box and type in your own name.

- **Description** For simple queries, the name generated by Discoverer is more than adequate for identifying what will happen when a condition is selected. There are occasions, however, when using complex conditions, that the name alone will not be sufficient. When the name generated by Discoverer does not accurately convey what will happen when the condition is selected, you should type in a description here.

- **Location** In case you have forgotten in which workbook you are working, Discoverer Desktop inserts the name of the current workbook here. Discoverer Plus also has a Location, but it is not labeled. You will see the workbook name under the Case-sensitive button.

- **Item** A drop-down list of available items, upon which you can base the condition. You must select something here; otherwise, Discoverer will be unable to create your condition. A full explanation of the options open to you is given in the next section. An example of an item is the ship date.

■ **Condition**   A drop-down list of expressions, from which you have to select one. A full
list of all available expressions is given in the next section. An example of an expression
is the = symbol, such that the condition now looks like "ship date =."

■ **Value(s)**   Another drop-down list. This time, there is a list of values, from which you
must select one or more in order to complete the condition. For example, we could enter
the date 01-AUG-2004, thus completing our condition to be ship date = 01-AUG-2004.
A full explanation of all available values is given in the next section.

NOTE
*The previous three components are the three required elements of
any Discoverer condition. The next section explains each of these in
detail. Remember also that when you enter values that are dates or
text, you must enter them inside single quotes.*

■ **Advanced**   Click this button if you want to access the advanced features associated with
creating conditions. These are explained in detail later in this chapter.

■ **Match case/Case-sensitive**   Uncheck this box only if you do not want Discoverer to
match the case values in your query. Normally, you would not want to uncheck this,
especially if you have selected from a list of values to begin with.

NOTE
*Queries will take much longer if you uncheck this box. In the authors'
experience, it is not uncommon to find query times increasing by
200 percent or more. This is because Discoverer is creating the query
exactly as instructed, by ignoring match case, and therefore causing
the database to search for all possible combinations of the value.
For example, say we were searching for the name 'Michael' in our
condition but did not check the "Match case" or "Case-sensitive" box.
The database would scan for 'Michael', 'michae', 'MICHAEL', and
all combinations of the uppercase and lowercase values of the seven
letters in the name! You can see how long this would take and how
much of an impact this would have on your own queries.*

Basically, the burden is being switched to the database. Discoverer itself does not scan for all
combinations, but you will add a burden to the database. Look at the following sample code:

The original SQL:

```
WHERE (i100155 IN ('Central','East'))
GROUP BY i100155, i100195, i100203
```

With the Match Case unchecked:

```
WHERE (UPPER(i100155) IN (UPPER('Central'), UPPER('East')))
GROUP BY i100155, i100195, i100203
```

Building a Simple Condition Using the Workflow

Following the previous workflow, we will show you how to create a simple condition using the New Conditions dialog box in Plus. We will follow each step exactly as specified.

We have a query that reports, for all products and statuses, the total quantity shipped and the margin. There are no conditions in this query so far, but we want to add one that shows the margin only when the product has shipped.

Step 1 of the workflow requires us to launch the New Condition dialog box. If possible, you should have placed the focus into the cell on which you want to place the condition. In this example, we want the condition to be on the Status. The following illustration shows the New Condition dialog box with the item we selected already populated:

New Condition

What would you like to name your condition?

☑ Generate name automatically

What description would you like to give your condition?

Formula

Item	Condition	Values
⋮ Gs Sales.Status ▾	= ▾	▾

Advanced >>

☑ Case-sensitive

This condition is located in the workbook 'Workbook 2'.

Help   OK   Cancel

Step 5 says that if the item displayed is not the item that we want to base the condition on, we should pick another item. In this case, the item that we want is the Status, so we will proceed to Step 6.

Step 6 of the workflow is where we set the expression. As Discoverer has already inserted the default of =, there is no need for us to pick an expression, so we will proceed directly to Step 7.

In Step 7, we have to open the drop-down list and select the value that we want to constrain the status on. As we are not building a complex condition, only a simple condition, we will just select the status SHIPPED from the list of values. As you can see in the following illustration, when we opened the drop-down list, we were presented with a number of options, below which is the list of values from which we selected SHIPPED.

Values
'SHIPPED' ▾
Create Calculation...
Select Item...
New Parameter...
Select Multiple Values...
☐ ◉ CANCELLED
☐ ◉ HOLD
☐ ◉ OPEN
☑ ◉ SHIPPED

NOTE

For an explanation of all of the options in the drop-down list, please read ahead to the section that explains the basic components of a condition.

Step 8 requires us to make sure that Match case in Desktop or Case-sensitive in Plus is checked. By default, it is checked. The next three steps—for creating advanced conditions, naming the condition, and giving the condition a description—are not required. Therefore, we will proceed directly to finishing the condition. All that remains now is for us to click OK. At this point, Discoverer will rerun the query and apply the condition that we have just created.

If you follow the preceding workflow, you will quickly master the art of building simple conditions. Advanced conditions are more difficult and are dealt with later in this chapter.

The Basic Components of a Condition

As stated in the previous section, three basic components must be supplied for all Discoverer conditions. Without these components, Discoverer will be unable to build your condition. The three components are as follows:

- The item upon which the condition is based

- The expression being applied to the item

- A value (not always required)

In this section, we will take an in-depth look at these three basic components.

Basic Component 1: The Item

When building a condition, you must specify the item you want Discoverer to use. You do this in one of two ways:

- Outside the New Condition dialog box

- Inside the New Condition dialog box

Specifying an Item Outside the New Condition Dialog Box

How to specify the item that Discoverer must build the condition on from outside of the New Condition dialog box depends on whether you are using Desktop or Plus.

In Desktop you must select the item from the drop-down list of the Conditions dialog box. After that, you should click New. Discoverer will then open the New Condition dialog box and populate the Item field with whatever item you chose.

In Plus you need to make sure that the item has the focus before you click the New Condition button. Discoverer will then open the New Condition dialog box and populate the Item field with whatever item you chose. We showed you how to do this in the preceding section.

NOTE

The drop-down list of items in the Desktop Conditions dialog box contains only the items that are used within the worksheet. However, in the drop-down list of items in the New Condition dialog box, you can select from all of the items contained in the folders used in the worksheet.

Specifying an Item Inside the New Condition Dialog Box

Specifying the item inside the New Condition dialog box gives you more flexibility. This method should be used in any of these cases:

- You are not 100 percent sure which item you want to use in your condition.

- You want to build the condition on an item that is not currently used within the worksheet.

- You want the item to be a calculation (advanced condition).

- You want the item to be a predefined or user-defined condition (advanced condition).

To build conditions based on the preceding types, use the drop-down list inside the New Condition dialog box. Doing this, you will always see at the top of the list an option to create a calculation. If you have other conditions available, whether they be predefined or user-defined, you will also see an option to use these. The list will also contain all of the available items in the query, whether or not you have included them in your worksheet selections.

For example, suppose you have a folder containing ten items, and you include five of these in your worksheet. Opening the drop-down list of items inside the New Condition dialog box will display all ten items.

Building conditions based on other conditions or calculations will be explained later in this chapter when we discuss advanced conditions.

Basic Component 2: The Expression

The second basic component that you must supply, when building a condition, is the expression. Table 12-1 lists all of the available expressions.

NOTE
The expressions IS NULL and IS NOT NULL do not require a value.
The Value field is removed when you select one of these expressions.

Discoverer will automatically change the expression if the value you subsequently pick is incompatible with the current expression. For example, if you select = and then select two or more items from the list of values, Discoverer will change the expression to IN. This is because = takes only a single value, whereas IN can take single and multiple values.

Basic Component 3: The Value

The third basic component of a condition is the value. As you have seen in the preceding section, most, but not all, conditions take a value. If you select the expression BETWEEN, Discoverer will expect you to provide two values, a lower or start value and a higher or end value. It is up to you to ensure that the end value is indeed higher than the start value, because Discoverer will not validate your condition. So if you build a condition where the start date is between 31-DEC-2005 and 01-JAN-2005, you will get no rows returned. If you do not spot this, for example when accepting begin and end values via parameters, your users could be fooled into thinking that there is no data.

Symbol	Description	Examples
=	The item must equal the value.	Ship Qty = 15000
<>	The item must not equal the value.	Ship Qty <> 15000
>	The item must be greater than the value.	Ship Qty > 15000
<	The item must be less than the value.	Ship Qty < 15000
<=	The item must be less than or equal the value.	Ship Qty <= 15000
>=	The item must be greater than or equal the value.	Ship Qty >= 15000
LIKE	The item must match the value. You can use wildcards to find like values. The value must be enclosed in single quotes. Wildcards are valid but can be used only with text strings. In Oracle, the % sign indicates that everything after this is ignored. For those familiar with Microsoft, the % character equates to the asterisk (*). In Oracle, the _ (underscore symbol) matches a single character. For those familiar with Microsoft, the underscore equates to the question mark (?).	City Name LIKE 'D%'. This will return both Dallas and Denver. Product LIKE 'B_t'. This will return both Bat and Bit but not Bet.
IN	The item must be in one of the values. The values must be separated by commas and enclosed in brackets.	City IN ('Madrid','San Francisco','Tokyo'). This will find data that is in at least one of these cities.
IS NULL	The item must equal the NULL value. This expression returns values only when the named item is null (no value whatsoever, not even zero).	Cancel Date IS NULL. This returns only rows of data that do not have a Cancel Date.
IS NOT NULL	The item must not equal the NULL value. This expression returns values only when the named item is not null.	Ship Qty IS NOT NULL. This returns only rows of data when there is a ship quantity.
NOT IN	The item must not be in the set of values. The values must be separated by commas and enclosed in brackets.	City NOT IN ('Madrid','San Francisco','Tokyo'). This will find data for all cities except those listed.
BETWEEN	The item must be within the range of values defined. All data that is between the two values will be returned.	Ship Date BETWEEN '01-JUN-2006' and '30-JUN-2006'. This will find all shipments that took place in the month of June. Note that both the start and end dates are included.
NOT BETWEEN	The item must be not fall within the range of values defined. All data that is outside of the two values will be returned.	Ship Date NOT BETWEEN '01-JUN-2006' and '30-JUN-2006'. This will find all shipments excluding those that took place in the month of June. Note that both the start and end dates are excluded.
NOT LIKE	The item must not match the value. You can use wildcards to omit like values. The value must be enclosed in single quotes. Wildcards are valid but can be used only with text strings.	City Name NOT LIKE 'D%'. This will exclude both Dallas and Denver.
!= ^= (Desktop only)	Identical to <>	This works the same as <>, but because some versions of SQL do not support SQL, Discoverer offers you these alternatives. You should always use <> if available.

TABLE 12-1 *Available Expressions*

Having selected the item on which to build a condition, and the expression, you should click in the Value field. Unless you created the condition using one of the condition buttons on the analysis bar, the Value field will be blank.

If you know the value that you want, you can type it in; otherwise, open the drop-down list. Depending on whether the data item has a list of values, the drop-down list does not always give the same options. When there is no list of values, the options are as follows:

- Create Calculation...

- Select Item...

- New Parameter...

- Create Subquery... (Desktop only)

When there is a list of values, the preceding options are supplemented by

- Select Multiple Values...

- The list of values

NOTE
Until you have selected an item upon which to base the condition, you will not be able to see the drop-down list options for values. This is because Discoverer needs to ascertain whether a list of values is associated with the item. Even with a list of values you can choose to ignore the LOV and select one of the other options.

Create Calculation

This option opens the Edit Calculation dialog. This box is identical to the New Calculation dialog box that was described in Chapter 5. Creating calculations as part of a condition is described later in this chapter, while stand-alone calculations will be dealt with when we show you how to refine calculations in Chapter 13.

Select Item

This option opens the Items dialog box. This box lists all of the items in the folders used in the worksheet. You could reverse the contents of the Item and the Value fields, by inserting, for example, 'SHIPPED' in the item, and selecting 'STATUS' from the list of items. You can also create conditions that use two items, such as shipped date equals ordered date, so that you can analyze all of the orders that shipped the same day that they were ordered.

New Parameter

This option opens the New Parameter dialog box. Use this box to convert a condition into a parameter, or define a new parameter for your worksheet. Defining parameters from the Workbook Wizard was covered in Chapter 5, while converting conditions into parameters will be covered in Chapter 13.

NOTE
The New Parameter option cannot be used unless you have chosen an item from a folder. If you have typed in a value, such as SHIPPED, into the item field, Discoverer will not allow you to create a parameter based on this.

Create Subquery (Available in Desktop Only)

This option opens the Create Subquery dialog box. You use this box to apply a condition on an item or value that is in another worksheet. Discoverer will let you associate a condition with an item in an existing worksheet, or it will allow you to create a brand-new worksheet for the purpose.

The use of subqueries can be thought of as an advanced form of condition. This topic is covered in detail later in this chapter.

NOTE
Oracle has not added subqueries to Plus, although they will be included in the next release Plus. However, subqueries created in Desktop will work in Plus. They cannot be edited or maintained in Plus, though, as only Desktop has this ability. In many instances, the use of hyper-drilling will eliminate the need for subqueries altogether. Please refer to Chapter 10 for details on how to set up and manage hyper-drills.

Select Multiple Values

This option, available only if a list of values has been defined for the item, opens up the Values dialog box, as seen earlier in Desktop in Figure 12-1 and in Plus in Figure 12-6. Use of the Desktop version of this dialog box was covered in the first part of this chapter when we explained creating conditions using Show Values. The difference between opening the Values dialog box using Show Values and doing so using Select Multiple Values is that Show Values checks the items that are currently in use, whereas Select Multiple Values displays all values unchecked.

In the Plus version, as seen in Figure 12-6, you select and deselect items by dragging them between the Available and Selected boxes. Alternatively, you can also use the paste buttons to move items between the boxes. If the list of items is large but you know the items that you want to select all begin with the same character(s), you should use the Search By and Search For boxes in conjunction with the Go button to restrict the list to only the subset that you want to work with.

FIGURE 12-6 *Discoverer Plus Select Values dialog box*

The exception to this is if you have already selected items from the list of values and then clicked Select Multiple Values—the values previously selected will remain selected. For example, we have selected from the list of values the status OPEN. We then clicked Select Multiple Values and, as you can see in the following illustration, OPEN has remained selected.

The List of Values

When an item has a list of values, in Desktop Discoverer displays all of the items, which could take a while if the list has a lot of values. In Plus, however, as you can see from this illustration, if the list contains more than 100 items, Discoverer displays the items in groups of 100 at a time. The forward and back buttons at the bottom of the screen will cause Discoverer to display the previous or next 100 rows. The number 100 is not cast in stone but is controlled by your Discoverer manager. As an organization, if you do not want to go with the default of 100, you should choose how many items should be fetched in any one set. Be careful not to set this too high; otherwise, Discoverer will time out while fetching the list of values.

NOTE
Remember, when you are using the BETWEEN expression, you must provide two values, a lower or start value, and a higher, end value. Discoverer does not check the validity of the start and end values. If you enter an end value that is lower than the start value, Discoverer will accept the condition but will return no data.

Editing an Existing Condition

Another technique commonly used when refining queries is to edit an existing condition. In this situation, you are neither adding nor removing existing conditions, just changing an existing definition. If you find that the same query constantly needs modifying just to edit a single condition, we recommend you change that condition into a parameter. Changing conditions into parameters is dealt with in detail in Chapter 13.

To edit an existing condition, use the following workflow:

1. Open the Conditions dialog box in Desktop or select the Conditions tab from the Available Items Pane in Plus.

2. From the list of conditions displayed, highlight the condition you want to edit.

3. Click the Edit button, or additionally in Plus right-click the condition and from the pop-up list select Edit. This opens the Edit Condition dialog box.

4. Change the condition as required.

5. Click OK to exit from the Edit Condition dialog box. In Desktop, click OK again to exit from the Conditions dialog box.

NOTE
As stated earlier, if you realize at this point that you have made a mistake and edited the wrong condition or changed it incorrectly, you can reverse the changes by clicking Edit | Undo Conditions or pressing CTRL-Z. Do not do anything else; otherwise, you will not be able to undo your mistake. This is because Discoverer allows you to undo, or redo, only the last action that you did.

When you have completed editing the condition, Discoverer will execute the query and display the new results. In Desktop you can change multiple conditions and the query will execute only when you exit the Conditions dialog box. In Plus, however, there is no Conditions dialog box, and unless you uncouple the database from the query or use the Edit Worksheet dialog box, the query will execute every time you change a condition.

To uncouple Discoverer Plus from the database, from the menu bar, select Tools and uncheck the box called Auto Refresh. You can now change as many conditions as you wish and Discoverer will requery the database only when you click the Refresh button on the tool bar.

Another way to maintain multiple conditions in Plus without executing the query every time is to launch the Edit Worksheet dialog box by using Tools | Conditions from the toolbar. As Discoverer opens the Edit Worksheet dialog box, it will navigate to the Conditions sub-tab on the Select Items tab. You can now change or create as many conditions as you wish. When you have finished working with your conditions, click OK to close the Edit Worksheet dialog box. Discoverer will now re-query the database.

Using Advanced Conditions

Probably the most daunting aspect of creating or editing conditions is knowing how to use advanced conditions effectively. Following the workflow given earlier in this chapter, it is very easy to create simple conditions. To fully master Discoverer, you need to spend time learning how Discoverer handles complex, advanced conditions.

Using Discoverer, we have identified the following four types of advanced conditions:

- Conditions based on calculations
- Conditions based on other conditions
- Conditions using Boolean operators
- Conditions using subqueries

Creating Conditions Based on Calculations

As you saw earlier in this chapter, when we discussed the three basic components of a condition, both the Item and the Value drop-down boxes have options to create calculations. In this section we will show you how this is done.

There are two ways of creating conditions based on calculations. These are

- Using an existing calculation
- Creating a new calculation as part of the condition

There, in a nutshell, is the reason why Discoverer allows you to create two types of conditions based on calculations.

Using an Existing Calculation

Existing calculations will appear in the list of items, even if they are not being displayed in the final output. If you base a condition on an existing calculation and then delete the calculation from the worksheet by deleting the column, the condition can still use the calculation. You can even create a new condition based on the calculation.

However, if you delete a calculation from the Calculations dialog box, it can no longer be used. Any conditions that used that calculation are also deleted. Conditions based on existing calculations are therefore vulnerable because the calculation could accidentally be deleted, unaware that it is used in a condition. Discoverer will not warn you that you are deleting a needed calculation. Unless you realize it in time and do an Undo (CTRL-Z), once the damage is done, you will have to start over!

To use an existing calculation within a condition, use the following workflow:

1. Open the New Condition dialog box.
2. In the Item field, open the drop-down list.
3. From the options provided, select the calculation.
4. Set the expression and value you require.
5. Click OK.

Let us give you an example. We built a query of shipments, showing order number and quantity shipped, sorted by order number. We next added a profit calculation, being defined as the sum of the selling price minus the sum of the cost price. The following illustration shows how this looks:

	▸ Order Number	▸ Ship Qty SUM	▸ Profit
1	1059	10000	113700.00
2	1060	1200	10848.00
3	1061	1000	9040.00
4	1062	1920	29702.40
5	1063	1920	29702.40
6	1064	48	301.44
7	1065	50	338.00
8	1066	10000	113700.00
9	1067	1600	18496.00
10	1068	8400	97104.00
11	1069	10000	115600.00
12	1070	15000	280650.00
13	1071	200	3742.00
14	1072	1200	11196.00
15	1073	1200	11196.00
16	1074	1200	13236.00

Next, we opened the New Condition dialog box. From the drop-down list of items we selected the profit, as you can see here:

Finally, as shown here, we selected the expression > (greater than) and entered a value of 20000.

After we clicked OK, Discoverer ran the query using the condition just created, and the query was constrained to show only orders with a profit greater than 20,000.

Creating a New Calculation as Part of the Condition

Calculations created as part of a condition will not appear in the list of items, nor will they be listed in the Calculations dialog box. They exist only as part of the condition and cannot be manipulated outside of the condition. Calculations created this way will be used only internally by the condition; they cannot be displayed as a column of the worksheet, nor can they be used in other conditions. If you delete the condition, the calculation is also deleted.

Because these calculations are created as part of the condition, they are not vulnerable to being accidentally deleted.

To build a condition, with a calculation created as part of it, use the following workflow:

1. Open the New Condition dialog box.

2. From the options provided, select Create Calculation. This opens the Edit Calculation dialog box.

3. Create the calculation.

4. Click OK. This returns you to the New Condition dialog box.

5. Set the expression and value you require.

6. Click OK.

Using the same query of shipments we used in the example for creating conditions based on an existing calculation, we will show you how to create the same condition. This time, however, we will create the calculation from within the New Condition dialog box.

After opening the New Condition dialog box, we selected Create Calculation from the Item drop-down list. In Plus, as you can see here, Discoverer opens the New Calculation dialog box:

NOTE
In Desktop the box is called the Edit Calculation dialog box.

Looking at the preceding illustration, you will notice that this box looks almost identical to the standard New Calculation dialog box. However, if you look closely and you are in Desktop, you will notice that the Name field is deactivated. In Plus, as shown in the illustration, Discoverer suppresses the name altogether. This is because the calculation belongs to the condition that created it. It cannot be used in any other context and, therefore, needs no name.

As you can see in the illustration, we have also created the profit calculation. This is the sum of the selling price minus the cost price. Looking at the illustration, you will see that we used the SUM function to build the calculation.

After clicking OK, we were returned to the New Condition dialog box. In here, we entered the expression > and a value of 20000. In the completed condition, the calculation displays in its entirety in the Item field, obviating the need to name the calculation, shown here:

After we clicked OK, Discoverer ran the query using the condition just created, and the query was constrained to show only orders with a profit greater than 20,000.

Creating Conditions Based on Conditions

The second of the advanced types of conditions is to create a condition based on an existing condition. Whether these existing conditions are administrator- or user-defined is irrelevant. The important thing you need to know is that Discoverer allows you to create these conditions. Extending your skill set to include creating conditions based on other conditions will greatly enhance your expertise in Discoverer.

Perhaps the simplest way to explain why you would even bother to build a condition based on another is as follows. If you have created, or have available to you, multiple existing conditions, and you are using more than one of them at the same time, Discoverer will apply an AND between each one.

For example, let's say you have two conditions in your worksheet, an administrator-defined one, which constrains the order quantity to be greater than 15,000, and a user-defined condition limiting the status to just SHIPPED. In the Conditions dialog box, you can only decide whether to use or not use these conditions. If you check both of them, Discoverer will select data only when both of the conditions are true. However, what if you want your query to return data when one or the other condition is true, such as order quantity > 15000 OR status = 'SHIPPED'? The only way to do this is to create a new condition, based on both of these conditions, combining them with the Boolean operator OR.

As you have seen in the Item drop-down list, one of the options is to use Select Condition. To build a condition based on another condition, use the following workflow:

1. Open the New Condition dialog box.

2. From the options provided, choose Select Condition. In Desktop, this opens a dialog box entitled Conditions. Don't confuse this dialog box with the Conditions dialog box. In Plus, the dialog box is more appropriately named Select Condition. The box that has been opened here merely contains a list of the available conditions upon which you can base another condition.

3. From the list, select the condition you want to use.

4. Click OK. This returns you to the New Condition dialog box, with both the Expression and Value fields removed. At this stage, you could click OK, but all this will do is create another condition with the identical functionality to the original. What you should do instead is use Discoverer's advanced features and use Boolean logic to combine the existing condition with something else, perhaps another condition.

5. Click Advanced. This opens an extended version of the Edit Condition dialog box, in which you should create a Boolean condition (see the next section for details on how to do this).

6. When you have finished creating the Boolean condition, click OK.

Using the example just outlined, the following illustration shows a worksheet with the two existing conditions, order quantity > 15000 and status = 'SHIPPED'. With both conditions checked, we would see only eleven rows of data. Discoverer has applied the Boolean operator AND between the two conditions.

However, we don't want to see only the rows that satisfy both conditions; we want to see all orders with an order quantity > 15000 OR a status of SHIPPED. By creating a new condition that combines both of the existing conditions, we can do just that.

Therefore, we will open the New Condition dialog box, and from the Item drop-down list we will take the option Select Condition. This opened the Select Condition dialog box shown in this illustration. As you can see, both of our existing conditions are available to use.

We selected the first condition and clicked OK. As you can see next, this inserted the condition into the New Condition dialog box and removed both the Expression and Value fields.

Next, we clicked Advanced. This opened the extended New Condition dialog box, as seen in the following illustration. This box, and all its functionality, will be explained in the next section when we deal with Boolean conditions.

In order to combine the two existing conditions, we need to add the second condition to the one that is already selected. To do this, we clicked the New Item button. In Desktop the button is labeled Add; however, the functionality is the same. Discoverer has changed the display of the dialog box and inserted another set of the three basic components of a condition, as you can see in the following illustration:

Not quite done. To add the second condition, from the new Item drop-down list we again chose Select Condition. From the list of available conditions, we selected the second one and clicked OK. This resulted in the following illustration. As you can see, Discoverer has now combined the two conditions into one, using the Boolean operator AND.

Almost there! We now have to change the Boolean operator to OR. To do this, we clicked the AND joining the two conditions, and from the drop-down list we selected OR. In Desktop you will need to click the Or button.

We then clicked OK to save this new condition. In Plus the new condition was added to the list of conditions in the Conditions tab and the query was re-executed. To complete our worksheet we right-clicked each of the two original conditions and from the pop-up menu selected Remove from Worksheet. Our final Conditions tab looks like this.

In Desktop, however, you will be returned to the Conditions dialog box without executing the query. All you need to do now is to deselect the two original conditions and then click OK.

As you can see in the next illustration, the result of running with this condition is quite different from the eleven rows that we started with:

	Status	Order Number	Order Qty SUM
1	OPEN	2822	16000
2		3134	24000
3		3392	34800
4		3394	30000
5	SHIPPED	1059	10000
6		1060	1200
7		1061	1000
8		1062	1920
9		1063	1920
10		1064	48
11		1065	50
12		1066	10000
13		1067	1600
14		1068	8400
15		1069	10000
16		1070	15000

Where the two conditions match exactly, we see all data values displayed. However, where only one or the other condition is true, the values that correspond to the false condition are displayed as NULL.

NOTE
Don't forget to deselect the existing conditions upon which you have created the new condition. If you forget this, Discoverer will give you a result based on the combination of all three conditions.

Using Boolean Operators

The third of Discoverer's advanced types of conditions uses Boolean operators. We touched on this subject in the previous section, when we showed you how to combine conditions using Boolean operators. In this section, we will explore the whole gamut of Boolean operators and show you how to make effective use of them.

First, if you are not familiar with Boolean operators, we will give you a brief explanation. Boolean algebra, a system of symbolic logic dealing with operands, was devised by G. Boole (1815–1864), an English mathematician. This system includes any logical operation in which each of the operands and the result take one of the two values, true or false. These operations form the basis of logic gates in computers.

Within Discoverer there are operands and operators. An operand is anything that equates to a true or false value, such as status=shipped, or quantity > 15000. An operator is a symbol that allows you to make a connection between operands, such as status=shipped AND quantity > 15000. Discoverer allows you to use the operators AND, OR, and NOT.

Now that you understand the concept of Boolean operators, it is a straightforward task to convert these into conditions. We will show you how to build both simple and complex Boolean conditions. Before you start building complex conditions, you should check that there are no existing conditions that will satisfy what you are trying to do.

Creating Boolean Conditions

When creating Boolean conditions, use the following workflow:

1. Open the New Condition dialog box.

2. Because you know you will be creating a Boolean condition, click Advanced. This opens the extended New Condition dialog box as shown in Figures 12-7 and 12-8.

3. Create a condition, or use the Item drop-down list to create a new calculation or select an existing condition. This step creates the first part of the Boolean condition.

4. Click Add in Desktop or New Item in Plus to create or insert another condition.

5. Set the Boolean operator you want to be applied between the conditions.

6. Repeat Steps 4 and 5, adding new conditions and operators, until you have created the desired complex condition.

7. Click OK.

FIGURE 12-7 *Desktop extended New Condition dialog box*

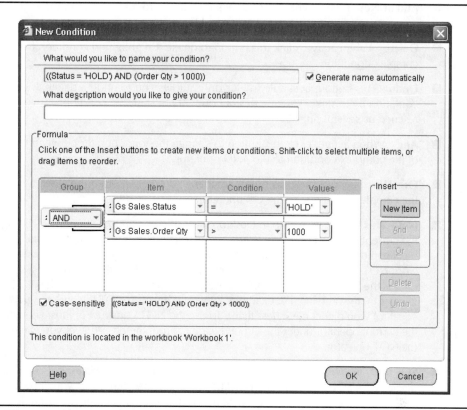

FIGURE 12-8 *Plus extended New Condition dialog box*

The Extended New Condition Dialog Box

Whenever you are creating complex conditions, Discoverer opens the extended New Condition dialog box. This dialog box has all of the fields from the New Condition dialog box, as seen in Figures 12-4 and 12-5, but in addition, it also has several more. As shown in Figures 12-7 and 12-8, this extended dialog box consists of the following additional features:

- **Group** An area containing the Boolean operators being used to join the elements of the complex condition together. Clicking one of the operators in this area highlights it. You can then click one of the Boolean operator buttons to change the join operator.

- **Row Selection button** Click this button to highlight a condition that is to become part of a sublevel.

NOTE
Sublevels are used to group together conditions that are to have different Boolean operators to the main conditions. This allows you to create complex conditions such as A = 1 or (A = 2 and B = 4), where conditions A = 2 and B = 4 are combined together in a sublevel using the AND operator, as compared to A = 1, which is joined to the sublevel using the OR operator. In essence, this query returns all rows where A = 1, or where A = 2 and B = 4.

- **Add or New Item**   When active, click this button to add a new condition to the complex condition you are creating or editing.

- **Delete**   When active, click this button to delete a highlighted condition from the complex condition.

- **Undo**   This button, available in Plus only, allows you to undo a delete. If you delete a condition by mistake, clicking this button will reinstate the condition. This has already rescued us several times!

- **And**   When active, click this button to change the join operator between two elements of the complex condition to the AND operator.

- **Or**   When active, click this button to change the join operator between two elements of the complex condition to the OR operator.

- **Not**   This button, available in Desktop only, allows you to negate the meaning of the current Boolean operator. When active, clicking this button negates the current highlighted item in the dialog box. With a join operator highlighted, Discoverer adds the word NOT as a prefix to the current join operator. Clicking the Not button a second time returns the join operator to its original state. With an expression highlighted, Discoverer negates that expression. For example, IN would become NOT IN, and >= (greater than or equal to) would become < (less than). To use the NOT construct in Plus, you need to click the current operator under the Group heading. From the drop-down, you can now insert the NOT operator.

- **SQL box**   As you create the condition formula, a box at the bottom of the dialog box displays the SQL syntax for the condition that you are entering. If you know SQL very well, you can use this box to validate that Discoverer is defining the condition as you would like it.

When you enter the extended New Condition dialog box for the first time, all of the Boolean operator buttons, apart from Not, are deactivated. This is because Add, Delete, And, and Or cannot be used until you have created at least one condition. Clicking Not would change the default condition to <>.

In Desktop, do not click OK until you have built at least one condition. If you click OK too early, Discoverer will give you this error message:

NOTE
In Plus, Discoverer disables the OK button until you have a valid construct.

Building a Simple Boolean Condition

Before building a Boolean condition, you need to work out in advance what you want to know and convert that into simple Boolean algebra.

For example, let's build a condition that constrains a query to orders that are on hold and have a quantity ordered in excess of 1,000. First of all, the Boolean algebra for this is as follows:

Order Status = HOLD AND Quantity Ordered > 1000

Having ascertained that there are no existing conditions that will satisfy what we want, we opened the New Condition dialog box and clicked Advanced. This opened the extended New Condition dialog box as seen in Figures 12-7 and 12-8.

Using the status to constrain the worksheet to only those orders that are on hold, we will now build the first condition. There are no illustrations for any of these steps, because by now you should know how to do this. Having created the first condition, all of the Boolean operator buttons are now activated.

Next, we clicked Add, opened another row of basic components, and built the second condition. The final complex condition is shown in Figures 12-7 and 12-8.

Building a Complex Boolean Condition

Once you know how to build simple Boolean conditions, building complex ones is straightforward. A complex Boolean condition takes three or more separate conditions and uses Boolean operators to join them together. Many people have asked the authors if it is possible to combine different Boolean operators in the same condition. The answer is yes, and in this section, we will show you how.

First of all, as always, we need to think out in advance what it is that we are trying to do. The complex Boolean that we are going to build uses the following logic to analyze our query of sales orders and quantities:

Order quantity > 10000 OR (order quantity between 7000 and 8000, AND the status is OPEN)

The portion in parentheses is to be considered a single condition, such that our result will display all orders that have an order quantity in excess of 15,000, along with all open orders that have a quantity between 7,000 and 8,000. Do you have a mathematical grounding? If so, you might want to think back to school and the principle of BODMAS. Here you determined the precedence of calculations as being: Brackets, Order, Division, Multiplication, Addition, and Subtraction. It is the same with conditions also.

NOTE

It is quite common for people to forget that parentheses always come first, which means you must calculate the answer of whatever is in the parentheses before you attempt to calculate the rest of the problem. Once you have worked out whatever is in the parentheses, usually the rest of the problem resolves easily!

So, where do we begin? As always with complex conditions, we need to proceed directly to the extended New Condition dialog box, by clicking Advanced in the normal New Condition box. By examining our documentation of the system, we discovered that there is already an administrator-defined condition for the order quantity being in excess of 15,000. Therefore, we opened the Item drop-down list and took the option to Select Condition. Doing this opened the following Select Condition dialog box. As you can see in this illustration, the condition we want already exists and, as it is the only condition available to use, it has been automatically highlighted for us to use.

Clicking OK returned us to the extended New Condition dialog box, placing the condition we just selected in the first row. Next, we clicked New Item, or Add if you are following along using Desktop, to add the second part of our complex condition, the order quantity between 7,000 and 8,000. When we opened the Item drop-down list this time, Discoverer had added another option to the list, the chance to Copy Condition.

As the second part of our condition uses the same item as the first part, so that we cannot possibly select the wrong item in error, we will copy the first condition and then change it. Taking the option Copy Condition reopens the Conditions dialog box, from where we once again selected the administrator-defined condition. This resulted in the following:

As you can see in the preceding illustration, Discoverer has added a second instance of the condition, but this time it has made it available for editing. Isn't that nice?

NOTE
Remember, you cannot edit administrator-defined conditions. By copying them, you are in effect creating a new condition, a condition that you can edit. You have used the original condition as a template.

We edited this second condition and changed it so that it now selected quantities between 7,000 and 8,000, as shown here:

NOTE
In order to show you the preceding illustration, we had to widen the extended New Condition dialog box. You can do this by clicking one of the sides and dragging it to the required size.

As you can see from the preceding illustration, the two parts of this condition are out of sync with each other. It is not possible to select order quantities in excess of 15,000 while at the same time selecting order quantities between 7,000 and 8,000. Discoverer will allow you to complete this condition, but the query will return no data.

We now have to add the third component of this complex condition, the bit that constrains the status to only orders that are on hold. We clicked New Item, or Add if you are using Desktop, and then added the third condition, so that our complex condition now looks as shown here.

You will notice that our current complex condition has three separate components joined together using AND. We need to convert the structure of our condition, such that it satisfies our original request for Order quantity > 15000 'OR' (order quantity between 7000 and 8000, 'AND' the status is open).

In order to accomplish this, we needed to create a sublevel within our condition based on the items that are in parentheses. Before we did that, we changed the overall Group item to be OR. To do this, we clicked the AND operator in the Group area and then clicked the Or button. This gave us the complex condition as seen next. In particular, notice how Discoverer has defined the SQL syntax.

In order to complete our condition, we need to insert the sublevel. To create a sublevel in a complex condition, use this workflow:

1. Determine which items need to be part of the sublevel.

2. Click the Row Selection button to the left of the first item that needs to be part of the sublevel. This highlights the Row Selection button (see Figures 12-7 and 12-8).

3. Hold down the CTRL key and click the row selection button for the next condition that needs to be part of the sublevel.

4. Click the Boolean operator button that you want to apply to the two conditions selected. Discoverer will now create a new sublevel to your condition.

5. Check that the Boolean operator linking the new sublevel to the remainder of the complex condition is correct. If not, click it and change it.

6. Repeat Steps 2–5 as many times as needed, creating as many sublevels as is necessary.

7. When you have finished creating sublevels, click OK.

Using this workflow, we clicked on the Row Selection button for the second order quantity condition (between 7,000 and 8,000), held down the CTRL key, clicked the Row Selection button for the status condition, and then finally clicked AND. You can see in the following illustration how our complex condition now contains a sublevel. Once more, notice how Discoverer has defined the SQL syntax.

Finally, when we clicked OK to complete the condition, Discoverer ran the query again and gave us the following result. As you can see in the next illustration, we do indeed have both conditions satisfied. We have a row containing an on-hold order with a quantity between 7,000 and 8,000, while at the same time we have several other rows containing quantities in excess of 15,000.

	▶ Status	▶ Order Number	▶ Order Qty SUM
1	HOLD	2818	8000
2	OPEN	2822	16000
3		3134	24000
4		3392	34800
5		3394	30000
6	SHIPPED	2404	18000
7		2414	15600
8		2559	26400
9		4395	16000
10		4748	26400
11		4810	15600
12		4924	18000
13		5649	18000
14		5923	16000
15		6831	15600
16		7015	26400

Using Subqueries

The final type of complex condition uses subqueries. These conditions use the results from another worksheet to determine the value or values to be used within the conditions. You can build very complex queries using this type of condition. In fact, you can even combine the results from different worksheets to be applied as values to be used within conditions of your current worksheet.

NOTE
Remember, you cannot create a condition based on a subquery in Plus, but conditions created in Desktop using subqueries can be used in Plus.

These types of queries are very easy to use and build, but they can dramatically increase the length of time it will take for your query to run. Many queries using subqueries could be rewritten as Boolean conditions. You should, therefore, use subqueries only when it is impossible to build a condition or conditions within the main query that would give you the result you are looking for.

There are two types of subquery conditions. These are

- Subqueries using single items

- Subqueries using correlated items

Whichever type of subquery condition you decide to build, you will use the Create Subquery dialog box.

Create Subquery Dialog Box

The only way to create a condition based on a subquery is to use the Create Subquery dialog box. This box, as seen in Figure 12-9, has the following features:

- **Subquery sheet selection** In this area, you can type in or use the associated drop-down list to tell Discoverer which sheet to use.

- **Item Match** In this area, you can type in or use the associated drop-down list to tell Discoverer which item to use in the sheet being linked to.

- **New** Click this button to create a new worksheet, in which you intend to build constraints to define the item you want your main query to link to.

- **Add** Click this button to add a pair of correlated items to the subquery.

- **Remove** Click this button to remove a pair of correlated items from the subquery.

Building a Condition Using a Subquery

Whether you decide to build a condition using a single value from a subquery or using correlated items, the way that you build the condition is the same.

To build a condition based on a subquery, use the following workflow:

1. Open the New Condition dialog box.

2. Select the item you want to use to link to the subquery, and then select an expression.

3. From the Values drop-down list, choose Create Subquery. This opens the Create Subquery dialog box shown in Figure 12-9.

4. Discoverer tries to find a link to the item you chose in Step 2 within an existing worksheet in the workbook. If a link can be found, Discoverer inserts both the sheet and item names into the dialog box. If multiple sheets exist, and the one you want is not the one Discoverer has defaulted to, use the drop-down list of worksheets to locate the worksheet that you want, and then use the drop-down list of items to locate the item.

5. If the worksheet does not exist, use the New button to create a new worksheet. This opens the Workbook Wizard, ready for you to build the new worksheet. After you have specified the new worksheet, Discoverer will return you to the Create Subquery dialog box.

6. If you are using correlated items, Discoverer will allow you to link to an item only in the same worksheet that you based the initial Subquery on.

7. Click OK. Discoverer applies the condition, creating any new worksheet that was defined in Step 5.

This workflow, while not having many steps, is complex. Take your time learning this workflow. Steps 4, 5, and 6, in particular, involve much more than the mere clicking of a button.

Please take it easy when building conditions based on subqueries, because the time taken to run the query could be very long. This is especially true if you are scanning the whole database against several values in a subquery. We have found that basing the subquery on items that have small lists of values, like sales channels, statuses, codes, or customer names, will improve the performance of these types of conditions. Using items that have large lists of values, such as sales order numbers, quantities, amounts, and dates, will take much longer.

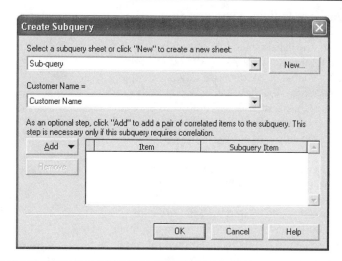

FIGURE 12-9 *The Create Subquery dialog box*

NOTE

If you edit a subquery and cause the values to change, Discoverer will not recognize that the values being linked to have changed, even if you manually make Discoverer rerun the original query. This limitation prevents us from building template queries that automatically work out, using subqueries, new sets of values based on time. The only way to make Discoverer refresh a link to a subquery is to edit the subquery condition itself. For details on how to force Discoverer to use the latest subquery data, refer to the section "Editing a Subquery" later in this chapter.

Subqueries Without Correlated Items

These are the simplest type of subquery condition to build and understand. Whether you build the subquery first or build it from within the main worksheet makes no difference to Discoverer. However, if the subquery requires some manipulations or extremely complicated mathematical computations, we advise you to create the subquery first. Spending time refining subqueries to make them efficient in terms of indexes and items being selected will prove to be time well spent.

A good example, and the one that we will show you here, makes sheet 1 (the subquery) return a list of all customers who have had a cancellation in the current month; then, using that list, it makes the current query return a list of those customers who also have outstanding orders not yet shipped. You might want to have a heads-up and be aware that these orders could be in risk of being cancelled as well. At the very least, you should have the salesperson call the customer and make sure the outstanding orders are still required.

The preceding query could be created both ways, either building the subquery first or building the main query and then building the subquery as part of the condition. We will show you both ways.

Example Subquery, Building Subquery First   First of all, we built the query that is destined to become the subquery. In this example, we selected the customer name, the fiscal cancellation month of April 2005, and the total quantity ordered. We don't need to use the status in this query because orders with a cancellation date are cancelled! When we ran this query, as you can see in this illustration, it returned a list of the 17 customers who had cancelled an order in April.

To make this example easier to follow, we have named this sheet "Sub-query."

Next, we opened a new sheet in the workbook (Sheet | New Sheet from the menu bar). In this sheet, we selected customer name (for the link), the fiscal order month of April 2005, the status OPEN, and the total quantity ordered for all customers who currently have a balance of 2,000 or more items. The status is required this time because we need to identify which orders are not shipped. When we ran this query, as you can see next, it returned a list of 15 customers with open orders.

Page Items: Month: APR-05 ▼

	Customer Name	Order Qty SUM
1	ABC WIDGET CO	50
2	BIG RIVER WIDGETS	1200
3	CASA DE WIDGETS	1300
4	CEBU WIDGET CO	10000
5	HONG KONG WIDGETS	15000
6	MOUNTAIN WIDGETS	10200
7	PATRIOT'S WIDGET CO.	50
8	RIO WIDGETS	2600
9	THING'S	1920
10	WE'VE GOT WIDGETS	700
11	WIDGET O THE MERSEY	2400
12	WIDGET SUPPLY CO.	4320
13	WIDGETS DE MEXICO	200
14	WIDGETS MARKET	2400
15	WIDGETS OESTE	100
16	WIDGETS R US	100
17	WILD WEST WIDGETS	1200

We now need to build a new condition restricting the main sheet to only the customers from sheet 1. In order to do this, we will follow the workflow that we gave you earlier.

First, we opened the New Condition dialog box, and then from the drop-down list of items we selected the customer name, set the expression to be =, and set the value to be Create Subquery. As you can see earlier in Figure 12-9, this opened the Create Subquery dialog box. Discoverer has already found another sheet in our query, the sheet entitled "Sub-query," and has also scanned all of the items in that sheet, locating an item called Customer Name. These values have automatically been inserted into the Create Subquery dialog box.

Page Items:	Month: APR-05 ▼	Status: OPEN ▼
	Customer Name	Order Qty SUM
▸ 1	ACE MANUFACTURING	3100
▸ 2	BIG RIVER WIDGETS	2700
▸ 3	CASA DE WIDGETS	14500
▸ 4	CEBU WIDGET CO	15700
▸ 5	LAST RAILWAY WIDGETS	8908
▸ 6	OXFORD WIDGETS	7400
▸ 7	PATRIOT'S WIDGET CO.	2360
▸ 8	THE LITTLE WIDGET	2400
▸ 9	THING'S	2680
▸ 10	WARSAW WIDGETS	2400
▸ 11	WE'VE GOT WIDGETS	11820
▸ 12	WIDGETS MARKET	4300
▸ 13	WIDGETS R US	10000
▸ 14	WILD WEST WIDGETS	5000
▸ 15	YAMATA WIDGET LTD.	9400

As all required items within the Create Subquery box were complete, we clicked OK. Discoverer returned us to the New Condition dialog box, where we could see the resulting condition was Customer Name = Sub-query. Clicking OK this time caused Discoverer to rerun the query using the condition that we had just defined, returning only those customers with current orders of 2000 or more items who placed an order in April 2005 and also had a cancellation in the same month.

As you can see here, we have nine customers who match the criteria that we defined.

Page Items:	Month: APR-05 ▼	Status: OPEN ▼
	Customer Name	Order Qty SUM
▸ 1	BIG RIVER WIDGETS	2700
▸ 2	CASA DE WIDGETS	14500
▸ 3	CEBU WIDGET CO	15700
▸ 4	PATRIOT'S WIDGET CO.	2360
▸ 5	THING'S	2680
▸ 6	WE'VE GOT WIDGETS	11820
▸ 7	WIDGETS MARKET	4300
▸ 8	WIDGETS R US	10000
▸ 9	WILD WEST WIDGETS	5000

Example Subquery, Building Main Query

First   This time we built the main query first, and then opened the New Condition dialog box. We will not show you any illustrations, because these are the same as in the preceding example. We again selected the Customer Name from the Item drop-down list, set the expression to be =, and set the value to be Create Subquery. This time when we entered the Create Subquery dialog box (see Figure 12-9), Discoverer was unable to populate any of its fields because there was no subquery within the workbook.

We therefore needed to add a new sheet. Clicking Add launched the Workbook Wizard. In there, we created a new query using the customer name and quantity ordered for April 2005. When we clicked Finish to complete this query, rather than running it, Discoverer returned us to the Create Subquery dialog box. As the subquery was now complete, we clicked OK and completed the condition.

Subqueries Using Correlated Items

Queries using correlated items are simply queries that link to more than one item in the subquery. For example, suppose you had a subquery that returned the average unit selling price for each product sold in the past month. Using correlated items, you could analyze the selling price of the same products by customer, returning a list of customers who had paid more than the average selling price for their goods. Obviously, last month these customers were willing to pay more than the average price for these items. Therefore, if you want to quickly increase your profits for the current month, all you need to do is have a salesperson contact these customers and see if they are willing to buy some more. You could even offer them a discount, yet still sell to them at above the average selling price!

We will show you how to create this query. We have chosen to build the subquery first, although we could just as easily have opted to build the main query first.

For the subquery, we selected the product name, the average selling price, and the average quantity shipped for January 2001. We then created a calculation to derive the average unit price, by dividing the average quantity shipped into the average selling price. This produced the list as shown here.

For the main query, we selected the customer name, average selling price, average quantity shipped, and product name for the same month. We also calculated the customer's unit price, and then we launched the New Condition dialog box. Here, we created a new condition where the customer's unit price was greater than the unit price in the subquery. We then clicked Add in the Create Subquery dialog box to add a correlated item.

	Product Name	Selling Price AVG	Ship Qty AVG	Unit Price
1	AB-2000	83025.00	6150	13.50
2	AB-2500	31316.55	2696	11.62
3	AB-3000	41898.93	2586	16.20
4	AVR-500	57478.96	2133	26.95
5	AVR-550	17524.24	700	25.03
6	AVR-800	106895.25	3085	34.65
7	AVR-900	26957.70	778	34.65
8	CD-100	18859.17	1237	15.25
9	CD-200	10556.05	884	11.94
10	CD-500	83396.80	3760	22.18
11	CD-550	26771.26	1207	22.18
12	CD-625	30715.27	1385	22.18
13	DS-1200	3667.96	686	5.35
14	QB-1000	9197.09	1392	6.61
15	QB-2000	56280.00	2400	23.45
16	QB-3000	19352.11	1425	13.58
17	QB-5000	38944.72	2245	17.35
18	QB-5500	6322.28	358	17.66
19	QB-6000	8280.02	880	9.41

Page Items: Month: JAN-01

In the following illustration, you can see both the New Condition and Create Subquery dialog boxes. In the New Condition dialog box, we selected the Cust Unit Price from the Item drop-down box, changed the expression to >, and then selected Create Subquery from the Values drop-down list. This opened the Create Subquery dialog box, in which Discoverer detected the existence of an existing sheet but was unable to detect a field called Cust Unit Price. We had to select the Unit Price from the drop-down list. After clicking Add to add a correlated item, from the drop-down list we selected Product Name. Discoverer, finding a matching item in sheet 1, automatically made the correlation.

Editing a Subquery

Unfortunately, as previously mentioned, Discoverer will not detect that the data being returned in a subquery has changed. Therefore, changing a subquery will have no impact on the main query that it is referenced by. This will produce totally unexpected results when comparing the output of the worksheets.

In the preceding example, when we showed you how to build a subquery excluding correlated items, we constrained the subquery to return a list of customers who had cancellations in April 2005. Editing the subquery by adding a new condition to show only those customers who had total cancellations with a quantity in excess of 3,000 will result in a smaller list of customers. This will cause the subquery result to change, but not the main query. Even if you refresh the main sheet, it will not recognize the new list and will continue to be constrained on the original subquery.

To compound the problem, if we share this query with someone who is not very proficient in Discoverer, that person will look at the conditions for the subquery and assume that the main query result is correct, totally unaware that there is a mismatch.

The only way to correct this is to edit the subquery condition. This will cause Discoverer to recognize that the subquery has changed. To show you how this works, we added a new condition to the subquery, where the order quantity is greater than 3,000. When we ran the query in the master sheet, as expected, Discoverer did not warn us that the subquery had changed.

As we were aware of the situation, we launched the Conditions dialog box, highlighted the Customer Name IN Sub-query condition, then clicked the Edit button. In the Edit Condition dialog box, we opened the drop-down list in the Value field. As you can see here, Discoverer had added another option to the list, an option to Edit Subquery:

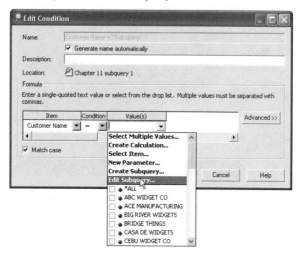

Taking the option Edit Subquery caused Discoverer to at last recognize that the subquery had changed. As you can see in the next illustration, we were given the following warning that the subquery had changed. We clicked Yes, then clicked OK in the Edit Subquery box, and completed the condition. This caused Discoverer to rerun the query correctly.

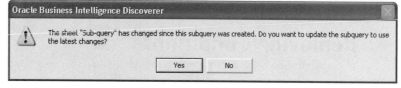

Subqueries and Discoverer Plus

As previously mentioned, in Discoverer Plus you cannot create, maintain, or edit conditions that are based on subqueries. However, you can execute worksheets that use subqueries. Look at the following illustration:

As you can see, we have run our report for April 2005 using Discoverer Plus and have obtained the correct answer. Looking now at the Conditions tab, shown here, you will see that Discoverer Plus correctly identifies that a subquery is in use:

However, if we try to edit the Sub-query condition, we will get the following message:

As you can see, Plus has reminded us that we cannot edit or view this condition because it contains a subquery. We can still activate and deactivate the condition, though.

Removing Conditions

There are three very good reasons you may want to remove a condition. These are

- To return a query to its original state following analysis or printing

- Because you made a mistake and created an incorrect condition

- Because you avoided "The Query from the Twilight Zone" and now wish to open up the query to produce some more meaningful results

There are two ways to permanently remove a condition from a query, and one way to deactivate a condition yet still leave it in situ in case of a future requirement.

Permanently Removing Conditions

As stated, there are two methods of permanently removing a condition from a query. These are

- Undo the last condition.

- Delete the condition from the query.

NOTE
Deleting a condition from a workbook removes it from all worksheets in the workbook. If you have multiple worksheets in your workbook, you should be very careful not to delete a condition that is used by a worksheet other than the one you are currently working with. Discoverer will not warn you, nor will it prevent you from doing this.

Permanently Removing a Condition by Undoing the Last Condition

If you made a mistake and created an incorrect condition, you can return your query to its original state very easily by either pressing CTRL-Z or from the menu bar selecting Edit | Undo Conditions.

Either of these methods causes Discoverer to automatically undo the condition that you just created. In fact, Discoverer actually deletes the condition.

NOTE
You can only use undo immediately following the creation of a condition, although it does not matter which method you used to create the condition.

Deleting a Condition from a Workbook in Desktop

To delete a condition from a workbook in Desktop, you should use the following workflow:

1. Open the Conditions dialog box.
2. From the list of conditions displayed, highlight the condition you want to delete.
3. Click the Delete button.
4. Click OK.

Deleting a Condition from a Workbook in Plus

To delete a condition from a workbook in Plus, you should use the following workflow:

1. Click the Conditions tab in the Available Items pane.
2. From the list of conditions displayed, highlight the condition you want to delete.
3. Right-click and from the drop-down select Delete.

Deactivating a Condition

Deactivating a condition does not delete a condition from a workbook. In fact, unless you are certain that you no longer require a condition, you would be better advised to deactivate it. This recommendation has even more merit when there are multiple worksheets in the workbook.

Deactivating a Condition in Desktop

To deactivate a condition in Desktop, use the following workflow:

1. Open the Conditions dialog box.
2. From the list of conditions displayed, uncheck the condition you want to deactivate.
3. Click OK.

Deactivating a Condition in Plus

To deactivate a condition in Plus, use the following workflow:

1. Click the Conditions tab in the Available Items pane.
2. From the list of conditions displayed, right-click the condition you want to deactivate.
3. From the drop-down select Remove from Worksheet.

Removing Columns Upon Which Conditions Are Based

At first sight, this may seem a rather dangerous thing to do. However, the ability to remove a column from the display, without impacting any condition based upon that column, is another of Discoverer's really useful features. Discoverer will remember the item and will continue using it. There are two types of columns that you can remove. These are

- Columns based on data items from the database
- Columns based on calculations

Removing a Database Item Used in Conditions

You are quite safe removing a database item from a query, even if that item is used in one or more conditions. This is because the item, being in the database, is still accessible. Discoverer will continue being able to apply conditions on that item, even if you no longer wish to display the item in the final results set.

Removing Calculations Used in Conditions

You can even remove calculated columns from the results set, and Discoverer will continue using those calculations within conditions. This is because when you remove a calculated column, Discoverer does not delete the calculation. Instead, Discoverer leaves the calculation in the workbook but marks it as being inactive. You can deactivate a calculation, yet still allow Discoverer to use that calculation in a condition.

Deactivating a Calculation Used in a Condition in Desktop

You have two ways to deactivate a Calculation used in a Condition in Desktop. These are as follows:

- Deactivate the calculation in the Calculations dialog box by removing the check mark alongside the calculation.

- Highlight the column heading and then press the DELETE key on your keyboard. This does not delete the calculation from the worksheet. The calculation is deactivated just as if you had unchecked it in the Calculations dialog box.

Deactivating a Calculation Used in a Condition in Plus

You have two ways to deactivate a calculation used in a condition in Plus. These are as follows:

- Deactivate the calculation in the Calculations tab of the Available Items pane by right-clicking the calculation and selecting Remove from Worksheet from the drop-down list.

- Highlight the column heading, then right-click, and from the drop-down select Remove from Worksheet.

- Highlight the column heading and then press the DELETE key on your keyboard. This does not delete the calculation from the worksheet. The calculation is deactivated just as if you had unchecked it in the Calculations dialog box.

Deleting Calculations Used in Conditions

Take care when deleting calculations from worksheets if those calculations are used in a condition. If you delete a calculation from a worksheet and that calculation is used in a condition, Discoverer also deletes the condition. You will not be warned that there is a condition dependent upon the calculation you are about to delete. The query will be rerun automatically, and the results you see will be minus both the calculation and the condition.

Summary

In this chapter, we have shown you how to build effective conditions, and how learning this skill will allow you to unleash the power of Discoverer. You have learned to add a condition using the analysis bar buttons to create a new condition. You have been shown how to use the Conditions dialog box to add a condition. We have introduced you to a workflow to create a condition and shown you how to effectively use the New Condition dialog box.

You were also shown how to put into practice the skills learned in the early part of the chapter, building skill by skill. We showed you real-world examples of building conditions using the workflow.

Next, you were taught the basic components of a condition: the item, the expression, and the value. Using these basic components, you learned to edit an existing condition. We also showed you how to take it a step further by using the Advanced button. This allows you to create conditions based on other conditions, conditions based on calculations, conditions using Boolean operators, and conditions using subqueries. We taught you how to create conditions using correlated items and how to edit a subquery.

Finally, we showed you how to remove conditions temporarily and permanently, as well as how to undo a condition. You learned how to delete a condition from a workbook and how to deactivate a condition. We also explained how you can remove items from a worksheet, while still allowing Discoverer to use those items in conditions.

In the next chapter, you will continue to learn important advanced techniques that will allow you greater and greater control of this powerful product.

CHAPTER
13

Refining Parameters, Calculations, Sorting, and Percentages

his, the third chapter in the advanced techniques section of the book, will deal with parameters, calculations, sorting, and percentages. As you become more expert in Discoverer, your queries will become more complex. A change in one data item could bring about the need to change a variety of query definitions. Chapter 12 took an in-depth look at conditions. By changing a condition, you may need to reevaluate one or more of the following items: parameters, conditions, sorts, and percentages.

In this chapter, you will learn to change a condition to a parameter, use dynamic parameters, activate and deactivate parameters, edit parameters, and rearrange the order of parameters. We will also show you how to define mandatory and optional parameters and to manage cascading parameters. We will show you how to refine calculations by defining the main components of a calculation and how to define the calculation in advance. You will learn how to convert an algorithm into a Discoverer script as well as how to avoid division by zero errors. For information about how to create calculations using analytic functions, please see Appendix B.

We will show you housekeeping techniques to use after editing a condition by reviewing conditions based on calculations, and reviewing the data items used in the edited calculation. We will explain how to use standard functions and show you how to define calculations for standard margin and markup. You will be taught how to place a final refinement on the sort order, as well as how to remove an item from the sort order. Finally, we will show you techniques for refining percentages, including how to change and how to remove them.

Refining Parameters

After dealing with conditions, as we did in Chapter 12, the next most common way to refine a query is to refine or define parameters. The ability to convert conditions into parameters is essential if you are going to build queries on behalf of your department.

Parameters can be considered as placeholders that are used instead of hard-coded values in the definition of a condition. Unlike normal conditions, which always return the same results each time the worksheet is executed, parameters offer you the chance to enter a value before the worksheet is executed. The value entered is then fed to the condition, with the net result that the same worksheet can produce a variety of results.

Parameters are particularly useful if many people have access to the same worksheet. Discoverer will then produce a result that is of interest only to a particular person or department. As you can see, the use of parameters can save time and money, allowing you the freedom to move on to other tasks. Later, when a change is required to this query, you have only one worksheet to worry about. If, however, you had built one workbook per user, you would have many queries to refine.

Chapter 5 has detailed instructions on creating parameters and explains the difference between parameters and conditions. We also showed you how to build a parameter. However, we did not show you how to convert a condition into a parameter. In this section on refining parameters, we will show you how to convert a condition into a parameter as well how to edit a parameter.

Changing a Condition to a Parameter

In Chapter 4, we advised you to avoid "The Query from the Twilight Zone" by applying strict conditions. Those hard-coded conditions need to be either replaced or converted into parameters to make the query more useful and flexible.

Workflow to Convert a Condition into a Parameter

To change a condition to a parameter, use the following workflow:

1. Open the Edit Condition dialog box and make any changes to the condition that may be required.

NOTE
If you want your users to be able to use wildcard characters in the Parameter Wizard, you must ensure that you build the condition using the LIKE expression. Creating conditions using expressions such as = and < will return no data and need changing.

2. From the Values drop-down list, select New Parameter. This opens the New Parameter dialog box, as seen in Figures 13-1 and 13-2. Refer to Chapter 5 if you are unsure how to use this box.

3. Enter a meaningful name if you so choose. This is not a required field, but if you do add your own name, we recommend that you use meaningful names. Later, when you are editing your conditions or placing them in the title of your worksheet, this will help you to differentiate between hard-coded conditions and parameters.

NOTE
The use of meaningful names in Parameters extends the power of Discoverer. In a Header, Footer, or Title if you type the ampersand character (&) followed by the name of a parameter or Page Item, you can make that object display exactly where you want.

New Parameter

What do you want to name this parameter?

Which item do you want to base this parameter on?

Gs Sales.Status

Create condition with operator: =

What prompt do you want to show for this parameter?

What description do you want to show for this parameter?

Do you want to allow different parameter values for each worksheet?

- Allow only one set of parameter values for all worksheets.
- Allow different parameter values for each worksheet.

What properties do you want to give this parameter?

- ☑ Require users to enter a value
- ☐ Enable users to select multiple values
- ☐ Enable users to select either indexes or values

What default value do you want to give this parameter?

Value

Do you want to filter the list of values for this parameter?

- Show all available values
- Filter the list of values based on the selected conditions:

Select	Name
☐	▽ Order Qty > 15000

Help   OK   Cancel

FIGURE 13-1 *Plus New Parameter dialog box*

FIGURE 13-2 *Desktop New Parameter dialog box*

4. Enter a helpful prompt for the end user. This needs to be text that will be easily understood by the end user. It may not be obvious what the choices for the parameter are. It doesn't hurt to be polite, and the words please, bitte, s'il vous plait, or por favor go a long way.

5. Enter a description if you choose. This is not a required field. However, this is an excellent extension of the prompt and can actually contain the list of values that the end user may choose from. We like to use this field as "context-sensitive help." In here we add comments such as "Select from the drop-down list or leave blank for ALL values."

6. Check the box for multiple values if you want the end user to be able to select multiple values for the parameter.

7. Enter a default value if you choose. If a drop-down list is available, you should select the default from that list. This is not a required field.

8. Decide whether you want the values entered into this parameter to be applicable to the current worksheet only or to the whole workbook. In Desktop, the radio buttons are labeled "Allow only one value for all sheets" and "Allow a different value in each sheet." In Plus, the radio buttons are labeled "Allow only one set of parameter values for all worksheets" and "Allow different parameter values for each worksheet." The default is to make the parameter values available across the whole workbook.

9. In Plus only, you can choose whether the parameter is mandatory or optional by checking or unchecking the box labeled "Require users to enter a value." We describe the use of mandatory and optional parameters later in this chapter.

10. Click OK and complete editing the condition. You will notice that Discoverer references the parameter by placing a colon followed by the parameter name.

NOTE
The workflow outlined here is different from the workflow given in Chapter 5. This workflow is based on an existing condition, which means the data item and operator are already selected for you. You cannot change them.

Converting a Condition into a Parameter Using the Workflow

In our database, we have an existing query that has multiple conditions and no parameters. Following the preceding workflow, we will show you how to change one of the conditions to a parameter. Once you have learned this skill, you will be able to convert any condition into a parameter.

Our example query displays the order number, product name, ship quantity, ship date, and status. The status is located on the page axis. We are editing the workbook in Discoverer Plus, and our current worksheet has two conditions:

- Order Qty > 15000 (an administrator-defined condition)

- Status = SHIPPED

Following the workflow, we opened the Edit Condition dialog box for the condition concerned, and then from the Values drop-down list we selected New Parameter. This opened the New Parameter dialog box, as seen in earlier Figure 13-1.

As you can see in the following illustration, we have completed the dialog box and given the parameter the name Status. We could have chosen not to add our own name, allowing Discoverer to create one for us, but we like to name our parameters. The rest of the fields are self-explanatory. When we add a default of SHIPPED, the parameter duplicates the original condition, thereby allowing the end user to run the query as it was originally built.

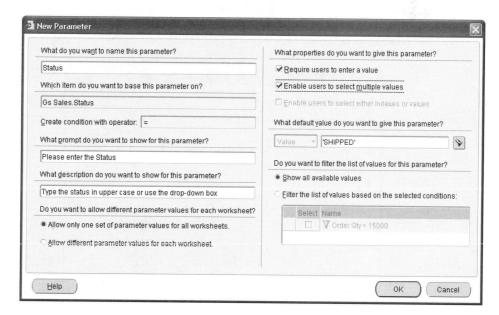

As the parameter is now complete, we click OK. This returns us to the Edit Condition dialog box shown next. As you can now see, Discoverer has changed the condition value to be the name of the parameter prefixed by a colon.

The condition is now complete, and we click OK to complete the condition. Discoverer now runs the query and, in Plus, presents us with the following Edit Parameter Values dialog box. In Desktop this is called the Parameter Wizard dialog box. As you can see, Discoverer has inserted the default and description that we specified. If the item that the parameter is based upon has a list of values, you can see that Discoverer has also added a flashlight button (this will be drop-down arrow in Desktop) alongside the default.

When we click the flashlight alongside the default, Discoverer opens the Select Values dialog box. As you can see, the list contains all of the values for the Status item, along with buttons for adding or removing items from the selected list. If you are using Desktop, and the user is allowed to select multiple values, this dialog box will have an additional item called Select Multiple Values at the bottom of the list.

In addition, and also only available in Plus, at the top of the box is a Search For area. Using this area, you can search for items within the list of values, thereby reducing the list to only those items that match your chosen search criteria. In our example we only have four values, so there is probably no need to search. However, you may easily have parameters that have hundreds of values. Your users can cut down the number of displayed values by making effective use of

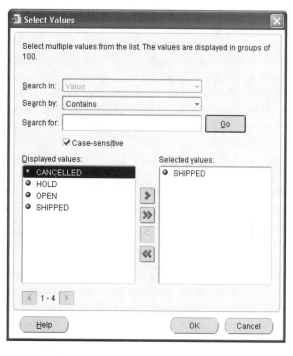

Discoverer's search technology. As an example, however, we keyed the following value, ED, into the Search for box and clicked Go. As you can see in the illustration that follows, Discoverer now only displays CANCELLED and SHIPPED.

Having selected one or more values from the list provided, clicking OK in the Select Values dialog box returns the user to the Edit Parameter Values dialog box. Clicking OK in Plus, or Finish in Desktop, causes Discoverer to run the query using the parameters entered.

NOTE
By the careful use of default values in parameters, you can force the query to run as it was originally built. If a user clicks OK in Plus, or Finish in Desktop when prompted, without changing the default, the query will return exactly the same result as if there were still a hard-coded condition.

Creating a Condition from a Parameter

By now, you should understand that while you are creating conditions, you can create an associated parameter. Perhaps you are not aware that you can also do the reverse. Discoverer also allows you to create an associated condition while you are creating a parameter. This is probably one of the least used features of Discoverer.

To create an associated condition while creating a parameter, use the following workflow:

1. Launch the New Parameter dialog box by selecting Tools | Parameters from the toolbar, or in Plus only by clicking the New Parameter button.

2. In the dialog box, click New. See Figure 13-1.

3. Give the parameter a meaningful name.

4. When prompted "which item do you want to base this parameter on," use the drop-down and select the item.

5. Check the box labeled "Create condition with operator."

6. Set the operator.

7. Discoverer will create a name for the condition based on the item, operator, and parameter name. You can either leave the name as defined by Discoverer or you can insert your own name. We generally leave Discoverer to create the condition name.

8. Enter a suitable prompt.

9. In the description box, provide some context-sensitive help.

10. Complete the rest of the dialog box using your own preferences.

11. Click OK to complete the parameter.

12. Click OK to close the Edit Worksheet dialog box, if open.

13. Discoverer will automatically create the condition, associate it with the parameter, and activate it for use.

14. Execute the worksheet.

Creating Instant Parameters

Another little known feature of Discoverer is its ability to create instant, quick and dirty parameters. These are parameters that are created "on the fly," either by design or by accident, by referencing as yet nonexistent parameters inside a condition. As you know, when working with calculations or conditions, parameters are indicated by a colon followed by the parameter name. For example, if you have a parameter called Status, you can use it in a calculation by typing **:Status**.

When creating or editing an existing condition, you can associate the condition with an existing parameter by choosing Select Parameter from the Values drop-down list. If you know the name of the parameter, you can also type it directly into the values box. However, you need to be very careful to make sure that you spell the name correctly, because if you type the name wrong, Discoverer creates another parameter.

Thus, if you have a parameter called Status and by mistake you type :stats, Discoverer creates another parameter. You will still be prompted only once, but you will probably be unaware that Discoverer is not using your original parameter. Your first inkling that something is wrong may come from a user who complains that there is no list of values. When you launch the Edit Sheet dialog box to try to solve the problem, you still may not be aware, especially if there are lots of parameters in the worksheet, that there are two parameters, one called Status and one called Stats. Editing the parameter that you originally created will show no issues because it will have a list of values, and you will be left scratching your head. It's at this point that you go to MetaLink and ask for help.

Unless you are an expert Discoverer user, do not create these instant parameters. Should you create one of these parameters and then edit it, you may be surprised to see that it is not in fact associated with a data item. Instead you will see that the parameter is based on the item called <NONE>. You have in fact just created a dynamic parameter by mistake!

Having created a dynamic parameter by mistake, we will now show you the correct way to create and use these useful parameters.

Dynamic Parameters

Dynamic parameters are not associated with any data item in the database. They are essentially free-form parameters that can later be "associated with" or "attached to" both calculations and conditions at will.

If required, these parameters can also be linked to multiple conditions in different worksheets within the same workbook. As mentioned, you can also create dynamic parameters that interact with calculations.

Here are a couple of examples of dynamic parameters:

■   A Y/N parameter that controls whether one course of action is followed or another.

■   A Percentage parameter that when passed to a calculation adjusts a sales amount by that percentage—useful for what/if analysis, extrapolation analysis, or simply applying discounts.

Using Dynamic Parameters

After you have created a dynamic parameter, it will not be applied to the worksheet until you have associated or attached the parameter to a calculation or condition and you have activated that calculation or condition. For more information relating to activating or deactivating parameters, please see the next section in this chapter.

There are, therefore, two types of dynamic parameter:

■   **Attached**   Parameters that are linked to a calculation or condition

■   **Unattached**   Parameters that are not linked to a calculation or condition

NOTE
You need to be aware that if the user executes a workbook that contains an unattached dynamic parameter, Discoverer will not prompt the user to enter a value for that parameter. There will be no impact to the worksheet results, and your user will be blissfully unaware that any such parameter should have been prompted.

To create a dynamic parameter, use the following workflow:

1.   Launch the New Parameter dialog box by selecting Tools | Parameters from the toolbar, or in Plus only by clicking the New Parameter button.

2.   In the dialog box, click New.

3.   Give the parameter a meaningful name.

4.   When prompted "which item do you want to base this parameter on," use the drop-down and select <NONE>.

5.   Enter a suitable prompt.

6.   In the description box, provide some context-sensitive help.

7.   Click OK.

8.   Attach the parameter to a calculation or condition.

We have an existing workbook that contains a customer name, a price, and a calculation named discount that is taking the price and multiplying it by 0.9, effectively applying a discount of 10 percent. Now, let's say we want to apply the discount only when a switch says Y. We therefore need a dynamic parameter for this switch. After reopening the worksheet, we launched the New Parameter dialog box and entered the following values:

1.   In Name, we entered **DiscParam**.

2.   We changed Item to <NONE>.

3. In Prompt, we typed: **Should we apply a discount?**

4. In Description, we typed: **Enter Y for Yes, any other character for No**.

5. We unchecked the option to allow users to enter multiple values.

6. In Default, we entered **N**.

NOTE
In case you forgot, you launch the New Parameter dialog box using Tools | Parameters and then clicking the New button. In Plus only, you can click the New Parameter button. This button is the third button from the right on the Toolbar.

The preceding settings can be seen in the following illustration:

After completing the New Parameter dialog box, we clicked OK. As expected, when we ran the query, the results did not change. The parameter is not being offered, and the discount of 10 percent is still being applied. To complete this parameter and bring it in to use, we have to edit the calculation for the discount.

In order to complete our calculation, we need to alter it such that the following logic is applied:

IF Discount Parameter = Y

THEN apply a 10% discount to the price

ELSE leave the price unchanged

The standard SQL set of functions that are available in Discoverer do not include a function called IF. However, either of these two functions, CASE and DECODE, which are both explained in depth later in this chapter, can be used to complete the calculation. When we changed our existing calculation:

```
SELLING PRICE SUM * 0.9
```

to

```
DECODE(:DiscParam, 'Y', SELLING PRICE SUM * 0.9, SELLING PRICE SUM)
```

Discoverer now prompts the user to enter the discount. If the user types a *Y*, the discount will be applied. If the user types any other character, including *y*, the discount will not be applied.

To make the parameter more user friendly, try altering the calculation as follows:

```
DECODE(UPPER(:DiscParam), Y', SELLING PRICE SUM * 0.9, SELLING PRICE SUM)
```

This alteration allows the user to type either an uppercase or a lowercase *Y*, thereby making the query much more user friendly.

NOTE
Don't worry about the syntax for the functions used in this example at this time. We cover advanced calculation in depth later in this chapter. There is also an appendix at the back of the book that lists all of the functions along with their syntax.

The worksheet used in the preceding example could easily be further refined. Let's say we no longer want to hard-code the discount of 10 percent but want to allow the user to key in the percentage amount from the keyboard. This is another excellent use of a dynamic parameter. To do this, we will need to create another dynamic parameter, this time prompting the user to enter the discount percentage. Having created the parameter, remember that it will not be brought into use until you attach it to a calculation or condition.

Therefore, let's say we have added a new dynamic parameter called DiscPct. All we need to do is make use of this in our discount calculation and we now have an extremely powerful worksheet. Not only do we ask whether we should apply a discount, but we even ask what percentage should be applied. If you are interested, the discount calculation has been further amended as follows:

```
DECODE(UPPER(:DiscParam),'Y', Selling Price SUM *
   (1-(:DiscPct/100)),Selling Price SUM)
```

After we amended the calculation and executed the worksheet, the following two parameters were prompted.

As you can see, Discoverer has now prompted us for the two parameters.

The use of dynamic parameters opens up a completely new set of possibilities. You no longer need to export data into a spreadsheet to perform complex what-if scenarios. A recent client of ours asked if we could help them with their payroll calculations. For years they had been extracting data to a spreadsheet and then applying calculations to generate the new pay rates. Using dynamic parameters, we were able to create a single Discoverer worksheet that prompted for the pay raise percentage for each of the different levels of employee and then applied those percentages to the current payroll data for each employee. The company is now able to try out various what-if scenarios without ever having to export their sensitive payroll data out of the system. Not only did we save time by simplifying the process but we helped their security by not having sensitive data stored outside of the database.

Mandatory and Optional Parameters

In all previous releases of Discoverer, parameters were mandatory. What this meant for your users is that until they had entered a value into every parameter the OK button remained grayed out. With this release of Plus you can now choose whether to create mandatory or optional parameters. Previously, your only other option was to pre-populate parameters with default values like '%'—which was never very appealing because it did not offer a great deal of control.

NOTE
A mandatory parameter can be recognized because Discoverer places a small asterisk alongside the prompt. If there is no asterisk, the parameter is optional and the user can leave the parameter blank.

Optional Parameters

As previously mentioned, the Discoverer 10.1.2 Plus release allows you to create optional parameters. Essentially, these are parameters that do not need to have a value entered in order for the worksheet to be executed. If you omit a value, in other words if you leave the box blank, Discoverer will assume that you want to query *all* values. Remember, Discoverer does not display an asterisk alongside optional parameters.

NOTE
Even though Desktop cannot edit or create optional parameters, it will allow their use, and it does use the asterisk to signify that the parameter is mandatory.

Defining Mandatory and Optional Parameters

By default, all parameters are mandatory. If you want to switch a parameter from being mandatory to optional, or vice versa, you need to alter its definition. This can be done only in Plus, where you can use either the New Parameter or the Edit Parameter dialog box. The switch itself is a check box that can be found in the top right-hand corner of the dialog box. As seen in the following illustration, it is labeled "Require users to enter a value."

Optional Parameters and Calculations

You cannot use optional parameters in calculations. Depending upon how you go about doing this, you will get a different error message.

If you create an optional parameter and then try to create a new calculation or amend an existing calculation using that parameter, Discoverer will give you the following error message.

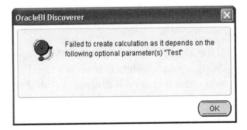

If you attach a mandatory parameter to a calculation and then try to alter the parameter to make it optional, you will get this error message:

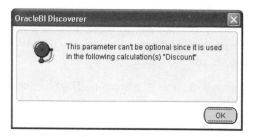

The bottom line, therefore, is that you can use only mandatory parameters in calculations. We like to use the term Purity Prevails. By allowing you to use only mandatory parameters, Oracle is ensuring that the final SQL that is submitted to the database is pure and does not contain any ambiguities that would otherwise prevent your worksheet from executing.

NOTE
When creating a new calculation or editing an existing calculation, Discoverer suppresses the display of optional parameters. While you cannot create calculations based on optional parameters, you can create conditions.

Parameter Support for Keywords

Discoverer will now accept the following keywords into a parameter:

- **SYSDATE** This inserts the current date. If you are prompting for a date and the user types SYSDATE, Discoverer will interpret this as the current date.

- **NULL** This inserts the NULL value.

- **USER** This inserts the name of the user who is logged in.

NOTE
Even though we show these keywords in uppercase, they are not case sensitive.

Of the three keywords that are available to you, the one that you will use most frequently is the SYSDATE. As mentioned, this keyword inserts the current date into a date parameter. It is very useful in parameter defaults when you want the query to default to the current date.

Activating and Deactivating Parameters

Parameters are not stand-alone objects within Discoverer. As mentioned previously, parameters become activated in the worksheet only when they are attached to a calculation or condition. This section deals with activating and deactivating parameters.

Activating Parameters

Before you can get Discoverer to prompt for a parameter, that parameter needs to be activated. Unlike other parts of Discoverer, such as Items, Conditions, Calculations, Totals, and Percentages, which all have a right-click drop-down capability to add or remove them from the worksheet, no such functionality exists for Parameters. Parameters are activated by association or by attachment to calculations or conditions. In other words, if you activate a calculation or condition that in turn uses a parameter, that parameter also gets activated. We will describe this in Plus.

To activate a parameter, use the following workflow:

1. From the toolbar, select Tools | Parameters. The Edit Sheet dialog box will now open at the Parameters tab.

2. Look at the text in the Order column. If is showing "n/a," the parameter is not active. If it is showing a number, the parameter is already active and you can exit this workflow.

3. Click the Select Items tab.

4. If the parameter is associated with a condition, click the Conditions subtab and add the condition to the worksheet.

5. If the parameter is associated with a calculation, click the Calculations subtab and add the calculation to the worksheet.

6. Click OK to close the Edit Sheet dialog box.

7. Execute the worksheet.

Deactivating Parameters

Because there is no right-click drop-down capability to add or remove parameters from a worksheet, the only way to deactivate a parameter is to deactivate the calculation or condition to which the parameter is associated. We will describe this in Plus.

To deactivate a parameter, use the following workflow:

1. From the toolbar, select Tools | Parameters. The Edit Sheet dialog box will now open at the Parameters tab.

2. Look at the text in the Order column. If is showing "n/a," the parameter is already inactive and you can exit this workflow. If it is showing a number, the parameter is active.

3. Click the Select Items tab.

4. If the parameter is associated with a condition, click the Conditions subtab and remove the condition from the worksheet.

5. If the parameter is associated with a calculation, click the Calculations subtab and remove the calculation from the worksheet.

6. Click OK to close the Edit Sheet dialog box.

7. Execute the worksheet.

Cascading Parameters

Cascading parameters are parameters that are constrained by having a filter on a pre-existing condition. That condition can either be a hard-coded condition or a condition that is associated with a previously prompted parameter. Using cascading parameters, you can ensure that lists of values are seeded so as to ensure that only the correct list is offered for selection.

We recommend that, in order to effectively use cascading parameters, you create these parameters on items that a) have lists of values and b) are contained within the same Discoverer drill hierarchy. This is simply for performance reasons and will not be enforced by Discoverer.

Oracle advises users not to create cascading parameters on non-drill-hierarchy items, though users can still go ahead and do so if they wish.

But what do we mean by a drill hierarchy?

Drill Hierarchies

According to Oracle, a Discoverer *drill hierarchy* is "a set of related items that provide a predefined path to help Discoverer users navigate worksheets." We understand that this description is a little difficult to follow at first, so we will help you by providing the following example.

In the next illustration, which is part of the Entity Relationship Diagram (ERD) for our database, you can see that our customer hierarchy is based on joins between the following four tables:

- Customer

- City

- District

- Region

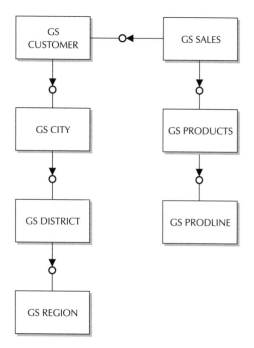

At the lowest level you can see that the Customer table joins to our Sales table. Using this information, our users can thus create worksheets that report sales by customer. To help us even further, our Discoverer manager has created a drill path that utilizes the joins between the four tables. Using this, our users can drill from Customers up to City, thus enabling them to create worksheets that are summarized by city. There is a similar link between City and District and, finally, another one between District and Region, which is our highest level. Our users can therefore now create reports that report sales only by region. This query will return significantly fewer rows of data than if they queried by customer.

Creating Cascading Parameters

Taking advantage of the drill hierarchy and lists of values that exist on each item within the hierarchy, if we create a parameter that prompts for the Region, and then have a second parameter that prompts for the District, we can force Discoverer to display only the districts that lie within the region we chose for the first parameter. This is what is called a cascading parameter.

To create a cascading parameter, use the following workflow:

1. Create a worksheet that uses two or more items from the same hierarchy.

2. Create a parameterized condition on the highest-ranked item in the hierarchy.

3. Create another parameterized condition on a lower-ranked item in the hierarchy.

4. When you create the second parameter, check the radio button labeled "Filter the list of values based on the selected conditions." See the illustration on the following page.

5. From the list of conditions that are now displayed, check one or more conditions that should be used as filters for this parameter.

6. Complete the condition.

7. Execute the worksheet.

We will now walk you through creating a worksheet that uses the preceding workflow to create cascading parameters. In this example, we will be using the same drill hierarchy that we outlined earlier in this section. We will create a worksheet that uses two parameters, one for Region and one for District, with the parameter for District being constrained by the values obtained from Region. Thus if the user selects "EUROPE" for the Region, the District list should only display "EU-EAST", "EU-NORTH", and "EU-SOUTH".

1. We will start a new workbook and select the following items:

    a. Order Qty from Sales

    b. District and Region from Customer

2. If we execute this worksheet without any constraints, the results that we get are as follows:

	▸ Region	▸ District	▸ Order Qty SUM
1	EUROPE	EU-EAST	493291
2		EU-NORTH	3203429
3		EU-SOUTH	1772980
4	FAR EAST	FE-ALL	2025531
5	NORTH AMERICA	NA-NORTH	6335702
6		NA-SOUTH	2576580
7	SOUTH AMERICA	SA-ALL	1459758

3. Create a parameterized condition on the Region.

4. When creating the parameter:

    a. In Name, type **Region**.

    b. In Prompt, type **Please enter the Region**.

    c. Allow multiple values.

    d. Do not set a default.

    e. Complete the parameter by clicking OK.

    f. Complete the condition by clicking OK.

5. Create another parameterized condition on the District.
6. When creating this parameter:

a. In Name, type **District**.

b. In Prompt, type **Please enter the District**.

c. Allow multiple values.

d. Do not set a default.

e. Click the radio button labeled "Filter the list of values based on the selected conditions."

f. Check the box alongside the Region condition.

g. Complete the parameter by clicking OK.

h. Complete the condition by clicking OK.

NOTE

If Discoverer detects that you already have created a condition on another item that is in the same hierarchy as the item that you are creating this parameter for, Discoverer will check that condition by default. This is a really clever feature and one that we recommend you take into account.

7. Execute the worksheet by selecting EUROPE when prompted for the Region.

8. As you can see in the following illustration, when we click the flashlight alongside the District, we can see only the districts that are within Europe.

You can see from this example just how easy it is to create cascading lists of values. There is no rocket science about this. The creation of cascading parameters works so well that you will wonder how you ever managed to use Discoverer without them.

Editing Parameters

Perhaps you want to add a bitmap to the Desktop Parameter Wizard entry screen. Maybe you want to place your newest parameter at the top of the Parameter list. Neither of these things can be done during the creation of a parameter. You will have to edit the parameter if you want to make changes like these.

If you allowed Discoverer to name the parameter, the name will contain the word "Parameter." If you named the parameter yourself, and you followed our recommendation, your name will also contain the word "Parameter."

If you want to edit a parameter that has been based on a condition, other than renaming the parameter, you have to amend the parameter definition in the Edit Parameter dialog box, available from the menu bar using Tools | Parameters, and the condition itself in the Edit Condition dialog box. This dual process can seem somewhat irritating at first, but in our experience, you will soon learn to handle this. However, if you only want to edit the name of the parameter, changing it in the Edit Parameter dialog box also changes it in the associated condition. The authors like this dynamic interaction that Discoverer has.

Workflow to Edit a Parameter

To edit an existing parameter, use the following workflow:

1. From the menu bar, select Tools | Parameters. In Desktop, this opens the Parameters dialog box. In Plus, this opens the Edit Sheet dialog box and places the focus on the Parameters tab.

NOTE
Unlike for Calculations and Conditions, there is no drop-down button alongside the New Parameter button.

2. Highlight the parameter you want to edit.
3. Click the Edit button. This opens the Edit Parameter dialog box.
4. Change the parameter as required.
5. Click OK.
6. If required, adjust the ordering of the parameters.
7. If required, and in Desktop only, you can optionally add your company logo by clicking Bitmap. This opens a drop-down list. From the list, select Set Bitmap, and then browse to the bitmap you desire and click Open. This causes Discoverer to display the logo to the left of the available parameters. It will also display on the Parameter Wizard screen.

NOTE
Attaching a bitmap to the dialog box is unique to Desktop. If you add a bitmap to the dialog box in Desktop, it will not display in either Plus or Viewer. However, if your organization does not use Plus or Viewer or you are a dyed-in-the-wool Desktop user, you will find this to be a really cool feature.

8. Click OK.

Rearranging the Order of Parameters

After adding a parameter that is based on a calculation or condition, or following an edit of an existing parameter, you need to review the order in which the parameters will be presented to the end user. The section entitled "Rearranging the Parameter Order" in Chapter 5 explains how to do this. We recommend that you position the most important parameters at the top of the list. If you have cascading parameters, you must place the highest-level parameter before any dependent parameter, with each of the dependent parameters being placed in descending order of their dependency. Discoverer does not enforce the sequential placement of cascading parameters, but it's actually a good idea to do so and a habit that we heartily recommend you adopt.

In the following illustration you can see that we have created a worksheet with four parameters. When a user runs this worksheet in Desktop, the Parameter Wizard opens and displays the first three parameters. The user has to input or select the required criteria for each of these three parameters and then click Next to set the criteria for the final parameter. This restriction of three parameters to a page in Desktop was not carried through into Plus or Viewer, where Discoverer dynamically expands the list to accommodate the parameters.

NOTE
Discoverer remembers the last set of criteria that you entered into the Parameter Wizard, and will insert these as the default the next time that the worksheet is run.

When the user runs this query, Discoverer opens one of the following parameter screens. First, in Desktop, as you can see in Figure 13-3, there is a Parameter Wizard. This wizard presents parameters to the user in the order in which they appear in the Parameters dialog box. Because there are more than three parameters, the Next button is active.

NOTE
As previously commented, the Desktop Parameter Wizard can show only three parameters per screen. If there are more than three parameters, Discoverer creates multiple three-parameter entry screens. Users can navigate between these screens using the Next and Back buttons. However, until all of the mandatory parameters have a value, the Finish button will be grayed out.

In the Plus screen, shown in Figure 13-4, the screen is called the Edit Parameter Values dialog box. The nice thing about this box is that there is no restriction on the number of parameters that will be prompted because the list will dynamically expand to accommodate the number of parameters that you have.

FIGURE 13-3 *Desktop Parameter Wizard*

NOTE
Do you see the small asterisk alongside some of the parameters?
This indicates that the parameter is mandatory. Optional parameters
have no asterisk and can be left blank. Discoverer will not activate
the Finish or OK buttons until you have entered something for each
mandatory parameter.

FIGURE 13-4 *Plus Edit Parameter Values dialog box*

Rearranging Cascading Parameters   When cascading parameters are in use, you need to take great care when rearranging your parameters. Do not move, or attempt to move, one of the dependent parameters above one of the parameters on which it depends. Doing this will cause Discoverer to generate the following warning:

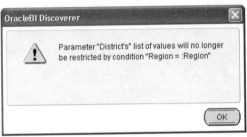

Unfortunately, Oracle does not provide a cancel button, so at this point you are up the creek without a paddle, or so you might think. Even though your only option at this point is to click OK, do not despair. Go ahead, click OK. When you do so, Discoverer rearranges the parameters and moves the dependent parameter above the one on which it depends. It appears as though you have lost your cascading parameter, and you may think that you have no choice but to rebuild the cascade, redefining the order of the parameters as you do.

We even tried clicking the X on the title bar to close the dialog box, but this did not work either. Discoverer still moves the parameter and we lost our cascade, or so we thought. Before you do anything else, click the Cancel button. This will restore the previous settings for the ordering of the parameters. The flip side of this is that if you had added or edited any parameters, these changes will also be lost, but we think this is a small price to pay for not losing the cascade.

Using Parameters in the Title, Header, or Footer

Placing parameters on the worksheet title, or in the header or footer, is a good way for users to see at a glance what parameters have been chosen. You can choose to globally insert all parameters, or if you can remember the names that you gave your parameters, you can place individual parameters in the title, header, or footer.

Do you recall our recommending that you give your parameters meaningful names? Apart from the fact that it makes good sense, this ability to place individual parameters into the title, header, or footer is a good enough reason in itself.

Be careful inserting parameters into the title, header, or footer when the parameter uses a keyword such as SYSDATE or USER. Even though, as you know, these are interpreted as the current date and current user, what Discoverer displays in the title, header, and footer will be the keyword itself, and not its interpreted meaning. To insert the current date, you should use &Date. Unfortunately, there is no shortcut or token that you can use for inserting the user name.

Inserting Parameters into the Title

First of all, if you cannot see the title to your worksheet, you need to make it visible.

In Desktop, this is done from the menu bar using Tools | Options followed by selecting the Table or Crosstab tab, depending upon the type of worksheet you are working with. Then you need to check the box called Title and click OK.

In Plus, the title is also made visible from the menu bar, but this time you only need to select View | Title. There is no check box and no need to click OK. You can see that it is much easier to turn on the title in Plus.

NOTE
To turn the title off, just reverse the preceding logic. However, please note that this does not delete the title. It is simply not being displayed. Re-enabling the title later will restore the title to its previous state. This smart feature of Discoverer works in both Desktop and Plus, even if you close and subsequently reopen the workbook later.

After having turned on the title, you can choose to insert all of the parameters or just selected parameters. First of all you need to launch the title editor. To do this, you simply double-click the title, which, by the way, kindly defaults to "Double click here to edit this title." This is a nice touch and one of the many reasons why Discoverer is a really pleasant tool to work with.

To insert parameters into the title, use this workflow:

1. If it is not already visible, display the title.

2. Launch the Edit Title dialog box by double-clicking the title.

3. To insert all parameters, click the Insert button, and from the drop-down list select Parameters. Discoverer inserts all of the parameter names and all of their associated values.

4. To insert a single parameter, type the ampersand character, **&**, followed by the name of the parameter. Be wary, though, because if you have parameters and Page Items in use at the same time, and you have named a Page Item the same as a parameter, it is the Page Item that takes priority.

NOTE
Remember, parameter names are also case-sensitive, so if you display individual parameters in the title, make sure to type the names exactly as they appear in the list of parameters.

5. Click OK.

Inserting Parameters into the Desktop Header or Footer

Just as with the title, you can insert parameter names and values into the header and footer. Unlike with the title, there is no activation step for editing headers and footers.

To insert parameters into the Desktop header or footer, use this workflow:

1. From the menu bar, select File | Page Setup.

2. Click either the Header or the Footer tab. As shown in this illustration, you will notice that there are three sections, left, center, and right.

3. Pick the section where you want the parameter(s) to be inserted by clicking in the appropriate area.

4. To insert all parameters, click the Insert button, and from the drop-down list select Parameters. Discoverer inserts all of the parameter names and all of their associated values.

5. To insert a single parameter, type the ampersand character, **&**, followed by the name of the parameter. Just like with the title, please remember that if you have parameters and Page Items in use at the same time, and you have named a Page Item the same as a parameter, the Page Item will take priority.

6. Click Preview to see what the page will look like with the parameter(s) inserted into the header and/or footer.

7. Click OK.

Inserting Parameters into the Plus Header or Footer

Just as with Desktop, you can insert parameter names and values into the Plus header and footer. Once again, there is no activation step for editing headers and footers.

To insert parameters into the Plus header or footer, use this workflow:

1. From the menu bar, select File | Page Setup.

2. Click the Header/Footer tab. As shown in the following illustration, you will notice that this tab has two areas, one for Headers and one for Footers. You will also notice that each area has three sections, left, center, and right.

3. Pick the area and section where you want the parameter(s) to be inserted by clicking in the appropriate section.

4. To insert all parameters, click the Insert button, and from the drop-down list select Parameters. Discoverer inserts all of the parameter names and all of their associated values.

5. To insert a single parameter, type the ampersand character, **&**, followed by the name of the parameter. Just as with Desktop, if you have parameters and Page Items in use at the same time, and you have named a Page Item the same as a parameter, the Page Item will take priority. We've repeated this warning several times now, so you won't forget, will you?

6. Click Preview to see what the page will look like with the parameter(s) inserted into the header and/or footer.

7. Click OK.

Refining Calculations

After dealing with parameters, the next most common way to refine a query is to refine the calculations. The ability to manipulate data by the use of both simple and complex calculations and the ability to create new items using calculations are very useful skills to master.

Main Components of a Calculation

Before we get too deep into the complexities of calculations, we feel it would be appropriate to remind you of the main components of a calculation. Whether you are creating or editing a calculation, Discoverer opens the New Calculation dialog box shown in Figure 13-5. This box allows you to give your calculation a meaningful name, and to build your calculation using a combination of items from the database, functions, and operators. In Chapter 5, we introduced you to calculations using the Workbook Wizard. Appendix B contains a full list of all the functions used within Discoverer, along with many useful practical examples, and we strongly recommend that you spend some time learning how to use these functions.

FIGURE 13-5   *New Calculation dialog box*

Define the Calculation in Advance

As with just about everything that we have taught you so far, once again we want to impress upon you the need to think ahead. Unless the calculation is very simple and can be obtained by adding one column to another, or something equally straightforward, we recommend that you work out the calculation in advance. Yes, even in this super-modern world, this is still a use for pencil and paper.

In our experience, even the simplest of algorithms can prove difficult to translate into a script that Discoverer can understand. In this section, we will outline a few fundamentals that you should bear in mind, which may help you when dealing with calculations. These are as follows:

- How to convert an algorithm into a Discoverer script

- How to avoid division by zero errors

- How to choose the correct level of aggregation for a calculation

How to Convert an Algorithm into a Discoverer Script

Converting an algorithm into a Discoverer script need not be daunting, yet many people make it so. This is because they don't remember, or don't know, that the basic language of all computers is a sequential series of zeros and ones. When working with a computer, you need to break everything down into its simplest form, and the same applies to Discoverer.

You need to remember that there is a hierarchy when dealing with Discoverer's mathematical operators. Put simply, this mathematical hierarchy is as follows:

1. Powers and square roots
2. Multiplication and division
3. Addition and subtraction

Normally, Discoverer will work out a calculation from left to right—exactly as you key it in, providing all of your operators are at the same level. If you have operators from mixed levels, Discoverer will evaluate the operators from the highest level first, again left to right, then the next level down, and so on. If you are not careful with your operators, you will end up with incorrect calculations.

For example, look at the following algorithm:

$$5 - 2 * 6 + 10 / 2$$

What do you think is the right answer, and how do you think Discoverer will evaluate this? Look at the algorithm again. A human will evaluate this expression literally from left to right and get the answer 14 in the process. This is the answer that we want Discoverer to generate.

In fact, the answer given by Discoverer is –2. Is this the answer that you got? What Discoverer did was to evaluate the multiplication and division parts first, followed by the subtraction and the addition.

If we insert parentheses into the formula, grouping the multiplication and division components together, and then evaluate the mathematics contained within those parentheses first, this may help you understand what Discoverer is doing:

$5 - (2 * 6) + (10 / 2)$, which evaluates to $5 - 12 + 5$, which is –2.

If you want to force Discoverer to evaluate an expression differently than its natural hierarchy, you have to use parentheses.

For example, suppose we wanted the preceding expression to be calculated exactly as written, that is: subtract 2 from 5, multiply by 6, add 10, and finally divide by 2. Inserting parentheses as follows

$$(((5 - 2) * 6) + 10) / 2$$

evaluates to 14 as required.

We hope this explanation helps you understand how Discoverer performs mathematical calculations and that you will be able to take advantage of this in your query building.

How to Avoid Division by Zero Errors

As with all things computational, you cannot divide by zero in Discoverer. You must be very careful defining expressions that use division, to ensure that the divisor does not evaluate to zero. A calculation that has worked for the last six months may suddenly stop working because the divisor has now evaluated to zero.

In Discoverer, if you attempt to create a calculation such as X divided by Y when Y is zero, the calculation will not work. As the report writer, it is your responsibility to look for and trap this error during the construction of the worksheet.

The authors think that it is folly to assume that a divisor will never be zero. Even the best-designed systems occasionally have glitches that cause erroneous data to get into the database. Perhaps an upload mechanism that was designed to add the cost price for new products did not run when it was supposed to, leaving those costs at zero! You cannot leave your users in the unenviable situation of having worksheets that will not run.

There may also be valid zero values in the database. Sales orders that have not yet shipped will genuinely have an invoiced amount of zero.

So, if you cannot guarantee that the divisor will never be zero, what can you do? There are two ways to overcome the divide by zero error:

■ Use a condition to omit the zero values.

■ Use functions to avoid divide by zero errors.

Use a Condition to Omit the Zero Values   This is the simplest way to avoid divide by zero errors. If you are going to use this method, you must ensure that the item you are going to place the condition on is in fact the same item that Discoverer is using within the calculation.

Sounds obvious, doesn't it? At first sight, we expect that you will say something like "That's obvious," and so it is, yet many users make the mistake of pulling the wrong item into the condition. For example, using our test database, we built a query that showed the total quantity shipped and the selling price by month for the third quarter of 2005, and then we calculated the unit price by dividing the price by the quantity. As you can see next, there are no zero values. But is this the right answer?

Page Items: Quarter: 2005-Q3 ▾

	▸ Month	▸ Selling Price SUM	▸ Ship Qty SUM	▸ Unit Price
1	APR-05	8448518.26	302340	27.94
2	MAY-05	6472950.80	289555	22.35
3	JUN-05	10116505.97	258283	39.17

Without investigating further, it would be very easy to take the answer at face value and assume that the unit price is correct. In fact, as we will show you, the answer is not correct. We first noticed we had a problem when we attempted to drill into the data for May 2005 and opted to view the Status for that month from the Sales Order folder. Discoverer Plus will not let us do this and reports the following divide by zero error:

However, when we tried the same thing within Desktop, we were able to execute the query, but we did not get the expected results. Looking at the drilled-down Desktop data that follows, you can see that we have a divide by zero error:

Page Items:	Quarter: 2005-Q3 ▾			
	Month	Status	Selling Price SUM	Ship Qty SUM	Unit Price
▸ 1	MAY-05	HOLD	29330.00	0	#DIV/0!
▸ 2	MAY-05	OPEN	1004343.06	0	#DIV/0!
▸ 3	MAY-05	SHIPPED	5147552.39	289555	17.78
▸ 4	MAY-05	CANCELLED	291725.35	0	#DIV/0!

Let's stay with Desktop for the time being. From the illustration, the logical condition to apply would seem to be to set the Ship Qty SUM not equal to zero. This would at least solve the divide by zero error. Doing just that resulted in the output you see next:

Page Items:	Quarter: 2005-Q3 ▾			
	Month	Status	Selling Price SUM	Ship Qty SUM	Unit Price
▸ 1	MAY-05	SHIPPED	5147552.39	289555	17.78

So far, so good. Having avoided our divide by zero error, we glanced at the unit price and wondered whey this was lower for May 2005 than in our query before we began drilling. Leaving the condition in place, we used Show Values on the Month heading to get back to the original selections, and we removed the Status. As you can see next, the result is identical to the result we had when we first started out:

Page Items:	Quarter: 2005-Q3 ▾			
	Month	Selling Price SUM	Ship Qty SUM	Unit Price
▸ 1	APR-05	8448518.26	302340	27.94
▸ 2	MAY-05	6472950.80	289555	22.35
▸ 3	JUN-05	10116505.97	258283	39.17

NOTE
Rather than use Show Values, which does not exist in Plus, you can just as easily use Edit | Undo Drill.

Have you spotted the error yet?

By applying the condition to be on the Ship Qty SUM, as opposed to applying it on the Ship Qty itself not being equal to zero, we have uncovered a fundamental flaw in our query. In fact, we should be excluding all items that have a ship quantity of zero because these items are causing our unit price calculation to be too high. We have been adding the selling price for items that have not shipped. After we refined the condition, the result looked as in the next illustration. Notice how the unit price for May is now the same as what we had when we drilled in to the data a few steps back!

Page Items:	Quarter: 2005-Q3 ▼			
	Month	Selling Price SUM	Ship Qty SUM	Unit Price
▶ 1	APR-05	5554173.83	302340	18.37
▶ 2	MAY-05	5147552.39	289555	17.78
▶ 3	JUN-05	4402298.59	258283	17.04

We hope the preceding example has shown you how critical it is to place the condition on the right item when trying to avoid the divide by zero error. At first glance, it appeared as though the condition should have been on the Ship Qty SUM, whereas in fact the correct condition needed to be applied to the Ship Qty itself.

Do not be drawn into believing that all divide by zero errors can be solved by placing the condition on the item, as opposed to the SUM, because they cannot. Databases that use negative values to store amounts and quantities to represent returns may require that the condition be placed on the SUM. For example, suppose you have a sales database where positive values are used to represent actual shipments, and negative values are used to store customer returns. You may not have any zero values in the individual items, yet you may still end up with zero values in the result. This is caused by the total amount for the returns exactly counteracting the amount of real shipments. If you place a condition on the individual items not being zero, the total amount will still be zero.

For example, suppose you had total shipments of 8,000 items to various customers during August 2006, and then you received a single return from a major customer, also for 8,000 items. As you can see, adding the two together, you will get a total stock movement of zero. You would be wrong to place a condition on the SUM because the answer is correct and this row should be included in the result. The only way to overcome this situation is to use either the CASE or DECODE function as described in the next section.

Use Functions to Avoid Divide by Zero Errors   As we showed you in the preceding section, there are times when a zero value belongs in a column that will be used as a divisor. In these cases, you cannot use a condition to omit the item because the end result will be wrong. Perhaps the calculation is the reason why, the raison d'être, the worksheet exists in the first place. If this is the case then you cannot use a condition to remove the items with zero. In order to avoid the divide by zero error and yet leave zero values in the divisor column, you must use some sort of SQL function.

We would like to say:

IF Y = zero

THEN zero

ELSE compute X / Y

Oracle does not have a direct IF . . . THEN construct. Instead, Oracle provides two functions that allow you to compute IF . . .THEN scenarios. These are

■ CASE

■ DECODE

Using the CASE and DECODE Functions to Overcome Divide by Zero Errors   What are the CASE and DECODE functions? These functions equate directly to the IF functions used in Excel and 1-2-3 spreadsheets and to the IF . . . THEN . . . ELSE constructs used in traditional programming languages.

To avoid the divide by zero error, we therefore need to tell the computer

■ **IF** the column being used as the divisor equals zero

■ **THEN** place a zero in the calculated column

■ **ELSE** perform the calculation

Let's take a simple case and calculate X divided by Y, and we want to trap the condition when Y equals zero using zero as the result in this case. In simple syntax this would be written as:

IF Y = 0

THEN 0

ELSE X / Y

In Discoverer, these would be written as:

```
CASE WHEN Y = 0
THEN 0
ELSE X / Y
END
```

or

```
DECODE(Y, 0, 0, X / Y)
```

You will notice that the CASE function is the closest thing we have to a genuine IF . . . THEN . . . ELSE construct. However, if you can master the syntax, you will find that the DECODE is an equally powerful function.

Please refer to Appendix B for a full description of the syntax of the CASE and DECODE functions, and see the section entitled "Using Standard Functions in a Query" later in this chapter for a basic overview of how to use functions within in your worksheet.

Data Type Manipulation with CASE and DECODE   When using CASE or DECODE, you need to be aware that the data type for the function takes its format from the first result obtained within the code. In the following examples, we use RESULT1 and RESULT2 to signify the two possible results that can be returned by these functions.

```
CASE WHEN X = Y THEN RESULT1 ELSE RESULT2 END
```

or

```
DECODE(X, Y, RESULT1, RESULT2)
```

Because RESULT1 is referred to first, Discoverer uses the format of that item for the overall format of the function. You therefore need to be very careful creating functions that look like this:

```
CASE WHEN X = Y THEN 'No Sales' ELSE A / B END
```

or

```
DECODE(X, Y, 'No Sales', A / B)
```

In actual fact, because Discoverer does not allow you to mix formats within a CASE statement, the first function, using CASE and 'No Sales', cannot be created. Discoverer will generate an error at this point informing you that inconsistent or invalid data types cannot be used in a CASE statement.

The latter function, DECODE, will compute, but the format of the ensuing calculation will be textual and not numeric as you would expect. Interestingly enough, although you cannot apply numeric formatting to the cells, such as adjusting the number of decimal places, you can still use totals and these will compute correctly.

Because of the error that will be generated by a CASE statement, and the wrong data type that will be generated by a DECODE, we therefore recommend not mixing data types in either of these functions. If you want to be clever and use a phrase such as 'No Sales' we recommend you use the NULL result and make use of Discoverer's NULL-replacement functionality. The following examples show both functions using the NULL result:

```
CASE WHEN X = Y THEN NULL ELSE A / B END
```

or

```
DECODE(X, Y, NULL, A / B)
```

Choosing the Correct Level of Aggregation for a Calculation

Similar to our advice to use care when applying conditions to avoid the divide by zero error, you must be careful when selecting items that will be used inside calculations. Be sure to select the data item that is being used within a column, rather than the data item that is within the database. We understand that this may be a little confusing at first, so please take the time to stay with us while we explain.

For example, let's say we have a worksheet in which we have created two calculations, both of which subtract the value in one column from another. The following illustration shows the end result, with both the correct and incorrect calculations, plus a column showing the factor of incorrectness. Looking at the factor for the first row of data, you can see that the incorrect calculation is 13 times higher than the correct calculation. This is because there are 13 sales orders on the system that have a selling price of 1,172.50 and a cost price of 621.00.

	► Selling Price	► Cost Price	► Correct Calc	► Incorrect Calc	► Factor
1	1172.50	621.00	551.50	7169.50	13
2	1161.00	620.92	540.08	540.08	1
3	1149.05	608.58	540.47	540.47	1
4	1134.00	606.48	527.52	1055.04	2
5	1125.60	596.16	529.44	4764.96	9
6	1110.00	790.00	320.00	11840.00	37
7	1109.00	531.00	578.00	15606.00	27
8	1108.80	510.08	598.72	1197.44	2
9	1098.00	447.12	650.88	1301.76	2
10	1080.00	577.60	502.40	9043.20	18
11	1078.00	459.20	618.80	6188.00	10
12	1071.00	503.16	567.84	567.84	1
13	1070.00	770.00	300.00	8700.00	29
14	1064.64	509.76	554.88	17201.28	31
15	1062.50	494.00	568.50	6822.00	12
16	1059.60	499.80	559.80	2799.00	5
17	1039.50	478.20	561.30	3367.80	6
18	1024.28	483.14	541.14	1082.28	2
19	1020.00	479.20	540.80	5408.00	10
20	1020.00	474.24	545.76	2183.04	4

As you can see in the following illustration, the correct calculation uses the data without any aggregation, so that we are subtracting the cost price detail from the selling price detail, not the SUM of these.

The incorrect calculation, shown next, uses the SUM of aggregation. This causes Discoverer to add all instances where the selling price is the same and the cost price is the same.

During the construction of the incorrect calculation, Discoverer recognized that there was a potential problem by giving us this warning.

Ignore these warnings at your peril, because there is always a good reason why Discoverer issues warnings like these.

Using COUNT in a Crosstab

Another of the less-used aggregations is the COUNT. Rather than select an item into a worksheet, click the plus key alongside the item and take a look at the options. You will find that if you use the COUNT on the item that is unique, such as an Employee ID or Sales Order Number, you can generate calculations such as Headcount and Number of Orders. We will build a simple crosstab for you to demonstrate this.

Let's start out by selecting the Order Status, the COUNT of the Order Number, and the Order Date Year. These three items on their own make for an interesting query, as you can see here.

	Number of Orders			
	▸ CANCELLED	▸ HOLD	▸ OPEN	▸ SHIPPED
▸ FY1998	7	0	0	370
▸ FY1999	43	0	1	681
▸ FY2000	129	35	430	1087
▸ FY2001	109	0	0	1058
▸ FY2002	119	0	0	1544
▸ FY2003	150	0	0	1628
▸ FY2004	160	0	0	1899
▸ FY2005	151	6	255	1567

We will save this workbook and come back to it when we visit percentages later in this chapter.

As we were creating this worksheet, notice how Discoverer warned us that it was only displaying the first 1,000 order numbers:

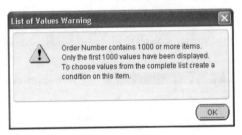

This setting is managed by the Discoverer administrator to protect the system from creating huge lists of values. By default this setting is set to 1,000. Many organizations consider this to be too high and set a much lower value, such as 50.

Housekeeping after Editing a Calculation

After you have edited a calculation, you should undertake some housekeeping measures to maintain the efficiency of the worksheet. There are two steps to take after editing a calculation:

- Review any conditions based on the edited calculation.

- Review the data items used in the edited calculation.

Review Conditions Based on Calculations

As we showed you in Chapter 12, one of the advanced condition types that Discoverer allows is to build a condition based on a calculation. If you create a condition based on a calculation and subsequently edit that calculation, you should evaluate whether the condition is still valid. Discoverer will automatically use the new calculation; however, the condition may no longer do what you wanted.

Review the Data Items Used in the Edited Calculation

After editing a calculation in which you have changed data items, you should check to see if the original data items are still needed in the worksheet. If they are no longer needed, delete them. If you have used additional items, you may need to add them. This will add to the integrity of the workbook as well as keep the query running efficiently.

For example, suppose you have a worksheet in which you are calculating the unit cost price for each sales order by dividing the order quantity into the cost price sum. For clarity, the worksheet will probably include both source items. If you now edit the calculation to base the unit price on the selling price, without changing the items displayed in the result, you could confuse the recipient of your report.

The following illustration perfectly demonstrates this situation. We have a query where the unit price was based on the cost price. The calculation has been changed, and the unit price is now based on the selling price. As you can see, you could easily be led into believing that the unit price is still based on the cost price. You should edit the worksheet, remove the cost price, and insert the selling price in its place.

	Order Number	Order Qty SUM	Cost Price SUM	Unit Price
1	1100	4800	50976.00	22.18
2	1200	2000	24840.00	23.45
3	1300	500	5310.00	22.18
4	1400	200	1242.00	15.25
5	1500	1000	8330.00	17.66
6	1600	500	7970.00	34.65
7	1700	20	248.40	23.45
8	1800	200	2124.00	22.18
9	1900	2400	17328.00	13.50
10	2000	2900	18009.00	15.25
11	2100	10	83.30	17.66
12	2200	960	15302.40	34.65
13	2300	2400	29808.00	23.45
14	2400	200	2124.00	22.18
15	2500	100	722.00	13.50
16	2600	2400	25488.00	22.18
17	2700	2400	25488.00	22.18
18	2800	2400	17328.00	13.50
19	2900	500	4165.00	17.66
20	3000	100	1242.00	23.45

Using Standard Functions in a Query

Perhaps the most difficult part about using calculations in Discoverer is learning how to use the functions that are available to you. When you open the New Calculation dialog box (see earlier Figure 13-2) and click the Functions button in Desktop, or in Plus select Functions from the drop-down of available options, Discoverer displays the folders shown here:

There are nine folders of functions available to you:

■ **All Functions**   Opening this folder displays all of the functions available to you, listed in alphabetical order.

■ **Analytic**   This folder displays all of the analytic functions available to you. These functions are all applied to the result of your query and are not calculated on a row-by-row basis. Please refer to Appendix B for more details on how to use these functions.

■ **Conversion**   This folder contains functions relating to converting data from one format into another. There are functions to convert strings into dates, dates into strings, and so on.

- **Database**   This folder contains user-defined functions that are specific to the database you are currently using. This folder will be empty unless your Discoverer administrator has created some functions for you.

- **Date**   This folder contains functions that manipulate dates. There are functions to generate the system date and time, functions to truncate the time, and so on.

- **Group**   This folder contains functions that work on groups of data. These functions include SUM, MAX, MIN, and so on.

- **Numeric**   This folder contains functions that are used in mathematical computations, such as +, −, *, /, and so on.

- **Others**   This folder contains functions that cannot be categorized into one of the other folders. Examples of these include NVL, CASE, DECODE, and so on.

- **String**   This folder contains functions that manipulate strings. Examples of these include UPPER, LENGTH, CONCAT, and so on.

In the remainder of this section, we will demonstrate the use of some of the more common, non-analytic, functions available to you in Discoverer. In particular, we will show you the following:

- Advanced use of the CASE and DECODE statements

- Manipulation of dates

- Use of TO_CHAR with the number format mask

NOTE
A full explanation of all the functions used in Discoverer can be found in Appendix B, along with many examples. Appendix B also contains a full listing of the format masks available to you.

Advanced Use of the CASE and DECODE Statements

Not a lot of people have harnessed the power of the CASE and DECODE functions, yet their usage is one of the most powerful features of Discoverer. Three of the best uses of these functions are

- Defining a list of new values

- Creating new data types

- Creating calculations based on data subsets

Defining a New List of Values   Few people understand that you can use the CASE and DECODE functions to change a list of values as defined in your database to one that is more meaningful. For example, in many Oracle Applications tables you will notice that Oracle uses the character *Y* for Yes but uses a null value for No. To make a report more meaningful and user-friendly, you might want to display the words Yes and No instead of *Y* and null. You can intercept the Oracle list of values and replace it with your own by using one of the following example pieces of code:

```
CASE WHEN Oracle field name = 'Y' THEN 'Yes' ELSE 'No' END
```

or

```
DECODE(Oracle field name, 'Y', 'Yes', 'No')
```

Using our example database, we will now show you how to replace one list of values with another. As you have seen in our test database, the original list of values for Status is

- CANCELLED

- HOLD

- OPEN

- SHIPPED

Let's say that our shipping department has decided that they want to use the value Pending instead of OPEN for the Status. Also, they want the remaining values to appear with the first letter capitalized and the rest in lowercase. In the following illustration, we have used a DECODE statement to give us the desired result.

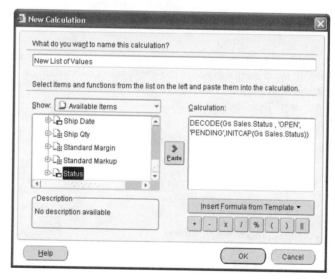

Running this calculation will produce the following list of values:

- Cancelled

- Hold

- Pending

- Shipped

Calculations and conditions can use either the original or amended list of values, but our report will always display the new list.

NOTE
When the current data cannot be sorted into the order that you desire, creating a sort using a new list of values will do the trick. This technique, very common in programming circles, is a very clever use of calculations. In the example just given, we created a new list of values. However, in our final report we want them sorted as Shipped, Hold, Pending, and then Cancelled. By prefixing the items using A-, B-, or 1., 2., and so on, you can reorder any list of values in any arrangement.

Creating New Data Types   You can use calculations to create new data types within your worksheet, but these new types will exist only within that worksheet. However, you can apply sorts and totals and even base other calculations on these data types.

Let's say we want to generate a new data type called Category, and that this category has three values:

■ High

■ Middle

■ Low

We want to analyze our sales and work out our top-ranking customers, such that customers with Sales greater than nine million are in the High category, customers with Sales greater than four million but less than nine million are in the Middle category, and customers with Sales less than or equal to four million are in the Low category.

Here is the basic syntax:

```
IF Sales > 9000000
THEN High
ELSE IF Sales > 4000000
THEN Middle
ELSE Low
```

Using a CASE statement, this translates into

```
CASE WHEN Sales > 9000000
THEN 'High'
ELSE CASE WHEN Sales > 4000000
THEN 'Middle'
ELSE 'Low '
END END
```

NOTE
If you use multiple CASE statements in the same calculation, you must remember that each statement is completed by the END clause. Thus in the preceding example, you can see that two END clauses are required. You can also see that the new data types are enclosed in single quotes.

We will now build this worksheet so that you can see the power of new data types. First of all, we started off by pulling in our Selling Price and Customer Name, and we added a condition such that the Status of the order is Shipped. This ensures that we produce statistics for only those customers to whom we have actually shipped widgets.

Next, we created a new calculation called Category, using the CASE statement outlined earlier. To help you, the following illustration shows the New Calculation dialog box:

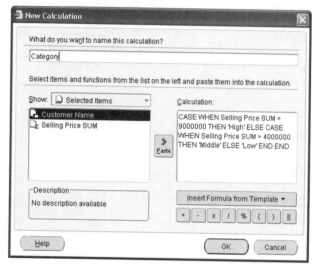

If you are comfortable with Discoverer, then you can use the WIDTH_BUCKET analytic function to create binning-type calculations on your data. Another very powerful way to perform best/worst kind of analysis on your data is to use the NTILE analytic function. You would use NTILE for rank-based bucketing, and WIDTH_BUCKET for value-based bucketing.

Manipulating New Data Types   As mentioned earlier, after you create a new data type you can manipulate it as if it were a normal data type. You can sort by the new data type, you can use it in Page Items, and you can even use it in other calculations or percentages. Your only restriction is your own imagination.

Using the new data type that we created earlier, in this illustration you can see that we successfully created a group sort on the category.

Next we enabled Page Items. Remember you do this by selecting View | Page Items from the menu bar. Finally, after enabling Page Items, as you can see next, we moved the category into the page axis.

Page Items: Category: High ▼

	▶ Customer Name		Price SUM
1	CASA DE WIDGETS	• High	706464.46
2	CEBU WIDGET CO	Low	208176.02
3	MUM'S WIDGET CO	Middle	086011.53
4	THING'S	<All>	087688.97
5	WIDGET SUPPLY CO.		9691684.08
6	WIDGETS DE MEXICO		9777165.68
7	WIDGETS ON THE WEB		9446731.49
8	WIDGETS R US		9301618.76
9	WONDER WIDGETS		10271449.63

	▶ Category	▶ Customer Name	▶ Selling Price SUM
1	High	CASA DE WIDGETS	11706464.46
2		CEBU WIDGET CO	12208176.02
3		MUM'S WIDGET CO.	9086011.53
4		THING'S	9087688.97
5		WIDGET SUPPLY CO.	9691684.08
6		WIDGETS DE MEXICO	9777165.68
7		WIDGETS ON THE WEB	9446731.49
8		WIDGETS R US	9301618.76
9		WONDER WIDGETS	10271449.63
10	Low	BRIDGE THINGS	2916150.18
11		PALMELA WIDGETS	1545422.77
12		RIO WIDGETS	3766134.83
13		WALKING HORSE WIDGET	3933731.69
14		WIDGETS OESTE	3852987.28
15		WILD WEST WIDGETS	2787306.77
16	Middle	ABC WIDGET CO	4814032.14
17		ACE MANUFACTURING	5855992.83
18		BIG RIVER WIDGETS	4256828.80
19		GATOR WIDGETS	5244876.37
20		HONG KONG WIDGETS	8575274.10

Our final worksheet now has a new data type called Category that has three values: Top, Middle, and Low. You can see that Discoverer is quite happy creating a list of values on this new category.

Creating a Calculation on the Subset of an Item   The third advanced use of the CASE and DECODE functions is a bit more tricky. In our database we have two sales channels: External and Internet. Discoverer will normally see these as being a subset of the channel and will not allow us to apply a calculation to one without it's being applied to the other. For example, suppose we want to see the unit price for the External channel only. Defining a calculation as we have done previously will cause Discoverer to show the unit price for both channels.

However, let's suppose we want to see the following output, in which we have displayed the unit price for the External channel, and N.A. for the Internet.

Page Items:	Month: JUN-05 ▼		

	Order Qty SUM	Cost Price SUM	Retail Unit Price
▶ Channel			
▶ EXTERNAL	150435	1404634.97	9.34
▶ INTERNET	415693	3536266.85	N.A.

The only way to do this is to use either CASE or DECODE. These code extracts show exactly how to do this:

```
CASE WHEN Channel = 'INTERNET' THEN NULL ELSE Cost Price Sum / Order Qty Sum END
```

or

```
DECODE(Channel, 'INTERNET', NULL, Cost Price Sum / Order Qty Sum)
```

Here is the calculation as a DECODE:

To complete the report, we made Discoverer display N.A. instead of the null value. This was done in Tool | Options. Refer to Chapter 15 for a full explanation of how to manipulate null values.

Manipulating Dates

There are many date functions available to you in Discoverer, and the skilled application of these coupled with other functions will greatly enhance your skill set. The ability to effectively manipulate and understand date logic is vitally important to your becoming proficient in Discoverer.

Manipulating the Current Date   Current date manipulation lies at the heart of most date manipulations. Once you have mastered it, you can apply the same techniques to other dates, creating more and more powerful queries as you advance your knowledge.

The SYSDATE function returns the current date *and* time. We have italicized the word "and" to draw your attention to the fact that this function returns the time as well as the date. The TRUNC(SYSDATE) function returns the current date alone, with the time portion truncated. It is vitally important that you remember these two uses of the SYSDATE function.

The addition of the time to the date means that you can apply both time and date formats to the SYSDATE, but you should not use it alone in calculations or conditions. To demonstrate this, look at the following illustration. In it we have a single item, the SYSDATE, which has been formatted to show the current date and time in the 24-hour-clock format.

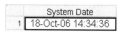

And here is the calculation:

As you can see, if you attempt to find all shipments using this date, you would find only shipments that took place at precisely 14:34 and 36 seconds! An unlikely scenario, we think you will agree. You might be lucky, but probably not.

To use the current date in calculations and conditions, you will apply the TRUNC function to all dates that you use. This will truncate the time portion from the date and allow you to do comparisons and computations safe in the knowledge that you are comparing apples with apples.

To find all shipments that have taken place today, you should use this construct:

TRUNC(SYSDATE)=TRUNC(Ship Date)

Most data warehouse applications will truncate transaction dates as they are being loaded into the warehouse. This will help you considerably because now your construct will become

TRUNC(SYSDATE)=Ship Date

NOTE
Unless you apply formatting criteria to the results of your calculation, the result of a date calculation will always be displayed in the default date format as specified by your Discoverer administrator. Most Oracle systems display the date as either DD-MON-YY or DD-MON-YYYY, meaning that 25 December, 2006, will display either as 25-DEC-06 or 25-DEC-2006.

Common Problems Associated with Not Using TRUNC   As the correct manipulation of the current date requires the application of the TRUNC function to all dates used when comparing one date with another, it is not surprising to find that users frequently run into problems with this. The most common errors encountered when users try to use this function are as follows:

- A condition such as Current Date = Ship Date returns no data. This is because one or both of the dates have a time portion associated with them. Some databases—data warehouses, for example—may be stored with dates already truncated, so you would only need to apply the TRUNC to the Current Date.

- A condition such as Ship Date < Current Date may return incorrect results by including some of the current day's shipments in the result. Suppose the current time is 4:30 P.M., and you last made a shipment at 4:00 P.M. This last shipment would be included in the result because the date and time combination on the shipment is prior to the current date and time combination.

- Ship Date <= Current Date returns data, but Ship Date = Current Date does not. We have seen this happen in data warehouse applications when the ship date has been truncated, but the user forgot to truncate the current date.

NOTE
If you are using Oracle Applications, you will generally find that the transaction dates are not truncated and that the time will be stored as well. You therefore have to be very careful with your date manipulations when using Apps to ensure that your end results are correct. The following example shows you how to search for all today's transactions when the time is stored as part of the transaction date.

Transaction Date BETWEEN TRUNC(SYSDATE) and TRUNC(SYSDATE + 1)

Manipulating Other Dates   We will conclude this section with some more examples of date manipulation. Suppose you wanted to find the date that an item first shipped. A combination of the DECODE, SUM, and MIN functions will give you the answer you are looking for, using this construct:

```
DECODE(SUM(Qty Shipped), 0, NULL, MIN(Ship Date))
```

If we take a closer look at this construct and break it down into plain English, you will be able to follow what is happening. Translating this into words, we get:

If the sum of the quantity shipped is 0, then return a null value; otherwise, return the earliest ship date on file. You may think that the MIN(Ship Date) alone would return the answer you are looking for, but it will not.

The following example will explain why not. Imagine that product A has three sales orders: one has not shipped, one shipped last moth, and one shipped this month. The MIN(Ship Date) will return a null value because it encountered a null value in the ship date. Null values anywhere in the set of results will cause the whole result to be null; therefore, we need to eliminate them.

Last, to find yesterday's date, the function TRUNC(SYSDATE -1) can be used irrespective of the current date. Some Discoverer administrators supply a prebuilt condition for their users in tables that require a lot of reporting on data from yesterday.

Using TO_CHAR to Manipulate Dates   There are three ways to use the TO_CHAR function in Discoverer: with dates, with numbers, and with labels. In the following section we will show you a practical use of the TO_CHAR function being applied to dates. Later in this section we will also show you how to manipulate numbers using the TO_CHAR function.

We have been asked many times how to display dates in various formats other than the format in which the database normally displays dates. For example, you may want to show and manipulate only the month component of the ship date. You might want to convert an Oracle E-Business Suite flex field into a date that you can use in other date manipulations.

First, of all, before we show you how to use the TO_CHAR function to manipulate the month, we recommend that you take a look at Appendix B, at the section that outlines all of the date formats. In there you will see other practical uses for what we are about to show you.

So let's manipulate the ship month so that we can find all sales orders that have shipped during the current month. As you know, the SYSDATE function returns the current date.

If we use TO_CHAR(SYSDATE,'MON'), this will convert today's date to the month. Comparing this with TO_CHAR(Ship Date, 'MON') will return all orders that have shipped in the current month. When you know how, it's simple.

Using TO_CHAR with the Number Format Mask   In this section we will show you a practical use of the TO_CHAR function being applied to numbers.

We have frequently been asked if there is a way to make Discoverer apply a grand total to a select number of columns in a single statement. The answer, as you will by now have realized, is no. You can either define individual totals to the columns you want to total, or you can apply the total to all of the data points. There is no middle ground; however, there is a work-around using the TO_CHAR function.

Let's assume you have three columns of data: one for quantity shipped, one for the local currency amount, and one for the regional currency amount. If you are using multiple currencies, you cannot apply a total to the local currency amount. However, you also do not want to create individual totals for the remaining columns, each with its own label. What you want is a way to apply the grand total to all of the data points, except the local currency, with a single label of 'Grand Total'.

The answer is simple. Well, simple if you know how! You create a new calculation, using TO_CHAR, based on the column or columns that you do not want to include in the grand total. For example, the syntax for converting the local currency amount into a string is:

```
TO_CHAR(local currency amount)
```

However, on its own, the TO_CHAR function will not retain any formatting that you applied to the original number. To do this, you must add a format mask to the calculation. Let's use the same example and assume you want the local currency to be formatted with leading zeros and two decimal places. The following is the revised syntax:

```
TO_CHAR(local currency amount,'999990D99')
```

For a full description of all of the format masks available to you, refer to Appendix B.

Calculating Standard Margin and Markup

If you are working in a manufacturing or order entry environment, these two mathematical formulae are arguably two of the most used formulas within Discoverer queries. The ability to be able to know how to create calculations for these is fundamental to becoming a master of Discoverer in this area.

There is a marked difference between margin and markup. Confusing the two may cause you to create an incorrect calculation or compute a quotation that is too low. Margin is defined as the percentage of the selling price represented by the gross profit. Markup is the amount (usually stated as a percentage of cost) that has to be added to the cost to achieve the selling price.

Standard Margin

Using the definition just outlined, the calculation for standard margin is therefore calculated by taking the difference between the selling price and the cost price, and then dividing this by the selling price.

In order to transform this into Discoverer format, we need to place in brackets the subtraction portion of this definition so that it now becomes: (selling price – cost price) / selling price. In other words, the Margin = (10 – 5) / 10, which works out to be 50 percent.

NOTE
Look closely at the calculation in the following illustration. You will see that once again we have used parentheses to force Discoverer to calculate the subtraction before we perform the division.

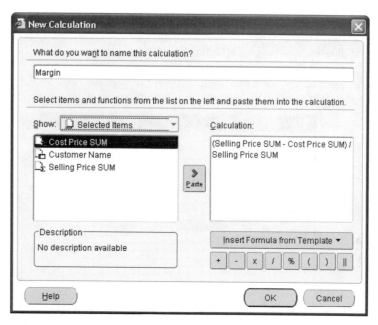

The final result of this calculation needs formatting as a percentage to two decimal places. When done, the Margin looks like this.

	Product Size	Status	Cost Price SUM	Selling Price SUM	Margin
1	LARGE	CANCELLED	5239287.26	10858018.30	51.75%
2		HOLD	194845.76	427691.46	54.44%
3		OPEN	3521376.21	7130347.90	50.61%
4		SHIPPED	51673187.71	105903161.93	51.21%
5	MEDIUM	CANCELLED	5941241.26	13308146.27	55.36%
6		HOLD	358324.01	775642.66	53.80%
7		OPEN	6499755.77	14109687.50	53.93%
8		SHIPPED	54244826.48	121726092.77	55.44%
9	MINI	CANCELLED	849188.58	1202512.05	29.38%
10		HOLD	804.00	1190.00	32.44%
11		OPEN	384185.40	539596.00	28.80%
12		SHIPPED	7231369.32	10289549.45	29.72%
13	SMALL	CANCELLED	1956923.31	3933474.55	50.25%
14		HOLD	69322.84	131146.90	47.14%
15		OPEN	1351942.50	2487595.15	45.65%
16		SHIPPED	18194814.19	36752039.75	50.49%

The calculation, Selling Price minus Cost Price, is generally referred to as the Profit. You could calculate the profit separately and then feed the result of that calculation into the margin as follows: profit / selling price.

Standard Markup

Using the definition outlined earlier, the calculation for standard markup is therefore calculated by taking the difference between the selling price and the cost price, and then dividing this by the cost price.

Again, in order to transform this into Discoverer format, we need to place in brackets the subtraction portion of this definition so that it now becomes: (selling price – cost price) / cost price.

Markup = (10 – 5) / 5, which works out to be 100 percent. Once again, if you have precalculated the profit, you could use this formula: profit / cost price.

Alternate Method to Create Margin or Markup   Assuming that you have already have a calculation called Profit, there is another way of performing either the Margin or Markup calculation that does not involve the use of the New Calculation dialog box. This method uses the analysis toolbar.

Let's start out with the following simple workbook:

	▶ Product Size	▶ Status	▶ Profit	▶ Cost Price SUM	▶ Selling Price SUM
1	LARGE	CANCELLED	5618731.04	5239287.26	10858018.30
2		HOLD	232845.70	194845.76	427691.46
3		OPEN	3608971.69	3521376.21	7130347.90
4		SHIPPED	54229974.22	51673187.71	105903161.93
5	MEDIUM	CANCELLED	7366905.01	5941241.26	13308146.27
6		HOLD	417318.65	358324.01	775642.66
7		OPEN	7609931.73	6499755.77	14109687.50
8		SHIPPED	67481266.29	54244826.48	121726092.77
9	MINI	CANCELLED	353323.47	849188.58	1202512.05
10		HOLD	386.00	804.00	1190.00
11		OPEN	155410.60	384185.40	539596.00
12		SHIPPED	3058180.13	7231369.32	10289549.45
13	SMALL	CANCELLED	1976551.24	1956923.31	3933474.55
14		HOLD	61824.06	69322.84	131146.90
15		OPEN	1135652.65	1351942.50	2487595.15
16		SHIPPED	18557225.56	18194814.19	36752039.75

As you can see in the figure, we have the Profit already calculated. Because the Margin is the Profit divided by the Selling Price, we can use the quick and dirty method for creating a calculation. You need to click the heading for the Profit and then, holding down the CTRL key on the keyboard, you need to next click the heading for the Selling Price. With these two columns selected, you click the Divide icon in the calculation drop-down, as shown next, to obtain the new calculation.

Finally, you need to rename the calculation to Margin and then format it as a percentage.

Activating and Deactivating Calculations

Calculations are stand-alone objects within Discoverer and as such can be activated and deactivated. This section deals with activating and deactivating calculations.

Activating Calculations

Before Discoverer can display a calculation, that calculation needs to be activated. To activate a calculation, use this workflow:

1. From the menu bar select Tools | Calculations, or in Plus click the Calculations tab.
2. Select the calculation that you wish to activate.
3. In Desktop, check the box alongside the calculation and click OK.
4. In Plus, right-click the calculation and from the drop-down list select Add to Worksheet.

NOTE
Some calculations are used as intermediary calculations for other calculations or within conditions. Even though these calculations may be displayed as being inactive, because another calculation or condition is using that calculation it is actually active.

Deactivating Calculations

Discoverer has the ability to deactivate a calculation without deleting its definition. To deactivate a calculation, use this workflow:

1. From the menu bar select Tools | Calculations, or in Plus click the Calculations tab.
2. Select the calculation that you wish to deactivate.
3. In Desktop, uncheck the box alongside the calculation and click OK.
4. In Plus, right-click the calculation and from the drop-down list select Remove from Worksheet.

Refining the Sort Order

After you have refined conditions, parameters, and especially calculations, the next logical step is to refine the sort order. Perhaps the addition of a new calculation has added a new column. Maybe the calculation was created specifically for the purpose of defining a new list of values. It is also likely that an erroneous data item was removed from the worksheet when you refined your calculations.

Therefore, after you have refined calculations, you will need to revisit sorting if one of the following is true:

■ You deleted a column upon which a sort had been created.

■ You added a new item that needs to be part of a sort.

■ You added a new list of values and a sort exists on the old list.

■ The new items that have been added to the worksheet fundamentally changed the essence and meaning.

In Chapter 5, we explained in detail how to sort, add group sorts, add multiple sorts, and rearrange the order. We even showed you how to add or remove sorts using the menu bar or from a drop-down list. If you are not sure how these are done, you should go back and read the section on sorting in Chapter 5 again.

Sort Order Manipulation

When you have multiple sorts in your worksheet, you can choose, using Tools | Sort, the order in which those sorts are applied. By default, Discoverer has a hierarchy for sorting. This hierarchy places group sorts above standard high-to-low or low-to-high sorts.

It is important to remember that Discoverer has this sorting hierarchy because adding or removing sorts with a different rank will cause the sort order to change. This may be what you intended or not.

In the following illustration, we have three sorts in operation. These are

■ A low-to-high group sort on Quarter

■ A low-to-high group sort on Channel

■ A high-to-low normal sort on Status

	▸ Quarter	▸ Channel	▸ Status	▸ Selling Price SUM
1	2005-Q2	EXTERNAL	SHIPPED	6389994.34
2			OPEN	64680.00
3			CANCELLED	126188.80
4		INTERNET	SHIPPED	15633998.25
5			OPEN	694614.00
6			CANCELLED	1499149.82
7	2005-Q3	EXTERNAL	SHIPPED	3739763.28
8			OPEN	2380532.75
9			HOLD	30485.00
10			CANCELLED	962248.20
11		INTERNET	SHIPPED	11364261.53
12			OPEN	4976441.78
13			HOLD	2254.64
14			CANCELLED	1581987.85
15	2005-Q4	EXTERNAL	OPEN	86613.00
16			HOLD	28140.00
17		INTERNET	OPEN	461901.70
18			HOLD	2125.00
19			CANCELLED	85878.00

In the Sort tab of the Edit Worksheet dialog box, the sort definitions look like this:

	Column	Direction	Sort Type	Hidden
Sort by	🔲 *Quarter*	▾ Low to High ▾	Group Sort ▾	☐
then by	🔲 *Channel*	▾ Low to High ▾	Group Sort ▾	☐
then by	🔲 *Status*	▾ High to Low ▾	Normal ▾	☐

Using one of the techniques shown to you in Chapter 5, we will change the group sort on the Quarter to become a standard low-to-high sort. If you recall, you do this by right-clicking in the column that has the sort you want to change, and from the drop-down list clicking Group Sort. This removes the Group Sort rule and changes the sort to become a standard sort. When we did this on our Quarter, this is what happened.

	▸ Quarter	▸ Channel	▸ Status	▸ Selling Price SUM
1	2005-Q2	EXTERNAL	SHIPPED	6389994.34
2	2005-Q2		OPEN	64680.00
3	2005-Q2		CANCELLED	126188.80
4	2005-Q3		SHIPPED	3739763.28
5	2005-Q3		OPEN	2380532.75
6	2005-Q3		HOLD	30485.00
7	2005-Q3		CANCELLED	962248.20
8	2005-Q4		OPEN	86613.00
9	2005-Q4		HOLD	28140.00
10	2005-Q2	INTERNET	SHIPPED	15633998.25
11	2005-Q2		OPEN	694614.00
12	2005-Q2		CANCELLED	1499149.82
13	2005-Q3		SHIPPED	11364261.53
14	2005-Q3		OPEN	4976441.78
15	2005-Q3		HOLD	2254.64
16	2005-Q3		CANCELLED	1581987.85
17	2005-Q4		OPEN	461901.70
18	2005-Q4		HOLD	2125.00
19	2005-Q4		CANCELLED	85878.00

As you can see, the Quarter is no longer group-sorted. You can also see that the Channel is no longer sorted after the Quarter but that the Quarter is now being sorted after the Channel. Looking at the Sort tab of the Edit Worksheet dialog box, the sort definitions now look like this.

	Column	Direction	Sort Type	Hidden
Sort by	🔲 *Channel*	▾ Low to High ▾	Group Sort ▾	☐
then by	🔲 *Quarter*	▾ Low to High ▾	Normal ▾	☐
then by	🔲 *Status*	▾ High to Low ▾	Normal ▾	☐

By comparing this illustration to the one given earlier, you can see that Discoverer has switched the sort order so that the Channel now sorts before the Quarter.

As an experiment, try highlighting the Quarter in the Sort tab and then clicking the Move Up button. If you do this, because you will be moving a standard sort above a group sort, Discoverer will change the sort on the Quarter to once again become a group sort.

Deleting a Sort Using the Sort tab

In Chapter 5 you were shown how to delete a sort using a drop-down list. However, you can also delete sorts from the Sort tab of the Edit Sheet dialog box.

If you have decided that a sort is no longer needed, you can delete it, using the Sort tab, by using the following workflow:

1. From the menu bar, select Tools | Sort, or you can also click the Sort tab on the Edit Sheet dialog box. This will open the Sort dialog box.

2. Highlight the sort you want to delete.

3. Click the Delete button.

4. Click OK.

Refining Percentages

Finally, the last component to refining a worksheet is refining percentages. Very little of the previous refinements will have had any significant impact on the percentages, which is why we have left this section till last. However, you may have changed the definition of a calculation that was used in a percentage. That change may now require you to either amend or remove the percentage definition.

In Chapter 5, we explained in great detail how to create percentages. We also gave you examples of all of the different types of percentage that you can create in Discoverer. In Chapter 9, we showed you many examples of percentages being used to analyze data. In this chapter, we will give you workflows for editing a percentage and for removing an unwanted percentage.

Using COUNT and Percentages in a Crosstab

Earlier in this chapter we created a worksheet that used the count of the sales orders. We will now refine that worksheet to add a percentage and show you how the different percentage options work.

Let's start out by reloading the worksheet that used the Order Status, the COUNT of the Order Number, and the Year. By clicking anywhere in the data for this worksheet and then clicking the New Percentage button, as you can see next, Discoverer automatically creates a percentage based on the order number count.

Editing the percentage shows that we have four main options for calculating the percentage:

- Grand total of all values

- Grand total for each column

- Grand total for each row

- Subtotal at each change in group sort

The next three illustrations show how this simple percentage worksheet looks when each of the first three options are selected.

The following illustration shows a percentage based on a grand total of all values.

	Number of Orders				Percent			
	▸ CANCELLED	▸ HOLD	▸ OPEN	▸ SHIPPED	▸ CANCELLED	▸ HOLD	▸ OPEN	▸ SHIPPED
▸ FY1998	7	0	0	370	0.06%	0	0	3.24%
▸ FY1999	43	0	1	681	0.38%	0	0.01%	5.96%
▸ FY2000	129	35	430	1087	1.13%	0.31%	3.76%	9.51%
▸ FY2001	109	0	0	1058	0.95%	0	0	9.26%
▸ FY2002	119	0	0	1544	1.04%	0	0	13.51%
▸ FY2003	150	0	0	1628	1.31%	0	0	14.24%
▸ FY2004	160	0	0	1899	1.40%	0	0	16.62%
▸ FY2005	151	6	255	1567	1.32%	0.05%	2.23%	13.71%
Percent	868	41	686	9834	7.59%	0.36%	6.00%	86.04%

The following illustration shows a percentage based on a grand total for each column.

	Number of Orders				Percent			
	▸ CANCELLED	▸ HOLD	▸ OPEN	▸ SHIPPED	▸ CANCELLED	▸ HOLD	▸ OPEN	▸ SHIPPED
▸ FY1998	7	0	0	370	0.81%	0	0	3.76%
▸ FY1999	43	0	1	681	4.95%	0	0.15%	6.92%
▸ FY2000	129	35	430	1087	14.86%	85.37%	62.68%	11.05%
▸ FY2001	109	0	0	1058	12.56%	0	0	10.76%
▸ FY2002	119	0	0	1544	13.71%	0	0	15.70%
▸ FY2003	150	0	0	1628	17.28%	0	0	16.55%
▸ FY2004	160	0	0	1899	18.43%	0	0	19.31%
▸ FY2005	151	6	255	1567	17.40%	14.63%	37.17%	15.93%
Percent	868	41	686	9834	100.00%	100.00%	100.00%	100.00%

The following illustration shows a percentage based on a grand total for each row.

	Number of Orders					Percent				
	▸ CANCELLED	▸ HOLD	▸ OPEN	▸ SHIPPED	Total	▸ CANCELLED	▸ HOLD	▸ OPEN	▸ SHIPPED	Total
▸ FY1998	7	0	0	370	377	1.86%	0	0	98.14%	100.00%
▸ FY1999	43	0	1	681	725	5.93%	0	0.14%	93.93%	100.00%
▸ FY2000	129	35	430	1087	1681	7.67%	2.08%	25.58%	64.66%	100.00%
▸ FY2001	109	0	0	1058	1167	9.34%	0	0	90.66%	100.00%
▸ FY2002	119	0	0	1544	1663	7.16%	0	0	92.84%	100.00%
▸ FY2003	150	0	0	1628	1778	8.44%	0	0	91.56%	100.00%
▸ FY2004	160	0	0	1899	2059	7.77%	0	0	92.23%	100.00%
▸ FY2005	151	6	255	1567	1979	7.63%	0.30%	12.89%	79.18%	100.00%

Workflow to Change a Percentage

To change a percentage definition, use the following workflow:

1. From the menu bar, select Tools | Percentages, or in Plus click the Calculations tab in the Available Items pane. In both versions you will see a list of percentages.

NOTE
Clicking the Percentage button on the Desktop analysis bar or the Plus menu bar does not open the Percentages tool. These buttons create a percentage based on the column currently highlighted.

2. Double-click the percentage that you want to change. Discoverer now opens the Edit Percentages dialog box.

3. Change the percentage definition (refer to Chapter 5 for an explanation of percentage definitions).

4. Click OK.

Workflow to Delete a Percentage

To delete a percentage definition, use the following workflow:

1. From the menu bar select Tools | Percentages, or in Plus click the Calculations tab. Either one of these methods displays the list of percentages.

2. Highlight the percentage that you want to remove, and then in Desktop click Delete or in Plus right-click the Percentage and from the drop-down menu select Delete.

3. In Desktop only, click OK.

Activating and Deactivating Percentages

Percentages are stand-alone objects within Discoverer and as such can be activated and deactivated. This section deals with activating and deactivating percentages.

Activating Percentages

Before Discoverer can display a percentage, that percentage needs to be activated. To activate a percentage, use this workflow:

1. From the menu bar select Tools | Percentages, or in Plus click the Calculations tab.

2. Select the percentage that you wish to activate.

3. In Desktop, check the box alongside the percentage and click OK.

4. In Plus, right-click the percentage and from the drop-down list select Add to Worksheet.

Deactivating Percentages

Discoverer has the ability to deactivate a percentage without deleting its definition. To deactivate a percentage, use this workflow:

1. From the menu bar select Tools | Percentages, or in Plus click the Calculations tab.

2. Select the percentage that you wish to deactivate.

3. In Desktop, uncheck the box alongside the percentage and click OK.

4. In Plus, right-click the percentage and from the drop-down list select Remove from Worksheet.

Summary

In this chapter you have learned to change a condition to a parameter, edit parameters, and rearrange the order of parameters. We have also shown you how to refine calculations by defining the main components of a calculation and how to define the calculation in advance. We have taught you how to convert an algorithm into a Discoverer script as well as how to avoid division by zero errors. We have shown you how to use DECODE to overcome divide by zero errors, as well as how to create custom lists of values. We have shown you to how review conditions based on calculations and review the data items used in the edited calculation. We have shown you how to use standard functions to define calculations for standard margin and markup.

We taught you how to refine the sort order, as well as how to remove an item from the sort order. And finally, we gave you workflows for refining percentages, including how to change percentages and how to remove them.

In the following chapter, we will teach you techniques for managing queries, including sharing, security, and understanding your access to the queries of others.

CHAPTER
14

Query Management

nce a workbook has been formatted into a valuable report, the decision needs to be made about who will have access to it. Will it be distributed in print only, or will others have access to it through Discoverer? Will it be e-mailed to your manager or even become a company-wide report used by many people every day? Is it destined to find its way into your enterprise portal as a Discoverer portlet? Since Discoverer 10.1.2 provides a great deal of new functionality in portlets, this is also a very attractive option.

In this chapter, you will learn a little about the role of the Discoverer manager, and how he or she is an important part of report management. You will need to know what access you have to any given report. A good relationship with your Discoverer manager plays an important role in that access. You might be given access to a report that has been developed by another person, perhaps a library manager or superuser. Perhaps the access you are given might be limited and you will be allowed only to view the report, not to make any changes to it.

We will talk about libraries in depth and show you how they can help you organize your workbooks. You will learn how to work with libraries and see how helpful they can be in avoiding duplication of workbooks.

We will show you how to share workbooks that you have created as well as how to open workbooks that have been shared with you. You will learn the benefits of sharing workbooks as well as the involvement of superusers in the management of shared workbooks. We will teach you how to use and edit shared workbooks.

Deleting unwanted or unused workbooks from the database is another important part of report management. An equally important facet is managing the properties of a report. This chapter will teach you how to perform these functions as well as why caution should be used. We will explain how security is set up to protect sensitive company data and how that affects you.

A section called "Worksheet Manipulation" will show you how to manage worksheets within your workbooks. We will show you how to reorder worksheets, how to rename worksheets, and how to delete unwanted worksheets. You will also learn how to find data within a worksheet and even how to copy or move worksheets between workbooks.

Use of the Workbook Scheduler will be covered, as well as the benefits to you of executing your workbooks at a scheduled time. You will learn how to schedule a workbook, how to view the results, and how to unschedule a workbook. You will also learn how to share the results of scheduled workbooks with other users.

We will show you the added flexibility that using a third-party scheduler provides by using the command line. We will further show you how to use XP's native scheduler to set up your own third-party scheduling.

We have also added a section on Discoverer's command-line utility, and will introduce you to the features that give additional power to the end user. An overview has been provided to give you the syntax of all of the command-line functions, along with many examples that will show you how to use the command line.

Another topic to be covered in this chapter is the management of SQL code: importing, exporting, and the use of structured SQL. You will also be shown how to send reports to others via e-mail.

The Discoverer Manager and the End User

Before you can begin to work with Discoverer, your Discoverer manager needs to have granted, or arranged for you to have been granted, various rights and privileges. The most important of these is the creation of a user account for the database(s) that you will be accessing. This setup will assign you a user ID and password and will create the basic database privileges that you will need. Your Discoverer administrator will convey these to you, probably in an e-mail.

NOTE
If you are using Oracle Applications, your user ID, password, and responsibility will probably have already been assigned to you by the system administrator. You need to liaise with the Discoverer manager as to what rights and privileges your particular responsibility has been granted. You may well need to be granted a separate responsibility for accessing Discoverer.

Having set up an account for you, your Discoverer manager will now grant you access to one or more business areas as well as specify your end-user privileges. The rights that you are assigned at this stage dictate whether you have the power to grant access for other people to share your queries, whether you have the power to save and delete queries to the database, and whether you have the power to schedule queries.

Managing Libraries

We introduced you to the concept of libraries in Chapter 2. If you are unsure as to the definitions of a Discoverer library and Discoverer manager, please go back and read those sections in Chapter 2. In this section, we expand on the concept and show you how we feel libraries should be an integral part of your Discoverer environment.

NOTE
The concept of a Discoverer library is not a "native" Discoverer concept but one that we advocate for more efficient management of Discoverer content.

Expanded Library Concept

The concept of a Discoverer library is a mechanism that we invented to help our clients better manage Discoverer. It is not restricted to 10.1.2, although 10.1.2 Plus, as you can see in this illustration, lends itself ideally to working with a library.

You can think of a library as a collection of Discoverer workbooks all based around a common theme. For example, you could have one set of workbooks dedicated to human resources, another dedicated to accounting, another dedicated to order entry, and yet another library dedicated to maintaining inventory. If you are using the Oracle E-Business Suite, in other words Oracle Applications, you can see how easy it would be to set up one library for each module of the system. Each library has a dedicated, generic user account such that you will create accounts called HR Library, OE Library, and INV Library.

Next you will create two sets of roles, or responsibilities if using Oracle Applications. One set will be for the library managers, with names such as HR Library Manager, OE Library Manager, and INV Library Manager. The second set is for end-user access, with names such as HR User, OE User, and INV User. Using the Discoverer Administrator tool, the Discoverer manager will assign these roles or responsibilities access to the required business areas.

Next, you assign the library manager role(s) to designated users. These users will be responsible for maintaining the workbooks inside their library. Logging into Discoverer Plus, the library manager can SHARE workbooks with the user roles or responsibilities, such that a person with the HR Library Manager role can share the HR Workbooks with the HR User role.

All that remains is to grant the HR role or responsibility to a real HR user. The user will then automatically have access to all of the workbooks in the HR library.

The use of libraries maintains sets of corporate workbooks that adhere to corporate standards, are documented, and are guaranteed to work. End users cannot modify these workbooks, because they are not the owner. Only the library manager has the power to add or remove workbooks and worksheets. The manager also controls which workbooks get shared and which do not.

As we hope you can see, a Discoverer library is a means of centrally managing and maintaining Discoverer workbooks. The concept is not restricted to 10.1.2, though, and can be used with every release of Discoverer. However, as explained earlier, the Discoverer 10.1.2 Plus release lends itself perfectly to the use of libraries.

In the next sections we will explain how libraries are used and give you some simple workflows for changing library reports and for gaining access to existing library reports.

There are six important features of a library report that make it different from a Discoverer workbook. Library documents are different to normal Discoverer workbooks in that they are

- Owned by a library manager

- Guaranteed to be accurate and perform efficiently

- Guaranteed to adhere to corporate standards

- Centrally documented

- Centrally maintained

- Secure, with access being strictly controlled

We will deal with each of these concepts in turn.

Library Reports Are Owned by a Library Manager

Perhaps the single biggest difference between a standard Discoverer workbook and a library report is that the library reports are centrally owned and controlled. The person who has this responsibility is the library manager. The manager account will not normally be a real user account but a database account, or Apps account, which is responsible for a set of workbooks. Adopting this method of working ensures the continued existence of the library following the departure of the manager, either from the company or from that position.

NOTE
By default, the Discoverer manager also has the library manager role for all libraries.

Library Documents Are Guaranteed to Be Accurate and Perform Efficiently

Candidate reports will have stringent user testing to confirm that they do what they are supposed to do. Before being put forward as candidates for the library, new reports will require user sign-off and documentation. The users need to confirm that the report indeed does what it sets out to do. However, not only must the report do what it is supposed to do, but it should do it effectively and efficiently without putting undue overhead on the system. In other words, where required, the report's underlying SQL will have been optimized for good performance. This may require the writing of special SQL code, as either a Custom folder or a database view.

Library Reports Adhere to Corporate Standards

These standards dictate the layout, style, and naming conventions that will be used. There should be an agreed list of abbreviations to which all library reports will conform. Standard headers and footers should be employed, and the data should be displayed in your organization's corporate colors. A confidentiality statement will be used where necessary. The adoption of these standards ensures that reports display a corporate image. The library manager is responsible for checking that the standards are being correctly used and that your corporate look and feel is being maintained. Reports that do not conform will be rejected and sent back to the report writer.

Library and Workbook Prefixing   Another standard you may want to consider is the use of prefixes in the naming of your libraries and workbooks. We like to use two- or three-character prefixes for all of our corporate libraries and workbooks. Using prefixes helps us keep track of which workbooks belong to which library and, if we similarly prefix our business areas and folders, which business area the workbook uses. For example, let's say we have a human resources business area. Using this standard, we would prefix the business area name with the letters HR, perhaps naming it HR – Human Resources. All folders within the business area will also get the same prefix; thus, for instance, our employee folder will be called HR – Employees. Following this theme, our library would be called HR – Human Resources Library, and all library reports will be prefixed similarly.

Library Reports Are Centrally Documented

Library reports will have meaningful descriptions for the report requirements, column names, and function definitions. Any special requirements such as parameter usage will be explained in detail. There should also be a set of example screenshots from the report. Users should be able to use this documentation to understand what the report does and thus make a decision as to whether it satisfies the need that they have.

Library Reports Are Centrally Maintained

Following a request for a change to a library report, the library manager will consult with the requesting end user or department head and that department's report writer. The end result of this consultation will be either acceptance or rejection of the request. When a change request is accepted, the library manager will release the workbook containing the report and assign it to a report writer. Following a change, the report will need user testing, sign-off, and updated documentation prior to acceptance back into the library.

Library Reports Are Secure, with Access Being Strictly Maintained

Access to a library report will require a request from either an end user or the end user's manager. No user will be allowed to change a library report. Following the approval of a request, the library manager will work with the Discoverer manager to ensure that the user has access to the relevant business area. When this confirmation has been received, the library manager will share the report with the user's role or responsibility. Finally, the user will be informed that their request has been accepted and that the report is now available to them.

NOTE
Some reports need to get assigned to a subset of the user base. In this case, we recommend that rather than sharing the report with the user direct, you create another role or responsibility for this purpose. Then, if another user needs to have access to the same report, the library manager only needs to ensure that the user gets granted the role or responsibility.

Creating New Library Reports

If you are working in an organization that is using libraries and you need to get a new report created and added to the library, use this workflow:

1. Raise a new report request, including a justification and specification for the new report, and send this request to the library manager.
2. The library manager checks existing library reports to see if such a report already exists.
3. If no report currently exists, a report writer is assigned the task.
4. After the report has been built, user acceptance testing must be completed.
5. The library documentation is produced by the report writer.
6. The report writer shares the new report with the library manager and requests that the report be included in the library.
7. Upon receipt of a request for a report to be included in the library, the manager

   ■ Checks that corporate standards have been met.

   ■ Checks that naming standards have been met.

   ■ Checks that the user requirements have been met.

   ■ Checks that the documentation is complete.

   ■ Accepts the new report into the library by using Save As.

   ■ Makes the report available to the end users using Discoverer's share functionality. The report will normally be shared with a role or responsibility, not with a named user.

8. The report writer deletes the report from his / her account.

Gaining Access to a Library Report

Before a user can log in and run a report contained within a Discoverer library, the following steps need to have been completed:

1. The user or the user's manager will need to request that access to Discoverer be made available. This request should specify to which database the user needs to have access and to which business areas access should be granted. The request should also contain the user's contact information, the user's position, and whether the user needs to have full Discoverer access (report writer) or just the ability to run prewritten reports (report viewer).

2. The library manager will take the request and coordinate it with the DBA, Apps administrator, and Discoverer manager. After the DBA or Apps administrator has created the user account and granted the appropriate roles or responsibilities, the Discoverer manager will complete his or her tasks by granting access to the required business areas or roles, and possibly arranging for the user to attend a training course.

3. After the Discoverer manager has completed his or her tasks, the request will be passed back to the library manager for completion. The library manager will ensure that all relevant reports to which the user needs to have access have been shared with that user's role or responsibility. Departmental training will also now be arranged.

4. Finally, when all of the preceding steps have been completed, the user will receive notification from the library manager that the account has been set up and has been activated.

Sharing Workbooks with Other Users

Sharing workbooks allows you to grant other people rights to run your workbooks. These other users will be allowed to view, analyze, and print the results from your workbook, but they will not be allowed to save any changes to your query. Users who execute shared workbooks will see that the Save option on the menu bar is disabled. However, users will be allowed to save the workbook under their own name, leaving the original intact.

Apart from the convenience of having the ability to share your workbooks with other users, there are a number of other benefits to sharing workbooks. Sharing gives users without the right to create workbooks the ability to run them and perform analysis on the data.

Another key benefit of sharing workbooks is the all-important matter of saving resources. There is nothing more frustrating to a manager than to find that two of that manager's staff have used time and effort creating virtually the same report. Communication among the Discoverer users in a department will keep staff members from "reinventing the wheel." Even when the reporting needs of two separate users are different, the same workbook may satisfy both needs as the foundation to build upon.

If you are using scheduling in your organization, you will be pleased to know that users using Plus can now share the results of scheduled workbooks with other users, thus disseminating information across your organization.

NOTE
A new feature of sharing in Plus is the ability to share not only with an individual user, but also with a role or responsibility. This is one of the ways that setting up libraries in Discoverer has been facilitated.

Superuser Involvement with Shared Workbooks

One of the real pluses of having a superuser is the ability to appoint him or her as your departmental workbook guru or report writer. Having a single person in this position can be extremely advantageous. Involvement with shared workbooks could then be the responsibility of the superuser in the following three ways:

■ **For development of shared workbooks**   Given that your superuser has increased knowledge of the database, he or she could be tasked with workbook development. These workbooks, once written, could then be shared with other members of your department or even company wide.

- **For support of shared workbooks**   If you have a superuser who has taken on the responsibility for creating your department's workbooks, the same person should be tasked with supporting those workbooks by essentially creating your first Discoverer library. They would become the first line of support for your department's users.

- **For maintaining documentation**   When shared workbooks are used, it is vitally important that documentation is provided about those workbooks. It is natural that the person who creates the workbooks also creates and maintains that documentation. When using libraries, this documentation becomes part of the central documentation.

How to Share a Workbook

In order to share a workbook, you need to have been granted the appropriate rights and privileges. If you do not have the correct privileges, both at the database and end-user layer levels, you will not be able to share a workbook. The privileges are set by the Discoverer administrator, and you will need to submit a request to have these set up for you.

You can share workbooks in one of two ways:

- You can allow one or more users, roles, or responsibilities to share one of your workbooks or the workbooks you are managing.

- You can allow one or more workbooks to be shared by one user, role, or responsibility.

Sharing a Workbook Using Desktop

To share a workbook in Discoverer Desktop, use the following workflow:

1. From the menu bar select File | Manage Workbooks | Sharing. This opens the Share Workbooks dialog box, as seen in Figure 14-1. As you can see, the Share Workbooks dialog box has two tabs: one for Workbook > User and one for User > Workbook.

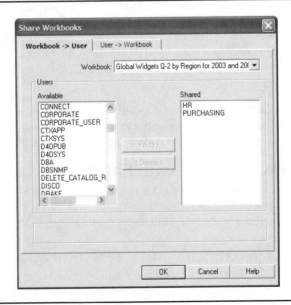

FIGURE 14-1   *Desktop Share Workbooks dialog box*

2. Select the tab Workbook > User.

3. The Workbook drop-down list displays all of the queries that you have created. From the Workbook drop-down list, select the workbook that you want to share.

4. The user list displays all of the users that have access to the same database as yourself, although they may not have access to the business area that the workbook is using. From the list of available users, click the user you want to share the workbook with.

NOTE

To highlight more than one user, hold down the CTRL key while clicking the user names. This allows you to share the workbook with multiple users at the same time.

5. Click Add. This moves the users over into the Shared box.

6. Click OK. This closes the Share Workbooks dialog box and completes the sharing of the workbook with the user(s) concerned.

Sharing a Workbook Using Plus

To share a workbook in Discoverer Plus, use this workflow:

1. From the menu bar, select Tools | Manage Workbooks. This opens the Manage Workbooks dialog box shown in Figure 14-2. Until you select a workbook to share, the Share button is grayed out.

FIGURE 14-2   *Plus Manage Workbooks dialog box*

2. Expand the list of workbooks that you own.

3. Click one of your workbooks. You will notice that the Share button has now been activated.

4. Click Share. This opens the Share Workbooks dialog box shown in Figure 14-3.

5. As you can see in Figure 14-3, the Plus Share Workbooks dialog box, like the Desktop equivalent, also has two tabs: one for Workbook > User and one for User > Workbook.

6. Unlike when using the Desktop dialog box, you now have the ability to share with a database Role or an Apps Responsibility.

7. Using the Workbook > User tab, you can share one workbook with one or more users, database roles, or Apps responsibilities. The workbook was already selected in Step 4. From the Available pane select the user, role, or responsibility you want to share the workbook with and move it over into the Shared pane.

NOTE
Users and roles are identified by different icons, as are scheduled workbooks.

8. Using the User > Workbook tab, you can share multiple workbooks with one user, database role, or Apps responsibility. Use the Select User button to choose one user, role, or responsibility and then from the Available pane select one or more workbooks that you want to share, moving them over into the Shared pane.

FIGURE 14-3 *Plus Share Workbooks dialog box*

NOTE
We recommend that, when working with Oracle Applications,
you always share with an Apps responsibility. Similarly, if you are
a library manager and you are sharing a library report, make sure
you share it with a database role or Apps responsibility and not
with an individual user.

9.   After you have made your selections, click OK to close the Share Workbooks dialog box.

10. Click Close to close the Manage Workbooks dialog box.

Using a Shared Workbook

If you have been granted permission to use a shared workbook, there are a number of things that you need to know, including the following:

■   How to recognize a shared workbook

■   How to open a shared workbook

■   How to manage missing items

■   How to edit and save a shared workbook

How to Recognize a Shared Workbook

When you log in to Discoverer to open an existing workbook, Discoverer prefixes shared workbooks with the name of the owner or library. In the following illustration, you can see that this user has many workbooks available from the database. The first two in the list are the user's own workbooks, and the last ones have been shared by library owners. In Desktop, shared workbooks always appear at the bottom of the list of available workbooks. In Plus, workbooks can be viewed either alphabetically or by owner.

How to Open a Shared Workbook

To open and execute a shared workbook, use the following workflow:

1.   From the menu bar, select File | Open.

2. Locate and click a workbook that has been shared with you.

3. Click Open. In Plus, Discoverer automatically opens and executes the workbook. In Desktop, Discoverer prompts you with the Workbook in Other Database Account dialog box.

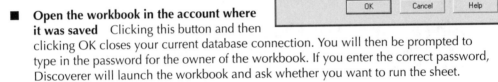

In the preceding box, you can see that you have three options:

- **Open the workbook in the account where it was saved**   Clicking this button and then clicking OK closes your current database connection. You will then be prompted to type in the password for the owner of the workbook. If you enter the correct password, Discoverer will launch the workbook and ask whether you want to run the sheet.

- **Open the workbook in the current database account**   Clicking this button (the default) and then clicking OK launches the workbook. Discoverer validates whether you have access to the required business area and then asks whether you want to run the sheet. If you do not have rights to the business area used by the workbook, you will be unable to open the workbook. See the following sections, "How to Manage Missing Items."

- **Do not open the workbook**   This option does just as it says and returns you to the workbook selection list, from which you should select another workbook.

How to Manage Missing Items in Desktop

When working in Desktop, every time you open a workbook that has been shared with you by another user or from a library, Discoverer validates that you have the rights to the business area used by the workbook. If this validation fails, you will see the following Missing Item or Condition dialog box. Unless you successfully manage these missing items, you will not be able to run the workbook that has been shared with you.

As you can see in the preceding illustration, this dialog box has a number of buttons. The first item that Discoverer is unable to find will be displayed in the box. You will be informed of the name of the folder and the name of the item. At this point, you have the following options:

- **Substitute**   Clicking this button opens the following Substitute Item dialog box. In this box, Discoverer will once again display the item that you do not have access to, along with all of the business areas and folders that you do have access to. You should select another item that will be substituted for the missing item. For example, many companies have business areas that are broken down by region or department. If you have been granted access to a workbook that was created using the European region and you have access only to the Middle East region, you should open the Middle East business area, locate the matching folder and item, and then substitute it. When done, click OK.

- **Ignore** Clicking this button ignores the current item and displays the next item that Discoverer could not validate.

- **Ignore All** Clicking this button causes Discoverer to ignore all invalid items.

- **Cancel** Clicking this button cancels the opening of the workbook.

- **Help** Clicking this button opens Discoverer's help system.

When you have completed substituting items, Discoverer either runs the query or displays the following "Item dependency" error message. This message means that you did not successfully substitute a new item for every item that was missing.

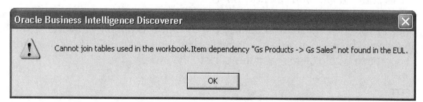

Clicking OK in the Item Dependency error box causes Discoverer to display the "failed workbook" error message. You will not be able to continue opening this workbook.

At this stage, you now have two options available to you. The first option is to speak with the person who owns the workbook. The owner, or library manager, may be able to share another workbook with you that uses a business area to which you do have access. The second option is to speak with your Discoverer manager, who may be able to grant you access to the business area that this workbook tried to open.

How to Manage Missing Items in Plus

When working in Plus, every time you open a workbook that has been shared with you, Discoverer validates that you have the rights to the business area used by the workbook. If this validation fails, you will see a message like this one:

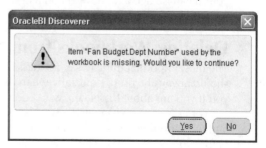

As you can see in the illustration, Plus warns you that you do not have access to an item that is used in the workbook and asks you if you want to continue. If you click No, Discoverer abandons the attempt to open that workbook. However, if you click Yes, unlike with Desktop, Plus does not offer you any chance to substitute for the missing item.

Instead, Plus now informs you about the next missing item, repeating the process for all of the missing items. Eventually, Plus will have no more items to check and will either open the workbook with all of the items missing or—and this is the more likely—will display the following error message:

As you can see in this illustration, Discoverer has given you the dreaded "Item dependency not found in the EUL" message. The opening of the workbook has failed. As with Desktop, you now have two options. Option 1 is to speak with the owner of the workbook and see if there is another workbook that they can share with you. Option 2 is to speak with the Discoverer manager and see if there is a way for you to be granted access to the business area that the workbook is using.

How to Edit and Save a Shared Workbook

As mentioned earlier in this chapter, you are not permitted to make permanent changes to workbooks that are owned by someone else. Therefore, you will notice that some of the menu items are deactivated. Notably, you will not be able to save any changes to the original workbook, nor will you be allowed to share it with anyone else. However, you will be allowed to schedule it. In older versions of Discoverer, you were also forbidden from turning page items on or off, but with both 10.1.2 Desktop and Plus you can now do so.

If you do want to make permanent changes to this workbook, you will have to save the workbook to your own database account using the Save As option. However, if you have spotted an error in the workbook—perhaps an incorrect calculation or a missing condition, for example—the correct approach would be to report this back to the owner.

NOTE
Do not try sharing a workbook that has been shared with you. You are not the owner, and you do not have the required sharing privileges. Discoverer will therefore not allow you to share that workbook with anyone else.

Workbook Manipulation

Managing the workbooks within your environment is an important aspect of Discoverer management. In this section we will show you how to delete unwanted workbooks from your database account, how to add a description to your workbooks, and how to manage the workbook identifiers.

Deleting Workbooks from the Database

The most important thing to say about deleting workbooks from the database is that caution should always be used, especially when deleting shared workbooks. Discoverer will not warn you if you are about to delete a workbook that is being shared with someone else.

Let's say you have created a workbook but no longer use it. Because you are conscientious and care about not wasting space on the database, your inclination is to delete it. However, before you do so, please check whether you have shared that workbook with someone else. That person may be using your workbook on a regular basis, and deleting it could be devastating. The situation is even more fraught with danger in Desktop, because Desktop does not even ask you to confirm whether you are deleting the correct workbook. If you click the Delete button, that will be the end of the workbook!

How to Delete a Workbook Using Desktop

To delete a workbook from the database using Desktop, use the following workflow:

1. From the menu bar, select File | Manage Workbooks | Delete.

2. The Delete Workbook from Database dialog box shown here will open. Notice that the Delete button is grayed out.

3. Select the workbook you wish to delete. The Delete button is now activated.

4. Click Delete.

NOTE
Be sure you really want to delete a workbook from the database before you click the Delete button, because Discoverer will delete it without any further prompting. There is no "undo" option! However, in Desktop, after deleting an open workbook, it is still open, so you have the option of resaving it. You will be prompted for the name when you try to save it.

How to Delete a Workbook Using Plus

To delete a workbook from the database using Plus, use the following workflow:

1. From the menu bar, select Tools | Manage Workbooks. This opens the Manage Workbooks dialog box shown in Figure 14-2. Unless you have a workbook highlighted, you will notice that the Delete button is currently grayed out.

2. Expand the list of workbooks that you own.

3. Select the workbook you wish to delete. The Delete button is now activated.

4. Click Delete.

5. Discoverer will now ask you to confirm that you want to delete this workbook.

6. If you click Yes, the workbook and all associated sharing will be deleted. If you click No, the workbook will be retained.

Managing Workbook Descriptions and Identifiers

For those of us that affectionately remember the DOS days with naming conventions that limited us to eight-character filenames with three-character extensions, long filenames are a real blessing. We have, however, gotten over our giddiness now and tend to be fairly utilitarian in the naming of our files. Discoverer gives you the added option of adding a description to your files that will help you keep track of queries and the purpose they serve. You can also control the identifier by which the workbook will be known to the system. Both of these are handled using what are known as the workbook properties.

To manage workbook properties, use the following workflow:

1. Open the workbook that you wish to manage.

2. From the menu bar, in Desktop select File | Manage Workbooks | Properties, or in Plus select File | Workbook Properties. This opens the Workbook Properties dialog box shown in this illustration:

3. Enter a meaningful description of the workbook in the Description field. Note that spaces are permitted in the description.

4. If desired, enter a meaningful identifier for the workbook. Spaces are not permitted in the workbook identifier. If you are a library manager, it is recommended that you enter the library prefix as a prefix to the workbook identifier to help associate it with the library that you are managing. Identifiers should be used very carefully, as they are used by Discoverer to uniquely identify every object in an EUL. This is also known internally as the developer key of an object. Discoverer by default will give every object—workbooks, worksheets, parameters, etc.—a unique identifier value.

5. Click OK.

NOTE
In Plus, using Tools | Manage Workbooks, selecting a workbook and clicking Properties allows you to view the properties for the chosen workbook. Even though you may own the workbook, you cannot edit its properties this way. You need to open the workbook and then use File | Workbook Properties.

Worksheet Manipulation

Managing the worksheets within a workbook is an important aspect of workbook management. In this section we will show you how to reorder your worksheets, how to rename worksheets, and how to delete unwanted worksheets. Then we will also show you how to add a description to your worksheets. After that, we show you how to copy and move worksheets between workbooks. Finally, we will show you how to find data in your worksheet results.

Reordering Worksheets

As you go about building workbooks, you will undoubtedly have workbooks that have multiple worksheets. The order in which you present those worksheets to your users may or may not have any importance. We have noticed that when worksheets have differing levels of data, users usually like to see the higher-level, or summarized, worksheets before they see the lower-level, detailed worksheets. This means you need to know how to rearrange the order of your worksheets. Because this is handled differently in Desktop and Plus, we will show you each separately.

Reordering Worksheets in Desktop

To rearrange the order of the worksheet in Desktop, use the following workflow:

1. Open the workbook that contains the worksheets you want to reorder.
2. Click the tab name of the worksheet that you wish to move.
3. Drag and drop the worksheet into its new position. Discoverer will reorder the worksheets.

NOTE
Older versions of Discoverer may require you to hold the CTRL key down while you drag the worksheet to its new position.

Reordering Worksheets in Plus

To rearrange the order of the worksheets in Plus, use the following workflow:

1. Open the workbook that contains the worksheets you want to reorder.
2. Right-click the tab name of any worksheet, and from the pop-up menu, select Move Worksheet.
3. As shown in this illustration, Discoverer now opens the Move Worksheets dialog box:

4. In the Move Worksheets dialog box, drag and drop worksheets or use the Promote and Demote buttons to rearrange the order of the worksheets in the workbook.

5. When you have rearranged the order of your worksheets, click OK. Discoverer now rearranges the worksheets.

NOTE
The Move Worksheets dialog box can also be launched from the menu bar by selecting Edit | Move Worksheet.

Renaming Worksheets

Throughout this handbook we have stressed the need to use meaningful names whenever you can. This naming standard applies to worksheets, too. Giving worksheets meaningful names will greatly help your users, allowing them to choose which worksheet to run by simply looking at its name.

To rename a worksheet, use the following workflow:

1. Open the workbook that contains the worksheets you want to rename.

2. Double-click the worksheet name. In Desktop this opens the Rename Worksheet dialog box, whereas in Plus this opens the Worksheet Properties dialog box.

3. Give the worksheet a suitable, meaningful name.

4. Click OK.

NOTE
In Plus, the Worksheet Properties dialog box can also be launched by right-clicking the worksheet name and from the pop-up list selecting Worksheet Properties. It can also be launched from the menu bar in Plus by selecting either Edit | Rename Worksheet or Edit | Worksheet Properties, or in Desktop by selecting Sheet | Rename Sheet.

Deleting Worksheets

As time goes by, you will find that some worksheets are either no longer needed or have been superseded by another worksheet, either in the same workbook or in another workbook. Rather than clog up your system with these unwanted worksheets, you should delete them. Thus, another essential aspect of worksheet manipulation is the removal of unwanted worksheets. Because this is handled differently in Desktop and Plus, we will show you each separately.

Deleting a Worksheet in Desktop

To remove an unwanted worksheet in Desktop, use the following workflow:

1. Open the workbook that contains the worksheet you want to delete.

2. Right-click the worksheet that you want to delete, and from the pop-up menu, select Delete Sheet.

3. When prompted "Are you want to delete the sheet?" click Yes or No.

NOTE
You can also delete a worksheet from the menu bar by selecting Sheet | Delete Sheet.

Deleting a Worksheet in Plus

To remove an unwanted worksheet in Plus, use the following workflow:

1. Open the workbook that contains the worksheet you want to delete.

2. Click the worksheet name that you want to delete, and wait for the name to become highlighted. The worksheet has now become the focus.

3. Right-click the worksheet name, and from the pop-up list, select Delete Worksheet.

4. When prompted "Are you sure you want to delete the worksheet?" click Yes or No.

NOTE

In Plus only, with the worksheet name highlighted, you can also press the DELETE key. You can also select Edit | Delete Sheet from the menu bar. Either of these methods causes Discoverer to pop up the same prompt referred to in Step 4 of the preceding workflow.

Adding a Description to a Worksheet

Another excellent way to help your users determine what a worksheet does is to provide a meaningful description. Unfortunately, you can add worksheet descriptions only in Plus. By the way, the requirement to expose a worksheet identifier is one of the reasons Oracle introduced the Worksheet Properties dialog box. The other reason is the need to cleanly separate workbook- and worksheet-level properties.

To add a description to a worksheet in Plus, use the following workflow:

1. Open the workbook that contains the worksheet for which you want to enter a description.

2. Double-click the tab for the worksheet name. This launches the Worksheet Properties dialog box.

3. Enter a suitable, meaningful description for the worksheet.

4. Click OK.

NOTE

In Plus, the Worksheet Properties dialog box can also be launched by right-clicking the tab for the worksheet name, and from the pop-up list selecting Worksheet Properties. It can also be launched from the menu bar by selecting either Edit | Rename Worksheet or Edit | Worksheet Properties. Either method allows you to change the description.

Copying and Moving Worksheets Between Workbooks

Another little-known feature of Discoverer is its ability to copy and move worksheets between workbooks. You can do this only in Desktop. The reason this will not work in Plus is that you can only open and work with one workbook at a time in Plus, whereas Desktop can open and manipulate several workbooks at the same time.

To copy or move worksheets between workbooks, use the following workflow:

1. Launch Desktop.

2. Open the two workbooks that you want to manipulate.

3. From the menu bar, select Window | Tile Horizontally. Discoverer places the workbooks one above the other with the first opened workbook at the top, and the last opened workbook at the bottom.

4. To initiate the copy process, press and hold down the CTRL key on your keyboard. To initiate the move process, press and hold down the SHIFT key on your keyboard.

NOTE
You cannot move a worksheet if it is the only worksheet in the workbook.

5. Holding down either the CTRL or SHIFT key, left-click the name tab of the worksheet that you want to copy or move and hold the mouse button down. You can now release the CTRL or SHIFT key.

NOTE
Make sure you keep holding the left mouse button down after you release the CTRL or SHIFT key

6. Drag the worksheet out of its current workbook and into the receiving workbook but do not release the mouse button until you have placed the worksheet alongside or on top of one of the worksheet names in the receiving workbook. Release the mouse button only when you see a small arrow appear above the worksheet name.

NOTE
Be very careful to make sure you place the worksheet correctly before you release the mouse button. If you release the mouse button before you have placed the worksheet in position, Discoverer creates a new workbook and places the worksheet in that workbook.

7. Discoverer now copies or moves the worksheet into the receiving workbook.

NOTE
You can place the new worksheet alongside an existing worksheet only when you are copying. If you are moving a worksheet, you must drag it on top of one of the existing worksheets in the receiving workbook. Discoverer will reorder the worksheets automatically.

8. You may want to check the names of conditions, parameters, and calculations. If the second worksheet has an identically named condition, parameter, or calculation, Discoverer does not share these objects. Instead, Discoverer creates a second object and appends the number 1 to its name.

Finding Data in Your Worksheet Results

When you execute a worksheet that has many pages of results, there are times when you would like to quickly find out whether a particular value or item was returned in the set of results. Fortunately, Discoverer provides such a mechanism.

To search for a value or item in a set of results, use the following workflow:

1. Open and execute the worksheet.
2. On the keyboard, press CTRL-F. This launches the Find dialog box shown in the following illustration.

3. In the Find dialog box, enter the value or name of the item that you wish to search for. In Desktop this is labeled "Search Text." In Plus, this is labeled "Search For."

4. You need to tell Discoverer how to perform the search. In Desktop this is labeled "Find Text That." In Plus this is labeled "Search By." By default this is set to Contains. Your valid options are

    ■ Exactly matches

    ■ Contains (this is the default and the one you most often use)

    ■ Begins with (in Plus this option is called Starts with)

    ■ Ends with

    ■ Is NULL

5. You now need to tell Discoverer whether to take the case of the value or item into account during the search. In Desktop, the button is labeled Match Case. In Plus, this button is labeled Case-Sensitive. By default this is unchecked and is the setting that you will use the most.

6. After you have made your selections, click Find Next. Because Plus has an additional button called Find Previous, you can click this instead if you wish.

7. Discoverer will now search for the value or item that you entered, using the search criteria that you set. If the value or item that you are searching for is found in the worksheet, Discoverer locates the first instance of that value or item, in the direction you are searching, and places the cursor on it. The Find dialog box will remain open and on top of the open worksheet. If the value or item that you are searching for cannot be found within the worksheet, a suitable message will be displayed.

8. To find further occurrences of the value or item, click Find Next or, in Plus only, click Find Previous.

9. When you have finished searching the worksheet, click Close.

NOTE
In Desktop, when Discoverer cannot find any more items matching the value or item you selected, a box saying "Cannot find the specified value in the sheet" will be displayed. In Plus, Discoverer simply returns you to the first or last found item, depending on whether you clicked Find Next or Find Previous.

Scheduling Workbooks

Scheduling workbooks is a way to run a report at a set time. These reports will probably not be the ones you use on a daily basis for analysis purposes. Scheduled reports are the ones that you want, for example, to run daily, weekly, or monthly. Good candidates for scheduled reports might be monthly profits or weekly sales.

Another reason to schedule a report is time. Some queries are complex and take a long time to run. A query of this type may take so long to run, in fact, that the time it takes exceeds the time that your Discoverer manager has allotted for you to run queries. Scheduling a workbook of this nature allows the query to run in the background during "off-peak" hours, when you are not under the same exacting time constraints. If you are using Desktop, another advantage to scheduling is that the scheduled workbook runs on the server. You don't even need to leave your PC on.

Discoverer's Scheduling Wizard is intuitive and easy to use; however, it does have some limitations. At the end of this section, we have included a discussion addressing some third-party scheduling applications and their use.

The Benefit of Scheduling Workbooks

There are a number of benefits to scheduling workbooks. The five main benefits of scheduling workbooks are as follows:

■ The user does not need to be logged in to Discoverer while the queries run.

■ If you have limited bandwidth or frequently see network congestion at peak times, scheduling workbooks to run off-peak will help.

■ The user can run key reports prior to the start of the working day at off-peak hours.

■ The user can run queries that normally exceed the time they are allowed by the Discoverer manager.

■ The user can schedule special reports to run as weekly or monthly reports. Such reports will run automatically without user intervention.

How to Schedule a Workbook

In order to schedule a workbook, you need to have been granted the appropriate rights and privileges. If you do not have the correct privileges, both at the database and EUL levels, you will not be able to schedule a workbook. These privileges are controlled by the Discoverer manager, and should you find that your scheduling options are grayed out, you will need to submit a request to have these set up for you.

Using the Desktop Schedule Workbook Wizard

To schedule a workbook in Discoverer Desktop using the Schedule Workbook Wizard, use the following workflow:

1. If the workbook that you want to schedule is the one that is currently open on your screen, from the menu bar select File | Schedule. This automatically opens the first part of the Schedule Workbook Wizard, as seen in Figure 14-4. Proceed to Step 7 of this workflow.

2. To schedule any other workbook, from the menu bar select File | Manage Workbooks | Scheduling Manager. This opens the Scheduling Manager dialog box.

3. Click Schedule. This opens the Schedule Workbook dialog box. This box, as you can see, has two selection buttons, one for My Computer, the other for Database.

4. Select the location where the Discoverer workbook has been saved.

5. Click Schedule. This either opens the Open dialog box, if scheduling a workbook that was saved to the file system, or the Schedule Workbook from Database dialog box.

6. From within either the Open or Schedule Workbook from Database dialog box, locate the workbook that you want to schedule, and then click Open or Schedule, respectively. Discoverer opens the first part of the Schedule Workbook Wizard, as seen in Figure 14-4.

7. Define which sheet or sheets are to be scheduled by clicking in the check box to the left of the worksheet name(s). Click Select All to include all of this workbook's worksheets. Click Select None to deselect all of the worksheets. Once all worksheets have been deselected, you should check the individual sheets that you want.

NOTE
All worksheets in the workbook will be listed by their name. This is another reason we recommend giving your worksheets meaningful names, because Sheet1, Sheet2, and so on might not be obvious.

8. Set the date and time you want the workbook to run.

FIGURE 14-4 *Desktop Schedule Workbook Wizard Step 1*

9. Define a repeat schedule, if required. Under the prompt "How often do you want to repeat this schedule?" there are two radio buttons, Never and Repeat Every. This is your opportunity to set this schedule up to run periodically, daily, weekly, or however often you choose. To do this, click Repeat Every, type in a number, and then select a time period from the drop-down list illustrated next. The default is Never, which will run the scheduled workbook only once.

10. Having completed Step 1 of the Schedule Workbook Wizard, click Next. Discoverer opens Step 2 of the wizard, as seen in Figure 14-5.

FIGURE 14-5 *Desktop Schedule Workbook Wizard Step 2*

11. Enter a unique name for the workbook that you are scheduling. This is an optional step, as Discoverer will automatically give your workbook a unique name; however, we recommend that you give it a name that is meaningful to you.

12. Enter a description for the workbook that you are scheduling. This is another optional step; however, again, we recommend that you take some time to give your scheduled workbook a description. This may seem like extra work, but we feel it is worth the effort. A description might include why you have scheduled the worksheet, and what is to be done with it after it has run. The description you enter will be displayed at the bottom of the Desktop Scheduling Manager dialog box seen later in Figure 14-8.

NOTE
Discoverer will automatically give your scheduled workbook a description, based on the original workbook name, the name you have given the scheduled workbook, and the date upon which the workbook is to run.

13. Define the delete criteria. Discoverer automatically deletes the results after 30 days.

14. Having completed Step 2 of the wizard, click Finish.

15. If you did not give your scheduled workbook a unique name, Discoverer issues the warning shown in the following illustration. Click Yes to force Discoverer to assign a unique name, or No to return to Step 2 of the wizard to enter your own unique name.

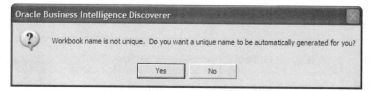

16. If there are any parameters in the worksheets within the workbook, Discoverer will now prompt you for those parameters. This illustration shows the sheet prompt. Enter the parameters that you want.

17. Click Finish.

The worksheets that you have just scheduled will be run on the date and time that you specified.

Using the Plus Schedule Wizard

To schedule a workbook in Discoverer Plus using the Schedule Wizard, use the following workflow:

1. If the workbook that you want to schedule is the one in active memory, from the menu bar select File | Schedule. This automatically opens the first part of the Schedule Wizard, as seen in Figure 14-6. Proceed to Step 5 of this workflow.

2. To schedule any other workbook, from the menu bar select Tools | Manage Schedules.

3. Click Schedule.

4. From the list of workbooks, locate the workbook that you want to schedule and click Select.

5. Enter a unique name for the workbook that you are scheduling. This is a mandatory step, as Discoverer requires that all workbooks have a unique name. If you do not enter a unique name, Discoverer displays the Scheduling Error box. In the box, you must either type a unique name or elect to have Discoverer keep the name but delete the existing workbook and its results. After you have made your choice, click OK.

FIGURE 14-6 *Plus Schedule Wizard Step 1*

6. Enter a description for the workbook that you are scheduling. This is another optional step; however, again, we recommend that you take some time to give your scheduled workbook a description. The description you enter will be displayed at the bottom of the Plus Scheduling Manager dialog box seen later in Figure 14-9.

7. Define which sheet or sheets are to be scheduled by clicking in the check box to the left of the worksheet name(s). Click Select All to include all of this workbook's worksheets. Click Select None to deselect all of the worksheets. Once all worksheets have been deselected, you should check the individual sheets that you want.

8. Having completed Step 1 of the Schedule Workbook Wizard, click Next. If everything has been defined correctly, proceed to Step 10. If you did not enter a unique name in Step 5, Discoverer displays the Scheduling Error box just shown.

9. In the Scheduling Error box, you must either type a unique name for the workbook or elect to have Discoverer keep the name but delete the existing workbook and its results. After you have made your choice, click OK.

10. Discoverer now opens Step 2 of the wizard, as seen in Figure 14-7.

11. Set the date and time you want the workbook to run. You can either choose Immediately or use the Calendar pop-up to select a date for when you want the workbook to be scheduled. You need to also set the time.

NOTE
If you choose not to schedule immediately, Discoverer automatically adds one day to the current date and sets the time to be one minute past midnight. Change this if need be.

FIGURE 14-7 *The Plus Schedule Wizard Part 2*

12. Define a repeat schedule, if required. Under the prompt "How often do you want to repeat this schedule?" there are two radio buttons, Never and Repeat Every. This is your opportunity to set this schedule up to run periodically, daily, weekly, or however often you choose. To do this, click Repeat Every, type in a number, and then select a time period from the drop-down list. The default is Never, which will run the scheduled workbook only once.

13. You next have to choose whether Discoverer should keep all results or just the latest set of results.

14. Define the delete criteria. Discoverer automatically deletes the results after 30 days.

15. Having completed Step 2 of the wizard, click Finish.

The worksheets that you have just scheduled will be run on the date and time that you specified. The schedule time is based on the database time when scheduling from Desktop and Plus. Thus, if the database is in California and the user is in Denver, this may cause some confusion.

The Scheduling Manager Dialog Box

The Desktop Scheduling Manager dialog box, as seen in Figure 14-8, and the Plus Scheduling Manager dialog box, as seen in Figure 14-9, have the following features:

- **Scheduled workbooks area** In this area, Discoverer displays details about all of your scheduled workbooks. This includes those scheduled to run, those that are running, and those that have already run. The Status column will tell you whether the workbook is Scheduled (Pending in Plus), running, expired, or completed (Report ready), or if it has encountered an error. It is also possible for you to see a status that your Discoverer manager has unscheduled your workbook.

  In addition to the Status column, there are columns for the date and time that the workbook is scheduled to run, and how long the workbook took to run. To the left of the workbook name are icons indicating the status of the workbook. The Clock icon indicates that the workbook is scheduled to run or is running. The icon without a clock indicates that the workbook has run and that the report is ready for viewing. In Plus, you must click the small plus sign alongside a workbook that has a status of Complete in order to see the actual results. These results will have the status "Report Ready."

- **Open** If your workbook has the status "Report Ready," this means that the workbook has run and that the results are ready to be viewed. Highlight the report you want to view and then click this button or double-click the report name to view the results. In Desktop, you may get prompted whether you want to see the results or leave the sheet empty.

- **Edit** Click this button to edit a report's schedule. Discoverer reopens the Schedule Workbook Wizard. When this opens you will see two tabs, one called General and one called Schedule. On the General tab you will find the name and description of the workbook. On the Schedule tab is where you alter the timings.

- **View Error** If your scheduled workbook is showing an error status, click this button to view the details. Viewing errors might be frustrating, because these generally describe database conditions, and these error messages can be difficult to understand. If you encounter errors with your scheduled queries, see your Discoverer manager.

■ **Delete**   Click this button to delete the output from a completed scheduled workbook. If the workbook was scheduled not to repeat, this also causes the scheduled workbook itself to be deleted.

NOTE
The original workbook is still intact because Discoverer uses a copy of the workbook within the scheduler. It is important for you to remember this when you change the original. It has changed, but the scheduled one has not. If you want the scheduled workbook to reflect the changes to the original, you will need to delete and reschedule the workbook.

■ **Schedule**   Click this button to schedule a new workbook.

■ **Unschedule**   Click this button to unschedule a currently scheduled workbook.

NOTE
In Desktop, Discoverer toggles between Delete and Unschedule depending upon the status of the report. In Plus, Discoverer has two different buttons, one for Delete and one for Unschedule.

■ **Refresh**   Click this button to refresh the status of all scheduled workbooks. Discoverer will not automatically refresh the statuses while you are in the dialog box. Therefore, if the status is "Running query" and you are waiting for the query to complete, keep clicking Refresh until the status changes to "Report ready."

■ **Close**   Click this button to exit from the Scheduling Manager dialog box.

■ **Description**   This area displays the description you typed in when you first scheduled the workbook.

■ **Share**   This button, available only in Plus, allows you to share a scheduled workbook with other users, roles, or responsibilities.

How to Share the Results of a Scheduled Workbook

The ability to share the results of scheduled workbooks is one of the most requested features in previous versions of Discoverer. The authors were delighted to find that this is now available as standard functionality in Plus 10.1.2.

To share the results of a scheduled workbook with other users, use this workflow:

1. From the menu bar, select Tools | Manage Schedules. This opens the dialog box shown in Figure 14-9.

2. Select the scheduled workbook that you want to share.

3. Click the Share button. This opens the Plus Share Workbooks dialog box shown earlier in Figure 14-3.

NOTE
The ability to share scheduled workbooks is available only in Plus.

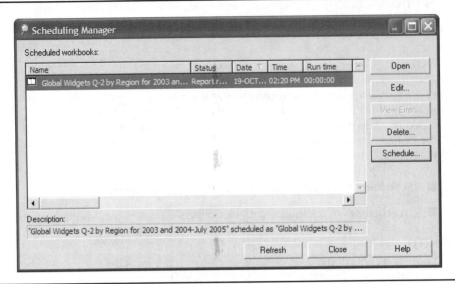

FIGURE 14-8 *The Desktop Scheduling Manager dialog box*

FIGURE 14-9 *The Plus Scheduling Manager dialog box*

Viewing Results

There are several ways to view the results of a scheduled workbook:

- In Desktop, from the menu bar use File | Open | Scheduling Manager or File | Manage Workbooks | Scheduling Manager.

- In Plus, from the menu bar use File | Open to launch the Open Workbook from Database dialog box. In this box, click the drop-down list labeled View and from the list select Scheduled Workbooks.

- Also in Plus, again from the menu bar, select Tools | Manage Schedules.

Viewing Results from the Open File Dialog Box

In both Desktop and Plus, to view the results of a scheduled workbook from the Open File dialog box, use the following workflow:

1. From the Desktop menu bar, select File | Open | Scheduling Manager. From the Plus menu bar, select File | Open and from the drop-down alongside View select Scheduled Workbooks. These launch the Open File dialog boxes seen in Figures 14-10 and 14-11.

2. Continue with Step 3 of the workflow in the following section.

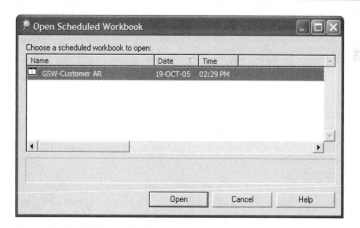

FIGURE 14-10   *The Desktop Open Scheduled Workbook dialog box*

FIGURE 14-11 *The Plus Open Workbook from Database dialog box*

Viewing Results from the Scheduling Manager Dialog Box

Both Desktop and Plus have the ability to view the results of scheduled workbooks using the Scheduling Manager. To view the results of a scheduled workbook from the Scheduling Manager dialog box, use the following workflow:

1. From the menu bar in Desktop, select File | Manage Workbooks | Scheduling Manager, whereas for Plus, select Tools | Manage Schedules. Either of these methods will open the Scheduling Manager dialog boxes as seen in Figures 14-12 and 14-13.

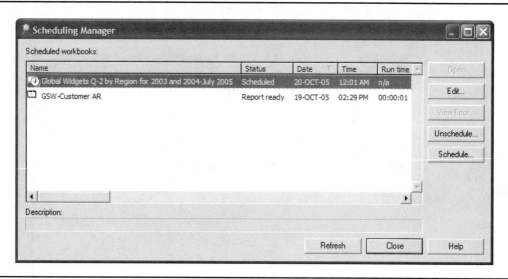

FIGURE 14-12   *Desktop Scheduling Manager dialog box*

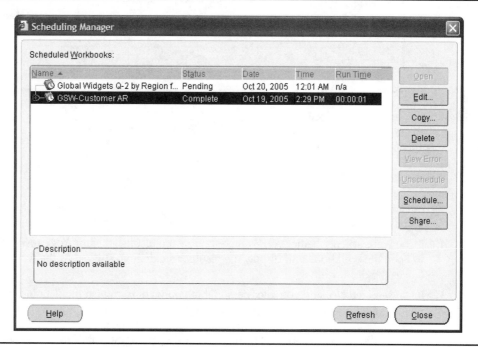

FIGURE 14-13   *Plus Scheduling Manager dialog box*

2. In Desktop highlight the worksheet result that you wish to view. In Plus, as shown here, you need to first click on the workbook name and then highlight the worksheet result that you wish to view:

NOTE
In Desktop the results are sorted by the order in which the results were generated so that the most recent set of results will be at the bottom of the list. However, Plus has a rather nice feature that sorts the results with the most recent first.

3. Click the Open button, or double-click the results that you want to view. You may be asked to confirm whether you want to view the results or leave the worksheet empty.

4. If you were asked whether you wanted to view the results, clicking Yes causes Discoverer to open the workbook and display the results. Clicking No still opens the workbook but leaves the display empty.

5. If you selected No, and you later decide that you want to refresh the data in the sheet, clicking the Refresh button causes Discoverer to ask whether you now want to re-query for the latest data or to continue viewing the results. Clicking Yes causes Discoverer to re-query the database and display the results using the latest data. Clicking No in Desktop now displays the results from the scheduled workbook. In Plus, clicking No continues to leave the worksheet empty.

NOTE
Discoverer will always keep the results of a scheduled workbook until you either refresh the data from the database or delete the output. Careful management of the results of scheduled queries will allow you to retain important results virtually indefinitely. We do not recommend that you keep results forever; however, retaining them for a couple of months should satisfy your need for the output. This is especially true if you want to manipulate the results in the future.

Unscheduling a Scheduled Workbook

Because the method used to unschedule a workbook is different in Desktop and Plus, we will show both methods separately.

Unscheduling a Workbook in Desktop

To unschedule a scheduled workbook in Desktop, use the following workflow:

1. Open the Desktop Scheduling Manager dialog box, as seen in Figure 14-8.
2. Highlight the scheduled workbook.
3. Click Unschedule. This opens the following Confirm Unschedule dialog box:

4. As you can see in the dialog box, you can choose to unschedule and keep the results, or you can unschedule and delete all of the results.
5. Click Yes to unschedule or No to leave the schedule unchanged.
6. Close the Desktop Scheduling Manager dialog box.

NOTE
In Desktop, clicking the Delete button with a set of results highlighted allows you to delete those results. As mentioned earlier, the Delete button is not available in Desktop when the workbook itself is highlighted. You must use Unschedule to remove the workbook.

Unscheduling a Workbook in Plus

To unschedule a scheduled workbook in Plus, use this workflow:

1. Open the Plus Scheduling Manager dialog box, as seen earlier in Figure 14-9.

2. Click on the workbook that you wish to unschedule.

3. Click the Unschedule button. This opens the Confirm Unschedule dialog box:

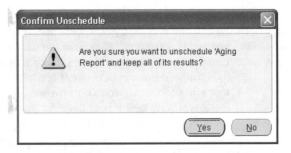

4. As you can see in the dialog box, your only choice is to unschedule the workbook while keeping all of the results.

5. Click Yes to unschedule or No to leave the schedule unchanged.

6. Close the Plus Scheduling Manager dialog box.

NOTE
In Plus, clicking the Delete button with the workbook selected gives you the chance to delete the workbook and all of the results. Clicking the Delete button with a set of results highlighted allows you to delete just those results.

Editing a Scheduled Workbook

Editing a schedule workbook allows you to adjust the settings that will be applied to the next run. To edit a scheduled workbook that has not yet run, use the following workflow:

1. Open the Desktop or Plus Scheduling Manager dialog box as seen in Figures 14-8 and 14-9.

2. Click the workbook that you wish to edit.

3. Click the Edit button. This opens the Schedule Workbook dialog box. As you can see, the Desktop box has two tabs: Schedule and General, whereas the Plus box has two or three tabs depending upon whether the scheduled workbook uses parameters.

NOTE

The preceding dialog boxes are almost the same as the Schedule Workbook Wizard that we showed you earlier in this chapter. It differs in that the dialog box has tabs instead of the Back and Next buttons that you saw earlier. In Desktop, there is also an additional button on the General tab for parameters, whereas in Plus there will be an additional tab called Parameter Values.

4. From the tabbed forms, make any edits that you require.

5. If you need to edit the parameters for the workbook, in Desktop click the Parameters button, and in Plus click the Parameter Values tab. Follow the instructions given earlier in this chapter for setting parameters in a scheduled workbook.

6. When you have finished editing, click OK.

Security

In order for a user to be able to schedule a workbook, the Discoverer manager must grant scheduling privileges to that user. The following illustration, from the Discoverer Administrator tool, shows the security privileges that are controlled by the Discoverer manager:

Among the privileges that are controlled are the following:

■ **Owner of the results**   The Discoverer manager dictates who owns the results of scheduled workbooks that you create. Normally, this is yourself; however, you may agree to transfer your viewing rights to a colleague. When your Discoverer manager deems that the database privileges required to schedule workbooks are beyond the level they wish you to possess, he or she can grant these privileges to another database user. This will enable you to still schedule and view reports as if the results were owned by you. This is different than allowing another user the ability to read the scheduled report.

■ **Maximum number of scheduled workbooks**   Your Discoverer administrator can restrict the number of workbooks that you are allowed to schedule. If you think you should have more, you must discuss this with your Discoverer administrator.

■ **Limits on scheduling time**   Your Discoverer administrator can limit the times between which you are allowed to schedule workbooks. Perhaps the peak hours will be off-limits, maybe during system backup, and so on.

Limitations of the Discoverer Scheduler

There are two major limitations of the Discoverer scheduler. These are as follows:

■ There is no export feature within the Discoverer scheduler.

■ There is no e-mail feature within the Discoverer scheduler.

NOTE
Oracle plans to review the entire scheduling functionality of Discoverer. Therefore, in a future release this could change.

There Is No Export Feature Within the Discoverer Scheduler   Using the previous weekly sales report scenario, you would love for the Discoverer scheduler to automatically export the results in a specified format into a specific folder. Then, your e-mail system could scan the folder, pick up the contents, and e-mail them to the sales force. The sales force would not even need to have access to Discoverer; instead, they would receive the reports via e-mail. Alas, Discoverer cannot do this. You will need to either do this manually or use a third-party scheduler.

There Is No E-Mail Feature Within the Discoverer Scheduler   For those of you who are used to scheduling jobs overnight and e-mailing the results to company managers, customers, vendors, and so on, you will be disappointed in Discoverer's scheduler. We know that there are many companies who have old legacy systems that allow this sort of scheduling, and we have heard complaints that Oracle's system does not allow this directly from within the scheduler.

All is not lost, though, as there are two ways of getting around this problem. The first is to use a third-party scheduler to export the results into a specified folder and then use an agent on the e-mail application to pick up the file and send it to a designated recipient. Lotus Notes, for example, can be set up very easily to do just this.

The second work-around is to export the SQL from your worksheet into an Oracle Report format and then get Oracle's Report scheduler to do the rest. To do this, you would export the file as an RDF file and then manually submit the file to the Reports server, from which the report can be run and the results e-mailed. In Plus and Viewer the Reports format is Reports XML and the export file contains both the query and the layout. From within Plus, use File | Export to launch the Export dialog box. In the second step of this box, use the drop-down alongside the format and from the list pick "Oracle Reports (*.xml)". From within Viewer, click the Export link. On the Choose export type page, use the drop-down to pick "Oracle Reports XML (*.xml)" from the list.

NOTE
There is no option to export to Oracle Reports from within Desktop.

Third-Party Scheduling

As you now know, Discoverer's own scheduler cannot output your data to a file, nor can the results be made available to other users. However, using the command-line interface, you can use third-party schedulers to run queries and create output automatically, without the intervention of the human hand.

The use of third-party schedulers can be advantageous because they offer more flexibility and allow users to open reports in formats like HTML without the need to have Discoverer installed. There are many scheduling products on the market, including the following:

- **Winat.exe**   The Windows NT native scheduler

- **Task Scheduler**   The Windows 98 native scheduler

- **Norton Program Scheduler**   The Norton Utilities scheduler

- **JIT Scheduler**   A freeware utility available from the Web

- **AT Scheduler**   The Windows XP native scheduler

Third-Party Scheduling Using XP

We have had many requests from clients asking about third-party scheduling and how to make it work. In the following sections we will show you how to use the Windows XP scheduler to set up some third-party Discoverer scheduling. We will cover

- The Scheduled Tasks dialog box

- Scheduling a new task in XP

- Setting advanced properties

- Modifying a scheduled task

- Removing a scheduled task

- Pausing and restarting scheduled tasks

The Scheduled Tasks Dialog Box   Windows XP has an extremely powerful, built-in scheduling tool that can be used to launch Discoverer and run workbooks via the command line. How to set up the command line to execute Discoverer workbooks and worksheets is explained later in this chapter.

To open Scheduled Tasks, use the following workflow:

1.   Click the Windows Start button.

2.   Navigate to Programs | Accessories | System Tools | Scheduled Tasks.

Scheduling a New Task in XP   To schedule a new task, use the following workflow:

1. Open Scheduled Tasks as just explained. This opens the Scheduled Tasks Wizard as shown here:

NOTE
Confirm that the system date and time on your computer are accurate. Scheduled Tasks relies on this information to run the tasks. To verify or change this information, double-click the time indicator on the Windows taskbar.

2. Double-click Add Scheduled Task to open the display screen of the Scheduled Task Wizard as shown here:

3. Click Next to display the file selection screen. As you can see in the next illustration, the Scheduled Task Wizard offers you a list of all the programs that are on your system. If you examine this list carefully, you will notice that Discoverer Desktop is among the list of available programs.

NOTE
Do not select Discoverer to run this way, because all that will happen is that the Desktop executable will launch!

4. Click Browse and navigate to a batch file that you have created to execute Discoverer via the command line.

5. Highlight the file you want to schedule and then click Open.

6. The wizard displays the following Frequency window:

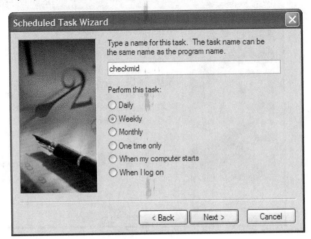

7. In the Frequency window give the task a suitable name, select a frequency for how often the task should run, and then click Next.

8. Depending upon what option you pick in the Frequency screen, you will be presented with either the Login screen or one of the optional Setup screens as displayed for Steps 10-12.

9. If you select "When my computer starts or When I log in," you will be taken to the Login screen as seen in Step 13.

10. If you selected Daily, you will be presented with the following optional setup screen:

11. If you selected Monthly, you will be required to complete a similar screen.

12. If you selected One Time Only, you will be required to complete this screen:

13. Having completed any optional setup steps, you will be presented with the following Login screen. If a username and password are required, enter it here and click Next.

NOTE
It is recommended that you always set the password for the user who should run this task.

14. To complete the scheduling of this task on the last screen, click Finish.

NOTE
If you want to set advanced properties for this task, make sure you check the box entitled "Open advanced properties for this task when I click Finish" before you click Finish.

Setting Advanced Properties If you checked the box called "Open advanced properties for this task when I click Finish" before you clicked Finish in the last section, you will be presented with the Advanced Properties dialog box for the task you have just scheduled. This box has three tabs:

■ Task tab

■ Schedule tab

■ Settings tab

Each of these will be described next.

■ **Task tab** Shown next, this is where you get an opportunity to confirm the file to be run, to state who to run the task as, and to specify whether the task should be run only when logged in and whether or not the task is enabled.

NOTE
If you leave the password blank and you want the task to run only when you are logged on, open the task. On the Task tab, select the Run only if logged on check box. The task will run at its scheduled time when the user who created the task is logged in to the computer.

■ **Schedule tab** The Schedule tab, shown next, is where you get an opportunity once again to specify how often the task should run and when it should run for the first time.

- **Settings tab**   The Settings tab, shown next, allows you to take great control over the scheduled task. You can control how long the task will run, whether it should start only if the computer is idle, or if the computer is a laptop, just what should happen should the computer be running on battery power or is in sleep mode.

Modifying a Scheduled Task   To modify a scheduled task, use the following workflow:

1. Open Scheduled Tasks.

2. Right-click the task you want to modify, and then click Properties.

3. Do one or more of the following:

   ■ To change a program being run, in Run, type the path for the new program.

   ■ To change the schedule for the task, click the Schedule tab.

   ■ To customize the settings for the task, such as maximum run time, idle time requirements, and power management options, click the Settings tab.

   ■ To set security for the task, click the Security tab, if present.

NOTE
If you change the user account or the program that is being run, you must supply the password for the user account.

Removing a Scheduled Task   To remove a scheduled task, use the following workflow:

1. Open Scheduled Tasks.

2. Right-click the task that you want to remove, and then click Delete.

NOTE
Removing a scheduled task only removes the task from the schedule. The program file that the task runs is not itself removed.

Stopping a Scheduled Task   To stop a schedule task that is running, use the following workflow:

1. Open Scheduled Tasks.

2. Right-click the task that you want to stop, and then click End Task.

NOTE
If a scheduled task is started and then stopped, End Task does not stop all of the other programs that the scheduled task might have started. You may experience a delay of several minutes before the actual task shuts down.

To restart a stopped task, right-click the task, and then click Run.

Pausing and Resuming Scheduled Tasks   The Pause Task Scheduler command is useful if you do not want scheduled tasks to run at the same time you are installing software or running another program (such as editing a workbook or loading data).

Tasks that are scheduled to run while Scheduled Tasks are paused will not be run until their next scheduled time.

To pause a scheduled task, use the following workflow:

1. Open Scheduled Tasks.

2. From the menu bar of the Scheduled Tasks dialog box, select Advanced | Pause Task Scheduler.

To resume the schedules for all tasks, use the following workflow:

1. Open Scheduled Tasks.

2. From the menu bar of the Scheduled Tasks dialog box, select Advanced | Continue Task Scheduler.

We hope that this section has shown you how easy it is to use XP's native scheduler to set up jobs to be run. In the next section we will deal with running Discoverer from the command line.

Running Discoverer Desktop from the Command Line

Perhaps one of the less-known capabilities of Discoverer Desktop is the ability to specify many of its functions directly from the command line. Using this command-line interface, you can, without opening Discoverer itself, run queries, automate printing, and export the results. You can also use third-party schedulers to control the running of queries outside of normal hours.

Running Discoverer from the Command Line

To run Discoverer from the command line, use the following workflow:

1. From the Windows Start button, select Run. This opens the Run dialog box as shown here.

2. Click Browse. This opens the following Browse dialog box:

3. Locate the Discoverer end-user run-time program, dis51usr.exe, and then click Open. As shown here, Windows now inserts the path and location of Discoverer into the Run dialog box:

4. Add the options that you require to pass to Discoverer, which will be explained in the following section.

5. Click OK. Windows now performs the command-line instructions, opening and running Discoverer.

Optional Command-Line Parameters

To increase the efficiency of the command-line interface, Discoverer will accept various parameters when launched this way. Each option begins with the forward slash character (/) and is preceded and followed by a space. The command-line options are as follows:

- **/apps_fndnam <foundation-name>** When working in Apps mode, this causes Discoverer to override the standard setting for the FNDNAM (foundation name) parameter, which can be found in the Connection tab after selecting Tools | Options. This is passed as a parameter to the /connect option. The standard foundation name is apps.

- **/apps_gwyuid <gwy-userid> / <gwy-password>** When working in Apps mode, this causes Discoverer to override the standard setting for the GWYUID (gateway user ID) parameters, which can be found in the Connection tab after selecting Tools | Options. This is passed as a parameter to the /connect option. The standard gateway user ID is *applsyspub,* and the standard gateway password is *pub.*

- **/apps_user** When you have an Apps-mode EUL, this switch tells Discoverer to log in as an Apps user.

- **/apps_responsibility** When this modifier is coupled with the above */apps*_user command, you can supply an Apps responsibility as part of the login information. Standard practice dictates that you should enter the responsibility name inside double quotes, especially if there are spaces in the name.

- **/batch** This causes Discoverer to run in batch mode. This mode does not wait for user interaction and will process one workbook after another, even if an earlier one fails. This mode is mandatory if you are scheduling workbooks using a third-party scheduler. When using this command, you must also include either an */export* or one of the two print, */pt* or */p,* commands; otherwise, you will get an error.

- **/cmdfile <filename>** This causes Discoverer to open the text file named in the command and execute it. Inside the text file, you should place all of the parameters that you need to run one job. To run multiple jobs one after the other, use DOS batch files.

- **/connect userid/password@database** This is a means for you to pass your login information to Discoverer. If the information that you specify is correct, in that you have provided a valid user ID, password, and database connect string, Discoverer will bypass the login screen and log you in. For example, if your user ID is 'Michael', your password is 'happy', and the database you want to connect to is 'odbc:polite', the following command-line option will log you in automatically:

```
/connect Michael/happy@odbc:polite
```

NOTE
If the information that you specify is incorrect, Discoverer will display the standard Desktop login screen populated with the information that you have entered and will wait for you to manually complete logging in.

- **/eul <eul-name>**   This allows you to specify the EUL against which you will be running. You must have access privileges to the EUL that you name. In the real world, this parameter is rarely used; if it is omitted, Discoverer will connect you to the default EUL.

- **/export <format><export-file-name>**   This exports the results of executing a worksheet to the file named, in the format specified. If you do not specify a worksheet on the command line, Discoverer exports the results from the active worksheet. If you nominate */sheet ALL* on the command line, Discoverer exports all of the worksheets in the workbook and names the output files as <file><sheet-name>.<ext>, identically to the behavior of the Export Data command.

- **/open <my-workbook>**   This opens a Discoverer workbook (.DIS) from the file system, My Computer. You need to specify the full path and location of the workbook and to combine this with a valid */connect* parameter.

- **/opendb <db-workbook>**   This opens the named workbook from the database.

- **/p<workbook-name>**   This opens a workbook, executes it, and prints a file located in My Computer to the default printer.

- **/pt <file><printer><driver><port>**   This opens, runs, and prints a file located in My Computer to a specified printer, with specified printer driver and port.

- **/parameter <parameter-name><parameter-value>**   This option is a means for you to pass a value to a parameter in a worksheet. If you do not pass a parameter value, Discoverer will use the default value. If you are running in */batch* mode, Discoverer will run the worksheet using the defaults; otherwise, it will prompt you when Discoverer opens.

- **/savedb <file>**   This copies a workbook from the file system, My Computer, and saves it to the database. Again, you need to specify the full path and location of the workbook, and you must have supplied a valid */connect* parameter.

NOTE
To copy and save multiple workbooks use multiple /savedb parameters in the same command line.

- **/sheet ALL**   This forces Discoverer to open and run all of the worksheets in the workbook.

- **/sheet <sheet-name>**   This forces Discoverer to open and run the worksheet specified by the worksheet name.

■ **/sheet <sheet-number>**   This forces Discoverer to open and run the worksheet specified by the worksheet number.

■ **/?**   This option displays the Command Line Help dialog box.

Command-Line Examples

The following is a list of command-line examples. Most of the commands can be mixed together, and Discoverer allows you to place them in any order.

Oracle Business Intelligence Discoverer

Command-line options:
<file-workbook>
/OPEN <file-workbook>
/OPENDB <db-workbook>
/CONNECT <username>/<password>[@<database>]
/P <file-workbook>
/PT <file-workbook> <printer> <driver> <port>
/EXPORT <format> <export-file>
/SHEET {<sheet-name> | <sheet-number> | ALL}
/BATCH
/PARAMETER <parameter-name> <parameter-value>
/?

[OK]

NOTE
If you make a mistake with any of the command-line options, Discoverer abandons the command and just launches the login screen. The username and database will be populated, but the password will be blank, even if you provided a valid password.

c:\oracle\BIToolsHome_1\bin\dis51usr.exe /connect bob/apple@report   This example logs the user Bob, using the password apple, into the report database. The login screen is bypassed, and Discoverer launches with the screen that asks whether the user should open an existing report or create a new one.

c:\oracle\BIToolsHome_1\bin\dis51usr.exe /connect darlene/motbo@prod /apps_user / apps_responsibility "HR User" /eul prod1   This example logs the Apps user Darlene, using the password motbo, into the prod database using the responsibility HR User. The user will be connected to the EUL called prod1.

NOTE
The preceding Apps login can also be entered as: c:\oracle\ BIToolsHome_1\bin\dis51usr.exe /connect "darlene:HR User/ motbo@prod" /apps_user /eul prod1.

c:\oracle\BIToolsHome_1\bin\dis51usr.exe /connect mark/swindon@prod /apps_user / apps_responsibility "Inv User" /apps_fndnam apps /apps_gwyuid applsyspub/pub   This example logs the Apps user Mark, using the password swindon, into the prod database using the Inv User responsibility. Because the */eul* parameter is omitted, the user will be connected to the default EUL. However, as you can see, we have provided the foundation name, the gateway user ID, and the gateway user password.

c:\oracle\BIToolsHome_1\bin\dis51usr.exe /connect john@odbc:polite /opendb workbook5 /sheet 1   This example connects john to an Oracle Lite database named polite, using ODBC connectivity. It opens the file workbook5 from the database and runs sheet 1. As this user has no password, the password component has been omitted.

NOTE
The preceding is an example of poor workbook and worksheet naming. Compare this with this example command line:

c:\oracle\BIToolsHome_1\bin \dis51usr.exe /connect michael/hidehi@disco10g /opendb "Product History" /sheet "Prod Summary" /parameter product_param AB-2000 This example logs in Michael using the password hidehi into the database called disco10g. It opens a worksheet called Prod Summary in the workbook called Product History and passes the value AB-2000 to the parameter called product_param. This time, Discoverer runs the query without prompting us for input. The parameter name that you specify must match exactly with the name you gave the parameter when you created the worksheet. If you recall, we recommended giving your workbooks, worksheets, and parameters meaningful names. This is one of the reasons why.

NOTE
Workbook and worksheet names are case sensitive, and if they contain spaces, you must enclose the name in double quotes as in the preceding example.

c:\oracle\BIToolsHome_1\bin \dis51usr.exe /connect michael/hidehi@disco10g /opendb "Product History" /sheet "Prod Summary" /parameter product_param AB-2000 /batch / export HTML prodlist This example, building on the preceding one, runs the query in batch mode and exports the result in HTML format to the file called prodlist.

NOTE
Discoverer recognizes the following format options in the command line: XLS for an Excel spreadsheet, WKS for a Lotus spreadsheet, TEXT for a text file, CSV for a comma-separated file, HTML for a file in HTML format, SYLK for a symbolic link file, FIXED for a PRN file, DIF for a data interchange file, SQL for an export of the SQL used in your worksheet, and RDF for an Oracle Report format file.

c:\oracle\BIToolsHome_1\bin\dis51usr.exe /connect byron/daisy@home /open c:\ myqueries\small_fry /sheet detail /parameter child_prompt RYAN /export SQL c:\export\ myexport.sql /batch This example logs in Byron using the password daisy into the database called home. It then opens the workbook called small_fry from the file system and executes the worksheet called detail, passing the value RYAN to the parameter called child_prompt. Running in batch mode, this command exports the SQL for the worksheet into the file called myexport.sql located on the file system at c:\export.

c:\oracle\BIToolsHome_1\bin \dis51usr.exe /connect bob/apple@report /opendb "bob's report" /sheet ALL This example opens the file "bob's report" from the database and runs all sheets. Notice how we have enclosed the filename in double quotes. This is because the filename contains spaces.

c:\oracle\BIToolsHome_1\bin \dis51usr.exe /connect byron/daisy@home /open c:\ myqueries\small_fry /sheet detail /parameter child_prompt 'RYAN','MADISON' This example shows you how to pass multiple values to a parameter and open a file from your hard disk. In this case, because we have not specified batch mode, the query will run online with the output being visible onscreen. When passing multiple values to a parameter, separate each value from the next with a comma, with no spaces. We have seen reports that Discoverer wants the parameters to be enclosed in double quotes, but we have not needed to do this with our system.

NOTE
When exporting results, you can either export one sheet or all sheets. If you want to export more than one sheet, but not all of them, you will have to create batch files for each sheet that you want to export.

Known Command-Line Problems

There are a number of known problems with the command line, three of which are

- Giving a parameter the name "prompt"

- Passing a parameter value to an unattached parameter

- Defining the parameter prompt to be the same as the parameter name

Giving a Parameter the Name "Prompt" While you may think of this as being obvious, Discoverer itself does not have a problem with this construct. However, running this from the command line, with older versions of Discoverer, results in either a Dr. Watson error or an illegal operation error. While this has been fixed in this release, we have left this warning here in case you are using an older version. We therefore recommend that you do not give any of your parameters the name "Prompt."

Passing a Parameter Value to an Unattached Parameter The illegal operation error message will also be caused when you have not associated a parameter with any particular item and you pass a value to that parameter in the command line.

Defining the Parameter Prompt to Be the Same as the Parameter Name During the normal course of worksheet development you can define a parameter prompt as being the same as the parameter name itself. However, under the following special combination of events you will also generate an illegal operation error message when you execute the workbook using the command line:

1. You have defined the parameter prompt to be the same as the parameter name itself.

2. You have not associated the parameter with any particular item.

3. You have used the parameter inside a calculation.

NOTE
We think you will agree that this is an interesting phenomenon. However, the situation gets more intriguing when you associate the parameter with a condition. This time Discoverer is quite happy to execute the code from the command line.

The following example shows you what happened when we associated a parameter with the name Example, and the prompt also defined as Example, with a calculation.

First, here is the parameter definition in which we defined the parameter prompt to be the same as the parameter name itself. Notice how we have chosen the value <NONE> for the item to associate the parameter with. When we executed this in Desktop, Discoverer had no issue.

Next, we created a calculation. As you can see, we have simply moved the value received from the parameter into the calculation. Running this from within Discoverer itself produces no error, but running this from the command line does.

To remedy this, change the prompt for the parameter to anything other than the name of the parameter itself.

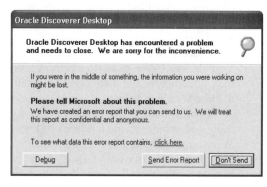

SQL Management

As we stated earlier in the book, when Discoverer runs a query, it converts it into SQL. This SQL is then submitted to the database. Discoverer allows you to view the SQL, view the Explain Plan, and export or import the SQL.

Viewing SQL

If you want to see what the SQL being used in your worksheet looks like, from the menu bar in Desktop select View | SQL Inspector, or in Plus select Tools | Show SQL. Discoverer now opens a two-tabbed dialog box in which you can see the SQL code. Here is the Plus dialog box with the SQL tab selected.

As you can see in the dialog box, there are two tabs. The first tab, called SQL, allows you to view the SQL used in your worksheet. The second tab, called Plan, allows you to look at the Explain Plan, as described next.

Both tabs have a Copy button and an OK button. In Desktop only, there is an additional Export button, which is active only while you are on the SQL tab.

Viewing the Explain Plan

To most end users the content being displayed within the Plan tab will be meaningless gobbledygook. If you are one of the 99 percent of end users to whom SQL is a big mystery and something that just happens, we recommend you take just a quick peek to see what excites the geeks in your company and then forget all about it. Here is an example:

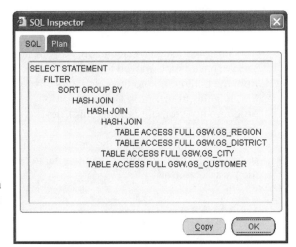

If you are one of the 1 percent of end users with a masochistic tendency to know everything that Discoverer can do, here is a brief description of what you see when you look at the Plan tab. The Explain Plan, as it is called by SQL tuning experts, is a mechanism that forces Oracle to explain how it plans to execute the SQL that you can see in the SQL tab. It is simply an aid to performance tuning and is something that your DBA may look at should you have a worksheet that is performing badly.

There, now you can go and bamboozle your friends with another piece of useless trivia!

Exporting SQL

Only Desktop allows exporting of the SQL code. To export the SQL code from your worksheet, use the following workflow:

1. From the Desktop menu bar, select View | SQL Inspector. This opens the following SQL Inspector dialog box:

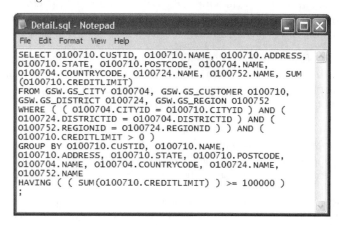

2. Click Export. This opens the Save As dialog box.
3. Select the location to which the code should be saved.
4. Give the export file a name.
5. Click Save.
6. Close the SQL Inspector dialog box.

NOTE
You can also use the Desktop command line to export SQL. Please refer to the section "Running Discoverer Desktop from the Command Line" earlier in this chapter for more details.

Importing SQL

Once again, only Desktop allows you to import SQL. To import SQL code into a worksheet, use the following workflow:

1. From the menu bar, select File | Import SQL. This launches the Open dialog box.
2. Locate the SQL file you want to import.
3. Click Open. Discoverer imports the code into a new worksheet.
4. If the code has parameters, Discoverer opens the Parameter Wizard dialog box. Enter the parameters. When you have entered all of the parameters, click Finish.

NOTE
Discoverer deactivates the Finish button until you have entered all of the parameters. When Discoverer imports code with parameters, it gives each prompt the same name as the name of the parameter. You will need to edit each parameter and give it a correct and meaningful prompt.

Structured SQL

If you are unfamiliar with SQL, looking at the code in the SQL Inspector dialog box might be daunting. No matter how complex and involved the SQL code appears, there are in fact only four basic components of an SQL query:

- **Select**   This command begins all SQL queries. Following it is a list of all of the items that are to be displayed in the final result of the query. Each item is usually prefixed by the name of the table or folder in which the item resides. Multiple items are separated from each other by a comma. There is no comma after the last item.

- **From**   This command follows the last selected item and starts on a new line. Following this command is a list of all of the tables and folders used in the query. Each folder or table is normally prefixed by the name of the owner of the object. Multiple entries are separated from each other by a comma. There is no comma following the last table or folder.

- **Where**   This command follows the last table or folder and again starts on a new line. In this section of the query, you will see the joins, conditions, and parameters. However, as Discoverer usually protects you from knowing the joins between folders, you will probably only see conditions and parameters in here. If there are multiple statements, each will be separated from the next by the word "AND."

- **Group By**   If used, this statement follows the last join, condition, or parameter. This construct allows aggregations to group by the items listed.

This illustration shows the example of SQL code that was exported from our database earlier in this section. As you can see, each of the four basic components starts on a new line:

While not pretending to even begin teaching you all about SQL, we hope this small section on the basic components of a SQL query will be of some help when you view the SQL.

E-Mailing Worksheets and Reports

An excellent way to share the results of worksheets and reports is by e-mail. This feature can be used only if your e-mail system supports this kind of linking, and it can be used only from within Desktop and Viewer. In Desktop, if you do not see the Send option on the file menu, your e-mail application does not support this feature. For e-mailing in Viewer, see Chapter 10.

Discoverer can send a workbook in a variety of formats, including the following:

- Discoverer Workbook (*.dis)

- Excel Workbook (*.xls)

- HTML (*.htm)

- Text File (Tab Delimited) (*.txt)

- CSV (Comma Delimited) (*.csv)

- Formatted Text (Space Delimited) (*.prn)

- Oracle Report Definition File (*.rdf)

- DIF (Data Interchange Format) (*.dif)

- SYLK (Symbolic Link) (*.slk)

- Lotus 1-2-3 (*.wks)

Available in Plus and Viewer are the following additional formats:

- **IQY**   Web query for Microsoft Excel 2000 and higher

- **XML**   Oracle Reports

- **PDF**   Native PDF export. This does not rely on the Reports DLLs

NOTE
Depending upon what software has been installed on your system, you may also see options to send workbooks in PDF and RDF formats. If you are using OLAP, you will see a slightly different set of export formats.

You can send these files as attachments to an e-mail. Or, message text can be sent directly in the body of the e-mail. This would be the recommended method only if the e-mail system you or the recipient uses does not support attachments. The following three formats can be sent as message text:

- Text File (Tab Delimited)

- CSV (Comma Delimited)

- Formatted Text (Space Delimited)

To Send a Discoverer Workbook via E-Mail

To send a Discoverer workbook or results via e-mail using Desktop, use the following workflow:

1. From the menu bar, Click File | Send.

2. This opens the Prepare Mail dialog box, shown here:

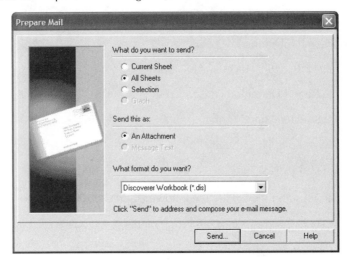

3. Tell Discoverer what you want to send. Will you send the Current Sheet, All Sheets, Selection, or Graph? Graph will be inactive if there is no graph in the workbook you want to send.

NOTE
To send a selection, you need to highlight the rows and columns you want to send before you launch the dialog box.

4. Choose whether you will send it as an Attachment or as Message Text.

5. Select the file type, the format, in which you will send the workbook or the results. If you select the type htm, and you are sending the results from only one worksheet, Discoverer inserts the HTML code directly into the e-mail as message text, irrespective of whether you chose to send it as an attachment or not.

NOTE
The drop-down menu is not available for graphs, as graphs are always sent as a WMF (Windows Metafile). This format is the recognized format for sending a graph. Do not worry if you have not exported a document in the format in which you want to send the attachment. Discoverer will create this for you when it sends the e-mail.

6. Click Send. Your e-mail application system will open. Depending on the selections that you made in the Prepare Mail dialog box, the worksheet or workbook will appear either as an attachment or in the message body itself.

NOTE
If you are e-mailing all sheets or a sheet that you have not yet run, Discoverer will prompt you to run those sheets before you e-mail the results.

7. Using your normal e-mail system, address the message and send the e-mail.

Known Problem with E-Mailing from Within Discoverer

Some e-mail systems are unable to decipher graph documents. If you see an error message when attempting to send a graph, this means that your e-mail application is unable to handle files sent as a WMF (Windows Metafile).

Summary

In this chapter, we have shown you the importance of the system administrator and his or her relationship with the end user. You have learned the security issues of access rights, sharing rights, and scheduling privileges, all of which are established by the Discoverer manager. We explained in depth how to make use of and manage libraries.

You have learned the benefits of sharing queries with other users and the importance of superuser involvement with shared workbooks. We have taught you how to share a workbook and given you a workflow for sharing a workbook with another user. You have learned how to use a shared workbook, and how to recognize a shared workbook. We have shown you how to open, edit, and save a shared workbook.

In this chapter, we taught you about manipulating workbooks, including how to delete workbooks from the database and the caution that should be used. We taught you how to add a description to the workbook properties.

In the section called "Worksheet Manipulation," we showed you how to manage worksheets within your workbooks. We showed you how to reorder worksheets, how to rename worksheets, and how to delete unwanted worksheets. You also learned how to find data within a worksheet and even how to copy or move worksheets between workbooks.

You were next taught the power of scheduling workbooks and the benefit of scheduling workbooks, and you got to try a workflow showing you how to schedule a workbook. We taught you how to view the results of a scheduled workbook, and how to unschedule a scheduled workbook. You have been taught how to edit a scheduled workbook and shown the security issues surrounding a scheduled workbook. You were introduced to the benefits of third-party scheduling, how to use XP's native scheduler, and how to use Discoverer's command-line utility for scheduling. We taught you how to run Discoverer from the command line and gave you many command-line examples that will help you set these up for yourself. We also outlined a few of the known command-line problems.

In this chapter, we taught you how to manage SQL code. We taught you about exporting, importing, and structured SQL. And finally, we showed you how to e-mail workbooks and reports and how to send a Discoverer workbook via e-mail. We also covered one of the known problems with e-mailing from within Discoverer.

In the next chapter, you will learn about some of your options in setting up user preferences. You will learn to customize some of Discoverer's features and establish defaults for some common formatting issues. We will also give you a more in-depth look at the Discoverer administrator.

CHAPTER
15

User Preferences, the Toolbar, and the Discoverer Administrator

here are a variety of user preferences that you can set up within Discoverer. Most of these are done using the Options dialog box. In this chapter, we will show you the various settings available to you for customizing Discoverer to suit your particular needs. Because Discoverer Desktop and Plus have enough differences, we will show you the Options dialog box in both versions.

In this chapter, we will also give you a quick reference guide to the Discoverer Desktop and Plus toolbars. We will describe each button's functionality and its location on the toolbar.

You will also learn more about your Discoverer administrator and his or her role in your successful use of Discoverer. We will teach you about the various tasks a Discoverer administrator needs to perform as well as what he or she can do for you.

Customizing User Preferences

Discoverer allows you to customize many of the day-to-day features you will be using. These features include setting file locations, how queries run by default, how your reports are set up, and many more. This customization is done using the Options dialog box. You have already been introduced to this dialog box in relation to creating reports and formatting queries, as well as in how your queries run. We want to be sure nothing is missed and so will take you through each section of the Options dialog boxes for both Desktop and Plus.

The Options dialog box is accessed through the Tools menu on the menu bar. To open the Options dialog box, select Tools | Options from the menu bar.

NOTE
The Options dialog box can also be accessed from a button in the Workbook Wizard. This button is active in all steps of the Workbook Wizard except Step 1. Before the button can be activated, you need to have chosen a table or crosstab layout. In Desktop, if you click Options in the Workbook Wizard, only the Query Governor, Table/ Crosstab Format, and Default Format tabs are available. In Plus, if you click Properties in the Workbook Wizard, only the General, Table/ Crosstab Format and Aggregation tabs are available.

Desktop Options

The Desktop Options dialog box consists of seven tabs, however, only five of them can be seen at the same time. There are left and right arrows in the upper-right corner that give you access to the additional tabs. The seven tabs are as follows:

- General
- Query Governor
- Sheet Format (Table or Crosstab)
- Default Formats
- Cache Settings
- Advanced
- EUL

Our tutorial on the Options dialog box will begin with the General tab.

General

The General tab in Desktop, as seen in Figure 15-1, is divided into three areas.

The first area, called Viewers, concerns how you want to view multimedia files. If the Discoverer workbook contains video, images, or sound items, click these boxes to have Discoverer's built-in viewers open and play these files.

The second area, called Workbooks, is for setting up preferences for how and when your workbooks run. As you can see in Figure 15-1, there are three radio buttons to choose from, a check box, and an input box. The radio buttons are as follows:

■ **Run query automatically**   When you open a workbook, Discoverer will automatically run the active worksheet if you select this option. Discoverer will not run any of the other worksheets until you click the corresponding worksheet tab.

■ **Don't run query (leave sheet empty)**   When you open a workbook, Discoverer will not run any of the worksheets if you select this option. You will, however, be in the active worksheet with no data displayed.

■ **Ask for confirmation**   When you open a workbook, Discoverer will ask for confirmation that you want to run the active worksheet. Clicking Yes will run the worksheet, and clicking No will not.

FIGURE 15-1   *The Desktop Options dialog box General tab*

NOTE
Because Discoverer has sticky features, it remembers the last worksheet that was opened in the workbook. This worksheet is called the active worksheet. We think the best option to choose is "Ask for confirmation." If you are anything like us, you don't remember which worksheet you last had open. By selecting this option, you have the chance to choose whether Discoverer runs the active worksheet. If you are not sure what the active worksheet does, click No when prompted, and then open the Edit Sheet dialog box and check it out. With the other options, you could be waiting for a query to run when it is not even the one you need.

NOTE
In Plus 10.1.2, users now have the option of selecting which workbook they want to open, so this makes life a bit simpler.

The remaining options in the Workbook area are as follows:

- **Display warning when opening workbook saved in a different database account** Check this box to display a warning if you are about to open a workbook that has been saved in a different database account. This is checked by default, and we think it is a good idea to leave it that way.

- **Workbooks in recently used list** This is a selection box to the right, near the bottom of this area. In this box, enter how many files you want to see in the recently used file list. The default is four, but you can select up to nine.

The last area in the General tab is a check box for showing graphics in the Workbook Wizard. If you have a slow-running computer or are querying over long distances, we recommend you deselect this option.

Query Governor

The Query Governor tab gives you options for how you want large queries to run. Figure 15-2 shows the Query Governor tab.

The Query Governor has two areas, one called Summary Data and one called Query Governor.

The Summary Data area has two radio buttons. These are as follows:

- **Always, when available** Select this option if you want to force Discoverer to always use summary data.

- **When summary data is more recent than** Select this option if you want to force Discoverer to only use summary data when the data is more recent than the number of days specified.

Later in this chapter, we will teach you about summary data and how it can be set up by your Discoverer administrator.

FIGURE 15-2   *The Options dialog box Query Governor*

The second area of the Query Governor tab allows you to customize the following five query options:

■ **Warn me if predicted query time exceeds**   This option allows you to ask Discoverer for a warning if the query will take more than a designated time to run. Select from one minute to 99 hours and 59 minutes. Your Discoverer administrator can set a maximum default time. If this has happened, you can only set lower time limits.

This option is only relevant if your company's Discoverer administrator has not disabled Discoverer's query predictor. Discoverer's query predictor is a clever feature that predicts approximately how long a query will take to run. To do this, Discoverer needs certain database settings to have been made by the DBA. When set correctly, Discoverer will maintain a log of past queries and compare your query with those results. If your query uses items that have been queried before, Discoverer will be able to give you an approximation of how long it will take this time. Unfortunately, the settings that Discoverer's query predictor needs are incompatible with Oracle Applications prior to 11*i*. If your Discoverer administrator has not disabled the query predictor, your queries will take much longer to run. Discoverer also utilizes the Oracle database's cost-based optimizer along with its own gathered query statistics to come up with the query prediction values.

- **Prevent queries from running longer than** This option allows you to create a time limit for your queries. Worksheets that reach this deadline are terminated. The Discoverer administrator can set a default time period. If this has happened, you can only set a lower time limit.

- **Limit retrieved data to** Here you can designate the maximum number of rows of data you want a query to retrieve. If your Discoverer administrator has set a maximum value, you cannot set a limit that is higher.

- **Retrieve data incrementally in groups of** Here you can select the number of rows of data you want Discoverer to retrieve at one time. The default is 100 rows. As each group of data is retrieved, Discoverer displays what has been retrieved so far. Assuming the data is good, you can continue by retrieving the next group.

- **Cancel value retrieval after** This setting is used by Discoverer when displaying lists of values. In order to display a list of values, Discoverer queries the databases to find a unique list. These queries can take a long time. If the search for a list of values exceeds the time allotted, Discoverer will abandon the search.

Table/Crosstab

The third tab in the Options dialog box is the Table or Crosstab tab. Depending upon the worksheet format you have chosen, this tab will be labeled either Table or Crosstab. In this tab, you can determine how the worksheet will be seen on the screen, and how it will look when printed. Most of the options for the Table and Crosstab are the same. When there is a difference, we will bring this to your attention. The tab for a Table is shown in Figure 15-3, while the tab for a Crosstab can be seen in Figure 15-4.

FIGURE 15-3 *The Options dialog box Table tab*

The options for the Table and Crosstab tabs are as follows:

- **Title**   Here you can turn on or turn off the title display of your worksheets. When checked, the worksheet title will be displayed.

- **Default Title**   Click this button to open the Edit Title dialog box. We covered the functionality of this box in Chapter 6, so we will not do so again here. When you create a title using the Default Title button, the title you create will become the default for all future workbooks. It will not, however, apply to any of the titles in the current workbook.

- **Page Items when Printing**   This option allows you to turn on or turn off the printing of page items. When checked, the page items will be printed.

- **Horizontal Gridlines**   This option allows you to turn on or turn off the horizontal gridlines. When checked, the horizontal gridlines will be displayed.

- **Vertical Gridlines**   This option allows you to turn on or turn off the vertical gridlines. When checked, the vertical gridlines will be displayed.

- **Gridline Color**   This button allows you to change the color of the gridlines in your worksheet. Click the button to open the color box, and then select the color you desire.

- **Column Headings (table only)**   This option allows you to turn on or turn off the column headings. When checked, the column headings will be displayed.

- **Row Numbers (table only)**   This option allows you to turn on or turn off the row numbers. When checked, the row numbers will be displayed.

- **Column Sizes (table only)**   This area has two radio buttons. You can choose between Use Default Width (Faster) and Auto-Size (Slower). We have tried both settings and have seen no appreciable difference in speed. However, if you are concerned about performance, you should use the default width as recommended by Oracle.

NOTE
This is likely to be an issue when working over the Web for very large data sets. When using "Auto-Size," Discoverer will attempt to size the column according to the width of the widest cell for that column, as opposed to the default option, where the width is set according to the heading width.

- **Axis Labels (crosstab only)**   This option allows you to turn on or turn off the side axis labels. When checked, the axis labels will be displayed.

NOTE
There is no option for turning off the column labels in a crosstab. These are always displayed.

- **Axis Gridlines (crosstab only)**   This option allows you to turn on or turn off the axis gridlines. When checked, the axis gridlines will be displayed.

FIGURE 15-4   *The Options dialog box Crosstab tab*

- **Gridline Style (crosstab only)**   This box contains two choices, 3D and Normal. 3D is the default setting. Selecting Normal will give a flat appearance to the axis gridlines. We don't see any performance issues either way. This is simply a user preference issue.

- **Style (crosstab only)**   This area gives you two radio buttons to choose from. The first, Inline, will lay out the Y axis labels (the side axis) side by side, as seen in Figure 15-5. This is the default for a crosstab style.

The second radio button is for an outline-style crosstab. This style of crosstab places the first side axis item above the second side axis item, and so on. It also creates a subtotal on the data items for the topmost side axis item. Figure 15-6 shows the same table seen in Figure 15-5, but this time as an outline crosstab. Notice how each item is indented from the previous one.

			Cost Price SUM			
		Status	CANCELLED	HOLD	OPEN	SHIPPED
Region	Customer Name					
EUROPE	ACE MANUFACTURING		152988.00		491161.56	2786172.27
	CASA DE WIDGETS		666475.72		531175.46	5496657.92
	LAC WIDGETS SA		237383.50	804.00	458501.08	3952848.58
	LONDON WIDGETS LTD.		408913.93		533361.93	4040804.09
	MUM'S WIDGET CO.		902114.47	467155.14	241500.33	4349893.29
	OXFORD WIDGETS		240924.59	118765.14	127734.00	3973799.49
	PALMELA WIDGETS		135196.80		65636.10	736353.65
	TRICOLOR WIDGETS		199630.49		382381.30	2784812.28
	WARSAW WIDGETS		467688.84		416425.30	3582467.97
	WIDGET O THE MERSEY		743489.56	509.76	418379.58	4008061.21
	WIDGETS ON THE WEB		258166.08		352292.08	4628065.82
FAR EAST	ABC WIDGET CO		212059.12		107426.14	2302044.71
	CEBU WIDGET CO		696967.92		436902.30	5847959.27
	HONG KONG WIDGETS		523218.56		311694.38	4086035.77
	YAMATA WIDGET LTD.		206217.73		194218.27	3251965.46
NORTH AMERICA	BIG RIVER WIDGETS		192796.03		130125.94	2045198.30
	BRIDGE THINGS		130815.40		44594.92	1367320.68
	GATOR WIDGETS		143900.90	14904.00	88641.76	2506754.62
	LAST RAILWAY WIDGETS		470256.12		283618.60	4088165.46
	LOTS OF WIDGETS		149420.98	14904.00	74884.77	3459003.10
	MOUNTAIN WIDGETS		392396.63		169848.77	3616683.18
	PATRIOT'S WIDGET CO.		594518.26		547331.40	4174559.36
	THE LITTLE WIDGET		64339.51		312218.00	3294699.07
	WALKING HORSE WIDGET		183486.80			1862634.98
	WE'VE GOT WIDGETS		289739.00	1242.00	304791.92	2988223.15
	WIDGET AIR		347525.49		359442.47	3770952.92
	WIDGET SUPPLY CO		482664.16		231797.37	4587464.09

FIGURE 15-5   *An Inline crosstab*

Formats

The fourth tab in the Options dialog box is the Formats tab. This tab allows you to view the currently defined formats for five of the most common worksheet options, and for determining what Discoverer will display when null values are returned in your query. The Formats tab is shown in Figure 15-7.

Oracle Business Intelligence Discoverer Desktop - [Workbook3]					
File Edit View Sheet Format Tools Graph Window Help					
			Cost Price SUM		
	Status	CANCELLED	HOLD	OPEN	SHIPPED
Region Customer Name					
EUROPE		4412971.98	587234.04	4018548.72	40339936.57
ACE MANUFACTURING		152988.00		491161.56	2786172.27
CASA DE WIDGETS		666475.72		531175.46	5496657.92
LAC WIDGETS SA		237383.50	804.00	458501.08	3952848.58
LONDON WIDGETS LTD.		408913.93		533361.93	4040804.09
MUM'S WIDGET CO.		902114.47	467155.14	241500.33	4349893.29
OXFORD WIDGETS		240924.59	118765.14	127734.00	3973799.49
PALMELA WIDGETS		135196.80		65636.10	736353.65
TRICOLOR WIDGETS		199630.49		382381.30	2784812.28
WARSAW WIDGETS		467688.84		416425.30	3582467.97
WIDGET O THE MERSEY		743489.56	509.76	418379.58	4008061.21
WIDGETS ON THE WEB		258166.08		352292.08	4628065.82
FAR EAST		1638463.33		1050241.09	15488005.21
ABC WIDGET CO		212059.12		107426.14	2302044.71
CEBU WIDGET CO		696967.92		436902.30	5847959.27
HONG KONG WIDGETS		523218.56		311694.38	4086035.77
YAMATA WIDGET LTD.		206217.73		194218.27	3251965.46
NORTH AMERICA		6443250.18	36062.57	5518477.81	64785326.23
BIG RIVER WIDGETS		192796.03		130125.94	2045198.30
BRIDGE THINGS		130815.40		44594.92	1367320.68
GATOR WIDGETS		143900.90	14904.00	88641.76	2506754.62
LAST RAILWAY WIDGETS		470256.12		283618.60	4088165.46
LOTS OF WIDGETS		149420.98	14904.00	74884.77	3459003.10
MOUNTAIN WIDGETS		392396.63		169848.77	3616683.18
PATRIOT'S WIDGET CO.		594518.26		547331.40	4174559.36
THE LITTLE WIDGET		64339.51		312218.00	3294699.07
WALKING HORSE WIDGET		183486.80			1862634.98
Sheet 1					

FIGURE 15-6 *An Outline crosstab*

If you want to amend the current default format of one of the five options described next, select the format you want to amend and click Change. This opens the relevant Edit dialog box. These were described in detail in Chapter 6.

To reset an option back to Discoverer's default, select the format you want to change and click the Reset button.

These five default options you can set are as follows:

■ **Data** Setting this controls how your data will look onscreen. You can set font, alignment, and background color. The Discoverer default is Arial 10 point, in a regular typeface, left justified, using black text on a white background.

- **Headings** Setting this controls how your column headings will look on screen. You can set font, alignment, and background color. The Discoverer default is Arial 10 point, in a regular typeface, center justified, using black text on a light-gray background.

- **Sheet Titles** Setting this controls how your sheet titles will look onscreen. You can set font and background color. The Discoverer default is Arial 10 point, in a bold typeface, center justified, on a white background.

- **Totals** Setting this controls how your totals will look onscreen. You can set font and background color. The Discoverer default is the same as for the data option (Arial 10 point, in a regular typeface, left justified, on a white background).

- **Exceptions** Setting this controls how your exceptions will look onscreen. You can set font and background color. The Discoverer default is Arial 10 point, in a regular typeface, left justified, on a red background.

The last option on the Formats tab, as shown in Figure 15-7, is for formatting null values. In the field entitled Show NULL values as, you can either select from the drop-down list or type in your default. Normally, a null value displays as nothing, but you can change this to any text value, number, or date that you want to see.

FIGURE 15-7 *The Desktop Options dialog box Format tab*

Cache Settings

The Cache tab is where you set the options for memory and disk caching. On the tab shown in the illustration that follows, Discoverer allows you to set various caching options. You should not change any of these settings without the approval of your Discoverer administrator.

If you encounter errors such as "Cannot create virtual memory swap file" or "No data can be retrieved because the disk is full," your settings may need changing. However, as stated, do not attempt to make these changes without consulting your Discoverer administrator.

Connection

The Connection tab is where you set the connection options. You choose whether to connect to standard or Oracle Applications EULs. There are three choices:

- Connect to standard EULs

- Connect to applications EULs

- Connect to both standard and applications EULs

If you choose to connect to an Oracle Applications EUL, you will need to give the application's Gateway User ID and password as well as the Foundation's name.

You should not change any of these settings without the approval of your Discoverer administrator.

Advanced

On the Advanced tab, as shown in Figure 15-8, Discoverer allows you to turn on or turn off automatic querying and the trapping of join errors.

The options for the Advanced tab are as follows:

- **Disable automatic querying**   Check this box if you want to prevent Discoverer from automatically requerying the database after you have made changes to the worksheet. With this box checked, you will need to manually refresh the worksheet. We do not recommend that you check this box without approval from your Discoverer administrator.

- **Disable fan-trap detection**   Check this box if you want to prevent Discoverer from detecting fan traps. Fan traps were covered in detail in Chapter 10. Unless you are using Discoverer version Desktop 4.1 or above, we do not recommend you check this box. In any case, you should not check this without approval from your Discoverer administrator.

- **Disable multiple join path detection**   Check this box if you want to prevent Discoverer from detecting multiple join paths. This topic was also discussed in detail in Chapter 10. Do not check this box without approval from your Discoverer administrator.

FIGURE 15-8   *The Desktop Options dialog box Advanced tab*

EUL

On the EUL tab, as shown in Figure 15-9, Discoverer allows you to change the End User Layer you are using. This feature is primarily used by the Discoverer administrator, who needs access to both development and production Discoverer End User Layers. Unless you are a very experienced user, you should not attempt to change the default setting. If you are unsure about what EUL should be the default, check with your Discoverer administrator.

Plus Options

The Plus Options dialog box has six tabs. The six tabs are as follows:

- General

- Query Governor

- Sheet Format

- Formats

- Advanced

- EUL

Our tutorial on the Plus Options dialog box will begin with the General tab.

FIGURE 15-9   *The Desktop Options dialog box EUL tab*

General

The General tab is for setting up preferences for how and when your workbooks run. The General tab in Plus is seen in Figure 15-10.

As you can see in Figure 15-10, there are three radio buttons to choose from. They are as follows:

- **Run query automatically**   When you open a workbook, Discoverer will automatically run the active worksheet if you select this option. Discoverer will not run any of the other worksheets until you click the corresponding worksheet tab.

- **Don't run query (leave sheet empty)**   When you open a workbook, Discoverer will not run any of the worksheets if you select this option. You will, however, be in the active worksheet with no data displayed.

- **Ask for confirmation**   When you open a workbook, Discoverer will ask for confirmation that you want to run the active worksheet. Clicking Yes will run the worksheet; clicking No will not.

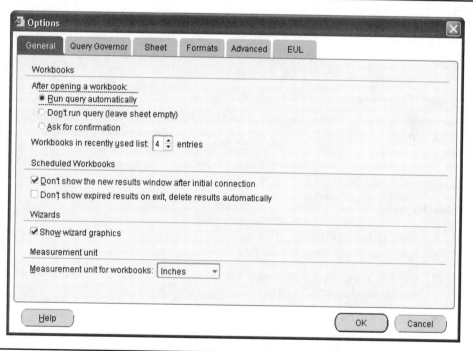

FIGURE 15-10   *The Plus Options dialog box General tab*

NOTE
Because Discoverer has Sticky Features, it remembers the last worksheet that was opened in the workbook. This worksheet is called the active worksheet. We think the best option to choose is "Ask for confirmation." If you are anything like us, you don't remember which worksheet you last had open. By selecting this option, you have the chance to choose whether Discoverer runs the active worksheet. If you are not sure what the active worksheet does, click No when prompted and then open the Edit Sheet dialog box and check it out. With the other options, you could be waiting for a query to run when it is not even the one you need. You can now use the slightly improved Workbook navigator in Plus to select the worksheet you want to open.

The last area in the General tab is a check box for showing graphics in the Workbook Wizard. Graphics use a tremendous amount of system resources and can seriously decrease performance. If you have a slow-running computer or are querying over long distances, we recommend you deselect this option.

Query Governor

The second of the Plus tabs is the Query Governor tab. This tab is identical to the Query Governor tab in Desktop in appearance and functionality. For details on the Desktop tab, please refer to the Desktop "Query Governor" section earlier in this chapter. You should also refer back to Figure 15-2 to see the Query Governor tab.

Sheet Format

The third tab in the Options dialog box is the Sheet Format tab. There are some differences in this tab, depending on whether the worksheet you have open is a table or a crosstab. When there is a difference, we will bring this to your attention. This tab is also used to determine what Discoverer will display when null values are returned in your query. The Sheet tab is shown in Figure 15-11.
The options for the Sheet tab are as follows:

Table Headers

- **Show Column Headings**   This option allows you to turn on or turn off the column headings. When checked, the column headings will be displayed.

- **Show Row numbers (table only)**   This option allows you to turn on or turn off the row numbers. When checked, the row numbers will be displayed.

- **Column Width**   This area has a drop-down list. You can choose between Use Default Width (Faster) and Auto-Size (Slower). We have tried both settings and have seen no appreciable difference in speed. However, if you are concerned about performance, you should use the default width as recommended by Oracle. Default width will size the columns by the column heading width, while Auto size will format the size by either the widest column heading or the widest data item in the column.

FIGURE 15-11   *The Plus Options dialog box General tab*

Crosstab Headers

- **Show Item Labels**   This option allows you to turn on or turn off the item labels. When checked, the item labels will be displayed.

- **Show heading gridlines**   This option allows you to turn on or turn off the heading gridlines. When checked, the heading gridlines will be displayed.

- **Crosstab Style**   This area has a drop-down list. You can choose between outline or inline crosstab styles. Figure 15-5 shows an inline crosstab where the first child record is on the same row as the parent record. Figure 15-6 show the same crosstab as an outline crosstab where the first child record is one row lower than the parent record.

- **3D heading gridlines**   Use this check box to display the crosstab heading gridlines in 3D. This check box is enabled only when the Show heading gridlines check box has been selected.

Table and Crosstab Detail Area

- **Show vertical gridlines**   Here you can turn on or turn off the vertical gridlines. When checked, the vertical gridlines will be displayed.

- **Show horizontal gridlines** Here you can turn on or turn off the horizontal gridlines. When checked, the horizontal gridlines will be displayed.

- **Gridline color** Here you can choose to use a color other than black for your gridline colors. Click the button to open a palette of colors or create a custom color for your gridlines.

Sheet Content Area

- **Title** Here you can turn on or turn off the title display of your worksheets. When checked, the worksheet title will be displayed. When you uncheck this box, the Title check box will be unchecked by default when you create new worksheets.

- **Text area** Here you can turn on or turn off the text area display of your worksheets. When checked, the worksheet text area will be displayed. When you uncheck this box, the Text area check box will be unchecked by default when you create new worksheets.

- **Null values** This option allows you to either select from the drop-down list or type in your default. Normally, a null value displays as nothing, but you can change this to any text value, number, or date that you want to see.

Formats

The fourth tab in the Options dialog box is the Formats tab. This tab allows you to view the currently defined formats for seven of the most common worksheet options. The Formats tab is shown in Figure 15-12.

FIGURE 15-12 *The Plus Options dialog box Formats tab*

If you want to amend the current format of one of the five options described next, click the Change button. To reset the option back to Discoverer's default, click the Reset button.

The seven default options you can set are as follows:

- **Data Format**   Setting this controls how your data will look onscreen. You can set font, alignment, and background color.

- **Heading Format**   Setting this controls how your column headings will look onscreen.

- **Total Format**   Setting this controls how your totals will look onscreen.

- **Conditional Format**   Setting this controls how your conditional formats will look onscreen.

- **Stoplight Color Format**   Setting this controls how your stoplight formats will look onscreen.

- **Title**   Setting this controls how your title will look onscreen.

- **Text area**   Setting this controls how your text area will look onscreen.

Advanced

The Advanced tab in Plus is identical to the Advanced tab in Desktop in both appearance and functionality. For details on this tab, please refer to the Desktop advanced section on page 13 of this chapter. Also, refer back to Figure 15-8 to see the Advanced tab.

EUL

The EUL tab in Plus is identical to the EUL tab in Desktop in both appearance and functionality. For details on this tab, please refer to the Desktop EUL section on page 14 of this chapter. Also, refer back to Figure 15-9 to see the EUL tab.

The Toolbar

For the sake of not wanting to miss anything, we are adding this section on the toolbar. We are the types who, when we get new software, point at all of the buttons on the toolbar to see what they are for. If you are used to working in a Windows environment, you may have done the same. If not, you might not be in the habit of "checking out" the toolbar.

Many of the buttons on the toolbar have been covered in the preceding chapters. However, we will show them all here as a reference guide.

The Discoverer Desktop Toolbar

The Discoverer Desktop toolbar buttons are grouped in a logical manner, and in a very similar order to other Windows programs. The toolbar has been divided into five sections, so we will show them to you by these sections.

Workbook Section of the Desktop Toolbar

The first section of the toolbar is used for managing workbooks: opening, saving, and printing. The following illustration shows the first section of the toolbar:

The workbook section of the Desktop toolbar has the following five buttons:

- **New Workbook**   Opens the Workbook Wizard.

- **Open Workbook**   Opens the Open Workbook dialog box.

- **Save**   Saves the workbook. If the workbook has not already been saved, the Save Workbook dialog box will open.

- **Print**   Prints the workbook.

- **Print Preview**   Displays how this workbook will print.

Worksheet Section of the Desktop Toolbar

The second section of the toolbar is used for managing worksheets: creating new worksheets, editing, copying, drilling, and refreshing. The following illustration shows the worksheet section of the toolbar:

The worksheet section of the Desktop toolbar has the following six buttons:

- **New Sheet**   Opens the New Sheet Wizard.

- **Duplicate as Table**   Opens the Duplicate as Table dialog box.

- **Duplicate as Crosstab**   Opens the Duplicate as Crosstab dialog box.

- **Edit Sheet**   Opens the Edit Sheet dialog box.

- **Drill**   Drills to the data for the column selected.

- **Refresh**   Refreshes the data in the worksheet.

Graph Section of the Desktop Toolbar

The third section of the toolbar has only one button and is used for managing graphs. The first time you click this button, the Graph Wizard will open. Once a graph has been created, the button will open the graph.

Sorting Section of the Desktop Toolbar

The fourth section of the toolbar is used for formatting exceptions and sorting. The fourth section of the toolbar is shown here:

The sorting section of the Desktop toolbar has the following four buttons:

- **Format Exceptions**   Opens the Exceptions dialog box.

- **Sort Low to High**   Sorts the data in the column selected in ascending order.

- **Sort High to Low**   Sorts the data in the column selected in descending order.

- **Group Sort**   Group-sorts the data in the column selected.

Excel Section of the Desktop Toolbar

The fifth section of the toolbar is used for exporting the data in the worksheet into an Excel worksheet. If there is more than one worksheet in a workbook, Discoverer will export the first sheet by the same name as the workbook. After the first worksheet has been exported, you will be prompted to name the additional worksheets to be exported.

The Discoverer Plus Toolbar

The Discoverer Plus toolbar buttons are grouped into five sections, much the same as the Desktop toolbar. There are a few differences in the Plus toolbar because of differences in the functionality of the two products. Just as we did when we explained the Desktop toolbar, we will show the Plus toolbar to you by sections.

Workbook Section of the Plus Toolbar

The first section of the toolbar is used for managing workbooks: opening, saving, printing and print preview. The illustration, as shown here, displays the first section of the toolbar.

The workbook section of the Plus toolbar has the following five buttons:

- **New Workbook**   Opens the Workbook Wizard.

- **Open Workbook**   Opens the Open Workbook dialog box.

- **Save**   Saves the workbook. If the workbook has not already been saved, the Save Workbook dialog box will open.

- **Print**   Prints the workbook.

- **Print Preview**   Shows a print preview of the workbook.

Worksheet Section of the Plus Toolbar

The second section of the toolbar has five buttons. These buttons are used for managing worksheets: creating new worksheets, editing, and copying. Unlike in Desktop, you cannot drill from the toolbar in Plus, and the Refresh button has been moved into its own section. Oracle has also added an extra button to this section. This extra button opens the Table Layout dialog box. The worksheet section of the toolbar is shown here:

The worksheet section of the Plus toolbar has the following buttons:

- **Add Worksheet**   Opens the New Sheet Wizard. It also has a drop-down with the following options as seen here:

- **Duplicate as Table** Opens the Duplicate as Table dialog box.

- **Duplicate as Crosstab** Opens the Duplicate as Crosstab dialog box.

- **Edit Worksheet** Opens the Edit Sheet dialog box.

- **Edit Table/Crosstab** Opens the Table/Crosstab Layout dialog box.

Refresh Data Section of the Plus Toolbar

The third section of the toolbar has only one button, which is used to refresh the data in the query.

Sort Section of the Plus Toolbar

The fourth section of the toolbar is used for sorting. The following illustration shows the sort section of the toolbar:

The sort section of the Plus toolbar has the following three buttons:

- **Sort Low to High** Sorts the column in ascending order.

- **Sort High to Low** Sorts the column in descending order.

- **Group Sort** Places a group sort on the column.

Tools Section of the Plus Toolbar

The fifth section of the toolbar is used for opening five of the various tool dialog boxes. The buttons also have drop-down list of common functions and can be used to create simple operations. The following illustration shows the tools section of the toolbar:

The tools section of the Plus toolbar has the following five buttons:

- **Totals** Opens the Totals dialog box.

- **Percentages** Opens the Percentages dialog box.

- **Calculations** Opens the Calculations dialog box.

- **Conditions** Opens the Conditions dialog box.

- **Parameters** Opens the Conditions dialog box.

Export Section of the Plus Toolbar

Plus has two export buttons in the sixth section of the toolbar. Using these buttons, you can export the data in the worksheet into an Excel worksheet or as an HTML page. The sixth section of the toolbar is shown here:

- **Export to HTML**   We like the HTML option for distributing a worksheet's results. It is basically a snapshot of the worksheet that keeps all of the formatting.

- **Export to Excel**   This option should be chosen when the data needs to be manipulated in some way. Most of the formatting is exported, but you may need to do some column resizing.

NOTE
More export formats are available using the File | Export feature of the menu bar.

The Plus Graph Toolbar

The graph toolbar is available when the graph is activated. As you can see, you can do all of your manipulation of the graph from the toolbar. We think it is a great tool and allows you to make changes on the fly without any cumbersome dialog boxes. The buttons of the graph toolbar are covered in Chapter 7.

The Discoverer Administrator

We cannot tell you everything that the Discoverer administrator does, but in this section we will try to give you a brief glimpse behind the scenes. We hope this will give you a better understanding and insight into the job that this person does. Later in this section, we will outline just what the Discoverer administrator can do for you. Here, you will find a list of all of the things that your Discoverer administrator can change on your behalf.

The Discoverer Administrator's Role

As far as Discoverer is concerned, the most important person that you will come into contact with is your Discoverer administrator. Without this person, there will be no Discoverer. The role of the Discoverer administrator is a very specialized role indeed. Each company has at least one, and all of the users are thankful that he or she is there. The Discoverer administrator understands how to design business areas that support your company's way of doing things. At least one of the Discoverer administrators is also a database guru. This is the person who knows all there is about your company's databases—where they are located, how they are stored, and how the data is all linked together. It is not required that every Discoverer administrator be a database guru or even a DBA. The only prerequisite is that they understand the portion of data (tables, views, and joins) for which they are responsible. In addition, users who understand the data can share some of the responsibilities of administering the Discoverer End User Layer. For example, a user who understands the business terms used by the rest of the user community could be responsible for defining descriptions for folders and items.

Being able to design business areas and being a database guru are just two of the roles. The third role of the Discoverer administrator is somewhat more abstract than the other two, both of which are primarily technical. This third role requires good interpersonal skills and a really good sense of business acumen, something not usually associated with "techies." The Discoverer administrator knows the decision-makers within your company. He or she is able to talk with users at their level and in their language, omitting the jargon and techno-babble that is the domain of programmers. We feel strongly that this third role of the Discoverer administrator is the most important and cannot be overemphasized. Having built a good rapport with the business management, the Discoverer administrator is in a perfect position to identify what data is needed within your business areas.

You Can Help Your Discoverer Administrator Identify the Data Needed

Before your company makes Discoverer available to you, the users, it is your Discoverer administrator's responsibility to identify the data that is needed. He or she does this by talking with you and your fellow coworkers.

If you are lucky enough to be selected as a key user during the analysis phase, you can help your Discoverer administrator by having answers to some of the following questions:

- What reports do you create today, and who do you send them to?

- What is wrong with the data that you have today, and how would you like to see it made better in the future?

- Do you know where the data is kept today? Is it kept in a database, or perhaps you use spreadsheets?

- Maybe you have an EDI system and you need Discoverer to take a feed from that?

- Are you able to define any corporate algorithms or calculations that you would like to see standardized?

Do not keep quiet at this point. If you do not understand something at this stage, be sure to ask. Waiting until you have access to Discoverer is far too late.

Once the data has been identified, your Discoverer administrator will design the business areas that you will eventually see inside Discoverer. These are designed on paper first and are refined many times before the Admin Edition is even touched! It is a very complex and expensive process to unbundle badly created business areas, even with a product as good as Discoverer. Time spent analyzing and designing will repay itself over and over again.

Once the business areas have been created and you have a working system, the fun really starts. No Discoverer system can ever be considered finished. It is your responsibility to ensure that the system delivers what you need. You must keep in touch with your Discoverer administrator and be aware what he or she can do for you.

What Can the Discoverer Administrator Do for You?

Perhaps the most interesting part of the interaction between yourself and your Discoverer administrator is knowing what he or she can do for you. Using this knowledge, you should be better able to make requests of your Discoverer administrator. He or she can then take your request, act on it, and make modifications on your behalf. These modifications will make your life easier and enable you to write more cost-effective queries.

The following is a list of all of the items that your Discoverer administrator has control over. Use this list to see what your Discoverer administrator can do for you.

■ **Adding new users**   The Discoverer administrator is responsible for adding new users to the system. Whether he or she does it, or whether the DBA is assigned the task, is irrelevant. Any request for access should initially be directed to the Discoverer administrator. If you are able to specify exactly what type of access is required, this will make the job that much easier.

■ **Granting access to business areas**   If you find that you do not have access to a business area that you need, you should raise a request to your Discoverer administrator to have that access granted. Perhaps you have changed your job, or maybe your responsibilities have been extended.

■ **Granting privileges within the user edition**   If you feel that your privileges are not sufficient, you should discuss this with your Discoverer administrator. On the Privileges tab of the Discoverer Admin Edition, your Discoverer administrator grants access to the User Edition. Having granted you access to run the User Edition, your Discoverer administrator also determines whether you can create or edit a query, whether you can drill, whether you can share or schedule workbooks, and whether you can save workbooks to the database. The Discoverer administrator Privileges tab is shown here:

■ **Adding meaningful descriptions to business areas, folders, and data items**   A very simple, yet very useful, means of helping you understand your data better is to add descriptions to the data objects. This adds no overhead to the processing of the system, yet it is incredible to us how many business areas and folders are not given meaningful descriptions. In the following illustration, you can see that a description has been created for the main business area of our tutorial database. Similar descriptions can be created for each folder, making it a lot easier for you to understand what the folder contains.

- **Adding new items to folders** If you think that there is an item missing from a folder, you should talk to your Discoverer administrator. He or she is able to add new items to folders. Adding items to a data warehouse folder, however, could be a lengthy process. If the item already exists in your warehouse and your Discoverer administrator has determined that it does not contain sensitive information, then it takes only a few minutes for the administrator to make this item available.

- **Creating new folders** Your Discoverer administrator can create new folders within Discoverer. These folders can be based on SQL statements, extracts from the database, or even items contained in existing folders.

- **Creating joins between folders** There will be times when Discoverer deactivates folders. This is because there is no join between the items you have chosen and the deactivated folder containing the item that you want. It may be possible for your Discoverer administrator to create a join for you, thus enabling you to choose the item that you want.

- **Creating lists of values** Many users do not know that the lists of values that you see inside Discoverer have actually been created by the administrator. It is a misconception that these lists are created by the database—they are not. If you see a data item in a folder and you think that there should a list of values, contact your administrator and request that one be created.

- **Creating alternative sorts**   Another way that your administrator can help you is by creating alternative sorts. An example of an alternative sort is sorting the months of the year into the order in which they occur. Month names are text values, and a text list would place 'January' after 'February'. Your Discoverer administrator can create a custom sort placing the months in the order in which they occur. You can even have the months sorted by fiscal year.

- **Creating new items based on calculations**   If you have standardized calculations within your company, it makes sense to include these as items in Discoverer. Your administrator can create these custom calculations and add them as items to folders. You can then select these new items, saving you the step of creating the calculation in the query.

- **Creating new conditions**   Another simple task for your Discoverer administrator is the creation of conditions. Perhaps you have a large list of part numbers, of which only a certain range of numbers are available for shipment to customers. The remainder could be components or for internal use only. Your Discoverer administrator can create a condition based on the part number, constraining the list to only those that are shippable. You would then be able to select this condition just as you would any item.

- **Creating drill hierarchies**   One of the least-used features of Discoverer is the use of hierarchical drilling. This type of drill uses a predefined hierarchy of items, within which you can drill up or down by a click of the mouse. Typical hierarchies used are dates and geographic data, such as ZIP Code drilling up to State, and State drilling up to Country, and so on. If you can define a drill of this type, your Discoverer administrator can build a hierarchy for you.

- **Modifying an item's type**   A little-used function available to your Discoverer administrator is the ability to change an item's data type. If you always need to be able to manipulate a date—for example, as a string—you can ask your administrator to change the item's type.

- **Creating summary data**   When reporting from transaction systems, you do not want to be querying from the detail tables if you can help it. This will cause long delays while querying and can seriously reduce the performance of your OLTP system. Your Discoverer administrator can create summary folders that contain preaggregated data. If these have been created for you, your Discoverer administrator will advise you of the correct setting to make in the summary data section of the Query Governor tab of the Options dialog box. By default, summary administration is transparent to users and probably does not require any action.

- **Rearranging the order of folders in a business area**   When you select items from folders, in a business area it is nice to see the folders arranged in an order that makes sense to you. For example, in an HR system, you always want to add the employee name and identification number from the Employee Info folder first, then you want to add salary information from the Salary folder, and last of all, you want to add training information from the Training folder. The Discoverer Manager can make this easier by putting the folders in that order in the business area.

■ **Rearranging the order of items in a folder**   When you are querying from a folder, you may notice that you are always scrolling down the list of items to get the one you want. You can ask your Discoverer administrator to change the ordering of the items within the folder. This has no impact on the system, yet it can be a tremendous timesaver.

■ **Changing refresh cycles**   Many Discoverer systems are based on either a snapshot of the OLTP system or data warehouses. Both of these types of databases use a refresh mechanism to update. If you believe that the refresh schedule is insufficient, you can ask your Discoverer administrator to change it. Perhaps you would like an extra collection during the lunch period. It is possible that your Discoverer administrator will be able to accommodate you, if your justification is strong. Always remember that it doesn't hurt to ask; your Discoverer administrator can only say no!

■ **Allowing scheduling of workbooks**   Not all users are granted permission to schedule workbooks. Not all users need to schedule workbooks. If you believe that you should be given permission to schedule, you should bring that to the attention of your Discoverer administrator. You may be asked to provide justification. The screen that your Discoverer administrator uses to control scheduling is shown here:

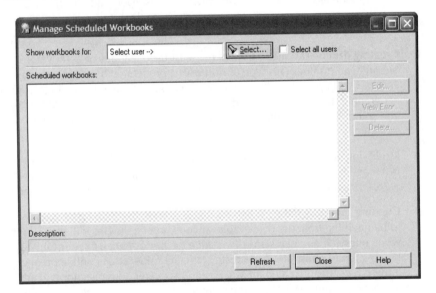

■ **Creation of new functions**   Discoverer already has a vast array of functions at your disposal. Refer to Appendix A for an alphabetical list of all of the functions. However, there may be times when you need a new function. Your Discoverer administrator has the ability to create new functions and make these available within the system. If you are familiar with SQL, you will notice that not all SQL functions are available in Discoverer. If there is a SQL function that you would like to use, your Discoverer administrator might be able to add it.

■ **Another source of help** Your Discoverer administrator is an expert in Discoverer, and you should treat him or her as a resource. If you are stuck with a tricky calculation or cannot define the right conditions, pick up the telephone.

Discoverer Desktop Directory Structures

There are two important directories that must be set in order for Discoverer Desktop to work correctly. Your Discoverer administrator is responsible for determining the location of these directories. The two vital directories are as follows:

■ **Discoverer's default directory for opening files** On the General tab of the Discoverer Desktop Options dialog box is a placeholder for entering the default directory for opening files. If this directory is located on a shared drive—such as on a network, on a terminal server, or on a shared PC—your Discoverer administrator will help you determine the correct entry for this placeholder. He or she is also responsible for ensuring that you have the correct read and write access to this directory. If the directory is to be located on your local PC, you should use a folder such as c:\temp.

■ **Discoverer's cache directory** On the Cache tab of the Discoverer Desktop Options dialog box is a placeholder for entering the default directory for disk caching. Unless advised by your Discoverer administrator, you should not change this directory.

NOTE
If you have many users sharing drives, particularly when using terminal servers, you may want to consider not sharing the same cache drive between all users. The reasoning behind this is that no one can determine exactly when Discoverer will need the disk cache. If two users swap to disk at the same time, it is possible that the caching may get impacted, with the resulting crash of the system.

Terminal Server Directories

This section is only applicable if your company uses terminal servers for accessing Discoverer. When using these shared machines, your network administrator will not take kindly to your saving files all over his or her server. Your Discoverer administrator, therefore, will work with the network administrator to create directories into which you can save workbooks.

If you have been advised to use a certain directory for your files, please use it. It is not just out of courtesy that we say this, although this is certainly a consideration. The biggest concern we have is that your saved workbooks may get deleted if they are stored outside of the agreed area. Having spent a great deal of time making a query work, we are sure that the last thing you want right now is to start all over again!

Summary

In this chapter, you have learned how to use the Options dialog box in both versions of Discoverer. We have shown you the various settings you can select to create defaults to customize Discoverer to meet your needs. Included in these options, you have learned how to create default formats for some of the most common data types. You have been shown how to format tables and crosstabs to present your data better. We have taught you which of these settings to use care in setting and when to contact your Discoverer administrator for assistance.

You have been given a quick reference guide to the Discoverer Desktop and Plus toolbars, with all of the functions. And finally, you have learned about your Discoverer administrator. You have learned about the privileges you can be granted, and how the Discoverer administrator provides you with them. You have also been taught how you can help the Discoverer administrator to determine the kinds of data and business areas you will need to create your queries and reports. We have shown you how a directory structure is set up in Discoverer, and why it is important to save your workbooks to the correct directory folders.

CHAPTER
16

Introducing Discoverer
OLAP

n this chapter we will introduce you to one of Discoverer's greatest new features, Discoverer OLAP. This chapter is intended as a taste to show you how Discoverer OLAP can be used as a part of your reporting solution. The range and depth of what Discoverer OLAP offers would require far more than we can put into this book, but we want you, the Discoverer user, to see it in action. Without at least one chapter dedicated to this tremendously powerful and versatile tool, we feel that our work would not be complete.

While we, unfortunately, have not had a lot of time to see Discoverer OLAP in action in a real-world setting, we are very excited by the possibilities that this new addition to the Discoverer family brings to the table. Discoverer OLAP can answer queries that can simply be impossible to create with a relational model. Coupled with the latest OLAP performance improvements in the 10.2 database, performance is an order of magnitude better than earlier versions. In this environment it runs very well indeed, and if you get a chance to try it out we are sure that you will be as impressed as we are.

OLAP Background

Imagine for a moment that you are the sales manager for Global Widgets. Your job is to increase sales revenue and profitability, so that the total revenue next year is 10 percent higher than last year, and margins over the same period are 5 percent higher. Given this challenge, how do you go about improving performance?

One of the first things you would think about is the factors that contribute to your performance over this period. The mix of products that you sell over the 12 months is obviously important, with some products selling for a higher price, some for a lower price, and of course different products attract different profit margins. Global Widgets sells both directly to customers via the Internet, and direct through distributors. Some customers will always be loyal, while others may defect to competitors if you try to raise prices. As a global organization, you have operations in many countries and you have historically had more success in selling in certain countries and territories.

You have been given twelve months in which to improve sales performance, but those twelve months are part of distinct seasons, each of which changes the demand for the products that you sell. These factors—the products that you sell, the customers that you sell to, the territories that you sell in, and the months in the year that you operate—can be thought of as dimensions to a business problem, and the outcomes that you are trying to influence—sales revenue and profit margin—are the measures that you wish to analyze.

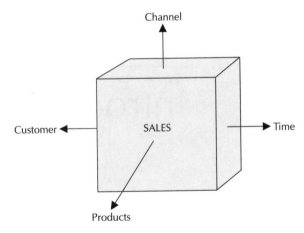

Imagine now that you are in charge of quality assurance at Global Widgets. Your task is to reduce the number of widgets that are returned by customers due to defects. Each month, you are presented with a report that gives an average defect rate for all widgets sold that month. As a general indicator of company performance this information is useful, but you suspect that this average figure might mask significant differences between the defect rates between the different types of widget the company produces.

Ideally, you would like to be able to break down this overall figure by the product lines that Global Widgets produces. You have heard that returns are greater in Asia than in North America, so you might want to instead take the overall average and break it down by region, and then further break down the Asian defect rates down to individual countries. To see whether this is a recent phenomenon, you might want to take the figures for Asia and break these down by season, and then by month.

What you are doing here is taking a measure, defects per thousand, and again using dimensions—geography, product, customer and time—to slice and dice your data in order to further determine why an outcome has been arrived at.

This form of analysis, taking a series of measures and analyzing them using different dimensions, is referred to as OLAP analysis. OLAP, short for online analytical processing, is a category of analysis that takes multidimensional data and manipulates it using a special type of database engine. Now, with Oracle 10*g* and Oracle Discoverer 10*g*, you can store multidimensional data directly in the Oracle database and analyze it with a new version of Discoverer, known as Discoverer Plus for OLAP, that is optimized for OLAP analysis.

The OLAP option was embedded directly into the Oracle database with the 9*i* R2 release (Oracle Database 9.2). While Discoverer in the 9.0.2 and 9.0.4 releases could access OLAP data through SQL views (ROLAP), with the 10.1.2 release it can directly access OLAP data through a dedicated multidimension API. As mentioned earlier, if you use the latest 10*g* R2 database, performance is amazing.

Oracle Business Intelligence Discoverer Plus for OLAP

Before we get too deep into showing you how to use Oracle Business Intelligence Discoverer Plus for OLAP, we will describe some of the key OLAP components. These are

- Discoverer Plus for OLAP

- The logical dimension model

- The Discoverer Catalog

Discoverer Plus for OLAP

Discoverer Plus for OLAP is a version of Oracle Discoverer 10*g* designed to generate native OLAP queries against multidimensional cubes of data. Part of the Oracle Business Intelligence Discoverer 10*g* family of reporting tools, Discoverer Plus for OLAP is new with version 10.1.2 and, like the standard Discoverer Plus, produces workbooks that can later be viewed using Discoverer Viewer and Oracle Application Server Portal. Discoverer Plus for OLAP complements Discoverer Plus and allows end users to produce sophisticated queries, calculations, and models against data described using a dimensional model of the organization.

To use Discoverer Plus for OLAP, your organization will need to license and install the OLAP Option to Oracle 9*i* or Oracle Database 10*g*, a pay-extra option to the Enterprise Edition of the Oracle database. The OLAP Option allows you to create multidimensional views of your data and store these models in either regular relational tables or specialized multidimensional data types held in Analytic Workspaces.

Up until recently, organizations that wanted to provide OLAP functionality for their users have had to purchase expensive, stand-alone OLAP servers and then integrate them into their existing data warehouse. Now, with the OLAP Option to Oracle 9*i* and Oracle Database 10*g*, this functionality has been incorporated into the core RDBMS, and tools such as Discoverer Plus for OLAP, together with Oracle Business Intelligence Beans and the Oracle Business Intelligence Spreadsheet Add-in, provide end-user access to this data.

If you have previously used Oracle's Express Server OLAP engine, or query tools such as Oracle Sales Analyzer, Oracle Financial Analyzer, or Express Web Agent, you will recognize much of the functionality from these tools within Discoverer Plus for OLAP. The OLAP engine that powers the OLAP Option to the Oracle Database is a direct descendant of the multidimensional engine used in the Express Server product line. Now, however, with the OLAP Option to Oracle 9*i* and Oracle 10*g*, the power of the Express Server engine has been embedded in the Oracle RDBMS, and new tools such as Discoverer Plus for OLAP are able to directly access this multidimensional data and perform high-end analysis and modeling.

The OLAP Option to Oracle 9*i* and Oracle Database 10*g*, like tools such as Discoverer Plus for OLAP, is typically used within organizations when they need to analyze, model, and perform forecasts on their data. These tools complement the more traditional form of relational analysis that you will have used with Discoverer Plus and Discoverer Desktop. Indeed, many organizations use both relational and OLAP query tools, and Discoverer Plus for OLAP and the relational version of Discoverer Plus are designed to work together to meet the complete reporting and analysis needs for an organization.

NOTE
The OLAP Option for Oracle Database 10g is a pay-extra option, and to use Discoverer Plus for OLAP in production, you will need to separately license this option. In addition, your database administrator will need to prepare data from your relational source systems or data warehouse and load it into a separate OLAP data store within the Oracle RDBMS before you can use Discoverer Plus for OLAP to analyze your data. For more details on preparing data for OLAP analysis, see the online documentation and download Analytic Workspace Manager, a free tool provided by Oracle to create and administer OLAP workspaces.

The Logical Dimensional Model

As a user of Discoverer Plus and Discoverer Desktop, you will be familiar with the concepts of End User Layers, business areas, folders, items, joins, hierarchies, and item classes. End User Layers and business areas allow administrators to remove the complexity from relational databases and present data items to users by using familiar business terms. This relational form of reporting is particularly suited to queries such as how many widgets did I sell last month, who are my customers within a particular region, and other such record-orientated reporting.

With its OLAP support, Discoverer Plus for OLAP presents data to users in the form of a logical dimensional model to reflect the way in which they picture their organization.

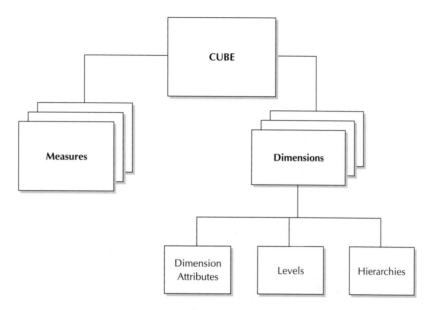

Within a logical dimensional model, data is organized into cubes that contain the following elements:

- **Measures**   These are the data items that you wish to track, measure, analyze, or forecast, such as, in our case, sales revenue or profit margin.

- **Dimensions**   These are the factors that categorize your measures, such as products, territories, and time periods. Dimensions can be thought of as containers for dimension members (as a folder is to individual items), and the group of dimensions that are used by a measure is known as the dimensionality of the measure.

- **Dimension members**   These are the individual elements of a dimension, such as individual products, months in the year, sales territories, or sales people.

- **Dimension hierarchies**   These are drill paths through dimensions that define the ways in which dimension members can be aggregated.

- **Dimension member attributes**   These are features of dimension members that can be used to create selections of dimension members.

A typical logical dimensional model consists of a number of dimensions and a number of cubes, with each cube containing measures that share the same dimensionality, each dimension having multiple dimension members with a number of attributes, and the dimensions having single or multiple hierarchies to define how data can be aggregated.

When you define a logical dimensional model for your data, you can formulate dimensional queries with terms familiar to users within the organization without worrying about how the data is actually stored in the database. For example, one query might be: What was the percent change in revenue for a grouping of the top 20 percent of our products during a rolling three-month time period one year ago, as compared to the current period this year for each region worldwide? Or, another query might be: Who are my top 10 customers?

The Discoverer Catalog

Instead of using an End User Layer to hold information on workbooks, calculations, and user permissions, Discoverer Plus for OLAP instead uses the Discoverer Catalog to perform the same function. The following illustration shows the two versions of Discoverer Plus along with the database objects that they work with.

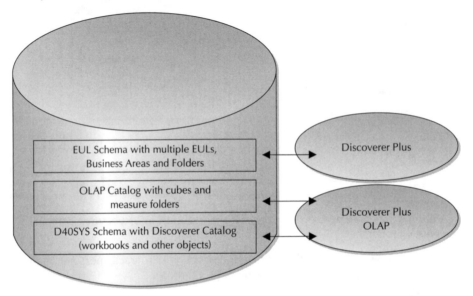

EUL Schema with multiple EULs, Business Areas and Folders

OLAP Catalog with cubes and measure folders

D40SYS Schema with Discoverer Catalog (workbooks and other objects)

Discoverer Plus

Discoverer Plus OLAP

The Discoverer Catalog is installed by the system administrator into the D40SYS schema and is maintained using Oracle Application Server 10g Application Server Control.

About the Examples

The sample schema that comes with this book includes OLAP data that you can analyze using Discoverer Plus for OLAP. The samples require Oracle Database 10g with the 10.1.0.4 patch set or higher, together with Analytic Workspace Manager II, available at the time of going to press as a free download from the Oracle Technology Network. Oracle's own OLAP samples can work with the following database combinations: 9.2.0.4 or higher with the OLAP patch and 10.1.0.3 or higher, also with the OLAP patch. The configuration guide has more details.

Using Analytic Workspace Manager, you can create an analytic workspace within your schema that will hold the data you wish to analyze. Then, using a graphical user interface, you can define the dimensions, levels, hierarchies, attributes, measures, and calculated measures that make up your logical dimensional model, after which you can take these definitions and create an OLAP cube for analysis.

The Global Widgets Logical Dimensional Model

You will recall from working with the relational version of Discoverer Plus and Discoverer Viewer that the GSW business area is comprised of a number of folders containing customer, product, channel, and sales data for Global Widgets.

The administrator creating these folders will have named them to reflect the purpose of the folder and the items that they contain, but other than those names, there is no obvious structure to these folders—no way to determine visually that products, customer, channel, and order date are dimensions, that the dimensions contain hierarchies, and so on. Discoverer Plus for OLAP, together with the OLAP Option, adds structure to your data in the form of the logical dimensional model, so that users are instead presented with a model that more accurately reflects their view of the business.

For the purposes of the examples within this chapter, we will take the data used in the GSW business area (see Figure 16-1), use Analytic Workspace Manager to create an OLAP cube, and then create workbooks using this data using Discoverer Plus for OLAP (see Figure 16-2).

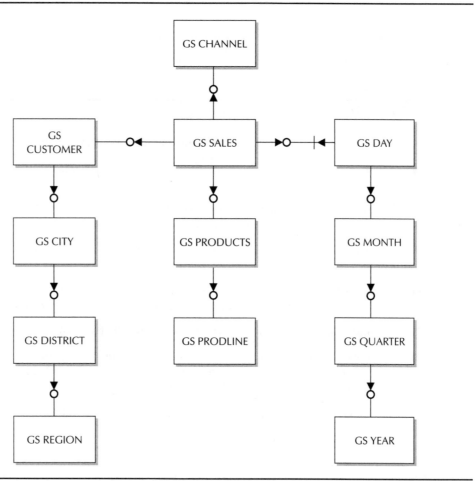

FIGURE 16-1   *The GSW relational folders*

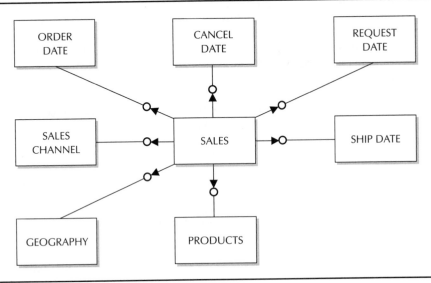

FIGURE 16-2 *The GSW dimensional folders*

The Global Widgets logical dimensional model has the following elements:

■ A cube, known as SALES, which acts as a container for the Global Widgets measures and dimensions

■ A Product dimension with three levels (products, product line, and all products), a single hierarchy, and an attribute (size) used to further refine product selections

■ A Time dimension with four levels (day, month, quarter, and year) and a single financial year hierarchy

■ A Customer dimension with four levels (city, district, region, and all customers), a single hierarchy, and four customer attributes (address, postcode, state, and credit limit)

■ A Channel dimension with two levels (channel and all channels) and a single hierarchy

■ Five measures: order quantity, ship quantity, order status, selling price, and cost price. All the measures except order status are defined as additive measures, with order status non-additive and only relevant at the lowest level of the cube's dimensions

To create the Global Widgets logical dimensional model, use the following workflow:

1. Grant the OLAP_USER role to the GSW user.

NOTE
*You will need to have installed the OLAP Option to Oracle
Database 10g for this grant to be allowed.*

2. Launch Analytic Workspace Manager 10.1 (AWM) and connect as the GSW user. As you can see in the following illustration, you will be presented with a dialog box of schemas.

3. Right-click the GSW user, and from the pop-up list, select Create Analytic Workspace from Template.

4. Select the GSW_AW XML template file provided with the Global Widgets samples.

5. Click Create. AWM will then take the definitions in the template file and create your OLAP cube.

NOTE
When the cube definition has loaded, you can examine the logical dimensional model within Analytic Workspace Manager (AWM). At this point, a logical dimensional model exists within AWM, and within an analytic workspace in turn within the GSW schema.

6. To load data from the Global Widgets tables into the analytic workspace, right-click the GSW_AW analytic workspace and from the pop-up menu select the option Maintain Analytic Workspace.

7. After a few minutes, your cube will have loaded.

8. Next, if you have not done so already, you will need to install the Discoverer Catalog and enable the GSW account for Discoverer Plus for OLAP. See the end of this chapter for details on how to do this.

Once you have installed the Discoverer Catalog, you will need to authorize schemas for use with Discoverer Plus for OLAP. The schemas you authorize will be those that contain OLAP data (either in relational tables or in analytic workspaces) and the schemas that will be granted access to this OLAP data.

To authorize the GSW schema for use with Discoverer Plus for OLAP, use the following workflow:

1. Navigate to the Application Server Enterprise Manager web site as before.
2. Click the link for Discoverer, and then Administration.
3. Under the Discoverer Catalog heading, click Manage.
4. Connect to the Discoverer Catalog using the connection details specified earlier.
5. Click Authorize Users and Roles.
6. Using the left-hand pane, highlight the GSW user.
7. Using the arrow buttons, move those users and/or roles into the right-hand pane.
8. Click Apply.

Connecting to Discoverer Plus for OLAP

To connect to Discoverer Plus for OLAP, first navigate to the Discoverer Plus URL, usually in the format http://*server*:*port*/discoverer/plus. Please refer back to Chapter 3 for instructions on logging in to Discoverer Plus.

After your username and password have been validated, you will be connected to Discoverer Plus for OLAP and presented with the first screen of the Plus Workbook Wizard.

NOTE
When connecting to Discoverer for OLAP, you need to specify the database connect information in the form host:port:sid *(e.g., ascserver. learndiscoverer.com:1521:orcl10g). This is different than when connecting to a relational EUL, where you have to specify either the SID or the full TNS entry.*

Creating Your First OLAP Plus Workbook

Now that you have connected to Discoverer Plus for OLAP, you are presented with the first screen of the Plus Workbook Wizard.

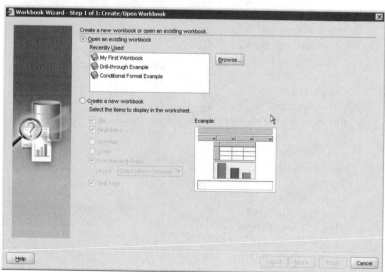

As you can see here, the Plus for OLAP wizard looks very similar to the standard Plus wizard that you have been working with so far. Just like the standard wizard, the OLAP wizard also has two options:

- Open an existing workbook, as stored in the Discoverer Catalog.

- Create a new workbook.

As there will initially be no workbooks in the Discoverer Catalog, we will use the second option to create a new workbook. Click the option to create a new workbook.

When you choose to create a new workbook, you are then presented with a series of options that determine how your initial worksheet will be laid out.

These are the default options for a new OLAP worksheet:

- The worksheet will have a title visible at the top of the page.

- The worksheet will have Page Items.

- The worksheet will contain a crosstab and a graph, with the graph below the crosstab.

- The worksheet will have a text area at the bottom of the page, for entering notes and comments.

NOTE
All Plus for OLAP worksheets are crosstabs; there is no facility for tabular worksheet layout as with the relational version of Discoverer Plus. This is due to the nature of OLAP data, which is multidimensional and therefore is usually displayed in a two-dimensional crosstab with one or more Page Items to provide access to additional dimensions.

For your first worksheet, you should accept the defaults, and then click Next.

As shown in the following illustration, you will now be presented with Step 2 of the wizard. In here, you select the measures and dimensions that will be the source of the data for your worksheet.

Take note of the Automatically Add/ Remove Dimensions check box at the bottom of the screen. This will automatically include the dimensions that are associated with measures you select in the item selection, and this tick box should usually be left selected.

Select selling price and order quantity from the list of measures (the items with the ruler icon next to them, i.e., ruler = measure) and note that the channel, customer, product, and time dimensions are then automatically selected.

Now that you have chosen the measures and dimensions to include in your worksheet, click Finish. This causes Discoverer to use the remaining default values for all the other settings for the wizard.

While Discoverer is creating the worksheet, the following message will be displayed:

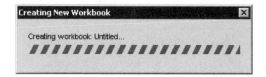

When the worksheet has executed, the message will clear, and you will then be presented with your first Discoverer Plus for OLAP worksheet, as shown in Figure 16-3.

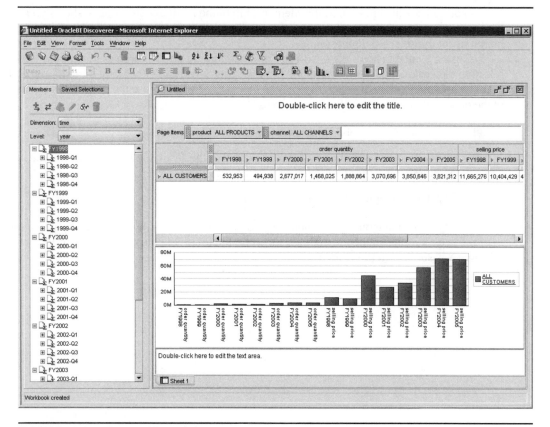

FIGURE 16-3 *First OLAP worksheet*

Exploring the Discoverer Plus for OLAP User Interface

Discoverer Plus for OLAP presents workbooks and worksheets in a similar format to the standard Discoverer Plus. Just as in standard Discoverer Plus, a Discoverer Plus for OLAP worksheet has the following areas:

- An Available Items pane, broken into two tabs, one entitled Members and one entitled Saved Selections

- A toolbar

- An area for displaying worksheets

- An optional pane for displaying filters or query steps

Available Items Pane

Looking again at the worksheet we have just created, your screen should look like the Figure 16-3.

As you can see in Figure 16-3, the Members tab of the Available Items pane shows you the list of members within the currently selected dimension, arranged according to the default hierarchy for the selected dimension.

Using the Available Items pane, you can navigate through the hierarchies in your dimension, selecting dimension members for addition to the crosstab. You can either drag dimension members from the available items pane directly onto the crosstab, or you can use the mini-toolbar at the top of the pane to do one of the following:

- Add dimension members to the crosstab.

- Swap dimension members you have selected in the Available Items pane with the existing members for that dimension in the crosstab.

- View the properties of a dimension member.

In addition to adding dimension members, you can also use the Available Items pane to add to or replace measures in the crosstab. As shown in the following illustration, you do this by selecting Measures from the Dimension.

When you display a list of measures in this pane, you can also use the toolbar to create and delete calculations based on these measures.

As shown in the previous illustration, the Available Items pane has a second tab, called Saved Selections. This tab allows you to recall and apply lists of saved dimension member selections.

You can also display a list of the query steps used in the worksheet by using View | Query Steps Pane from the toolbar. This causes Discoverer to split the left-hand pane into two parts, displaying the query steps below the list of available dimension members.

OLAP Toolbar

As seen next, the main OLAP toolbar is virtually the same as the toolbar provided with the standard Discoverer Plus interface, and it has all of the icons and buttons that you will be familiar with.

There are, however, new buttons for undoing and redoing your changes, and there is also a new top-level menu item called Window. You use the Window toolbar option to arrange worksheets within Discoverer Plus for OLAP's multiple document interface (MDI). Unlike Discoverer Plus, Discoverer Plus for OLAP allows you to display multiple worksheets simultaneously, so that you can compare the results from one crosstab with the results from another. If you have ever used Desktop, you will find this functionality behaves in a very similar manner. We like this feature and hope that one day this will be added to the standard Plus interface. As a sweetener, Oracle tells us that something even better is planned for the next major release of Discoverer. To find out, you will just have to wait and see and keep your eyes and ears open for announcements!

The following illustration shows the Plus for OLAP interface with two worksheets.

Saving a workbook in OLAP Plus is the same as saving in standard Plus, so we will not describe this in detail here. Suffice it to say that you do need to save the workbook that you have been working on.

Using the Workbook Wizard to Create OLAP Workbooks

As has already been explained, the Workbook Wizard can be used to create worksheets containing measures, dimension member selections, calculations, graphs, and conditional formatting. We will now look in more detail at how the Workbook Wizard is used.

Ensure that any open workbooks are closed, and then from the toolbar, select File | New. You will then be presented with the Workbook Wizard.

The Workbook Wizard has a number of steps and is used by Discoverer to collect the following information, prior to creating your worksheet:

■ The measures that you want to display on the worksheet

■ The dimensions with which you want to analyze your measures

■ The selection of dimension members for each of your chosen dimensions

■ The graph (if any) that you want to display

■ Whether you wish to include a text area for the worksheet, for comments and notes

After you have made your initial selection of measures and dimensions, you are free to exit the wizard at any stage, using the Finish button. The wizard will use default values for the rest of your choices. Using the Global Widgets OLAP dataset to illustrate these steps, we will now go through each of the pages in the wizard.

OLAP Worksheet Wizard Step 1

This step, which will be familiar to standard Discoverer Plus users, allows you to select whether your worksheet has a title, page items, and a text area, and whether the worksheet consists of a crosstab, a graph, or a crosstab and a graph.

NOTE
Whatever choice you make here can be altered later, either by stepping back in the wizard or manually by altering the layout of the worksheet using the toolbar.

As with standard Plus, as you alter the choices on this page of the wizard, the example layout on the right-hand side of the screen will change to reflect your choices. For the purposes of this example, we will leave the title, Page Items, and text area choices as the default, but change the current crosstab selection to Crosstab and Graph, and display the graph to the right of the crosstab. Having made your choices, click Next.

OLAP Worksheet Wizard Step 2

The second page of the wizard is where we choose what measures and dimensions we will include on the worksheet. As you can see here, Discoverer displays a list of these for you to select from:

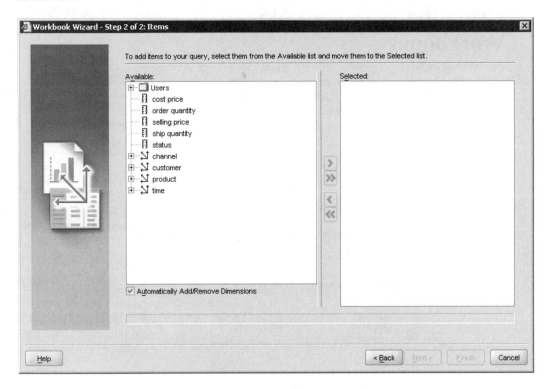

The list of measures that is offered here is the complete set that is available to you. There is no distinction between measures held in different Oracle schemas, because what you are seeing here is the list of all measures as available to you within the Discoverer Catalog.

To select an individual measure for inclusion in the worksheet, highlight the measure with your mouse and either double-click the measure or click the right-pointing single arrow button that is located between the two panes. As you can see here, Discoverer has started to build up the worksheet criteria:

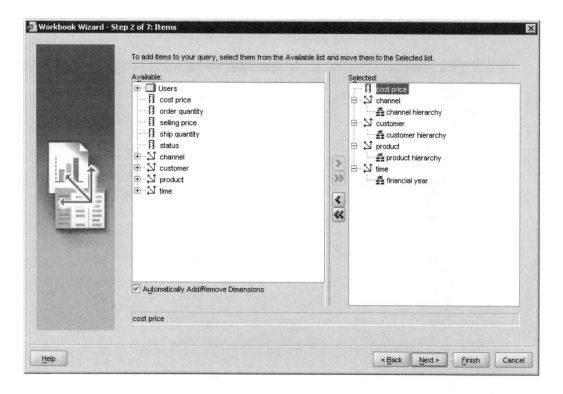

If you have left the Automatically Add/Remove Dimensions check box checked, the wizard will automatically bring across the dimensions that are associated with your measure, together with the default hierarchy for the measure. If you have unchecked this check box, you will need to bring across the dimensions yourself.

If you wish to exclude one or more dimensions from your report, you can select the dimension in the Selected pane and then either double-click it or click the left-pointing single arrow button to remove it from the selection. If you remove a dimension from the selection, later on in the wizard you will tell Discoverer how to provide values for this dimension. For the purposes of this example, we will remove the Channel dimension from the worksheet so that our selections look like this:

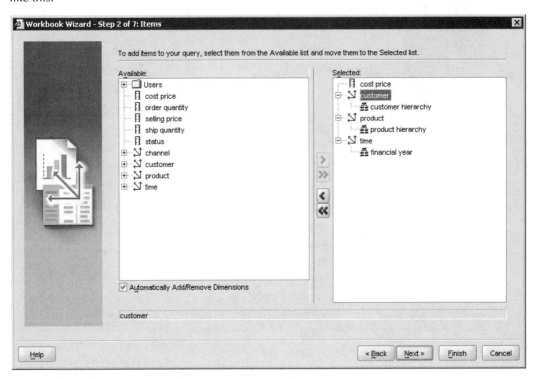

When you have completed making your item selections, click Next.

OLAP Worksheet Wizard Step 3: Graph Type

This next step in the wizard allows you to define what type of graph you would like to include in your worksheet. Note that the wizard step is now showing 3 of 8. This is because Discoverer has included additional steps in the wizard, following our selection of measures and dimensions, to allow us to further refine the member selection for our selected dimensions.

The list of graphs will be familiar to users of Oracle's other query and reporting tools; it is based on Oracle's Business Intelligence Beans technology.

For this example, as shown next, we will select the Bubble graph from the Scatter/Bubble graph group:

Again, you can come back to this page in the wizard should you wish to change your choice of graph, or you can change the graph from the main Discoverer Plus for OLAP toolbar after the wizard has completed. When you have made your graph selection, click Next.

OLAP Worksheet Wizard Step 4: Crosstab Layout

This part of the wizard, shown as Step 4 of 8, allows you to define where in the worksheet your dimensions and measures should be placed. For the purposes of a Discoverer Plus for OLAP crosstab, the set of measures that are available to you is itself treated as a dimension, and you can include this measures dimension in any changes you make to the layout of the crosstab.

For our example, we will swap the product dimension, which initially is the page item for the worksheet, with the time dimension, which is initially on the X axis for the crosstab, by dragging the product dimension tile and placing it on top of the time dimension tile.

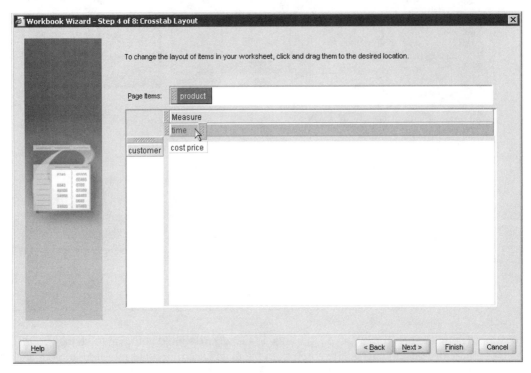

This action then swaps the time dimension with the product dimension as the dimension listed on the X axis of the worksheet.

Alternatively, you can drag the time dimension tile, which is now a Page Item, and drop it underneath the customer dimension tile to embed time as a nested dimension under the customer dimension. Alternatively, you may wish to drag and drop the time dimension tile and place it on top of the customer dimension tile. This latter operation has the effect of embedding the customer dimension as a nested dimension for the time dimension. However, for the purposes of this example, we will place the time dimension tile back into the Page Items area so that the customer dimension is the only dimension in the Y axis of the report.

When you have finished setting the layout, click Next.

OLAP Worksheet Wizard Steps 5–8: Dimensions

The remaining steps of the Workbook Wizard are created dynamically depending upon how many dimensions you selected. Each step allows you to pick the dimension members that will be included in the workbook. In our example, as you can see next, the first dimension that the wizard displays is the Time dimension:

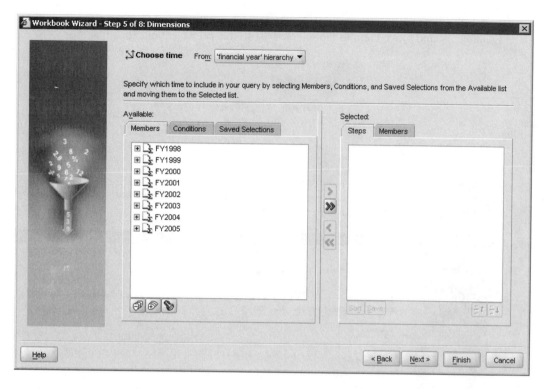

As you can see, at the top of the wizard there is a drop-down list with all of the hierarchies for this dimension. In our example there is only one hierarchy, Financial Year. Some dimensions may have multiple hierarchies, and when you select an alternate hierarchy, this will affect the list of available dimension members that you can select from.

On the left-hand pane of the wizard there are three tabs:

- **Members**   This tab displays the list of available dimension members that you can select from.

- **Conditions**   This tab lists any dimension member conditions you have specified.

- **Saved selections**   This tab lists the groups of dimension members that you have selected and then saved for later use.

The right-hand pane of this screen wizard is used to list those dimension members that have been selected for the worksheet. It has two panes:

- **Steps**   This is used to show the steps used to build up your list of dimension members.

- **Members**   This lists the dimension members that you have selected.

For the Time dimension, we will simply select the FY2003 and FY2004 values from the available list and move them to the selected list so that our selections look like this:

When you have finished with a dimension, click Next.

For the Customers dimension, we will select a group of customers and move them to the selected list, and save these customers as a saved selection.

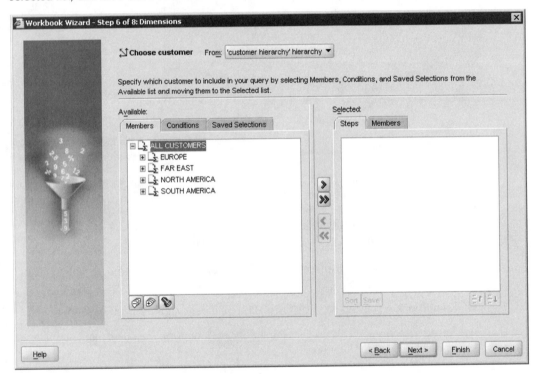

The left-hand pane initially lists the highest level in the dimension, which in the case of the Customer dimension, as you can see in the illustration, is All Customers. Expand the list of customers by clicking the plus key alongside the All Customers member. This causes Discoverer to drill down to the next lower level, which in our case is Regions. In OLAP terminology, the All Customers member is called the *parent,* while Regions are referred to as *children.* If we drill down further from Regions to Districts, Regions is considered the parent, and Districts the children.

Let's drill down from the Far East region, to the FE-All member, and on into our customers, finally expanding the city of Tokyo to see that we have one customer named Yamata Widget Limited. You can see this drill here:

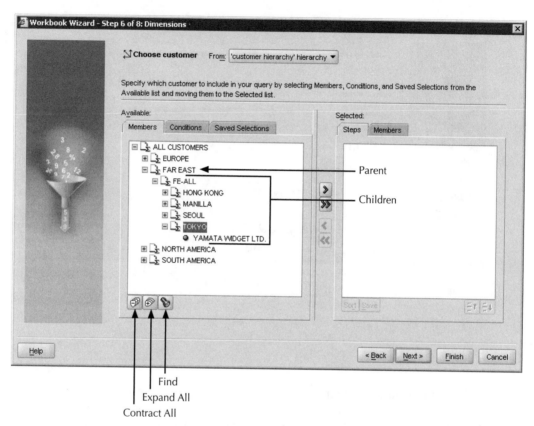

We want to spend a little time explaining the difference between navigating a dimension using Discoverer Plus for OLAP and navigating a folder using Discoverer Plus. In Discoverer Plus for OLAP a dimension has an embedded structure that clearly shows the relationship between the members within that dimension. In our case, as you have seen, our dimension consists of cities, districts, and regions. In Discoverer Plus there is no obvious relationship between the members except that they happen to be contained within the same folder and that our administrator has created a hierarchy on these items.

Using the Expand All and Contract All buttons located beneath the Available Members pane, you can display all members in all levels or revert back to a view of just the top level in the dimension hierarchy. Here, we have expanded the whole dimension:

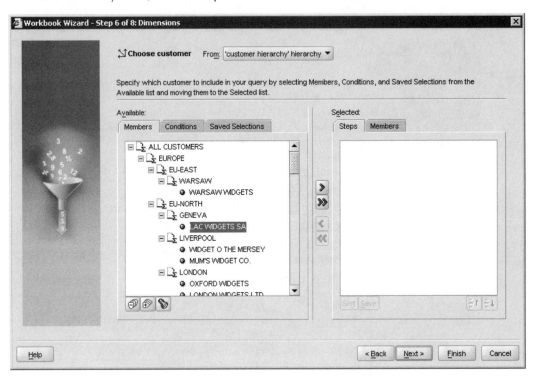

Finding Dimension Members

Discoverer provides a search mechanism that allows you to find members that match particular criteria. To launch the Find Members dialog box, click the Find button, shown as a flashlight, that you will find located immediately below the Available members pane.

As you can see next, to search for all dimension members with the word "widget" in their name, enter **widget** into the Find Members dialog box and click Find Next.

After you click Find Next, you will then be taken to the first dimension member that has "widget" in the name. If this is not the member that you want, click Find Next again to locate the next dimension member that meets your search terms.

For this example, we wish to select all customers who are within the Far East region, together with the dimension members that these customers are aggregated up to. This will allow us to produce a report on our selected customers, together with totals for the dimension levels directly above these dimension members.

To select these dimension members, use the following workflow:

1. Click the Collapse All button to return to the All Customers dimension member.

2. Expand All Customers to display the list of Regions.

3. Using the Far East region, drill down into FE-All.

4. At this point you are presented with a list of cities. Taking each city in turn, drill down again until you are displaying all of the customers within this district. You should now see this screen:

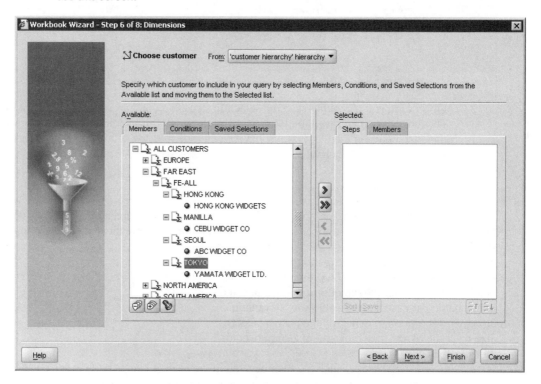

5. Starting with All Customers, select each dimension member and move it across to the Selected list. Do the same for the Far East, and then FE-All. Finally, add the four customers that are part of this district.

At this point, you might decide that you would like to save this selection of dimension members for later use.

To save a selection for later use, follow this workflow:

1. Click the Save button that is located under the list of selected items.

2. Discoverer displays the following Save Selection As dialog box:

3. At this point, you can either save the selection steps that you carried out to arrive at this selection, or you can save the members themselves. For this example there is no practical difference between the two options, but we will look in more detail at the significance of this option later in the chapter.

4. Having made your option and named the selection, click OK. Discoverer now moves on to the next page in the wizard.

Still, within the dimension member selection screens, we need to make our selections for Products. In this case, we will apply a simple condition to include only those products whose size is Medium. To do this, click the Conditions tab in the Available Items pane and expand the Match entry. As you can see next, you will be presented with a list of all the attributes for the dimension that we selected. In our particular case, the Size attribute is available, along with an option to match on the Name. Select Size = MEDIUM and then move the selection over to the Selected pane.

Having selected the size, click the Members tab in the Selected items pane to see a list of the products that meet this condition. As you can see here, there are seven products that are MEDIUM in size:

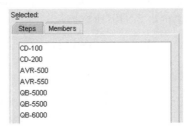

Click Next to move on to the final page of the wizard.

The final page of the wizard allows you to specify a value for the Channel dimension.

NOTE
This final step is required because the Sales cube is dimensioned by all four dimensions—products, customers, channel, and time—and you need to provide selections for all four dimensions even if you only want some of them to appear on the worksheet.

Here is the final step of the Workbook Wizard:

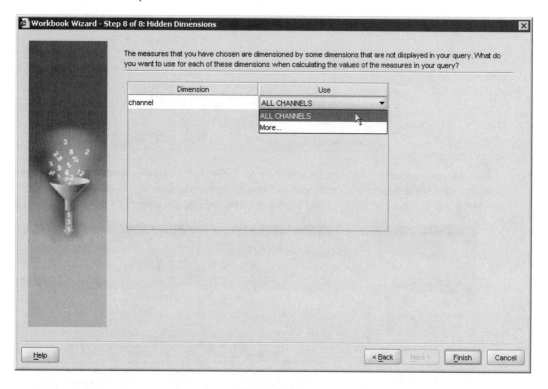

As you can see, there is a drop-down list available for the channel. At this point, the usual choice would be to select All Channels from the Use drop-down list. This would cause all of the available channels to be included within our calculations.

However, if you wish to select a particular channel dimension, you should select More from the drop-down list and select the channel dimension member that you want to use. For the purpose of this exercise, we will not select a channel dimension member, but we will show you what the Select Member dialog box looks like.

As we said, we will not in fact be selecting an individual channel member. We therefore selected All Channels and clicked Finish to execute the worksheet.

Here you can see the result of the worksheet that we just created:

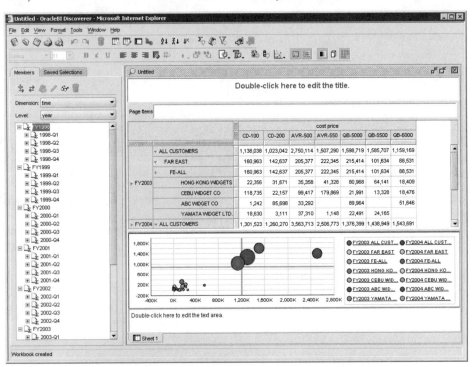

We hope this exercise shows you the power of the OLAP engine and how easy it is to create worksheets using Discoverer Plus for OLAP.

Creating OLAP Conditions or Query Steps

In Discoverer Plus for OLAP terms, conditions are called *query steps*; they are used to create selections of dimension members for displaying on your crosstab report.

You can create a query step in one of the following three ways:

- Using the Workbook Wizard, as you define the worksheet

- Using the Edit Worksheet dialog box

- Using the Filter button on the toolbar

A query step is an action that you perform on a dimension member selection, such as keep all of the products whose color is "red", or add those customers whose profitability is in the top 5 percent for the company.

In this respect then, a query step is similar to a Discoverer Plus condition, where you might, for example, exclude products that are not in a particular category. However, one key difference between query steps and Discoverer Plus conditions is that query steps are cumulative for a dimension and are applied in the order that you specify, allowing you to progressively refine a dimension member selection according to the query steps that you specify.

Let's explain this point using an example.

Creating Query Steps

As mentioned previously, a query step can be created using the Workbook Wizard, the Edit Worksheet dialog box, or the Query Steps dialog.

The Workbook Wizard is displayed when you create a new workbook. As you have seen, the wizard has multiple pages where you can in turn select the measures and dimensions for your worksheet, select a graph and the layout of the crosstab, and at the end of the wizard, select dimension members and apply conditions.

The Edit Worksheet dialog box is displayed by selecting Worksheet from the Edit menu. As you can see next, the Edit Worksheet dialog box looks very similar to the pages in the Workbook Wizard and allows you to select measures and dimension members.

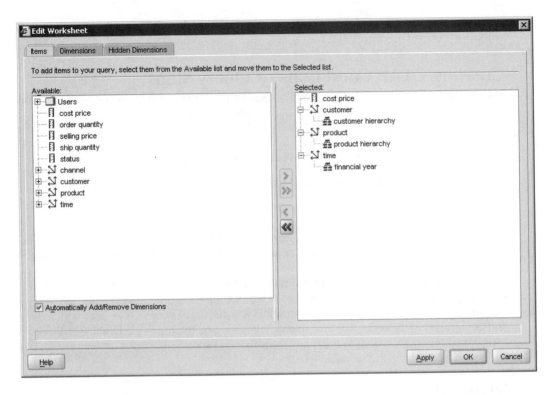

The Edit Worksheet dialog box has the following three tabs:

- **Items**   Use this tab to change the selection of measures used in the worksheet.

- **Dimensions**   Use this tab to change the selected dimension measures.

- **Hidden Dimensions**   Use this tab to provide values for hidden dimensions.

To illustrate how the Edit Worksheet dialog box can be used to create a condition, we will create a series of query steps that will answer the question "For our customers that are part of the Far East region, excluding those who in 2004 were in the bottom 10 percent of order quantity, what were the units sold last year broken down by product line?" Phew, what a query, you might say, and at first glance, you would be correct. However, we will now proceed to show you how easy this sort of query is using OLAP.

First of all, using the Global Widgets sample data, we created a worksheet that includes the order quantity measure, ensuring that all of the dimensions are included in the workbook. We left all of the remaining items with their defaults and clicked Finish. If you are following along with us, your worksheet should look like this:

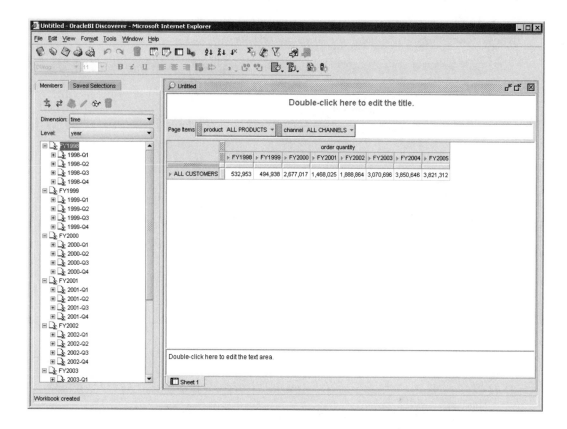

Our first query step will be to replace the All Customers dimension member that is currently on the worksheet with the individual customers that are part of the Far East region.

We could in fact do this in two ways. The first way would be to use the Available Items pane on the left-hand side to manually drill down through the customer hierarchy, highlight those customers who are in the Far East region, and then use the Available Items toolbar to swap those customers with the All Customers dimension member currently displayed in the crosstab. The second, and more efficient, way is to take advantage of the hierarchy that has been defined for our customer dimension and create a query step instead.

Using the Edit Worksheet dialog box, click the tab for Dimensions and select the Customer dimension. Initially it will display All Customers as the dimension member selected. Select this dimension member and move it back to the Available Items list.

Next, click the Conditions tab. In the Available Items pane, as you can see next, there are five types of conditions that you can use in your worksheet:

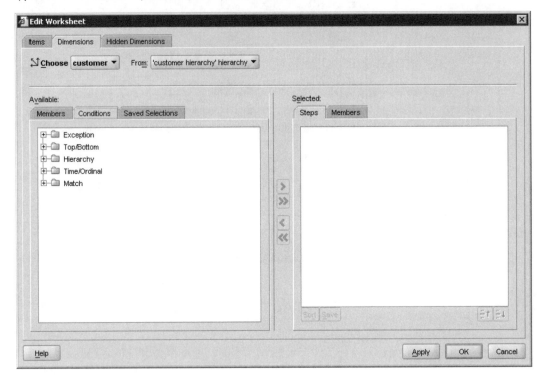

- ■ Exception
- ■ Top/Bottom
- ■ Hierarchy
- ■ Time/Ordinal
- ■ Match

As you can see, the icon alongside each condition type is the folder icon. This means that there must be subitems. Clicking any of these condition folders will cause Discoverer to display the full range of condition templates that are available within each type. Condition templates help you to build up a condition using familiar business terms.

Exception Conditions Folder Next we have expanded the Exception conditions folder:

Exception conditions allow you to add, remove, or keep dimension members using comparisons of values for measures. You would use an exception condition if, for example, you wanted to include all of those customers who had an order quantity this year greater than 10,000.

Top/Bottom Conditions Folder   Next we have expanded the Top/Bottom conditions folder:

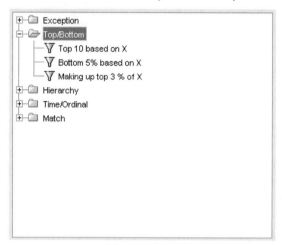

Top/Bottom conditions add, remove, or keep a specified number of dimension members after ranking the members by the specified measure. You might, for example, use one of these condition templates to remove all customers who are in the bottom 10 percent of order quantity for the last year.

Hierarchy Conditions Folder   Next we have expanded the Hierarchy conditions folder:

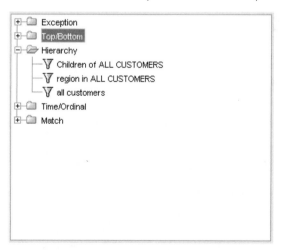

Hierarchy conditions are conditions that select dimension members based on hierarchical relationships—the hierarchies that your OLAP cube administrator would have defined when putting together your OLAP data source. Hierarchies are an important, powerful concept in OLAP and allow you to make dimension selections such as add all the last descendants of All Customers.

Within a hierarchy, you can refer to dimension members in terms of their position in a family tree relative to another dimension member. To take our example, we are going to select dimension members relative to the Far East region. Now, if we look at the customer hierarchy, we can see where the Region is positioned.

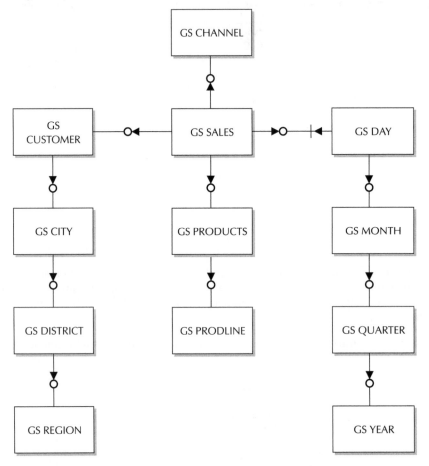

When we make selections based on hierarchical relationships, we can select members that are the

- **Children of a member**   In our case, this would be just the FE-All district.

- **Parent of a member**   Our dimension member rolls up into the one above it in the hierarchy, which for the Far East region would be All Customers.

- **Siblings**   In the case of the Far East region, the other dimension members in the hierarchy that have the same parent and therefore roll up into the same dimension member would be the other regions, Europe, North America, and South America.

- **Ancestors**   These include the parent of the dimension member, plus its parent, and its parent, and so on until the topmost dimension member in the hierarchy is reached. For the Far East region, this would just be the All Customers member.

■ **Descendants**   These are all of the dimension members that are directly descended from a dimension member, which for the Far East dimension member, would be the FE-All district and all the cities and customers that belong to this district.

■ **First Ancestor**   This is the dimension member within the hierarchy that our dimension member eventually rolls up into, which for all members in the customer hierarchy would be All Customers.

■ **Last Descendents**   These are the descendents for this dimension member that are at the very bottom of the hierarchy, which for the Far East region, would be all customers that eventually roll up into the Far East region.

In the case of our example, then, we would therefore want to add to our dimension member selection those dimension members that are Last Descendents of the Far East Region.

Time/Ordinal Conditions Folder   In this illustration we have expanded the Time/Ordinal conditions folder:

Time/Ordinal conditions are particularly suitable for time dimensions. These allow you to make time selections such as the last three months or six days starting from 27th September 1997.

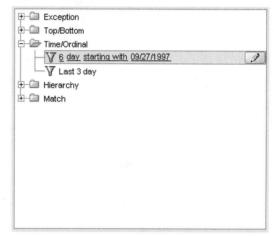

Match Conditions Folder   In the next illustration we have expanded the Match conditions folder:

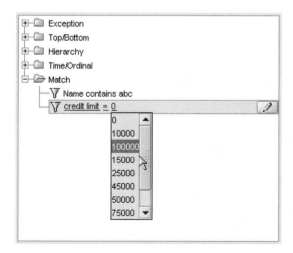

Match conditions are those that select dimension members according to matches with text strings and attribute values. We might, for example, wish to select those customers who have Widget in their name, or those with a credit limit of 25000, or those days that are a public holiday.

Qualifying Conditions

Another powerful concept with Discoverer Plus for OLAP conditions is the ability to qualify a condition. Whenever you create a condition using a condition template, you will notice a pencil icon at the end of the template line. If you click the pencil, you will be able to further qualify the condition.

In our example, we wish to exclude those customers who are in the bottom 10 percent of order quantity for 2004. Beforehand, we created this condition using a Top/Bottom template, but currently we will consider all values of order quantity for all time periods. If, however, we create the condition again but this time select the pencil icon next to the condition, we can then further qualify the condition. This causes Discoverer to open the following Edit Step dialog box:

The Edit Step dialog box allows you to change all aspects of the condition, but it has the following two key features that are relevant here:

- Narrowing the levels
- Qualifying a condition

Narrowing the Levels The first key feature of the Edit Step dialog box is that it allows you to narrow down the levels that your condition will consider. For example, we could ask Discoverer to consider only those dimension members that are in the Customer level.

NOTE
Please remember that dimension members at higher levels will also have aggregated values for measures, but in our case, we only want to consider actual customers.

Qualifying a Condition The second key of the Edit Step dialog box is that it allows you to qualify the condition, so that we can select a particular dimension member value (a particular year, a dimension member at a level lower than All Customers, for example) for your query. In our case, we only want to consider orders from 2004, but we want to consider all products and all channels, so we will use the Qualify button to make the necessary changes. Clicking the Qualify button causes Discoverer to display the Qualify Measure dialog box as shown here:

After you have made your dimension member selection, you can include it in the selected member list by moving it from the left-hand side of the dialog to the right-hand side. We will first move across the condition that adds all customers who are last descendants of the Far East region, such that our first step says Start with Last Descendants of FAR EAST.

Next, we will add our second, qualified condition, this time using it to remove those customers from our selection who make up the bottom 10 percent of our order quantity. The resulting Selected Items pane looks like this:

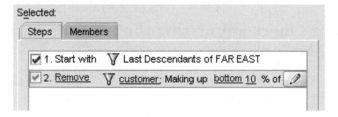

If you now click the Members tab, you will see a list of the members that match the two query steps that we have defined. In our example we have only three customers remaining.

Executing this worksheet, the resulting crosstab, with 2005 selected as the value for the Year, looks like this:

Creating a Query Step Using the Filter Button

An alternative way to create a query step without using the Workbook Wizard or the Edit Worksheet dialog box is to click the Filter button on the Discoverer Plus for OLAP toolbar. This brings up a dialog that allows you to select a dimension to work with, and then steps you through the creation of one of the following:

■ A Member Step

■ A Condition Step

■ A Saved Selection Step

Selecting any of these options will present you with a cut-down version of the Edit Worksheet dialog, focused on the creation of a new dimension member step, a new condition step, or a new saved selection step. You can think of the New Query dialog as a query step wizard that walks you through the process of refining your Discoverer Plus for OLAP query.

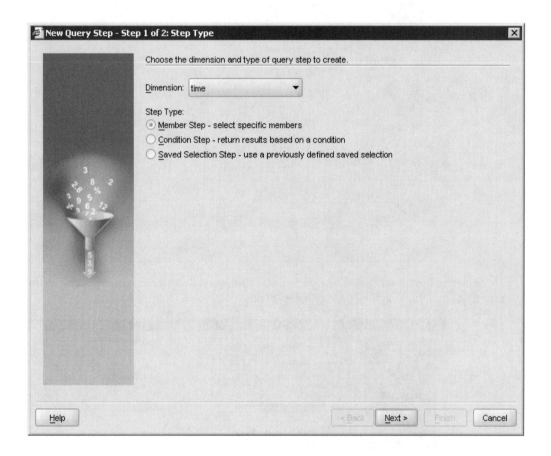

If you choose to create a Member Step, you will then be presented with an available items list and a selected items list, allowing you to add, remove, replace, or keep the dimension members you select.

Selecting Condition Step allows you to add a new condition to your query, using a similar process to that found in the Edit Worksheet dialog.

If you choose to create a Saved Selection step using the New Query Step dialog, you will then be presented with a list of previously saved selections, so that you can then apply one of them to your current worksheet.

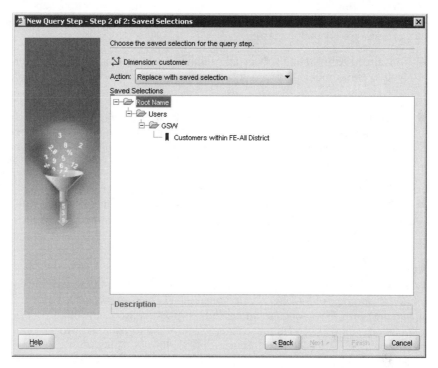

Whether you choose to use the Workbook Wizard, the Edit Worksheet dialog, or the New Query Step Wizard is down to personal preference. If you know what conditions you wish to apply at the time you create your workbook, the Workbook Wizard is a convenient place to define them. Once the workbook has been created, the New Query Step Wizard will help you create a new condition if you are unfamiliar with the process, and once you are more used to Discoverer Plus for OLAP, you may well find that you use the Edit Worksheet dialog more, as it offers more options and allows you to edit conditions that you previously created and applied.

Creating Calculations

Using Discoverer Plus for OLAP, you can create calculations that are based on the measures in your worksheet. Calculations are formulas that are calculated when you refresh your worksheet, and once defined, they can be included in worksheets and graphs just like any other measure.

Calculations are defined using the Calculation Wizard. You can display the Calculation Wizard using one of three methods:

- ■ Select Tools | Calculations from the menu bar.

- ■ Click the New Calculation button on the toolbar.

- ■ Select Measures as the dimension in the Available Items pane, and then click the New Calculation button.

When you first display the Calculation Wizard, you will be asked which calculation you wish to create. Discoverer Plus for OLAP supports four types of calculation:

- **Basic Arithmetic** Basic arithmetic calculations include addition, subtraction, division, multiplication, and ratios; they allow you to, for example, add one measure to another or add a number to a measure.

- **Advanced Arithmetic** Advanced Arithmetic calculations are more powerful and allow you to perform calculations such as cumulative total, index, percent variance, rank, and share.

- **Prior/Future Comparison** Prior/Future comparison calculations are used when you have time-series data and leverage the time-series calculation capabilities of the Oracle OLAP option. Using calculations such as Percent Difference from Prior Period, you can easily calculate the difference for a measure between two different time periods, or calculate the future value of a measure.

- **Time Frame** Similar to Prior/Future Comparisons are Time Frame calculations. Time Frame calculations give you the ability to quickly create moving averages, moving totals, or year-to-date totals.

NOTE
With the 10.1.2 version of Discoverer Plus for OLAP you are currently limited to adding, subtracting, multiplying, or dividing a maximum of two measures; if you need to add a third or more measures to your calculation, you will need to first calculate according to your first two measures, then use the product along with your third measure, and so on.

Both Prior/Future Comparisons and Time Frame calculations require at least one of your dimensions to have been defined as a time dimension. A *time* dimension is a special sort of OLAP dimension that contains additional attributes used for time-series analysis. Time dimensions are created using tools such as Analytic Workspace Manager. If your OLAP cube contains a dimension relating to time but these calculation types are not available, speak to your administrator, who will be able to create the required metadata.

Example Calculations

In this example, we are going to create two calculations:

- A profit margin calculation, based on the Selling Price and Cost Price measures

- The percentage change for Order Quantity compared to this time last year

To create our first calculation, use the following workflow:

1. Select Calculations from the Tools menu. The New Calculation Wizard is displayed.

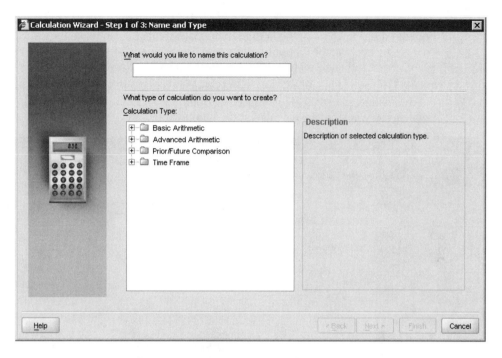

2. You can now enter the calculation name as Profit Margin and select Subtraction from the Basic Arithmetic calculation type folder.

3. Select Selling Price as the value, and Cost Price as the measure that is subtracted. Using this page in the wizard, you can also overtype a measure name and replace it with a number, for example: Minus: 50.

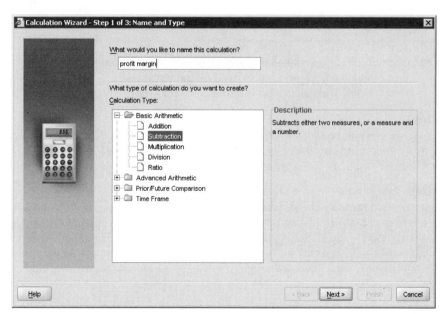

4. You can change the format of the number used to hold the calculation by selecting from the drop-down list at the bottom of the page, and you can make further formatting changes by clicking the Options button. In our case, we wish to subtract Cost Price from Selling Price and leave all formatting settings as the default values.

5. On the last page of the wizard, you can further specify the long and short labels for the calculation, give the calculation a description, and decide where in the Discoverer Catalog you will store the calculation definition.

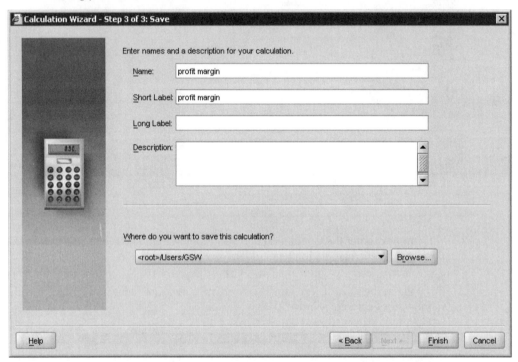

6. Once you have completed the wizard, click Finish to store the calculation. Now, the Profit Margin calculation is displayed on the worksheet alongside any other measures or calculations. The calculation is also available to select from in the Available Items pane.

NOTE
Calculations can be scoped within the Discoverer Catalog so that only certain users can select them. We will look in more detail about access rights and the Discoverer Catalog later in this chapter.

Sorting

Using the sort buttons on the standard toolbar, you can sort the rows and columns on your crosstab from either high-to-low, or low-to-high, and the sort you apply will also apply to a graph if you have one displayed. Sorting using Discoverer Plus for OLAP is slightly different from sorting within Discoverer Plus, as sorting takes place within the dimension hierarchy, and so to illustrate how sorting works we will work through two examples, one for sorting rows, and one for sorting columns.

Sorting Rows   For this example we will start with a workbook that shows quantity broken down by time, by customer, and by product. Initially, the regions within each year are ordered by the default ordering in the dimension, which in this case is alphabetical. All Customers will be at the top of the list of each set of customers because it is at a higher level in the customer hierarchy.

If you wish to sort customers by order quantity, first click the measure you wish to sort by, in this case order quantity, and then click the Sort High-to-Low button on the standard toolbar.

Now, as you can see below, the regions within the crosstab are sorted in descending order of order quantity.

NOTE
The All Customers dimension member is still displayed above the regions, as this is at a higher level in the customer hierarchy.

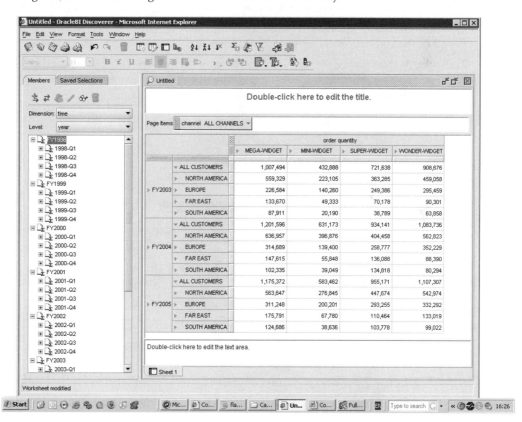

Sorting Columns   As well as sorting rows, you can also sort worksheet columns. When you sort columns, you first have to select a crosstab row that will provide the order for the columns.

Select the FY2004 time dimension member, and then select the Sort High-to-Low button from the standard toolbar. Your worksheet columns will be sorted by the measure values for FY2004, All Customers. If you wish to sort by a FY2004 and a specific region, select the region required within the FY2004 row, rather than FY2004 itself, and the column sort will be based on this region instead.

Sorting Dimension Members   As well as sorting worksheet rows and columns, sometimes you might wish to sort the members within a dimension, for example when you are producing a Pareto graph.

To sort dimension members, use the following workflow:

1. Open a worksheet.

2. Select Worksheet from the Edit menu, or click the Edit Worksheet button on the standard toolbar.

3. Select the Dimensions tab, and choose the dimension for which you want to sort members.

4. Select the dimension hierarchy required.

5. Using the available member list or using a condition, add dimension members to the selected items list.

6. Click the Sort button under the selected items list.

7. Using the Sort dialog, specify whether the dimension list is sorted by hierarchy or by reference to a measure value, and optionally then move dimension members up and down the sort order as required as seen here:

8. Click OK to confirm the new sort order, and click OK again to close the Edit Worksheet dialog.

Creating Totals

Totals are calculated rows or columns that you can add to a worksheet to summarize measures for a dimension. Using the Totals feature, you can add grand totals and subtotals to a worksheet, using any of the following aggregations:

- Sum

- Average

- Minimum

- Maximum

To illustrate how totals can be calculated, we will use a simple worksheet. The initial worksheet looks like this:

You now wish to add a grand total that adds together order quantity for each customer, for each year displayed on the crosstab. To create a total, use the following workflow:

1. Select Totals from the Tools menu, or select the New Total icon on the toolbar. The Totals dialog will then be displayed.

2. To create a new Total, click the New button. Discoverer opens the following New Total dialog box:

3. As we wish to calculate the SUM for order quantity for our customer dimension, we will change the value of the dimension drop-down list to Customer. The Level drop-down list lets you pick a particular level within the customer dimension for totaling; however, for the purposes of this grand total, we can leave this as All Levels, as we just wish to total up all of the customer dimension members (regions, in this instance) on the crosstab. You can also specify the header for the total (the description that will accompany the total) and the format, should you wish to alter the color of the cell or text used to display the total.

4. When you click OK, the total will be displayed on the worksheet as seen next.

NOTE
*In the same way, you can add a total for the Time dimension,
calculate the average, and display this as a new column in the
worksheet.*

Nested Totals   If you create a worksheet that nests one dimension inside another, you can use
the Totals feature to create subtotals at the nested dimension level. Using our original example,
we will nest the Product dimension inside the Customer dimension.

To create both a grand total and subtotals for order quantity, based on the customer and
product dimensions, use the following workflow:

1. Open the Create Total dialog. The first total should be for the product dimension, and you
    should ensure this time that the product line rather than All Levels is selected as the level;
    if you left the level selection as All Levels, you would end up double-counting orders, as
    you would include the values for All Products in your subtotal.

2. Once this total has been defined, you should then define the total for the customer
    dimension as before.

One useful feature of Totals with Discoverer Plus for OLAP is that you can use it to calculate aggregations using arbitrary selections of dimension members. For example, Global Widgets may create a promotion that applies to one Region, two districts, and a number of cities, and thereafter, it may wish to create a sales summary report for just these customer dimension members.

If you had to manually create a grand total for these dimension members, this would be a difficult process, as each of these customer dimension members are at a different level in the customer hierarchy and do not naturally aggregate, but with Discoverer Plus for OLAP you can add these dimension members to a selection and then easily create a grand total for them.

Editing Worksheet Properties

Selecting Worksheet Properties from the Edit menu lets you alter the properties of your workbook. The Worksheet Properties dialog has two tabs: one for entering a description and keywords for your worksheet, and one for setting view options for your worksheet.

The description that you enter for the worksheet will be displayed alongside the worksheet name whenever you display a list of worksheets. Any keywords you enter will be stored, along with the worksheet description, in the Discoverer Catalog, and you will be able to search for worksheets using these keywords with a future release of Discoverer Plus for OLAP.

The View Options tab (seen next) allows you to define the way that your worksheet handles null and zero value settings, and whether drill links have a visual indicator.

You can use the null and zero value settings to show rows and columns in your worksheet that contain null or zero values. By checking or unchecking the Show Drill Icon check box on this page of the dialog, you can decide whether Discoverer Plus for OLAP displays link icons to indicate links to other workbooks or URLs.

Creating Links to Discoverer Worksheets

One of the key features of Oracle Discoverer 10*g* is the ability to work with both relational and OLAP data. Using Discoverer Plus for OLAP, you can create a worksheet based on summarized data in an OLAP cube, and then drill through to a transactional-level tabular report using Discoverer Plus or Discoverer Viewer.

Discoverer Plus for OLAP can link to a Discoverer Plus relational worksheet, a Discoverer Viewer relational worksheet, or a separate Web page that you have previously created. You cannot link through to another Discoverer Plus for OLAP worksheet.

When you link from a Discoverer Plus for OLAP worksheet, you can pass to the relational worksheet the current value of the selected cell's dimension values. When you define parameters for your relational worksheet, you can use these values as inputs into the relational worksheet and then show only those values that correspond to the selected item in the OLAP worksheet.

Creating an Example Worksheet Link

To illustrate how worksheet links can be created, you will now create a worksheet link from an OLAP worksheet holding summarized orders data to a relational tabular report showing a breakdown of those orders. The example worksheets use the Global Widgets OLAP cube and the Global Widgets relational business area.

For the OLAP worksheet, the crosstab holds order quantity data dimensioned by product and by time as seen in Figure 16-4. Right-clicking in a cell causes Discoverer to display a drop-down menu from which you can select New Link.

FIGURE 16-4 *OLAP worksheet showing order quantity dimensioned by product*

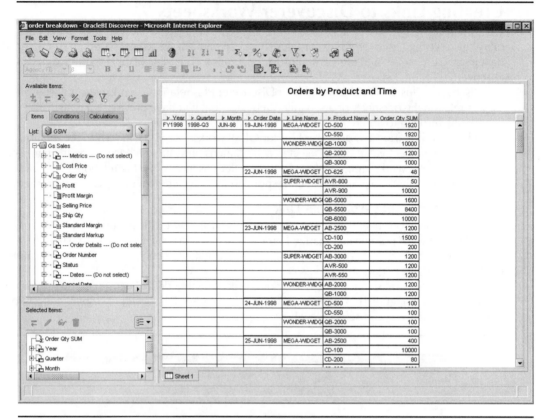

FIGURE 16-5 *Relational worksheet showing order details by product and time*

The relational worksheet contains a table that lists orders along with details of the products sold and the time period the order was placed. This is shown in Figure 16-5.

When you create the link to the relational worksheet, you will pass across the currently selected values for the worksheet dimensions to worksheet parameters that you have previously defined, so that only those transactions relating to the currently selected cell are displayed in the table. In the example OLAP worksheet in Figure 16-4, the current value for the product dimension is SUPER-WIDGET, while for the Time dimension it is FY2001.

SUPER-WIDGET is a product dimension member from the product-line level of the product dimension, and if passed as a parameter to our relational worksheet, it would usually map to a parameter based on the Line Name item in the GS Products folder. FY2001 is a time dimension member within the Year level and would map to a parameter based on the Year item in the FS Order Date folder.

But what would we do if our user had instead right-clicked on a crosstab cell that was for an individual product, rather than a product line? In this case, the dimension value for the product dimension that we passed across would be that of a product and would need to be mapped to a parameter based on the Product Name item in the GS Products folder, rather than Line Name. Effectively, where a dimension has multiple levels, the value passed across for the dimension selection could map to any one of multiple items in our business area.

To address this issue, you will have to create parameters for the relational worksheet for each possible item that could be the match for our dimension values, and then create a separate condition that checks the incoming parameter values against each of these worksheet parameters to find a match.

With the example OLAP worksheet, the cell that the user will link from will be dimensioned by product and time. Product, in the Global Widgets OLAP cube, has three levels (Product, Product Line, and All Products) while Time has four levels (Day, Month, Quarter, and Year).

Looking now at the Global Widgets business area, there are two folders, GS Products and FS Order Date, that contain items that the OLAP dimension will map to.

■   The product dimension–level Product will map to GS Products.Product Name.

■   The product dimension–level Product line will map to GS Products.Line Name.

■   The time dimension–level Year will map to FS Order Date.Year.

■   The time dimension–level Quarter will map to FS Order Date.Quarter.

■   The time dimension–level Month will map to FS Order Date.Year.

■   The time dimension–level Day will map to FS Order Date.Day.

However, there is one additional product dimension level, All Products, that does not have an item in the Global Widgets business area to map to. We will look at how this special value is handled later in the example.

The creation of a workbook link is a two-step process. Step 1 is to create the parameters, and a condition that uses these parameters, for your relational worksheet. Step 2 is to define a link for your OLAP worksheet. To illustrate the process, we will use the two example worksheets shown in Figures 16-4 and 16-5.

Creating Relational Workbook Parameters and Conditions

To create the parameters and condition for the relational worksheet:

1.   Open the relational worksheet using Discoverer Plus.

2.   Select Parameters from the Tools menu.

3.   Click New to create the first parameter.

4. Name the parameter **product_name**, select GS Products.Product Name, open the drop-down list, and ensure that the Create condition with operator check box is unchecked.

5. Repeat this step to create parameters based on the GS Products.Line Name, FS Orders. Year, FS Orders.Quarter, and FS Orders.Month items. Make sure that you have unchecked the Create condition with operator check box for each parameter.

6. Finally, create a day parameter, but select <NONE> rather than base it on the FS Order Date item, as this would cause Discoverer to error if we try to pass a non-date value to it, which we will do later on. The complete set of parameters should look like the following illustration:

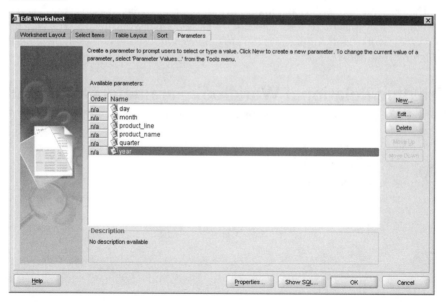

7. The next step is to create a condition that will take these parameters and use them to select the correct relational data.

8. Select Conditions from the Tools menu.

9. Create a New condition using the Advanced button.

10. You will now create a Boolean condition comprising multiple comparisons. For the first comparison, select GS Products.Product Name as the item, = as the condition, and the : product_name parameter you created earlier as the value.

11. Click the OR button to create a new condition line.

12. Do the same again, but this time comparing the GS Products.Line Name item with the : product_line parameter that you created earlier. Your condition should then look like this:

13. You now need to create a condition to handle the possibility of All Products being passed to the workbook as the product dimension member. To do this, add another condition, again joined with an OR operator, but this time specify the item as a calculation that returns the literal value "ALL PRODUCTS".

14. For the value that this item will be compared to, select New Parameter from the drop-down list. Give the parameter the name **all_products**, entering a prompt if desired, and click OK to close the New Parameter dialog box.

15. Now that you have created conditions to handle each of the possible product dimension values, you need to create another set of conditions, joined by an AND operator to the product dimension conditions. This new set will handle the time dimension values. To do this, click the OR operator that joins the product dimension conditions, and click the AND button.

16. Then, add conditions for the Year, Quarter, and Month parameters to this condition group, joining them using OR operators.

17. Finally, create a condition to compare the FS Order Data.Order Date item, which we will need to wrap with a TO_CHAR calculation.

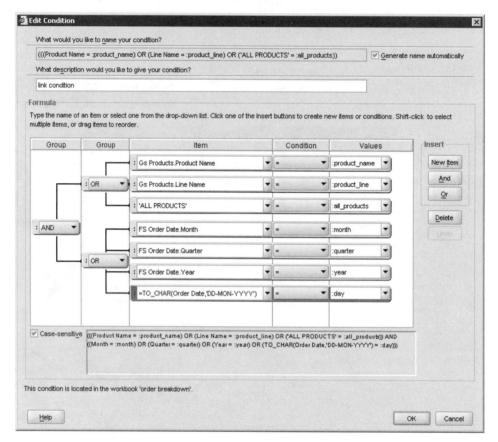

18. To do this, create a new calculation for the condition item and create it as TO_CHAR(FS Order Date.Order Date,'DD-MON-YYYY'), and then manually enter the **:day** parameter name into the values text box (just type this in; don't select from the list of available parameters).

When your condition has been created, you can run the worksheet with some sample values to check that it is all correct. Enter **'FY2004'** for every parameter that will be accepting a date dimension input, and **'SUPER-WIDGET'** for every parameter that will be accepting a product dimension input. The following illustration shows the Edit Parameters Values dialog box:

Creating the OLAP Worksheet Link

Now that you have chosen a relational worksheet to link to, and created parameters to accept the dimension values from the OLAP worksheet, you can open your OLAP worksheet and create the link.

1. Open the required worksheet, select a cell containing order quantity (this is all cells in the example worksheet), and then right-click the cell and select New Link.

2. Specify the name of the link. This name will be displayed when the user right-clicks the cell in the future.

3. Select which cells in the worksheet the link applies to. When you create a link, you can either link from the particular worksheet cell that you right-clicked, all of the cells for a particular measure, or all measure cells. To specify for what cells the link applies, select the required value from the Apply Link To drop-down list.

4. Using the Type drop-down list, select Plus Relational Worksheet.

5. Click the Worksheet button that has now appeared.

6. In the Specify Worksheet dialog, enter your connection information to connect to Discoverer Plus, together with the name of the worksheet.

7. To test that you have entered the connection details, workbook name, and worksheet name correctly, click the Test Link Connection button. This will attempt to start Discoverer Plus with your selected workbook and worksheet, and if the correction details are correct, you will see your worksheet.

NOTE
The workbook and worksheet names, together with the End User Layer name, are case-sensitive.

8. When you have successfully created your connection, click the Parameters button to map the OLAP worksheet parameters to the parameters of the relational worksheet that you have specified.

9. Enter the names of the relational worksheet parameters that you previously defined, and map them to the parameters of either the down or across dimensions in your crosstab.

10. After you click OK to accept these parameter settings, you will be able to see the link URL that Discoverer Plus for OLAP creates to enable the worksheet drill.

11. Click OK to save the link definition.

Managing the Discoverer Catalog

The Discoverer Catalog stores the definitions of workbooks, calculations, and saved selections that users create when working with Discoverer Plus for OLAP. These definitions are held as objects within the Discoverer Catalog, and security is provided at the object level so that administrators and users can specify which users and which roles have access to these objects. The Discoverer Catalog can be thought of as the equivalent of an End User Layer but for OLAP data, although there can be only one Discoverer Catalog per Oracle database, and it is held in the D4OSYS schema.

This section of the chapter will therefore look at the tasks you may want to carry out when installing and maintaining the Discoverer Catalog.

Installation and Removal of the Discoverer Catalog

If you have already been working with Discoverer Plus for OLAP, your administrator will have already installed the Discoverer Catalog for your database, as this is a prerequisite for Discoverer Plus for OLAP.

Discoverer Plus for OLAP requires a Discoverer Catalog to be installed in each Oracle database that it connects to. Therefore, if you wish to connect your copy of Discoverer Plus for OLAP to another database, you will need to install the Discoverer Catalog on this database.

You can install the Discoverer Catalog using either Oracle Enterprise Manager 10*g* Application Control or Oracle Enterprise Manager 10*g* Grid Control, or else you can install the Discoverer Catalog using a command-line Java utility.

To use Oracle Enterprise Manager, use the following workflow:

1. Connect to the Enterprise Manager web site for the Application Server 10*g* that contains your Discoverer installation.

2. Click the link for the Discoverer system component.

System Components

Enable/Disable Components | Create OC4J Instance

Start | Stop | Restart | Delete OC4J Instance

Select All | Select None

Select	Name	Status	Start Time	CPU Usage (%)	Memory Usage (MB)
☐	Discoverer	⇧	Dec 5, 2005 9:53:41 AM	0.00	9.84
☐	home	⇧	Dec 5, 2005 9:53:41 AM	0.23	25.38
☐	HTTP_Server	⇧	Dec 5, 2005 9:53:41 AM	0.03	58.02
☐	OC4J_BI_Forms	⇧	Dec 5, 2005 9:53:41 AM	0.06	82.38
☐	Web Cache	⇧	Dec 5, 2005 9:53:41 AM	0.00	60.90
☐	Management	⇧	Dec 5, 2005 9:55:54 AM	1.80	184.07

☑ **TIP** This table contains only the enabled components of the application server. Only components that have the checkbox enabled can be started or stopped.

3. Click the Administration tab.

4. Locate the section of the web page for the Discoverer Catalog.

5. Click the Install link to install the Discoverer Catalog.

Discoverer

Home | Performance | Administration

Page Refreshed **Dec 14, 2005 10:35:00 PM**

Discoverer Catalog

Install
Uninstall
Manage

Configuration

Public Connections
Private Connections
Services Logging

Discoverer Catalog Overview

The Discoverer Catalog is a repository for storing and retrieving definitions of workbooks, worksheets, and other objects that are created with Discoverer Plus OLAP. These objects are used by Discoverer Plus OLAP, Viewer, and Portlet Provider when accessing data from OLAP data sources. You can also use the Discoverer Catalog as the Catalog for a BI Beans application, leveraging both the content and user community.

6. Enter the connection details for the database that you wish to install the Discoverer Catalog in, and the username and password for the SYSTEM user (or another user with the DBA role).

Install Catalog

Cancel | Continue

When you install the Discoverer Catalog, a D4OSYS user is automatically created and populated with the schema objects that are needed by workbooks, worksheets, and other objects in Discoverer Plus OLAP. A database can contain only one Discoverer Catalog. Enter the database connection information.

∗ Indicates a required field

∗ Host	
Port	
SID	
∗ DBA Username	
∗ DBA Password	

7. Click Continue to confirm that you wish to install the Catalog. The Discoverer Catalog will now be installed.

Adding and Removing Users from the Discoverer Catalog

You can add users to the Discoverer Catalog either using Oracle Enterprise Manager or using the Java command-line utility. Users have to be added to the Discoverer Catalog before they can connect to Discoverer Plus for OLAP.

To add or remove a user from the Discoverer Catalog using Oracle Enterprise Manager 10g Application Control or Grid Control, use the following workflow:

1. Connect to the Discoverer Catalog home page within Oracle Enterprise Manager as before.

2. Click the Manage link.

3. Enter the connection details for the Discoverer Catalog.

4. Click Authorize Users and Roles.

5. You will then be presented with a list of available database users and roles, and a list of those users and roles that are currently authorized to access the Discoverer Catalog.

6. Select the users and roles that you want to access the Discoverer Catalog. If you add a role, all users with that role automatically have access to the Catalog. Any users or roles that you authorize for Discoverer Catalog use are assigned the D4OPUB role, which provides access to the objects stored in the catalog.

Managing Objects in the Catalog

Workbooks that you create are by default only available for you to use. If you wish to share a workbook you have created, you can do this using Manage Catalog from the Tools menu of the Discoverer Plus for OLAP applet.

To share a workbook with another user, use the following workflow:

1. Select Manage Catalog from the Tools menu.

2. Locate the workbook that you wish to share within the list of objects within your folder.

3. Select the workbook you want to share and click Copy.

4. Navigate to the Shared folder.

5. Click OK to move the workbook. The workbook is now sharable with other users.

6. Use the Location drop-down list to move to the shared folder. Locate the workbook that you just moved.

7. To share the workbook, right-click it and select Properties.

8. On the properties dialog, click the Privileges tab.

9. Click Add. Select those Discoverer Catalog users and roles that you would like to grant access, and select whether they have read, write, or full control privileges on the object.

10. Click OK to save these changes. Note that you can use this process to grant access to any Discoverer Catalog object that you own.

Exporting the Discoverer Catalog

If you have created Discoverer Plus for OLAP workbooks, worksheets, or calculations on one database and then wish to transfer these objects to another database, you can export the Discoverer Catalog from one database and then import it into another. You can export the Discoverer Catalog either using Oracle Enterprise Manager, or using the Java command-line utility.

To export the Discoverer Catalog from a database using Oracle Enterprise Manager 10g Application Control or Grid Control, use the following workflow:

1. Connect to the Discoverer Catalog home page within Oracle Enterprise Manager as before.

2. Click the Manage link.

3. Enter the connection details for the Discoverer Catalog on the database that you wish to export from.

4. Click the Export Catalog link.

5. Enterprise Manager will now present an XML file for download. This file contains an XML export of the Discoverer Catalog. Click Save to save this file to the file system.

To import a Discoverer Catalog, use the following workflow:

1. Connect to the Discoverer Catalog home page within Oracle Enterprise Manager as before.

2. Click the Manage link.

3. Enter the connection details for the Discoverer Catalog on the database that you wish to import to.

4. Click the Import Catalog link.

5. Use the Browse button to locate the Discoverer Catalog XML file that you previously exported.

6. Click the Import button to import the Catalog.

Importing BI Beans Crosstabs and Graphs

If you have created a crosstab or graph using an Oracle Business Intelligence Beans application, you saved that crosstab or graph to a BI Beans Catalog, and this BI Beans Catalog is also being used as the Discoverer Catalog, then you can import these objects into a Discoverer worksheet. Any imported BI Beans crosstab or graph will preserve any links to calculations or saved selections.

To import a BI Beans crosstab or graph into a worksheet, use the following workflow:

1. Select Import from the File menu.

2. In the Import dialog, navigate to the folder that contains the object.

3. Select the crosstab or graph that you wish to import.

4. Click OK to import the object.

Summary

In this chapter we have introduced you to the power of Discoverer OLAP. You have seen how Discoverer OLAP can become a useful reporting tool. We have introduced you to dimensions and the Discoverer Catalog. You have been taught how to install and configure OLAP and how to create workbooks using the Workbook Wizard.

You have also learned how to manipulate the data by moving the columns, using Page Items, and adding formatting. You have seen how Discoverer OLAP workbooks can be hyperlinked to relational workbooks created in Discoverer Plus. We have taught you how to create parameters for greater end-user control and for use in hyperlinks.

In this chapter we also taught you about the Discoverer Catalog and how to use the Oracle Enterprise Manager to take control of your workbooks.

PART

IV

Using the Discoverer
Administration Edition

CHAPTER
17

Getting Started in the
Administration Edition

elcome to the first of the chapters dedicated to the Discoverer Administrator tool. If you have never used the Discoverer Administrator tool before, you are going to be surprised at how easy it is. In this chapter we will teach you about the main features of the tool. We will then devote the rest of the chapter to showing you how to install the End User Layer and then build the business area that has been used throughout the end-user sections of this book. We will show you how to pull in objects from the database and then show you how to check the items that are used within the folders, making use of item separators to break up the items into logical groups or sets. In this chapter you will also learn how to hook Discoverer up to an E-Business Suite database using Apps mode.

NOTE
You need the Administrator edition only when working with relational data. If you are working with OLAP data, you should take a look at Chapter 16.

Key Definitions

Before we get into using the tool, we will give you a brief description of some of the key definitions as used in Discoverer administration. You should read this section in conjunction with Chapter 3, where we explained the key definitions of the following:

- Workbooks and worksheets

- Queries

- Reports

- Libraries

End User Layer

Commonly referred to as the EUL, the End User Layer is a metadata repository that stores all of the object definitions used by Discoverer. Using the EUL, you hide the complexity of the underlying system from the users, allowing them to interact with the database using familiar business language and terms. A well-designed End User Layer means that users do not need to know the underlying structure of the database.

The End User Layer also protects and preserves the integrity of the database. This integrity is preserved because using Discoverer, neither the Discoverer manager nor any Discoverer end user can change the underlying database. The only thing the Discoverer manager can change is the End User Layer itself, access to the underlying database being read only.

But what does the End User Layer look like? The End User Layer is a series of approximately 50 tables and views that all begin with the characters EUL5. For example, the table that stores the users is called EUL5_EUL_USERS, while the table that stores the workbooks is called EUL5_WORKBOOKS.

The main way to maintain the End User Layer is to use the Discoverer Administrator tool when logged in as an administrator. You can also use the EUL Command Line Utility for Java to manage the Discoverer EUL. While not as powerful as the Discoverer Administrator tool, this Utility will allow you to perform many of the standard maintenance tasks such as authorizing users to access the EUL, exporting/importing EUL objects, and others. We do not cover the Command Line Utility in this book. If you want to learn more about this utility, we recommend you take a look at the *Oracle Business Intelligence Discoverer EUL Command Line for Java* user guide, which you can find on OTN.

As the administrator, you are responsible for maintaining the EUL and the conceptual view of the database. This conceptual view helps the end user navigate through the data more easily when performing queries. The EUL contains enhanced definitions of folders and their items, as well as the relationships between the folders, and other constructs that help users explore their data.

Business Areas

A *business area* is a set of common, related information with a single business purpose in mind. One business area, for example, might be created for Accounting, while another might be created for Purchasing, with yet another created for Human Resources. End-user access is maintained by the Discoverer administrator. Business areas are organized into

- **Folders** These are a collection of related items. Each folder can be thought of as being like a table in a database. There are three types of folders:

    - **Simple** A simple folder maps directly to a database object such as a table or a view.

    - **Custom** A custom folder is a single SQL statement that you type directly into Discoverer.

    - **Complex** A complex folder is used to group items together from other folders.

- **Joins** These map the links between folders. Each join can be thought of as being like a join between tables in a database. Joins can either be predefined or user-defined. If the folders are based on database objects and if foreign-key / primary-key constraints exist between the objects, you can import the predefined joins for use within Discoverer. If no predefined constraints exist, you can manually create them. Joins can be either one-to-many or one-to-one. Discoverer also supports the concept of outer joins, although performance can deteriorate if they are used.

- **Items** These are components of a folder or worksheet. Each item can be thought of as being like a column in a database table. Folder items can either be predefined or user-defined. Predefined folder items are loaded from the database as part of the folder definition. User-defined folder items are manually created by the Discoverer administrator, as either a calculation or a condition. To the report writer, both of these are regarded as predefined and therefore reusable. Predefined worksheet items are loaded from the EUL. A user-defined worksheet item is manually created by the report writer, and can either be a calculation, condition, or parameter. Items can be made to appear on various axes.

NOTE
Discoverer as yet has no concept of a predefined parameter, and these must be created by the report writer directly within the workbook. As such, these parameters are not reusable and must be defined on a workbook-by-workbook basis. In a future release of Discoverer, Oracle plans to add administrator-defined parameters.

Axes

You can think of an *axis* as being a placeholder into which an end user can position data within a worksheet. As part of the setup and maintenance of business areas, the Discoverer administrator gets to choose the default location for every item. During the creation of a report, the report writer chooses the axes where the data should be displayed, overriding the default assigned by the Discoverer administrator if need be. During the execution of a report, a report viewer can further customize the output to see the data displayed on yet a different axis. Every item must have a default axis, and every item used within a worksheet must be displayed on an axis. Discoverer uses four axes:

- **Page axis** This axis is used to break up a report into multiple pages. If you place, for example, a customer name in the page, Discoverer will display that customer's details only on the current page of the report. Discoverer will dynamically create a list of values (LOV) for every item that is placed on the page axis.

- **Top axis** This axis can be thought of as the column headings in a report. Moving an item to the top axis causes Discoverer to place the item's name in the column heading with each data value displayed in a different row.

- **Side axis** In a Table worksheet, this is where Discoverer places the row numbers. In a crosstab this is where the row headings are displayed. A user can drag an item from the top or page axis and place it on the side axis to create a crosstab or a pivot table. Such a worksheet must have at least one item on the side axis; otherwise, it cannot be constructed. Moving an item to the side axis causes Discoverer to place the item's name in the row heading with each data value displayed in a different column.

NOTE
In reality, a top axis and a side axis don't really make a lot of sense in the case of a table, but we hope you understand what we are getting at.

- **Data points** This axis is used to hold items that can be used for aggregation, such as totals and averages. A crosstab worksheet must have at least one data point; otherwise, it cannot be constructed.

Figure 17-1 shows the relationship between the various axes. It also shows the location of the title and text areas.

FIGURE 17-1 *Axes used in Discoverer*

Item Classes

These are lists of values—drop-down lists that aid users when they are selecting items for a query. Lists of values are predefined and are created by the Discoverer manager. Not all items get a list of values to begin with, and if users see an item that does not have a list of values that they believe should have one, the user should contact the Discoverer administrator. We will discuss these in depth in Chapter 18.

Hierarchies

A hierarchy, in Discoverer terms, is a default drill path between related items in a folder. Hierarchies can be used in Discoverer even when there is no relationship between the items in the database. Users can then roll up to see aggregated data or drill down to see detail data. Hierarchies are created by the Discoverer administrator and as such are predefined. Using a hierarchy, for example, a user could roll up from all the months in a year to just the year itself, or drill down from one particular month to see all of the daily transactions for that month. In Discoverer, there are two types of hierarchy:

■ **Item hierarchies**   These map the relationship between items such as City, State, and Country, thus allowing end users to drill between those items.

■ **Date hierarchies**   These map the relationship between key time elements of a date such as Day, Month, Quarter, and Year. Date hierarchies work best when the fiscal year that you are using corresponds to the calendar year, such that Q1 runs from January to March, Q2 runs from April to June, and so on. While you can use a modified date hierarchy to create fiscal time hierarchies, we like to use item hierarchies to create hierarchies based on fiscal years that do not correspond to calendar years, such as when using a 4-4-5 notation, where quarters are determined by the number of weeks in the period.

The use of hierarchies is explained in detail in Chapter 18.

Summaries

These are preaggregated tables of results against which Discoverer can query. In database terms these are Materialized Views (MV) and, if they exist, the Oracle database optimizer will rewrite a user's query to go after an MV if it can be determined that it will satisfy the requirements. Discoverer can work with a preexisting MV, or it can even build it for itself, provided that the Discoverer administrator has been granted the required database privileges by the DBA. Within the Discoverer Administrator tool there is a Summary Wizard that allows the Discoverer administrator to analyze user queries to determine whether a summary table, MV, will help. Using this wizard, Discoverer can even create the materialized view and set up the automated refreshes for it. Discoverer has the ability to preaggregate data that is being used by user queries into prebuilt tables. Essentially, you are creating materialized views. You use these summary folders to improve query response time for your end users. The response time is improved because the query will use preaggregated and prejoined data rather than accessing the underlying database tables at run time. Summary management is discussed in detail in Chapter 22.

Properties

Most of the components of the End User Layer have properties. These are placeholders for you to define additional characteristics about the component that you are working with. Properties exist for business areas, folders, and items. We will discuss properties in detail in Chapter 18, with further comments in Chapter 19.

Sticky Features

The Discoverer Administrator tool has a memory. From time to time, Discoverer will make a note in the system Registry of "last used" options. The next time you are given a choice for one of these options, Discoverer will remember what you last did and default to that setting. We call this Discoverer's Sticky Feature.

The Steps to a Successful Discoverer Implementation

There are six steps that you must follow if you are to implement Discoverer successfully:

1. Understand and anticipate user requirements.
2. Create the End User Layer.
3. Create a business area.
4. Refine the business area.
5. Grant access to the business area.
6. Deploy.

Understand and Anticipate User Requirements

The Discoverer administrator should understand and anticipate user requirements, have knowledge of the application database, and be able to set up the relational structure in the EUL to best display the application data.

Of these tasks, perhaps the most difficult is to understand and anticipate user requirements. You need to be able to work with your users to analyze their data requests. At the very least, you will probably need to conduct interviews with your users to determine what it is that they are asking for. You need to be able to understand your business using the terminology of the end users, essentially being able to use user-speak when talking with your users and geek-speak when talking with others in your IT department.

Be wary, though, because users will usually demand everything and insist that it is delivered at breakneck speed. You will need to be a good mediator, setting reasonable expectations. Perhaps the best approach is to deliver the data in bite-sized chunks as opposed to trying to deliver everything all at the same time.

During the discussion phase you should encourage your users to show you how they use the information that they currently have and what they have to do to make good reports out of it. Perhaps they cannot get any reports at the moment, which is why they approached you in the first place!

Create the End User Layer

You must have an End User Layer before you can create a business area. We will walk you through the steps in creating your first End User Layer later in this chapter.

Create a Business Area

You must create at least one business area. In a real-world implementation, you will consider using several business areas, each with its own particular business purpose. You will point these business areas at particular tables and views of the data within the database, thus ensuring that each business area covers one succinct business purpose. While you can create business areas that cover multiple business purposes, this is not good practice, because it makes life difficult when you come to manage the user access to those areas.

Later in this chapter, we will walk you through the steps in creating your first business area, the business area that is used in the end-user sections of this book.

Refine the Business Area

After you have created a business area, the business of maintaining that business area begins. This is where you refine the business area to add new folders, new calculated items, conditions, and lists of values. This is covered in Chapters 18 and 19, when we discuss editing the business area and how to interact with the users.

Granting Access to the Business Areas

As you go about determining the user requirements. you should also have had a pretty good idea of what type of access the users would need. The lowest level of control that you have within Discoverer relates to a business area. User access is therefore managed at the business area level. You cannot restrict access to a particular folder. This is one of the reasons why we recommend restricting business areas to one particular business purpose. The granting of access to a business area is discussed in Chapter 19.

Deploy

If your organization is like most organizations, you will be considering a 70:30 split between report viewers and report writers. The report writers will need to be able to create workbooks and therefore will need to have access to Discoverer Plus, while your report viewers will want to run only workbooks that have been created for them by someone else. These users need to have access to Discoverer Viewer.

In Chapter 19 we will show how you to interact with the users and how to grant access to the business area.

Source to Destination

Before we begin, we need to think a little about what we are going to do. We are going to take a set of relational data definitions from a source database and load these into our End User Layer as a business area. That business area will then be worked on to produce the final result that we will present to our users. The final result, our destination schema, will be a new set of data definitions that our users can understand.

Source Database

Our source database, as shown in Figure 17-2, has twelve tables. As you can see in the figure, our twelve database tables are all based around a single Sales table. From the Sales table there are joins to the Date, Channel, Customer, and Product folders.

Source Hierarchies

If you take a close look at the database schema in Figure 17-2, you may be able to spot some of the hierarchies that we will eventually be using in our business area. At first glance you should be able to spot three: Date, Customer, and Product.

FIGURE 17-2 *Source database*

The Date table joins to a hierarchy of interrelated tables containing Month, Quarter, and Year data. The Customer table joins to a hierarchy of tables containing City, District, and Region data. The Product table joins to a Product Line table, thus in effect producing a small product hierarchy. Because the Channel table links to no other tables, it is not part of any hierarchy and will thus end up becoming a single folder inside our business area.

Destination Schema

In Figure 17-3 we show you the design for our final business area. The hierarchy based around the Customer table has become a single complex folder called Geography. The hierarchy based around the Product table has become a single complex folder called Products. The hierarchy that is based around the Date table has become four complex folders, one each for our Cancel Date, Order Date, Request Date, and Ship Date. Do not worry about how you create these complex folders and hierarchies at this stage. This will all be explained in Chapter 18.

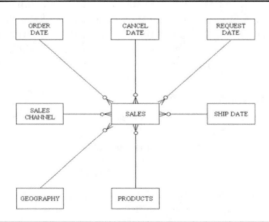

FIGURE 17-3 *Destination schema*

As mentioned earlier, because the Channel table is not part of any hierarchy, it will become its own folder in the final business area. Oh yes, we must not forget the Sales table, which is at the heart of the source database. This will become the key folder in our new business area, in which our users will find the metrics.

Take a close look at the destination schema in Figure 17-3. If you are familiar with data warehousing, you should recognize this as being a star schema. Wherever possible, you should always try to design relational business areas using star schemas. These types of schema make for excellent performance within Discoverer and, as an added bonus, are the easiest for end users to understand. They are what we like to call less join intensive. By this we mean that users do not have to open numerous tables in order to find the joins that they need.

Take a look at Figure 17-2 again. Let's say you build the End User Layer exactly as per this diagram, with twelve folders joined using the primary and foreign key constraints defined within the database. If a user wants to build a worksheet that uses something from the Sales folder along with Region and Year, can you see that there are numerous ways to do this? You could start in the Sales folder, but then where would you go next? The only folders available to you at this time are Channel, Customer, Products, and Day. You cannot see the Region or the Year folder because you need to make joins between several other folders to get where you want to be. This type of worksheet is join intensive and something that you need to avoid.

Unfortunately, many companies do exactly this, and as consultants we spend a great deal of time explaining why this is not a good idea. As we have stated before, what starts right, stays right. A good conceptual model minimizes the number of joins a user needs to make to find the data that he or she needs. Take another look at Figure 17-3. Can you see that if the user starts by pulling something, anything, from the Sales folder, that all of the other folders are instantly available? This is a good design and one that you should strive to follow. We have also mentioned that a good design hides the complexity of the database from the end user. This is what we mean. Behind the scenes the user does not need to know that we have overlaid the database with six complex folders to create the business area.

All you need to do is tell your users that they should select something from the fact or metric folder first and then select one or more items from the dimension folders. You will find that your users have a greater chance of understanding your model and thus making use of the business area that you have built for them.

For example: Let's say that a user wants to build a query that selects the total quantity shipped by channel by product, I can easily explain that the two BY clauses, by channel and by product, are both dimensions. If I now teach the user that all of the metrics, such as total quantity shipped, can be found in the Sales folder and that they should begin their selections in there, the user will find this easy. Imagine how much easier it becomes when the Sales folder is right at the top of the list of folders. If we place all of the other dimension folders beneath the main metric folder, it now becomes very easy for the user to a) understand the model, and b) make the necessary selections for the query.

Creating the End User Layer

Before you can begin creating business areas, you need to have an End User Layer. So let's start at the very beginning and assume that you do not have an End User Layer. So where do you begin? Well, first of all you need to create a new database user for the End User Layer.

New User Privileges

Whether you have the ability to do this yourself or you need to ask your DBA to do it for you, the standard database privileges that you will need are as follows:

CONNECT	CREATE TABLE
RESOURCE	CREATE VIEW
ALTER ANY MATERIALIZED VIEW (9i and 10g databases)	DROP ANY MATERIALIZED VIEW (9i and 10g databases)
ALTER ANY SNAPSHOT (8i database)	DROP ANY SNAPSHOT (8i database)
ANALYZE ANY	EXECUTE ANY PROCEDURE
CREATE ANY MATERIALIZED VIEW (9i and 10g databases)	GLOBAL QUERY REWRITE
CREATE ANY SNAPSHOT (8i database)	SELECT ANY TABLE (optional, see the following note)
CREATE PROCEDURE	UNLIMITED TABLESPACE
CREATE ROLE	EXECUTE ON SYS.DBMS_JOB
CREATE SEQUENCE	SELECT ON SYS.V_$PARAMETER
CREATE SESSION	

NOTE
Your DBA may consider the SELECT ANY TABLE privilege to be too powerful and may not want to let you have it. If this is the case, then you will need to assign SELECT rights over the individual objects that you need.

The ALTER, CREATE, and DROP ANY MATERIALIZED VIEW, or SNAPSHOT, privileges are required if you want to use Discoverer's Summary Management capabilities. Having the less powerful ALTER, CREATE, or DROP MATERIALIZED VIEW, or SNAPSHOT, without the word ANY, is not sufficient. This is because Discoverer will create the materialized view directly in the database schema that owns the objects upon which the materialized view is based. When this has been done, the database optimizer will be able to rewrite queries correctly. This is another reason why the EUL owner needs to have the unqualified UNLIMITED TABLESPACE privilege as opposed to the lesser privilege that would grant unlimited space against a named tablespace.

Another privilege that you may have access to is CREATE USER. If you do have this privilege, the Discoverer Administrator tool will make use of it, as you will see later in this chapter. Some organizations also grant the DBA privilege to the EUL owner. This is not really necessary and can be very dangerous in the wrong hands. However, if your Discoverer administrator is also your DBA, you won't have to worry.

For more information relating to privileges, particularly for the privileges needed for scheduling, please see Chapter 19 and Appendix A.

For demonstrating the creation of an End User Layer in this book, we are using a user called BOOK, which was created using the standard privileges mentioned earlier.

Software Installation

Having created your new user account, you need to install the Discoverer Administrator software on your PC into a new Oracle home. The default home that the software wants to use is called

BIToolsHome_1. We recommend you leave this as the default if you can. As the installation is easy, we will not cover it in any detail here. Please see Appendix A for an explanation about how to install both the Administrator and Desktop tools at the same time.

Create the EUL

Having installed the Discoverer Administrator software, you will create your first EUL. Assuming you installed it into the default Oracle home, from the Windows Start button, select Start | Programs | Oracle Business Intelligence Tools - BIToolsHome_1 | Oracle Discoverer Administrator. This launches the login screen shown here:

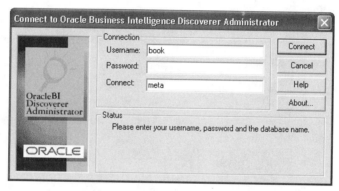

You should key in your username, password, and database. In our case we will connect using the BOOK user that we created earlier.

Assuming you enter a valid username, password, and database, Discoverer checks whether any End User Layer exists for the user that you entered. If the EUL does exist, Discoverer opens it. However, in our case the EUL does not exist and so we were given the message shown here:

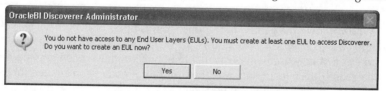

As you can see, the only options you have are to click Yes to create the EUL, or No to not create the EUL. When we clicked Yes, Discoverer opened the EUL Manager dialog box.

Discoverer prompts "What do you want to do?" Once again, you really have only one option. You should click the Create an EUL button; Discoverer will then take you into Step 1 of the Create EUL Wizard.

Create EUL Wizard

The Create EUL Wizard itself has three steps:

1. Select the owner and type of EUL (if you are installing a standard EUL, this is the only wizard screen that you will see).

2. Select the schema containing the FND tables (Apps mode only).

3. Select the tablespaces to be used in the installation (only available if creating a new user).

Create EUL Wizard: Step 1   The first step, to select the owner and type of EUL, illustrated here, has the following areas:

- **Who will own the EUL?**   In response to this question, you have two choices. The first choice is to select an existing user, while the second is to create a new user. The option to create a new user will be available only if you have been granted the CREATE USER database privilege. In our case, the user has already been created for us, and so we clicked the radio button called Select an existing user. If you do have the CREATE USER privilege, you will be required to enter a name and password for the new user. You will be required to provide the default tablespaces for the user later.

NOTE
You can have only one Discoverer EUL in a user's schema. This is because all of the EUL tables and views, from version 9.0.2 onward, begin with the characters EUL5.

- **Grant access to PUBLIC**   This box is checked by default. In most cases you will leave this box checked, as this will allow any user of the system to have access to the EUL that you have created. Should you wish to create a private EUL, you should uncheck this box.

- **New EUL is for use by Oracle Applications users ONLY**   Check this box only if you are creating an Apps-mode EUL. In our case we are not creating an Apps-mode EUL, so will leave this box unchecked.

NOTE
If you check this box, the Next button on the bottom of the screen will become active.

- **Select**   Click this button to display a list of users against whom you can create the EUL. If you pick a user other than the user who you logged in as, or you are creating a new user, you will be required to supply that user's password. For this example we chose the existing BOOK user.

- **Finish**   If you are creating a standard EUL and you are creating it in an existing user's schema, having made all of your selections on screen 1 of the wizard, your only option will be to click Finish.

- **Next**   If you are creating an Apps-mode EUL or are creating a new user for the EUL, your only option will be to click Next.

Create EUL Wizard: Step 2   The screen that displays at this point varies, depending upon whether you are creating an Apps-mode EUL and whether you are creating a new user. If you are not creating an Apps-mode EUL but are creating a new user, in this step of the wizard, as you can see in the illustration that follows, you will be required to tell Discoverer which default and temporary tablespaces should be used for the new standard EUL owner. To tell Discoverer which tablespace to use, you need to click it to highlight it. Having specified which tablespaces Discoverer should use, your only option is to click Finish.

NOTE
Even if there is only one temporary tablespace available, the Finish button will not activate until you highlight both the default and temporary tablespaces. If you are new to Discoverer and the Finish button is grayed out, you now know why.

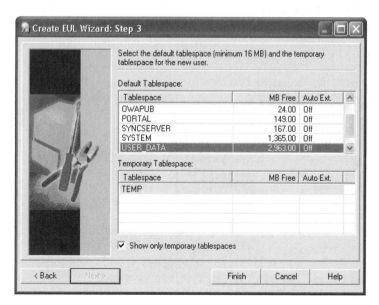

If you are creating an Apps-mode EUL, in this step of the wizard, as shown in the following illustration, you will be required to tell Discoverer the username and password of the database schema that contains the Apps foundation tables. In most cases, this will be the APPS user. Having provided this information, your only option is to click Next.

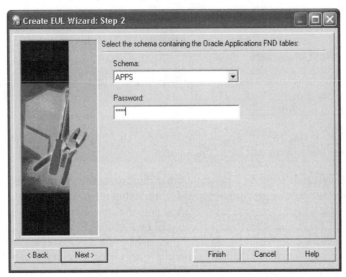

Create EUL Wizard: Step 3   You will see a third step to the Create EUL Wizard only if you are creating an Apps-mode EUL and a new user at the same time. In this step you will be required to tell Discoverer which default and temporary tablespaces should be used for the new Apps mode owner. Even if there is only one temporary tablespace available, the Finish button will not activate until you highlight both the default and temporary tablespaces.

Creating the EUL for Real

Once you have clicked Finish in the Create EUL Wizard, Discoverer will now create the End User Layer. As the install progresses, you will see a series of three identically sized message screens. The install goes through three stages:

- Creating tables and views

- Populating tables with default data

- Granting access on EUL tables

NOTE
As a bit of fun, watch the jigsaw gradually fill in as the status moves toward 100 percent.

When the installation has completed, you will be given the message saying that the EUL has been successfully created.

As you can see here, your only option is to click OK. At that point, Discoverer might present you with the following screen.

This screen will be prompted only if Discoverer detects that a database user called VIDEO5 exists in the database or that the user does not exist but you have the CREATE USER privilege. This is the schema used by Oracle's Video Store tutorial. If you wish to have this tutorial installed, click Yes. If you have the CREATE USER privilege and the VIDEO5 user does not exist, during the install of Oracle's sample data, Discoverer will create the user and give it the default password VIDEO5. We don't need this for our EUL, so we clicked No.

Finally, to complete the installation of the End User Layer, close the EUL Manager dialog box by clicking Close.

If you installed the EUL into a new user account, you will now be prompted to connect as that user. When prompted "Do you want to connect as the owner of the EUL which you just created?" click Yes.

If you are creating an Apps-mode EUL, you have not yet finished and need to follow the steps in the next section. However, if you are creating a standard EUL, well done, you are finished. Please move on to the section entitled "Creating Your First Business Area."

Completing the Apps-Mode EUL

The remainder of this section is only required if you are creating an Apps-mode EUL.

After the EUL has been created, Discoverer will display the box shown in Figure 17-4 later. As you have not yet completed setting up Discoverer to operate in Apps mode, you should click Cancel and then follow the instructions.

To complete setting up an Apps-mode EUL, use the following workflow:

1. From the toolbar, select Tools | Options, and then, as shown in the following illustration, click the Connection tab.

2. As you can see, the Connection tab has three radio buttons and an area called
   Applications EUL Settings. The three radio buttons are

   ■ **Connect to standard EULs** Check this if your organization will only ever be using
   Discoverer in standard mode.

   ■ **Connect to applications EULs** Check this if your organization will only ever be
   using Discoverer in Apps mode.

   ■ **Connect to both standard and applications EULs** Check this if your organization
   will be using Discoverer in both Apps and standard modes. If you are wondering
   how this can be, let us explain. Some organizations use Discoverer in Apps mode
   against their Oracle Apps database but use it in standard mode against another
   database, such as a data warehouse. Because there is only one Administrator tool,
   the same tool needs to be able to administer Discoverer in both modes, hence the
   third option on the screen.

3. Having enabled Discoverer in Apps mode and specified whether you will only be
   administering Apps EULs or a combination of standard and Apps EULs, you are now
   required to provide the information in the Applications EUL Settings area:.

   ■ **Gateway User ID (GWYUID) / password** Enter applysyspub/pub as one string.

   ■ **Foundation Name (FNDNAM)** Enter apps or whichever user your organization is
   using for the ownership of the Apps foundation tables.

4. When you have completed this screen, click OK.

5. From the menu bar, select File | Connect. The Discoverer Administrator login screen
   will be displayed, and you should reconnect as the owner of the EUL. There is now an
   additional check box called Oracle Applications User. Do not check this box at this time.

6. When prompted with the standard load screen shown in Figure 17-4, click Cancel.

7. From the menu bar, select Tools | Privileges and grant the SYSADMIN user the following privileges by checking the boxes alongside each privilege:

   ■ Administration Privilege, plus all subprivileges

   ■ Desktop and Plus Privileges, plus all subprivileges

8. When you have completed assigning privileges to the SYSADMIN user, click OK.

9. From the menu bar, select File | Connect. The Discoverer Administrator login screen will be displayed once more, but this time you should reconnect as the SYSADMIN user. You will, of course, need to know the SYSADMIN password, and you must make sure that you check the box called Oracle Applications User.

10. Discoverer will now authenticate the SYSADMIN user against the Oracle Applications E-Business Suite. If the credentials are correct, you will be presented with the following Choose a Responsibility screen.

11. Select the System Administrator responsibility and click OK.

12. From here on, you should log in to the Administrator tool only as the Apps SYSADMIN user.

NOTE
Do not attempt to administer an Apps-mode EUL as the EUL owner. This account is used to store the EUL tables and views, but it is not an Apps account. You will run into serious trouble if you start administering the EUL with it, so please do not try.

Creating Your First Business Area

Once you have created your empty End User Layer, Discoverer displays the first screen of the Load Wizard. You will use this wizard to create business areas. The Load Wizard has the following five steps:

1. Create or open a business area.
2. Select the schema.
3. Select the objects to use.
4. Define the import options.
5. Name the business area and provide final preferences.

Load Wizard Step 1: Create or Open a Business Area

On the first screen of the Load Wizard, seen in Figures 17-4 and 17-5, you are asked whether you want to create a new business area or open an existing business area.

NOTE
*Having created your EUL, from now on, each time you log in
to Discoverer Administrator, this is the screen that you will see.*

There are two buttons on Screen 1 of the Load Wizard. As you can see in Figures 17-4 and 17-5, the screen changes, depending upon which button you click. As we do not have any existing business areas, we will show you how to create one.

Creating a New Business Area

Having decided that you want to create a new business area, take a look at Figure 17-4. On that screen you will see that there are two ways to create a business area:

- **On-line dictionary**   Use this to select objects from the database data dictionary. This is the most common way of bringing objects into a business area.

- **Gateway**   Use this to select objects from a gateway. A gateway is a link between another application and Discoverer. For example, if you are using Warehouse Builder, you might create a gateway between the Warehouse metadata repository and Discoverer.

As we do not have a gateway installed, we clicked the On-line dictionary radio button and then clicked Next. Discoverer will now open the second screen of the Load Wizard.

FIGURE 17-4   *Load Wizard Part 1: Create a new business area*

FIGURE 17-5 *Load Wizard Part 1: Open an existing business area*

Load Wizard Step 2: Select the Schema

In this the second step of the Load Wizard you need to pick the user that owns the database objects that you want to use within the business area. If there is a database link in use, you should select it first. In most cases, there will not be a database link and you will be selecting objects directly from the database in which the End User Layer has been created.

In our case the user that we will be using is called GSW, short for Global Sales Widgets. At the bottom of the screen you will notice a box called "Load user objects that match." If you are aware of the name of the table or view that you want to load or know that there is a prefix that you can use, enter the name of the object or the prefix into this box immediately prior to the wildcard character. In our case, because all of the tables that we want to load begin with the letters GS, we entered these characters into the match box.

Having made your selections for Step 2, click Next. Discoverer will now open the third screen of the Load Wizard.

Load Wizard Step 3: Select the Objects to Use

As you can see in the next illustration, the third screen of the Load Wizard has an Available items box and a Selected items box. In the Available items box, Discoverer presents you with a list of the objects that are available for selection into your End User Layer. In the Selected items box, Discoverer lists the objects that you have already selected for inclusion in your End User Layer.

NOTE
Discoverer does not remember what items you have previously selected for your End User Layer. So if your EUL already contains a table called Sales and you reopen the wizard, the wizard will not place Sales in the Selected items list. You have to remember that you have already done this.

In the third screen of the Load Wizard, Discoverer displays a list of the objects owned by the user that you selected in Step 1, constrained by the match criteria that you entered in Step 2. As you can see in the preceding illustration, the GSW user owns a number of objects that all begin with the characters GS.

NOTE
Discoverer initially displays an empty screen with just the user name(s) that you selected. If you click the plus character alongside the user name, Discoverer will now display the objects owned by that user.

If you look back at Figure 17-2, you can see that we want all of the objects that begin with GS. Therefore, drag and drop or push each object from the Available items list to the Selected items list, and then click Next. Discoverer will now open the fourth screen of the Load Wizard.

Load Wizard Step 4: Define the Import Options

The fourth screen of the Load Wizard has the following areas:

- **Do you want to create joins?**   Check the box called Yes if you want Discoverer to automatically create joins for you. You have the option to create joins from Primary/Foreign key constraints, or Matching by column names. If we are aware that Primary/Foreign key constraints exist in the database, we will generally allow Discoverer to go ahead and create the joins for us. However, be wary of allowing Discoverer to create joins based on matching column names, because in that case you are relying on whoever created the database to have designed it with this in mind.

NOTE
When using Discoverer against Oracle Apps, take NOTE that Oracle does not generally use Primary/Foreign key constraints, so all that you will have to go on is the column names. Make sure the joins really do exist before allowing Discoverer to create them.

- **Summaries based on folders that are created**   Check this box if you want Discoverer to create summaries, materialized views, based on the folders that are being created. You will rarely use this feature. We recommend that you not check this box at this time. You can always create summaries later, and unless you really know what you are doing, you could easily overpower your system with materialized views.

- **Date Hierarchies**   Check this box if you want Discoverer to create date hierarchies for every date that is being imported into the business area. Having checked the box, you next need to tell Discoverer which hierarchy type it should use to create the new hierarchies. Again, we do not recommend that you check this box at this time. As not all dates will warrant a hierarchy, it is better to create hierarchies later, when you have had a chance to look at the data.

■ **Default aggregate on data points** Check this box if you want Discoverer to assign a default aggregate to each of the data points that are being imported into the End User Layer. We like this feature and recommend that you keep this box checked. Having checked the box, you now need to tell Discoverer what default aggregate it should use. The default, SUM, is the one that you will most often use.

■ **List of values for items of type** Check this box if you want Discoverer to automatically create lists of values for the imported objects. If you check the box, you also need to tell Discoverer which objects should have lists of values associated with them. You can associate lists of values with the following types:

   ■ Character

   ■ Integer

   ■ Decimal

   ■ Date

   ■ All keys

NOTE
We recommend not letting Discoverer create its own item classes (lists of values) because you a) cannot control the name of the item class and b) cannot prevent Discoverer from creating duplicate item classes should the same item exist in multiple folders.

Having made your choices for Step 4, click Next. Discoverer will now open the fifth and final screen of the Load Wizard.

Load Wizard Step 5: Name the Business Area and Provide Final Preferences

The fifth screen of the Load Wizard, shown next, is a screen for inputting the name of the business area plus setting a number of preferences.

It has the following areas:

- **What do you want to name this business area**? Give the business area a meaningful name that fits in with your corporate naming standards. In our case we will call it GSW, which is short for Global Software Widgets.

- **What description do you want to give this business area**? Provide a meaningful description of the business area to help your users understand what it is used for. In our case we entered "This is the tutorial business area associated with the Discoverer 10*g* Handbook."

- **Replace all underscores with spaces** This setting is down to user preference and will be part of your corporate standards. In our case, we always replace underscores with spaces, such that the name order_qty will become order qty.

- **Remove all column prefixes** This setting is down to user preference, but if it is checked, Discoverer will remove any prefixes that it finds in the column names.

- **Capitalize** This setting is also down to user preference and will be part of your corporate standards. In our case, we always capitalize the first letter of every word, but you can use the associated drop-down list to capitalize only the initial letter if you so wish.

- **Sort folders** This preference allows you to alphabetically sort all of the folders. We do not recommend doing this, as you will be placing folders exactly where you want them in a later step.

- **Sort items** This preference allows you to alphabetically sort all of the items within the folders. We do not recommend doing this, as one of the important steps to good business area design calls for the placement of items in the order that we choose.

At this stage you are ready to create your business area. If you are unsure as to any of the settings that you have made, use the Back button to go back and check. You can use the Back and Next buttons to navigate through all of the wizard steps.

When you have made all of your choices, come back to the fifth screen of the wizard and click Finish. Discoverer will now create the business area, loading the data objects that you have selected and setting the preferences and options that you input to the wizard. Once again, Discoverer will create a jigsaw, gradually filling in more and more pieces as the business area is created.

Congratulations, you have now created your first business area.

Key Business Area Objects

There are three very important objects that must have unique names within Discoverer:

- Business area
- Folders
- Joins

Discoverer cannot have duplicate business area, folder, or join names anywhere within the End User Layer. These objects must have unique names. Part of your job as the Discoverer manager is to make sure that these are unique. If you do not ensure uniqueness using names that are under your control, then Discoverer will do it for you. However, Discoverer does this by appending a number to the end of the name. If you are not proactive and do not take control of the names, this can have disastrous consequences for exporting and importing objects between End User Layers when Discoverer will not be able to import objects using the name that they were originally assigned.

In addition to names, Discoverer uses unique object identifiers. These unique identifiers are initially assigned by Discoverer but can be changed by you. The authors recommend that you should always make sure that you have both meaningful names and identifiers for the three objects just listed.

Let us explain why.

When Discoverer saves a workbook, it saves both the object names and the object identifiers for the business area, folders, and joins used within each worksheet. When that workbook is subsequently opened either in the same End User Layer or in a new End User Layer, Discoverer first of all looks for the objects by name. If it cannot find the objects by name, it will look for the objects by their identifiers. If it finds either the name or the identifier, the workbook will open. If neither the name nor the identifier can be found, workbook validation will fail and the workbook will not open.

If you have been sloppy and allowed Discoverer to name folders as FOLDER_1 and so on, then during an export of objects from one End User Layer to another, Discoverer may already have a folder called FOLDER_1 in the new EUL and will thus rename the second one to something like FOLDER_11. Any workbook using that folder will fail validation when it looks for the name and will then try to find the folder using the identifier. If you have also not taken care to assign meaningful identifiers, it is possible that an existing folder had the same identifier as the one you were trying to import and that the identifier also got renamed. At this point the workbook will fail to open.

Thus it is essential that after you have created a new business area or added new critical objects to a business area, you make checks on the business area.

Checking a Business Area

Having created a new business area or added new critical objects to a business area, such as folders or joins, you need to check the business area. We check it by doing the following:

- Check the business area name, description, and identifier.

- Check the folder names, descriptions, and identifiers.

- Check the order of the folders.

- Check the names of the items.

- Check the order of the items.

- Check or create lists of values.

- Check the names and identifiers for the joins.

Check the Business Area Name, Description, and Identifier

As previously explained, the business area's name and identifier must be unique and meaningful. You should already have assigned the new business area a meaningful name and description during the creation stage. However, this is the first time that you have had a chance to look at the identifier.

To check the identifier for a business area, use the following workflow:

1. Right-click the business area name.
2. From the pop-up menu, select Properties.
3. Make sure that the name, description, and identifier meet your standards.
4. If not, change the name, description, and / or identifier.
5. When done, click OK.

NOTE
Folder names can use a combination of upper- and lowercase characters and the space character. Identifiers are all in uppercase and can have no spaces.

Check the Folder Names, Descriptions, and Identifiers

Many times, especially when importing objects from the database, you will find that the name of the table is not user friendly. We therefore need to rename all non-user-friendly folder names. In our case, the folder names are okay, so we will not rename them. However, there are two other things that should be checked at this point. These are the folder descriptions and identifiers.

To change the name, description, or identifier of a folder, use the following workflow:

1. Right-click the folder that you want to check.

2. From the pop-up menu, select Properties.
3. Make sure that the name, description, and identifier meet your standards.

4. If not, change the name, description, and / or identifier.

5. When done, click OK.

If you do decide to change the name of an identifier, you will be presented with the following warning:

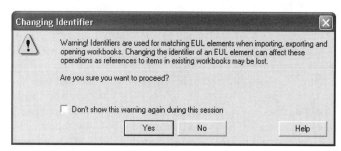

Discoverer is warning you that changing an identifier after workbooks have been created can cause those workbooks not to open. Be careful therefore when renaming identifiers to do so only during the object creation stage and not after the users have started creating workbooks against the business area.

NOTE
Click the Dependents tab to view all items that reference this folder. Discoverer will list all of the other folders, items, summaries, and workbooks that reference the folder you are working on.

Check the Order of the Folders

As mentioned earlier, it is important that you place folders in the most logical order in which they will be used by users. In particular, you should place folders in this order:

1. Place Fact or Metric folders first.

2. Place non-date dimension folders next, in alphabetic order.

3. Place date dimension folders next, in either alphabetical or business use order.

In our case, because the Sales folder contains the metrics for our business area, we will move this "fact" folder to the top of the list of folders. Because all of the other folders, apart from the Channel folder, will be used to create hierarchies. we will move the Channel folder to be second in the list beneath the Sales folder.

To move the location of a folder, use the following workflow:

1. Left-click the folder that you want to move and hold the mouse button down.

2. Move the mouse cursor to the location where you would like this folder to be.

3. Wait until Discoverer highlights the destination folder.

4. Release the mouse button.

5. The folder will now move to the chosen position.

This illustration shows our business area with the Sales folder at the top of the list and the Channel folder next. The position of the remaining folders does not matter because these will all be used to define hierarchies.

Grouping Folders

The business area that we are building is a relatively simple business area that will have less than ten folders in the final iteration. However, some business areas can have as many as twenty or even thirty folders. If you have more than thirty folders, we recommend you consider breaking the business area up into two or even three smaller areas.

However, there are times when your business will dictate that you have a lot of folders. In this case you may want to consider grouping your folders together into logical sets. One way to group folders is to group them using a theme, where aggregate folders are listed first followed by detail folders. Another way to group folders is to group them by type, with all of the metric folders first followed by all of the dimension folders. A third grouping method consists of grouping the folders by subject area, with all of the folders relating to sales in one group and all of the folders relating to invoices in another group. Of course, you might say that these should be in their own business area, and from the purist perspective so would we. However, we cannot dictate for the business area design of all companies, and where this style would not work for your company, for another company this may be exactly what they need.

Whichever method you choose for grouping folders together, we believe you ought to use separator folders to split the folders into separate groups.

Separator Folders   A *separator* folder is really an empty folder that is being used to group sets of folders together. Users cannot select anything from these folders, but that is exactly what we want.

To create a separator folder, use the following workflow:

1. Right-click the name of the business area into which you want to insert a separator folder.

2. From the pop-up menu, select New Folder. Discoverer now adds a new folder, called NewFolder1, to the bottom of the list of folders. The identifier for this new folder will also be NEWFOLDER1, all in uppercase.

3. Using the Folder Properties dialog box, give the folder a new name and a new identifier. Use something like **--- GSW Metrics ---** for the name and **GSW_METRICS** for the identifier.

4. Move the separator folder to its new position.

This illustration shows the use of separator folders in our own business area. As you can see, we have inserted one separator for our metrics and one for our dimensions.

Check the Names of the Items

Even though we told Discoverer to replace underscores with spaces and to remove prefixes from our item names, we need to check the names to ensure that they have meaningful names. Many times, especially when importing objects from the database, you will find that the name of the item is not user-friendly.

If you look here at the names of the items in our Sales folder, you will notice that many of these are cryptic with no spacing and the occasional use of a not-so-obvious abbreviation. These need to be changed:

To rename an item, use this workflow:

1. Right-click the item that you want to rename.

2. From the pop-up menu, select Properties.

3. Single-click in the field called Name.

4. Enter a more business-friendly name.

5. Optionally, provide a description.

6. Click OK.

As you can see in the next illustration, we have renamed all of the items, except the items that are used as joins, in the Sales folder.

If you have downloaded the database and are following along with us as we create this business area, you need to rename the item names for all of the other folders in the database. The following table lists the items, folder by folder, indicating which need to be renamed and which should be left as they are.

Folder	Original Name	New Name	Comment
GS Channel	Name	Channel	Ignore Channelid
GS City	Name	City	Ignore Cityid, and Districtid
	Countrycode	Country Code	
GS Customer	Name	Cust Name	Ignore Custid, Cityid
	Contactname	Contact Name	
	Creditlimit	Credit Limit	
	Postcode	Post Code	

Folder	Original Name	New Name	Comment
GS Day	Dayid	Calendar Date	Ignore Monthid
GS District	Name	District	Ignore Districtid and Regionid
GS Month	Monthid	Fiscal Month	Ignore Sequenceno and Quarterid
	Enddate	Month End Date	
GS Prodline	Name	Prod Line	Ignore Lineid
GS Products	Name	Prod Name	Ignore Prodid, and Lineid
	Prodsize	Prod Size	
	Cost	Item Cost	
	Sell	Item Price	
GS Quarter	Quarterid	Fiscal Qtr	Ignore Yearid
	Enddate	Qtr End Date	
GS Region	Name	Region	Ignore Regionid
GS Year	Yearid	Fiscal Year	
	Enddate	Year End Date	

Check the Order of the Items

After you have renamed all of the items within the folders, it is now time to check the order of the items. We need to open each folder and look at the ordering of the items, rearranging the order to make selections for users easier.

We move metrics to the top, followed by descriptor items, dates, and finally nonessential identifiers. After we have moved the items into their correct positions, we use item separators to break up the items into logical sets or groups.

To change the position of an item, use this workflow:

1. Left-click the item that you want to move and hold the mouse button down.
2. Move the mouse cursor to the location where you would like this item to be.
3. Wait until Discoverer highlights the destination item.
4. Release the mouse button.
5. The item will now move to the new position.

In the following illustration, you can see how we have reordered the items in Sales folder:

As you can see, we have split the items up into the following four groups:

- **Metrics**   Cost price, selling price, order quantity, and ship quantity

- **Descriptor items**   Order number and status

- **Dates**   Cancel date, order date, requested date, and ship date

- **Identifiers**   Channelid, custid, and prodid

Using Item Separators

Item separators are used to break up and group sets of items together. These help the users to understand about the different data sets that are in our folders. We can also use the Description field of these items to provide more generic help about how to use the folder.

To insert an item separator, use this workflow:

1. Right-click the name of the folder into which you want to insert an item separator.

2. From the pop-up menu, select New Item. Discoverer opens the New Calculation dialog box.

3. Give the item a separator Name such as **--- Metrics ---**.

4. In Calculation use NULL.

5. Click OK to complete the calculation.

6. Move the item to its correct position.

Take a close look at this illustration to see how we have inserted item separators into the Sales folder to logically break up the folder into groups:

The Remaining Folders

Because the rest of the folders, with the exception of the Channel, will be used to create hierarchies and complex folders, there is no need to alter the order of the items in these folders. Even the Channel folder does not need reordering, because it contains only two items, the channel ID and the channel name. In our final business area, the channel ID will be hidden from the end user, leaving just the channel name, and as only one item will then be visible to the user, there is no need to reorder.

It is hoped that this discussion gives you a good idea when items should be reordered and when they should not. Here are a few simple rules that should help you decide:

- Reorder when the folder will be visible to the user and more than one item in the folder will be visible to the user.

- When reordering, place items in the following order:

  - Metrics

  - Descriptor items

  - Dates

  - Identifiers

- Do not reorder folders that will be used as the basis for complex folders, but don't forget to reorder the items in the actual complex folders. We won't get to this step until later in this chapter.

Check Default Positions

Having worked out the positions for all of the items in our folders, we need to look at the default positions that have been assigned to those items. In particular, we need to pay close attention to items that could have mathematical possibilities.

By default, when Discoverer imports data items, they are assigned the following default positions:

Data Type	Default Axis
Dates	Top axis
Integers	Top axis
Numbers with decimal places	Data point
Strings	Top axis

As you can see in the table, most of the default positions are fine, except for integers. By default, Discoverer assigns integers to the top axis. This is because most integers in a database are items such as identifiers, order numbers, line numbers, and units of measure that do not need to be summed. However, integers such as order quantity and ship quantity do need to be summed and therefore need to have their default format changed.

To change an item's position, use this workflow:

1. Right-click the item whose position you want to change.

2. From the pop-up menu, select Properties.

3. Single-click in the field called Default Position, and from the drop-down menu, select the new position.

4. Your options are Data Point, Page, Side, Top, Top, or Side.

5. When done, click OK.

NOTE
To change the default position of multiple items at the same time, hold down the CTRL key while clicking each item with the mouse. When you right-click any of the highlighted items, all will be selected at the same time.

Whenever we change an item's default position like this, we will change it to become a data point, thus allowing us to manage aggregations on the items.

In our business area, two items in the Sales folder need to have their default position changed. These are the Order Qty and the Ship Qty. This illustration shows the metrics area of the Sales folder as it stands following the change of these two default positions.

Note how the icon alongside both Order Qty and Ship Qty has changed to look like a small calculator.

Check Item Aggregation

Having reassigned the default position for our items, we need to look at the default aggregation properties of these items. This is because when you change an item's position to become a Data Point, Discoverer sets the aggregation property to Detail.

However, if you recall, when we first imported the data definitions from the database, we told Discoverer to set the default position to SUM. Unfortunately, while Discoverer Administrator has many "sticky" features, this is not one of them. When you change an item's default position to Data Point, Discoverer *always* sets the new aggregation to Detail. Therefore, after you have changed an item's default position, you now have to also check the default aggregation.

NOTE
The same situation applies when you bring in a new Data Point item from the database. Discoverer assigns the default aggregation of these items to Detail also.

To change an item's default aggregation, use this workflow:

1.   Right-click the item whose property you want to change.

2.   From the pop-up menu, select Properties.

3.   Single-click in the field called Default Aggregate, and from the drop-down menu, select the new aggregate.

4.   Your options are AVG, COUNT, Detail, MAX, MIN, and SUM.

5.   When done, click OK.

NOTE
To change the default aggregate of multiple items at the same time, hold down the CTRL key while clicking each item with the mouse. When you right-click any of the highlighted items, all will be selected at the same time.

In our business area, there are two items in the Sales folder that need to have their default aggregation changed. These are the Order Qty and the Ship Qty. The following illustration shows the Properties dialog box as it looks after we selected SUM from the drop-down menu:

NOTE
In the preceding dialog box, NOTE how the name of the database column is blank. This is because we changed the default aggregate for more than one item at the same time.

Check Default Formats

When Discoverer imports data items from the database, it automatically assigns the default format of the data items as follows:

- **Dates**   DD-MON-RRRR, or to whatever is the default NLS date format

- **Integers**   As defined within the database, e.g., 9999999999

- **Numbers with decimal places**   As defined within the database, e.g., 999999D99

- **Strings**   As defined in the database

So if the item formats have been defaulted to the way in which they were defined within the database, why do we need to check them? We check the format for a number of reasons, among which are these:

- To allow for leading zeros in numbers that have decimals

- To increase the number of decimal places to allow for better mathematical accuracy

- To increase the number of places before the decimal to allow for summations

- To insert comma separators

- To truncate dates

- And many other reasons

To change an item's default format, use this workflow:

1. Right-click the item whose format you want to change.

2. From the pop-up menu, select Properties.

3. Single-click in the field called Format.

4. Change the format.

5. When done, click OK.

In our business area we need to change the format of two data items. We will change the following:

- Cost Price and Selling Price, from 999999D99 to 999999990D99, thus increasing the number of places to the left and inserting a leading zero. This will allow users to compute summations on the total cost or revenue without worrying that the computation will fail.

Summary

In this chapter we have introduced you to the Discoverer Administrator tool. You have learned the key components of the tool as well as your responsibilities as an administrator. We have shown you how to build an End User Layer and a business area based on the Global Sales Widgets database. We have described to you the importance of understanding and anticipating end-user requirements and the six steps to a successful Discoverer implementation.

We also showed you all of the steps required to make Discoverer work in Apps mode.

You have learned how to refine the business area by arranging the folders and items in a meaningful way. You have also learned how to change an item's properties in order to improve performance. We have taught you how to create folders that hide the complexities of the database from the users and hierarchies to improve drilling capabilities.

Using Discoverer Admin is truly an art and not just a science. In the next few chapters we will show you how to create an environment for reporting that is truly exceptional.

CHAPTER
18

Editing the Business Area

n this chapter we will expand on what you learned in Chapter 17 and show you how to continue with the remaining business area checks. We will show you how to manage lists of values and joins. Later we will show you how to add new folders, followed by managing hierarchies. Finally we will show you some of the more advanced mechanisms for item management, culminating in an explanation of how to manage descriptive lists of values.

Remaining Business Area Checks

The last two checks that we need to make on a new business are

- Managing lists of values
- Managing joins

Managing Lists of Values

The next stage to successful business area management is to create lists of values. Depending upon whether you allowed Discoverer to create its own lists of values during the import stage determines whether you will have to create your own list of values or check existing lists of values. As we advised you not to allow Discoverer to automatically create lists of values, we will start by showing you how to create these.

Defining Lists of Values

If you followed our advice and did not allow Discoverer to create its own lists of values during the import stage, you get to have some fun and create them now. Just as when riding the Tour de France, you have come over that monstrous climb in the middle of the stage to find that you have a long downhill section before the next climb, so creating lists of values following all that checking comes like a breath of fresh air. This is a chance to catch your breath before the next climb.

In Discoverer's language a list of values is an item class. According to the 10.1.2 Discoverer Administration Help guide, *item classes* are "groups of items that share some similar properties. An item class enables you to define item properties once, and then assign the item class to other items that share similar properties."

Now that you have set up the business area with the items you want, it is time to create the lists of values that your users will need when creating their worksheets. Before we show you the steps required to create a list of values, we will discuss how they will be used.

Lists of Values Usage

You do not need to place a list of values on every item in a folder. We have rarely seen an occasion when users need to query lists of identifiers. They usually don't need to see lists of values on dates either. If you recall from our discussions with the Plus tool, Discoverer Plus will display a calendar pop-up whenever a user is offered a parameter that is a date. You, as the administrator, do not need to do anything to enable this behavior, so why go to the trouble of creating a list of values on the date?

Another reason for not allowing Discoverer to automatically create its own lists of values is that during the automatic creation stage Discoverer does not check to see if an existing item class already exists. For example, let's say you create a new business area and import two objects, one for the Purchase Order header and one for the Purchase Order detail. Both objects may well contain identical items. At the very least you will probably have the PO Number in both. If you allowed Discoverer to automatically create its own lists of values, it would have created two, one for the PO Number in the Header folder and one for the PO Number in the Detail folder. This may not sound like too big of a deal, but imagine that you have created a large business area that has ten folders, each of which contains a Product Number. Discoverer will create ten item classes, not a very efficient way of working.

NOTE
We have deliberately used the word "object" in the preceding paragraph because we can import data definitions based on tables, views, or materialized views.

Continuing with the usage of lists of values, we will give you another very good reason not to automatically allow Discoverer to create its own lists of values. Let's say you have a table that contains ten million rows, not an uncommon scenario. Let's say the table contains a column called Gender that has two values, Male and Female. If you allow Discoverer to create a list of values based on the Gender column in this table, every time a user clicks the list of values, SQL will execute a select distinct gender clause from that table. In essence you are forcing the database to look for two values out of a ten million row table. Later in this chapter we will show you how to overcome this by using a custom folder to generate this list of values.

Creating a List of Values

Now that we have explained why you should not allow Discoverer to automatically create its own list of values, we will walk you through creating manual lists of values.

To create a manual list of values, use the following workflow:

1. Determine the item for which you want a list of values.

2. Navigate to and right-click the item, and from the pop-up menu, select New Item Class.

3. Discoverer launches the Item Class Wizard and starts at Step 2.

NOTE
If you want to create a list of values using an Alternative Sort or for use in Drill to Detail, these switches can be found on Step 1 of the wizard. To get to Step 1 of the wizard, click the Back button. For this exercise, we will create a standard list of values.

4. The item that you right-clicked in Step 1 of this workflow will be selected automatically. Although you can change it if you wish, we don't recommend you alter the settings once you have started. Having confirmed that the item checked is the one that you want to use for generating this new list of values, click Next.

NOTE
If you have opted to create a list of values using an alternative sort, Discoverer inserts an additional step into the wizard at this point. Because we will discuss alternative sorts later in the chapter, you should not see this screen at this time.

5. You are in Step 3 of the wizard, or Step 4 if you are creating an alternative sort. In this step, as you can see next, you can optionally associate the new list of values with other items in the business area. Unless you are an experienced Discoverer administrator, we don't recommend you do this, because you can easily make a mistake and assign the list of values to the wrong item.

6. Click Next.

7. Step 4 of the wizard (Step 5 if you created an alternative sort) is where you assign advanced options. As you can see in the following illustration, you can assign five options:

- **Retrieve values in groups of**   This defaults to 100, and unless you have a real need to alter this value, you should leave this setting as is.

- **Sort the values and remove duplicates**   This is checked by default because this option guarantees that the list will be sorted and will not contain duplicates. We do not recommend that you uncheck this option unless you have good reason.

- **Show values in "Select Items" page of Worksheet Wizard**   This is checked by default. If you uncheck this, your users will not be able to expand the list of values when creating worksheets. We do not recommend that you uncheck this option.

- **Require user to always search for values**   This is unchecked by default. If you check this, Discoverer will launch the Search dialog box whenever a user clicks the list of values. Should you have a large list of values, you may want to consider turning on this option.

- **Cache list of values during each connection**   This is checked by default because caching is the most efficient way of retrieving lists of values. If you do not want to cache the values but want to force Discoverer to dynamically re-create the list every time the users access it, you should uncheck this box. If you are worried about security and are using a virtual private database, you might want to consider unchecking this.

8. After you have assigned your advanced options, click Next.

9. Step 5 of the wizard (Step 6 if you created an alternative sort) is where you assign a meaningful name and optional description. We recommend you name these ChannelLOV, ProductLOV, and so on. While not mandatory, we recommend you make use of the description box if you have changed any of the default options. It is acceptable to have spaces and mixed case in the names; however, since the end user will not see

these names, we don't add spaces. It is really a holdover from the days when few applications allowed spaces, and we have become accustomed to omitting spaces when they are not needed. This step is shown here.

10. When done, click Finish. Discoverer creates the list of values, which you should test by clicking the plus icon alongside the item.

NOTE
If Discoverer gives you a warning saying that this could take a long time, ignore it. As the administrator you need to test that your list of values a) works and b) is efficient! If the retrieval times out, the limit can be increased by going to the Tools | Options Query Governor tab and increasing the default value.

Removing a List of Values

From time to time it will become necessary for you to remove a list of values from the system. This is very easy.

To remove a list of values, use the following workflow:

1. Click the Item Classes tab in the main Administrator window.

2. Locate and right-click the list of values that you want to remove, and from the pop-up menu, select Delete Item Class.

3. The Confirm Delete dialog box will open.

4. When prompted "Are you sure you want to delete this," you have four options:

- **Yes** Click this to delete the item class.

- **No** Click this to cancel.

- **Impact** Click this to see what impact deleting this item class will have. If Discoverer displays only one item in the Impact dialog box, you are probably safe in deleting the item class. If Discoverer displays more than one impacted item, you might want to reconsider.

- **Help** Click this to open context-sensitive help in a browser window.

5. If you click Yes, the item class will be deleted.

Checking Lists of Values

If we had allowed Discoverer to automatically create its own lists of values, or if you need to undertake a cursory examination of an existing list, you will need to examine the item class settings.

To check a list of values, follow this workflow:

1. Click the Item Classes tab in the main Administrator window.

2. Locate and right-click the list of values that you want to check, and from the pop-up menu, select either Edit Item Class or Properties.

3. If you selected Edit Item Class, as you can see next, Discoverer opens the Edit Item Class dialog box.

NOTE
The Edit Item Class dialog box is a multitabbed box that corresponds to the steps in the Item Class Wizard. After making any changes that are required, click OK.

4. If you selected Properties, as you can see in Figure 18-1, Discoverer opens the Item Class Properties dialog box.

The Item Class Properties dialog box is a form that allows you to view or change the properties of a list of values. If you take a close look at this box, you will notice that there are a couple of additional properties that cannot be set anywhere else. These are explained in the following section.

Additional Item Class Properties
In the preceding section we showed you how to examine the properties of an item class by launching the Item Class Properties dialog box, seen in Figure 18-1. In this box there are two additional properties that cannot be set anywhere else:

■ **Auto generate name** This is a most interesting property. By default it is set to No, which means that Discoverer allows you to assign your own name for the item class. If you change this to Yes, Discoverer replaces your name with an auto-generated name consisting of the folder name and the item name upon which the item class is based. Unless you switch this property back to No, you will not be allowed to edit the name again. Furthermore, although we cannot show this to you in a black-and-white illustration, Discoverer colors the name of the item class on the Item Classes tab. If you

FIGURE 18-1 *Item Class Properties dialog box*

redisplay the Item Class Properties, you will notice that the name is now grayed out. This is to indicate that the item class name is non-editable.

■ **Identifier** Discoverer assigns unique identifiers to item classes. By default, this is the uppercased value of the item class name. There is no need to change this name unless your corporate standards dictate.

NOTE
Even though setting the Auto generate name property to Yes causes Discoverer to rename the item class, this has no impact on the Identifier. The Identifier can be changed only manually.

Required Lists of Values

In our tutorial business area, we need to create 14 lists of values. The following table shows the lists of values we will create:

Folder Name	Item Name	List of Value Name
Sales	Status	StatusLOV
Channel	Channel Name	ChannelLOV
City	CityName	CityNameLOV
	Country Code	CntryCodeLOV
Customer	Cust Name	CustNameLOV
	State	StateLOV

Folder Name	Item Name	List of Value Name
District	District Name	DistrictNameLOV
Month	Monthid	FMonthLOV
Products	Product Name	ProdNameLOV
	Product Size	ProdSizeLOV
Prod Line	Line Name	ProdLineLOV
Quarter	Quarterid	FQuarterLOV
Region	Region Name	RegionNameLOV
Year	Yearid	YearLOV

Having created the lists of values, click the Item Classes tab. You should see the lists displayed as seen here.

Issues with Lists of Values

These are the most common issues that occur with lists of values:

- Lists of values take too long to generate and time out.
- Lists of values show the data in the wrong sort sequence.

If users report that the list of values is timing out or it is not producing the full list, you have the following three possible solutions.

Increase the Time Out Limit   If the user is using Desktop or Plus, tell him/her do the following:

1. Launch Discoverer Desktop.
2. From the Tools menu, select Options | Query Governor.
3. Change the option called "Cancel value retrieval after" to a higher value.
4. Click OK.

If the issue is occurring in Plus, do the following:

1. Launch Discoverer Plus.
2. From the Tools menu, select Options | Query Governor.
3. Change the option called "Cancel list-of-values retrieval after" to a higher value.
4. Click Apply.

If the issue is occurring in Viewer, do the following:

1. Launch Discoverer Viewer.
2. The user should click the link called Preferences.
3. Change the option called "Cancel list-of-values retrieval after" to a higher value.
4. Click Apply.

NOTE
Between Plus and Viewer there is only one set of preferences, so if a user changes the retrieval value in one, it is automatically reflected in the other the next time the user connects.

If the issue is occurring in the Administrator edition, do the following:

1. Launch Discoverer Administrator.
2. From the Tools menu, select Options | Query Governor.
3. Change the option called "Cancel value retrieval after" to a higher value.
4. Click OK.

Force the Use of the Search Dialog Box   Launch the Item Class Properties dialog box and set the property called Display Search Dialog to Yes. This will force the Discoverer end user to be prompted for the item that he or she wants rather than displaying a large list of values.

Use Another Data Item to Create the List of Values   If neither of the preceding two options rectify the situation, you should try creating the list of values on an alternate item, perhaps from another table. You might also want to consider using a custom folder for this purpose.

NOTE
Another option for improving retrieval times is to optimize the database table by adding an index.

When checking lists of values, you need to be aware that Discoverer creates these based on the following underlying data types:

■   Date

■   Number

■   Varchar or Varchar2

Sorts based on dates and numbers will always be in the correct order. Sorts based on Varchar or Varchar2 data types, strings to you and me, can create problems because they will sort alphabetically. Sometimes this is not the order that we wish them to sort in. The following section on alternative sorts addresses this issue.

Using Alternative Sorts

Sometimes, when you look at a list of values, you will see that it is not in the order that you would like. To overcome this, you can use what is called an *alternative sort*. In order to use an alternative sort, you must have another unique item available in the folder that contains the item on which you created the list of values.

This alternative item must be one of the following:

■   Another unique and available item, such as month end date

■   An artificially created sequence number

Among the most common data elements that sort in the wrong order are days of the week and months of the year. For both of these you will need to create an alternative sort if you want your users to see the list displayed in the right order.

For example, look at the following table:

Natural Order	Logical Order
April	January
August	February
December	March
February	April
January	May
July	June
June	July
March	August
May	September
November	October
October	November
September	December

Creating an Alternative Sort   Let's look at the Month data in the sample database. Open the Month folder and click the plus character alongside the Fiscal Month data item. This opens the current list of values which, as you can see next, is displayed in alphabetical order.

To add an alternative sort, use the following workflow:

1. Click the Item Classes tab.

2. Expand the list of item classes.

3. Locate the list of values that needs the alternative sort. In our case we are looking for the MonthLOV.

4. Right-click the item class, and from the pop-up menu, select Edit Item Class.

5. In the Edit Item Class dialog box, click the Alternative Sort tab.

6. Select the item that will be used to generate the new alternative sort. In our case, we can use the Month End Date because for any one month there is only one month ending date. As mentioned previously, because dates always sort correctly, this is an excellent item on which to sort.

7. Click OK.

8. Recheck the list of values. As you can see in this illustration, the months are sorted correctly.

NOTE
Days of the week are trickier because there is no obvious alternative item that you can use to sort by. However, if we think outside the box, we can create an artificial sort using a sequence number as the alternate item. We will show you how to do this when we discuss custom folders later in this chapter.

Removing an Alternative Sort   If you make a mistake by setting an alternative sort for an item that does not need this type of sort, you can remove the alternative sort. This is a new feature. If you have used previous versions of Discoverer, you will know how hard it was to remove an alternative sort until now.
To remove an alternative sort, use the following workflow:

1. Right-click the item class that has the alternative sort you want to remove, and from the pop-up menu, select Edit Item Class.

2. Click the Alternative Sort tab.

3. Click the Remove Alternative Sort button.

4. Click OK.

Managing Joins

The next thing we need to do in working with a newly created business area is to create the joins that we need between our folders or check the joins that already exist. As we hope you recall from the creation of our business area, we asked Discoverer to automatically create joins for us based on the primary and foreign key constraints in the database. Looking at Figure 18-2, of the data model that we used for the tutorial database, you see that there are twelve tables, interlinked by a series of one-to-many (1:N) relationships.

Defining Joins

In Discoverer, a join relates two folders using one or more matching items, whereas in the database a join relates two tables using one or more matching columns. Just like in the database, where the DBA has to know which table is the parent and which is the child, Discoverer needs to know which folder is the master and which is the detail. What we are looking for are one-to-many (1:N) or one-to-one (1:1) relationships. A many-to-many (N:N) relationship cannot be handled by Discoverer, so these need to be resolved in some other way.

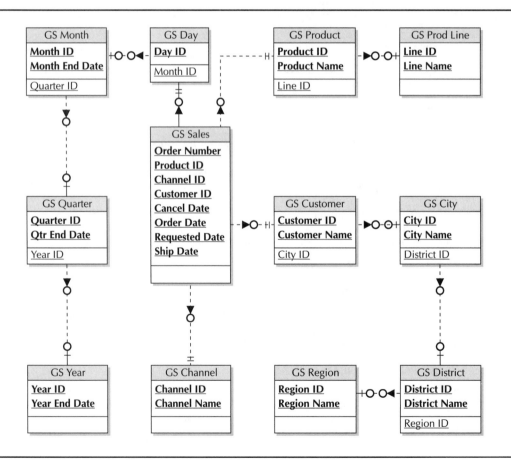

FIGURE 18-2 *Tutorial database schema*

When you create a join between two folders, Discoverer gives end users the rights to pull items out of both folders into the same worksheet. The user does not need to know how the join was created or which folder is the master. This complexity is hidden from the end user by the End User Layer's metadata. Our job, as Discoverer administrators, is to make life as easy as possible for our end users. We should be looking for ways to make it easier for the end users to build the queries that they need. One of the best ways we can do this is to create joins between folders. Users do not have this power, so if we do not create joins, our end users will have a difficult time.

If you look back at Figure 18-2, which outlines the GSW data model, you will see that there are twelve tables, interlinked by a series of one-to-many (1:N) relationships.

Data Types

Discoverer has a rule that the data items on both ends of a join must be of the same data type and size; otherwise, it cannot create the join. The prime responsibility therefore rests with the data designer and the DDL creator to ensure that the items are the same. However, as the Discoverer administrator, if you find that the data items do not match, what can you do?

The real question is—what should you do? Our first piece of advice is to take a deep breath and not panic. These things happen from time to time, and hopefully this data mismatch is just an oversight. Go back to the data designer and the DDL creator to see if they are aware of this situation and ask whether this was intentional. Tact will dictate that you should not use the words bug or bad design when discussing a data model with your data designer. You do need to find out if a data model revision is planned. If the answer is No, and the data model cannot be changed, the question is—what can you do?

Correcting this situation in Discoverer is not the most effective way and will almost certainly cause performance issues. However, by using a function to convert the data type and size of one of the items to match the data type and size of the other item, you can at least create the join. Should you do this? Ideally, no—but sometimes you will have no choice. Workarounds are one of our greatest weapons!

But which item should you change? Speaking logically, you need to change the one that has the least impact. In most master/detail relationships you will typically be joining from the primary key of a master folder to an item in the detail folder that may or may not be associated with an index. You do not need Primary/Foreign key constraints enabled in the database to make this work.

Applying a function to change the data type of an item in the primary key of the master folder could have serious consequences for performance. Doing this will probably negate searches on the primary key and cause the Oracle database to do a full table scan, something you want to avoid if you can. We therefore need to look at the other end of the relationship, at the properties of the detail item. We will cover this later in this section when we discuss creating a complex join.

Creating a Simple Join

Let's focus on one pair of tables, the GS_Prodline and GS_Products folders. Looking at the data model, we can see that the primary key of the GS_Prodline table is the column called Lineid. When we look inside the GS_Products table, we can see that there is also a column called Lineid. There is a 1:N join between these tables, and the parent table is the GS_Prodline.

Looking inside Discoverer, we have folders that correspond to these two tables. The Discoverer folder corresponding to the GS_Prodline table is called Product Line, while the folder corresponding to the GS_Products table is called Products. We therefore need to create a join from the Product Line folder to the Products folder.

To create a join, use the following workflow:

1. Determine the two folders that need to be joined.

2. Determine the names of the items that need to be joined.

3. Determine which folder is the master and which folder is the detail.

4. Navigate to and open the folder that contains the master item.

5. Navigate to and right-click the master item, and from the pop-up menu, select New Join.

6. Discoverer opens the Join Wizard. Looking at the first screen of the Join Wizard, you can see that it has the following seven areas:

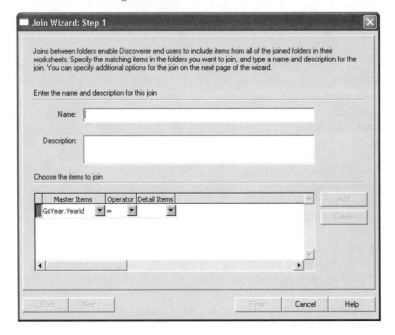

■ **Name**   Join names are critical to the successful operation of Discoverer workbooks. Every join must have a unique name, not only in the business area but across the entire EUL. Discoverer will auto-generate a name if you leave this blank.

■ **Description**   This is a placeholder for you to type a description about the join.

■ **Choose the items to join**   This area comprises three components: a Master Item, an Operator, and a Detail Item. These components are the heart of the join and tell Discoverer exactly how the join is put together.

■ **Add**   Use this button to add additional join items, in effect creating a composite join between multiple items. For example, in Apps you might have both a Category Code and a Category Item Code in use joining the two tables together.

- ■ **Delete**   Use this button to delete the secondary components that are in use in a composite join.

- ■ **Next**   Use this button to navigate to the second screen of the Join Wizard. It will be active only when the three join items, the Master item, the Operator, and the Detail item, have been entered.

- ■ **Finish**   Use this button to complete the join. It is active only in Step 2.

7. Discoverer starts to create the join by inserting, under the heading Master Items, the folder and item names of the item that we selected. Click the drop-down icon under the heading Detail Items. This opens the New Join dialog box.

8. In the New Join dialog box you need to select the business area, folder, and detail item required to complete the join, and then click OK.

9. When control is passed back to the wizard, you should notice that the folder and item name of the detail item have been filled in.

10. While a join name is mandatory, Discoverer will auto-generate the name for you based on the names of the folders. Therefore, you should notice that the Next key is now active. You should also note that the Finish button is still grayed out.

Choose the items to join		
Master Items	Operator	Detail Items
GsYear.Yearid	=	GsQuarter.Yearid

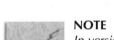

NOTE
In version 9.0.4, and continued with 10.1.2, Oracle added a number of SQL optimizations to the SQL generation capabilities of Discoverer. One of these is join trimming, which means that in a query that joins two or more tables, if the query can be answered and still satisfy all constraints by not including a table at all in the SQL, then Discoverer will drop that table from the SQL that it sends to the database. The Next screen when defining a join is for that purpose: to force the Discoverer administrator to make a choice and not simply rely on the defaults. It is therefore good practice to pay more attention to this second screen than ever before.

11. Click Next to proceed to the second screen of the wizard.

12. In Step 2 of the Join Wizard you need to provide information about the join details and set any optional configurations you need. These are the two main areas of this screen:

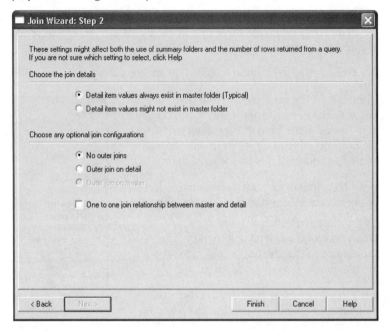

- **Choose the join details** In this area you must tell Discoverer whether the detail items always exist in the master folder or whether these are optional. You must check one of the two radio buttons. Typically, you will nearly always encounter the situation where the detail items do exist in the master folder. This is the default.

- **Choose any optional configurations** In this area you must tell Discoverer about the join itself, whether there is an outer join, whether the outer join is on the detail or the master, or if the join is a one-to-one (1:1). Normally the configuration is such that the join is not an outer join. This is the default.

NOTE
The option for "Outer join on master" is grayed out. This option is available only when you check the button called "Detail item values might not exist in master folder" in the join detail section. Unless you really need to and you know what you are doing, take care adjusting these settings. Making incorrect join settings will result in worksheets that at best run slow or at worst give incorrect results.

13. Click Finish.

14. Discoverer completes the join and closes the wizard.

Creating Complex Joins

A complex join occurs in two situations:

- When one of the data types is wrong.

- When multiple items are used to join the folders together.

What follows is a fictitious example of a multi-item join. This is a join between a Product folder and a materialized view that has been created against Sales. After speaking with the data modeler, it was determined that the items shown in the following table make up this join:

Master Folder	Master Item	Detail Folder	Detail Item	Join Type	Join Order
Product	Org ID	Sales MV	Org ID	Complex	First
Product	Prod ID	Sales MV	Prod ID	Complex	Second

As mentioned earlier, the only stipulation that Discoverer has is that the data types of all the items in the join must match. However, in our situation we have a further complication. As defined in the database, the data type of Prod ID in the Product table is NUMBER(4), whereas in the Sales materialized views it is defined as VARCHAR2(4). The lengths are the same, but the data types are not. When we tried building this join, Discoverer responded with this error message:

Clicking OK returned us to the Join Wizard, and we cannot continue with the join. One of the data types must be changed.

Changing Data Types for a Join   Whenever you have a situation where the data types are not the same and you need to create a join, you need to change the data type for one of the join items.

To change the data type, use the following workflow:

1. Click the heading for the folder that contains the data type you want to change, in this case the Sales MV.

2. From the pop-up menu, select New Item.

3. Discoverer displays the following New Item dialog box:

4. Enter a meaningful, unique name for the item. In our case we will name it New Prod ID.

5. Expand the list of items in the Show box and locate the item you want to change.

6. Paste or push the item into the Calculation box and use a converter function to make the change. Your calculation should look like this:

7. Click OK to close the Edit Calculation dialog box.

8. Because the new item was created using the TO_NUMBER function, it will have been created with a default position of Data Point. Using the Properties dialog box, change the default position to Side.

Now you can use this new item in the join.

Creating a Multi-Item Join   Now that we have added a new item with the data type we need for the complex join, we can create the join. We are referring to the new item in the Sales MV folder.

Master Folder	Master Item	Detail Folder	Detail Item	Join Type	Join Order
Product	Org ID	Sales MV	Org ID	Complex	First
Product	Prod ID	Sales MV	New Prod ID	Complex	Second

To create the complex multi-item join, use the following workflow:

1. Use the workflow that was outlined earlier in this section and create a simple join on the Org ID between the Product and Sales MV folders. Do not click Next after you have added this first element, but click Add.

2. Add a second join item between the Prod ID in the Product folder and our new item. Call this second item New Prod ID in the Sales MV folder.

3. The screen should look like this:

4. Click Next, and then click Finish.

NOTE
*Do not forget that when you bring
tables into Discoverer, each table equates to a folder, and the columns
in the table equate to items within the folder.*

Checking Joins

From time to time it may become necessary for you to check a join.
Let's expand the Channel folder so that we can see all of the items.

As you can see in this illustration, this folder has only two items,
a channel and a channel ID. The channel ID is in bold, while below
it is another item with a "crows foot" icon. These are the join items.
The channel ID is in bold because it is the primary key in the primary/foreign key relationship.

NOTE
*The corresponding foreign key in the Sales order will be italicized.
Discoverer bolds all primary keys and italicizes all foreign keys.*

Let's take a closer look at the join. To examine a join, use the following workflow:

1. Right-click the join you want to examine and from the pop-up menu, select Edit Join.

2. Discoverer displays the following Edit Join dialog box:

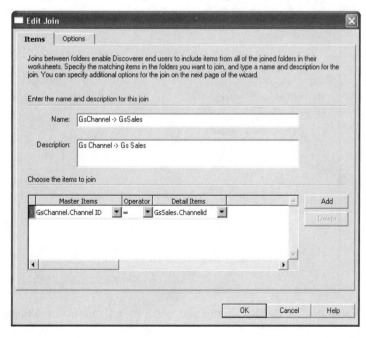

As you can see in the illustration, the Edit Join dialog box has two tabs: one called Items and one called Options.

The Items Tab   The Items tab has the following five areas:

■ **Name**   Join names are critical to the successful operation of Discoverer workbooks. Every join must have a unique identifier, not only in the business area but across the entire EUL. Even though join names can be duplicated within the business area, we recommend giving joins unique names to match the identifiers. You will find this to be extremely helpful if you need to debug the system at a later date.

■ **Description**   This is a placeholder for you to type a description about the join.

■ **Choose the items to join**   This area comprises three components: a Master Item, an Operator, and a Detail Item. These components are the heart of the join and tell Discoverer exactly how the join is put together.

■ **Add**   Use this button to add additional join items, in effect creating a composite join between multiple items. For example, in Apps you might have both a Category Code and a Category Item Code in use joining two tables together.

■ **Delete**   Use this button to delete the secondary components that are in use in a composite join.

The Options Tab   The Options tab, illustrated here, has two main areas:

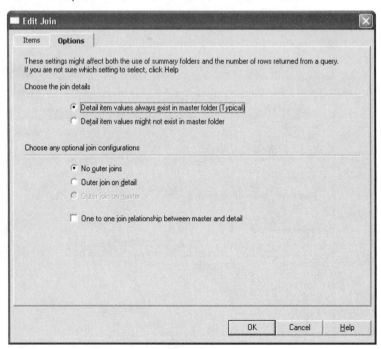

■ **Choose the join details**   In this area you must tell Discoverer whether the detail items always exist in the master folder or whether these are optional. You must check one of the two radio buttons. Typically, you will nearly always encounter the situation where the detail items do exist in the master folder.

■ **Choose any optional configurations** In this area you must tell Discoverer about the join itself, whether there is an outer join, whether the outer join is on the detail or the master, or if the join is a one-to-one (1:1). Normally the configuration is such that the join is not an outer join.

NOTE
You will notice that the option for "Outer join on master" is grayed out. This option is available only when you check the button called "Detail item values might not exist in master folder" in the join detail section. Do not adjust any of these settings unless you really need to and you know what you are doing. Making incorrect join settings will result in worksheets that at best run slow or at worst give incorrect results.

Now that you know how to look at the join settings, you need to check that Discoverer has correctly created all of the joins that you were expecting. If all of your joins are in place, well done, you have successfully completed checking your new business area. We will discuss joins in more detail in the next section when we discuss maintaining business areas.

Enhancing Business Areas

After you have created a new business area and made all of the necessary checks to ensure that the items you imported and their associated properties are correct, you can begin your enhancements. Unfortunately, many inexperienced Discoverer administrators think that they have finished at this point. You would be amazed at some of the horror stories that we could tell about poorly designed business areas.

We will outline the enhancements that need to be made to complete your business area. We have identified five major areas of work still needed:

■ Folder enhancements

■ Hierarchy enhancements

■ Item enhancements

■ User access

■ Testing

For the remainder of this chapter we will discuss the first three of these major work areas in some detail.

Folder Enhancements

The folder enhancements that we will discuss primarily concern adding new folders. There are three types of new folders:

■ **New** This type of folder is the sort that we will use when we wish to create a new, complex folder. A complex folder is one that is made up of items from existing folders. You will use these folders often.

- **Custom** This type of folder allows you to key the SQL yourself directly into Discoverer. We use these folders for manually adding lists of values or alternative sorts.

- **From Database** This type of folder is associated with an object from the database. These objects could be a table, a view, or a materialized view.

Creating New Folders

To create a new folder, follow this workflow:

1. Single-click the business area heading such that the business area name is highlighted.

2. Right-click the business area name; Discoverer will pop up a context menu.

3. From the context pop-up menu, click the type of folder that you want to create.

Paste
New Folder
New Folder from Database...
New Custom Folder...
Delete Business Area...
Security...
Refresh...
Properties...
Sort Folders

NOTE
An alternate method for Step 2 is to select Insert | Folder from the menu bar.

Adding Complex Folders

Complex folders are folders that combine data from one or more other folders in the End User Layer. They enable your users to see data from multiple folders at the same time, somewhat similar to the way a view works in the database. You use complex folders to simplify what the user sees when logging in. Rather than seeing numerous interlinking folders, the user will see one folder. If your company has strict rules for creating database views, you may want to consider complex folders because you do not need the CREATE VIEW privilege to create a complex folder. You can also use complex folders to create subsets of the data for different parts of your organization, leaving the original folders intact.

NOTE
To combine data from multiple folders, just as with a database view, there must be joins in place between the folders.

Choosing New Complex Folders How do you choose when to use a complex folder? Take a look back at Figure 18-2, which gives you an entity-relationship diagram for the database that we are using in this book. While this may look like a star schema, it is actually a snowflake schema.

NOTE
You will find information concerning star and snowflake schemas in Appendix C.

Look at the joins that radiate out from the GS Sales folder. You can see that there are four, one each to GS Channel, GS Customer, GS Day, and GS Product, respectively. Beyond the GS Customer, GS Day, and GS Product folders, there are more folders. Beyond Products, there are

Product Lines, while beyond Customer there is a complete geographic hierarchy linking to Cities, Districts, and Regions. Looking beyond the Day folder, you can see a time hierarchy linking to Months, Quarters, and Years. We will use complex folders based around each of these hierarchies so that our end users will see one Geographic folder containing all of the items from Customer, City, District, and Region; and one Products folder containing all of the items from Products and Product Lines.

You might ask, "What about the time hierarchy, shouldn't we create a complex folder on this too?" The answer is yes, we will do this, but we will not build one complex folder but four, one folder for each of the dates that we have in our Sales folder: Cancel Date, Order Date, Requested Date, and Ship Date. Why four complex folders, wouldn't one suffice? The answer is no. If we want our users to build queries such as "show me how many of the sales orders that were ordered in Q3 did not ship until Q4," they cannot do this if we have one date folder. However, if we have a separate folder for Order Date, containing our month, quarter, and year data along with the calendar dates, and we have another, similarly defined folder for the Ship Date, our users can build such a query.

NOTE
GSW, our fictitious retailing company, uses a fiscal time calendar running from October to September. Our Q1 is therefore October to December, while Q2 is January to March of the following fiscal year. We thus cannot use the standard Discoverer date hierarchy.

We need to create six complex folders. The data model shown in Figure 18-3 shows the business area model after we have added the new folders. If you think that this looks like a star schema, you would be right. Discoverer works well with star schemas, and this is what you should be trying to do with your models. If you cannot create a star schema in the database, you should try to use complex folders to do this for you in the tool. Users understand star schema data models better than any other kind of data model.

Fiscal Date Complex Folders   As mentioned previously, and as seen in Figure 18-3, in our Sales folder there are four dates, one each for

- Cancel Date

- Order Date

- Request Date

- Ship Date

We will create one new folder for each date and populate it from the existing Day, Month, Quarter, and Year simple folders. We will describe only the process for the new Cancel Date folder in detail. Having shown how to do this for Cancel Date, we will then show you how to create the other three folders by copying and pasting what you have just done.

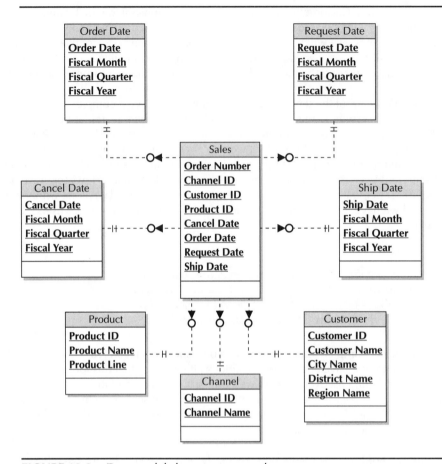

FIGURE 18-3 *Data model shown as a star schema*

NOTE
As shown in the following illustration, it is much easier to do the next tasks if you split the screen into two windows using Window | Split Window from the menu bar.

To create the Cancel Date complex folder, use the following workflow:

1. In the right-hand window, right-click the business area name, and from the pop-up menu select New Folder.

2. As you can see next, Discoverer creates a new empty folder named NewFolder1, expands the list of existing folders, and places the new folder at the bottom of the list.

3. Right-click the new folder, and from the pop-up menu select Properties. The Folder Properties dialog box will open. Using the General tab, rename the folder to **Cancel Date** and change the Identifier to **CANCELDATE**.

4. Click OK when warned that changing identifiers can be risky.

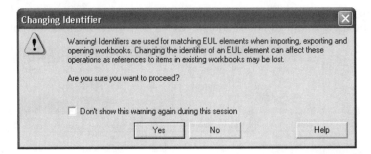

5. If there is already a folder in the EUL by the name that you are trying to use, Discoverer will give this warning telling you that the name must be unique:

NOTE
It is perfectly safe to change the identifier when creating a new folder. Waiting until later, however, when users may well have workbooks based on the folder, increases the risk that workbooks will no longer open and is not recommended.

6. In the left-hand window, expand the Day folder.

7. Click the item called Calendar Date and drag it across the window separator into the new folder.

8. In the left-hand window, minimize the Day folder and expand the Month folder.

9. Click the items called Fiscal Month and Mth End Date and drag these across the window separator into the new folder.

NOTE
To drag multiple items at the same time, left-click one of the items to highlight that item, and hold down the CTRL key while you left-click the other items. With all items highlighted, you can drag the set across the window separator into the new folder.

10. In the left-hand window, minimize the Month folder and expand the Quarter folder.

11. Click the items called Fiscal Quarter and Qtr End Date and drag these across the window separator into the new folder.

12. In the left-hand window, minimize the Quarter folder and expand the Year folder.

13. Click the items called Fiscal Year and Year End Date and drag these across the window separator into the new folder.

NOTE
Existing lists of values are maintained and remain attached to the items as they are dragged into the new folder.

14. Your new folder should look like this:

NOTE
As you become more comfortable with highlighting and dragging items between folders, you may well find it easier to highlight the items in all of the simple folders first and then drag them all over at the same time.

After creating our base complex folder, we need to make it ready for use. If the items in the new folder do not have meaningful names, these should be renamed. To help our users, we will rename the item called Calendar Item to Cancel Date.

Having created a new folder, we need to join it to the Sales folder. The new folder that we created is for the Cancel Date, so it makes sense to create a join from here to the Cancel Date item in the Sales folder. This is shown here.

To finish the remaining date folders, we need to create three more complex folders, one each for the Order Date, Requested Date, and Ship Date. This process is much easier than creating the Cancel Date folder because we can take advantage of what we have just done by copying the new Cancel Date folder and pasting a replica of its definition into the business area three times.

Replicating a Folder   To replicate a complex folder, use the following workflow:

1. Click the name for the folder you want to copy so that the name is highlighted.
2. Right-click the folder, and from the pop-up menu, select Copy.
3. Right-click the heading for the business area, and from the pop-up menu, select Paste.
4. Give the new folder a meaningful name and identifier.

Completing the Date Folders   To complete our complex data folders, use the following workflow:

1. Use the workflow in the previous section to copy the Cancel Date folder three times.
2. After you have made these three copies, rename the new folders to **Order Date**, **Request Date**, and **Ship Date**, respectively.
3. Make sure you assign a unique identifier to each new folder.
4. Rename the Cancel Date items in these folders to be **Order Date**, **Request Date**, and **Ship Date**, respectively.
5. Add one join from each new folder to the Sales folder. As you do this, make sure you join on the correct items, with the Order Date folder joining to the Orderdate item, the Request Date joining to the Reqdate item, and the Ship Date joining to the Shipdate item.
6. Expanding the Sales folder, it now looks like this:

As you can see in the illustration, there are now seven joins into the Sales folder.

Creating a New Complex Geographic folder   We will create one new folder for the geographic rollup, containing all of the customer data, along with the city, district, and region data.

In our Sales fact folder there is a customer ID, which has a N:1 (many-to-one) join to the customer folder. The customer folder, in turn, has a N:1 join to the city, which in turn joins to district, which joins to region.

To create the Geographic rollup, use the following workflow:

1. Create a new complex folder.
2. Name both the new folder and its identifier **Geography**.
3. Drag the Cust ID from our Customer folder into the new folder.
4. Drag the remaining customer items.
5. Drag the City Name from the City folder.
6. Drag the District Name from the District folder.

7. Drag the Region Name from the Region folder.

8. Create a new join from the new folder to the Sales folder, joining on the Customer ID.

9. Hide the Customer ID in the Sales folder.

10. Hide the four original folders.

Creating a New Complex Products Folder   We will create one new folder for the product rollup, containing all of the product and product line data. In our Sales folder there is a product ID, which has a N:1 (many-to-one) join to the product folder. The product folder, in turn, has a N:1 join to the product line.

To create the Geographic rollup, use the following workflow:

1. Create a new complex folder.

2. Name both the new folder and its identifier **Product**.

3. Drag the Prod ID from our Products folder into the new folder.

4. Drag the remaining product items.

5. Drag the Line Name from the Prod Line folder.

6. Create a new join from the new folder to the Sales folder, joining on the Product ID.

7. Hide the Product ID in the Sales folder.

8. Hide the two original folders.

Notes about Complex Folders   Whenever you use complex folders, note these points:

■   Lists of values are copied, and the item classes are shared with the original items.

■   Joins are not copied, they must be created manually.

■   Complex folders make great candidates for creating hierarchies.

■   Hierarchies make great candidates for cascading parameters. A prerequisite of being able to create cascading parameters is that the items must belong to a hierarchy.

Adding Custom Folders

A custom folder is based on SQL that you key directly into Discoverer. While there are many reasons for using custom folders, there are three that we would like to discuss here:

■   To create a new list of values

■   To create an alternative sort sequence for a data set that does not have a natural sort

■   To pull data from a database link

We will discuss each of these in turn, but first let us show you how easy it is to create a custom folder.

To create a custom folder, use the following workflow:

1. Single-click the business area heading such that the business area name is highlighted.

2. Right-click the business area name; Discoverer will pop up a context menu.

3. From the context pop-up menu, select New Custom Folder. Discoverer opens the following Custom Folder dialog box:

4. Key or paste the SQL code into the box.
5. Give the folder a unique Name.
6. Click the Validate SQL button to check if the SQL is okay for Discoverer's use.
7. If the SQL is invalid, you will see the following message:

NOTE
The actual ORA error message will vary depending upon what is wrong with your code. In this situation, the ORA 00936 means that we have forgotten to include a required element. We actually forgot to SELECT anything from our SQL!

8. Please note that not all SQL that is valid in SQL Plus is valid in Discoverer. We will explain this in the next section. You may have to keep plugging away until Discoverer says it is valid.
9. If the SQL is valid, you will see the following message:
10. Whether you have entered valid or invalid SQL, so long as you enter a unique name for the folder, Discoverer will allow you to click OK and save the folder.

NOTE
*Discoverer will allow you to create a custom folder with invalid SQL.
This is done for development purposes, allowing you to save what
you have done so far and come back to it later when you have figured
out what the problem is. This also allows you to create some SQL and
then ask a colleague to take a look at it to see if he or she can figure
out why it is not working.*

If you have a custom folder that has invalid code, perhaps you should save what you have
done so far and come back to it later. When the code is invalid and you click OK, Discoverer
displays the following message:

If you click Yes, Discoverer will save the folder. Don't worry, your users will not be able
to select from this folder while it is in an invalid state.

If you have a custom folder that is currently valid and you add some additional code that
makes it invalid, you will see this message:

Getting the SQL Valid in a Custom Folder   One of the most common complaints that we see
from inexperienced administrators is that Discoverer says that their SQL is invalid. As mentioned
in the preceding section, not all SQL that is valid in SQL Plus will compile inside Discoverer.
You have to remember that Discoverer needs to have a unique name for every item in the SELECT
statement.

Look at the following code, which is valid in SQL Plus but not valid in Discoverer. Because
Discoverer strips off table prefixes from custom code, it will not be able to differentiate between
the two HEADER_ID columns.

```
SELECT
SOH.HEADER_ID,
SOL.HEADER_ID
FROM
SO_HEADERS_ALL SOH, SO_LINES_ALL SOL
WHERE
SOL.HEADER_ID = SOH.HEADER_ID
```

Changing the code as follows is valid:

```
SELECT
SOH.HEADER_ID SOH_HEADER_ID,
SOL.HEADER_ID SOL_LINE_ID
FROM
SO_HEADERS_ALL SOH, SO_LINES_ALL SOL
WHERE
SOL.HEADER_ID = SOH.HEADER_ID
```

Using a Custom Folder to Create a New List of Values   We mentioned earlier in this chapter that you should not be creating lists of values from tables that have millions of rows of data. This is because of the performance hit on the database by Discoverer executing a SELECT DISTINCT from a million-row table. To overcome this, the solution is to use a custom folder.

To use a custom folder to create a list of values, use the following workflow:

1. Determine what the list of values should be. You can do this either by selecting from a separate dimension folder or by using DUAL.

2. Create a custom folder using the SQL that you have developed.

3. Create a new list of values based on the item in the custom folder.

4. Attach the list of values to the original item by right-clicking the item and, from the pop-up menu, selecting Properties.

5. In the Item Properties box look for the property called Item Class. When you click in here, you will be presented with a list of the valid item classes that Discoverer thinks could be suitable.

6. Select the new item class from the list presented.

NOTE
Discoverer does some filtering on the item classes to not show you the lists of values that are not suitable. For example, if the column you are working on is defined as being a Number, Discoverer will offer you only numeric lists of values. It won't offer you anything based on a VARCHAR or DATE, because it knows these would not work!

7. Click OK.

From here on, every time a user clicks the plus icon alongside the item in the original folder, Discoverer will execute the code contained in the custom folder to generate the list of values. The following two examples show this to good effect.

Custom Folder Based on a Dimension Table
Let's say you have an Oracle Applications system and you need to get a list of values based on the currency contained in your PO Lines, but you have millions of purchase orders and it takes too long to get the list by querying the PO Lines. The following code will give you a list of just the active currency codes contained in the system:

```
SELECT CURR_CODE
FROM APPS.FND_CURRENCIES_ACTIVE_V
```

If you place this code inside a custom folder, you will see a single item called CURR_CODE. Creating a list of values on this item will produce the list in seconds.

Custom Folder Using DUAL

Let's say you have a system that has ten million rows, and you have a column called Active that has only two values, a Y to indicate Yes and N to indicate No. The following code will give you a list containing just two values, Y and N:

```
SELECT 'Y' ACTIVE_STATUS FROM DUAL
UNION
SELECT 'N' ACTIVE_STATUS FROM DUAL
```

Placing this code within a custom folder will cause Discoverer to generate a new folder containing a single item called ACTIVE_STATUS. Creating a list of values on this item will produce the list in a fraction of a second.

Using a Custom Folder to Create an Alternative Sort Sequence   Earlier in this chapter we mentioned that we would show you how to use a custom folder to generate the days of the week list of values. The following code will give you a new folder containing two items, one called DOY and one called SEQUENCE:

```
SELECT 'SUNDAY' DOY, 1 SEQUENCE FROM DUAL
UNION
SELECT 'MONDAY' DOY, 2 SEQUENCE FROM DUAL
UNION
SELECT 'TUESDAY' DOY, 3 SEQUENCE FROM DUAL
UNION
SELECT 'WEDNESDAY' DOY, 4 SEQUENCE FROM DUAL
UNION
SELECT 'THURSDAY' DOY, 5 SEQUENCE FROM DUAL
UNION
SELECT 'FRIDAY' DOY, 6 SEQUENCE FROM DUAL
UNION
SELECT 'SATURDAY' DOY, 7 SEQUENCE FROM DUAL
```

If you create a new list of values based on the DOY, using the SEQUENCE as the alternative sort item, the list will be generated in the order you want.

Using a Custom Folder to Pull Data from a Database Link   Sometimes when working with data, you may find that the piece of data you need is located in another database. Once again, let's say we are working in an Oracle Applications environment and that you have a data warehouse that has pulled in the SALESREP ID but somehow not the SALESREP NAME, and your users want to see the name. You ask your Oracle Warehouse Builder team if they can correct the code, and they say they can but not for another six months. Rather than telling your users that the request will have to wait, you use the following code to pull both the SALESREP_ID and SALESREP_NAME:

```
SELECT DISTINCT
RSA.RA_SALESREP_ID SALESREP_ID,
RSA.NAME SALESREP_NAME
FROM
APPS.RA_SALESREPS@DW_TO_PROD RSA
```

Adding New Folders from the Database

You can add new folders from the database very easily. In fact, this is what we did to create the business area in the first place.

To create a new folder from the database, use the following workflow:

1. Single-click the business area heading so the business area name is highlighted.
2. Right-click the business area name; Discoverer will open a pop-up menu.
3. From the context pop-up menu, select New Folder from Database.

Discoverer reopens the Load Wizard that we used at the beginning of Chapter 17.

Managing Folder Properties

Like all other objects in Discoverer, folders have properties. These properties are managed from the Folder Properties dialog box.

To display the Folder Properties dialog box, use the following workflow:

1. Right-click the folder whose properties you want to maintain, and from the pop-up menu select Properties.
2. Discoverer displays the Folder Properties dialog box, as shown in Figures 18-4 and 18-5.
3. Having changed any property, click OK to commit the change.

As you can see in Figures 18-4 and 18-5, there are four tabs to the Folder Properties dialog box:

- **General** On this tab, shown in Figure 18-4 for a complex folder and in Figure 18-5 for a folder based on a database object, you will find the following general properties:

  - **Name** This is the name of the folder and must be unique in the EUL.

  - **Description** This is an optional property and one that is greatly underused. When an end user clicks a folder that has a Description, Desktop or Plus displays the text that is contained in it. You should therefore make good use of this property.

  - **Visible to User** This is a Yes/No property. When set to No, the folder will not be visible to the end user. Be careful making folders invisible after the fact because this can upset users and even prevent existing workbooks from opening.

  - **Database** If the folder is based on a database object, Discoverer displays the name of the database where the object is located.

  - **Owner** If the folder is based on a database object, Discoverer displays the name of the owner of the object here.

  - **Object** If the folder is based on a database object, Discoverer displays the name of the object here.

  - **Optimizer Hints** If you are used to working with optimizer hints and you find that end-user performance is bad, you might want to try adding optimizer hints here. In the authors' experience, if you find that hints are necessary, you may well need to create a database view instead and base the folder on that view.

  - **Identifier** This is the unique identifier for the folder in the EUL.

FIGURE 18-4   *Folder Properties dialog box for a complex folder*

■   **Dependents**   On this tab Discoverer will display a list of all the secondary objects that are dependent upon this folder. Examples of secondary objects are

   ■   Item classes (lists of values)

   ■   Joins

   ■   Workbooks

FIGURE 18-5   *Folder Properties dialog box for a folder based on a database object*

The following illustration shows the Dependents tab for our Sales folder. We recommend that you always check for workbook dependencies whenever you are about to make a major change to a folder, such as to remove a join or disable reach-through to a base folder.

NOTE
If you do not check for dependent workbooks, and you proceed with your change, the workbooks will no longer open and it will be your fault. We can almost guarantee that when the user complains that a workbook no longer opens, you will not connect the two events and will be left scratching your head.

- **Components** On this tab, which is displayed only for a complex folder, Discoverer displays a list of the objects that are being used to create the complex folder. These objects include:

  - Folders
  - Items
  - Joins

Here, you can see the Components tab for our Cancel Date folder:

- **Reach-Through** On this tab, which is also displayed only for a complex folder, Discoverer allows you to define the objects that can be reached through this folder. We will describe reach-through in detail in the next section.

Using Reach-Through from a Complex Folder
One of the really clever features of Discoverer is *reach-through*. This features allows

Desktop and Plus users to add items to their worksheets from the base folders that were used to create the complex folders. A base folder can be any of the following:

■ A simple folder based on a database object

■ A custom folder based on SQL

■ Another complex folder

If reach-through is enabled, when a user selects from one of the complex folders, all of the enabled reach-through folders from which the complex folder was created become available for selection.

You may say that you could already achieve this by adding joins from the complex folder back to its base folders. This is true, except it is not very elegant and not very efficient. For a start, you have all those extra joins to maintain, and it can also affect performance. The best way is to enable reach-through.

To enable reach-through from a complex folder back to one or more of its constituent base folders, use the following workflow:

1. Right-click the complex folder that you want reach-through to enable, and from the pop-up menu, select Properties. Discoverer displays the Folder Properties dialog box.

2. Click the Reach-Through tab.

3. Click the check box against the base folder(s) that you want to allow the users to reach.

4. Click OK to complete the reach-through.

The illustration shows the Reach-Through tab for our Cancel Date folder with reach-through enabled back to the original Month and Quarter folders.

Canceling Reach-Through While canceling reach-through is a very simple task, you need to be very careful. If you cancel reach-through to a folder that has been used in a user's workbook, the user will no longer be able to open that workbook.

To cancel reach-through, use the following workflow:

1. Right-click the complex folder that is currently reach-through enabled, and from the pop-up menu, select Properties. Discoverer displays the Folder Properties dialog box.

2. Click the Reach-Through tab.

3. Uncheck the box against the base folder that you no longer want to allow users to reach.

4. Discoverer understands that disabling reach-through can have disastrous consequences for your users and displays the Remove Reach-Through dialog box:

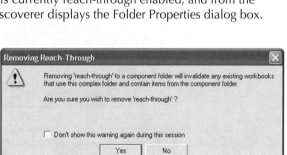

5. When prompted "Are you sure you wish to remove reach-through," clicking Yes confirms your understanding of the consequences, while clicking No abandons the reach-through removal. If you continue with the removal and there was a workbook using the reach-through-enabled folder, the user will get this message in Desktop:

The user will get this message in Plus:

To rectify this situation, all you have to do is re-enable the reach-through, if you can remember what you did. Perhaps it is better that you check dependencies first!

Even if you clicked Yes in the previous step, it is still not too late to abandon the removal. Clicking Cancel will abort what you have started.

If you are sure that you want to remove the reach-through, click OK.

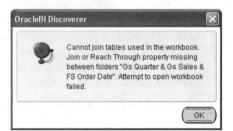

Reach-Through Restrictions   As an administrator, there are several restrictions that you need to be aware of when working with the reach-through capability of Discoverer:

■ The Discoverer Administrator tool will not allow you to enable reach-through if there is a join in existence between the base folder and the complex folder. Discoverer will generate the following error message:

■ The Discoverer Administrator tool will not allow you to create a join between a base folder and its associated complex folder if reach-through has been enabled. Discoverer will generate the following error message:

■ When you have a reach-through-enabled folder, and you are using Discoverer's automatic summary management (ASM) feature to create summary folders, Discoverer will not generate summary folder information on the folders that are reach-through enabled.

■ Items that are in folders that are joined to the reach-through-enabled folder are not available for selection by the end user. The reach-through works only to the folder that is reach-through enabled using the implied join.

■ There must be at least one item from the base folder in the complex folder for reach-through to work. In other words, if you edit a complex folder and remove all the items from a reach-through-enabled base folder, the implied join between the two folders will be removed. Any user workbook that was using the implied join to get data from the base folder will fail.

■ If you remove a join between a complex folder and a base table in order to enable reach-through and a user's workbook was using that join, the workbook will no longer open and the user will see the dreaded "Cannot join tables used in the workbook. Item dependency" error message. Therefore, before removing any join, please check the impact.

Hiding a Folder

After you have created complex folders, it is common practice to hide the non-reach-through-enabled base folders upon which the complex folder has been created.

To hide a folder, use this workflow:

1. Right-click the folder you want to hide.
2. From the pop-up menu select Properties.
3. Change Visible to user from Yes to No.
4. Click OK.

Hierarchy Enhancements

A hierarchy allows a user to drill through the data. Typically we use 1:N relationships to define hierarchies in a business area so that users can roll up data or drill down. In a database, there are two types of drill:

■ **Roll Up**   This reduces a query by allowing a user to include data from a higher level of the hierarchy, essentially summarizing the data. For example, you could roll up from a Month to a Quarter to see the whole quarter's revenue.

■ **Drill Down**   This expands a query by allowing a user to include data from a lower level, essentially bringing in more detail items to the query. For example, you could drill down from a Quarter to a Month to see the revenue for all of the months in the quarter.

In both types, Discoverer may requery the database. As well as the two database hierarchy types, there are two kinds of Discoverer hierarchy:

■ **Item hierarchies**   According to Oracle, these are hierarchies on anything that is not a date; however, we will show you how to use these for dates too.

■ **Date hierarchies**   These work only on dates. When you opt to allow Discoverer to create a date hierarchy, you need to be aware of what Discoverer will do and how this can impact performance. We will cover this later in the chapter.

Date Hierarchy or Item Hierarchy?

We are frequently asked where we stand with regard to using date hierarchies. To be truthfully honest, we rarely use date hierarchies and never use them for anything other than the simplest of folders. Let us explain.

As a concept, Oracle's implementation of date hierarchies in Discoverer is clever, really clever. What happens is that Discoverer creates a hierarchy of date format masks, inserting new items into the folder, one for each time element. At run time, Discoverer applies those format masks, using the TO_CHAR function, to evaluate each element of the hierarchy. The problem here is that these functions have to be evaluated against every row of the data in order to determine whether a filter that is being applied against one of those elements is true or false.

During the early summer of 2005, we had cause to visit a client of ours who was having trouble with performance. They complained that a worksheet running against a single table was taking over ten minutes to run. The first thing we noticed is that they had defined a date hierarchy on every date in the transaction folder. There were ten dates in that folder, and every one was using five different time elements. This made us step back and think. Our curiosity aroused, we wondered how many rows of data there were in that table. When we looked at the database, we were amazed to find that the table in question had more than two million rows. To make things worse, the users had constructed workbooks that used all of the time elements for all of the dates. In effect, 50 TO_CHAR functions were being performed on every row of the data, and of course the users were filtering on non-indexed items.

The first thing we did was to drop all of the date hierarchies. We then created a new materialized view that had all of the time elements prebuilt and pre-indexed. Next we created individual date folders, as you have seen us do in our tutorial, for each of the important dates. Finally, we created new item hierarchies, one per date folder, to replace the old date hierarchies. The time filter was applied against an index in this folder, joining back to an index in the main folder. When we ran a workbook against this setup, it ran in less than one minute.

You may think this is an extreme case. Believe us, it is not. There are organizations out there with billions of rows of data in single tables. If you attempt to create a date hierarchy on these, you will be asking for trouble. Our recommendation is to use a materialized view for your date elements using an item hierarchy that simply links the elements together. No functions, no TO_CHAR, no hassle.

Date Hierarchies and Indexes   We recommend that you not create date hierarchies on dates that are indexed. This is an area of great concern to us and one that we have seen affect performance so many times.

According to Oracle, "If you apply a date hierarchy to a date item from an indexed table, a query that includes one of these date items will not use the indexes (which can reduce performance)." We will qualify this statement by saying that this *will* affect performance, big time. The index will not be used, and Oracle will undertake full table scans every time.

We will show you how to create both types of Discoverer hierarchy. In both cases we will use the Cancel Date for the hierarchy.

Creating an Item Hierarchy

To create an item hierarchy, use the following workflow:

1. Click the Hierarchies tab.

2. Right-click the business area in which you wish to create the hierarchy, and from the pop-up list, select New Hierarchy. This opens the Hierarchy Wizard as seen in Figure 18-6.

FIGURE 18-6   *Hierarchy Wizard Step 1*

3. Check Item Hierarchy.
4. Click Next. This opens the second screen of the Hierarchy Wizard.

5. Locate and open the folder containing the items that will be in the hierarchy. As you can see in the preceding image, we have selected the Cancel Date, Fiscal Month, Fiscal Quarter, and Fiscal Year.
6. Select the lowest-level drill item and move or paste it in the right-hand side.
7. Select the next items, in order, until you have selected all of the items you need.

8. When all items are selected, click Next. This opens the third and last screen of the Hierarchy Wizard.

9. Give a meaningful name and optional description to the hierarchy.
10. Click Finish.

Creating a Date Hierarchy

To create a date hierarchy, use the following workflow:

1. Click the Hierarchies tab.
2. Right-click the business area in which you wish to create the hierarchy, and from the pop-up list, select New Hierarchy. This opens the Hierarchy Wizard as seen in Figure 18-6.
3. Check Date Hierarchy.
4. Click Next. This opens the second screen of the Hierarchy Wizard.

5. Select the hierarchy items that you want to include by expanding the group elements and pasting the required time element into the right-hand side.

6. If the time element that you need is not among the available elements in a group, click the New Format button. This opens the New Date Format dialog box. Select the Group that you want to define a new element for, and in the New Format box type the format mask for the new time element. When done, click OK. The new element will be available in the chosen group.

NOTE
In the preceding box, we have defined a new element called YYY in the Year group. For a list of all the valid date format masks, please refer to Appendix B.

7. Select the time elements, in descending order of Group, until you have selected all of the elements that you need

8. In the following example, you can see that we have chosen 'YYYY' from the Year group, "Q"Q from the Quarter group, "Mon-RR" from the Month group, and "DD-Mon-YYYY" from the Date group.

NOTE
The Promote, Demote, and Description boxes in the Hierarchy Wizard will be grayed out until you click one of the elements that you have chosen. Then you can provide a description for the element and manipulate the hierarchy by demoting and promoting elements.

9. When all elements have been selected, click Next. This opens the third screen of the Hierarchy Wizard.

10. Optionally select the date item that you want to associate with this hierarchy. As you can see in the preceding example, we have used the Cancel Date.

NOTE
You do not need to select any date item in this step. If you leave the Selected box empty, you will be creating a new template. For more information on date templates, see the next section.

11. When you have finished with Step 3, click Next. This opens the fourth and last screen of the Hierarchy Wizard.

12. Give a meaningful name and optional description to the hierarchy.

13. Click Finish.

14. Discoverer creates and adds one new item per time element to the folder, as you can see in this example:

Date Hierarchy Templates

In the preceding section we commented that if you left the third screen of the Date Hierarchy Wizard empty, you would in effect be creating a new date hierarchy template. But what is a date hierarchy template? Put in its simplest form, according to Oracle, "A date hierarchy template enables you to define a date hierarchy that you can apply to date items. A date item uses information that specifies the date, month, year, and time. Discoverer uses this information to calculate, for example, quarter, week, and days of the week. A date hierarchy template automatically creates items based on a date item, for example to represent the year or month."

It is far more efficient to reuse a date hierarchy than to have to redefine the hierarchy every time you want to create a new one. This is where the template comes in. By saving a set of date hierarchy elements as a date hierarchy template, you can reuse this any number of times.

Creating and Selecting Your Hierarchies

How many hierarchies do you need in your business area? The number will vary depending upon how many rollups or drills you need. However, in our case, we need to create one item hierarchy for each of the six new complex folders that we have created:

- Cancel Date

- Order Date

- Request Date

- Ship Date

- Geography

- Product

We have already shown you how to create the Cancel Date hierarchy using both Item and Date hierarchies. Because we are using a custom fiscal calendar that has been prebuilt and pre-indexed, we will use item hierarchies for all of our dates. Simply following the instructions given earlier for creating an item hierarchy, we created the three other time hierarchies on the Order Date, Request Date, and Ship Date folders.

Turning to the Geographic and Product hierarchies, these are simple to build. They are both item hierarchies.

Geographic Hierarchy

Our geographic hierarchy is based on the Geography folder. At the lowest level this folder joins on the Customer ID to our Sales folder. The customer is the lowest-level item in the hierarchy. Looking at the available items, we can see that the Customer Name is available to use in the

Geography folder. In turn, we need to pick something from the other base folders that make up our complex Geography folder. If you recall, we have four 1:N folders making up the complex folder:

- Customer
- City
- District
- Region

It makes sense, therefore, that because the tables that these base folders are based on have a primary/foreign key relationship, we select one City item, one District item, and one Region item. In our final hierarchy we chose the following:

- Customer Name
- City Name
- District Name
- Region Name

Any sort of drilling on these items will perform very fast.

Product Hierarchy

We will turn our attention to the product hierarchy that will be based on the Product complex folder. At the lowest level this folder joins on the Product ID to our Sales folder. The product is therefore the lowest-level item in this hierarchy. Looking at the available items, we can see that both the Product Name and the Product Size are available to us in the Product folder. However, the join between the base Products folder and the Sales folder is on the Product ID, which in turn is linked to the Product Name. Therefore, the Product Name becomes the lowest element in our hierarchy. We need to pick something from the other base folder that forms part of our complex Product folder. If you recall, we have two 1:N folders making up this complex folder:

- Products
- Product Line

It makes sense that, because the tables that these base folders are based on have a primary/foreign key relationship, we should select the Product Line. In our final hierarchy we have the following:

- Product Name
- Product Line

Item Management

Why do we create new items? We create new items in the End User Layer to enable our users to

- Make better sense of the data

■ Avoid mistakes

■ Have guaranteed working algorithms

For these reasons, we will always look to create new algorithms in the business area whenever possible. If you look back to the early part of this chapter where we created a new item to convert a string into a number for use in a complex join, you already know how to add a new item to a folder. We therefore will not dwell on this point, other than to say that you will be using the New Item dialog box.

In this section we will not belabor how to create new items but concentrate instead on the following:

■ Types of items

■ Useful algorithms

■ Sorting items

■ Assigning indexes to an item

Types of Items

Discoverer understands three types of items:

■ **Columns**   These items are based on columns from objects in the underlying database.

■ **Components**   These items are based on the components of a custom folder.

■ **Calculations**   These items are based on calculated items that you, the administrator, create on behalf of your users.

Useful Algorithms

A number of useful, standard algorithms can be created in Discoverer. We will describe three of these:

■ **Profit**   Calculated as the Selling Price minus the Cost Price

■ **Standard margin**   Calculated as profit divided by SUM of the selling price

■ **Standard markup**   Calculated as profit divided by SUM of the cost price

When creating calculated items using division, we must make sure that we allow for and ensure that we do not introduce divide by zero errors. This subject was covered in depth in Chapter 13, where we described the techniques that you must use to avoid these errors.

Adding Items to a Complex Folder

If you are creating new items in a complex folder, Discoverer lists all of the folders that were used to create the complex folder. Discoverer also displays all of the items in the original base folders, irrespective of whether they are being used in the complex folder. This is very useful to know, especially if you are adding calculated items to the complex folder.

This allows you to build new items on any item from the base folders, not just on the items in the complex folder itself.

Sorting Items

Should you wish to sort the items in a folder, Discoverer provides a means to do so. To sort the items in a folder, use the following workflow:

1. Right-click the folder that you wish to sort.

2. From the pop-up menu, select Sort Items.

3. Discoverer displays the following Alphabetical Sort dialog box:

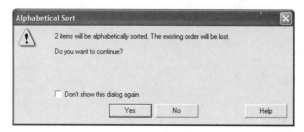

4. As you can see in the preceding illustration, Discoverer tells you how many items are to be sorted and prompts "Do you want to continue?" Click Yes to sort, or No to cancel.

Descriptive Lists of Values: Assigning Indexes to an Item

Another new feature of Discoverer is the ability to add an indexed item to another item to improve parameter selection performance in the end-user tools. So long as both items exist in the same folder, and neither is hidden, you can tell Discoverer to search an index rather than the original item.

Let's explore this some more by using the following example. Suppose you have a base table that has a Product Name and a Product ID, with the Product ID being indexed and the Product Name not indexed. Most users will know a product by its name, not by its ID value, and so will want to create parameters based on the name. However, because the name is not indexed, the query could take a long time. To overcome this poor performance, Oracle has introduced the concept of *descriptive* lists of values. The list of values, in the parameter selection screen, is shown along with its associated ID. However, when the query is executed, Discoverer uses the ID.

To set up a descriptive list of values, use the following workflow:

1. Open and expand a folder that contains both the item and the indexed item.

2. Right-click the item, and from the pop up menu, select Properties.

3. Navigate to the property called Indexed Item. It is located toward the bottom of the list.

NOTE
In order for this to work, the item must have a list of values associated with it before the Indexed Item property is available. If you do not have a list of values associated with the item, the property will be grayed out.

4. Click the Indexed Item property and from the pop-up list, select the indexed item that you wish to use.

5. As you can see in the preceding illustration, Discoverer inserts a marker alongside any indexed item that it finds in the folder.

6. Select the indexed item that matches one-to-one with the original item and click OK.

7. As you can see next, Discoverer prompts "Setting an indexed item requires a new LOV to be created" and offers you OK or Cancel.

8. Click OK to complete the attachment of the index.

In Discoverer Plus, whenever the user creates a parameter on the customer name, he or she will be given the opportunity to search by name or by the index. Searching by the index will greatly improve performance.

Using Descriptive Lists of Values in Plus

Having set up the descriptive lists of values, perhaps you might be interested in seeing how an end user can take advantage of this in Discoverer Plus. For this example, we created a descriptive list of values on the Channel using the Channel ID as the indexed item.

We created a new workbook using the Channel and then started to create a new condition using a parameter. As you can see in the illustration that follows, Discoverer now allows the user to check the box named "Enable users to select either indexes or values."

With the indexes or values box checked, the boxes immediately below are enabled. The first, as you can see in the preceding image, is a drop-down that allows the user to specify that an Index or a Value should be used as the default. As you can see, we have opted to use the index as the default and have selected "(2) INTERNET" from the drop-down.

When this parameter is presented to a user in a working query, Discoverer displays the revised Edit Parameter Values dialog box.

In the preceding dialog box, you can see that Discoverer is allowing the user to choose whether he or she wants to input the index value or the actual value. Many users actually know the index values or codes that are being used on the system and may prefer to key in the code value when selecting parameters. The preceding explanation shows you how to enable this.

Summary

In this chapter you learned how to continue with the remaining business area checks. You learned the value of a well-designed business area as it affects the end user. We demonstrated how to manage lists of values and joins. We showed you how to add new folders, followed by managing hierarchies. Finally we showed you some of the more advanced mechanisms for item management, culminating in an explanation of how to manage descriptive lists of values.

CHAPTER
19

Interacting with
the End User

his chapter, another in the series of chapters dedicated to the Discoverer administrator, is packed with useful workflows that will help you interact with your end users. The intention of this chapter is to complement the last section of Chapter 15. If you look back at that section, entitled "What Can the Discoverer Administrator Do for You?," you will see that it contains a list of approximately twenty topics. This chapter will take each of those topics, in turn, and describe or provide you with a workflow that will tackle the topic.

Several of the workflows that are needed to answer questions posed by the users have already been given in previous chapters. We will not repeat those workflows here but simply direct you to the relevant chapter. However, in this section you will find some totally new concepts being introduced or explained for the first time. Among the new topics that you will find in this chapter are managing access, managing privileges, creating predefined conditions, and managing scheduling.

In many of the workflows used within this chapter, you will be asked to click Cancel when the first screen of the Load Wizard appears. To understand what we are suggesting, please take a look at Figure 19-1.

Adding New Users

If you receive a request for a new user, you need either to ask your DBA to create an account or, if using Oracle Applications, to direct the user to the applications system administrator. For a standard EUL, the DBA will also need to know which privileges and roles should be granted. For an Apps-mode EUL, the system administrator will need to know which responsibilities should be granted.

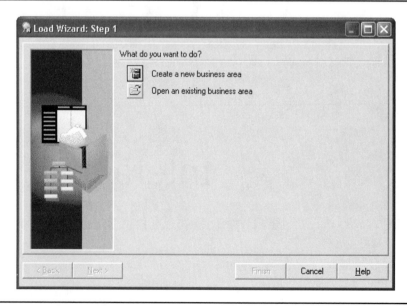

FIGURE 19-1   *Load Wizard Step 1*

Special database privileges are required for scheduling. These are dealt with later in this chapter.

In some cases, the user that you will be creating will have all or partial access to some of the features of the Discoverer Administrator tool. You need to work with the user to determine how much administration is required. If the user is to be a second administrator, you will need to ask your DBA to create a user that has the identical database privileges that you have.

Having created the user accounts, you need to assign the Discoverer privileges and grant access to the required business area. These are dealt with later in this chapter.

Granting Access to Business Areas

Having received a request from a user for access to a business area, before you log in to the Administrator tool to do the work, there are some other tasks you need to do first.

Presumably, the user already has an account. If not, you need to address this issue first. So, let's assume that the user has an account but does not have access to the business area that he or she is requesting. It is not your responsibility as the Discoverer administrator to decide who gets access to what. Your job is only to ensure that you obtain the necessary approval or rejection, and that the access is maintained on an ongoing basis.

There are two types of access for you to consider. These are

- Open

- Restricted

Open Access

Some business areas are considered open. By this we mean that anyone can have access without the need for higher-level approval. The only consideration should be, does the person need to have this access to do their job? If the answer is yes—and usually the manager can confirm this—the access should be granted.

Restricted Access and Insider Trading

However, many organizations have what are called "restricted" or secure business areas. These business areas need higher-level approval. All you need to do is submit the request to the person responsible. An example of a "restricted" business area is one that contains revenue information. If you are in an organization that releases periodic results to your shareholders, access to the revenue business area should be restricted to only those people who are allowed to see the results prior to publication. Using this data, an unauthorized user could use that information to buy or sell stock in your company or influence others to do so. This practice, called *insider trading,* is prohibited by law. It is therefore essential that those sensitive business areas are protected.

NOTE
If you grant access to secure data to a role or responsibility, you are in effect delegating the access for that secure data to whoever is responsible for managing those roles or responsibilities. Unless you have created special roles or responsibilities for this purpose, we strongly recommend you grant secure access to user accounts only.

Workflow to Grant Access

Assuming the user has been approved for access to a business area, to grant access to that business area, use the following workflow:

1. Launch the Discoverer Administrator tool.

2. When the Load Wizard displays, as seen in Figure 19-1, click Cancel.

3. From the menu bar, select Tools | Security. Discoverer opens the Security dialog box.

4. The Security dialog box has two tabs:

    ■ **Users -> Business Area**   This tab allows you to grant a single user or role to have access to one or more business areas.

    ■ **Business Area -> User**   This tab allows you to grant access to a single business area for one or more users or roles.

5. On the Users -> Business Area tab, you first need to select the user that you want to work with. Having selected the user or role, as shown next, Discoverer shows you the access currently assigned to that user or role.

NOTE
When working in Apps mode you will be working with responsibilities instead of roles. The label in the above box will therefore change to allow you to choose between users and responsibilities.

6. Using the Available and Selected business area boxes, adjust the access for the user, role or responsibility and then click OK.

7. On the Business Area -> User tab, use the drop-down alongside the Business Area box to select the area you want to work with.

8. Using the Available and Selected users/roles or users/responsibilities boxes, adjust the access for the business area and then click OK.

9. Inform the user that the access has been adjusted.

Granting User Edition Privileges

If a user comes to you and suggests that their Discoverer privileges are insufficient, you should discuss this with the user. Having determined what additional privileges the user needs, you should use the Privileges tab of Discoverer Administrator.

To grant additional user edition privileges, use the following workflow:

1. Launch the Discoverer Administrator tool.

2. When the Load Wizard displays, as seen in Figure 19-1, click Cancel.

3. From the menu bar, select Tools | Privileges. Discoverer opens the Privileges dialog box. As you can see in Figure 19-2, the Privileges dialog box has four tabs:

   ■ **Privileges** This tab allows you to assign multiple privileges to a single user or role.

   ■ **User/Role** This tab allows you to assign multiple users, roles or responsibilities to a single privilege.

   ■ **Query Governor** This tab to assign query governor privileges to a single user, role or responsibility.

   ■ **Scheduled Workbooks** This tab allows you to maintain the scheduling privileges for a single user. Scheduling is dealt with later in this chapter.

NOTE
In Apps mode the User/Role tab is labeled User/Responsibility.

We will deal with the Privileges, User/Role, and Query Governor tabs separately in the following sections.

Working with the Privileges Tab

To work with the Privileges tab, use the following workflow:

1. Launch the Privileges dialog box, shown in Figure 19-2, and click the Privileges tab.

2. Click the Select button. Discoverer opens the Select User/Role or Select User/ Responsibility search box.

3. Type or search for the user, role or responsibility for whom you want to assign privileges.

FIGURE 19-2 *Privileges dialog box*

NOTE
*If you have used previous versions of Discoverer, you may notice that
this box has changed. Whereas in older versions this used to be a
drop-down, it has now become a field that you have to search for first.
This has been done to improve performance. Oracle tell us that they
had cases where the user population ran into tens of thousands, and
populating a drop-down with ten thousand or more values takes time,
sometimes a lot of time. Hence, Oracle has provided this new search-
then-assign workflow.*

4. Click OK to close the Select User/Role or Select User/Responsibility search box.

5. As shown in Figure 19-3, Discoverer displays the current privileges for the user, role
   or responsibility.

NOTE
*For an explanation of what each privilege allows, please read ahead
to the section entitled "Discoverer Privileges Explained."*

6. Grant the privileges that are needed by checking the appropriate privilege boxes.

FIGURE 19-3 *Privileges tab*

7. Having worked with the privileges, use one of the following options:

■ **Apply** Click this to apply the privileges you have set and stay within the tab.

■ **OK** Click this to apply the privileges you have set and exit the tab.

■ **Cancel** Click this to exit the tab without applying privileges.

Working with the User/Role or User/Responsibility Tab

To work with the User/Role or User/Responsibility tab, use the following workflow:

1. Launch the Privileges dialog box, shown earlier in Figure 19-2, and click the User/Role or User/Responsibility tab.

2. Note the different areas of this tab, as shown here and described after these steps.

3. Having worked with the privileges, use one of the following options:

■ **Apply** Click this to apply the privileges you have set and stay within the tab.

■ **OK** Click this to apply the privileges you have set and exit the tab.

■ **Cancel** Click this to exit the tab without applying privileges.

These are the options available to you within the User/Role or User/Responsibility tab:

■ **Show users/roles with this privilege** Use the drop-down to select the privilege that you want to administer.

■ **A Show area** This contains two check boxes:

■ **Users** Check this box to show only users who have the privilege.

■ **Roles** Check this box to show only roles who have the privilege.

■ **A list of users** Use the check boxes alongside the user or role to grant or remove the privileges.

NOTE
In Apps mode, the word User is replaced by the word Responsibility.

Working with the Query Governor Tab

To work with the Query Governor tab, use the following workflow:

1. Launch the Privileges dialog box, shown in Figure 19-2, and click the Query Governor tab.

2. As you can see in the preceding illustration, this tab has the areas described next.

NOTE
*Using the Discoverer Viewer Preferences tab, or the Query Governor
tab from Tools | Options in both Desktop and Plus, a user can apply
his or her own query governor settings. However, a user can apply
only settings that are lower than or equal to the settings that the
administrator has set.*

3. Having made the query governor settings for the user, use one of the following options:

    ■ **Apply**   Click this to apply the settings you have set and stay within the tab.

    ■ **OK**   Click this to apply the settings you have set and exit the tab.

    ■ **Cancel**   Click this to exit the tab without applying the settings.

These are the options available to you within the Query Governor tab:

■ **Show query limits for**   Use the Select button to pick the user that you want to
administer.

■ **A Query Governor area**   This contains three check boxes:

- **Warn user if predicted time exceeds** Check this box and then use the Seconds box to set a query limit for the user. When set, with the query predictor enabled, Discoverer will estimate how long a query will take and warn the user if the predicted time exceeds this limit.

- **Prevent queries from running longer than** Check this box and then use the Seconds box to set a maximum query limit for the user. When set, with the query predictor enabled, Discoverer will estimate how long a query will take and prevent the user from running any query that is predicted to exceed this time limit.

- **Limit retrieved data to** Check this box and then use the Rows box to set a maximum query limit for the user. When set, Discoverer prevents the user from pulling more than the number of rows defined here.

Discoverer Privileges Explained

In this section we will give a detailed explanation of both the administration and the user privileges that are under your control.

Administration Privileges Explained

The Privileges tab of the Privileges dialog box, shown in Figure 19-3, shows all of the administration privileges that you can grant. Table 19-1 gives a detailed explanation of each of these privileges.

Privilege	Description
Administration Privilege	Checking this allows a user or role to log in to the Discoverer Administrator tool. Until this box is checked, you will not be able to assign the individual administrator privileges.
Format Business Area	Grant this privilege if you want to allow the administrator to edit formatting information in an existing business area to which they have access. Such formatting information includes folders, summary folders, joins, and items. Granting this privilege allows the user or role to specify names, descriptions, default format masks, and placement.
Create/Edit Business Areas	Grant this privilege if you want to allow the administrator to create and modify business areas, folders, summary folders, joins, calculations, conditions, hierarchies, and item classes.
Create/Edit Summaries	Grant this privilege if you want to allow the administrator to create summary folders using the Discoverer Administrator tool. The use of this privilege also requires database privileges for materialized views.
Set Privilege	Grant this privilege if you want to allow the administrator to maintain and modify user privileges using this dialog box. You cannot grant this privilege to a role.
Manage Scheduled Workbooks	Grant this privilege if you want to allow the administrator to monitor and maintain the schedule for scheduled workbooks.

TABLE 19-1 *Administration Privileges*

User Privileges Explained

The Privileges tab of the Privileges dialog box, shown in Figure 19-3, also shows all of the user privileges that you can grant. Table 19-2 gives a detailed explanation of each of these privileges.

Privilege	Description
Desktop and Plus Privilege	Checking this allows a user or role to log in to Discoverer Desktop and Discoverer Plus. Until this box is checked, you will not be able to assign the individual privileges. A user who has been authorized to use Discoverer will always be able to log in to Viewer—you cannot revoke this privilege.
Create/Edit Query	Grant this privilege if you want to allow the user or role to create new worksheets and workbooks. Without this privilege, the user will be able to run only existing workbooks. You should therefore unset this if the user only needs to run Viewer and does not need to make changes.
Collect Query Statistics	Grant this privilege if you want Discoverer to maintain statistics about how the user's queries perform.
Item Drill	Grant this privilege if you want to allow the user or role to be able to drill to detail within a worksheet. If you want to grant this privilege, you must also grant the Drill Out privilege.
Drill Out	Grant this privilege if you want to allow a user or role to be able to launch another application to see related information. Before a user can use this privilege, the administrator must create the drill using the Item Class Wizard, or edit the item properties and set the Content Type to <FILE>.
Grant Workbook	Grant this privilege if you want to allow a user or role to be able to share their workbooks with other users so that they can run and view them.
Schedule Workbooks	Grant this privilege if you want to allow a user to schedule a workbook to run at a later time and at regular intervals (i.e., daily, weekly, monthly). You cannot grant this privilege to a role, and the user must have certain database privileges; otherwise, this will not work.
Save Workbooks to Database	Grant this privilege if you want to allow a user or role to save their workbooks to the database. By default, Discoverer Desktop workbooks are saved on the user's hard drive. If the user is using Plus and you have not checked this box, the user will be unable to save.
Change Password	This privilege is not used in this release.
Create Link	This privilege, new to 10.1.2, allows you to control who is allowed to create their own drill links. A drill link is a way to access another worksheet or URL from a particular worksheet cell value.

TABLE 19-2   *User Privileges*

Adding Meaningful Descriptions to Business Areas, Folders, and Data Items

A very simple, yet very useful, means of helping users understand the data better is to add descriptions to the data objects. This adds no overhead to the processing of the system, yet many administrators do not assign meaningful descriptions. Of particular help to end users is the addition of meaningful descriptions to the following EUL objects:

■ Business areas

■ Folders

■ Items

Adding a Meaningful Description to a Business Area

To assign a meaningful description to a business area, use the following workflow:

1. Launch the Discoverer Administrator tool.

2. When the Load Wizard displays, as seen in Figure 19-1, click Open an existing business area.

3. Open the business area that needs a description.

4. Right-click the business area, and from the pop-up menu select Properties. Discoverer opens the Business Area Properties dialog box.

5. Enter a meaningful description for the business area.

6. Click OK.

Adding a Meaningful Description to a Folder

To assign a meaningful description to a folder, use the following workflow:

1. Launch the Discoverer Administrator tool.

2. When the Load Wizard displays, as seen in Figure 19-1, click Open an existing business area.

3. Open the business area that contains the folder.

4. Expand the business area and locate the folder.

5. Right-click the folder, and from the pop-up menu select Properties. Discoverer opens the Folder Properties dialog box.

6. Enter a meaningful description for the folder. Take a close look at the identifier. It looks like we should change this as well!

7. Click OK.

Adding a Meaningful Description to an Item

To assign a meaningful description to an item, use the following workflow:

1. Launch the Discoverer Administrator tool.

2. When the Load Wizard displays, as seen earlier in Figure 19-1, click Open an existing business area.

3. Open the business area that contains the folder.

4. Expand the business area and locate the folder that contains the item.

5. Expand the folder and locate the item.

6. Right-click the item, and from the pop-up menu select Properties. Discoverer opens the Item Properties dialog box.

7. Enter a meaningful description for the item.

8. Click OK.

Adding New Items to Folders

If you are approached by an end user who believes an item is missing from a folder, you need to sit down with the user and talk it over. You will probably also need to take a look at the user's worksheet to see whether you can pull the item in from another folder.

Having determined that the item is currently not available within any of the folders that the user currently has access to, you first need to determine whether the item exists within the EUL. If it does exist but is not accessible to the user's worksheet, you should look to create a join to the folder that contains the item. To do this, please look at the section called "Managing Joins" in Chapter 18.

At this stage, you have determined that the item does not exist within the EUL, so you need to add it. There are still some decisions that need to be taken, and these differ depending upon what type of folder you are working with.

Adding New Items to Simple Folders

As you know, a simple folder is one that is based on an underlying database object, where that object is a table, a view, or a materialized view. You need to examine these objects to determine whether the required item already exists within the object. If it does, all you need to do is refresh the folder. If the item does not exist, you will need to add it. However, adding a new item to a table can be difficult, especially if you are working in an Oracle Applications or data warehousing environment. If the item that is required can be evaluated using items that already exist, you might want to consider adding a calculated item to the folder. To do this, please look ahead to the section entitled "Creating New Items Based on Calculations."

If the item cannot be evaluated using items that already exist but the underlying object is a view or materialized view, you have a much better chance of getting the object changed. Assuming that you have been able to get the object changed, to make the new item available within the EUL, you need to refresh the object. If the object is a table and you are forbidden from altering it, we recommend you consider creating a view and then switching the folder to point at the view instead of the table. We will show you both of these two workflows.

Refreshing a Folder

To refresh a folder in order to bring in a new item, use the following workflow:

1. Launch the Discoverer Administrator tool.

2. When the Load Wizard displays, as seen earlier in Figure 19-1, click Open an existing business area.

3. Open the business area that contains the folder you want to refresh.

4. Locate the folder, right-click it, and from the pop-up menu select Refresh.

5. Discoverer will open the Refresh Wizard.

6. In Step 1 of the Refresh Wizard, shown next, you need to tell Discoverer from where it should refresh the folder.

7. Having determined where the folder will be refreshed from, click Finish.

8. Discoverer will now analyze the folder by comparing the contents of the folder with the contents of the database object.

9. When the analysis is complete, Discoverer will either tell you that no changes were found or display a dialog box of the changes. If any changes were uncovered, Discoverer will display the Refresh Business Area dialog box.

10. Use the check boxes alongside the changed items to signify whether you accept or reject the change.

11. Having made all of your selections, click OK.

12. Discoverer will make the necessary changes to your folder.

13. Before opening up the folder to the user, you need to check the properties of the new item to make sure that it is correct. At the very least, you need to check the following:

- **Default Position**   You need to determine whether this is a data point, or whether it should by default be located on the Top, Side, or Page axis.

- **Default Aggregate**   If the item is a data point, Discoverer will assign the default aggregate as being Detail. If this is not what you want—and it probably is not—you should change it.

14. Determine the position in the folder where the new item should be and move it to its final position.

15. Having completed all of your checks and made any adjustments, you should now inform the user that the item has been successfully added.

Switching a Folder from a Table to a View

To switch a folder from a table to a view, use the following workflow:

1. Create a new view in the database containing all of the original items.

2. Launch the Discoverer Administrator tool.

3. When the Load Wizard displays, as seen earlier in Figure 19-1, click Open an existing business area.

4. Open the business area that contains the folder you want to refresh.

5. Locate the folder, right-click it, and from the pop-up menu select Properties. Discoverer will open the Folder Properties dialog box.

6. In the Object property, click the object that you want to change. Discoverer will open the Choose Table or View dialog box.

7. Having chosen the new object, click OK. Discoverer does not validate that the new object contains all of the items, so you need to be very careful not to pick the wrong object.

8. Follow all of the steps in the preceding section to refresh the folder. Discoverer should locate the new item but should not detect any other changes.

9. If any additional changes are found, you should revisit the view and then restart this workflow.

Renaming a New Item and Using Headings

New items will come through from the database using the name of the column as it exists in the source table or view. Therefore, having added a new item from the database, you should check the name to make sure it complies with your organization's naming standard. If the name does not comply, you should change it.

As you know, when a user creates a worksheet, by default Discoverer takes the name of the item and uses that as the column heading. However, there are times, especially when the name is long, that you will want to use a different heading. Fortunately, Discoverer has a mechanism for doing just this.

To force Discoverer to use a different heading to the item's name, use the following workflow:

1. Right-click the item, and from the pop-up menu select Properties. Discoverer will open the Item Properties dialog box.

2. Scroll down to the property called Heading.

3. Change the value for the heading.

4. Click OK.

NOTE
By default, the item's heading is linked to the item's name; thus, if you change the name the heading will also change. However, if you edit the heading the link is broken, and the two properties must now be managed separately.

Adding New Items to Complex Folders

As you know, a complex folder is one that is based on one or more joined base folders. A base folder can be a simple, complex, or custom folder. Adding a new item to a complex folder is a simple task.

To add a new item to a complex folder, use the following workflow:

1. Determine which base folder contains the item that needs to be added to the complex folder.

2. Launch the Discoverer Administrator tool.

3. When the Load Wizard displays, as seen earlier in Figure 19-1, click Open an existing business area.

4. Open the business area that contains the complex folder to which you want to add the new item.

5. Open a second window by using Window | New Window on the menu bar.

6. Expand the base folder that contains the item that needs to be added to the complex folder.

7. Click the item and drag it into the complex folder.

8. Before opening up the folder to the user, you need to check the properties of the item to make sure that it is correct. At the very least, you need to check the following:

   ■ **Default Position**   You need to determine whether this is a data point, or whether it should by default be located on the Top, Side, or Page axis.

   ■ **Default Aggregate**   If the item is a data point, Discoverer will assign the default aggregate as being Detail. If this is not what you want—and it probably is not—you should change it.

9. Determine the position in the folder where the item should be and move it to its final position.

10. Having completed all of your checks and made any adjustments, you should now inform the user that the item has been successfully added.

Adding New Items to Custom Folders

As you know, a custom folder is a SQL script that you have created. This script is stored in the EUL and can be edited using the Custom Folder Properties dialog box.

To add a new item to a custom folder, use the following workflow:

1. Launch the Discoverer Administrator tool.

2. When the Load Wizard displays, as seen earlier in Figure 19-1, click Open an existing business area.

3. Open the business area that contains the custom folder to which you want to add the new item.

4. Right-click the custom folder, and from the pop-up box select Properties. Discoverer opens the Custom Folder Properties dialog box.

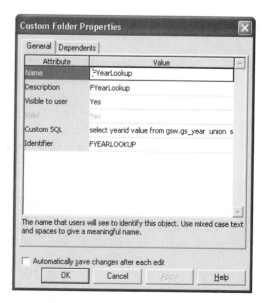

5. Click the Custom SQL property. Discoverer opens the following Edit Custom Folder dialog box:

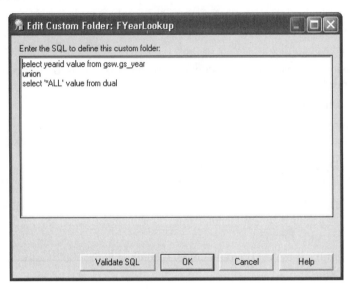

6. Change the SQL.

7. Use the Validate SQL button to confirm that the SQL is valid.

8. When you have valid SQL, click OK.

9. Click OK to close the Custom Folder Properties dialog box.

10. Before opening up the folder to the user, you need to check the properties of the item to make sure that it is correct. At the very least, you need to check the following:

   ■ **Default Position**   You need to determine whether this is a data point, or whether it should by default be located on the Top, Side, or Page axis.

   ■ **Default Aggregate**   If the item is a data point, Discoverer will assign the default aggregate as being Detail. If this is not what you want—and it probably is not—you should change it.

11. Determine the position in the folder where the item should be and move it to its final position.

12. Having completed all of your checks and made any adjustments, you should now inform the user that the item has been successfully added.

Creating New Folders

Your Discoverer administrator can create new folders within Discoverer. These folders can be based on SQL statements, extracts from the database, or even items contained in existing folders. If, as the administrator, you want to create a new folder, please look at the section called "Creating New Folders" in Chapter 18.

Creating Joins Between Folders

In both Desktop and Plus, Discoverer will gray out a folder if there is no join to it from any other folder that has been used as the basis for a worksheet. Sometimes this is just an oversight and there really should be a join. Perhaps you have just added a new folder to the EUL and you now need to join to the other folders. In either case, you need to manually add this join.

To create joins, please look at the section called "Managing Joins" in Chapter 18.

Creating Lists of Values

Most business areas are created with either none or the minimum number of lists of values. As time goes by and more and more users begin to use the system, the demand for additional lists of values will increase. As users cannot add lists of values, they will come to you, the administrator, and ask you to do this for them.

Adding a list of values to an existing data item is a very simple process. Please look at the section called "Managing Lists of Values" at the beginning of Chapter 18.

Creating Alternative Sorts

If a user comes to you and says that the list of values is not sorting in the right order, you need to add what is called an *alternative sort*. An example of an alternative sort is sorting the months of the year into the order in which they occur. Because month names are text values, a text sort would place 'January' after 'February'.

Adding an alternative sort to an existing list of values is a very simple process if you have an item that can be used for the alternative sort.

Please look at the section called "Using Alternative Sorts." You will find this in the section "Managing Lists of Values" of Chapter 18.

Creating New Items Based on Calculations

If you have standardized calculations within your company, it makes sense to include these as items in Discoverer. You can create these custom calculations on behalf of your users and then add these as items to folders. Users can then select these new items, saving themselves the step of creating the calculation in the query.

To create a new item based on a calculation, use the following workflow:

1. Determine which folder needs to have the calculated item.
2. Launch the Discoverer Administrator tool.
3. When the Load Wizard displays, as seen earlier in Figure 19-1, click Open an existing business area.
4. Open the business area that contains the folder to which you want to add the new item.
5. Locate and right-click the folder, and from the pop-up box click New Item.
6. Discoverer opens a box called New Item. You use this box in exactly the same way that an end user would create calculations. You should therefore continue this workflow by looking at the section called "Workbook Wizard Step 6: Creating User-Defined Calculations" in Chapter 5.

7. After you have created the new item, you need to determine the position in the folder where the item should be and move it to its final position.

8. You should also make sure to check the format and aggregation properties.

9. Having completed all of your checks and made any adjustments, you should now inform the user that the item has been successfully added.

Creating New Conditions

Another simple task for you, as the Discoverer administrator, is the creation of predefined conditions. We can best show you how to do this by using an actual example. Let's say we want to allow users to create reports that use only sales orders that are past due. But what is the formula for past due, and how do you ensure that users comply with this definition?

First of all, here is our formula. An order is past due when it is still open and the order date is more than two weeks in the past. If we allow users to create their own conditions, they could easily get this wrong. To avoid this, we will create the condition for them.

Before we show you how to create an administrator-defined condition, we need to tell you about mandatory and optional conditions. In Chapter 4 we showed you how an end user could create conditions, and we also discussed the use of predefined conditions. When, as an administrator, you create a condition, you have the ability to specify whether this condition is mandatory or optional. If you create a mandatory condition, it will always be applied and the user will have no choice whether to use that condition or not. If you create an optional condition, the user will get a choice and will be allowed to decide when to use it.

To create our administrator-defined condition, use the following workflow:

1. Launch the Discoverer Administrator tool.

2. When the Load Wizard displays, as seen earlier in Figure 19-1, click Open an existing business area.

3. Open the GSW business area.

4. Expand the GS Sales folder.

5. To begin the condition, we need to locate the first item for the condition. In our case this is the Status. Right-click the Status and from the pop-up box select New Condition. Discoverer opens the New Condition dialog box with the item Status selected.

6. Use the drop-down button under Value(s) and select OPEN.

7. Take a close look at the dialog box. You will notice that there is an area of the screen called Type. This area is where you specify whether the condition is mandatory or optional. In our case we will leave it set to the default of Optional.

8. We need to extend this condition to also include the fact that the order date must be more than seven days in the past. To do this, click Advanced. Discoverer opens an extended dialog box.

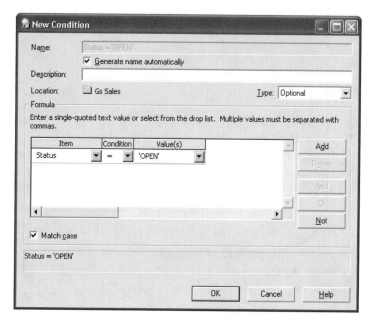

9. Just as with end user conditions, the extended dialog box allows you to add extra components to the condition. Click the Add button and then under the Item drop-down, select Create Calculation.

10. In the New Calculation dialog box, enter this algorithm: **TRUNC(SYSDATE) - 14**.

11. Upon return to the extended Condition dialog box, complete the condition by setting the condition itself to greater than, and then select the Order Date in the Value(s) box.

12. Name this condition **Past Due Orders** by unchecking the Generate name automatically box and typing the name. The final condition looks like this:

13. Complete the condition by clicking OK.

14. At the bottom of the list of items for the folder, as shown in the following illustration, you will see a new item called Past Due Orders (Optional):

When an end user opens the folder for item selection, that user will now see this new condition and can select it into his or her worksheet just like any other item. Users are not permitted to edit predefined conditions, so if any changes are required, these will have to be done by the administrator.

Deleting Predefined Conditions

Deletion of predefined conditions must be done by the administrator. However, you must be very careful because deleting a predefined condition that has already been used by a user in a workbook will cause that workbook to return incorrect results. Before you delete a predefined condition, you need to check the impact of the deletion.

To correctly delete a predefined condition, use the following workflow:

1. Locate the predefined condition that you want to delete.

2. Right-click the condition and from the pop-up menu select Delete Condition. Discoverer will display the Confirm Delete dialog box.

3. In the Confirm Delete dialog box, click Impact. Discoverer will display the Impact dialog box. As you can see, Discoverer will let you know if there are any workbooks that use the condition. You should not delete the condition if it is in use.

4. Click OK to close the Impact dialog box and return to the Confirm Delete dialog box.

5. If there will be no impact, click Yes; otherwise, click No.

If you did not check the impact or if you ignored the impact and you deleted a predefined condition, the next time the user tries to open a workbook that uses the condition, he or she will see this warning.

The workbook will continue to open, but the results will be wrong.

Creating Drill Hierarchies

As we have mentioned before, one of the least-used features of Discoverer is hierarchical drilling. In this type of drill a user navigates up or down a predefined hierarchy of items. Over the years, we have received many requests for drill hierarchies from users who do not understand the relationships that must exist between the component items in a hierarchy. Unless you fully understand the intricacies of a hierarchy, you can easily create Discoverer hierarchies that result in erroneous drills.

When a user comes to you and asks you to create a hierarchy, you need to take your time and not rush into creating it. First of all, you need to determine whether there are one-to-many relationships between all of the items in the proposed hierarchy. There can be no ifs or buts, no maybes, and no exceptions. There has to be a one-to-many relationship between every item, period! Do not allow someone in a position of authority to browbeat you into creating a hierarchy when the relationships are wrong. Equally, do not be tempted to insert an additional item into an existing hierarchy when that item is not unique within the entity that it comes from.

Let's look at one of our hierarchies: the geographic hierarchy. As we have explained several times in this book, there are one-to-many relationships between the Region and the District, the District and the City, and the City and the Customer. Conversely, there are many-to-one relationships going the other way. This sounds obvious, we hear you say, but it is these relationships that lie at the heart of the hierarchy. For every many-to-one relationship there must be a value for the entity that is on one end of the relationship. This cannot be an optional item, and the join cannot be an outer join. In our case, our joins are mandatory and thus the unique items within each table—the Customer Name, City Name, District Name, and Region Name—are the perfect candidates for a hierarchy.

NOTE
You must pick a unique item from within every one of the entities for the hierarchy to work. There is no point trying to create a hierarchy from the Customer to the City using the Contact Name because there is no guarantee that there are not two people with the same name, albeit in different companies.

Having found the unique items that can be used to form a hierarchy, the next step, if you have not already done so, is to make sure that these items exist within a single Discoverer folder. Sometimes the best way to do this is to use a predefined object in the database. Views and materialized views are perfect candidates for hierarchy generation. However, many times you will have to use a complex folder. In Chapter 18 we showed you in detail how to create both complex folders and hierarchies.

If you are using Oracle Applications, you are probably aware that the table called GL_PERIODS is the one that contains your organization's fiscal time calendar. Time and time again, we have seen organizations make the base GL_PERIODS table available to end users. This is wrong and will cause your queries to perform badly. You need to create a materialized view of GL_PERIODS and prebuild all of the hierarchical information against each date. Allowing users to dynamically manipulate GL_PERIODS is asking for disaster. We have a client who was doing just this. They had daily reports that were taking over seven hours to complete. Following our recommendation, they created a hierarchical materialized view. The same reports now run in five minutes.

Modifying an Item's Type

A little-used function is the ability to change an item's data type. If one of your users comes to you and says that he or she always has to change the data type of a certain item, you should create another item whose data type and format has been set the way the user needs it. Let's say the user has said that he or she wants to be able to display the order date as a string and that it is to be formatted differently. Rather than the system showing 01-JAN-2006, the user wants to print January 1, 2006. Now we know what you may be saying. You are saying that the user could do this without your help. While this is true, the art to being a good administrator is to make the user's life a little easier. Why make the user do this when you could do it for him?

To add a new item for the order date with a different item type, use the following workflow:

1. Open the GSW business area and expand the list of folders.

2. Locate and right-click the heading for the Sales folder. From the pop-up menu, select New Item.

3. Complete the New Item dialog box as follows and then click OK:

   ■ **Name**   Enter New Order Date.

   ■ **Calculation**   Enter TO_CHAR(Gs Sales.Order Date,'Month D, YYYY').

4. Move the new item to its correct location within the folder.

NOTE
Please look at the back of Appendix B for a listing of all the available format masks that can be used with dates.

Creating Summary Data

Performance is the reason we use summary tables. Please look at Chapter 22 for full details on managing summary tables. In this chapter we give you workflows for managing Discoverer's automated summary management feature and show you how to manually manage summary tables.

Rearranging the Order of Folders in a Business Area

In Chapter 17 we recommend that you order the folders in a business area in a way that makes sense to your users. With all the best will in the world, we can still have folders in the wrong order. If a user comes to you with a request to change the order of the folders within a business area, it is an easy task to change it. However, before you jump in and start changing things, you might want to step back and think about what the user is asking for.

Perhaps the user is unaware that the organization has a standard for the way that folders are presented. Perhaps the user is relatively new to the company and is not yet fully on board with the reasons a business area has been set up the way it is being presented. You may need to arrange for the user to get some training.

Notwithstanding all of these points, it could be that the user's idea really is a good one and that the order does need changing. We have already given you a workflow for rearranging the order of the folders in a business area. You will find this in Chapter 17.

Rearranging the Order of Items in a Folder

In Chapter 17 we recommend that you order the items in a folder in a way that makes sense to your users. We also recommend that you set up a corporate standard for this ordering, making use of item separators to group items together into logical sets. Even with all our planning and standards, we can still have items in the wrong order. If the user's idea really is a good one and the order does need changing, you should take a look at the workflow that we have already provided in Chapter 17.

Changing Refresh Cycles

Many Discoverer systems are based either on a snapshot of the OLTP system or on data warehouses. Both of these types of databases use a refresh mechanism to update. If a user comes to you with the belief that the refresh schedule is insufficient, you are in the perfect position to do something about it.Perhaps the users would like to see an extra data warehouse collection during the lunch period. Perhaps the users need to have materialized views refreshed more frequently. Perhaps the business needs to have an additional copy of the OLTP database to coincide with the start of the business day in another part of the world.

NOTE
Some organizations keep a backup copy of the database and apply the database logs from the production environment to bring the copy up to date.

Some Discoverer managers will have more power than others, and some of you will be directly responsible for one or more of the refreshes that we have outlined. However, before you set off making wholesale changes, remember that these refreshes could have a bigger impact than just the user or business unit that requested them. You may need to liaise with other IT departments, perhaps the data warehouse production team. Even if you don't have responsibility over these areas, you will surely have input and be required to provide feedback from the end user community.

Allowing Scheduling of Workbooks

Not all organizations make use of scheduling. Assuming your organization is making use of scheduling, not all users are automatically granted permission to schedule workbooks. In fact, not all users need to schedule workbooks. If a user asks for permission to schedule, you will need to either validate the request with the user's manager or discuss this in more depth with the user.

Scheduling Privileges

In order for a user to be able to schedule workbooks, that user needs to have the following database privileges:

- CREATE PROCEDURE
- CREATE TABLE
- CREATE VIEW
- EXECUTE ANY PROCEDURE
- UNLIMITED TABLESPACE
- EXECUTE ON SYS.DBMS_JOB
- SELECT ON SYS.V_$PARAMETER

We have been asked many times, especially by DBAs, just why these privileges are required. The answer to this, and much more, can be found in Appendix A.

NOTE
With 10.1.2, scheduled workbooks can be shared, so these privileges can be provided to only a few users. These users can then share scheduled workbooks with other users. Of course, with shared scheduled workbooks, the data that a user sees is the data that the owner of the scheduled workbook would have seen. Your users therefore need to be very careful not to share secure data!

Enabling Scheduling

Having determined that the user's request is valid, to allow the user to schedule, use the following workflow:

1. Make sure that the user has the necessary database privileges outlined in the preceding section.

2. Launch the Discoverer Administrator tool.

3. When the Load Wizard displays, as seen earlier in Figure 19-1, click Cancel.

4. From the menu bar, select Tools | Privileges. Discoverer opens the Privileges dialog box.

5. As you can see in Figure 19-2, the Privileges dialog box has four tabs. These are

    ■   **Privileges**   This tab allows you to assign multiple privileges to a single user or role. The Privileges tab was dealt with earlier in this chapter; however, we need to use it again now.

    ■   **User/Role**   This tab allows you to assign multiple users or roles to a single privilege. The User/Role tab was dealt with earlier in this chapter.

    ■   **Query Governor**   This tab allows you to assign query governor privileges to a single use or role. The Query Governor tab was dealt with earlier in this chapter.

    ■   **Scheduled Workbooks**   This tab allows you to maintain the scheduling privileges for a single user. This tab will be used in this section.

6. Click the Privileges tab.

7. Click the Select button. Discoverer opens the Select User/Role search box.

8. Type or search for the user for whom you want to manage scheduling.

9. Click OK to close the Select User/Role search box.

10. Check the box entitled Schedule Workbooks. The Schedule Workbooks privilege can only be assigned to a user. It cannot be assigned to a role or an Apps responsibility. If you attempt to do so, you will receive this error message.

11. Click Apply. The user now has the power to schedule. However, you have not finished yet, as you need to make sure that the user has the correct scheduling powers.

12. Click the Scheduled Workbooks tab. As you can see in the following image, this is a rather busy screen. However, it is a very important screen and one that you need to master.

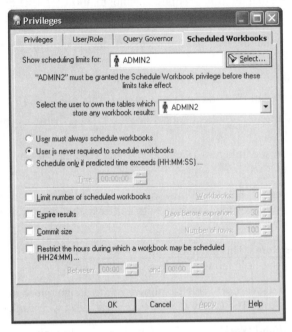

13. If you want another user to own the tables that store the workbook results, use the drop-down alongside and select another user. A discussion on this topic follows at the end of this section.

14. In the middle of the screen are the following three radio buttons:

- **User must always schedule workbooks**   Check this radio button if you want this user to be forced to always schedule their workbooks. The user will not be able to run workbooks inside Plus or Viewer, unless the workbook has been scheduled.

- **User is never required to schedule workbooks**   Use this radio button if you do not want to force the user to have to schedule. The user will then be able to choose. This is the default option and the one you will use most often.

- **Schedule only if predicted time exceeds**   Use this radio button if you want to force the user to have to schedule if the predicted time for the query exceeds the limits set here. After checking the box, you need to define the time limit.

15. At the bottom of the screen are the following check boxes:

- **Limit number of scheduled workbooks**   Check this box if you want to limit the number of scheduled workbooks that the user can have at any moment in time. After checking the box, you need to define the maximum number that the user can use.

NOTE
This option allows you to prevent users from submitting so many scheduled workbooks that no other jobs in the DBMS_JOB queue can run.

- **Expire results** Check this box if you want to limit the length of time that the user's results will be retained within the database. After checking the box, you need to define the time limit. This is typically set to 30 days but can be set lower or higher depending upon user and organizational needs. Following expiry, the results are deleted the next time the user exits the EUL.

- **Commit size** Contrary to popular belief, this box does not restrict the number of rows of data that can be saved in a scheduled workbook. This check box is to set the commit frequency. For example, if this is set to 100, then Discoverer will issue a commit every time 100 rows of data have been retrieved. After checking the box, you need to define the commit size. According to Oracle, little gain will be achieved by setting this higher than 1000.

- **Restrict the hours during which a workbook may be scheduled** Check this box if you want to restrict the hours during which the user can schedule. This will be of particular importance to organizations that have users all across the globe. By restricting the hours that a user can schedule, you can, for example, prevent a user in the United States from being able to schedule during the European hours of operation. After checking the box, you need to define the start and end times. You can go across midnight; thus, if you set the start time to 23:00 and the end time to 03:00, the user will be able to schedule only between 11 P.M. and 3 A.M.

16. Having set all of the scheduling privileges, click Apply or OK to make the changes take effect.

User Selection

If you have used previous versions of Discoverer, you may notice that the Privileges dialog box has changed. Whereas in older versions the user selection used to be a drop-down, it has now become a field that you have to search for first. As commented elsewhere, this has been done to improve performance.

Oracle tell us that there were cases where the user population ran into tens of thousands, and populating a drop-down box, as you will appreciate, with ten thousand or more values takes time, sometimes a lot of time. Hence, Oracle has provided this new search-then-assign workflow that you will see used throughout the Privileges dialog box.

Storing Workbook Results

When a scheduled workbook is run, Discoverer stores the results in database tables. Discoverer's default behavior will be to store the scheduled workbooks in the EUL owner's schema. Before an end user can schedule a workbook, you must decide which database user is to own those tables. The results can be stored in one of two places:

- The schema of the user who is running the scheduled workbook

- A scheduled workbook results schema

Storing the Results in the Owner's Schema

The main advantage to storing the results of scheduled workbooks directly in the owner's schema is that a database limit can be specified on the maximum amount of data that the user can store in the database. The DBA can control the maximum amount of space that the user can fill with their results. If that user should fill their allotted space, this will affect only that user.

> **NOTE**
> *The previous option should not be taken if you are using Discoverer in Apps mode.*

Storing the Results in a Scheduled Workbook Results Schema

The advantage of storing the results in a separate schema is that individual users do not need to have the special database privileges that are needed to run scheduled workbooks. Some organizations think that it is easier to manage the data when it is stored in a central repository than when there are multiple user schemas to manage.

Of course, the disadvantage of storing the results in a central repository is that one user could run a scheduled workbook that fills the available storage space, thus preventing other scheduled workbooks from running. The storage space quota is thus shared and could easily be used by a single user.

> **NOTE**
> *If you are working in Apps mode, you need to use the APPS schema for this purpose.*

Setting up a Scheduled Workbook Results User

To set up workbook scheduling using a centralized repository schema, you must log in to the database as a SYSDBA and run the batchusr.sql script that can be found at $ORACLE_HOME/discoverer/util.

> **NOTE**
> *If you are using Discoverer in Apps mode, you must use the batchusr_app.sql script.*

This script creates a new user who is granted the appropriate privileges. In addition the user will be granted the SELECT ANY TABLE database privilege. If you do not want the user to have this powerful privilege, you will need to manually revoke it later. You will also need to make sure the user has appropriate SELECT privileges to all the objects that will be needed. In our opinion, this is one of the times when you should use the SELECT ANY TABLE privilege.

In addition to creating the user, the Discoverer manager must also use the Scheduling Privileges screen to point the results of all users who will schedule as this new user.

If the scheduled workbook user is to be a user's real schema, then it is sufficient to grant the appropriate privileges. You do not have to run the batchusr.sql script in this case.

Managing Scheduled Workbooks

As the Discoverer manager you have the ability to monitor the jobs that users have scheduled. This is done from the menu bar by selecting Tools | Manage Scheduled Workbooks. You can use the Manage Scheduled Workbooks dialog box to

- Edit the user's scheduled workbook

- Delete a scheduled workbook from the processing queue

- View the status of a scheduled workbook

- Read an error message that a scheduled workbook has incurred

NOTE
You must have the Manage Scheduled Workbooks administration privilege to access the Manage Scheduled Workbooks dialog box.

To manage scheduled workbooks, use the following workflow:

1. Launch the Discoverer Administrator tool.

2. When the Load Wizard displays, as seen earlier in Figure 19-1, click Cancel.

3. From the menu bar, select Tools | Manage Scheduled Workbooks. Discoverer opens the Manage Scheduled Workbooks dialog box.

4. You need to either check the box called Select all users or use the Select button to choose one user.

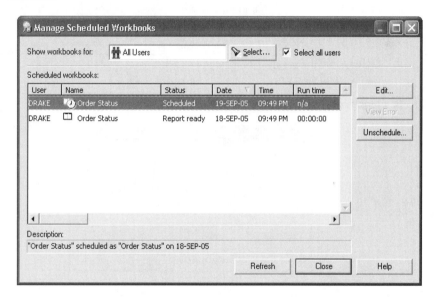

5. As you can see in the preceding image, Discoverer displays the scheduled workbooks for the user(s).

6. When you have completed your management, click Close.

These are the components of the screen just shown:

■ **Show workbooks for** This displays the user(s) that you are managing.

■ **Select** Click this button to locate a single user.

■ **Select all users** Check this box to display the schedules for all users.

■ **Scheduled Workbooks** This box displays the actual scheduled workbooks, along with their names, statuses, and when to run. At the end of this section, you will find a list of the possible statuses.

■ **Edit** Click this button to edit the scheduled workbook.

■ **View Error**   If the results show that there was an error, click this button to get more information about the error.

■ **Unschedule**   Click this button to unschedule a workbook that has not yet run. You will see this screen and two additional options. Select your option and click Yes to cause Discoverer to take the requested action; otherwise, click No.

■ Unschedule but keep all results.

■ Unschedule and delete all results.

■ **Delete**   Click this button to delete a workbook that has already been run. You will see the following screen and two options. Select your option and click Yes to cause Discoverer to take the requested action; otherwise, click No.

■ Delete only the results run for the date you clicked on.

■ Unschedule and delete all results.

■ **Refresh**   Click this button to refresh the list of scheduled workbooks.

NOTE
On the Manage Scheduled Workbooks screen you will not see the buttons Delete and Unschedule at the same time because they use the same position on the screen and are mutually exclusive. Delete applies only to already executed workbooks, while Unschedule applies only to schedules that have not yet executed.

List of Scheduled Statuses

This is the list of possible statuses that you could see when managing scheduled workbooks:

Status	Description
Could not schedule	The workbook could not be submitted to the processing job queue.
Error while running query	Running the query produced an error. You will need to click the View Error button for more details.

Status	Description
EUL has changed, reschedule report	A change occurred in the EUL that has affected the workbook; for example, a folder was deleted.
Number of rows limit exceeded	The "Limit retrieved data" threshold set in the Scheduled Workbooks tab has been exceeded.
Report deleted by Administrator	This workbook has been set for deletion by the administrator.
Report expired	The workbook has expired and will be deleted the next time the user exits from the EUL.
Report ready	The workbook ran successfully and the report is ready. As the administrator, you cannot see the results; only the user can do this using Plus or Viewer.
Running query	The workbook is running, and the result set is being built.
Scheduled	The workbook is scheduled to run at a future time.

Creation of New Functions

Discoverer already has a vast array of functions at your disposal, and you should refer to Appendix B for an alphabetical list of all of the available functions. However, there may be times when you need a new function.

For the purposes of this exercise, we have created the following very simple function:

```
CREATE OR REPLACE function f_eul_month
    (day date)
return varchar2 is month varchar2(6) := 'JAN-10';
begin
    select monthid into month
        from gsw.gs_day
        where day = dayid;
    return (month);
    exception
        when no_data_found then
        return (month);
end f_eul_month;
/
```

If you execute this function in SQL Plus using

```
select f_eul_month('29-AUG-2004') from dual
```

the database will reply with SEP-04. The function takes a date, as an argument, and returns the fiscal month.

To make a new function available inside Discoverer, use the following workflow:

1. Use SQL Plus to create the function in the database.
2. Launch the Discoverer Administrator tool.
3. When the Load Wizard displays, as seen earlier in Figure 19-1, click Cancel.

4. From the menu bar, select Tools | Register PL/SQL Functions. Discoverer opens the following PL/SQL Functions dialog box:

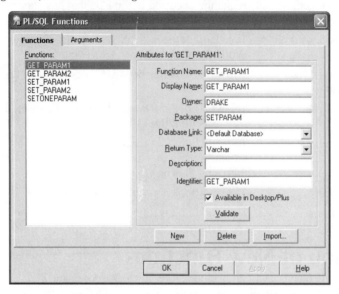

5. Click Import. Discoverer displays the second screen of the Import PL/SQL Functions Wizard.

6. In the preceding screen, you need to select the user that you want to work with and then locate the function that you want to import.

7. Having located the function, click OK. As shown next, Discoverer imports all of the features about the function and displays them back in the main screen.

8. Click the Arguments tab to look at the arguments that Discoverer needs to supply to the function. As you can see at the bottom of the screen, there is a Usage area that has two radio buttons: Optional and Required. Discoverer has correctly recognized that our function has a single, mandatory (Required) date argument.

9. Return to the Functions tab and Click Validate. This causes Discoverer to validate that the function is okay to work within the EUL.

10. Hopefully, if you have done everything correctly, you will see this box.

11. Close the box informing you that the function is valid and then click OK to complete the importation of the function. The function is now available for use within Discoverer.

Working with Optional Arguments

There appears to be a bug within Discoverer when importing PL/SQL functions with optional arguments in that Discoverer can sometimes see these as being required. You will need to check these manually and switch those which were imported with the wrong usage definition.

NOTE
You should therefore make a point of checking every argument when you are importing new functions.

Summary

In this chapter, you have learned how to interact with your end users. The intention of this chapter is to be complementary to the last section of Chapter 15. If you look back at that section, entitled "What Can the Discoverer Administrator Do for You?" you will see that it contains a list of approximately twenty topics. This chapter took each of those topics in turn and provided you with a workflow that will tackle the topic.

Several of the workflows that are needed to answer questions posed by the users have already been given in previous chapters. These were not repeated here, but we simply directed you to the relevant chapter. However, in this chapter we did introduce or explain to you some totally new concepts for the first time. Among the new topics that you found in this chapter are managing access, managing privileges, creating predefined conditions, and managing scheduling.

CHAPTER
20

Configuring Discoverer

his chapter is intended for a different audience than the rest of this book. This discussion is aimed at the technical team member who is responsible for configuring the Oracle Application Server, and in particular for the administrator who needs to control the Discoverer environment. In this section we will describe the basic components of a Discoverer installation and show you how to configure all of the various components. We will show you how to use Oracle Enterprise Manager (OEM) to configure Discoverer for a corporate look and feel. We will also show you how to configure Discoverer for use with Single Sign-On. After describing all of the preferences that you can set for the Discoverer mid-tier, we will show you how to use Web Cache and how to configure it to load balance multiple Discoverer servers.

The 10*g* Release 2 Business Intelligence Application Server provides three primary Discoverer components:

- Plus

- Viewer

- Portlet Provider

As the application server administrator, it is your responsibility to guarantee that these three components are available, performing correctly, and configured appropriately to your organization's business intelligence needs. To be able to accomplish this goal, you must be familiar with Discoverer and the components that it depends on.

Architecture

Discoverer has the following three-tier architecture:

- The end user

- A middle tier, which may include the following two components:

    - The Discoverer server

    - The Application Server infrastructure

NOTE
It is called the Discoverer Server because it is not really an application server. The Discoverer Server resides inside the Oracle Application Server.

- The database, which includes the EUL and the data that Discoverer will be reporting on

The application server includes many different components that all work together to deliver a rich business intelligence environment to the user. When an end user makes a web request to Discoverer, the first component that user will reach is Oracle Web Cache, which is a caching reverse proxy server, designed to accelerate mid-tier performance. If enabled for use and if Web Cache does not have the content that the user needs in its cache, it intelligently makes an additional request to the Oracle HTTP Server (OHS). OHS is responsible for routing all HTTP requests to the appropriate component. In the case of Discoverer, all requests are routed to Oracle Containers for J2EE (OC4J), which is the heart of the server. OC4J runs Discoverer Viewer, Discoverer Plus, the Discoverer Portlet Provider, and OLAP. To maintain high availability, every Application Server install includes Oracle Process Management and Notification (OPMN). OPMN is essentially a heartbeat process that keeps every component up and running. Oracle Enterprise Manager (OEM) Application Server Control is also provided so that the administrator can easily make common configurations without touching configuration files or the database. This chapter will acquaint you with the configuration and usage of these components.

Take a look at Figure 20-1. This diagram should help simplify the components of the Oracle Application Server. With regard to Discoverer, the key points to understand are

- Web Cache is optional

- SSO is optional

- In 10.1.2, even the infrastructure is optional

Previous releases of Discoverer Plus and Viewer required an install of the Application Server infrastructure. With 10.1.2, this is no longer true. However, if you implement an infrastructure with Discoverer, you will be adding a powerful set of identity management and security features. The infrastructure includes a simple Oracle database (metadata repository, MR), Oracle Single Sign-On (SSO), Oracle Internet Directory (OID), and the Delegated Administration Service (DAS). We will briefly discuss these components and the configuration needed to use them with Discoverer.

FIGURE 20-1 *Application Server components*

Oracle HTTP Server (OHS)

Oracle HTTP Server uses standard Apache 1.3 with some additional Oracle-supplied modules underneath the covers. Apache has been the most popular web server on the Internet since April of 1996. According to the February 2005 Netcraft Web Server Survey (http://news.netcraft.com/archives/web_server_survey.html), more than 68 percent of the web sites on the Internet are using Apache, making it more widely used than all other web servers combined.

OHS receives all requests from Oracle Web Cache (if used) and then routes the request to OC4J_BI_Forms. Apache has many sophisticated features and configuration options that you can explore. These configurations can either be found in $ORACLE_HOME/apache/apache/conf/httpd.conf, or files referenced in the httpd.conf file using the Include directive. Here are some of the key Apache directives:

- **Timeout** This is the maximum number of seconds allowed for a command to complete. The default value is 300.

- **KeepAlive** Setting this to On allows Apache to keep the connection open for that client when the client requests it. Because the connection has to be set up only once, this can improve performance. The trade-off is that the server process cannot be used to service other requests until the client disconnects, the connection times out (as controlled by the KeepAliveTimeout directive), or the MaxKeepAliveRequests value has been reached. The default value for KeepAlive is On.

- **MaxKeepAliveRequests** This is the maximum number of requests to allow during a persistent connection. Setting this to 0 allows an unlimited amount, which is not recommended. If you have long client sessions, you might want to increase this value. See the preceding item, KeepAlive, for additional comments. The default value is 100.

- **KeepAliveTimeout** This is the number of seconds that the system will wait for the next request from the same client on the same connection. Once again, please see the previous item **KeepAlive** for additional comments. The default value is 15.

- **MaxRequestsPerChild** This is the number of requests that each child process is allowed to process before the child dies. The child will then exit, thus avoiding the problems that can occur after prolonged use when Apache memory leaks happen. On most operating systems this is not really an issue, however, Solaris is renowned for leaks in its libraries. For Solaris we therefore recommend setting this to a number such as 10000. If you set this to 0, which is usually the default, your setting will be unlimited. According to Oracle, if you use Windows, you should set this to 0 because in Windows there is only one server process.

- **ThreadsPerChild** This setting specifies the number of requests that each child process is allowed to handle before the child process dies. Requests in excess of this number will be required to wait in the TCP/IP queue. Allowing such requests to wait in the TCP/IP queue often results in the best response time and throughput. While setting this value high will allow more requests to be active at the same time, you need to be aware that this could seriously affect performance as the requests end up being handled more slowly. According to information from Oracle on some in-house testing that they have done, "A setting of 20 ThreadsPerChild per CPU produces good response time and throughput results. For example, if you have four CPUs, set ThreadsPerChild to 80. If, with this setting, CPU utilization does not exceed 85%, you can increase ThreadsPerChild, but ensure that the available threads are in use." Thus, as you can see, altering this setting can help with performance tuning. The default for this is 50. According to Oracle, the ThreadsPerChild setting in Windows works like the MaxClients setting in UNIX.

- **MinSpareServers**   The MinSpareServers and MaxSpareServers (see the next item) settings allow the HTTP server to dynamically adapt to the system load as it sees fit. It will maintain enough processes to handle the load, keeping a few in reserve just in case. The server does this by periodically checking how many clients are waiting for a request. If that number is below MinSpareServers, it will create a new spare, whereas if there are more than the MaxSpareServers, some of them will be killed off. Unless you really need to alter these settings, we recommend you leave these set with their default. The default for MinSpareServers is 5.

- **MaxSpareServers**   See the preceding item for a description of this setting, the default for which will either be 10 or 20.

- **MaxClients**   This sets a limit on the total number of clients that can connect simultaneously. If this limit is ever reached, then subsequent clients will be locked out and will be unable to connect. Thus, please do not set this too low! Oracle has designed this to be used as a brake to stop a runaway server from taking the system down with it. The default for this setting is 150 and has been set by Oracle following exhaustive tests. According to information obtained from the Application Server Performance Guide, "Tests on a 2-processor, 168 MHz Sun UltraSPARC on a 100 Mbps network showed that saturation of the network occurs when MaxClients is set to 150. Even on 4- and 6-processor, 336 MHz systems, there was no significant performance improvement seen by increasing the MaxClients setting from 150 to 256, based on static page and servlet tests with up to 1000 users." You should therefore understand that increasing MaxClients when system resources are saturated will not improve performance. In fact, when the system is overloaded, we recommend that you reduce the number of MaxClients to force requests to stay in the network queue. It might be better to have requests time out and get the system to retry rather than having long response times. According to Oracle, the MaxClients setting in UNIX works like the ThreadsPerChild setting in Windows.

- **Listen**   This is the default HTTP listener port and is set during the installation of the Application Server. The default is usually 7777 or 7778 but can be 7780 or higher if you have previously installed a database or other Application Server components, such as 9.0.4, prior to installing 10.1.2.

- **Port**   This is the port to which the stand-alone server listens. If you encounter issues, please disable any firewall, security, and other services. The default port is 80.

Here is an example Include directive:

```
include "C:\oracle\BIHome_1\Apache\Apache\conf\mod_oc4j.conf"
```

For further information regarding the OHS settings, please take a look at the B14001-02 Oracle Application Server Performance Guide 10*g* Release 2 (10.1.2), which you will find available on OTN. Please also review the httpd.conf file and www.apache.org for a discussion about these directives. Unless you really have cause to do otherwise, we recommend that you leave all of Apache's configurations set to the default. Apache scales really well and, in most cases, will be the least of your problems. Any initial changes that you make will relate to enabling the Secure Sockets Layer (SSL) and Single Sign-On (SSO), or disabling Web Cache. It is important to know that any change to Apache's httpd.conf file requires a restart. Instead of going into detail about Apache's standard directives, which is a complete topic by itself, let's discuss the procedure that you must follow to make changes to Apache's configuration. You will use a tool called DCM (Distributed Configuration Management).

Oracle HTTP Server Configuration

To perform Oracle HTTP server configuration, use the following workflow:

1. Locate the httpd.conf file, which you will find in $ORACLE_HOME/Apache/Apache/conf.

2. Take a backup of this file.

3. Make any changes you want to make.

4. Save the file.

5. Update the configuration by executing the following command:

   ```
   $ORACLE_HOME/dcm/bin/dcmctl updateconfig
   ```

6. Stop OPMN by executing the following command:

   ```
   $ORACLE_HOME/opmn/bin/opmnctl stopall
   ```

7. Restart OPMN by executing the following command:

   ```
   $ORACLE_HOME/opmn/bin/opmnctl startall
   ```

NOTE
The Oracle Application Server automatically creates snapshots of configuration histories, so you may be able to roll back to a specific configuration. It also keeps the configurations in multiple locations.

When you run dcmctl updateconfig, the following actions occur:

■ A backup of the present configuration (all OHS, OC4J, and OPMN configuration files) is taken.

NOTE
It is important to note that Discoverer's pref.txt is not managed by DCM.

■ All configuration files are checked for errors.

■ If the configuration files are error-free, their contents are copied into the $ORACLE_HOME/dcm directory. The contents in this location must be the same as the various configuration files. If they are not, you will receive synchronization errors and the server will not start again.

Another advantage of DCM is that you may detect and troubleshoot configuration errors before restarting Apache, thus avoiding unnecessary downtime.

NOTE
If Apache fails to restart, you may elect to roll back.

To roll back, use the following workflow:

1. Open a command shell and navigate to the $ORACLE_HOME/dcm/bin folder.
2. Execute the following command:

   ```
   $ORACLE_HOME/dcm/bin/dcmctl listarchives
   ```

3. Note the name of the archive and now execute the following command:

   ```
   $ORACLE_HOME/dcm/bin/dcmctl applyarchiveto <archivename>
   ```

For more details about dcm, enter **dcmctl help**. Most of dcmctl's commands relate to managing OC4J applications. On a Discoverer server, you may use dcmctl to deploy your own J2EE application. Therefore, for a very high-quality business intelligence environment, you may develop and deploy your own J2EE business intelligence web site that complements Discoverer.

Key Oracle HTTP Server Modules

The Oracle HTTP Server has over 50 modules, among which the following three are considered key to Discoverer:

- **mod_oc4j**   This module routes requests from OHS to OC4J. The protocol that mod_oc4j uses to communicate with the OC4J instance is AJP (Apache Jserv Protocol). This module is enabled by default. OC4J instances are started and stopped by Oracle Process Manager and Notification Server (OPMN).

- **mod_osso**   This module redirects requests for protected content to Single Sign-On for authentication and authorization. In other words, this module enables Single Sign-On for the OHS.

- **mod_ossl**   This module provides the facilities to support HTTPS (SSL) requests. It enables cryptography for the OHS. The module is a plug-in to the OHS that enables the server to use SSL.

Configuring Oracle HTTP Server Using Oracle Enterprise Manager

To configure HTTP Server using Oracle Enterprise Manager (OEM), use the following workflow:

1. From a browser, enter **http://*fully_qualified_domain_name*:1810**.

NOTE
The OEM port depends upon your installation and may not be 1810. It may be anywhere in the range 1810–1829.

2. In Username, enter **ias_admin**.

3. In Password, enter the ias_admin password.

NOTE
As you work with the Oracle Application Server, you will notice that there are numerous times when you will be asked for a password. The password that is associated with many of the key components is the password that you provided for ias_admin during the install of the server. You should not lose this password. Equally, you should not lightly give it away.

4. The Application Server farm page shown in Figure 20-2 will appear if you are joined to an infrastructure. On this page you will see all of the clusters and instances in your farm.

5. From the Application Server farm page, select the Discoverer instance that you want to administer. The Application Server home page shown in Figure 20-3 will open.

6. From the home page, click the link called HTTP Server. The HTTP Server home page shown in Figure 20-4 will open.

7. From the HTTP Server home page, click the link called Administration. The HTTP Server Administration page shown in Figure 20-5 will open.

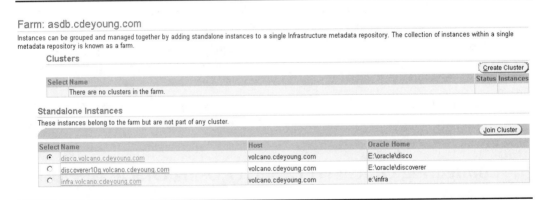

FIGURE 20-2 *OEM Application Server Control farm page*

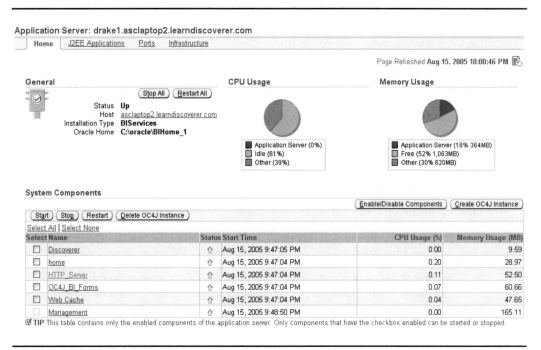

FIGURE 20-3 *OEM Application Server Control home page*

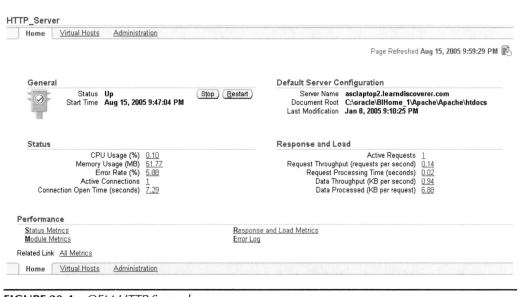

FIGURE 20-4 *OEM HTTP Server home page*

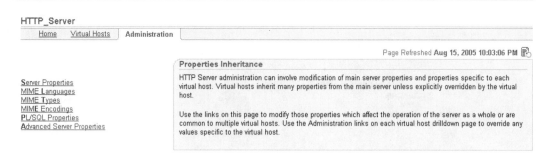

FIGURE 20-5 *OEM HTTP Server administration page*

8. On the HTTP Server Administration page you can perform many OHS configuration tasks:

- ■ **Server Properties**   Clicking this link opens the HTTP Server Properties page shown in Figure 20-6.

- ■ **MIME Languages and Types**   Use these two areas to manage the Multipurpose Internet Mail Extension (MIME) languages and types. This is where you associate file extensions with language codes, so that, for example, the extension fr is associated with France, and the extension zh_CN is associated with China.

- ■ **PL/SQL Properties**   This is not used by Discoverer. It is used only with a PL/SQL-developed web site. You can safely ignore this.

- ■ **Advanced Server Properties**   This area allows you to edit the httpd.conf and its referenced files through the OEM interface. The advantage of using OEM to edit these files instead of editing them directly is that the dcmctl updateconfig command will run behind the scenes. Also, OEM prompts you to restart OHS. There is less chance of error if you manage your httpd.conf this way.

9. Click Apply.

As partly seen in Figure 20-6, the HTTP Server Properties dialog box has the following areas:

- ■ **Listening Addresses and Ports**   Use this area to define the default listening port, usually 80, as well as the other listening ports used by the server.

- ■ **Administrator E-Mail**   Use this area to enter your admin e-mail address.

- ■ **Logging**   Use this area to manage the server logging location and filename.

- ■ **Client Request Handling**   Use this area to set both the maximum number of requests that can be processed simultaneously and the request timeout, which is entered in seconds. These equate to the ThreadsPerChild and Timeout settings in the httpd.conf file.

- ■ **Client Connection Handling**   Use this area to tell HTTP Server whether it is allowed to handle multiple requests per connection. You can qualify this by setting further switches to control the connection timeout (in seconds) and, if checked, what the request limit per connection should be. These equate to the KeepAlive, MaxKeepAliveRequests, and KeepAliveTimeout settings in the httpd.conf file.

Server Properties

General

Version	**10.1.2**
Server Root Directory	**C:\oracle\BIHome_1\Apache\Apache**
Configuration File	**C:\oracle\BIHome_1\Apache\Apache\conf\httpd.conf**
Process ID File	**logs/httpd.pid**

* Document Root	C:\oracle\BIHome_1\Apache\Apache\htdocs
Administrator E-Mail	you@your.address

Listening Addresses and Ports

Default Port 80

Select Item and... (Remove)

Select All | Select None

Select	Listening IP Address	Listening Port
☐		4444
☐		7778
☐	127.0.0.1	7200

(Add Another Row)

Port Dependencies

Changing a listening port number or IP address affects HTTP Server virtual hosts and other components (e.g. Web Cache, Portal, Internet Directory, etc.). Updates to one or more of these dependent components may be required. For more information, see help topic: Configuration Dependencies for HTTP Server

FIGURE 20-6   *OEM HTTP Server Properties dialog box*

NOTE
There is a great deal of information in the preceding section, and we appreciate that some of these settings do not directly affect Discoverer. However, we have provided this information as a direct response to requests that we have received from system administrators who wanted to know just what settings can and cannot affect Discoverer.

Oracle Containers for J2EE (OC4J)

This is a J2EE (Java 2 Enterprise Edition)–compliant container that executes Java code on the Application Server. This is the component that actually runs your Discoverer web site, so if you are the system administrator for your company, you will find the following section to be invaluable.

All J2EE applications are bundled and delivered to Application Servers using .EAR (Enterprise Application Archive) or .WAR (Web Application Archive) files. When the Discoverer Application Server is installed, the discoverer.ear file is deployed to OC4J in the OC4J_BI_Forms instance. Each OC4J instance executes Java code in the instance using one or many Java processes.

Overview of the OC4J Configuration Files

First of all, as mentioned earlier, there will be an Include statement in the httpd.conf file for the mod_oc4j.conf file, as shown in this example:

```
Include "/Discoverer/apache/apache/conf/mod_oc4j.conf"
```

NOTE
The httpd.conf file can be found in the $ORACLE_HOME/Apache/ Apache/conf folder.

In the mod_oc4j.conf file you will find the following directives:

```
<IfModule mod_oc4j.c>
<Location /oc4j-service>
SetHandler oc4j-service-handler
Order deny,allow
Deny from all
Allow from localhost qualified_hostname hostname
</Location>
Oc4jMount /j2ee/*
Oc4jMount /webapp home
Oc4jMount /webapp/* home
Oc4jMount /IsWebCacheWorking home
Oc4jMount /IsWebCacheWorking/* home
Oc4jMount /Discoverer OC4J_BI_Forms
Oc4jMount /Discoverer/* OC4J_BI_Forms
</IfModule>
```

NOTE
In the preceding listing, the qualified_hostname and hostname will be taken from the HOSTS file on your own system.

Look at the Oc4jMount Discoverer directives shown in bold in the preceding listing. This is how OHS and mod_oc4j know how to route requests that have /Discoverer in the URL to the OC4J_BI_Forms instance.

Next we will explore the OC4J configuration files. These can be found in

$ORACLE_HOME/Discoverer/j2ee/OC4J_BI_Forms

Four primary directories need to be discussed:

- **applications/discoverer/META-INF**   This folder contains the web site and JAR files. If you have the time, you will find it interesting to explore the application.xml and orion-application.xml files, especially if you have an understanding of J2EE application development.

- **applications/discoverer/discoverer/WEB-INF**   This folder contains further web site and JAR files. In this folder, you will find the web.xml and orion-web.xml files.

- **applications-deployment**   This folder and its subfolders contain essentially the same configuration files as the files found in the applications subfolders. The difference is that the files in the applications-deployment folders are generated by the Application Server when the application is first deployed. After deployment, OC4J only reads the configuration files in the application-deployment directory. Therefore, post-deployment, the Application Server does not use the application.xml and web.xml files that are located in the applications subfolders.

- **config**   This folder contains configurations that are global to the entire OC4J_BI_Forms OC4J instance. In this directory you will find the default-web-site.xml, http-web-site.xml, and server.xml files.

Here is an excerpt from default-web-site.xml:

```
<web-app application="discoverer" name="discoverer" load-on-startup="true"
root="/discoverer" />
```

Here is an excerpt from server.xml:

```
<application name="discoverer" path="../applications/discoverer.ear" auto-start="true"
/>
```

Notice that the application name (application="discoverer") in the default-web-site.xml file matches the application name provided in the server.xml file. By having the identical name in both of these files, OC4J knows how to route the URL (root="/discoverer") to the application code (path="../applications/discoverer.ear"). The server.xml file also points to all of the major configuration files for the OC4J_BI_Forms instance. The auto-start attribute designates that we want this application to automatically start when OC4J_BI_Forms starts.

Understanding the OC4J Request Flow

Understanding the request flow of Discoverer gives an administrator the ability to accurately pinpoint where a problem exists, when one occurs.

To summarize the request flow:

1. A user enters http://*fully_qualified_domain_name*:7778/Discoverer/Plus in their browser.

2. After a DNS lookup, the request will be routed to Oracle Web Cache. Web Cache checks its site-to-server mapping and routes the request to the appropriate Oracle HTTP Server (OHS).

3. OHS identifies the presence of /Discoverer in the URL, looks at the Oc4jMount directive in the mod_oc4j.conf file, and routes the request to OC4J_BI_Forms.

4. OC4J_BI_Forms looks at the default-web-site.xml and server.xml files, identifies that the URL contains /Discoverer, and routes the request to the applications directory.

Configuring OC4J Using Oracle Enterprise Manager

To configure OC4J using OEM, use the following workflow:

1. From the Application Server Home page, shown earlier in Figure 20-3, select OC4J_BI_Forms. Discoverer opens the OC4J BI Forms Home page seen in Figure 20-7.

2. Click Administration. Discoverer opens the OC4J BI Forms Administration page shown in Figure 20-8. From this page you can perform many OC4J configuration tasks. It is infrequent, yet occasionally vital, to make changes to the OC4J_BI_Form instance.

The changes you can make include the three areas described next.

Instance Properties

Instance properties consist of the following:

- Server Properties

  - Number of Processes

  - Ports

OC4J: OC4J_BI_Forms

Home | Applications | Administration

Page Refreshed **Aug 18, 2005 9:47:07 PM**

General

Status	**Up**	
Start Time	**Aug 18, 2005 9:34:29 PM**	[Stop] [Restart]
Virtual Machines	1	

Status

CPU Usage (%)	**0.07**
Memory Usage (MB)	**51.55**
Heap Usage (MB)	**9.62**

JDBC Usage

Open JDBC Connections	**0**
Total JDBC Connections	**0**
Active Transactions	**0**
Transaction Commits	**0**
Transaction Rollbacks	**0**

Response - Servlets and JSPs

Active Sessions	**0**
Active Requests	**1**
Request Processing Time (seconds)	**0.008**
Requests per Second	**0.17**

Response - EJBs

Active EJB Methods	**0**
Method Execution Time (seconds)	**0.00**
Method Execution Rate (per second)	**0.00**

FIGURE 20-7 *OC4J BI Forms home page*

- ■ Command Line Options

  You may be called on to change the command options. For example, -Xms128M and -Xmx512M specify the minimum and maximum heap memory to be allocated for Discoverer's Java processes.

- ■ Website Properties

  Here you can see the URL mappings for all of the current web modules within the OC4J container. One of these will be Discoverer. You should see a setting indicating that Discoverer loads on startup.

OC4J: OC4J_BI_Forms

Home | Applications | Administration

Page Refreshed **Aug 18, 2005 11:46:21 PM**

Instance Properties

Server Properties
Website Properties
JSP Container Properties
Replication Properties
Advanced Properties

Application Defaults

Data Sources
Security
JMS Providers
Global Web Module

Related Links

ADF Business Components

OC4J Inheritance

OC4J applications have a hierarchical parent-child relationship to facilitate administration through inheritance. A child application inherits certain attributes from its parent application such as principals and JNDI objects including data sources, JMS providers and EJBs. When an OC4J application is deployed, you specify the parent application. The Default Application is the top of the parent hierarchy.

FIGURE 20-8 *OC4J BI Forms administration page*

- JSP Container Properties

- Replication Properties

- Advanced Properties

On this page you will see a list of the configuration files for the OC4J server. You can edit any of these by clicking the appropriate link.

Application Defaults
Application defaults consist of the following:

- Data Sources

- Security

- JMS Providers

- Global Web Module

Related Links
Related links consist of the following:

- ADF Business Components

- BC4J (This will be available only if you have installed BC4J in the Application Server.)

- UDDI Registry (This will be available only if you have an infrastructure database and you have performed the post-installation of the UDDI registry.)

NOTE
For more information regarding these areas please navigate to the appropriate page and click the Help link.

OEM Application Server Control
This browser-based tool allows you to start, stop, monitor, and configure many of the Application Server components. To launch OEM, open a browser window and enter **http://fully_qualified_domain_name:1810**, or whatever is your OEM port. OEM will ask you to log in.

NOTE
You may investigate the actual port number assigned by looking at the port numbers listed in ORACLE_HOME/install/portlist.ini.

If your Discoverer installation is using a metadata repository, then you will next see a farm page. A *farm* is a collection of Oracle Application Servers using the same infrastructure. If your Discoverer installation is stand-alone, then you will be taken directly to the Application Server management page. The Application Server home page contains performance metrics and indicates which components are running and how they are performing. From here you can configure Discoverer, OC4J_BI_Forms, Web Cache, and the Oracle HTTP Server by clicking the respective links.

Configuring Discoverer Using OEM

From the OEM main page click the Discoverer link. This opens the Discoverer control page. On this page you will find the following three tabs:

■ **Discoverer Home tab**   On this tab you can enable or disable the three Discoverer components (Discoverer Plus, Discoverer Viewer, and Discoverer Portal Provider). To enable or disable a component, check the box adjacent to the particular component and then click the appropriate Enable or Disable button.

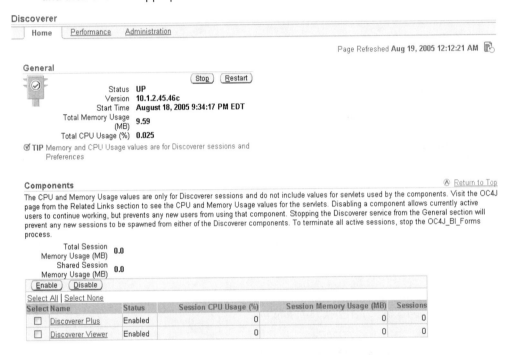

■ **Discoverer Performance tab**   On this tab you can see how well the Discoverer sessions are performing. You can filter the display to show only the top *N* sessions based upon their usage of memory or CPU resources.

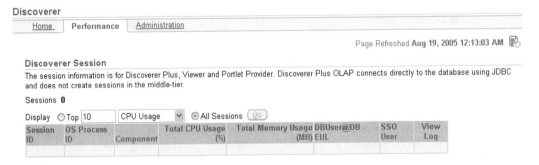

■ **Discoverer Administration tab**   This tab is described next.

Discoverer Administration Tab

On the Administration tab, illustrated here, you manage the Discoverer Catalog and the Discoverer Configuration. Both of these are described in the following sections.

Discoverer

| Home | Performance | **Administration** | |

Discoverer Catalog

Install
Uninstall
Manage

Configuration

Public Connections
Private Connections
Services Logging

Discoverer Catalog Overview

The Discoverer Catalog is a repository for storing and retrieving definitions of workbooks, worksheets, and other objects that are created with Discoverer Plus OLAP. These objects are used by Discoverer Plus OLAP, Viewer, and Portlet Provider when accessing data from OLAP data sources. You can also use the Discoverer Catalog as the Catalog for a BI Beans application, leveraging both the content and user community.

Managing the Discoverer Catalog

In the Discoverer Catalog area of the Administration tab, you manage the Discoverer catalog for OLAP. As you may recall from Chapter 16, Discoverer OLAP does not use an End User Layer but rather uses a catalog for storing workbooks, worksheets, and all of the Discoverer OLAP metadata.

The Discoverer Catalog area of the Administration page has three links:

- **Install** As seen next, you will use this link to install the Discoverer Catalog. You must provide a Host name (fully qualified domain name), DBA username (we use SYSTEM), and Password in order to install the catalog. In our experience, you will probably also need to provide the port and database SID as well. You will find the catalog under the D4OSYS schema.

Install Catalog

When you install the Discoverer Catalog, a D4OSYS user is automatically created   (Cancel)   (Continue)
and populated with the schema objects that are needed by workbooks, worksheets,
and other objects in Discoverer Plus OLAP. A database can contain only one
Discoverer Catalog. Enter the database connection information.

* Indicates a required field

* Host	asclaptop2.learndiscoverer.com
Port	1521
SID	laptop
* DBA Username	sys
* DBA Password	••••••••

- **Uninstall** As seen here, you will use this link to uninstall the Discoverer Catalog. In addition to the required parameters that you used when installing the catalog, you will also need to provide the D4OSYS password.

Uninstall Catalog

When you uninstall the Discoverer Catalog, the D4OSYS user is removed from the   (Cancel)   (OK)
database. As a result, all workbooks, worksheets, and other objects that were created by
Discoverer Plus OLAP are also removed. If you want to save these objects, then export the
Discoverer Catalog before uninstalling it.

* Indicates a required field

* Host	asclaptop2.learndiscoverer.com
Port	1521
SID	laptop
* DBA Username	sys
* DBA Password	••••••••
* D4OSYS Password	••••••••

After you have provided the uninstall credentials, click OK. You will be prompted whether you really want to uninstall the Discoverer Catalog. Click Yes to remove the catalog, or No to leave it in place.

■ **Manage** As seen next, you will use this link to manage the Discoverer Catalog.

You must provide the Hostname, Port, SID, and password for the D4OSYS schema. After you click the Login button, Discoverer validates your credentials and, if successful, displays the following Manage Catalog page:

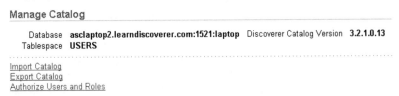

On the Manage Catalog page there are the following three links:

■ **Import Catalog** When you click this link, you will be asked to provide the name of a file that contains the information you want to import. You can use this mechanism to import workbooks, worksheets, or other objects into the catalog.

■ **Export Catalog** When you click this link, Discoverer automatically generates an export file called d4o_export.xml. If you are using Windows XP, you may well see the following download box being displayed. Back in OEM you will also see a message saying that the catalog has been successfully exported.

■ **Authorize Users and Roles** When you click this link, Discoverer displays the following Authorize Users page. Use this page to grant or revoke users and roles access to the catalog.

Managing the Discoverer Configuration

In the Discoverer Configuration area of the Administration tab, you manage the Discoverer connections and logging.

The Discoverer Configuration page, as seen in the preceding illustration, allows you to manage the public and private connections, as well as the Discoverer services logging.

■ **Discoverer Connections** A Discoverer connection stores the user ID, password, connect string, and EUL that are needed to log in to the database. This allows a user to log in to an EUL at the click of a button. Connections are not used with Discoverer 10*g* unless you have associated the mid-tier with an infrastructure. Discoverer connections have two types, public and private. The difference between the two is that only the Application Server administrator can create public connections, connections that are available to all users. Private connections, however, are created by the end user and, unless you are using SSO, are stored as cookies on the end user's computer. If you are using SSO, the connections are stored within the infrastructure. This allows the user to keep their connections as they move from one computer to another. It is also quite annoying for users to lose their Discoverer connections when they clear their cookies, but this is what will happen unless you enable SSO. From the Discoverer configuration page you may create public connections and allow or disallow users to create their own private connections.

■   Without SSO, as mentioned, a user's private connection is stored as a cookie. Because non-SSO URLs are unprotected, anyone who has access to the PC has access to the cookie, thus exposing the Discoverer URL to just about anyone. In this situation, even though the user provided a password when creating the connection, the password will always be prompted, thus affording Plus and Viewer the same protection as Desktop.

■   **Manage Logging**   This is where you enable logging for the Discoverer services tier.

NOTE
Enabling logging on this page does not enable logging for the individual Discoverer components (Plus, Viewer, and Portal Provider) but only for the Discoverer service itself. Logging for the components is managed from the individual component's home page.

Connection Tip for Bypassing the Connection Screen   If you want to bypass the Discoverer connection screen, use the following workflow:

1.   Create a public connection using OEM.

2.   Enter the URL to launch Discoverer, e.g., http://ascserver.learndiscoverer.com:7778/ discoverer/viewer.

3.   Expand the details for the public connection and note the connection key.

4.   Add the connection key to the URL as a parameter; e.g., if the connection key you noted in Step 3 was cn=cf_a105, your URL will now become http://ascserver.learndiscoverer. com:7778/discoverer/viewer?cn=cf_a105.

Discoverer Plus Configuration Page

From the component area of the main Discoverer home page, select the Discoverer Plus link. This displays the Discoverer Plus Configuration Page seen in Figure 20-9.

Selecting the link for Discoverer Plus allows you to view a performance page dedicated to just Discoverer Plus. This page has the following areas:

■   **Logo**   This area allows you to manage your corporate logo for both the standard and OLAP versions of Discoverer Plus. This area has the following radio buttons:

■   **None**   Check this button if you are not using a logo.

■   **URL**   Check this button if you want to use a URL address for the logo. You must then complete the box alongside by providing a valid URL.

■   **File**   Check this button if you want to use a logo contained within a file. Use the Browse button to locate the file.

Discoverer Plus Configuration

Discoverer Plus and Discoverer Plus OLAP are ad hoc query and reporting tools that allow users to create workbooks and calcuations, perform drill downs (Cancel) (OK)
and drill outs, pivot, sort, and change layout. Users can share and publish workbooks to Discoverer Viewer and Discovererer Portlets.

Logo

Change the logo used in Discoverer Plus and Discoverer Plus OLAP.

○ None

○ URL [   ]

◉ File [   ] [Browse...]

Look And Feel   Ⓐ Return to Top

Change the look and feel for Discoverer Plus and Discoverer Plus OLAP. To use the Plastic look and feel, use Sun Java Plugin 1.4 or higher. If Oracle Jinitiator is used,
the Plastic look and feel will default to Browser.

Look And Feel   [Plastic ▾]

Java Plugin   Ⓐ Return to Top

Select the Java plug-in for launching Discoverer Plus and Discoverer Plus OLAP.

Java Plugin   [Sun Java Plugin (1.4) ▾]

Communication Protocols   Ⓐ Return to Top

Discoverer Plus is a Java applet that runs on the user's machine and communicates with the Oracle Application Server. This setting does not apply to Discoverer Plus
OLAP.

◉ Default

   Discoverer will first attempt to make a direct connection using JRMP. A direct connection will only work within a firewall. If a direct connection cannot be established, Discoverer will automatically
   attempt to use the tunneling methods defined below.

○ Tunneling

   This method supports access via firewalls. If the Discoverer URL uses http, then Discoverer will use http tunneling, which is not secure. If the Discoverer URL uses https, then Discoverer will use
   the secure tunneling method defined below.

○ Secure Tunneling

FIGURE 20-9   *Discoverer Plus configuration page*

NOTE
*The logo that you set here is only applied to the Discoverer Plus
screens. It is not applied to the Plus for OLAP or the Viewer screens.*

- **Look And Feel**   This feature allows you to change the general appearance of the
  Discoverer Plus applet. The choice you make here applies to both the standard and OLAP
  versions of Discoverer Plus. You can pick from one of four types: Browser, Oracle, Plastic,
  and System. However, if you intend to use Oracle JInitiator, please note that the Plastic look
  and feel will default to the Browser. The main differences between the types are as follows:

  - **Browser**   This type picks up the colors from your Windows theme.

  - **Oracle**   This type uses dark gray for the background of the Plus screens and a
    medium gray for the background of the menus and the nonfocused tab names.
    Whenever the focus is placed in a cell, the outline of the cell becomes dark gray.
    When a tab receives the focus, the background for the tab changes to the same
    medium gray as the background for the menus. Slider bars are in the medium gray.

  - **Plastic**   This type uses a very light gray color for both the background of the Plus
    screens and the background of the menus. Nonfocused tabs get a more medium gray
    background for the tab names. Whenever the focus is placed in a cell, the gridlines
    for that cell become orange. When a tabs receives the focus, the background for the
    tab changes to the same light gray color as the remainder of the backgrounds. Slider
    bars are in blue.

- **System** This type uses the same light gray colors for the background of the Plus screens and the background for the menus as the color used in the Plastic type. Whenever the focus is placed in a cell, the bottom gridline of the cell becomes a series of dots in the same color as the main gridline color. Tabs that have the focus get a small orange bar on the outer edge of the tab name. Slider bars are in blue.

  Once you have changed the look and feel of Discoverer Plus using OEM, in order for your users to see the change, they only need to launch Plus. The system will automatically pick up the new look and feel without the need to restart the Discoverer services.

- **Java Plugin** This area allows you to choose to use either Oracle JInitiator or Sun's Java plug-in. The choice you make here applies to both the standard and OLAP versions of Discoverer Plus. Your selection will determine which Java plug-in your user downloads from the Application Server the first time the user connects to Discoverer. In our experience, most companies seem to be using the Sun Java plug-in, and this is the default.

- **Communication Protocols** This area allows you to control how your standard Discoverer Plus communicates with the Oracle Application Server. You have the following three protocols to choose from:

  - **Default** If you check this button, Discoverer will communicate using JRMP (Java Remote Method Protocol) unless it fails to connect due to the existence of a firewall. Upon failure, it will attempt to connect via HTTP or HTTPS. You should use this option if none or very few of your users connect to Discoverer through a firewall.

  - **Tunneling** If you are using a firewall, checking this button will cause Discoverer to initially attempt to communicate with the server using HTTP. If this fails, Discoverer will then try to use the secure tunneling protocol of HTTPS. You should use tunneling if a firewall exists between your users and Discoverer, and you mainly use HTTP. It will allow much faster connectivity.

  - **Secure Tunneling** If you are using a firewall, checking this button will cause Discoverer to always use HTTPS for all connections. You should use Secure Tunneling only if a firewall exists and you use only HTTPS. Your connections will be fast.

- **Logging** This allows you to specifically enable logging for the standard Discoverer Plus. The logging that you set here has no effect on Plus for OLAP. When managing logging, you can choose between None, Error, Warning, Notification, and Trace. Obviously, if you choose None, you will get no Plus logging. The remaining options log activity in greater and greater detail starting with Error and going up to Trace. You should enable Trace logging only when you already have serious issues and you are trying to find out what is going wrong. Under normal situations we recommend you either use None or Error.

Discoverer Viewer Configuration Page

Some of the greatest enhancements with the Discoverer 10g Release 2 edition relate to the configuration of Discoverer Viewer. If you take time and care setting up these configurations, you can set up Discoverer Viewer so that it looks and feels like part of your corporate web site.

From the Application Server home page select Discoverer Viewer. The Discoverer Viewer home page will open. This page has the following three tabs:

- Home

- Performance

- Customization

Discoverer Viewer Home Tab

The Discoverer Viewer home tab is shown in Figure 20-10.
On the Discoverer Viewer home tab, you can set the following:

- **Caching**   Check this box as the first of several steps that you must perform if you want to allow Web Cache to cache your Discoverer Viewer pages. Please refer to the section "Web Cache" later in this chapter for more details.

- **Printing Paper Sizes**   One of the weakest areas in previous releases of Discoverer Viewer was its printing features. Now, you can preselect a variety of different paper sizes that Discoverer end users are allowed to use. Using the two boxes in this area of the Viewer Configuration page, you can enable or restrict the paper sizes that users can pick for printing. You will generally find that all of the available paper sizes have already been enabled for use. If you see a page size that you know will not be needed, you should move it back into the available box using the remove buttons.

NOTE
In the 10.1.2.0.0 release of Discoverer, users have no means of changing the paper size that they are using. From 10.1.2.0.2, this has been changed and a new drop-down box allows uses to select the paper size. These sizes are saved with the worksheet, and so any page size set in Plus will be seen in Viewer, and vice versa.

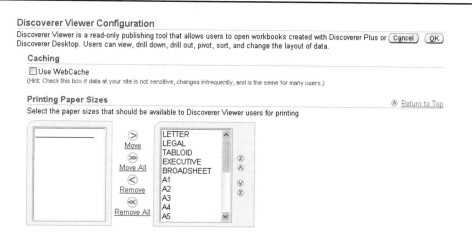

FIGURE 20-10   *Discoverer Viewer home tab*

■ **PDF Generation**   You can set the resolution of the PDF (Portable Document Format) documents, the maximum memory used to generate the PDFs, and the maximum number of concurrent users allowed to create PDFs. The defaults for these are a resolution of 200 pixels (your options are 100 to 600), a maximum memory of 64MB, and a maximum number of two users. The latter two options are free-form, and you can set these to any reasonable value that will support your configuration.

PDF Generation

Viewer PDF Generation options

* Indicates a required field

PDF Resolution (pixels) | 200 ⌄ |

* Maximum Memory (MB) | 64 |

☑ TIP Specify the maximum amount of memory to be used for PDF generation.

* Maximum Users | 2 |

☑ TIP Specify the maximum number of concurrent users that are allowed to generate PDF.

NOTE
If your users report difficulty generating PDFs, the most common problem is that their Discoverer output is larger than what fits on a page. You need to ask them to make the report smaller. You may also want to allocate more memory to your OC4J_BI_Forms instance. Please refer to the OC4J discussion in this chapter for details.

■ **Email**   This is where you set the SMTP server, the timeout, and the maximum attachment size. During the install of the Discoverer mid-tier, you would have been asked for the SMTP server to use for your e-mail application. Whatever SMTP server you entered at that time will be displayed here. However, as you know, the completion of the SMTP server screen of the installer is optional, and you can install the mid-tier without setting your e-mail server. If you did not have an e-mail server or could not remember the name of your e-mail server when you installed the mid-tier, here is where you enter it.

NOTE
Later in this section we will show you how you can set up Discoverer's e-mail so that it always sends from the same e-mail address.

Email

Viewer Email options

* Indicates a required field

SMTP Server | mailserver.com |

* Maximum Attachment Size (KB) | 4096 |

* Timeout (seconds) | 60 |

■ **Viewer Delay Times** This is where you specify how long Discoverer Viewer should wait before displaying the Query Progress page. You can also set the frequency (in seconds) that Viewer waits before checking to see if the report is finished. Internet Explorer's default timeout is 60 seconds, so please do not set the delay to be higher than this. Should you do this, we will leave you to guess what will happen! We recommend lowering the default from 6 seconds to 1 second. Otherwise, a page that would normally take 4–9 seconds will always take 10 seconds.

Viewer Delay Times

Specify the amount of delay time.

∗ Indicates a required field

∗ Query Progress Page (seconds) [3]

Time to wait before returning the initial query progress page.

∗ Request (seconds) [6]

Frequency to check for request completion. This should typically be just less than the browser's timeout specification.

■ **Viewer Logging** This is where you set the logging level for Discoverer Viewer. When managing logging, you can choose between None, Error, Warning, Notification, and Trace. Obviously, if you choose None, you will get no Plus logging. The remaining options log activity in greater and greater detail starting with Error and going up to Trace. You should enable Trace logging only when you already have serious issues and you are trying to find out what is going wrong. We recommend that under normal situations you either use None or Error.

Discoverer Viewer Performance Tab

The Discoverer Viewer Performance tab is shown in Figure 20-11. You use this tab to see all Discoverer Viewer activity and the resources used.

Discoverer Viewer

| Home | Performance | Customization |

Page Refreshed **Oct 6, 2005 8:33:58 PM**

Discoverer Viewer Sessions

Sessions **1**

Display ○ Top [10] [CPU Usage ▼] ◉ All Viewer Sessions (Go)

Session ID	OS Process ID	Total CPU Usage (%)	Total Memory Usage (MB)	DBUser@DB - EUL	SSO User	View Log
200510062033131504	1504	1.77	14.04	drake@laptop		📋

FIGURE 20-11 *Discoverer Viewer Performance tab*

On the Discoverer Viewer Performance tab, you have the following areas:

- **Sessions**   This displays the total number of current Viewer sessions.

- **Display**   Select this radio button to specify that you want to see information about the top N Viewer sessions. Having selected this button, you use the Top box to enter a value for the number of sessions that you want to view and then use the drop-down box alongside to specify whether you want to see information about CPU Usage or Memory Usage.

- **All Viewer Sessions**   Select this radio button to tell Discoverer that you want to see information about all of the current Viewer sessions. The drop-down box for CPU Usage and Memory Usage is still available.

- **Go**   Click this button to view the session details.

- **Session ID**   This is the session ID of the Discoverer Viewer session.

- **OS Process ID**   This is the operating system process ID.

- **Total CPU Usage %**   This is the total percentage of CPU that is currently being used by the session.

- **Total Memory Usage**   This is the total amount of memory that is currently being used by the session.

NOTE
The CPU and Memory Usage statistics shown here do not include the CPU and Memory being consumed by the servlets. To see the amount of resource being used by the servlets, you need to view the usage statistics of the individual servlet. You do this by navigating to the Discoverer page from the OC4J_BI_Forms home page.

- **DBUser@DB**   This displays the database user, database name, and EUL for the session.

- **SSO User**   If SSO is enabled, this displays the name of the SSO that is using the session.

- **View Log**   Discoverer maintains logs of the session according to the log requirements that you specified on the Discoverer Viewer home tab. Most of the time you will have the logging set to only log errors, so when you click this icon, you will usually get a message to say that there is no error log. This is normal.

Discoverer Viewer Customization Tab

This tab has two sections, both of which are activated by selecting the section you want to work on and then clicking the Go button. The two sections that are available for customization are

- Look and Feel

- Layout

Look and Feel   This section, as you can see next, has two main areas.

The two areas you can manage are Colors and Fonts.

Use the Colors area to type hex codes or use palette buttons to set the colors; for example, #000000 is white, meaning 00 for red, 00 for green, and 00 for blue. There are five colors you can set:

- **Core**   This is used to define the following colors:

    - The Actions and Worksheet headings

    - The Arrow icons

    - The Column headings

    - The Connected To text

    - The Crosstab or Table heading

    - The Header panel

    - The Last Run date

    - The text color of the header cells for the Connections table on the Connections page

    - The Tools headings

    - The Worksheet name

- **Accent**   This is used to define the following colors:

    - The background color of the Connections table on the Connections page

    - The background color of the Workbook Explorer

    - The text background for the Actions and Worksheets

- **Foreground**   This is used to define the following colors:

    - The Connections table

    - The final breadcrumb text: the text that displays the current location within Viewer

    - The text used in drop-down lists, e.g., lists of values

    - The Workbook Explorer

- **Background**   This is used to define the main background color used in all Discoverer Viewer pages.

- **Links**   This is used to define colors for all link texts used in Viewer.

Use the Fonts area to define the base font size and font family that Viewer will use.

- **Base Font Size**   You use this field to specify the font size for most of the text displayed within the Viewer user interface. It does not control the following:

    - The Actions heading

- The Exit, Help, and Preferences links in the header

- The Go button

- The text used for crosstab tools and layout controls

- The Worksheet name

- **Font Family** Use this field to specify the font family that is to be used for text displayed within Viewer. You can choose one of the following:

  - Arial (this is the default)

  - Courier

  - Times New Roman

As you make changes to the look and feel, use the Preview button to see what your settings will look like. Discoverer maintains an example screen to the right of your selections, as seen in the next illustration, of how the changes will look. When you have the set of colors and fonts that you want to use, click the Apply button. There is no need to restart the mid-tier, because these changes are applied immediately.

NOTE
If you select the Reset to Minimal button, then Viewer pages will be assembled faster. This is because Discoverer will have to perform the minimum amount of rendering to put a worksheet screen together.

Customize Layout   As you can see next, this section has four main areas.

Customize Layout

(Preview) (Apply)

Corporate Branding

☑ Logo
  ⦿ Default (Viewer Logo)
  ○ URL [   ]
  ○ File [   ] (Browse...)

Global Buttons

If URLs specified below do not start with http://, ftp://, and
so on, then they are assumed to be relative to
http://host:port/discoverer.

☑ Exit   URL [   ]
☑ Help   URL [   ]
☑ Logout
☑ Preferences

Action Links

☑ Rerun Query   ☑ Print Options   ☑ Export
☑ Send as email   ☑ Save/Save As   ☑ Revert
☐ Link/Unlink Layout ☑ Worksheet Options

Others

☑ Last Run   ☑ Connected To
☑ Tool Bars ☑ Worksheets

These four main areas are as follows:

- **Corporate Branding**   In this area, you can tell Discoverer that it should use your corporate logo rather than use the generic logo that is normally displayed. As in Plus, this area has the following radio buttons:

  - **None**   Check this button if you are not using a logo.

  - **URL**   Check this button if you want to use a URL address for the logo. You must then complete the box alongside by providing a valid URL.

  - **File**   Check this button if you want to use a logo contained within a file. Use the Browse button to locate the file.

NOTE
The logo that you set here is applied only to the Discoverer Viewer pages. It is not applied to the Discoverer Plus pages.

- **Global Buttons**   Both the top right and very bottom of the Viewer screen have placeholders for the following five buttons. You can choose whether to individually hide or display these buttons. In addition, Oracle has provided a way for you to customize the behavior of the Exit, Logout, and Help buttons by allowing you to enter your own URLs for these three buttons.

  - **Exit**   Use this check box to display or hide the Exit link that normally displays at the top right and immediately below all Discoverer Viewer worksheets. If you select this check box, you can optionally define a target URL. If you decide not to define a target URL and a user clicks the Exit link, Discoverer Viewer will display a standard exit page.

■ **Help**   Use this check box to display or hide the Help link that normally displays at the top right and immediately below all Discoverer Viewer worksheets. If you select this check box, you can optionally define a target URL for your own help. If you decide not to define a target URL and a user clicks the Help link, Discoverer Viewer will display the appropriate help page for the page that they are currently in.

■ **Logout**   Use this check box to display or hide the Logout link that that normally displays at the top right and immediately below all Discoverer Viewer worksheets. If you select this check box, you can optionally define a target URL. If you decide not to define a target URL and a user clicks the Logout link, Discoverer Viewer will log the user out of Discoverer.

■ **Preferences**   Use this check box to display or hide the Preferences link that that normally displays at the top right and immediately below all Discoverer Viewer worksheets. The Preferences page enables end users to specify their own values for several of the Discoverer Viewer settings (e.g., the query governor). If this box is not checked, your users will not be able to set their own preferences.

■ **Return to Portal**   Use this check box to display or hide the Return to Portal link that normally displays at the top right of Discoverer Viewer worksheets that have been reached from a Discoverer Portlet.

NOTE
If you have not attached Discoverer to an infrastructure, you will not see the Return to Portal button. If you have not enabled SSO, your users will not see the Logout button but will see the Exit button instead.

■ **Action Links**   On the left-hand side of the main Viewer screen your users will be presented with a box of actions. This box is a placeholder for the following eight options. You can choose whether to individually hide or display these buttons.

■ **Rerun Query**   If this is enabled, your users will see a link called Rerun query. When a user clicks this link, that user will be able to rerun the query to obtain the latest information from the database.

■ **Save/Save As**   If this is enabled, your users will see links called Save and Save As. Turning this feature off does still not prevent a user from saving. You will need to remove the user's Save to Database privilege in the Administrator edition to completely prevent a user from saving within Viewer.

■ **Revert**   If this is enabled, Viewer will display a link called Revert to Saved. When a user clicks this link, Discoverer will rerun the query from the database, restoring any formatting or layout changes to the way that they are set within the saved workbook.

■ **Print Options**   If this is enabled, your users will see a link called Printable Page. When a user clicks this link, Discoverer will display a page called Printable Page Options, where users can set up their own preferences for things such as whether the headers and footers should print and whether to show the title on the first page or all pages. Users will also get the chance to use Page Setup to determine the page size, margins, and scaling.

■ **Export**   If this is enabled, your users will see a link called Export. When a user clicks this link, Discoverer will allow the user to export the data from the report in a number of different formats.

■ **Send as email**   If this is enabled, your users will see a link called Send as Email. When a user clicks this link, Discoverer will allow the user to send the results via e-mail, provided of course that you have specified your SMTP e-mail settings.

■ **Link/Unlink Layout**   If this is enabled, and in OLAP only, your users will see a link called Link or Unlink Layout. When a user clicks this link, Discoverer will allow the user to link or unlink the screen layout from the query.

■ **Worksheet Options**   If this is enabled, your users will see a link called Worksheet Options. When a user clicks this link, Discoverer will display a page that allows the user to decide whether the title, graph, table, or crosstab should be displayed.

NOTE
You will be asked to hide several of these buttons if you choose to enable Oracle Web Cache. See the section on "Web Cache" later in this chapter for more details.

■ **Others**   You can hide or display the toolbars, the connections the user is connected to, the date the query was last run, and the available worksheets by using these buttons:

  ■ **Last Run**   If this is enabled, your users will see when the query was last run. This information will be displayed at the top left corner of each worksheet.

  ■ **Connected To**   If this is enabled, your users will see a label at the top right-hand corner of each worksheet informing them of their connection information.

  ■ **Tool Bars**   If this is enabled, your users will see the Layout, Format, and Sort tools links on the screen, which will allow them to modify and analyze the data. By default these are enabled.

  ■ **Worksheets**   If this is enabled, your users will see the list of available worksheet links on the left-hand side of each worksheet.

Just as with the look and feel section, as you make changes to the layout, use the Preview button to see what your settings will look like. Discoverer maintains an example screen to the right of your selections showing how the changes will look. When you have defined the layout that you want to use, click Apply. Once again there is no need to restart the mid-tier, because these changes are applied immediately.

Customizing Viewer Manually   We are frequently asked whether it is possible to customize Discoverer Viewer further. The answer to this is yes. In order to customize Discoverer Viewer even further than is allowed using OEM, you need to edit the Discoverer UIX files. You will appreciate that we cannot give you all of the customizations possible. This would require a complete book to itself! However, just to show you what is possible, we will show you how to manually suppress the display of the Export Types.

NOTE
*Before you jump in and start editing your UIX files, please read ahead
to the next section called "Warning Concerning Editing UIX Files" and
make sure you understand all of the warnings.*

To hide the display of the Display Types, use the following workflow:

1. Locate this file:

```
$ORACLE_HOME/j2ee/OC4J_BI_Forms/applications/Discoverer/Discoverer/ExportTypes.uix
```

2. Make a safe backup of ExportTypes.uix.
3. Delete the following lines:

```
<choice name="${uix.data.constants.EXPORT_TYPE_PARAM}"
selectedValue="${uix.eventResult.selectedExportTypeValue}">
<contents childData="${uix.eventResult.exportTypeList}">
<option value="${uix.current.exportTypeValue}"
text="${uix.data.nls[uix.current.resourceKey]}" />
</contents>
<primaryClientAction>
<fireAction event="refreshExportUI"
formSubmitted="true"/>
</primaryClientAction>
</choice>
```

4. Examine the following lines. Each line you add represents the export type you would
   like available to your users. Add these lines in the same location where you deleted the
   previous set of lines:

```
<option value="1" text="${uix.data.nls['export.type.excel']}"/>
<option value="1" text="${uix.data.nls['export.type.excel.pivot']}"/>
```

5. Save the file.
6. Take a backup of the modified file and place it somewhere safe.
7. Restart OC4J_BI_Forms.

Warning Concerning Editing UIX Files   Before you jump into editing the UIX files and make
wholesale changes to your underlying configurations, we need to give you the following words
of warning:

- *Never* make any changes without first backing up the UIX file that you intend to work
  on. You need to go slowly and carefully, making backups as you go and trying out your
  modifications on a test system first.

- Any changes you make to a UIX file will not be supported by Oracle, and if you run into
  any problems with changes that you make to a UIX file, you will be on your own, hence
  the need for a backup.

- If you need future support, you will need to be able to prove that the issue you are
  encountering is not due to any changes that you have made. You will basically need
  to have a clean instance to prove that the issue is still there.

■ Any upgrades or patches that you subsequently apply may overwrite any custom changes that you have made to the UIX files. It will be your responsibility to keep copies of any changes that you have made, and it will be your responsibility to make sure that these changes are still valid after any upgrade or patch.

■ Oracle does not guarantee that they will continue using UIX in future releases. Therefore, any effort you spend in gaining UIX expertise for the purpose of customizing Discoverer could be useless in the future.

NOTE
The authors cannot be held responsible or liable if you tamper with your UIX files and mess up your system. You have been warned!

E-Mail Tip

If you want to force users to send Discoverer reports from a pre-specified e-mail account, use the following workflow:

1. Locate this file:

   ```
   $ORACLE_HOME/j2ee/OC4J_BI_Forms/applications/Discoverer/Discoverer/Email.uix
   ```

2. Make a safe backup of Email.uix.

3. Find the following line and add the information in bold:

   ```
   <contents>
   <messageTextInput required="yes" name="sender" disabled="true"
   tip="john.doe@company.com" columns="40"
   prompt="${uix.data.nls['email.text.sender']}" text="Discoverer@company.com"/>
   ```

4. Find the following line and add the line in bold below it.

   ```
   <formValue name="event" value="sendEmail" />
   <formValue name="sender" value=Discoverer@company.com />
   ```

NOTE
Make sure that the domain name you provide is the same domain that you are using for the SMTP server; otherwise, your Discoverer Viewer users will not be able to send e-mail.

5. Take a backup of the modified file and place it somewhere safe.

6. Restart the OC4J_BI_Forms component.

NOTE
Once again, we cannot overstress the need for you to read the section in this chapter called "Warning Concerning Editing UIX Files." Please make sure you understand all of the warnings and make all recommended backups before you start.

Discoverer Portlet Provider Configuration Page

The Discoverer Portlet Provider Configuration page, illustrated next, allows you to manage how portlets are displayed in Portal.

Discoverer Portlet Provider Configuration

The Discoverer Portlet Provider generates portlets for use on OracleAS Portal pages. Discoverer portlets can be created when setting up a Portal page.   Cancel   OK

Discoverer Session

The Discoverer Portlet Provider uses Discoverer sessions to update cached data for Discoverer Portlets. These Sessions can be pooled for reuse by different Discoverer Portlets, saving CPU and memory.

Specify the maximum number of Discoverer sessions to pool.

* Indicates a required field

  * Maximum Sessions `20`

☑ TIP A small number of maximum sessions in the pool saves memory but causes requests to be queued for a short time if all sessions are in use.

  * Maximum Session Inactivity (minutes) `17`

☑ TIP The maximum number of minutes a session is allowed to be inactive in the pool before being removed.

  * Maximum Session Age (hours) `35`

☑ TIP The maximum number of hours a session is allowed to be in the pool even if it is active.

  * Maximum Wait Time (minutes) `1`

☑ TIP The maximum number of minutes to wait for a session to become available before cancelling a portlet refresh

▲ Return to Top

Portlet Generic Parameters

Discoverer Worksheet Portlet uses generic portlet parameters in order to support Portal Page parameters. Specify the number of generic parameters that you want Discoverer Worksheet Portlet to expose.

* Indicates a required field

  * Maximum Generic Parameters `10`

☑ TIP Typically the maximum number of generic parameters should be equal to the maximum number of query parameters that may be present in any Discoverer worksheet that is published as a portlet.

To manage portlets, use the following workflow:

1. From the application home page select Discoverer Portlet Provider.

2. You can manage the following:

  ■ **Maximum sessions value**   If you are using Discoverer to provide portlets to Oracle portal, you can control the number session pools by changing this value. The default is 20, but Oracle recommends setting this to the number of CPUs on your application server.

  ■ **Maximum Session Inactivity and Maximum Session Age**   These settings determine how long the session that served the portlet will remain alive.

  ■ **Maximum wait time**   This setting determines how long Portal will wait for Discoverer to provide the portlet.

  ■ **Portal Generic Parameters**   If you so choose, you can pass parameters that Portal maintains to Discoverer Portlets. The Portal Generic Parameters setting sets the maximum number of generic parameters that may be mapped. The default value of 10 should be sufficient unless workbooks have been developed with more than 10 user-defined parameters to which Portal needs to provide values.

  ■ **Portlet Provider Logging**   This setting controls the amount of logging done for the Portlet Provider.

Single Sign-On (SSO)

SSO provides a great deal of flexibility and allows for easier integration with Discoverer and Oracle Portal. You must decide whether using SSO with Discoverer is cost-effective. Deciding on whether or not your organization is interested in investing in an Identity Management server is another discussion. If you already have implemented OID and SSO for other Oracle products, like *Portal*, then this discussion is for you.

SSO is installed with the Application Server's infrastructure install type. It allows a user to employ a single login and password for all web applications (Oracle and otherwise) in your organization. Thus, for example, when a user enters http://ascserver/learndiscoverer.com:7778/discoverer/plus, the Oracle HTTP server's mod_osso module identifies that the /Discoverer/plus/ is protected and redirects the user to the SSO login page, as seen in Figure 20-12, that is served from the infrastructure's HTTP server.

After the user provides his or her name and password, SSO checks with the Oracle Internet Directory (OID) to see if that is a valid user. If so, SSO places a temporary cookie in the user's browser indicating the user has been authenticated. Then, the user is redirected back to the Oracle HTTP Server (OHS) that the original request was made to. Upon returning, SSO still identifies that /Discoverer/plus is protected, but this time because the cookie exists, mod_osso allows the user to access Discoverer Plus.

From here on, if the user clicks a link to another web site, like /Discoverer/viewer, the SSO server will automatically authenticate them. Another advantage of using Single Sign-On is that users have their own set of Discoverer connections that can follow them wherever they log in, versus storing the connections as cookies.

Configuring Single Sign-On

To configure SSO, use the following workflow:

1. Launch a web browser and enter the URL to manage SSO, e.g., http://infraserver. learndiscoverer.com:7777/orasso.

2. Log in using orcladmin and the ias_admin password that you provided during installation.

3. As you can see next, you have the following three choices:

Edit SSO Server Configuration
Maintain the configuration information for the SSO Server. These configuration settings include the SSO Server's session settings.

Administer Partner Applications
Create or edit configuration information for partner applications. Partner applications are applications that have delegated authentication processing to the SSO Server.

Administer External Applications
Create or edit configuration information for external applications. External applications are web-based applications that perform their own user name/password authentication through HTML login forms. The SSO Server will login to these applications on behalf of the user.

Sign In

Enter your Single Sign-On user name and password to login

User Name orcladmin

Password ●●●●●●●●

Login   Cancel

FIGURE 20-12 *SSO Login page*

- **Edit SSO Server Configuration**   Set the Single Sign-On session duration. This is how long a user may stay logged into Single Sign-On. Also, verify the IP addresses for requests made in the SSO server. This security check compares the IP address of the browser to the IP address provided in the HTTP request. Do not check this if you are using Portal.

- **Administer Partner Applications**   A partner application is any application that delegates authentication to Single Sign-On. The implication here is that the web application does not have its own login mechanism and will solely depend upon using SSO to protect its content. If you configure SSO using mod_osso configuration, you have configured a partner application.

- **Administer External Applications**   An external application is one where SSO maintains the additional username and password for the other application, and then upon navigation to the other application, SSO submits the username and password. It is very simple to set up an external application. All you need to provide is the URL to submit the username and password to and the field names for the username and password. You can easily find this information by exploring the HTML source of the applications login page.

Enabling Discoverer with SSO

As explained earlier, it is actually the mod_osso module in OHS that is configured to protect an application like Discoverer.

To enable Discoverer to use Single Sign-On, use the following workflow:

1. Ensure you are joined to an infrastructure.

2. Navigate to mod_osso.conf file located in $ORACLE_HOME/Apache/Apache/conf.

3. Make a backup copy of mod_osso.conf.

4. Edit mod_osso.conf and locate these lines:

    ```
    #
    # Insert Protected Resources:
    #
    ```

5. Insert the following lines:

    ```
    <Location /Discoverer/plus*>
     require valid-user
     AuthType Basic
     </Location>
    <Location /Discoverer/viewer>
     Header unset Pragma
     OssoSendCacheHeaders off
     require valid-user
     AuthType Basic
    </Location>
    ```

    You will notice that Discoverer Viewer's parameters are different from Discover Plus. This is to due to a Microsoft Internet Explorer problem that occurs when exporting data from viewer.

NOTE
*In the changes just outlined, an asterisk (*) must follow the word plus,
e.g., /discoverer/plus*.*

6. Save mod_osso.conf.

7. In a command shell, navigate to $ORACLE_HOME/dcm/bin.

8. Run this command: **dcmctl updateconfig**.

NOTE
*This step can take several minutes, so please be patient while it runs
and make sure you do nothing else at this time. Well, maybe get a
coffee!*

9. When the dcm step has finished, start a browser and launch the Discoverer OEM.

10. Connect to the Discoverer mid-tier.

11. Restart the Oracle HTTP Server.

12. After SSO has been enabled, you should test it using the ias_admin username.

13. When you are happy that SSO is working, you can use any SSO login to create Single
    Sign-On users using OIDDAS. Please refer to the section "Oracle Internet Directory"
    later in this chapter for an explanation on how to connect to OID to add SSO users to
    your system.

OPMN (Oracle Process Management and Notification)

This component of the Oracle Application Server is used to start, stop, and monitor many of the
components in the server, including Discoverer. It will ping Discoverer and all other components
on a configurable interval. If it determines that a component has crashed or no longer responding,
it will notify MOD_OC4J to stop routing requests to that component, and then attempt to restart
the component. When the component is running again, the component itself will notify MOD_
OC4J that it is able to accept request again.

OPMN Basic Commands

The Oracle Process Manager and Notification Server (OPMN) uses the opmnctl utility to manage
all Oracle Application Server 10g server processes. The powerful **startall** and **stopall** commands
will manage all server components. Unless a tier consists of a stand-alone component such as the
Web Cache, opmnctl should be used rather than the separate component control program. Below
is a listing of the basic OPMN commands.

- **Opmnctl start**   Use this command to start OPMN.

- **Opmnctl shutdown**   Use this command to shut down OPMN and all of its managed
  processes.

- **Opmnctl startall**   Use this command to start OPMN and all of the managed processes.

■ **Opmnctl stopall**   Use this command to stop OPMN and all of the managed processes.

■ **Opmnctl status**   Use this command to list the status for each of the OPMN components. Adding the additional switch -I after the command causes the system to display an extended status showing the uid, memory used, and ports used. The following is a sample output from this command:

```
Processes in Instance: main.learndiscoverer.com
-------------------+-------------------+-------+---------
ias-component      | process-type      |   pid | status
-------------------+-------------------+-------+---------
DSA                | DSA               |   N/A | Down
LogLoader          | logloaderd        |   N/A | Down
dcm-daemon         | dcm-daemon        |  3524 | Alive
WebCache           | WebCacheAdmin     |  1680 | Alive
WebCache           | WebCache          |  4092 | Alive
OC4J               | home              |  1088 | Alive
OC4J               | OC4J_BI_Forms     |  1136 | Alive
HTTP_Server        | HTTP_Server       |  1464 | Alive
Discoverer         | ServicesStatus    |  1684 | Alive
Discoverer         | PreferenceServer  |  1732 | Alive
```

NOTE
The Log Loader process is always down after installation. Log Loader is a feature that compiles log messages from various log files into a single repository. You can start Log Loader after installation if you wish.

■ **Opmnctl startproc process-type=ServicesStatus (Discoverer Component)**   Use the startproc command to start an individual process. If no process attribute is supplied to this command, all opmn managed processes except components with id-matching=true will be started. The command above will start the Discoverer Services Status process.

■ **Opmnctl startproc process-type=PreferenceServer (Discoverer component)**   This command starts the Discoverer Preference Server.

■ **Opmnctl help**   Use this command to display a brief description of all the commands available for use with opmnctl.

■ **Opmnctl usage**   Use this command to display a detailed description of all the commands available for use with opmnctl. Adding an optional switch of the command name displays just the description for that command. For example, using **opmnctl usage start** displays a full description of the usage for the **start** command.

OPMN is primarily configured using opmn.xml. If you explore this file, you will recognize many key parameters. In the following section we will list several of the key parameters. However, please note that there are many more parameters than those that we list in the text that follows. The goal of this discussion is to identify OPMN as a key Discoverer component that deserves exploration whenever problems occur.

You should also explore the $ORACLE_HOME/opmn/logs as a first priority when troubleshooting Discoverer.

OPMN.XML Example

The opmn.xml file, found in $ORACLE_HOME/opmn/conf, is used to tell opmn the processes that it manages. The file is quite long. However, the file is broken up into sections beginning with the command **ias-component id=**. In a typical opmn.xml file you will find the following components:

- ias-component id="DSA"

- ias-component id="LogLoader"

- ias-component id="dcm-daemon"

- ias-component id="WebCache"

- ias-component id="OC4J"

- ias-component id="HTTP Server"

- ias-component id="Discoverer"

These IDs set the respective environment variables. If you look back in this chapter to the section called "OPMN Basic Commands," you will notice that the example output in that section contains entries that equate to the ias components listed above.

The section of the opmn.xml that manages Discoverer is shown here:

```
<ias-component id="Discoverer">
    <environment>
        <variable id="PREFERENCE_PORT" value="16001"/>
        <variable id="DISCO_DIR" value="$ORACLE_HOME"/>
        <variable id="DCLOG_CONFIG_FILE"
value="C:\oracle\BIHome_1\discoverer\util\ServerLogParams.txt"/>
        <variable id="LD_LIBRARY_PATH"
value="\usr\lib;C:\oracle\BIHome_1\discoverer\lib;C:\oracle\BIHome_1\lib"
append="true"/>
        <variable id="DC10_REG" value="C:\oracle\BIHome_1\discoverer\"/>
        <variable id="FND_TOP" value="C:\oracle\BIHome_1\discoverer\"/>
        <variable id="FND_SECURE" value="C:\oracle\BIHome_1\discoverer\secure"/>
    </environment>
    <process-type id="ServicesStatus" module-id="Disco_ServicesStatus"
status="enabled">
        <process-set id="ServicesStatus" numprocs="1"/>
    </process-type>
    <process-type id="PreferenceServer" module-id="Disco_PreferenceServer"
working-dir="$ORACLE_HOME/discoverer" status="enabled">
        <process-set id="PreferenceServer" numprocs="1"/>
    </process-type>
    <process-type id="SessionServer" module-id="Disco_SessionServer"
status="enabled">
        <start timeout="180" retry="0"/>
        <port id="ses" range="3801-3950"/>
        <process-set id="SessionServer" minprocs="0" maxprocs="50"
        restart-on-death="false" parallel-requests="true"/>
    </process-type>
</ias-component>
```

In the extract above, you will notice various switches and settings:

- **range="3801-3950"** This identifies the ports used by the Discoverer Session servers. You must have enough ports to handle the number of processes.

- **minprocs="0"** This identifies the number of session processes that are started when Discoverer is started. You may choose either 0 or 1.

- **maxprocs="50"** This is the maximum number of Discoverer sessions. Set this as high as your server's resources will permit.

- **restart-on-death="false"** If a process dies, this tells OPMN whether it should restart it or not. For the session server this must remain at false.

- **parallel-requests="true"** This tells OPMN whether it should process requests in parallel or serially.

Oracle Internet Directory (OID)

This is Oracle's LDAP (Lightweight Directory Access Protocol)–compliant server. It stores all of its data in an Oracle 10g database, but it maintains additional processes in front of the database to respond to LDAP requests. If Single Sign-On is being used with Discoverer, you will also be using OID. For the greatest convenience to your users, you may use external authentication for Single Sign-On.

For example, you could have your users log in to their Windows domain. Then, upon opening a web browser and typing the Discoverer connection URL, a user will not be given the Single Sign-On web page, but instead the Single Sign-On server will check with OID, which will in turn check with Microsoft Active Directory to determine whether the user is able to access Discoverer.

Therefore, using a Windows network domain, SSO, and OID, web users will never need to log in to Discoverer, just Windows. For further reference, please check the Oracle Internet Directory documentation for External Authentication. OID also has command-line tools that allow you to bulk-load all of your users into OID for use with Discoverer.

Delegated Administration Service (DAS)

This web site, illustrated next, allows your users to self-service manage their user account information. It also allows the OID administrator to add, delete, and alter user account information. It is essentially an easy-to-use graphical interface for Oracle Internet Directory.

This component is relevant to a Discoverer implementation only if Discoverer has been configured to use Single Sign-On.

To add a user to OID using DAS, use the following workflow:

1. Launch a web browser and enter the URL to connect to OIDDAS, e.g., http://ascserver. learndiscoverer.com:7777/oiddas.
2. Log in using orcladmin and the ias_admin password that you provided during installation.
3. Click the Directory tab.
4. Click Create.
5. Enter the user's information.
6. Click Submit.

Metadata Repository

The metadata repository (MR) is an Oracle 10g database that maintains metadata for the Application Server. Discoverer primarily uses the MR to maintain information about the portlets it provides for Oracle Portal. However, customers are licensed to also use the MR for their Discoverer EUL by using it to host the Discoverer metadata. If Discoverer is using Single Sign-On, then it will also indirectly use all the OID schemas. It is important to note that you cannot place any user data in the MR without purchasing a separate license. We would go further than this and say that we do not recommend the placement of any user data in the MR. The MR has been designed so that it should require virtually no tuning and be relatively hands-off. If you start placing data in this database, then the database may grow to be quite large and thus require tuning.

NOTE
We recommend you place the infrastructure on a separate machine from any of your middle-tier application servers. Placing the infrastructure and middle-tier servers on the same machine will place an unnecessary strain on the machine.

To be able to use any of the following additional features, Discover must be joined to both a metadata repository and an identity management server:

- Single Sign-On

- Discoverer Portlet Provider (via Oracle Portal)

- Discoverer Connections management page

- Private and public connections

- SSL functionality

- OracleAS Web Cache

- Oracle Identity Management (OID)

Joining a Discoverer Mid-Tier to an Identity Management Server and a Metadata Repository

To join a Discoverer mid-tier to an identity management server and MR, use the following workflow:

1. Install the metadata repository (otherwise known as the infrastructure) in a separate ORACLE_HOME either on the mid-tier Discoverer Server or on a separate server dedicated to this purpose.

NOTE
Unless you are really short of processing power and disk space, we recommend you keep your metadata repository away from the Discoverer mid-tier by installing the two on separate machines.

2. Launch the OEM AS Control for the Discoverer Server mid-tier, e.g., http://ascserver. learndiscoverer.com:1810.

3. Click the Infrastructure tab.

Identity Management

User identities and groups are administered using Internet Directory.   [Configure]

    Internet Directory Host   **Not Configured**
    Internet Directory Port

Grid Control Management

To centrally manage this application server with Oracle Enterprise Manager 10g Grid Control, the Management Agent installed on the application server host must be configured to connect to a Management Service.   [Configure]

    Management Service Host   **Not Configured**
    Management Service Port

Metadata Repository

Components' metadata are stored in database schemas in the Metadata Repository.   [Configure]

    Default Metadata Repository   **Not Configured**

4. As you can see in the preceding illustration, neither Identity Management nor the metadata repository has been configured. You must configure Identity Management first. To start this process, click the Configure button in the Identity Management area of the Infrastructure page.

5. Step 1 of the Configure Identity Management screen will open. To complete this step, do the following:

   ■ **Host**   Enter the fully qualified hostname of the identity management server, e.g., oidserver.learndiscoverer.com.

   ■ **Port**   Enter the OID port. You can determine the OID port by accessing OEM for the infrastructure in another web browser window and clicking the Ports tab. The component you are looking for is called Oracle Internet Directory and is located at the bottom of the list. If you are not using SSL, use the Non SSL Port number; otherwise, use the number corresponding to the SSL Port.

6. Click Next when you are done.

NOTE
When you click Next, Discoverer checks to see whether there is an OID host at the Port location that you specified. If no OID can be detected, you will get an error message. You will not be able to continue until you provide the correct connection information.

7. Once you have entered the correct connection information, Step 2 of the Configure Identity Management screen will open. To complete this step, do the following and then click Next:

   ■ **Username**   Leave this as defaulted to cn=orcladmin.

   ■ **Password**   Use the ias_admin password.

8. Step 3 of the Configure Identity Management screen will open. Because you are ready to make the changes permanent, click Finish. This may take some time, so do not worry. At the end of this step, you will be returned to the main Infrastructure page.

9. Click the Home link at the top of this screen to return to the Discoverer AS OEM main page.

10. Having configured OID or the metadata repository, before you continue you will need to restart all of the components of the Discoverer Server. You should notice that all components apart from Management are down. To restart all of the components, click the Start All button.

11. While the components are being restarted, OEM will display a message saying that this step may take a while to complete.

12. When all of the components have been started, you will see a green up arrow against each component with the stop light now showing a green arrow on a white background. You will also see a message at the top of the screen telling you which components were restarted.

13. Having configured and attached OID for use with the Discoverer Server and restarted all of the components, you now need to configure and attach the metadata repository. To start this process, from the Discoverer Server main page, click the Infrastructure link to display the Infrastructure tab.

14. As you will see, Identity Management is configured, but the metadata repository is not. You configure the metadata repository by clicking the Configure button in the metadata repository area of the Infrastructure page.

NOTE
If you try to configure the metadata repository before you have configured your Identity Management, Discoverer will generate an error.

15. Step 1 of the Configure Repository screen will open. To complete this step, review these settings and then click Next:

   ■ **Username**   Leave this as defaulted to cn=orcladmin.

   ■ **Password**   Use the ias_admin password that you provided during the install.

16. Step 2 of the Configure Repository screen will open. To complete this step, make this setting and then click Next:

■ **Repository** From the drop-down list of available repositories, select the metadata repository that you want to use.

NOTE
Unless you have multiple metadata repositories, OEM will already have populated the Repository box.

17. Step 3 of the Configure Repository screen will open. To complete this step, click Finish. Once again, it may take some time to complete. At the end of the step, you will be returned to the main Infrastructure page, where you will see that both Identity Management and the metadata repository have been configured. From here, you are almost done!

18. Click the Home link at the top of the Infrastructure page to return to the Discoverer AS OEM main page.

19. You should once again notice that all of the Discoverer Server components apart from Management are down. You will need to restart all of the components of the Discoverer Server.

Discoverer Preferences

Discoverer has a sophisticated component called preferences. These preferences can be set three ways:

■ You can set global defaults for all of your Discoverer users using the pref.txt file.

■ You can set individual preferences for a specific user using the dis51pr command-line utility.

■ Users can set their own preferences using Discoverer itself.

All preferences are stored in a hidden file called .reg_key.dc, which is usually located in the $ORACLE_HOME/Discoverer folder. In this file you will get all the defaults as set by pref.txt along with any individual preferences that have been made by users in Plus and Viewer. The system first of all reads the default settings and then overrides these with individual user settings.

NOTE
Even though .reg_key.dc looks like a file that could be edited manually using a standard text editor, do not be tempted to do so. This file is intended for system use only, and editing it manually could cause Discoverer to no longer work correctly. Please also note that its name begins with a period.

When a user makes adjustments to his or her preferences, Discoverer contacts the preference server, which has its own process, called dis51pr. It even has its own port. But why do preferences need to be a separate process? The primary reason is for Discoverer load balancing. Let's say you have two or more Discoverer servers, and that one of your users has set their background color to be light green. Unless we have a preference server, the next time the user logs on, if that user is directed to another Discoverer server, he or she would lose the light green background.

Therefore, in a multiple host Discoverer environment, you will start the preferences server on one host. The preferences will then be stored in the hidden .reg_key.dc file on this single mid-tier.

NOTE
Using a single preference server is a potential high-availability issue, because this server now becomes a single point of failure.

Changing Global Preferences Using pref.txt

To change Discoverer's global preferences, use the following workflow:

1. Open and edit $ORACLE_HOME/Discoverer/util/pref.txt.

2. In Unix or Linux, run applypreferences.sh or enter **dis51pr -apply -file pref.txt**; while in Windows, run applypreferences.bat. The applypreferences file can be found in the same folder as pref.txt.

3. Restart the Discoverer mid-tier server.

Changing User Preferences Using the Command Line

To change Discoverer's preferences via the command line, use the following workflow:

1. Navigate to the $ORACLE_HOME/bin folder.

2. Execute **dis51pr -user username@eulname -setpref *areaname prefname* *pref setting***.

For example, to set the default EUL for user michael on myeul to Marketing, use the following:

dis51pr -user michael@myeul -setpref "Database" "DefaultEUL" \\"Marketing\\"

Changing User Preferences as a User

An end user can set his or her own individual preferences from within Discoverer Plus using Tools | Options or from within Discoverer Viewer by clicking the Preferences link on the main Viewer page.

Table 20-1 contains a listing of the preferences that can be set inside the pref.txt file.

Preference	Default Setting	Description
Timeout	1800	Discoverer Plus, the web applet, will warn the user, and if the user does not respond, it will close the session after the number of seconds indicated. Upon installation the default is 1800 seconds (30 minutes). The minimum allowed is 180.
		Take care raising the timeout limit, as this will cause Discoverer to hold sessions open for longer.
		To set the timeout for Discoverer Viewer, you need to edit the session-timeout tag in the $ORACLE_HOME/j2ee/OC4J_BI_Forms/applications/Discoverer/Discoverer/WEB-INF/web.xml file. In this file the setting is stored in minutes, with the installed default being 30.
RowsPerHTML	25	This setting controls the number of rows per page that should be used to display the results on a report. The range is 1–999, with the default being 25. Be careful, because if you set this number too high, it will have an adverse affect on performance
EuroCountries	"de,de_AT,de_DE,de_LI,de_LIECHTENSTEIN,de_LU,de_LUXEMBOURG,el,el_GR,en_IE,es_ES,fi,fi_FI,fr,fr_BE,fr_FR,fr_LU,fr_LUXEMBOURG,it,it_IT,nl,nl_BE,nl_NL,pt,pt_PT,sv_FI"	This setting controls the list of countries that use the EURO as their unit of currency.
PrintHeadersOnce	0	This setting controls whether headers will print only once or for each printed page. It has two valid settings: 0 – Print the header only once. 1 – Repeat the heading on each printed page. The default is 0.
PrintPercentageOfTitle	60	If the title does not fit on a printed page, use this setting to automatically show a percentage of the title. The range is 20–60, and the default is 60. When used, the remaining part of the title will be truncated.
GraphAxesAutoScaledFromZero	1	This setting controls whether Discoverer will scale graphs from zero. It has two valid settings: 0 – Scale graphs from zero. 1 – Scale graphs automatically. The default is 1.
CacheFlushPercentage	25	This setting determines the percentage of cache that Discoverer will flush when the cache fills up. The range is 0–100, with the default being 25.
MaxVirtualDiskMem	1024000000	This setting specifies that maximum amount of virtual memory, in bytes, to use for the data cache. You need to make sure that this is greater than MaxVirtualHeapMem. The setting alongside equates to 1 Gb.

TABLE 20-1 *Discoverer Preferences*

Preference	Default Setting	Description
MaxVirtualHeapMem	5120000	This specifies the maximum amount of heap memory, in bytes, to make available for the data cache. The setting alongside equates to 5MB.
QueryBehavior	0	This setting controls what Discoverer will do when a workbook is opened. It has three valid settings: 0 – Automatically run the query when the workbook is opened. 1 – The query will not run automatically, and the user needs to click the refresh button to run the query. 2 – Discoverer will prompt the user every time the user opens this workbook to see if he or she wants to run the query. The default is 0.
ShowDialogBitmaps	1	This setting controls whether Discoverer shows images inside the wizard dialogs. It has two valid settings: 0 – Do not show images. 1 – Show the images. The default is 1.
SaveLastUsedParamValue	0	When a user enters a parameter value, this setting determines what the default will be the next time that user enters a parameter value. It has two valid settings: 0 – Use the default value that was set by the report writer. 1 – Save the value the user just entered and use that as the default. The default is 0.
NotifyNewRunsOnConnect	0	This setting controls whether a user will be alerted to scheduled jobs when logging in. It has two valid settings: 0 – The user will not be alerted to scheduled jobs that have finished when the user logs in. 1 – The user will receive a message notifying the user that his or her scheduled jobs are completed. It causes Discoverer to launch the New Schedule Runs dialog box on login. The default is 0.
ShowExpiredRunsAtExit	1	This setting controls whether the user will be notified about expired and deleted jobs when logging out. It has two valid settings: 0 – The user will not be notified about expired and deleted scheduled jobs when logging out. 1 – The user will be notified about expired and deleted scheduled jobs when logging out. The default is 1.
GraphShowRollupAggregates	1	This setting controls whether graphs that are associated with an outline crosstab show rollup values. It has two valid settings: 0 – Do not show the rollup values. 1 – Show the rollup values. The default is 1.

TABLE 20-1 *Discoverer Preferences* (continued)

Preference	Default Setting	Description
ExportGroupSortedItemsAsBlank	1	This setting controls how group-sorted items are exported when users export to a .CSV or TXT file. It has two valid settings: 0 – Export the first group-sorted value and then send the remainder of the values as blanks. 1 – Export all group sorted values. The default is 1.
AxisLabelBehavior	1	This setting controls how axis labels are managed. It has three valid settings: 1 – Always show the axis labels. 2 – Never show axis labels. 3 – Let the Discoverer desktop user control whether or not axis labels are displayed. The default is 1.
Data Format	"<fontFormat fontName="Dialog" pitch="11" bold="false" italic="false" underline="false" strikethrough="false" foreground="0,0,0" background="255,255,255" halign="right" valign="top" wordWrap="true"></fontFormat>"	This is where you may provide HTML to control how the data in the worksheet cells are displayed. End users can override this setting by using Tools | Options | Formats from the toolbar and setting their own default data format.
Heading Format	"<fontFormat fontName="Dialog" pitch="11" bold="false" italic="false" underline="false" strikethrough="false" foreground="0,0,0" background="247,247,231" halign="left" valign="top" wordWrap="true"></fontFormat>"	This is where you provide HTML to control how the headings appear in the worksheet. End users can override this setting by using Tools | Options | Formats from the toolbar and setting their own default heading format.
Totals Format	"<fontFormat fontName="Dialog" pitch="11" bold="false" italic="false" underline="false" strikethrough="false" foreground="0,0,0" background="247,247,231" halign="right" valign="top" wordWrap="true"></fontFormat>"	This is where you provide HTML to control how totals appear in the worksheet. End users can override this setting by using Tools | Options | Formats from the toolbar and setting their own default totals format.
NullValue	"NULL"	This specifies what Discoverer should display when a value is null.
NonAggregableValue	""	This specifies what Discoverer should display when a value cannot be aggregated.
ExcelExportWithMacros	1	This setting controls whether Discoverer will export macros when exporting to Excel. If this is disabled by changing the value to 0, no formats or macros will be exported. It has two valid settings: 0 – Do not export macros to Excel. 1 – Export macros to Excel. This causes Discoverer to also export the formats to Excel. The default is 1.

TABLE 20-1   *Discoverer Preferences* (continued)

Preference	Default Setting	Description
CellPadding	1	This setting determines how many pixels will be padded around cells. The range is 0–5. The default is 1.
ShowGraphToolBar	true	This setting controls whether the graph toolbar is displayed. It has two valid settings: false – Do not show the graph toolbar. true – Show the graph toolbar. The default is true.
ShowFormatToolBar	true	This setting controls whether the format toolbar is displayed. It has two valid settings: false – Do not show the format toolbar. true – Show the format toolbar. The default is true.
ShowStandardToolBar	true	This setting controls whether the standard toolbar is displayed. It has two valid settings: false – Do not show the standard toolbar. true – Show the standard toolbar. The default is true.
ShowJoins	false	This is a really cool setting, and a much-awaited feature. The default is false, meaning the joins will be hidden from Discoverer Plus users. Sometimes more sophisticated users become frustrated, as they do not know which folders are related. Changing this to true will allow the join icons to appear in Plus as they do in the Administrator tool. It has two valid settings: false – Do not show the joins to the user. true – Show the joins to the user. The default is false.
ShowDrillIcon	false	This setting controls whether or not to show the drill icons in worksheets. It has two valid settings: false – Do not show the drill icon. true – Show the drill icon. The default is false.
ColumnWidth	100	This setting controls the default column width. The default is 100.
DefaultExportPath	""	This setting controls the default export path for Discoverer Plus. The default is no path.
RowsPerPage	25	This setting controls the number of rows per scrollable page that are available within Discoverer Viewer. Each page down will move down the RowsPerPage. The default is 25.
ColsPerPage	128	This setting controls the number of columns per scrollable page in Discoverer Viewer. The default is a very large 128.
ScatterGraphDataMode	1	This setting controls how to display a scatter graph. It has three valid settings: 0 – Use the Discoverer Plus design. 1 – Use the Discoverer Desktop design. 2 – Use the Excel design. The default is 1.

TABLE 20-1 *Discoverer Preferences* (continued)

Preference	Default Setting	Description
Cell Gridcolor	0	This setting controls the default cell color. The value entered must be entered as a Hex value using the RRGGBB format, where RR is the value for red, GG for green, and BB for blue. The default is 0 – black.
Show Text Area	1	This setting controls the default display of the text area at the bottom of the Plus screen. It has two valid settings: 0 – Do not show the text area. 1 – Show the text area. The default is 1.
Show Title	1	This setting controls the default display of the title. It has two valid settings: 0 – Do not show the title. 1 – Show the title. The default is 1.
Cell XGridline	1	This setting controls the default display of the horizontal and vertical grid lines. It has two valid settings: 0 – Do not show the gridlines. 1 – Show the gridlines. The default is 1.
Cell YGridline	1	This setting controls the default display of the horizontal and vertical grid lines. It has two valid settings: 0 – Do not show the gridlines. 1 – Show the gridlines. The default is 1.
Default Title	""	This setting controls what will be displayed as the default title. You can set this to anything you like. The default is null.
Default Text Area	""	This setting controls what will be displayed as the default in the text area. You can set this to anything you like. The default is null.
Measurement Units	0	This setting controls the default for the unit of measure. It has three valid settings: 0 – Use pixels. 1 – Use inches. 2 – Use centimeters. The default is 0.
DisableClassicExports	0	This setting controls whether the classic export formats of DIF, SLK, and WKS will be displayed. It has two valid settings: 0 – Do not enable these export formats. 1 – Allow users to export in these formats. The default is 0.
AggregationBehavior	0	This setting controls whether Discoverer linearly aggregates values that otherwise cannot be computed or not. It has two valid settings: 0 – Disallow linear aggregation. 1 – Allow Discoverer to linearly aggregate values that it could not have done otherwise. The default is 0.

TABLE 20-1   *Discoverer Preferences* (continued)

Preference	Default Setting	Description
AllowAggregationOverRepeatedValues	0	This setting controls whether Discoverer is allowed to aggregate repeated values. It has two valid settings: 0 – Do not allow aggregation over repeated values. 1 – Allow aggregation over repeated values. The default is 0.
AdjustPlusFontSize	false	This setting controls whether Discoverer is allowed to adjust the font size to handle a Java bug. It has two valid settings: false – Do not adjust the font size. true – Adjust the font size. The default is false.
MRUEnabled	1	This setting controls whether Discoverer will keep a list of the most recently used (MRU) workbooks. It has two valid settings: 0 – Do not keep the most recently used workbooks. 1 – Keep a list of the most recently used workbooks. The actual number of workbooks that will be kept in the list is under user control and can be set from within the Tools | Options menu of the Plus screen. The default is 1.
DisableFanTrapDetection	0	This setting controls Discoverer's fan trap protection. It has two valid settings: 0 – Enable fan trap detection. 1 – Disable fan trap detection. The default is 0.
DisableFanTrapResolution	0	This setting controls whether Discoverer is allowed to resolve fan traps. It has two valid settings: 0 – Turns on Discoverer's fan trap resolution. 1 – Turns off Discoverer's fan trap resolution. The default is 0. Discoverer uses a patented mechanism for resolving fan traps. For more information on this, you should take a look in Chapter 10. We do not recommend you turn off Discoverer's fan trap resolution mechanism.
DisableMultiJoinDetection	0	When multiple joins between folders are detected, this setting controls whether Discoverer prompts a user as to which join should be used. It has two valid settings: 0 – Ask the user which join to use. 1 – Discoverer will select the first join it finds, even if it is incorrect. The default is 0.
DisableAutoQuery	0	This setting controls whether Discoverer should automatically run a query when the user opens a new worksheet. It has two valid settings: 0 – Turns off automatic querying. 1 – Turns on automatic querying. The default is 0.

TABLE 20-1 *Discoverer Preferences* (continued)

Preference	Default Setting	Description
DisableAutoOuterJoinsOnFilters	0	This setting controls how Discoverer uses outer joins when conditions or filters exist. It has two valid settings: 0 – When a query has a filter, a setting of 0 will disable outer joins. 1 – Enable outer joins. The default is 0.
EnhancedAggregationStrategy	1	This feature dictates how the database executes the group by clause. It has five valid settings: 0 – Use ordinary Group By, which is the slowest. 1 – Use the Grouping Sets command on the Group By clause. 2 – Optimize grouping sets by possibly submitting multiple queries to the database. 3 – Use cube and rollup commands as well. 4 – Let Discoverer decide the fastest way to execute the query. Whichever version of the application server you are using will determine what the current default level of this switch is. In 10g, it is usually defaulted to 1, whereas in 9i, it is usually defaulted to 4. If you are using 10g, we recommend leaving this set to 1; however, if you are using 9i, we would first of all try switching it from 4 to 1. If performance is still poor, you can then try switching it to 0. We have to say that performance in 10g Plus is better than in 9i Plus, and so you should have fewer issues. Nevertheless, we have seen complex crosstabs run for a long time in 10g initially, only for these to run in just a few seconds when we set this switch to 0. In some rare cases (e.g., a complex query where a CUBE aggregation strategy is chosen), an Enhanced AggregationStrategy of 4 can lead to Discoverer becoming unresponsive while it generates a large number of aggregation combinations. Accordingly, we endorse Oracle's recommendation to set this to 1.
ItemClassDelay	15	This setting controls the maximum number of seconds that Discoverer is allowed to use when determining a list of values. If the LOV takes longer than this setting, it will time out and not display the list. The default is 15.
PredictionThresholdSeconds	60	If enabled, this setting controls the number of seconds after which Discoverer will warn the user that the query might take a while. The default is 60. The minimum value that you can set is 1.
PredictionThresholdSecondsEnabled	1	This setting controls whether the query predictor threshold is enabled. It has two valid settings: 0 – Do not enable the query prediction threshold. 1 – Enables the query prediction threshold. If your database does not have a cost-based optimizer (i.e., it is a non-Oracle database or older than Oracle 8), then you must set this to 0. The default is 1.

TABLE 20-1 *Discoverer Preferences* (continued)

Preference	Default Setting	Description
QueryTimeLimit	1800	If enabled, this setting controls the maximum number of seconds that a query is allowed to run. If the query exceeds this limit it will time out, discarding all work. The default is 1800 seconds, 30 minutes. The minimum value that you can set is 1.
QueryTimeLimitEnabled	1	This setting controls whether the query time limit is enabled. A setting of 1 enables the query time limit; 0 disables the time limit. It has two valid settings: 0 – The query time limit is disabled. 1 – The query time limit is enabled. The default is 1.
RowFetchLimit	10000	If enabled, this setting defines the maximum number of rows a query is allowed to fetch. This setting is designed to protect the database from bad queries and Cartesian products. The default is 10000. The minimum value you can set is 1.
RowFetchLimitEnabled	1	This setting controls whether the row fetch limit is enabled. It has two valid settings: 0 – The row fetch limit is disabled. 1 – The row fetch limit is enabled. The default is 1.
MaxRowsPerFetch	250	This setting determines the maximum number of rows that be delivered with each fetch. The default is 250. The minimum value you can set is 1. The maximum value you can set is 10000.
RowsPerFetch	250	This setting determines how many rows are delivered per fetch. The default is 250. The minimum value you can set is 1. The maximum value you can set is 10000.
SummaryThreshold	60	If enabled, this setting controls how summary folders are used: 0 means do not use summaries. Any other value determines how many days old a summary can be and still be used.
SummaryThresholdEnabled	1	This setting controls whether the summary threshold is used. It has two valid settings: 0 – The summary threshold is disabled. 1 – The summary threshold is enabled. The default is 1.
MaterializedViewRedirectionBehavior	0	This setting controls how Discoverer uses materialized views. It has three valid settings: 0 – This setting means always use materialized views. 1 – This setting means use the materialized view only if the source data has not changed (not stale). 2 – This setting means never use materialized views. The default is 0.
DefaultEUL	"VIDEO5"	This identifies the default End User Layer. When installing a new EUL, Discoverer sets this to VIDEO5, the EUL for the Oracle sample data. You should change this setting for your own system.

TABLE 20-1   *Discoverer Preferences* (continued)

Preference	Default Setting	Description
DisableAlternateSortOptimisation	0	This setting controls whether Discoverer will write alternate queries for sorts. It has two valid settings: 0 – Do not disable alternate sort optimization. 1 – Disable alternate sort optimization. You should set this only if you are using unregistered external summaries. The default is 0.
SQLFlatten	1	This setting controls whether Discoverer will avoid inline views by flattening the SQL. It has two valid settings: 0 – Discoverer will not flatten the SQL, thus not avoiding inline views. 1 – Discoverer will avoid inline views (subqueries in the FROM clause) by flattening the SQL. The default is 1.
SQLItemTrim	1	This setting controls whether Discoverer includes nonrequired items in the query. It has two valid settings: 0 – Discoverer might include extra items in a query. 1 – Discoverer will not include items the user does not want. The default is 1.
SQLJoinTrim	1	This setting controls whether Discoverer includes joins to items that are not used in the query. It has two valid settings: 0 – Discoverer might include extra joins in the query. 1 – Discoverer will not join items the user does not need. The default is 1.
AppsGWYUID	"APPLSYSPUB/PUB"	This is the default setting if you are querying an Oracle 11i application database through a gateway. Unless you are using different settings, there will be no need to change this setting.
AppsFNDNAM	"APPS"	This is the foundation name, or main Apps user, of the Oracle E-Business 11i Application. This is used for connecting Discoverer in Apps mode. Unless you are using a different foundation username, there will be no need to change this setting.
BusinessAreaFastFetchLevel	1	This setting controls how much caching occurs when loading business areas. In general terms, the lower the value, the fewer folders and items are fetched into the Navigator dialog immediately. It has five valid settings: 0 – No fast fetch is performed. 1 – Discoverer will cache only the business area when it opens it. This makes for a faster opening of the business area. If you are not constantly changing business areas and trust that they are valid, you can safely use this setting. 2- Discoverer will cache the business area and all items within the business area that are used by the users. 3 – Discoverer will cache the business area and all items within the business area that are used by the administrator tool. 4 – Discoverer will cache the business area and all items within the business area. The default is 1.

TABLE 20-1   *Discoverer Preferences* (continued)

Preference	Default Setting	Description
ObjectsAlwaysAccessible	1	This setting controls whether objects are to be assumed always accessible to the users. It has two valid settings: 0 – This setting causes Discoverer to check that the objects exist and that the user has access to the objects every time the user opens up the items in a folder. 1 – If every user can access every folder, set this to 1. The security checks will then be deferred until query execution time, thus causing the business areas to load much faster. The default is 1. By default, in any of the user editions, whenever folders and items are displayed in the Navigator, Discoverer validates that the tables/views that they refer to exist and that the user has access to them. If you wish, you can switch this validation off by setting this registry setting to be any number greater than 0. This will speed up the display of folders and items in the Navigator. However, if the database objects do not exist or the user does not have access to them when this setting is greater than 0, the user will see an error when they execute the query.
SummaryObjectsUseCachedAccessibility	0	This setting controls whether summary data should be accessed using Discoverer's results cache. It has two valid settings: 0 – Use summary data from Discoverer's results cache. 1 – Do not use the cache. The default is 0.
AvoidServerWildcardBug	0	The database has a wildcard bug that Discoverer can avoid by setting this to 1.
RdbFastSQLOff	0	If you are using RDB, set this to 1.
QPPEnable	1	This setting controls query prediction. It has two valid settings: 0 – Query prediction is disabled. 1 – Query prediction is enabled. In fact, any nonzero value enables query prediction. The default is 1.
QPPCreateNewStats	1	This setting determines whether Discoverer will record new statistics in the EUL for query performance and prediction. A value greater than 0 enables the capturing of new statistics, while a setting of 0 turns it off. The statistics are stored in a table called EUL5_QPP_STATS. It has two valid settings: 0 – Do not capture statistics. 1 – Enable the capture of statistics. Any nonzero setting will work. The default is 1.
QPPLoadStatsByObjectUseKey	1	This setting controls whether Discoverer will load statistics for same objects first before others. It has two valid settings: 0 – Do not load same objects first. 1 – Load same objects first. The default is 1.

TABLE 20-1   *Discoverer Preferences* (continued)

Preference	Default Setting	Description
QPPUseCpuTime	1	This setting controls whether the CPU time should be included within the prediction estimates. It has two valid settings: 0 – Do not include the CPU time when predicting. 1 – Include the CPU time when predicting. The default is 1.
QPPMaxObjectUseKey	30	This setting determines how many statistics to cache in memory. The default is 30.
QPPCBOEnforced	2	This setting determines whether the use of the cost-based optimizer is enforced. It has three valid settings: 0 – The use of the cost-based optimizer is not enforced. 1 – The use of the cost-based optimizer is enforced. 2 – The use of the cost-based optimizer will be enforced only for an Oracle 8.1.6 or newer database. The default is 2. Setting QPPCBOEnforced to be 1 forces Discoverer to use the cost-based optimizer, but setting it to 0 does not turn if off. To stop Discoverer using CBO altogether, you need to turn off query prediction, which is done by setting QPPEnable to 0.
QPPObtainCostMethod	1	If the cost-based optimizer is enabled, this setting controls how the costs are estimated. It has two valid settings: 0 – Use the explain plan for the estimates. 1 – Use dynamic views for the estimates. The default is 1. Because of a bug in the Oracle 10g database (4024370) as recorded in a posting on MetaLink on 15-JAN-2005, we need to use a work-around for Discoverer that will force Discoverer to use explain plan instead of dynamic views. Therefore, when using a 10g database, you must set this setting to 0.
QPPMinCost	0	The setting controls how many statistics to record. A setting of 0 means to record all statistics, no matter how low the cost. The default is 0.
QPPMaxStats	500	This setting controls how many previous statistics to load. The default is 500.
QPPMinActCpuTime	0	To use CPU time or not to use CPU time, that is the question. A value of 0 is yes; anything above is no.
QPPMinActElapsedTime	0	A setting of 0 will record all statistics. Any number above 0 means record statistics only if the actual elapsed time is greater than the setting.

TABLE 20-1   *Discoverer Preferences* (continued)

Preference	Default Setting	Description
QPPMinEstElapsedTime	0	This setting controls whether you will record statistics only if the actual elapsed time is less than this setting. The default is 0.
UseOptimizerHints	0	This setting controls whether optimizer hints can be added to the SQL. It has two valid settings: 0 – Do not add optimizer hints. Any other value – Add optimizer hints to SQL. The default is 0.
QuerySQLFastFetchLevel	1	This setting controls how much SQL precaching occurs. Set this to 4; it is the fastest.
SQLTrace	0	This setting controls whether a SQL trace is maintained of every query sent to the database. It has two valid settings: 0 – SQL tracing is turned off. 1 – SQL tracing is turned on. The default is 0.
Axis Label	0	This setting controls whether axis labels are displayed in a crosstab. It has two valid settings: 0 – Do not display crosstab axis labels. 1 – Show the crosstab axis labels. The default is 0.
Axis Style	2	This setting controls the axis style for a crosstab worksheets. It has two valid settings: 1 – Display Crosstabs using the inline method. 2 – Display Crosstabs using the outline method. The default is 2.
Column Headings	1	This setting controls whether column headings will be displayed. It has two valid settings: 0 – Do not display column headings. 1 – Display column headings. The default is 1.
Row Headings	0	This setting controls whether row numbers will be displayed in a Table. It has two valid settings: 0 – Do not display row number for tables. 1 – Display the row numbers. The default is 0.

TABLE 20-1 *Discoverer Preferences* (continued)

Discoverer 10.1.2.0.2 Preferences

As mentioned already in this book, Oracle introduced the next version of Application Server, 10.1.2.0.2, during the late summer of 2005. More preferences have been added, and some have been removed. We recommend that you take a look at the 10.1.2.0.2 configuration guide for an updated list: Chapter 1, "1.2 What are the new configuration features in OracleBI Discoverer 10*g* Release 2 (10.1.2)," of the *Oracle Business Intelligence Discoverer Configuration Guide, 10g Release 2 (10.1.2.1) for Microsoft Windows and Solaris Operating System (SPARC)*, part no. B13918-03.

The release notes for 10.1.2.0.2 will also contain any last-minute changes made to preferences. Some of the preferences new in 10.1.2.0.2 are shown here:

Preference	Default Setting	Description
EUL Object Navigator	1	This setting controls the Available Items pane in Discoverer Plus. It has two valid settings: 0 – This hides the Available Items pane for new users or for users who have never set their own preferences. 1 – This enables the Available Items pane for new users and for users who have never set their own preferences. The default is 1. If the user changes his or her own settings, this will override whatever is set inside pref.txt.
Selected Object Navigator	1	This setting controls the Selected Items pane in Discoverer Plus. It has two valid settings: 0 – This hides the Selected Items pane for new users or for users who have never set their own preferences. 1 – This enables the Selected Items pane for new users and for users who have never set their own preferences. The default is 1. If the user changes his or her own settings, this will override whatever is set inside pref.txt.
QPPEnableEstimateWithNo Stats	0 – if set	This preference controls how query prediction works during the first execution of a new workbook. When a query is run, statistics are collected, and are then used the next time the query time is predicted. However, the first time a query is run, there will be no historical statistics available. In this case, Discoverer will try to get its information from the database using the explain plan. However, if the tables have not recently been analyzed, even the database may not be able to give the correct information the first time. This preference has two valid settings: 0 – Query estimation is not based on statistics. Discoverer returns a predicted time of 1 second and does not waste time

trying to predict the query run time. The users will not see any warning and the query will run immediately.

1 – Query estimation is based on the database explain plan.

In Discoverer 3.1.X the following prediction message appeared even if the Discoverer workbook was being run for the first time: "This query will take approximately X seconds."

In Discoverer 4.1.X the workbook must be run at least once to collect statistics for query prediction and after the workbook is saved, closed and re-opened, the query prediction message appeared.

Many Oracle customers found this change in behavior inconvenient and wanted to have control over it. This preference was introduced in 4.1.46 for the first time, went away in 9.0.2, returned in 9.0.4, and has been retained in 10.1.2. You will not find this preference within the existing pref.txt, so if you want to use it you will need to add it under the [Database] section, setting the preference to 0. You also need to ensure that QPPEnable is set to 1; otherwise query prediction will not be enabled.

NOTE
The preceding preferences exist in 10.1.2.0.0 as well but were not exposed for modification in the pref.txt file.

Web Cache

The number one question that most people ask us is, will Web Cache help Discoverer? The answer is, it depends. You see, Web Cache provides web content compression, load balancing, and of course, caching. Web Cache caches static and dynamically generated files in memory. You can configure the caching rules and expiration schedules for Web Cache content.

For example, a data warehouse that is refreshed every Saturday can have Discoverer Viewer pages expire on Saturday also.

However, because Discoverer Plus is a web applet, Web Cache will not provide any performance benefit through caching. The Java plug-ins, JInitiator and Sun Java Client, cache the applet on the client machine. On the other hand, Web Cache can provide significant benefits for both Discoverer Viewer and Discoverer Portlets. Therefore, in the following discussion we will show you how to configure Discoverer Viewer to use Web Cache.

Configuring Viewer with Web Cache

To configure Discoverer Viewer to use Web Cache, use the following workflow:

1. Launch OEM Application Server Control for the Discoverer mid-tier.

2. Click the Discoverer link.

3. Click the Discoverer Viewer link.

4. Click the Caching link.

5. Check the box called Use Web Cache.

6. Further down the same page, locate the section entitled Viewer Delay Times.

7. Set both Query Progress Page and Request to a high value such as 60.

8. Click OK. You may have to wait a couple of minutes for this to take effect.

NOTE
If Single Sign-On has been enabled, disable it. Please see the following section for more information.

9. Click the Discoverer Viewer link on the top of the screen.

10. Click the Customization tab located just underneath the heading Discoverer Viewer.

11. Select Layout from the Customize drop-down list and click Go to display the Customize Layout page. Oracle recommends that you deselect as many of the Actions check boxes as possible. Now that you are using Web Cache, their usefulness may be limited. For example, deselecting the Rerun Query box is a good idea because if a user tries to rerun a query, all that will happen is that the page will reload from the cache. However, if you are using Discoverer with a combination of secure and insecure web pages, you cannot use Web Cache.

12. Click OK to return to the Discoverer Viewer Home page.

13. Start Web Cache using OEM by calling your application server with the Web Cache Administration port, e.g., http://ascserver.learndiscoverer.com:4000.

14. Log in using the username ias_admin and the password that you provided during the application server install.

15. Select Expiration Policy Definitions, located in the section called Rules for Caching.

Expiration Policy Definitions

Use this page to define expiration policies. Expiration policies can be applied when creating Caching Rules

Select	Expire
○	as per HTTP *Expires* Header
○	after 300 seconds in cache
○	after 3600 seconds in cache
○	after 604800 seconds in cache

Add... | Edit Selected... | Delete Selected...

16. Check an existing policy or click Add to create your own expiration policy. After you
have added your own policy, click Submit.

Create Expiration Policy

This new policy currently does not apply to any rule. After creating this
policy (click Submit when you are done), you can add rule(s) to be
associated with this policy.

When to Expire:

- ○ Expire object 7   days ▾ after cache entry
- ○ Expire object [   ] seconds ▾ after object creation
- ○ Will expire as per HTTP *Expires* header

After Expiration:

- ◉ Remove immediately

- ○ Refresh on demand as application web server capacity permits
  AND no later than: [   ] seconds ▾ after expiration.

Submit   Cancel

17. Select Caching, Personalization, and Compressions Rules. It is also located in the section
headed Rules for Caching.

Caching, Personalization, and Compression Rules

For Site: volcano.cdeyoung.com:7779 ▾   View

Edit Selected...   Delete Selected   Insert Above...   Insert Below...   Move Up   Move Down

Create Site Specific Rule...   Create Global Rule...

Site Specific:

			Selectors					
Select	Priority	Name	Expression Type	URL Expression	HTTP Method(s)	URL and POST Body Parameters	POST Body Expression	Caching Policy
○	1	cache_wireless_rm	Regular Expression	/ptg/rm	GET, GET with query string	N/A	N/A	Cache

18. Complete the Caching, Personalization and Compression Rules page as follows:

- In the table called For All Sites, select any radio button, and then click the Insert
  Above button.

Edit/Add Caching, Personalization, and Compression Rule

For Site: *All Sites*

Name	Discoverer
Expression Type	Regular Expression ▾
URL Expression	/discoverer/app

HTTP Method(s)   ☑ GET ☐ GET with query string ☐ POST (WARNING!)

The following option will only be used if you set the Expression Type to 'Path Prefix' or 'File Extension' and select either the 'GET with query string' or 'POST' HTTP Method.

URL and POST Body Parameters   Name: [   ] = Value: [   ]   [Add ->] [Delete]

The following option will only be used if you set the Expression Type to 'Regular Expression' and select the 'POST' HTTP method.

POST Body Expression   [   ]

(You can restrict the POST body with a POST body expression and/or with the URL parameters in the table above. Otherwise, any POST body is accepted.)

Caching Policy   ☑ Cache ☐ Don't Cache

- In the URL Expression field, enter **/Discoverer/app**.

- Select the expiration policy you just created.

- Click Submit.

19. Restart Web Cache. At this point, Web Cache will maintain all Discoverer Viewer content for the amount of time that you specified after the data enters the cache. If you have many users running the exact same report, you will see significant performance improvement with Web Cache enabled.

Cache Operations

[Refresh Now]

Auto Refresh: [Never ▾] [Set]

Select	Cache Name	Uptime	Operation Needed
◉	volcano.cdeyoung.com-WebCache	01:32:16	Restart Web Cache

[Start] [Stop] [Restart]

Web Cache and Single Sign-On

It is vitally important that you not attempt to use Web Cache with sensitive data. This is because Web Cache has no mechanism to protect its content. When a request is made to Web Cache for a page that is cacheable (as defined by the caching rules) but has not yet been cached, then Web Cache makes a request on behalf of the user to the Oracle HTTP Server (Apache). OHS has the mod_osso add-on module, whose job it is to guarantee that a user must be authorized to view a page.

The first time such a request is received, the Single Sign-On connection screen will appear and the user will need to provide his or her SSO username and password. But, because the page is cacheable, Web Cache will keep a copy of it in memory. Then, any subsequent request from any user will deliver the user the page without authentication. This is why Oracle explains that you must cache only Discoverer Viewer content delivered through a Discoverer Public connection. The long and the short of this is that you should not cache pages in Web Cache unless it is okay for everyone to see them.

Configuring Discoverer for High Availability

Two fundamental advantages exist to having multiple Discoverer middle tiers. One is high availability; the other is load balancing. If your organization does not have a hardware load balancer, you can configure Oracle Web Cache to perform the load balancing for you. The fundamental challenge to load balancing Discoverer is that each user must stay connected to the same Discoverer server for their entire session. Fortunately, Oracle Web Cache has a feature called session binding that will guarantee this. If you are going to use a hardware load balancer, this is known as "sticky-bit" configuration.

Load-Balancing Multiple Discoverer Servers Using Web Cache

To load-balance multiple Discoverer servers using Web Cache, use the following workflow:

1. Install each Discoverer mid-tier.

2. Use the portlist.ini file from the first mid-tier during the installation of the second and subsequent mid-tiers. This will guarantee that the port numbers are the same for all installations.

3. Configure the tnsnames.ora files to be the same on all of the Discoverer servers.

4. Determine which Discoverer server will be used as the centralized "preference server" and note the hostname.

5. On the server that is now the preference server, locate and open this file: $ORACLE_HOME/opmn/conf/opmn.xml and find an entry like this one:

   ```
   <variable id = "PREFERENCE_PORT" value = "16003">
   ```

   Take note of the number after value="#####". This is your preference server's listening port. In the example just listed, and illustrated next, this is 16003.

Process Management

⚠ Warning
No validation is done on the correctness of any edits you make to the opmn.xml file. Be sure you carefully check your edits. You may want to back up this file before proceeding.

Process Management is done by editing the opmn.xml configuration file. Check the Help for more information on the content of this file, which is located at: E:\oracle\discoverer\opmn\conf\opmn.xml

```
      </ias-component>
      <ias-component id="Discoverer">
        <environment>
          <variable id="PREFERENCE_PORT" value="16003"/>
          <variable id="DISCO_DIR" value="$ORACLE_HOME"/>
          <variable id="DCLOG_CONFIG_FILE" value="E:\oracle\discoverer\discoverer\util\ServerLogParams.txt"/>
          <variable id="LD_LIBRARY_PATH" value="\usr\lib;E:\oracle\discoverer\discoverer\lib;E:\oracle\discoverer\lib"
append="true"/>
          <variable id="DC10_REG" value="E:\oracle\discoverer\discoverer\"/>
          <variable id="FND_TOP" value="E:\oracle\discoverer\discoverer\"/>
          <variable id="FND_SECURE" value="E:\oracle\discoverer\discoverer\secure"/>
        </environment>
        <process-type id="ServicesStatus" module-id="Disco_ServicesStatus" status="enabled">
          <process-set id="ServicesStatus" numprocs="1"/>
```

6. Launch OEM Application Server Control on each Discoverer server, e.g., http://ascserver. learndiscoverer.com:1810.

7. From the home page, select OC4J_BI_Forms to access the OC4J_BI_Forms page.

8. Select the Administration tab.

9. Select Server Properties.

10. Scroll down to the Command Line Options area.

11. In the Java Options field, append the existing text with the following text:

```
-Doracle.disco.activation.preferencePort=<portno>
Doracle.disco.activation.preferenceHost=<hostname>
```

NOTE
Make sure there is a space character between the existing text and the new text. Enter the hostname and port you obtained in Steps 4 and 5.

12. Click Apply.

13. Click Yes to restart the OC4J_BI_Forms component.

14. Identify which web cache you would like to use, as it has been installed on both mid-tiers. You may also choose to use Web Cache installed independently on another host.

NOTE
Web Cache is available for download as a stand-alone installation from OTN.

15. Launch the administration tool for this Web Cache, e.g., http://ascserver.learndiscoverer. com:4000.

16. From the Web Cache welcome page click OracleAS Web Cache Manager, located in the Managing Web Cache box at the top right of the screen.

17. When prompted to log in, use the username ias_admin and the password that you provided during the application server installation.

18. Select the Origin Servers option from the list of options at the left. It is located in the section headed Origin Servers, Sites, and Load Balancing.

Origin Servers

Use this page to configure application Web server or proxy server settings. These settings are required for load balancing, failover, and site-to-server mappings (Site-to-Server Mappings page).

Component Dependencies: Modifying an origin server port number on this page also requires changing the port number in the origin server's configuration.

Application Web Servers

Select	Host	Port	Routing	Capacity	Failover Threshold	Ping URL	Ping Interval (seconds)	Protocol
○	asclaptop2.learndiscoverer.com	7778	ENABLED	100	5	/	10	HTTP

[Add...] [Edit Selected...] [Delete Selected]

Proxy Servers

There are currently no Proxy Servers defined.

[Add...]

19. Click Edit Selected, then configure each of the Discoverer origin servers as follows:

- **Hostname**   This is the hostname of the server Web Cache will make requests to.

- **Port**   This is the Oracle HTTP Server's listening port.

- **Routing**   You may disable routing when performing maintenance on a server.

- **Capacity**   This is number of concurrent requests Web Cache will submit to a specific origin server.

- **Failover Threshold**   Web Cache will routinely ping the origin server. Failover Threshold is the number of failed pings that can occur before Web Cache automatically stops routing to the server.

- **Ping URL**   This is the URL that Web Cache will use to check the origin server. Be sure to enter a URL that calls one of the Discoverer web applications, e.g., http://ascserver.learndiscoverer.com:7778/Discoverer/viewer.

NOTE
The default tests only the Oracle HTTP Server.

- **Ping Interval**   This is the number of seconds between pings.

- **Protocol**   This indicates whether you are using secure HTTPS or just HTTP.

20. When you are done editing the Discoverer origin servers, click Submit.

21. Select the Site Definitions option from the list of options at the left. It is also located in the section headed Origin Servers, Sites, and Load Balancing.

Site Definitions

Use this page to configure site definitions and aliases (virtual hosting). Site definitions enable Web Cache to apply different caching rules to different sites. Requests for different sites can also be routed to specific origin servers through Site-to-Server Mappings.

A separate response is cached for each unique request URL. If two requests are identical except for a URL parameter value, and they yield identical responses, you can instruct the cache to ignore the parameter value and cache only one copy. You may specify site-specfic parameters to ignore here.

Alias definitions enable the mapping of multiple host names to a single site. For example, site www.company.com:80 may have an alias of company.com:80. By specifying the alias of company.com:80 for site www.company.com:80, Web Cache can cache the same content from either company.com:80 or www.company.com:80. Site and alias definitions also affect Error Pages configuration.

Note: When a site definition is deleted, the mapping for that site is not automatically removed from the Site-to-Server Mapping page.

Site								Aliases			
Select	Host Name	Port	URL Path Prefix	HTTPS Only Prefix	URL Parameters to Ignore	Client-Side Certificate	Default	Select	Host Name	Port	URL Path Prefix
○	asclaptop2.learndiscoverer.com	80				Not Required	Yes	N/A	None	N/A	N/A

[Add Site...]   [Edit Site...]   [Delete Site]   [Add Alias...]   [Edit Alias...]   [Delete Alias]

22. Select Add Site. This opens the Add Site dialog box.

Add Site

Host Name: *(hostname.domain)*	☐ (Example: www.company.com)
Port Number:	☐ (Examples: 80 for HTTP; 443 for HTTPS)
URL Path Prefix:	☐ (Example: /tech/)
HTTPS Only Prefix:	☐
Client-Side Certificate:	○ Required ◉ Not Required
URL Parameters to Ignore:	☐
	(Example: name, employee_id)
Default Site:	○ Yes ◉ No
Create Alias from Site Name with/without www:	○ Yes ◉ No

[Submit] [Cancel]

23. Complete the Add Site dialog box as follows:

- **Hostname**   This is what your users will enter to access Discoverer, e.g., www. learndiscoverer.com.

- **Port Number**   Enter 80 if using HTTP, or 443 if using HTTPS. Make sure that you select a port number in here that Web Cache is listening on. Selecting the Web Cache port number is a different step.

- **URL Path Prefix**   Enter this only if Web Cache is routing to other components than Discoverer, e.g., /tech/.

- **HTTPS Only Prefix**   Enter this only if you are using HTTPS.

- **Client-Side Certificate**   This setting has two choices, Required and Not Required. You should select Required only if you are using client-side certificates for authentication.

- **URL Parameters to Ignore**   You should use this box if you want Web Cache to ignore certain parameters when determining the uniqueness of a page.

- **Default Site**   If an HTTP request is made without a host in the header, Web Cache will route the request to the default site.

- **Create Alias from Site Name with/without www**   Check the Yes button if you want the system to respond to learndiscoverer.com as well as www.learndiscoverer.com. The default for this is No.

NOTE
When creating a site definition, make sure that your host's file and DNS server are configured appropriately to deliver requests to the name you enter here. A site definition in Web Cache is very similar to a virtual host in Apache.

24. When you are done adding the new site, click Submit.

25. Select the Site-to-Server Mapping option from the list of options at the left. It is also located in the section headed Origin Servers, Sites, and Load Balancing. The main screen of this option is shown here:

Site-to-Server Mapping

Use this page to map requests for sites defined in the Site Definitions page to origin servers configured in the Origin Servers page. Mappings are required for virtual host sites and are optional for ESI provider sites.

Note: Prior to creating mappings, ensure that site definitions and origin server settings have been created in the Site Definitions and Origin Servers pages. When a site definition is deleted from the Site Definitions page, the mapping for that site is not automatically removed from the Site-to-Server Mapping table.

		Site				Origin Server		
Select	Priority	Host Name	Port	URL Path Prefix	ESI Content Policy	Host Name	Port	Proxy
○	1	asclaptop2.learndiscoverer.com	80		Unrestricted	asclaptop2.learndiscoverer.com	7778	No
○	2	*	80		Exclude Fragments	asclaptop2.learndiscoverer.com	7778	No
○	3	*	*		Exclude Fragments	asclaptop2.learndiscoverer.com	7778	No

[Edit Selected...] [Delete Selected...] [Insert Above...] [Insert Below...] [Move Up] [Move Down]

26. Complete the Site-to-Server Mappings as follows:

- Select any radio button (the top if Web Cache is used only for Discoverer).

- Select Insert Above.

- Select the second radio button, Select from Site Definitions, and choose the site you created in the previous step, e.g., learndiscoverer.com:80.

- Check the box by each of the Discoverer origin servers.

27. When you are done setting the site to server mappings, click Submit.

28. Select the Session Binding option from the list of options at the left. It is also located in the section headed Origin Servers, Sites, and Load Balancing. The main screen of this option is shown here:

Session Binding

Use this page to create session binding settings. Before using this page, configure session definitions in the Session Definitions page.

Note: If you are using a cache cluster, in addition to configuring sessions and session binding mechanism for each site, be sure to enable the global session binding cookie feature at the bottom of this page.

Select	Site Name	Session	Session Binding Mechanism
○	asclaptop2.learndiscoverer.com:80	*(default session binding)*	n/a
○	*Default Session Binding*	Session Binding Disabled	n/a

[Edit Selected...]

29. Complete the Session Binding as follows:

■ Select the radio button for the site name you created earlier.

■ Click Edit Selected.

■ In the box entitled "Please select a session," from the drop-down list of values, select JSESSIONID.

■ In the box entitled "Please select a session binding mechanism," from the drop-down list of values, select Cookie-based.

NOTE
If your users cannot accept cookies, select OC4J-Based.

30. When you are done setting the session binding, click Submit.

31. On the top of the Web Cache page, click Apply Changes.

32. Click Restart.

Summary

We have traveled through the architecture of Oracle Application Server 10*g,* starting with the HTTP server and progressing through each of the major components used to run Discoverer. As you have observed, the Discoverer Server presents a great many configuration options designed to fit into your enterprise's landscape. In this section we described the basic components of a Discoverer installation and showed you how to configure all of the various components. We showed you how to use OEM to configure Discoverer for a corporate look and feel. We also showed you how to configure Discoverer for use with Single Sign-On. After describing all of the preferences that you can set for the Discoverer mid-tier, we showed you how to use Web Cache and how to configure it to load-balance multiple Discoverer servers. The only way to really become familiar with configuring the Discoverer mid-tier is to explore and test different options. Don't worry, though, because you can always roll back—that is, if you remembered to take backups when we told you!

CHAPTER
21

Setting Up Portal for Use
with Discoverer

elcome to the chapter dedicated to Discoverer portlets. If you have never used Oracle Portal with any of Discoverer's portlets, you should take a look. In this chapter we will first of all describe Oracle Portal and then introduce you to the three portlets made available with Discoverer. Following this we will show you how to use Portal to administer the Discoverer portlets by setting up the Discoverer Portlet Provider (DPP). With the DPP in place and working, we will show you how to publish a Discoverer portlet to Portal. Once it is published, you need to configure the portlet to make it work. We will describe in detail how to configure all three of Discoverer's portlets. With the portlets configured and running, we will show you how to link to Discoverer Viewer from the portlet's Analyze button. Finally, we will show you how to customize the three Discoverer portlets.

Using Portal

As you may recall from our discussions earlier in the book when we talked about installing Discoverer, we said that you can install the Oracle Business Intelligence middle tier as a stand-alone instance. However, in order to use Discoverer with Portal, you will need to install two more components of the Application Server. These are

- The infrastructure database

- The Portal middle tier

Infrastructure Database

You need to install or create an infrastructure database, into which you can install the metadata repository (MDR) and Oracle Internet Directory (OID). We say install or configure because you can either install the Infrastructure into an existing database or use Application Server to create a database for you.

If you want to install the MDR into an existing Oracle database, you need to have a 9.2.0.6 or 10*g* database available. If you allow the 10.1.2.0.2 Application Server to create a database for you, it will install a 10.1.0.4 database, fully configured with the Infrastructure, MDR, and OID. Don't worry about licensing, because Oracle allows you to use this 10.1.0.4 database at no extra cost so long as you use it only for storing the infrastructure components. If you intend to use this seed database for anything other than this use, you will need to purchase or hold a separate 10*g* license.

Installing the infrastructure into an existing database is straightforward but can be tricky if you have never worked much with Oracle databases before. There are lots of prerequisite checks that need to be made, and you should be prepared to spend approximately one day getting this working. Allowing the Application Server to install its own seed database is the easier of the two options available to you and is the one we recommend.

If you are working on a new machine, make sure that you have a fully qualified domain name (FQDN) installed in your hosts file. In AIX and UNIX you will find this file in the /etc folder. In Windows you will find it in the Windows\System 32\drivers\etc folder. If you attempt to install the infrastructure database without an FQDN, you will run into problems and you will not be able to correctly attach the Discoverer and Portal middle tiers.

Portal Middle Tier

After you have installed the infrastructure, the next step is to install Oracle Portal itself. This component, also available from the main Application Server installer, is a middle-tier component just like Discoverer. You can choose to install the Portal components onto the same machine as used by Discoverer, or you can place it somewhere else. Whether you choose to install Portal on the same machine as Discoverer or not, in a production environment, we recommend you keep the infrastructure on its own machine. At the very least, therefore, you will have two machines, and possibly three. If you use the 10.1.2.0.2 installer Portal and Discoverer are installed into the same mid-tier.

Configuring the Discoverer Server

With the infrastructure and Portal installed and configured, you will now need to configure the Discoverer Server to make it attached to the same farm as the other components. To do this, follow the instructions in Chapter 20 in the section entitled "Joining a Discoverer Mid-Tier to an Identity Management Server and a Metadata Repository."

Types of Portlet

Discoverer has three types of portlets:

- Discoverer Gauges portlet
- Discoverer List of Workbooks portlet
- Discoverer Worksheet portlet

Discoverer Gauges Portlet

The Discoverer Gauges portlet contains worksheet data displayed as one or more semicircular gauges. The gauges have a very similar look and feel to a speedometer dial on a car. When you are setting up a Gauges portlet, similar to the way that you would use stoplight conditions in a worksheet, you get the opportunity to define low, acceptable, and high thresholds.

At run time, Discoverer will then generate a gauge with the three ranges colored separately. Using gauges, you define Key Performance Indicators (KPI) for your worksheet. Users can then look at a gauge to determine whether a measure is on target, below target, or above target. Most commonly, you will find these types of portlet being employed in dashboard applications where senior executives want to see only KPIs and how the company is doing.

The Discoverer Gauges portlet is new to 10.1.2 and is one of the best of the new additions that were added by Oracle during this release.

NOTE
Only crosstab worksheets can be used as the source for a Gauges portlet.

Discoverer Worksheet Portlet

A worksheet portlet allows you to display individual worksheet content, data and graph, in a portlet. The portal user sees the results within a portlet.

Discoverer List of Worksheets Portlet

The Discoverer List of Worksheets portlet allows you to display a list of worksheets to the end user. If the user clicks a worksheet, then that worksheet is displayed inside Discoverer Viewer. When you are setting up a List of Worksheets portlet, you get the opportunity to filter the list so that only the worksheets that you want to make available will be shown in the list. You also get the opportunity to define how many worksheets will be displayed in the list and the order in which you want the worksheets offered to the user.

Analyze Link

If enabled, at the bottom-left corner of a configured Gauges or Worksheet portlet is a button called Analyze. If a user clicks this button, Discoverer launches Viewer and allows the user to see the worksheet as it normally appears inside Viewer. A link called "Cancel and return to Portal" will be displayed on the top right of the Viewer screen. If the user clicks this link, Viewer will close and the user will be returned to Portal. Any changes made within Viewer will be abandoned.

If the user has the Save privilege, then an additional link called "Save and return to Portal" will be available inside Viewer. Any changes made in Viewer will now be displayed back in Portal. If the user does not have the necessary Save privilege, then the only link that will display is "Cancel and return to Portal." Both links can be seen in Figure 21-1.

Portal Administration

There are three steps to setting up Portal for use with Discoverer:

- Register the Discoverer Portlet Provider (DPP) with your portal instance.

- Publish a Discoverer portlet to Portal.

- Configure the Discoverer portlet.

NOTE
The DPP is only registered with Portal; it is not created.

Register the Discoverer Portlet Provider (DPP) with Your Portal Instance

Registering the Discoverer Portlet Provider (DPP) with Portal is a one-off step that is done by your Portal administrator. To register the DPP for use with Portal, use the following workflow:

1. Connect to Portal as the Portal user. The default password is the same as ias_admin password that you entered when Portal was installed.

NOTE
If your screen does not display correctly, click your browser's Refresh button. Portal makes heavy use of caching, and you could easily be fooled into thinking that the options you are looking for are not available.

2. Click the Administer tab.

3. On the top-left side of the page, you will see three tabs, Portal, Portlets, and Database.

<u>Preferences</u>   <u>Save and return to Portal</u>   <u>Cancel and return to Portal</u>   <u>Help</u>

FIGURE 21-1   *Portal links within Viewer*

4.   Click the Portlets tab. It is the middle of the three tabs.

Portlets tab

Remote Providers box

5.   Locate the Remote Providers box.

6.   Click Register a Provider.

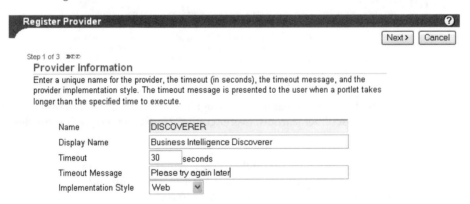

7.   In Provider Information, enter the following:

■   **Name**   For example, **Discoverer**.

■   **Display name**   For example, **Business Intelligence Discoverer**.

■   **Timeout**   For example, **30** seconds.

■   **Timeout message**   For example, **Please try again later**.

■   **Implementation Style**   Here, select Web.

NOTE
In the preceding section, you cannot use spaces in the Provider Name, and do not set the Timeout too low. The Display name does not have to be the same as the Provider Name, but you should use a meaningful name, because this is what your users will see when they try to create Portlets.

8.   Click Next.

9.   In General Properties, enter the following: http://*hostname:port*/discoverer/portletprovider (e.g., **http://ascserver.learndiscoverer.com:7778/discoverer/portletprovider**).

NOTE
If you copy and paste the URL from the address bar at the top of the browser, you can then replace everything from the right of the port number with /discoverer/portletprovider. Make sure you type this exactly as shown here, and do not add an additional forward slash at the end of the URL.

10.   Check the box Web provider in same cookie domain as the portal.

Chapter 2 of the *Oracle Business Intelligence Discoverer Publishing Workbooks in Oracle Application Server Portal,* 10g Release 2 (10.1.2.1), Part no. B14465-02, specifically states not to clear the "Web Provider in same cookie domain as the portal check box." According to the document, this can have unintended consequences, even if the Portal and Discoverer middle-tier servers are on the same domain.

However, while we recommend you do adopt this policy as your starting point, there are times when you will need to uncheck this box. MetaLink document 295708.1 covers two such instances when the box should be unchecked:

- The user gets the "An error occurred while handling the request in the controller" message during selection of a worksheet. The note says that this occurs with an OLAP connection, but we have seen it happen with standard EUL connections as well.

- A page will load twice or a folder will need expanding twice, even though the user clicked Next.

We have encountered both of these situations on our own server, both of which were corrected when we unchecked the "Web provider in same cookie domain as the portal" box. Leave the other defaults as they are and scroll down to the section called User/Session Information.

User/Session Information

Specify the type of information the provider requires.

Select Public, if no user or session specific information should be sent to the provider and if no calls are to be made to the providers for session initializations.
○ Public

Select User, to send user specific information to the provider.
◉ User
    Specify the frequency by which the call to the provider for session initialization is performed.
    Login Frequency [Once Per User Session ▾]

    Select the checkbox, if session specific information is to be sent the provider. Session specific information includes information such as session id and login time.
    ☐ Require portal user specific session information.

In User/Session Information, check User and specify that the frequency should be Once per user session.

When setting the preceding properties, if you are unsure as to which port number to enter, use the following workflow:

1. Launch a second browser window.

2. Type **http://hosntame:1811** and press ENTER.

NOTE
Depending upon what you have installed on your server, the port number may not be 1811, but it will be in the range 1810–1829. It can even be something like 18100, 18101, or the like.

3. For the username, enter **ias_admin** and the associated password.

4. When authenticated, you will be at your Application Server Farm main page. Click the Portal mid-tier instance (you may need to enter your ias_admin username and password again).

Farm: iasdb10g.learndiscoverer.com

Instances can be grouped and managed together by configuring standalone instances in a common repository. This collection of instances is known as an Oracle Application Server Farm.

Repository Type **Database**

Clusters

(Create Cluster)

Select	Name	Status	Instances
	There are no clusters in the farm.		

Standalone Instances

These instances belong to the farm but are not part of any cluster.

(Join Cluster)

Select	Name	Host	Oracle Home
⦿	disco10g.w2kserverv1.learndiscoverer.com	w2kserverv1.learndiscoverer.com	E:\oracle\10gdisco
○	infra10g.w2kserverv1.learndiscoverer.com	w2kserverv1.learndiscoverer.com	E:\oracle\10ginfra
○	prtal10g.w2kserverv1.learndiscoverer.com	w2kserverv1.learndiscoverer.com	E:\oracle\10gprtal

5. Click the Ports link alongside the word Home at the top of the screen.

6. Note the port number for your HTTP Server Listen (non-SSL) port. It will generally be in the range 7777–7877.

When you are done with General Properties, click Next to navigate to the Control Access page and follow these steps:

1. In Grant Access, leave this alone and click Finish.

2. If you get a warning about the cookie domain, click OK.

3. Exit Portal.

You have now successfully created a portlet provider for Discoverer.

Testing the Provider Connection

To test that your provider connection is working, enter this in your browser window: **http://*hostname:port*/discoverer/portletprovider**.

The system should respond with the message "Congratulations! You have successfully reached your Provider's Test Page" and display the portlets that it recognizes.

Congratulations! You have successfully reached your Provider's Test Page.

Recognizing Portlets...

default_gauges_portlet_name
default_worksheet_portlet_name
default_list_of_worksheets_portlet_name

Recognizing initialization parameters...

oracle.portal.log.LogLevel : 7

Recognizing component versions...

ptlshare.jar version: 10.1.2.0.2
pdkjava.jar version: 10.1.2.0.0

Creating a Connection

In order to test your connection for Portal, you need to have a connection. To create a connection, use the following workflow:

1. Make sure that you have created an EUL in your chosen database.
2. Note the TNS connection information.
3. Edit the TNSNames.ORA file for the Portal mid-tier that you are using and make sure you have a valid entry for the connection to your Discoverer instance.

NOTE
If you have both the infrastructure and your mid-tier instance on the same machine, you will have two TNSNames.ORA files. The one you need to edit is the one in the mid-tier instance. It is located at [Mid Tier Home]\network\admin.

4. Launch a browser.
5. Type **http://hosntame:1811** and press ENTER.
6. In username, enter **ias_admin** and the associated password.
7. When authenticated, you will see the form for your infrastructure and mid-tier.
8. Click the mid-tier instance (you may need to enter your ias_admin username and password again).
9. In the System Components section, click the link for Discoverer.
10. In the General section, click the link for Public Connections.
11. In the middle of the screen, you will see a message that says "No Public Connections Exist."
12. Click the button called Create Connection.
13. In the Create Public Connection window, enter the following:

   ■ **Connection Name**   Enter something like **CONNECT1**.
   ■ **Description**   Enter an optional description.

- **End User Layer**   Enter the name of the EUL in uppercase.

- **User Name**   Enter the name of a user who has access to Discoverer.

- **Password**   Type the user's password.

- **Database**   Enter the connect link that you used inside TNSNames.ORA.

14. Click OK; you have now created a Public Connection.

15. Close the Enterprise Manager.

You should now be able to test that it is working by entering **http://*hostname:port*/discoverer/plus** in a browser window on the mid-tier server.

Publish a Discoverer Portlet to Portal

Before a user can publish a Discoverer Portlet to a Portal page, you need to ensure that the following elements are in place:

- You need to have registered the Discoverer Portlet Provider with Portal.

- The user needs to know his or her login credentials for Portal.

- The user needs to have been granted Portal privileges that allow that user to create, edit, or customize Portal pages.

- Either you need to have created a public Discoverer connection or the user needs to have access to a Discoverer private connection.

- One or more workbooks need to have been saved to the Discoverer database. These workbooks can have been created by either Discoverer Plus, Discoverer Plus for OLAP, or Discoverer Desktop.

NOTE
Private connections will be available inside Portal only if Single Sign-On has been enabled. Without Single Sign-On, only public connections will be available to your users.

To publish a Discoverer Portlet to a Portal page, use the following workflow:

1. Launch a suitable web browser.

2. Launch Portal using http://*hostname:port*/pls/portal.

3. Log in as a Portal user. In this example, you will log in as the Portal user.

4. Click the Navigator link on the top right of the screen.

5. We will add a simple portlet to the Portlet Builder Build page to let us see a list of available workbooks.

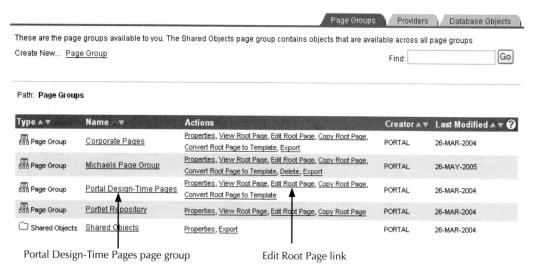

Portal Design-Time Pages page group   Edit Root Page link

6. On the Portal Navigator page, look for the Page Group called Portal Design-Time Pages and click the link called Edit Root Page.

7. Click the tab called Build.

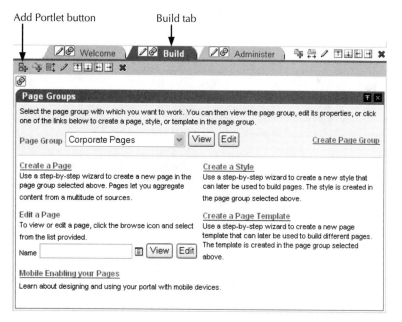

8. You will see a heading called Page Groups, and just above that you will see a set of nine icons, the first of which looks like a filing cabinet with a plus sign. This is the Add Portlet button.

NOTE
If you do not see the icons, you must not be in Edit mode. To enter Edit mode, click the Edit button that is located as the leftmost link on the second row of links at the top right of the page.

9. Click the Add Portlet button.

10. In the Add Portlets To Region screen, look for the area called Portlet Repository.

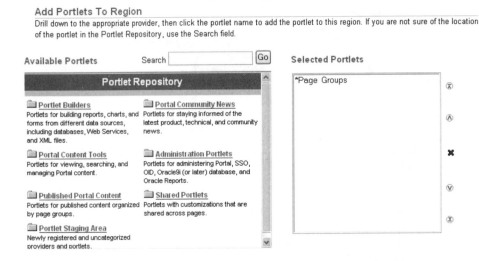

11. In the Portlet Repository dialog box, click the link called Portlet Staging Area.

12. In the Portlet Staging Area dialog box, click the link for Discoverer. It will be named by whatever Display Name was assigned when the DPP was registered. In our case, as you can see, it is called Business Intelligence Discoverer.

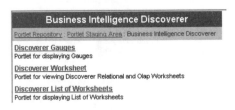

13. In the Discoverer portlets box, as you can see in the Available Portlets pane, there are three Discoverer portlets that you can use:

   ■ Discoverer Gauges

   ■ Discoverer Worksheet

   ■ Discoverer List of Worksheets

14. Click the portlet(s) that you want to use. Discoverer places a copy of the portlet(s) in the Selected Portlets pane. As you can see here, we have chosen to add one portlet of each type.

NOTE

You can publish multiple copies of the same portlet into the same area. Just keep clicking the portlet link. Each portlet will need to be configured separately.

15. Click OK at the top right of the screen. The portlet(s) will now be published to the Portal.

Having published your portlet(s), you will find that they are not yet available for use, because they need to be configured. Our three published portlets currently look like this.

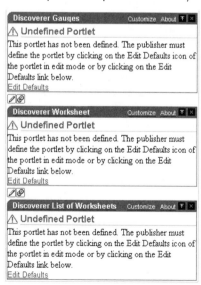

Configuring Discoverer Portlets

Once you have successfully published a Discoverer portlet to the Portal, before the portlet can be used it needs to be configured. As previously explained, there are three types of portlet that can be published, and we will describe how to configure each in turn in the following order:

- Configuring a Discoverer Gauges portlet
- Configuring a Discoverer Worksheet portlet
- Configuring a Discoverer List of Worksheets portlet

Configuring a Discoverer Gauges Portlet

To configure a Discoverer Gauges portlet, begin with the following workflow:

1. Locate the nonconfigured Discoverer Gauges portlet, and click the Edit Defaults link.

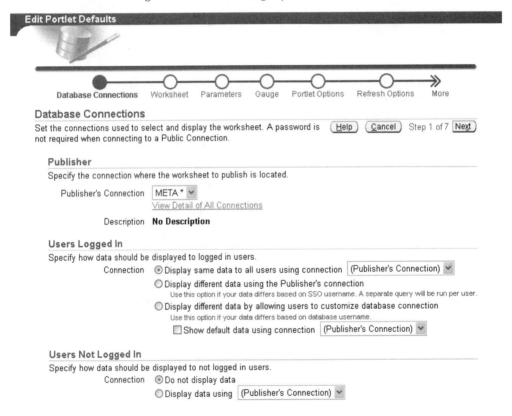

2. The Gauges portlet has the following seven pages. Select the connection you want to use and click Next.

- Database Connections
- Worksheet
- Parameters

- Gauge

- Portlet Options

- Refresh Options

- Review Portlet Defaults

3. Discoverer displays a list of the workbooks that contain crosstab worksheets. From the list of workbooks you need to determine the one that contains the worksheet that you want to work with. Having determined the workbook that you will be using, expand the workbook and check the box alongside the worksheet that you will be using.

○	⊕	▶ Example Hyper Drill Detail	Workbook
○	⊕	▶ Example Hyper Drill Lowest	Workbook
○	⊕	▶ Example Hyper Drill Master	Workbook
○	⊕	▶ Example Traffic Lighting and Typing	Workbook
○	⊕	▼ Example Year on Year	Workbook
◉		Crosstab	Crosstab

Selected workbook ────────→ Example Year on Year
Selected worksheet ────→ Crosstab

4. Click Next; you will be taken either to the Parameters page or to the Gauge page.

5. If the worksheet uses parameters, you will be asked to provide them. Having provided your parameters, click Next.

6. On the Gauge page there are three main areas. Set each area according to the descriptions that follow, and then complete portlet and refresh options and review your settings as further described in the text. Click Next after completing each page.

- Data Options

- Display Options

- Customization

7. Having completed the configuration of the Gauges portlet, click Finish. Discoverer will now execute the portlet, and you should see the results onscreen. Here are the results of the portlet that we just configured.

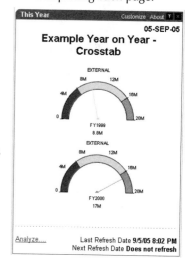

Data Options In the Data Options area, Discoverer executes the worksheet and, as you can see in Figure 21-2, displays the results. You are then required to supply the following:

- **Data for Gauge** As shown in the following illustration, you need to select the measure, the columns, and the rows the gauge will be based on. The number of gauges that will be generated depends on the number of columns and rows that you select. For example, if you select two columns and three rows, the number of gauges that will be generated is six.

Data for Gauge

The value of the selected measure is plotted on each gauge. The number of gauges displayed depends on the number of column items and row items selected. For example: if you select 3 column items and 2 row items, you will see 6 gauges arranged in 3 columns and 2 rows.

Measure [This Year ▾]
 Value plotted on the gauge.

* Column Items [   ] ✎
 Items represented as rows in the gauge set.

* Row Items [   ] ✎
 Items represented as columns in the gauge set.

Gauge

Set the gauge options.

(Help) (Cancel) (Back)

* Indicates required field

Data Options

▼ Hide Crosstab

⊙ Up | 25 Rows ▾ | Down ⊙   Rows 1-25 of 38

	EXTERNAL			INTERNET		
	This Year	Last Year	Diff	This Year	Last Year	Diff
FY1998	11,120,113	NULL	NULL	NULL	NULL	NULL
1998-Q3	1,996,801	NULL	NULL	NULL	NULL	NULL
1998-Q4	9,123,312	NULL	NULL	NULL	NULL	NULL
FY1999	8,758,203	NULL	NULL	1,033,398	NULL	NULL
1999-Q1	4,653,005	NULL	NULL	NULL	NULL	NULL
1999-Q2	1,963,930	NULL	NULL	381,072	NULL	NULL
1999-Q3	1,672,702	1,996,801	-324098.11	461,286	NULL	NULL

FIGURE 21-2   *Gauge page with worksheet results displayed*

- **Measure**   Discoverer will generate a list of values of the data points in the worksheet. You need to select one of them. For this example, we will select This Year.

- **Column Items**   Take a look at Figure 21-2. The columns that are available are the EXTERNAL and INTERNAL sales channels. Clicking the flashlight icon alongside Column Items causes Discoverer to display a list of the column items. In this example case, we will select EXTERNAL.

- **Row Items**   Take a look at Figure 21-2. The rows that are available are all of the values down the left-hand side, including the group headings. Clicking the flashlight icon causes Discoverer to display a list of the available row items, as you can see in this illustration. For this example, we will select FY1999 and FY2000.

Available Values

FY1998
FY1998>1998-Q3
FY1998>1998-Q4
FY1999
FY1999>1999-Q1
FY1999>1999-Q2
FY1999>1999-Q3
FY1999>1999-Q4
FY2000
FY2000>2000-Q1
FY2000>2000-Q2
FY2000>2000-Q3
FY2000>2000-Q4

- **Range**   As shown in the following illustration, you need to provide two range values for the gauge:

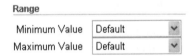

Range

Minimum Value | Default ▾
Maximum Value | Default ▾

- **Minimum Value**   Use this drop-down list to specify the minimum scale value that will be used in the gauge.

- **Maximum Value**   Use this drop-down list to specify the maximum scale value that will be used in the gauge.

The drop-down lists provided for both Minimum and Maximum Values have the same options:

- **Default**   Select this if you want Discoverer to use zero for the minimum value or automatically select the maximum value based on the values in the worksheet.

- **Map to Measure**   Select this if you want Discoverer to use one of the measures in the worksheet for the value. If you select this option, Discoverer redraws the page and displays another box from which you need to select the measure.

- **Specify**   Select this if you want to specify a value for the range yourself. For example, looking at the worksheet output in Figure 21-2, you might be aware that the minimum value is just over 8 million and that the maximum value is under 20 million. You could then specify 8 million for the minimum range value and 20 million for the maximum range value. If you select this option, as shown in the following illustration, Discoverer redraws the page and displays another for you to manually type in the value that you want.

For this example, we will allow Discoverer to use its default for the Minimum Value, but we will define a Maximum Value of 20 million.

- **Thresholds**   As shown in the following illustration, you have the option to enable thresholds for the gauge. Thresholds are used to split the gauge into regions. Typically, you would use these in a similar way as to using Stoplight Formatting, where you define a Low, usually unacceptable value and a High, usually desired value. Discoverer will use colors to color the unacceptable quadrant red, the acceptable quadrant in yellow, and the desired quadrant in green. Please note that because the Enable Thresholds box is unchecked, you cannot edit any of the threshold options move up.

The Thresholds area of the page is used as follows:

- **Enable Thresholds**   Use this check box to enable or disable the use of thresholds. If you check this box, Discoverer will redraw the screen to make the other options available.

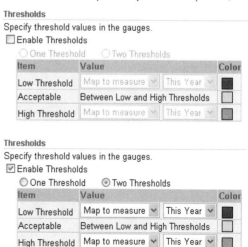

- **One Threshold/Two Thresholds** These radio buttons allow you to specify how many thresholds will be displayed in the portlet. Check One Threshold if you want to create two categories, a lower and an upper, or Two Thresholds if you want to create three categories, the typical lower, acceptable, and upper. If you check One Threshold, you will be able to define only the lower, red threshold.

- **Low Threshold** So long as you have checked Enable Thresholds, you can always define the lower threshold. Use the drop-down list to select and define the lower threshold.

- **High Threshold** This is available only if you have checked Enabled Thresholds and you have chosen to define Two Thresholds. Use the drop-down list to select and define the upper threshold.

These drop-downs are available for both Low and High Thresholds:

- **Map to Measure** Select this if you want Discoverer to use one of the measures in the worksheet for the value. Unlike the Range setting, where Discoverer redraws the page and displays another box from which you need to select the measure, the Map to Measure option is displayed by default.

- **Specify** Select this if you want to specify a value for the threshold yourself. If you select this option, Discoverer redraws the page and displays another box for you to manually type in the value that you want.

In our example, as you can see next, we chose to manually specify that the lower threshold is 6 million with the upper threshold being 16 million. You can also see the settings that we set for the other options.

Data for Gauge

The value of the selected measure is plotted on each gauge. The number of gauges displayed depends on the number of column items and row items selected. For example: if you select 3 column items and 2 row items, you will see 6 gauges arranged in 3 columns and 2 rows.

Measure This Year ▾
Value plotted on the gauge.

∗ Column Items EXTERNAL
Items represented as rows in the gauge set.

∗ Row Items FY1999; FY2000
Items represented as columns in the gauge set.

Range

Minimum Value Default ▾

Maximum Value Specify ▾ 20000000

Thresholds

Specify threshold values in the gauges.
☑ Enable Thresholds
○ One Threshold   ⦿ Two Thresholds

Item	Value		Color
Low Threshold	Specify ▾	6000000	■
Acceptable	Between Low and High Thresholds		□
High Threshold	Specify ▾	16000000	■

NOTE
According to the Help that is available from Oracle, you are supposed to be able to click each of the colors in the threshold area to manually select a chosen color from a palette. This did not work in our version of the product, 10.1.2.45.46; however, we have been informed by Oracle that this does work in the latest version, 10.1.2.48.18.

Display Options   In the Display Options area, shown next, you are required to supply the following options:

Display Options

Gauge Height/Width   200 (Gauge Set Size = **200x400**)
Used to calculate the Gauge Set size.
Background Color □
Plot Color □
Indicator Type ○ Arrow
□ Apply Threshold Colors to Arrow
⦿ Line
Measure Label ☑ Show Label
Font Size 9 ▾
Font Color ■
Range Labels □ Threshold Values
☑ Value Ticks
☑ Minimum Value
☑ Maximum Value
Font Size 9 ▾
Font Color ■

- **Gauge Height/Width**   Use this field to specify the size of the gauge in pixels. Discoverer then uses this setting to calculate the size of each gauge. For example, if you are using two rows and one column, as we are, a setting of 100 will produce a gauge size of 200 × 400 pixels.

NOTE
Discoverer automatically calculates the size of each gauge and displays this in bold alongside the Gauge Height/Width option.

- **Background Color**   Use this link to display a palette from which you can select the background color for the gauge.

- **Plot Color**   Use this link to display a palette from which you can select the plot color for the semicircular gauges.

- **Indicator Type**   Use these radio buttons to specify whether Discoverer should use an Arrow or a Line as the value indicator on the gauges. If you check Arrow, you can also specify whether the arrow should be displayed in the same color as the underlying threshold.

- **Measure Label**   Use this check box to specify whether Discoverer should show the Measure Label on the gauge. In most cases, you will want to do this. Having checked the box, you can now specify the Font Size and Font Color for the label.

■ **Range Labels** Use the Threshold Values and Value Ticks check boxes to specify whether you want these to display. You can also specify the Font Size and Font Color for the label.

Customization In the Customization area, shown next, you are required to set the following options:

Customization
☑ Allow Users to Customize Data Options
☑ Allow Users to Customize Display Options

■ **Allow Users to Customize Data Options** Use this check box to specify whether end users will be allowed to customize the data options for the portlet.

■ **Allow Users to Customize Display Options** Use this check box to specify whether end users will be allowed to customize the display options for the portlet.

Portlet Options On the Portlet Options page, as shown in the following illustration, there are two main areas:

Portlet Options
Select settings for these portlet options (Help) (Cancel) (Back) Step 5 of 7 [Next]

Display Options
Set options to display Worksheet in Portlet.
Portlet Title This Year
Portlet Content ☑ Title
☑ Text Area

Analyze Options
Set options for viewing worksheet in Viewer.
Analyze Options ☑ Allow user to analyze the worksheet in Viewer.
☐ Launch Worksheet Viewer in a new window

■ **Display Options** Use this area to define a title for the portlet. There are also check boxes for you to specify whether the worksheet's Title and Text Area will be displayed within the portlet. The default is to display both the Title and the Text Area.

■ **Analyze Options** Use the check box to specify whether end users can launch the worksheet in Viewer by clicking the Analyze button that will appear at the bottom left of the portlet. Having determined that an end user can launch Viewer, you can also specify whether Viewer should launch in another browser window. The default is to allow end users to launch Viewer but do so in the same browser window.

Refresh Options On the Refresh Options page, as shown in the following illustration, you can specify when the portlet should first refresh and how often it should refresh thereafter.

Refresh Options
Specify refresh schedule and refresh frequency for this (Help) (Cancel) (Back) Step 6 of 7 [Next]
portlet
First Refresh Time 21 ▼ : 15 ▼
First Refresh Date 2/4/06 ▦
2/4/06
Refresh Frequency ⦿ Never repeat
○ Refresh data every 1 Day(s) ▼

Review Portlet Defaults On the Review Portlet Defaults page, as shown in the following illustration, you get a chance to review all of the settings that you have set. If you have specified something wrong, you need to click the Back button and return to the appropriate page(s) to make your correction(s).

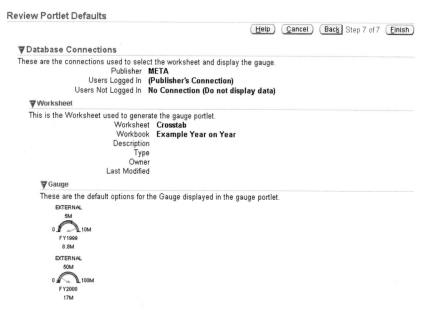

Configuring a Discoverer Worksheet Portlet

To configure a Discoverer Worksheet portlet, use the following workflow:

1. Locate the nonconfigured Discoverer Worksheet portlet and click the Edit Defaults link.

2. The Discoverer Worksheet portlet has the following six pages. Select the connection you want to use and click Next.

■ Database Connections

■ Worksheet

■ Parameters

■ Portlet Options

■ Refresh Options

■ Review Portlet Defaults

3. Discoverer displays a list of all the workbooks that are available. From the list of workbooks you need to determine the one that contains the worksheet that you want to work with. Having determined the workbook that

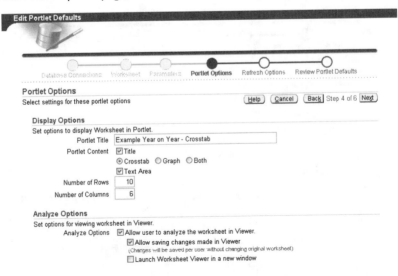

○	⊕	▶ Example Hyper Drill Detail	Workbook
○	⊕	▶ Example Hyper Drill Lowest	Workbook
○	⊕	▶ Example Hyper Drill Master	Workbook
○	⊕	▶ Example Traffic Lighting and Typing	Workbook
○	⊕	▼ Example Year on Year	Workbook
⦿		Crosstab	Worksheet
○		Table	Worksheet

you will be using, expand the workbook and check the box alongside the worksheet that you will be using.

As you can see in the preceding illustration, we will be using the same worksheet that was used in the gauges portlet example. Some organizations do this deliberately, displaying a gauge alongside its data, particularly in the case when end users have been prevented from analyzing the worksheet in Viewer.

4. Click Next; you will be taken either to the Parameter page or to the Portlet Options page.

5. If the worksheet uses parameters, you will be asked to provide them. Having provided your parameters, click Next.

6. On the Portlet Options page, as shown in the following illustration, there are two main areas:

■ **Display Options**   Use this area to define a title for the portlet. There are also check boxes for you to specify whether the worksheet's Title and Text Area will be displayed within the portlet. The default is to display both the Title and the Text Area. There are also radio buttons for you to specify whether the portlet should display the Crosstab, the Graph, or Both. The default is Both, but in our case we will display only the data. Finally, you can specify how many rows and columns of data should be displayed within the portlet.

■ **Analyze Options**   Use the check box to specify whether end users can launch the worksheet in Viewer by clicking the Analyze button that will appear at the bottom left of the portlet. Having determined that an end user can launch Viewer, you can also specify whether a user is allowed to save his or her changes in Viewer and whether Viewer should launch in another browser window. The default is to allow end users to launch Viewer in the same browser window but not to save. In our example, we will allow users to save, because in a later section we will show you how changes that are made in Viewer will be reflected back in Portal.

7. When you have set all of the Portlet Options, click Next.

8. On the Refresh Options page, as shown in this illustration, you can specify when the portlet should first refresh and how often it should refresh thereafter.

9. When you have set all of the Refresh Options, click Next.

10. On the Review Portlet Defaults page, as shown in the following illustration, you get a chance to review all of the settings that you have set. If you have specified something wrong, you need to click the Back button and return to the appropriate page(s) to make your correction(s).

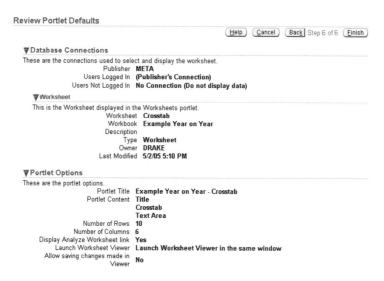

11. Another small but very useful enhancement in 10.1.2 is the presence of a small button at the bottom of the review page, named Refresh Page. After you have published a portlet for the first time, if you want to force a refresh of the portlet, you can simply go to this page and click the button.

12. Having completed the configuration of the Discoverer Worksheet portlet, click Finish. Discoverer will now execute the portlet, and you should see the results on screen. Here are the results of the portlet that we just configured.

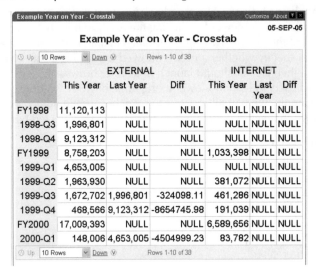

	EXTERNAL			INTERNET		
	This Year	Last Year	Diff	This Year	Last Year	Diff
FY1998	11,120,113	NULL	NULL	NULL	NULL	NULL
1998-Q3	1,996,801	NULL	NULL	NULL	NULL	NULL
1998-Q4	9,123,312	NULL	NULL	NULL	NULL	NULL
FY1999	8,758,203	NULL	NULL	1,033,398	NULL	NULL
1999-Q1	4,653,005	NULL	NULL	NULL	NULL	NULL
1999-Q2	1,963,930	NULL	NULL	381,072	NULL	NULL
1999-Q3	1,672,702	1,996,801	-324098.11	461,286	NULL	NULL
1999-Q4	468,566	9,123,312	-8654745.98	191,039	NULL	NULL
FY2000	17,009,393	NULL	NULL	6,589,656	NULL	NULL
2000-Q1	148,006	4,653,005	-4504999.23	83,782	NULL	NULL

Configuring a Discoverer List of Worksheets Portlet

To configure a Discoverer List of Worksheets portlet, use the following workflow:

1. Locate the nonconfigured Discoverer List of Worksheets portlet and click the Edit Defaults link.

2. The List of Worksheets portlet has the following five pages. Select the connection you want to use and click Next.

   ■ Database Connections

   ■ List of Worksheets

   ■ Portlet Options

   ■ Refresh Options

   ■ Review Portlet Defaults

3. Discoverer displays a list of all the workbooks that are available. In addition, Discoverer has the Worksheet Selections area shown here.

List of Worksheets

Select the worksheets to be displayed in the list.

Worksheet Selections | Specific Worksheets |

List of Worksheets will display only selected worksheets

☐ Allow users to change selected worksheets

4. Using the drop-down list of options, you can choose one of the following:

   ■ **Specific Worksheets**   Using this option, you manually choose which worksheets will be available within the portlet. If a new worksheet is added to any of the workbooks from which you made the worksheets available, the new worksheet will not be available within the portlet. Likewise, if you remove a worksheet, it will not be removed from this list. Therefore, you need to be very careful not to delete a worksheet that has been made available in a portlet using the Specific Worksheets option.

   ■ **All Worksheets from Selected Workbooks**   Using this option, you manually choose which workbooks will be available within the portlet. All worksheets within those workbooks will be available to the end user. If a new worksheet is added to any of the workbooks that you made available, the new worksheet will also be available within the portlet. Likewise, if a worksheet is deleted, it will also be deleted from the list.

   ■ **All Worksheets from All Workbooks**   Using this option, you will allow all worksheets in all workbooks to be available within the portlet. If a new worksheet or workbook is added to the system, the new worksheet or workbook will also be available within the portlet. Likewise, if a worksheet or workbook is deleted, it will also be deleted from the list.

5. Also in the Worksheet Selections area is a check box called Allow users to change selected worksheets. If you check this box, end users will be able to customize their own view of the portlet by changing the worksheets that are displayed in the list. Having determined the workbooks or worksheets that you will be allowing, check the box alongside the workbook(s) or worksheet(s). In this example, as you can see next, we will allow our end users to select any worksheet from the example workbooks in our end user layer.

☑	⊕	▷ Example Cascading Parameters	Workbook
☑	⊕	▷ Example Graph	Workbook
☑	⊕	▷ Example Hyper Drill Detail	Workbook
☑	⊕	▷ Example Hyper Drill Lowest	Workbook
☑	⊕	▷ Example Hyper Drill Master	Workbook
☑	⊕	▷ Example Traffic Lighting and Typing	Workbook
☑	⊕	▷ Example Year on Year	Workbook

6. Having completed the List of Worksheets page, click Next.

7. On the Portlet Options page, as shown in the following illustration, there are two main areas:

- **Display Options**   Use this area to define a title for the portlet. There are also radio buttons for you to specify whether the portlet will Show All worksheets or limit the display to a number that you specify. There are check boxes that allow you to specify whether the following will be displayed within the portlet: Description, Modified Date, Creation Date, Owner.

- **Analyze Options**   Use the check box to specify whether end users can save any changes that they make in Viewer. You can also specify whether Viewer should launch in another browser window. The default is to allow end users to save their changes but launch Viewer in the same browser window. For this example, we will allow users to save their changes.

8. When you have set all of the Portlet Options, click Next.

9. On the Refresh Options page, as shown in the following illustration, you can specify when the portlet should first refresh and how often it should refresh thereafter.

10. When you have set all of the Refresh Options, click Next.

11. On the Review Portlet Defaults page, as shown in the following illustration, you get a chance to review all of the settings that you have set. If you have specified something wrong, you need to click the Back button and return to the appropriate page(s) to make your correction(s).

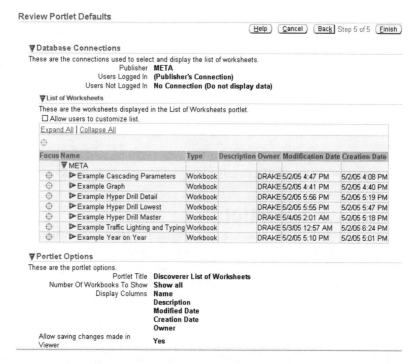

12. Having completed the configuration of the Discoverer Worksheet portlet, click Finish. Discoverer will now execute the portlet, and you should see the results on screen. Here are the results of the portlet that we just configured.

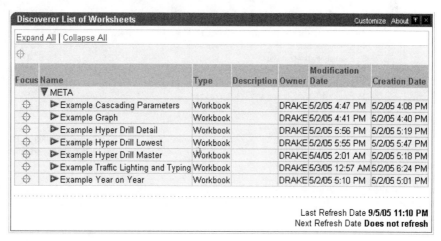

13. Click Next. The system will search for and generate a list of all worksheets that are available to the user.

For more information regarding publishing Discoverer content in Portal, please take a look at this Oracle document: B14465-01, Publishing Workbooks in Oracle Application Server Portal, which you find at this location on OTN: http://www.oracle.com/technology/documentation/discoverer.html.

NOTE
For 10.1.2 phase 2, the document part number has changed to B14465-02.

In this section we have shown you how to set up Discoverer's Portlet Provider for use within Portal. We have also walked you through adding a Discoverer Portlet to a Portal page.

Working with Portlets

As an end user, you may have access to Oracle Portal and subsequently to the Discoverer portlets. In this section we will show you how to work with Discoverer portlets. In particular, if you have been given permission, we will show you how to customize a portlet for your own use. Before we show you how to use the Analyze and Customization links, we want to draw your attention to another clever new feature of the Discoverer portlets. This is the ability to expand a list of worksheets from within the portlet itself.

Look at the Discoverer List of Worksheets portlet, shown here.

Discoverer List of Worksheets					Customize About ⊤ ⊠
Expand All | Collapse All					
⊕					
Focus	**Name**	**Type**	**Description**	**Owner**	**Modification Date**	**Creation Date**
	▼ META					
⊕	▶ Example Cascading Parameters	Workbook		DRAKE	5/2/05 4:47 PM	5/2/05 4:08 PM
⊕	▶ Example Graph	Workbook		DRAKE	5/2/05 4:41 PM	5/2/05 4:40 PM
⊕	▶ Example Hyper Drill Detail	Workbook		DRAKE	5/2/05 5:56 PM	5/2/05 5:19 PM
⊕	▶ Example Hyper Drill Lowest	Workbook		DRAKE	5/2/05 5:55 PM	5/2/05 5:47 PM
⊕	▶ Example Hyper Drill Master	Workbook		DRAKE	5/4/05 2:01 AM	5/2/05 5:18 PM
⊕	▶ Example Traffic Lighting and Typing	Workbook		DRAKE	5/3/05 12:57 AM	5/2/05 6:24 PM
⊕	▶ Example Year on Year	Workbook		DRAKE	5/2/05 5:10 PM	5/2/05 5:01 PM
					Last Refresh Date **9/5/05 11:41 PM**	
					Next Refresh Date **Does not refresh**	

We want to draw your attention to the top-left corner of the portlet. Do you see the two additional links called Expand All and Collapse All? Let's click the link for Expand All and see what happens.

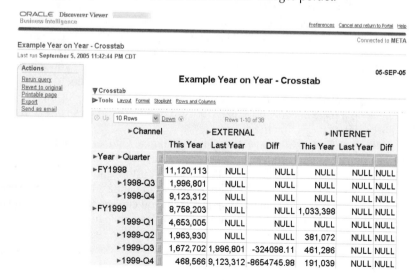

As you can see here, Discoverer has expanded the list to now display all of the worksheet names. Clicking any worksheet name causes Discoverer to launch Viewer. You will find that this ability to expand the list of workbooks directly within Portal is a terrific enhancement and one that you will wonder how you ever managed to live without.

Using Analyze

On the bottom left of Discoverer Gauges and Worksheet portlets, you may see an Analyze link in the bottom left-hand corner of the portlet. If you click this link, Discoverer Viewer will launch. To show you how this works, we followed the link from our Gauges portlet.

Look at the preceding illustration. As you can see, we are inside Discoverer Viewer. However, if you look carefully, you will notice a few changes from the usual Viewer interface. For a start, at the top right there is a new link called "Cancel and return to Portal." Clicking this link does exactly that and returns you to Portal without saving any changes that you may have made. If you have been granted permission to save your changes, then an additional link will appear. In the following illustration, taken from another linked worksheet, you can see that in this case we have a link called "Save and return to portal."

Also missing in "single Worksheet Viewer" mode are

- Save or Save As from the Actions pane

- Worksheet Options from the Actions pane

- The Worksheets pane

- The breadcrumb for Connect > Workbooks

Preferences   Save and return to Portal   Cancel and return to Portal   Help

The preceding illustration is taken from Viewer after we followed the link from the worksheet portlet that we created earlier. You will recall that in this case we allowed our users to save their changes. These are the sort of changes that you can make and save:

- You can change the layout.

- You can format.

- You can add Stoplight and Conditional Formatting.

- If a graph is included within the worksheet, you also have the ability to save changes made to the graph itself, such as the graph type, graph size, and other properties, such as gradient and 3-D effects.

Customizing Portlets

Another feature of portlets is the ability for an end user to customize a portlet for his or her own use. Customizations done this way will be saved under the user's own account, thus making the customizations unique to that user. End users can customize all three of the Discoverer portlets. If you look back at the headings for all of the portlets that we created, you will see that there is a small link called Customize. Clicking this link in the List of Worksheets or Worksheet portlet opens up a page called Review Portlet Customizations. Clicking the Customize link in a Gauges portlet opens up a page called Customize Gauges Portlet. It is on these pages that the end user applies the customizations that they want.

On the Review Portlet Customizations and Customize Gauges Portlet page, wherever there is something that a user can customize, Discoverer will add a button called Update. When a user clicks this button, that user will be taken to the actual customization pages.

On the Customize Gauges Portlet page, as shown in Figure 21-3, and on the Review Portlet Customizations, as shown in Figures 21-4 and 21-5, you can see that the user can also customize the Portlet Options. The exact list of things that a user can change differs from portlet to portlet, but if you look back earlier in this chapter to the configuration sections for the three portlet types and look at the Portlet Options page for each portlet, you will see what can be changed. All portlets allow an end user to customize these Portlet Options.

Customizing the Discoverer Gauges Portlet

If you have the ability to customize a Discoverer Gauges portlet, you will be pleased to know that, in addition to the Portlet Options, you also have full power to customize the Data Options and Display Options. This means you can specify your own settings for the data, the ranges, and all of the thresholds.

To customize a Discoverer Gauges portlet, use the following workflow:

1. Click the Customize link at the top right of the portlet. This opens the Customize Gauges Portlet page, shown in Figure 21-3.

2. At the right-hand side of the Gauge area, click the button called Update. Discoverer opens up a large page called Gauge. On this screen there are two areas that you can customize:

   ■ **Data Options**   In here you can change just about every single facet of the gauge definition. In fact the options that you can customize are the same as those described earlier when we showed you how to create the gauge in the first place.

   ■ **Display Options**   Once again you can customize all of the same options that were first set up when the Gauges portlet was created. Please look back to the section called "Configuring a Discoverer Gauges Portlet."

3. When you have made your changes, click Continue. Discoverer redraws the gauge.

4. If you want to customize the Portlet Options, click the Update button alongside that area.

FIGURE 21-3   *Discoverer Gauges – Customize Gauges Portlet page*

5. Having made any adjustments to the portlet options, such as the Portlet Title, and whether to include or exclude the worksheet title or text area, click Continue.

6. If all of the customizations look right, click Apply.

Customizing the Discoverer Worksheet Portlet

On a Discoverer Worksheet portlet, in addition to the ability to customize the Portlet Options, you can also provide your own Formats and Stoplight Formatting.

To customize a Discoverer Worksheet portlet, use the following workflow:

1. Click the Customize link at the top right of the portlet. This opens the Review Portlet Customizations page shown in Figure 21-4.

2. At the right-hand side of the Formats area, click the button called Update. Discoverer opens up a small Tools area just below the word Formats. In this area there are links for Format and Stoplight.

3. Click the Format link. Discoverer displays the following submenu of format options:

4. The amount of formatting that you can do is limited to the ability to Embolden, Italicize, or Underline particular data values. Using the mouse, highlight the cells that you want to format and then click the format that you want to apply. In 10.1.2.0.2 you can also customize the background and font colors.

Formats

Select the formatting properties.

▼**Tools Format** Stoplight

[B] [*i*] [U] | Number 99 ▼ (Go) |

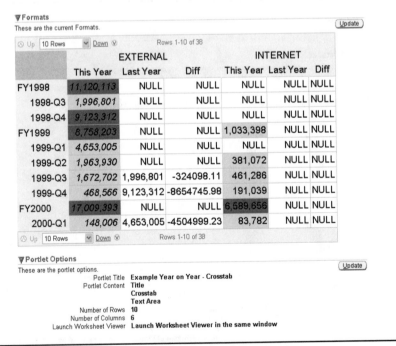

FIGURE 21-4 *Discoverer Worksheet - Review Portlet Customizations page*

5. If you want to apply stoplight formatting, continue with Step 6; otherwise, if you have finished applying formats, click Go and proceed to Step 11.

6. To apply stoplight formatting, click the Stoplight button. Discoverer displays the following submenu of stoplight options:

▼ **Tools** Format **Stoplight**

Format | This Year ⌄ | | Unacceptable | ☐ | ■ - Acceptable ☐ - Desirable | | ■ | Go

7. Pick the column that you want to format.

8. Set the Desirable and Unacceptable values.

9. Click Go.

10. If you want to apply stoplight formatting to another column, repeat Steps 7–9.

11. Click Continue to close the Formats page and return to the Review Portlet Customizations page to see the result of the formatting.

12. If you want to customize the Portlet Options, click the Update button alongside that area.

13. Having made any adjustments to the portlet options, such as the Portlet Title, whether to include or exclude the worksheet title or text area, or how many columns or rows should be displayed, click Continue.

14. If all of the customizations look right, click Apply.

Customizing the Discoverer List of Worksheets Portlet

As you may recall from our discussions on creating the Discoverer List of Worksheets portlet, we commented that we would allow our users to customize their own list.

To customize the Discoverer List of Worksheets portlet, use the following workflow:

1. Click the Customize link at the top right of the portlet. This opens the Review Portlet Customizations page for the List of Worksheets, as shown in Figure 21-5.

2. As you can see in Figure 21-5, there is an Update button alongside the List of Worksheets. Clicking this causes Discoverer to reopen the master list of worksheets and allow the user to modify the list. The list is modified using the same steps that were used earlier in this chapter when we showed you how to create a customized list of worksheets. Please refer to the section called "Configuring a List of Worksheets Portlet."

3. Having modified the list, click Continue. The List of Workbooks page will close, and you will be returned to the Review Portlet Customizations page.

4. If you want to customize the Portlet Options, click the Update button alongside that area.

5. Having made any adjustments to the portlet options, such as the Portlet Title, whether to limit the list to a specified number of workbooks, or whether to include the Description, Modified Data, Creation Date, or Owner, click Continue.

6. At the bottom of the Review Portlet Customizations page is a button called Refresh Page (Refresh Portlet Now in 10.1.2.0.0). Clicking this will refresh the list of worksheets within the portlet immediately.

7. If all of the customizations look right, click Apply.

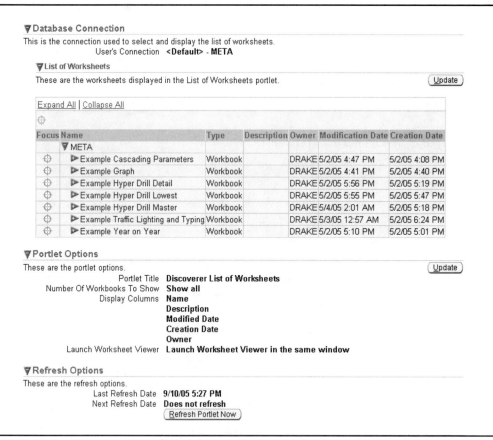

FIGURE 21-5 *Discoverer List of Worksheets – Review Portlet Customizations page*

As you can see from the modified list shown next, we have removed the Example Graph workbook and included the Drill to File workbook. Comparing this list of workbooks with the list in Figure 21-5 confirms that the list has changed.

NOTE
*When customizing a portlet, please note that any customizations you
make will be applied to the portlet only as you see it. In other words,
all portlet customizations are user specific, so you need not worry that
your customizations will affect what other users see. This is a great
feature that we recommend you make use of.*

Summary

This chapter introduced you to Discoverer portlets. You learned about Oracle Portal, and we
introduced you to the three portlets made available with Discoverer. Following this, we showed
you how to use Portal to administer the Discoverer portlets by setting up the Discoverer Portlet
Provider (DPP). With the DPP in place and working, we showed you how to publish a Discoverer
portlet to Portal. After this, we described in detail how to configure all three of Discoverer's
portlets. With the portlets configured and running, we showed you how to link to Discoverer
Viewer from a portlet's Analyze button. Finally, we showed you how to customize the three
Discoverer portlets.

CHAPTER
22

Summary Management

his chapter, another in the series of chapters dedicated to the Discoverer administrator, will show you how to manage summary tables. We talk about the background for summary tables and explain why you need them. After this, we talk about the setup requirements for the database and for the user privileges. We then discuss materialized views, the objects that lie at the heart of summary management. Next, we get to the heart of the chapter, where we discuss managing the summary tables. We show you the two ways to manage summaries: using Discoverer's automated summary management feature and manually configuring your own summary tables. After this, we discuss a strategy for managing summary combinations. Next, we show you how to use summary tables with the Oracle E-Business Suite and close off the chapter by looking at the end user options for managing summary data.

Background

Performance is the reason we use summary tables. But what is a summary table? In database terms, a *summary table* is a materialized view, which is really just a table that contains presummarized data. The clever thing about a materialized view, though, is that the Oracle database's optimizer will redirect a query to use a materialized view if all of the components that the query is looking for are contained within the materialized view.

NOTE
The differences between materialized views and other objects are discussed in depth later in this chapter.

When reporting from transaction systems, you do not want your users to query directly from the detail transaction tables if you can help it. This will cause long delays while querying and can seriously reduce the performance of your OLTP system.

Summary management is one of the most important features of Discoverer. When used correctly, it can speed query response time significantly, resulting in queries that take seconds rather than hours. Managing summaries is the key to good performance with Discoverer implementations.

Summary tables hold preaggregated and prejoined data. A query directed to a summary table may return results in a few seconds, whereas that same query directed against the base data tables may require a three- or four-table join and an aggregation over millions of rows, which would take considerably longer. Both queries, however, would produce the same results. Summary tables are used to provide a rapid response time for commonly run queries.

The process is automatic from the end user's view; that is, to the user it is not apparent that the query is being handled by a summary folder, rather than the base data tables. The net result is quick response times for queries and accurate results.

When Discoverer redirects to a summary folder, you will be able to detect this by looking at the execution plan and/or the SQL that Discoverer generates. However, if a query is rewritten to a materialized view by the database optimizer, this may not be detected by Discoverer. We therefore recommend you allow Discoverer to take control of, or at the very least be made aware of, the materialized views in the database.

Performance Overview

As mentioned earlier, the reason we use summary tables is for performance. By calculating the answers to difficult questions once, and only once, you can greatly reduce the load on your database. The performance gains can be summarized, pardon the pun, in the following four areas:

- **Physical reads**   Because there is less data to scan, there will be fewer physical reads.

- **Database writes**   Because you will not be causing the database to sort or aggregate as frequently as it would when querying against the base tables, there will be fewer database writes.

- **CPU consumption**   Because you will not be calculating aggregates and functions on the base tables, there will be decreased CPU consumption.

- **Response times**   Markedly faster response times will become the norm. Improved response times by many orders of magnitude are not out of the question.

Summary Setup

In order to set up summary management within your database, you need to handle the following:

- Database setup

- Database privileges

- Table analysis

Database Setup

In order for your database to fully support materialized views, you need to make sure that the following three init.ora settings are in situ:

- **COMPATIBLE**   This is a mandatory requirement for materialized views to function. It should be set to 8.1.0 or above.

- **QUERY_REWRITE_ENABLED**   This needs to be set to TRUE. If this is set to FALSE no query rewrites will take place. The default is FALSE.

- **QUERY_REWRITE_INTEGRITY**   This parameter controls how Oracle rewrites queries and can be set to one of the following three values:

    - **ENFORCED**   Queries will be rewritten using only those constraints and rules that are enforced and can be trusted by the Oracle database. Unless the relationship between items is being enforced by the database, even though a relationship existed, it would not be used. If you are unsure as to which setting to apply, use this one.

    - **TRUSTED**   Queries will be rewritten using the constraints that can be enforced by Oracle, as well as any additional relationships that exist within the database that we have told Oracle about but are not being enforced.

    - **STALE TOLERATED**   Queries will be rewritten to use materialized views even if the data in those views is old and out of date. This type of setting might be okay if you are using data that does not have to be completely up to date. For example, you do not need to have up-to-the-minute data when trending or data mining, so in these cases you might be okay using this setting.

Most databases we have seen use the ENFORCED setting.

Database Privileges

Before you can use summary management, you need to have certain database privileges. The following privileges are required if you want to create summary tables from within Discoverer:

- ANALYZE ANY
- ALTER ANY MATERIALIZED VIEW
- CREATE ANY MATERIALIZED VIEW
- DROP ANY MATERIALIZED VIEW
- CREATE PROCEDURE
- CREATE SESSION
- CREATE TABLE
- CREATE VIEW
- GLOBAL QUERY REWRITE
- UNLIMITED TABLESPACE
- SELECT ON SYS.V_$PARAMETER

You also need to make sure that your database is using the Cost Based Optimizer (CBO). If you do not use the CBO, no query rewrites will take place.

If you intend using external summary tables, you do not need to create these, because these will have been created for you. However, you will need to have been granted the SELECT privilege on those materialized views. These privileges must be granted to a user, not to a role.

Oracle provides a script to create these privileges. You will find it at $ORACLE_HOME/discoverer/util.

NOTE
$ORACLE_HOME is the home directory where you installed the Discoverer Administrator software. Logging in as SYSDBA and executing the script grants the necessary privileges.

Table Analysis

One of the most common summary table mistakes made by Discoverer administrators is not ensuring that the materialized views have been analyzed. No matter how good you are at creating summary folders, the database's Cost Based Optimizer (CBO) will not redirect queries to a materialized view if it has not been analyzed. This is one of the reasons the ANALYZE ANY privilege needs to be granted.

Unless you are a DBA, you will probably not have permission to analyze existing tables or materialized views. However, in case you are curious, here is a sample analyze statement:

```
analyze table my_best_mv compute statistics;
```

Materialized Views

As mentioned earlier, materialized views are actually tables in the Oracle database. However, a number of features of materialized views set them apart from standard database views:

- **Storage space** Unlike ordinary views, materialized views consume storage space within the database. You may well need to increase your permanently allocated disk space in order to use summary tables effectively. However, with the cost of disk space coming down all the time, we see no reason for you not to use materialized views whenever you can.

NOTE
If you are having difficulty convincing your organization to make more storage space available, please see Appendix A. The answer given to the second question might help you make your case. Although the question was about scheduling, you will find its content very appropriate.

- **Indexing** Materialized views can be indexed. Try doing this with a Discoverer custom folder or with a database view.

- **Refresh cycle** Oracle maintains the data in materialized views by refreshing them after changes are made to the detail tables. The refresh method can be incremental or complete.

  - **Incremental refresh** This refreshes incrementally by updating the materialized views with the changes in the detail tables as they occur.

  - **Full refresh** A full refresh refreshes by recalculating the full result set from the detail tables. Using Discoverer, materialized views can be refreshed either on demand or when the Discoverer manager manually executes a refresh. They can also be scheduled to refresh at regular time intervals. Alternatively, a materialized view in the same database as the detail tables can be refreshed whenever a transaction commits its changes to the detail tables.

- **Transparency to users** Oracle's query rewrite mechanism transforms a SQL statement expressed in terms of the detail tables into a statement accessing one or more materialized views that are defined on the detail tables. This transformation is transparent to the users.

Managing Summary Tables

In a Discoverer environment there are two ways to create and manage summary tables:

- **Automated Summary Management (ASM)** Discoverer recommends and manages the summary tables for you.

- **Manual specification of summaries** You create and maintain your own summaries either from within Discoverer or by registering external materialized views with Discoverer.

We are often asked, particularly by DBAs, which method we prefer and which we recommend. First and foremost, the choice is yours and Discoverer is quite happy working with whichever method you pick. However, if we have to recommend one method over another, without reservation we would always choose to allow Discoverer to manage its own summary tables.

Whichever method you choose, the entry point within Discoverer is the same. You need to launch the Summary Wizard. This can be done in one of four ways:

■ From the menu bar, select Insert | Summary.

■ From the Discoverer Administrator task list, select Create Summary Folders.

■ From the Summaries tab, right-click a business area and from the pop-up menu, select Create Summary.

■ Click the Summary button on the toolbar.

Whichever method you choose, Discoverer opens the Summary Wizard (see Figure 22-1). As you can see in Figure 22-1, you have two choices:

■ **Have Discoverer recommend and create the best summaries**   This is ASM.

■ **I want to specify the summaries myself**   This is the manual process.

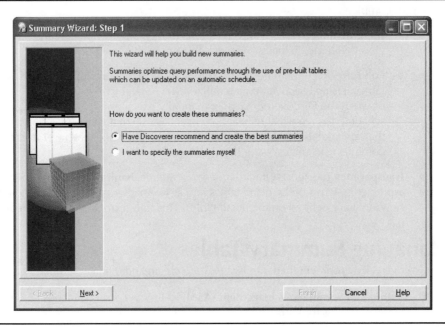

FIGURE 22-1   *Summary Wizard Step 1*

Automated Summary Management (ASM)

ASM is a feature that allows Discoverer to automatically manage summary folders.

To use ASM, you first make some settings and then have Discoverer perform an analysis. To make the settings, use the following workflow:

1. From the Summary Wizard main screen, shown in Figure 22-1, check Have Discoverer recommend and create the best summaries, and then click Next.

2. Discoverer opens the Analyze Folders screen, which has the following buttons (see Figure 22-2).

    ■ **Start**   Click this to start the analysis.

    ■ **Advanced Settings**   Click this to specify the settings for the analysis.

NOTE
If you do not specify any analysis settings, Discoverer will analyze every folder that is in the EUL. Unless you have a very small EUL or are prepared to sit and wait for a very long time, we do not advise clicking Start before you have at least specified some of the advanced settings.

FIGURE 22-2   *ASM Summary Wizard Step 2*

3. To specify the settings for the analysis, click Advanced Settings. Discoverer opens the Change Default Settings dialog box, which has the five tabs described next:

■ Analyze

■ Folders

■ Query User

■ Query Usage

■ Deletion

Complete each tab in turn, as described in the next five sections. When you are done, click OK to return to the Summary Wizard Step 2 screen, where you can launch the analysis, as we explain following the descriptions of the tabs.

The Analysis Tab

You use the Analysis tab to specify how folders should be analyzed. It has the following areas:

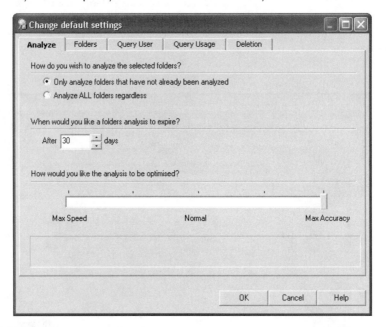

■ **A set of two radio buttons:**

   ■ **Only analyze folders that have not already been analyzed**   Use this option when you have recently analyzed some of your folders. If the remaining folders were analyzed longer ago than the period specified in the After Days box, they will be included anyway. This is the default option.

   ■ **Analyze ALL folders regardless**   Use this option to force Discoverer to analyze all folders regardless of when they were last analyzed.

- **An After Days box**   It is entitled "When would you like a folders analysis to expire?" This box is available only if you are analyzing folders that have not already been analyzed. The default is 30 days, and generally we recommend you leave this set to its default.

- **A slider bar**   It is entitled "How would you like the analysis to be optimized?" As you can see, the slider bar has three levels:

  - **Max Speed**   At this level approximately 10 percent of the folders are analyzed. This level produces a basic set of summaries without taking too long. According to Oracle, you may want to use this level if you have a large data warehouse and you don't want the analysis to take too much time.

  - **Normal**   At this level, you get an equal balance between speed and range.

  - **Max Accuracy**   This is the default level, at which 100 percent of folders are analyzed. This setting enables the widest range of summaries to be created by ASM. According to Oracle, you may want to use this level if you have a small data warehouse or you don't mind how long the analysis takes.

The Folders Tab

You use the Folders tab to specify which folders should be analyzed. The Folders tab has the following areas:

- **Available**   This box shows you the folders that are available but that have not been selected for inclusion within the analysis.

- **Included**   This box shows the folders that have been selected for analysis.

NOTE
If you have not analyzed for a while, Discoverer will place all folders in the Included box. You should be careful not to include too many folders within the analysis. We like to analyze folders on an individual business area basis, including only those folders that are used within the business area we want to analyze.

The Query User Tab

You use the Query User tab to specify which user schemas should be analyzed. The Query User tab has the following areas:

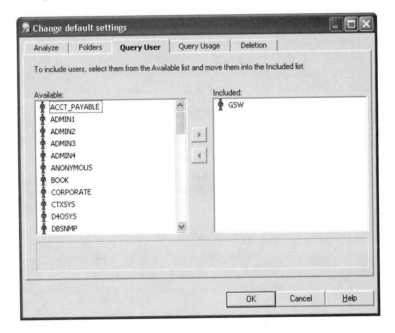

- **Available**   This box shows you the schemas that are available but have not been selected for inclusion within the analysis.

- **Included**   This box shows you the schemas that have been selected for analysis. By default Discoverer will include all schemas. However, if you know which schemas are used by the folders you selected, you should select those schemas only.

The Query Usage Tab

You use the Query Usage tab to specify which queries should be used within the analysis. The Query Usage tab has the following areas:

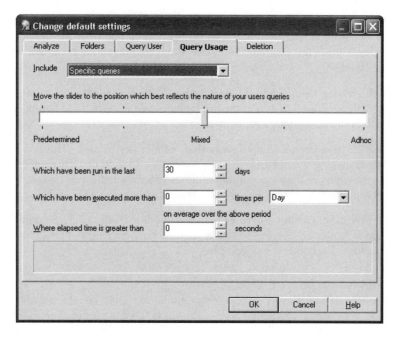

■ **Include** Use this drop-down box to select one of the following three settings:

   ■ **All queries** Use this to tell Discoverer to make summary recommendations for all queries that have been run.

   ■ **Queries since last execution** Use this to tell Discoverer to make summary recommendations based upon those queries that have run since the last time ASM was run.

   ■ **Specific queries** Use this to tell Discoverer which queries should be included within the analysis. With this setting selected, use the boxes in the lower half of the screen to specify which queries should be included.

■ **A slider bar** It is entitled "Move the slider to the position which best reflects the nature of your users queries." As you can see, the slider bar has three levels:

   ■ **Predetermined** Use this setting to optimize the summaries maintained by ASM to reflect the historical significance of your user's queries. Put another way, you can get great performance improvements for those queries that stay unchanged over long periods of time.

   ■ **Mixed** Use this, the default setting, to obtain a balance between predetermined and ad hoc queries.

■ **Ad hoc**   Use this setting to increase the coverage for a summary, thus allowing for possible queries that have not yet been run. The downside of applying too much weight to this setting is that not enough coverage may be allowed for your existing queries.

■ **Which have been run in the past *x* days**   This is available only if you are analyzing specific queries. Use this setting to include only queries that have been run within the number of days that you specify here.

■ **Which have been executed more than *x* times per period**   This is available only if you are analyzing specific queries. Use this setting to include only queries that have been executed more than the number of times specified here. You can set the period to be any of Minute, Day, Week, Month, and Year. The default is Day.

■ **Where elapsed time is greater than *x* seconds**   This is available only if you are analyzing specific queries. Use this setting to include only queries that have taken longer than the number of seconds specified here.

The Deletion Tab

You use the Deletion tab to specify how long summaries should be retained and which ones should be regarded as permanent. The first area of the tab is "Delete specific summary folders if." It has the following options:

- **Last queried more than**   Check this box to tell Discoverer that it can delete summary tables that have not been used for querying for longer than the period specified. You also need to enter a value for the period. This setting is not checked by default, but if you do enable it, the default period is 30 days.

- **Created more than**   Check this box to tell Discoverer that it can delete summary tables that were created more than the number of days specified. You also need to enter a value for the period. This setting is not checked by default, but if you do enable it, the default period is 30 days.

- **Average usage less than *x* times per period over the last *x* period**   Check this box to tell Discoverer that it can delete summary tables that have been used less than the settings you enter here. You need to enter a value for the following four items:

  - **Times**   Use this to enter a threshold value for the number of times a summary table must have been used.

  - **First Period**   Use this to enter a time period for the number of times a summary table must have been used. You can set this to be any of Minute, Day, Week, Month, and Year. The default is Day.

  - **Over the last**   Use this to enter a threshold value for the period that should be used for the usage of the summary table.

  - **Second Period**   Use this to enter a time period for the usage of the summary table. You can set this to be any of Minute, Day, Week, Month, and Year. The default is Day.

The next area of the tab covers summaries to retain. It includes a check box and a couple of additional boxes:

- **Always retain the following summaries**   Check this box if you want to always keep one or more of your existing summary tables. No matter what thresholds have been specified earlier, with this box checked you can force Discoverer to retain summaries.

- **Summaries to be retained**   With the above box checked, all summaries that are listed in this area will be retained irrespective of whether they have been used or not. If you have summaries that you want to keep, even if they are not currently being used, you should make sure to include those summaries here. Should you decide that a summary is no longer needed you should move it into the Available summaries box.

- **Available summaries**   This area lists those summaries that have not been slated for retention. These summaries will not be kept and will be removed. Should you decide that a summary should be kept, you should move it into the Summaries to be retained box.

Performing the Analysis

Now that you have made preliminary settings, it's time for Discoverer to perform the actual analysis to enable ASM. You should continue with the following workflow:

1. Upon your return to the Summary Wizard Step 2 screen shown earlier in Figure 22-2, click Start. Discoverer will now perform the analysis. Upon completion, the screen will look like this. Do not click Finish!

2. Click Next.
3. Discoverer opens one of the Summary screens shown in Figures 22-3 and 22-4.

4. If you see the summary screen shown in Figure 22-3, this means that Discoverer has been unable to recommend any summaries. You should click the Back button to go back and adjust your parameters.

5. If you see the summary screen shown in Figure 22-4, this means that Discoverer has been able to recommend at least one summary. On this screen you will see an overview of the effects that the summaries Discoverer is recommending will have, should you continue. Discoverer will show you the amount of storage available to you, how much disk space will be consumed by the summaries selected, and how much of a performance gain can be made by creating these summaries.

6. Complete the Summary screen as described next.

FIGURE 22-3 *Summary screen with no summaries recommended*

FIGURE 22-4 *Summary screen with summaries recommended*

Here is how to interpret the results shown on the Summary screen:

■ **Performance vs. Space**   Use this graph to evaluate the performance gain achieved by using the specified amounts of tablespace. To adjust the tablespace, click on the red slider with your mouse and move the slider line left and right. As you adjust the amount of tablespace, you will see the performance impact displayed as a factor.

■ The dotted line indicates the mount of available tablespace, the red line indicates the amount of tablespace selected and is the line that you click to manipulate the performance gain and space used, and the plot line shows the performance gain achieved by selecting various amounts of tablespace.

■ You can change the selected space setting by doing one of the following:

  ■ Click the graph area and drag the red line to the left or right.

  ■ Drag the triangle above the Space (KB) axis to the left or right.

  ■ Click the graph area to the left or right of the red line.

  ■ Directly enter the amount of tablespace you want to use, in KB, in the Create Summaries to fill field.

■ **Tablespace to use for summaries**   Use this drop-down list to select which tablespace you want to use to store the summary tables.

■ **Created summaries to fill**   Use this box to tell Discoverer how much tablespace you want allocated to summary tables. You can experiment by entering values here and then evaluating the performance gain for the various settings.

■ **Estimates performance gain**   This represents a factor by which Discoverer estimates how much of a performance gain can be achieved if you allow ASM to create the summaries that it is recommending.

■ **Recommended Summaries**   Clicking this button displays the Recommended Summaries dialog box. This box shows you the summaries that Discoverer intends to use. You can change the intended list if you wish. When you have completed specifying which summaries Discoverer should create, click OK.

■ **Advanced Settings**   Click this button to once again see the Change default settings dialog box that we worked with earlier in this workflow.

Viewing the Recommendations

It is time now to view the summaries the wizard recommends. To do so, use the following workflow:

1.   Click the Recommended Summaries button to see the summary tables that Discoverer recommends.

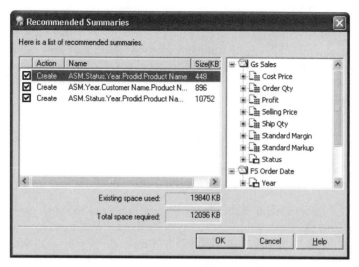

The Recommended Summaries screen has the following areas:

■ A box containing a list of the recommended summaries. This box lists each summary that Discoverer recommends. As you navigate from summary to summary, Discoverer will show you the folders and items against which the summary will be created. Use the check boxes alongside the summaries to indicate to Discoverer whether you want the specified action, Create or Delete, to take place.

■ The amount of existing space used for summaries.

■ The total amount of space needed for the summaries. As you check and uncheck summaries, this number will change.

2. When you have completed the Recommended Summaries screen, click OK to return to the main Summary screen.

3. When you have completed examining the Summary screen, click Finish. Discoverer will now create or delete the summary tables, depending upon the Action to be taken.

4. If you see the following message, this means that you already have an optimized database and there are no summary tables that can be used to help performance.

NOTE
As you will see, the law of diminishing marginal returns applies in the relationship between space and performance improvement, so you have to decide the sweet spot!

Running ASM after a Bulk Load

If you recall, in the Load Wizard that we used to create the EUL there was an option to allow Discoverer to automatically create summaries for the folders that were being created. As you may further recall, we also recommended that you not check this box at that time. Now that you have just learned about ASM, you are now in a position to start using this option. This is because if you do select this option, it is the ASM process that Discoverer will use.

> **NOTE**
> *Step 4 of the Load Wizard is where you choose whether to include summaries, using ASM, based on the folders that Discoverer will create. There is a check box, called "Summaries based on folders that are created", located half-way down the screen.*

If you think for a moment, it should be obvious that there won't be any query statistics for any of the folders that get created during this initial load of the business area. In this case, the ASM will be forced to try using structural statistics for the database objects upon which a candidate summary will be based. However, generating these statistics using the ANALYZE command could take a very long time. This could significantly reduce the performance of your load. The Discoverer ASM process will therefore use only tables that have already been analyzed and will only look at the tables and joins to determine possible candidate objects.

Manually Specifying Summaries

In addition to ASM, Discoverer also allows you to manually manage and create summary folders. To use the manual method for summary table management, use the following workflow:

1. From the Summary Wizard main screen, shown earlier in Figure 22-1, check "I want to specify the summaries myself."

2. Click OK.

3. Discoverer opens the screen shown in Figure 22-5.

4. There are three ways to manually create summary tables. All three ways can be accessed from this screen. These are the three ways:

   - Using items in the End User Layer

   - Using query performance statistics—the default

   - Registering an external summary table

We will describe each method separately.

Creating Summary Tables from Items in the EUL

To manually create summary tables using items in the EUL, use the following set of workflows to work through settings screen by screen:

1. On the Summary Wizard Step 2 screen, shown in Figure 22-5, check the button called From items in the End User Layer.

2. Click Next.

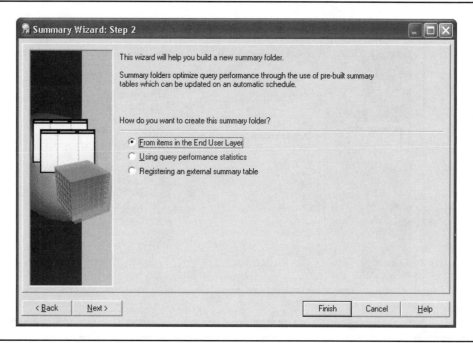

FIGURE 22-5 *Manual Summary Wizard Step 2*

3. Discoverer opens the Select Items screen shown in Figure 22-6. The Select Items screen
    has the following areas:

    ■ **Available items** This box shows you the folders and items that are available but
       have not been selected for inclusion in a summary table.

    ■ **Selected items** This box shows you the folders and items that have been selected
       for inclusion in a summary table. By default Discoverer preselects nothing, and it is
       up to you to pick what you want.

4. Expand the folder(s) that you want to use, and from the folders select the items you need.
    In our case, as you can see, we have chosen the following:

    ■ Cost Price SUM

    ■ Selling Price SUM

    ■ Customer Name

    ■ Ship Month

5. Having specified the items that you want, click Next.

The Combinations Dialog Box Discoverer next opens the fourth screen of the Summary
Wizard, shown in Figure 22-7, otherwise known as the Combinations dialog box.

FIGURE 22-6 *Manual Summary Table Step 3*

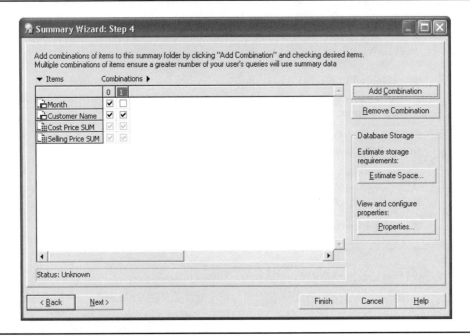

FIGURE 22-7 *The Combinations dialog box*

By default, Discoverer creates a single combination, number 0, and includes all of the items that you manually selected on the previous screen. As you can see in Figure 22-7, we have also included a second combination.

NOTE
A combination is a set of items that will be included within a summary folder. Discoverer will create one summary table, or materialized view, for each combination that you define.

The Combinations dialog box has the following areas:

■ **Items**   This shows you the items that have been selected for inclusion within each combination. All metrics are included by default and cannot be deselected. However, you are free to check and uncheck dimension items.

■ **Combinations**   This shows you how many combinations have been selected.

■ **Add Combinations**   Click this button to add a new combination.

■ **Remove Combination**   When you have more than one combination, you can remove combinations by clicking this button.

■ **Estimate Space**   Click this button to see a pop-up display that will estimate how much space will be consumed should you build this summary table.

■ **Properties**   This opens a new multitabbed dialog box where you can set the physical characteristics of the summary table.

To work with combinations, use the following workflow:

1. Create the combinations that you want using the Add Combination button. After you add a new combination, use the check boxes against each item in that combination to define a unique set of items. As you go, you should periodically check the amount of space that will be consumed by clicking the Estimate Space button.

2. When you have defined all of the combinations that you want, click the Properties button.

3. Discoverer opens the Database Storage Properties dialog box.

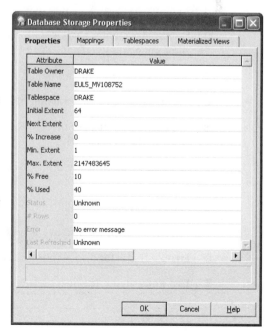

As you can see, the Database Storage Properties dialog box has four tabs. These are:

- **Properties**   Use this tab to set physical characteristics for the materialized view that will be created.

- **Mappings**   Use this to view the mappings that will be employed.

- **Tablespaces**   Use this to see the tablespaces that will be used.

- **Materialized Views**   Use this to set further characteristics about the materialized view that will be created.

The Properties tab has a lot of technical options that you can set:

- **Table Owner**   By default Discoverer inserts the current user. You can use the drop-down list to select a different database owner for the summary table.

- **Table Name**   By default Discoverer generates a table name beginning with the characters EUL5_MV. You can change this to any name you choose. Most organizations have naming standards for table names, so you should make sure you are aware of the standards employed by your company.

- **Tablespace**   By default Discoverer will use the default tablespace for the current user. You can use the drop-down list to select a different tablespace. If you would like to see how much space is available within the tablespaces, click the Tablespaces tab.

- **Initial Extent**   Enter an initial extent for the summary table. The default is 10KB. You will get a chance to enter the value in either KB or MB.

- **Next Extent**   Enter a next extent for the summary table. The default is 10KB. You will get a chance to enter the value in either KB or MB.

- **% Increase**   Enter a value for the percentage increase. By default Discoverer inserts zero. The values you can set are in the range 0–100.

- **Min Extent**   Enter the minimum number of extents that can be used.

- **Max Extent**   Enter the maximum number of extents that can be used.

- **% Free**   Enter the free percent to allow. The default is 10 percent, but you can set any value in the range 1–100.

- **% Used**   Enter the amount of used space. The default is 40 percent, but you can set any value in the range 1–99.

- **Status**   This is for display purposes only and cannot be changed.

- **# Rows**   This is for display purposes only and cannot be changed.

- **Error**   This is for display purposes only and cannot be changed.

- **Last Refreshed**   This is for display purposes only and cannot be changed.

The Mappings Tab   Having specified the Properties, click the Mappings tab. The Mappings tab is purely for display purposes only and cannot be changed. While you cannot manually change the mappings here, you should use this tab to confirm that you have chosen the correct combination of items. If you spot something wrong you should go back to the Combinations dialog box.

The Tablespaces Tab   Having looked at the Mappings, click the Tablespaces tab.

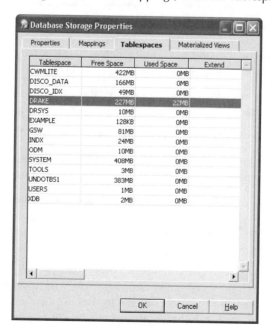

The Tablespaces tab shows all of the tablespaces within the database with the tablespace selected for this summary table selected. This tab is for display purposes only and should be used to check tablespaces before you manually set a tablespace on the Properties tab. One of the most common reasons we have seen for summary folder construction to fail is because the selected tablespace does not have enough space.

The Materialized Views Tab   Having looked at the Tablespaces, click the Materialized Views tab.

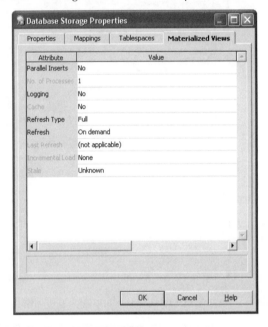

The Materialized Views tab has the following items:

■ **Parallel inserts**   Use this to choose whether to use parallel inserts when refreshing summary folders. Your options are No, Yes, and Default.

■ **No. of processes**   If you chose to use parallel inserts, you can use this box to tell Discoverer the number of parallel processes to be used when refreshing summary folders.

■ **Logging**   Use this Yes/No property to enable or disable database logging.

■ **Cache**   If you chose to use database logging, you use this Yes/No property to tell Discoverer whether to enable or disable database caching.

■ **Refresh Type**   Use this property to tell Discoverer whether to use a Full or Incremental refresh type. A Full refresh type means that the summary table will be completely rebuilt. An Incremental refresh type means that only rows that have been changed will be applied to the summary table.

■ **Refresh**   Use this property to tell Discoverer whether to use an On Demand or On Commit refresh strategy. An On Demand strategy means that the summary table will be refreshed manually or via scheduled refreshes. An On Commit strategy means that the summary table will be refreshed every time the base tables are updated. In this mode, there is no need to set up a refresh schedule, and the scheduling option of the Summary Wizard will not be available.

■ **Last Refresh**   This is for display purposes only and cannot be changed. Use this to see when the summary table was last refreshed.

■ **Incremental Load**   This is for display purposes only and cannot be changed. Use this to see the type of inserts that can be incrementally refreshed. The possible options that you could see are:

   ■ **None**   The materialized view cannot be incrementally refreshed.

   ■ **Direct Load**   Only direct loads can be handled.

   ■ **DML**   Only DML (Data Manipulation Language) statements can be handled.

   ■ **Direct Load and DML**   Both direct load and DML statements can be handled.

   ■ **Direct Load and Limited DML**   Direct loads and a subset of DML can be handled. Oracle recommends that you look at the database documentation for more information about which DML statements can be handled.

   ■ **Stale**   This is for display purposes only and cannot be changed. This property indicates whether the detail tables have changed since the summary table was last refreshed.

Summary Wizard Final Steps   In this final sequence of steps, you specify how your summary folder is to be refreshed and provide a name, description, and build time to the folder. Use the following workflow:

1. Having completed the Materialized Views tab, click OK.
2. Click Next.
3. Discoverer opens the Summary Wizard Step 5 shown in Figure 22-8.
4. As you can see in Figure 22-8, there are two areas to this screen. These are:

   ■ The top area, where Discoverer shows you when this summary folder was last updated

   ■ A bottom area, controlled by a check box where you can tell Discoverer when to automatically refresh the folder

5. If you want to enable automatic refreshes of a summary folder, check the box entitled Automatically refresh this summary folder, starting on, and then complete the rest of the settings:

   ■ **Date**   Enter the date when the summary folder should first refresh.

   ■ **Time**   Enter the time when the summary folder should first refresh.

   ■ **Repeat every x periods**   Enter a value for the Repeat Every and then select a period from the pop-up list. The valid periods are Day(s), Hour(s), Minute(s), Month(s), Week(s), and Year(s).

6. Click Next. Discoverer opens the Summary Wizard Step 6, shown in Figure 22-9.

FIGURE 22-8   *Manual Summary Wizard Step 5*

FIGURE 22-9   *Manual Summary Wizard Step 6*

7. As you can see in Figure 22-9, you complete this screen as follows:

- **Name**   Enter a meaningful name for this summary folder.

- **Description**   Enter an optional description.

- **Build immediately**   Check this box if you want Discoverer to build this summary table immediately.

- **Build at**   Check this box if you want to set a date and time when Discoverer should build this summary.

8. When done, click Finish. Discoverer will now build the summary folder.

Creating Summary Tables Using Query Statistics

To manually create summary tables using query statistics, use the following workflow:

1. On the Summary Wizard Step 2 screen, seen earlier in Figure 22-5, check the button called Using query performance statistics.

2. Click Next. Discoverer opens the Summary Wizard Step 3, shown in Figure 22-10.

3. As you can see in Figure 22-10, this screen has three main areas, as described after this workflow.

4. Having chosen a candidate query, click Next.

FIGURE 22-10   *Items Summary Wizard Step 3*

5. The remaining steps in this workflow are identical to the final steps in the workflow for creating summary tables using items in the EUL. Please continue from Step 3 of that workflow. It can be found in the section called "Creating Summary Tables from Items in the EUL."

These are the three main areas of Summary Wizard Step 3:

■ **A search area** In this area, use the boxes provided to define some search criteria that Discoverer will use to find queries that might be suitable for summarization. When you have set the search criteria, click Search. You can specify any or all of the following:

   ■ **Show query statistics from within the last *x* days** Use the up/down arrows to set the number of days that Discoverer should use when searching for queries. For queries to be selected, this must have been executed within this time period.

   ■ **Average CPU time exceeds** If you want to constrain the search by CPU time, check this box and then set the time period.

   ■ **Average elapsed time exceeds** If you want to constrain the search by elapsed time, check this box and then set the time period.

   ■ **Number of query runs exceeds** If you want to constrain the search by the number of times a query has been run, check this box and then set the search value.

■ **A selection area** After a search has been run, this box displays a list of the queries that satisfy the search criteria you entered. The list will be ranked with the most likely candidates at the top of the list.

■ **An item area** As you click the queries in the selection area, Discoverer shows you the items that are in that query.

Registering an External Summary Table The previous examples use Discoverer to populate the data in the summary tables. For very large systems, however, there may be more optimal ways of refreshing summary data, depending on the application. Some implementations may already have created summary tables and programs to refresh them and simply require Discoverer to know about these tables, so that they can be used to improve query performance.

Registered external summary folders map to tables that are created and populated by a method external to Discoverer. Data values in external summaries are not controlled or managed by the EUL. They are updated independently by some other application. External summaries are created by mapping to an existing summary table in the database.

Before you begin using this method, if you are going to be using tables created in another schema, you need to have been granted select access to that table with the grant option. You may need to ask your DBA to do this for you. If you attempt to access a table without this option, you will see this message:

To manually create summary tables by registering external summary tables, use the following workflow:

1. On the Summary Wizard Step 2 screen, shown earlier in Figure 22-5, check the button called Registering an external summary table.

2. Click Next.

3. Discoverer displays the Summary Wizard Step 3.

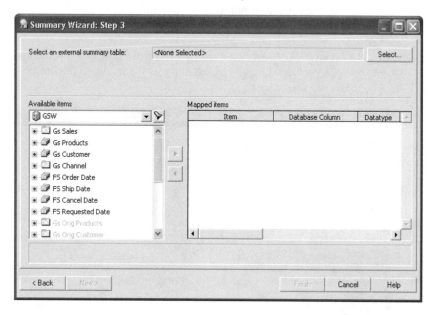

4. Click the Select button and select one table from the list of schemas and tables offered. Discoverer will display the name of the table and the incomplete mappings on the following screen.

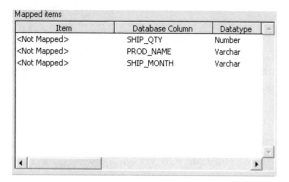

5. You need to complete this screen by specifying the mappings. This is done by opening up folders in the Available items box and linking them with items in the Mapped item box.

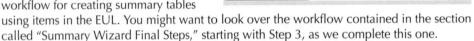

Item	Database Column	Datatype
Ship Qty SUM	⇨ SHIP_QTY	Number
Product Name	→ PROD_NAME	Varchar
Month	→ SHIP_MONTH	Varchar

6. After you have completed all of the mappings, click Next.

7. The remaining steps in this workflow are almost identical to the final steps in the workflow for creating summary tables using items in the EUL. You might want to look over the workflow contained in the section called "Summary Wizard Final Steps," starting with Step 3, as we complete this one.

8. Discoverer displays the next step of the wizard.

9. As you can see on the top of the screen, there is a box called Manage the refresh of this summary folder. If you check this, you will take over the refreshes. However, in our case we will allow the external folder to retain control.

10. Click Next.

11. All you need to do now is give this folder a name and an optional description, and you are just about done.

12. When done, click Finish. Discoverer will now build the summary folder.

Summary Combination Strategy

If you are going to build summaries manually, you will need to have some good summary combination strategies. Building summaries and summary combinations in layers is usually an efficient process. Implement the following summary combination strategies for a single summary folder:

■ For frequent queries, you should provide a number of summary combinations that combine only a few (three or four) axis items. Storage space is minimized and the performance gains are maximized.

■ For a wider variety of queries, you should provide a smaller number of summary combinations that combine a medium number (five to seven) of axis items. Using this approach, more storage space is required, but significant performance gains will still be realized. In essence, the larger the number of items in each combination, the better able Discoverer is to serve a wide variety of queries.

■ One of the summary combinations should contain all of the items in the summary folder. This type of combination will then provide a summary that works for any combination of items in the folder.

We are frequently asked by Discoverer managers, "How much space do I need for my summaries?" The answer, of course, depends on the number of types of queries, the number of items, and the performance gains that are required. According to Oracle, an additional fifty percent of storage space for storing summary tables is not unreasonable. In most cases, though, you will use significantly less space, but in some cases you may need more. Providing you have the space, it is generally not the space taken by the summary tables that is the problem, as much as the time taken to refresh summary tables if they are large.

Discoverer optimizes a summary refresh by using what is called *pyramid* refreshing. This is where summary combinations with the largest number of axis items are created first. Other combinations are created from the new summaries in sequence, depending on the number of axis items in the combination. For this reason, it is always best to include all the combinations of a particular summary in the same summary folder and not split them across multiple summary folders, where this optimization cannot be performed.

Using Summary Tables with Oracle Applications

When you are working with Oracle Applications, if you recall from our discussions in previous chapters, we told you to manage the EUL using the SYSADMIN user. Because this user is not a database user, and does not have access to the underlying storage space, you can only use external summaries when working in Apps mode.

You therefore need to make sure that the summaries that will be used in Apps mode are not managed by Discoverer.

If the external summaries that you will be using contain items that are based on Applications secure views or Applications business views, you can still use external summaries. Once again, the Discoverer manager needs to ensure that summaries based on Apps secure views or Apps business views are not managed by Discoverer. You also need to make sure that the external summaries have been analyzed.

End-User Options

In Discoverer Plus, Viewer, and Desktop, end users can control whether they access summary or detail data by setting one of the three options available in the Summary Data section of the Query Governor area. Settings made in either Plus or Viewer will be reflected in the other tool. However, settings made in Desktop are restricted to Desktop only. If users have the ability to use both Plus and Desktop, this should be brought to their attention.

This illustration is taken from Plus, but both Desktop and Viewer have similar screens. As you can see in the section called Summary Data, an end user has three options:

■ **Always, when available** This is the default. When selected, Discoverer will automatically use summary tables where possible.

■ **Only when summary data is not out of date (stale)** When selected, Discoverer will use summary tables only if they are up to date.

■ **Never** When selected, Discoverer will not use summary tables. Do not allow your users to choose this unless you have good reason for not wanting summary tables to be used.

NOTE
To access the Summary Data section in Plus or Desktop, a user should select Tools | Options from the menu bar and then click the Query Governor tab. To do this in Viewer, a user should click the Preferences link and navigate to the Summary Data section, which can be found towards the bottom of the screen.

Summary

In this chapter, you have learned about the background for summary tables and why you need them. After this we talked about the setup requirements for the database and for the user privileges. We then discussed materialized views, the objects that lie at the heart of summary management. In the heart of the chapter we discussed managing summary tables and showed you the two ways to manage summaries: using Discoverer's automated summary management feature and manually configuring your own summary tables. After this, we discussed a strategy for managing summary combinations. Next we showed you how to use summary tables with the Oracle E-Business Suite, and finally we closed off the chapter by looking at the end-user options for managing summary data.

PART

V

Appendixes

APPENDIX
A

Michael's Gold Mine of
Answers to FAQs

n this appendix I have included 70 of the tips and tricks that I have picked up over the last eight years of working with Discoverer. This is not an exhaustive list by any means, and I have tried to include tricks on all aspects of Discoverer. These tricks are not in any particular order and should make for interesting bedtime reading.

QUESTION: *I have access to two EULs, a 10.1.2 and a 9.0.2. Recently I set my default EUL to the wrong one. After this, every time I try to launch Desktop I get a message saying, "You must upgrade your EUL tables to use this software release. Please contact your Discoverer manager." I am the Discoverer manager—please help.*

ANSWER: When you are in Desktop and are presented with a list of EULs that you can connect to, make sure you pick one of the 10.1.2 EULs. If you pick an older EUL, you will not be warned but you will also no longer be able to connect to Discoverer without editing your Registry.

If you do this, you will be told that you need to reconnect in order to use this new EUL. However, when you do so, you will get a message saying "You must upgrade your EUL tables to use this software release. Please contact your Discoverer manager." You can no longer connect to Discoverer Desktop, and to add insult to injury you will probably get a memory issue warning when you try to exit from Desktop.

The only way to fix this is to edit this Registry setting on your machine:

[HKEY_CURRENT_USER]/ Software/Oracle/Discoverer 10/Database/UEUL_*username_database*

Here, *username* is your name, and *database* is the database that you connect to. You need to change this setting to the correct one.

QUESTION: *Our DBA says that we cannot use scheduling because he is afraid that we won't have enough disk space. Can you help with our case?*

ANSWER: We did some research on the Web and found that a really fast (15,000 RPM) 150GB SCSI drive will cost you about $1,200 retail. On average, a scheduled workbook will consume around 2MB of disk space, but for argument's sake let's say they take 5MB of disk space. Some are larger, but if well built, most will be smaller. As a worst-case scenario, if you enable 500 users and allow them to create three 5MB scheduled workbooks per day with a 30-day retention period, you will consume 450GB. Let's be more reasonable. In your case, let's assume you have ten libraries and that you allow each library to have ten scheduled reports daily that will be retained for 14 days. The amount of disk space consumed is only 6.8GB (10 libraries * 5MB * 10 workbooks * 14 days).

The reason for scheduling in the first place is to avoid making users waste time by waiting for large workbooks (in excess of 15 minutes) to run online. By allowing the same workbooks to be scheduled, you will save 45 minutes per user per day. But of course, library documents will be used by multiple users every day. If we conservatively say that each of the ten library workbooks will be used by five users per day, then the amount of time wasted by these ten users will be 225 minutes a day, equivalent to 18.75 man-hours per week per library, or about half of one full-time employee per year. If you have ten libraries, this equates to lost productivity of five full-time employees. In effect, not enabling scheduling will cost you half a person per library per year in lost productivity. Bear in mind that over time, the cost of disk space will go down while the cost of employees will go up.

If we compare employee cost to the cost of disk space, around $1,200 per 150GB (and remember that we need only 6.8GB for those same reports), you can see why we suggest that disk space should never be an issue. Somehow this equation needs to be brought to the attention of senior management so that the issue over disk space is eliminated from all future discussions. The same disk space issue will prevent you from harnessing all of Discoverer's power by not enabling materialized view management. One of the biggest incentives to using ad hoc tools is performance gain. Users should never complain that the tool is too slow. If this happens, you are taking the risk that Discoverer will not be embraced by the user community.

NOTE
In the answer above, the price of $1200 is the price as of
January 2006.

QUESTION: *We recently upgraded one of our Desktops to XP Service Pack 2. The user is using Internet Explorer and Discoverer Plus and can export to Excel fine because Discoverer writes the file. However, usually after it exports, it launches Excel for her to see the output. It is not doing this. I have checked her file associations and these are correct. Do you know what we are doing wrong?*

ANSWER: Microsoft, as always, does not quite tell you everything that they have changed. The big one this time is that Service Pack 2 sets a Registry switch that by default prevents Internet Explorer from transferring applications between zones. To Microsoft, running something from a web server (Discoverer) and then running something on your PC (Excel) means running applications in two different zones. With that switch set, your PC cannot switch zones when running Internet Explorer and so cannot open Excel from within Discoverer Plus or Viewer.

To allow Discoverer Plus to call a local copy of Excel, you need to reset the switch so that it once again allows zone switching, like the old XP. The switch should be set to 0. To reset this switch, use the following workflow:

1. From the Windows Start button, select Run to open the Run dialog box.

2. Type **regedit** and click OK.

3. Navigate to this folder: [HKEY_LOCAL_MACHINE]/SOFTWARE/Microsoft/Internet Explorer/Main/FeatureControl/FEATURE_ZONE_ELEVATION.

4. Locate and click the item called iexplore. It is probably set to 1 but should be set to 0.

5. Right-click iexplore and from the pop-up select Modify.

6. In the Edit DWORD Value dialog box, change the value from 1 to 0.

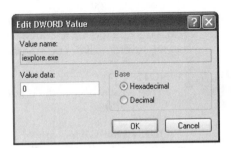

7. Click OK to close the Edit dialog box.

8. Close the Registry Editor.

9. Open Windows Explorer.

10. From the toolbar, select Tools | Folder Options.

11. Click the File Types tab.

12. Select the Extension XLS (or HTML) and then click Advanced.

13. At the bottom of the screen are three settings that use check boxes. If either of the following two are checked, un-check them:

    ■ Confirm open after download

    ■ Browse in same window

14. Select OK.

15. Click Apply.

16. Re-boot the PC.

QUESTION: *I am using page items in my report, but I don't want all page items to display in my title. Is there a way for me to display just one page item in the title?*
ANSWER: Yes, a little known feature of Discoverer is the ability to display single page items and parameters in the title, header, or footer. You need to know the exact name of the page item or parameter that you want to display and then type an ampersand (&) followed by the name.

For example, let's say you have a page item called Cust Name. You type **&Cust Name** in the title. Discoverer will display just that page item. When you use this construct, the title will dynamically change to reflect what is being displayed onscreen. As your users switch from one page item to another, they will see the title change.

Similarly, if you have a parameter called From that is being used to store the start date, you can use **&From** in your title, header, or footer.

QUESTION: *We have many materialized views in our EUL, and for one of them, when I try to open the lists of values, I get the following message: "The folder for this item class is inaccessible or invalid." The DBA checked in the database and did not find any invalid objects. Do you have any idea what I should look for?*

ANSWER: What this usually means is that the object upon which the item class is based has somehow become inaccessible to the user. You may want to check that your user has been granted SELECT on the necessary underlying database objects. Another possible cause is that the item class is using a COUNT function. An item class needs to be able to return the same set of values every time; in other words, the item code that produces the list of values must be deterministic. Functions can be used to generate lists of values but only if they are deterministic. In this case, the COUNT returns different values and so is considered to be non-deterministic. When you stop to think about it, it makes sense. In order to establish a stable list of values, each value in the calculated column must contain a known and consistent value. If the values might differ every time the row is examined, then the list will be invalid.

Another possible cause of this issue arises when you are accessing the data via a database link and one of the following situations occur:

- The database link has become invalid; perhaps the password has changed.

- The object on the other end of the link has been deleted or renamed.

- The user account being used for the database link no longer has the appropriate select privileges.

QUESTION: *We are using E-Business Suite with Discoverer and have written our own views for our reports. Several of these make recursive joins to the GL_PERIODS table, and our performance is poor. One of our reports takes over seven hours. Can you help?*

ANSWER: GL_PERIODS, as you know, is the Apps table that contains your organization's calendar. However, because you can have recursive joins between the elements of this table, report performance can be seriously impacted.

You should create a materialized view of your GL_PERIODS date hierarchy. After you have created the materialized view, you should place a unique index on the calendar date, with nonunique indexes on the months, quarters, and years. After you do this, inside your view you can now join your transaction date to the date in the materialized view and read off the hierarchy.

Most DBAs are rightly concerned about adding materialized views to E-Business Suite. In this case, because GL_PERIODS is updated only once a year, you have a perfect candidate for a materialized view. You just need to make sure that you refresh the materialized view after you add the dates for the next year.

NOTE
During a follow-up conversation with this client, they reported that the seven-hour report is now being produced in five minutes. They were busy similarly converting all of their long-running reports.

Here is a sample script that you can use as the beginning of a materialized view. This script builds a view of GL PERIODS using recursive joins to get the Month, Quarter, and Year information. It pulls the calendar data, starting from 01-OCT-1998, and runs against a fictitious calendar called GSW CALENDAR. To make this work in your organization, you will need to change the name of the calendar and the start date. You may also need to add data for the calendar dates.

```
CREATE OR REPLACE VIEW V_FISCAL_TIME
AS SELECT DISTINCT
gl_mth.period_name            month,
gl_mth.period_set_name        set_name,
gl_mth.start_date             mth_start_date,
gl_mth.end_date               mth_end_date,
gl_mth.period_num             mth_number,
gl_mth.last_update_date       mth_last_update_date,
(gl_mth.end_date -
   gl_mth.start_date) +1      mth_timespan,
gl_qtr.period_name            quarter,
gl_qtr.start_date             qtr_start_date,
gl_qtr.end_date               qtr_end_date,
gl_qtr.quarter_num            qtr_number,
gl_qtr.last_update_date       qtr_last_update_date,
(gl_qtr.end_date -
   gl_qtr.start_date) + 1     qtr_timespan,
gl_yr.period_name             year,
gl_yr.start_date              yr_start_date,
gl_yr.end_date                yr_end_date,
(gl_yr.end_date -
   gl_yr.start_date) + 1      yr_timespan,
gl_yr.last_update_date        yr_last_update_date,
gl_yr.period_year             period_year,
gl_qtr.entered_period_name    actual_qtr
FROM
apps.gl_periods gl_mth,
apps.gl_periods gl_qtr,
apps.gl_periods gl_yr
WHERE
gl_mth.PERIOD_SET_NAME = 'GSW CALENDAR'
AND gl_mth.period_type = 'Month'
AND gl_mth.start_date >= '01-OCT-1998'
AND gl_qtr.quarter_num = gl_mth.quarter_num
AND gl_qtr.period_year = gl_mth.period_year
AND gl_qtr.period_type = 'Quarter'
AND gl_yr.period_year  = gl_mth.period_year
AND gl_yr.period_type  = 'Year';
```

If you are using BOM (Bills of Material), there is another table that you might want to consider using. This is the BOM_CALENDAR_DATES table. Here is a simple script:

```
CREATE OR REPLACE VIEW V_DISCO_DAYS
AS SELECT ALL
trunc(bcd.calendar_date) calendar_date,
trunc(f_dis_week(trunc(bcd.calendar_date))) week_end_date,
substr(f_dis_month(trunc(bcd.calendar_date)),1,15) month,
bcd.last_update_date  last_update_date
FROM
apps.bom_calendar_dates bcd
WHERE
bcd.calendar_code = 'ABC'
AND bcd.exception_set_id = -1
AND bcd.calendar_date >= '01-APR-2005'
AND bcd.calendar_date <= '31-MAR-2006'
```

The preceding script uses a number of constructs, which need explaining:

- **F_DIS_WEEK**   This function returns the week end date for the date given. You need to create this function yourself to match your organization's requirements. If the week end date can be calculated using a combination of the TO_DATE and TO_CHAR functions, you should change the code accordingly. Some organizations end their week on a Friday, some on a Saturday, and some on a Sunday; hence it is impossible to give you a definitive answer.

- **F_DIS_MONTH**   This function returns the month name for the date given. Once again, you need to create this function yourself to meet your organization's requirements. Some organizations use constructs such as MON-YY; others use MON-YYYY and so on. If the month can be calculated using the TO_CHAR function, you should change the code accordingly. You need to make sure that the month you assign here corresponds to the month that you will find in GL_PERIODS. If you do this, you will be able to combine these two scripts into one materialized view.

- **CALENDAR_CODE**   Oracle E-Business Suite has the capability to use multiple calendars, especially if you are using multiple organizations. To avoid pulling multiple copies of the same calendar date, you need to choose one calendar as the base calendar for use within the reporting system.

- **DATE RANGE**   This is optional but is demonstrated here for an organization whose fiscal year runs from April through March.

QUESTION: *I seem to remember you mentioning that I could use a custom folder for the generation of lists of values. We are using E-Business Suite, and I need to get a listing of the customer master from the system. Do you have the code that I should use?*

ANSWER: Here is the script you asked for:

```
SELECT
cust.customer_id          customer_id,
cust.customer_name        customer_name,
cust.customer_number      cust_number,
cust.status               cust_status,
cust.customer_type        cust_type
FROM
apps.ra_customers cust
```

If you use this script in a custom folder, you will be able to create a list of values on the customer name. As a bonus, I have also included the code that generates the customer ID, customer number, status, and type. You can then create lists of values on the customer number, status, and type using the same custom folder.

QUESTION: *We are using lots of tablespaces. Our DBA says that it is a pain to keep checking the tablespace on the system. Do you have a script that will help us look at just the tablespaces that we need to look at?*

ANSWER: I've seen a lot of scripts that tell you about all the tablespaces in a database, but very few show only the ones that are going to give you problems. A colleague of mine has been using the following script for a few years now, and it has really saved him from dialing in at nights and on the weekends. He uses it as a cursor for a procedure and has it build an e-mail and/or page notification that is sent to him and others.

This script is useful because it drills down to what is going to give you a problem. My colleague does not have a lot of time to wade through pages of report to find out which tablespace is running out of space. The following script is short and sweet and allows him to get on with his day. He tells me that he has run the script on 8, 8*i*, 9*i*, and 10*g*, and that it has just one proviso: You need to make sure that you are using SYS, SYSTEM, or another user that has access to read the data dictionary.

```
SELECT
TSP.TABLESPACE_NAME T_NAME,
TSP.TOTAL_SPACE      TOT_SPACE,
FREE.TOTAL_FREE,
ROUND(FREE.TOTAL_FREE /TSP.TOTAL_SPACE*100)   PCT_FREE,
ROUND((TSP.TOTAL_SPACE - FREE.TOTAL_FREE),2) TOT_USED,
ROUND((TSP.TOTAL_SPACE - FREE.TOTAL_FREE)/TSP.TOTAL_SPACE*100) PCT_USED,
NEXTEXT.MAX_NEXT_EXTENT
FROM
(SELECT
TABLESPACE_NAME,
SUM(BYTES)/1024/1024 TOTAL_SPACE
FROM DBA_DATA_FILES
GROUP BY TABLESPACE_NAME) TSP,
(SELECT
TABLESPACE_NAME,
ROUND(SUM(BYTES)/1024/1024,2) TOTAL_FREE,
ROUND(MAX(BYTES)/1024/1024,2) MAX_FREE
FROM DBA_FREE_SPACE
GROUP BY TABLESPACE_NAME) FREE,
(SELECT
TABLESPACE_NAME,
ROUND(MAX(NEXT_EXTENT)/1024/1024,2) MAX_NEXT_EXTENT
FROM DBA_SEGMENTS
GROUP BY TABLESPACE_NAME) NEXTEXT
WHERE
TSP.TABLESPACE_NAME = FREE.TABLESPACE_NAME (+)
AND TSP.TABLESPACE_NAME = NEXTEXT.TABLESPACE_NAME (+)
AND ((ROUND(FREE.TOTAL_FREE/TSP.TOTAL_SPACE*100)) < 10
OR NEXTEXT.MAX_NEXT_EXTENT > FREE.MAX_FREE);
```

The following illustration shows a screenshot from SQL*Plus.

T_NAME	TOT_SPACE	TOTAL_FREE	PCT_FREE	TOT_USED	PCT_USED
EXAMPLE	148.75	0.13	0	148.62	100
USERS	176.25	3.69	2	172.56	98
XDB	46.875	2.63	6	44.25	94

QUESTION: *The following error messages are displayed whenever we try to submit a scheduled workbook:*
Database Error - ORA-04068: existing state of packages has been discarded
ORA-04063: package body
"<SCHEMA>.EUL5_BATCH_USER" has errors
ORA-06508: PL/SQL: could not find program unit being called
ORA-06512: at line 2.
Do you have any ideas?
ANSWER: It sounds like the EUL5_BATCH_USER package body is invalid because the V_$PARAMETER cannot be accessed.
To fix this situation, use the following workflow:

1. Using SQL Plus, connect to the database where the EUL is located and log in as the SYS or SYSTEM user.

2. Execute the following script:

```
GRANT SELECT ON SYS.V_$PARAMETER TO <eul_owner>;
```

NOTE
You need to replace <eul_owner> with the name of the user who owns the EUL in your environment.

3. You now need to recompile the EUL5_BATCH_USER package, by logging in to SQL PLUS as the EUL owner, and execute the following:

```
ALTER PACKAGE EUL5_BATCH_USER COMPILE PACKAGE;
```

4. Finally, you need to confirm that there are no issues by executing this SQL:

```
SELECT OBJECT_NAME, OBJECT_TYPE, STATUS FROM
USER_OBJECTS
WHERE STATUS LIKE 'INVALID';
```

QUESTION: *We have disabled the Save option in Oracle Enterprise Manager, yet Discoverer Viewer is still prompting the user to save the changes. It gives these messages:*
Do you want to save your changes before closing this worksheet?
You have not saved the changes you made to this worksheet. This worksheet must be closed to continue. Click "Yes" to save changes and continue, "No" to continue without saving changes, or "Cancel" to return to this worksheet. If you choose "Yes" and you do not own the workbook, you will be prompted to save it under a new name.
Can you help?
ANSWER: Customization to remove the Save link will only remove the Save and Save As links from the Viewer layout, but this does not stop the user from having the privilege to save. I am guessing, but you probably created a public EUL. Creating an EUL this way grants the option Save workbooks to Database to the public role, which in turn is granted to all users.

Your users will therefore be getting this warning message to save the workbook whenever some changes have been made to the formatting or the layout.

To disable this warning, use the following workflow:

1. Connect to the Discoverer Administrator.

2. Navigate to Tools | Privileges.

3. Click Select, provide the username that you want to administer, and click Go.

4. In the Desktop and plus privileges section uncheck the option Save workbooks to Database.

5. Click Apply.

NOTE
This will remove the privilege to only that particular user. To remove this privilege from all users, select the public role and revoke the privilege.

QUESTION: *How can I completely remove the Discoverer 10.1.2 applet and Java Runtime Environment (JRE) from a user PC?*

ANSWER: The first time that a user accesses the Discoverer Plus URL, the Discoverer applet will be downloaded. This applet includes a Sun JRE and a signed VeriSign Class 3 Certificate. These items are required for any subsequent access to Discoverer Plus.

If these need to be removed, use the following workflow:

1. From the Windows Start button, select Settings | Control Panel.

2. Double-click Add/Remove Programs.

3. Locate and click the item titled "Java 2 Runtime Environment SE, v1.4.2_04."

4. Click the Remove button.

NOTE
The default JRE that ships with Discoverer 10.1.2 is version 1.4.2_04. The version on the client machine may be higher if the Application Server Administrator has changed the Discoverer server-side configuration. You may need to remove more than one.

5. Windows may alert the user to restart the computer to completely remove the Sun JRE.

6. The Discoverer security certificate is in the browser and can be removed only by opening Internet Explorer and editing the Internet Options. If you have not already done so, launch Internet Explorer.

7. From the toolbar, select Tools | Internet Options.

8. Click the Content tab.

9. Click the Publishers button.

10. Click the Trusted Root Certification Authorities tab.

11. Scroll through the list of certificates and remove any certificates issued to "VeriSign Trust Network" and issued by "VeriSign Trust Network" that display a "friendly name" of VeriSign Class 3 Primary CA.

12. Click Close to exit the Certificates dialog box.

13. Click OK to save and exit from the Internet Options settings.

14. When all actions are completed, reboot the PC. The Discoverer 10.1.2 applet components will be completely removed from the client PC.

QUESTION: *Why does a user need to have the CREATE PROCEDURE, CREATE TABLE, and CREATE VIEW database privileges in order to schedule?*
ANSWER: In order for a user to be able to schedule workbooks, he or she needs to have all of the following database privileges:

- CREATE PROCEDURE

- CREATE TABLE

- CREATE VIEW

- EXECUTE ANY PROCEDURE

- UNLIMITED TABLESPACE

- EXECUTE ON SYS.DBMS_JOB

- SELECT ON SYS.V_$PARAMETER

For all of this to work, the user needs to be able to create a procedure that will execute the job at the allotted time. The create table and create view privileges are needed for the storage of the results. Every time the query is executed, Discoverer creates a table to store those results.

In standard Discoverer, when you create and run a worksheet the results are created dynamically. This means that the data is available only within the session that is running the worksheet. More important, the data is *not* available to any other worksheet whether within that session or not.

However, if you use a scheduled workbook, then the results from the worksheet are held in a temporary table until you remove the results or you delete the scheduled workbook.

NOTE
This temporary table is stored within the schema of the user who owns the workbook—not within the standard EUL schema.

A typical table has a name in the form EUL5_ B *YYMMDD HHMISS* Q*N* R*N,* such as EUL5_B050918214946Q1R3, which can be broken into six separate pieces as follows:

- EUL5_ is a constant

- B means Batch and is a constant.

- *YYMMDD* is the date that the scheduled worksheet was created, e.g., 050918 to mean 18 September 2005.

- *HHMISS* is the time when the scheduled worksheet was created, given in the 24-hour clock format, e.g., 214946 to mean 9:49:46 P.M.

■   Q*N* is the letter Q followed by a number, e.g., Q1, which signifies the query number. I believe Oracle has some plans to allow multiple queries, but for now this is always Q1.

■   R*N* means this is the letter R followed by a number, e.g., R1, R2, and so on. This is the run number.

Using the preceding logic, therefore, this is a valid example: EUL5_B051129151025Q1R1— this is result set number 1 for query 1, which was set up at 3:15:25 P.M. on 29 November 2005.

Something else that adds interest here is that the column names within the table do not match the column names in your original query. The scheduled results column names use generic names such as BRVC1, BRVC2, BRD1, BRD2, BRN1, and BRN2. These are codes and can be interpreted as follows:

■   BRCV1 and BRCV2 mean Batch Result Var Chars 1 and 2.

■   BRD1 and BRD2 mean Batch Result Dates 1 and 2.

■   BRN1 and BRN2 mean Batch Result Numbers 1 and 2.

So why do you need the CREATE VIEW privilege? This is used at run time to populate the latest table of results. For every scheduled workbook that you create, Discoverer will create one view. When the appointed time arrives for the execution of the query, Discoverer executes a CREATE TABLE xyz AS SELECT * FROM VIEW.

A typical view has a name like EUL5_B050918214946Q1V3, which, as you can see, looks almost identical to the format for the table name. This is deliberate and corresponds to the date and time when the schedule was first set up.

By the way, did you realize that what you are seeing is basically the forerunner to today's materialized views? In a materialized view Oracle is able to combine a view definition with a table to store the results. Discoverer has been able to do this for years; albeit the view and the table are stored as separate objects.

QUESTION: *Could you please explain the tables that are used by scheduling?*

ANSWER: Apart from the tables and views created by the user at the time of scheduling, Discoverer uses a set of predefined tables to manage scheduling. These are as follows:

■   **EUL5_BATCH_REPORTS**   This table contains one row per scheduled worksheet and contains all of the base information that the user assigned when the schedule was set up. Of particular importance are the following columns:

  ■   **BR_ID**   Is the unique ID assigned to this scheduled worksheet.

  ■   **BR_EU_ID**   Is the user ID of the owner of the schedule. This links to the EU_ID in the EUL5_EUL_USERS tables, where the EU_USERNAME column will tell you the actual user.

  ■   **BR_NEXT_RUN_DATE**   Contains the date and time of the next run.

  ■   **BR_EXPIRY**   Contains the number of days to keep the results.

  ■   **BR_NUM_FREQ_UNITS**   Contains the number of units to be used between refreshes as qualified by BR_RFU_ID.

- **BR_RFU_ID**   Contains a code indicating the frequency, where 2000 stands for minutes, 2001 stands for hours, 2002 stands for days, 2003 stands for weeks, 2004 stands for months, and 2005 stands for years.

- **BR_AUTO_REFRESH**   Contains a 0 or a 1, where 1 means automatically refresh and 0 means execute just once.

- **EUL5_BR_RUNS**   This table contains one row for each execution of the schedule. Of particular importance are the following columns:

  - **BRR_ID**   This is the unique ID assigned to this run.

  - **BRR_BR_ID**   This is the ID of the scheduled worksheet being run. This corresponds to the BR_ID in the EUL5_BATCH_REPORTS table.

  - **BRR_RUN_NUMBER**   This is a sequential number corresponding to the number of times the worksheet has been scheduled to run.

  - **BRR_STATE**   This is a code to indicate the status of the run, whose possible values include 1, which means this worksheet is still scheduled, and 9, which means this worksheet has been executed successfully.

  - **BRR_RUN_DATE**   This is the date and time when the schedule was run. It will be null if BRR_STATE is 1.

- **EUL5_BATCH_SHEETS**   This table contains one row per scheduled worksheet and contains a cross-reference to the actual worksheet. Of particular importance are the following columns:

  - **BS_ID**   This is the unique ID assigned to this run.

  - **BS_BR_ID**   This is the ID of the scheduled worksheet being run. It corresponds to the BR_ID in the EUL5_BATCH_REPORTS table.

  - **BS_SHEET_NAME**   This is the name of the sheet to be executed.

  - **BS_SHEET_ID**   This is the ID of the worksheet being scheduled. It is usually encrypted.

- **EUL5_BATCH_QUERIES**   This table contains one row per scheduled worksheet and contains the actual SQL that is to be executed. Of particular importance are the following columns:

  - **BQ_ID**   This is the unique ID assigned to this query.

  - **BQ_BS_ID**   This is the ID of the sheet being run. It corresponds to the BS_ID in the EUL5_BATCH_SHEETS table.

  - **BQ_RESULT_SQL_1–4**   These four columns contain the SQL that will be run to produce the results. Most of the time, the SQL can be contained in the first column. If there is more SQL than will fit in the first column, Discoverer will concatenate the columns into one string before executing the code.

■ **EUL5_EUL_USERS** This table stores information about EUL users. Of particular importance are the following columns:

■ **EU_ID** This is the unique ID assigned to the user.

■ **EU_NAME** This is the name of the user or role as stored within the database.

The following script will show you all the scheduled worksheets within your EUL, including those that have already run. You need to make sure you are logged in to SQL as the EUL owner.

```
SELECT
A.EU_USERNAME        "User Name",
B.BR_EU_ID           "User ID",
B.BR_WORKBOOK_NAME   "Workbook",
B.BR_ID              "Workbook ID",
R.BRR_RUN_NUMBER     "Run Number",
R.BRR_RUN_DATE       "Run Date"
FROM
EUL5_BATCH_REPORTS B,
EUL5_BR_RUNS        R,
EUL5_EUL_USERS      A
WHERE
A.EU_ID      = B.BR_EU_ID and
R.BRR_BR_ID = B.BR_ID
ORDER BY
B.BR_ID, R.BRR_RUN_NUMBER;
```

Here is what the output looks like.

This script will show you the scheduled worksheets within your EUL that have not yet run. You

User Name	User ID	Workbook	Workbook ID	Run Number	Run Date
DRAKE	100000	Order Status	108885	28	10/17/2005 9:49:05 PM
DRAKE	100000	Order Status	108885	29	
DRAKE	100000	Scheduled Order Status	111253	22	10/12/2005 2:38:51 PM
DRAKE	100000	Scheduled Order Status	111253	23	10/13/2005 2:38:48 PM
DRAKE	100000	Scheduled Order Status	111253	24	10/14/2005 2:38:52 PM
DRAKE	100000	Scheduled Order Status	111253	25	10/15/2005 2:38:50 PM

need to make sure you are logged into SQL as the EUL owner.

```
SELECT
A.EU_USERNAME        "User Name",
B.BR_NAME            "Workbook Name",
B.BR_CREATED_DATE    "Created Date",
B.BR_NEXT_RUN_DATE  "Next Scheduled Run Time",
'Every ' || B.BR_NUM_FREQ_UNITS || ' ' ||
DECODE(B.BR_RFU_ID,
    2000,'Minutes',
    2001,'Hours',
    2002,'Days',
    2003,'Weeks',
    2004,'Months','Years') "Often"
FROM
EUL5_BATCH_REPORTS B,
EUL5_EUL_USERS      A
WHERE B.BR_EU_ID=A.EU_ID;
```

Here is what the output looks like.

User Name	Workbook Name	Created Date	Next Scheduled Run Time	Often
DRAKE	Scheduled Order Status	9/20/2005 2:37:52 PM	10/19/2005 2:38:47 PM	Every 1 Days
DRAKE	Order Status	9/18/2005 9:49:45 PM	10/18/2005 9:49:00 PM	Every 1 Days
DRAKE	Analytic Function Examples with exceptions1	9/26/2005 2:26:20 PM	10/24/2005 2:26:00 PM	Every 1 Weeks

QUESTION: *I need a Discoverer workbook that shows the top 15 airlines in terms of passenger count. More specifically, the top 15 should each be listed in the report with their respective percentage share (highest to lowest), with any count less then 15 being totaled on the last line. Can you help?*

ANSWER: In order to give you the result that you want, you will need to use some rather clever calculations. Let me give you an example based on Airline and SUM.

1. Create a table worksheet that has Airline Name and Passenger SUM.

2. Rename Passenger SUM to Passengers and sort the rows high to low based on Passengers.

3. Create an analytic ranking calculation that looks like this:

   ```
   RANK() OVER(ORDER BY Passenger SUM DESC)
   ```

4. Create another analytic calculation called Grand Total that looks like this:

   ```
   SUM(Passenger SUM) OVER(ORDER BY Passenger SUM DESC RANGE
   BETWEEN UNBOUNDED PRECEDING AND UNBOUNDED FOLLOWING )/15
   ```

5. Create a calculation called Remainder that looks like this:

   ```
   Grand Total - Passenger SUM
   ```

6. Create a total on Passengers using SUM, and give this total the label Totals.

7. Create a total on Grand Total using Cell SUM; assign no label to this total.

8. Create a total on Remainder using Cell SUM; also assign no label to this total.

9. Format the data in both Grand Total and Remainder so that the background color is the same as the foreground color. This effectively hides the intermediate values, leaving just a single row at the bottom containing the Total Count for the 15 airlines, a Total for all airlines, and a Total for the difference between all airlines and the 15 selected in the ranking. Here is what the output looks like.

Rank	Airline	Passengers	Grand Total	Remainder
1	CD-625	1,750,997		
2	AVR-500	1,258,289		
3	CD-100	881,911		
4	QB-5000	829,052		
5	QB-5500	826,217		
6	QB-6000	819,342		
7	AB-2000	798,849		
8	AB-3000	783,452		
9	CD-200	775,574		
10	AVR-550	729,518		
11	AB-2500	702,475		
12	MS-1200	668,871		
13	AVR-900	542,121		
14	QB-3000	497,296		
15	DS-1200	480,295		
		Totals: 12,344,259	15,034,172	2,689,913

QUESTION: *Can you give me a script that allows me to query the database tables and views and find out which business areas use them within my EUL?*

ANSWER: Here is the script you requested:

```
SELECT DISTINCT
BA.BA_NAME            "BA Name",
OBJ.SOBJ_EXT_TABLE   "Table Name",
OBJ.OBJ_EXT_OWNER    "Owner",
FROM
EUL5_BAS             BA,
EUL5_BA_OBJ_LINKS    BOL,
EUL5_OBJS            OBJ
WHERE
BA.BA_ID        = BOL.BOL_BA_ID
AND OBJ.OBJ_ID  = BOL.BOL_obj_ID
AND OBJ.OBJ_EXT_OWNER IS NOT NULL
ORDER BY 1,2;
```

QUESTION: *What we want to do is know how long a person has been sick by subtracting the end date from the start date. However, if the sickness lasts from Friday till Monday, then only 1 day should count. In other words, we want an algorithm that works out the number of non-working days between any two dates, excluding Saturday and Sunday. Do you have a nice work-around for this?*

ANSWER: This can be done, but you have to use four calculations. Let's assume you have two dates: a Start Date and an End Date. The following example will show you how to do it. Of course you can always combine calculations into one algorithm, but for clarity I will break them out here so that you can see exactly what is going on. The algorithms can be tricky, but if you copy them into Discoverer exactly as they are shown here, they will work:

- **Calc 1: Base Diff** This counts the base number of days between the start and end dates, assuming of course that the end date is later than or equal to the start date. I add 1 because if the end date equals the start date, we still have to allow for one day's sickness.

   TRUNC(End Date) – TRUNC(Start Date) + 1

   In your example, where the end date is Monday and the start date is Friday, the base diff will be 4.

- **Calc 2: Weeks** This counts the number of whole weeks between the start and end dates. Therefore, if the Base Diff is 4, the number of whole weeks will be 0.

   TRUNC(ABS((Base Diff) / 7), 0)

- **Calc 3: Variance** This works out how many odd days there are between the base number of days and the total number of weeks. Therefore, if the Base Diff is 4, the variance will be 4.

   TRUNC(Base Diff – (Weeks * 7), 0)

- **Calc 4: Actual Diff** This works out how many working days there are between the start date and the end date, assuming that Saturday and Sunday are not to be counted. Basically this works out the day of the week for the end date and calculates the exact number of days the person has been sick.

   Base Diff – (2 * Weeks) – DECODE(DECODE(SIGN(TO_NUMBER(TO_CHAR(End Date, 'D')) – Variance),1,'N','Y'),'Y',2,0)

Let's look at this last algorithm in a bit more detail. It starts with the base difference and then subtracts two times the number of whole weeks. Once again, in the example provided, where the start date is a Friday and the end date is a Monday, the number of whole weeks is zero, and so nothing is subtracted, with the number of days remaining at 4.

Next, the algorithm subtracts an additional two days if the day of the week is greater than the variance. Let's see how this works:

DECODE(DECODE(SIGN(TO_NUMBER(TO_CHAR(End Date, D')) Variance), 1, 'N', 'Y') ,'Y',2,0) is the heart of the algorithm.

TO_CHAR(End Date, 'D') returns the Day of the Week integer in a string. This needs converting to a number before we can use the SIGN function, hence the TO_NUMBER function. In our example, Monday will return the number 2.

Consider the inner DECODE statement,

DECODE(SIGN(TO_NUMBER(TO_CHAR(End Date, 'D')) – Variance),1,'N','Y')

This is explained as:

IF the Day of the Week minus the Variance is positive

THEN return the value 'N' (nothing to add)

ELSE return the value 'Y'

In our example, where the variance is 4 and day of the week is 1, because the day of the week minus the variance is negative, the algorithm will return a 'Y'.

The outer decode simply says,

IF the value returned by the inner decode is 'Y'

THEN subtract an additional 2 days

ELSE subtract 0 additional days

In our example: because the inner DECODE returned a 'Y', we now subtract 2 additional days from the base difference, making the overall answer 2.

In the final worksheet the only calculation that you would have visible to the user would be the final one for Actual Diff.

QUESTION: *We need an algorithm that calculates the difference between two dates, with the result being displayed as Days, Hours, Minutes, and Seconds. Do you have an algorithm that can do this?*

ANSWER: This can be done, but once again you need to use several calculations. In this case, there are four. Let's assume you have two dates: a Higher Date and a Lower Date. The following example will show you how to do it. Of course, you can always combine calculations into one algorithm, but for clarity I will break them out here so that you can see exactly what is going on. The algorithms can be tricky, but if you copy them into Discoverer exactly as they are shown here, they will work:

■ **Calc 1: Base Diff** This calculates the base number of days between the higher and the lower dates, assuming of course that the higher date is later than or equal to the lower date. This time, unlike the answer given to the previous question, we do not use the TRUNC command:

Higher Date – Lower Date

- **Calc 2: New Mins**   This calculates the number of odd minutes between the times given:

  TRUNC(Base Diff * 1440) – (TRUNC(Base Diff) * 1440) – (TRUNC(MOD(Base Diff, TRUNC(Base Diff)) * 24) * 60)

- **Calc 3: New Secs**   This calculates the number of odd seconds between the times given:

  TRUNC(Base Diff * 86400) – (TRUNC(Diff) * 86400) – (TRUNC(MOD(Base Diff, TRUNC(Base Diff)) * 24) * 3600) – (New Mins * 60)

- **Calc 4: New Time**   This calculates the final display:

  TRUNC(Base Diff) || ' Days, ' || TRUNC(MOD(Base Diff, TRUNC(Base Diff)) * 24) || ' Hours, '|| New Mins || ' Minutes, ' || New Secs || ' Seconds'

Using the preceding calculations, if the Higher Time is 17:05:20 on Monday 26 September and the Lower Time is midnight on 20 September, the individual calculations come out as follows:

- **Calc 1: Base Diff**   5.7120 rounded to 4 decimal places

- **Calc 2: New Mins**   5

- **Calc 3: New Secs**   20

- **Calc 4: New Time**   5 Days, 17 Hours, 5 Minutes, 20 Seconds

Once again, you would make only the final calculation visible to the user.

QUESTION: *Do you have a script that will show us the business areas and folders as well as the items that are used in each folder?*

ANSWER: The following script will give you what you want:

```
SELECT DISTINCT
BA.BA_NAME              "BA Name",
OBJ.OBJ_NAME            "Folder Name",
EXP.EXP_SEQUENCE        "Item Order",
EXP.IT_HEADING          "Item Heading",
DECODE(EXP.EXP_DATA_TYPE,
    1, 'VARCHAR2',
    2, 'NUMBER',
    4, 'DATE',
    EXP.EXP_DATA_TYPE) "Data Type",
DECODE(EXP.IT_HIDDEN,
    '0', 'No', 'Yes')  "Item Hidden",
OBJ.OBJ_ID              "Folder ID",
BA.BA_ID                "BA ID"
FROM
EUL5_BA_OBJ_LINKS BOL,
EUL5_BAS          BA,
EUL5_OBJS         OBJ,
EUL5_EXPRESSIONS  EXP
WHERE
```

```
BOL.BOL_BA_ID   = BA.BA_ID
AND BOL.BOL_OBJ_ID = OBJ.OBJ_ID
AND EXP.IT_OBJ_ID  = OBJ.OBJ_ID
AND EXP.EXP_TYPE    IN ('CI','CO')
ORDER BY BA_NAME, OBJ_NAME, EXP_SEQUENCE;
```

QUESTION: *Do you have a script that shows who has access to each business area? Can you also let me know who are the administrators?*

ANSWER: Here is the script you asked for:

```
SELECT
BA.BA_NAME        "Business Area",
DECODE(PRIVS.AP_PRIV_LEVEL,1,
   'Yes','No')   "Administrator",
USR.EU_USERNAME "User Name"
FROM
EUL5_EUL_USERS    USR,
EUL5_ACCESS_PRIVS PRIVS,
EUL5_BAS          BA
WHERE
USR.EU_ID = PRIVS.AP_EU_ID AND
BA.BA_ID  = PRIVS.GBA_BA_ID;
```

QUESTION: *Can you provide me with a script to show me who has workbooks that they have saved to the database?*

ANSWER: As you know, the tables used by Discoverer 10.1.2 are all prefixed with EUL5. The users are stored in a table called EUL_USERS, and the workbooks themselves are stored in a table called DOCUMENTS, so in this version the tables are called EUL5_EUL_USERS and EUL5_DOCUMENTS. The following SQL query, when logged in as the EUL owner, will tell you which workbooks are owned by which users:

```
SELECT
EU_USERNAME      "Doc Owner",
DOC_NAME         "Doc Name"
FROM
EUL5_EUL_USERS     USRS,
EUL5_DOCUMENTS     DOCS
WHERE
USRS.EU_ID = DOCS.DOC_EU_ID
ORDER BY
"Doc Owner", "Doc Name";
```

By the way, to see who has shared what with whom, use this script in SQL when connected as the owner of the EUL:

```
SELECT
AP_CREATED_BY "Doc Owner",
DOC_NAME      "Doc Name",
EU_USERNAME   "Shared With"
FROM
EUL5_EUL_USERS     USRS,
EUL5_DOCUMENTS     DOCS,
```

```
EUL5_ACCESS_PRIVS PRIVS
WHERE
PRIVS.GD_DOC_ID = DOCS.DOC_ID AND
USRS.EU_ID = PRIVS.AP_EU_ID
ORDER BY
"Doc Owner", "Doc Name", "Shared With";
```

QUESTION: *We are using Discoverer in Apps mode and have too many workbooks assigned to too many responsibilities. We want to clean up the workbooks and the responsibility assignments. Can you provide us with a script that shows all of the workbooks and all of the responsibility assignments? Also, just how does the Discoverer metadata link to Apps?*

ANSWER: Here is a script that may well be of some use. In order to use it you will need to find out the name of the schema owner for your particular EUL. You then insert that name into this script at the five locations identified by *EUL_OWNER*. Finally, I recommend you log in to the Apps database as the APPS user in order to run this script. If you look carefully in this script, you will see exactly how the Discoverer metadata links to Apps.

```
SELECT
USER_NAME || ':' || DOCS.DOC_NAME "Doc Name",
RESP.RESPONSIBILITY_NAME           "Resp Name",
FROM
EUL_OWNER.EUL5_EUL_USERS      USRS,
EUL_OWNER.EUL5_ACCESS_PRIVS PRIVS,
EUL_OWNER.EUL5_DOCUMENTS      DOCS,
EUL_OWNER.EUL5_EUL_USERS      OWN_USR,
APPS.FND_RESPONSIBILITY_VL    RESP,
APPS.FND_USER                 CRTD_BY
WHERE
PRIVS.AP_TYPE = 'GD'
AND PRIVS.AP_EU_ID = USRS.EU_ID
AND PRIVS.GD_DOC_ID = DOCS.DOC_ID
AND OWN_USR.EU_ID = DOCS.DOC_EU_ID
AND RESP.RESPONSIBILITY_ID(+) =
    SUBSTR(USRS.EU_USERNAME,2,INSTR(USRS.EU_USERNAME,'#',2)-2)
AND CRTD_BY.USER_ID = SUBSTR(DOCS.DOC_CREATED_BY,2)
AND OWN_USR.EU_USERNAME NOT IN ('EUL_OWNER','PUBLIC')
ORDER BY 1,2
```

QUESTION: *I am trying to create a parameter where the users can pass one of the following parameters:*

- **'All' (i.e., all values)**

- **'003' (i.e., a specific value)**

- **'003','001' (i.e., multiple values)**

So my condition looks like this:

domain IN DECODE(:p_domain,'All',Domain,:p_domain)

I have checked the "Let user enter multiple values" check box for the domain parameter. With the preceding setup the query works correctly when I provide "All" and single values. However, when I execute the report with multiple parameters (i.e., '003,'001'), I only get records related to the first parameter, which in this case is '003'. How can I get this to work?

ANSWER: You need to create a complex condition like this:

domain = DECODE(UPPER(:p_domain), 'ALL', Domain)

OR

domain IN :p_domain

By the way, you might be interested to know that in the first part of this condition, when we refer to domain = DECODE, this works equally well with domain IN DECODE. This is because Discoverer silently changes to the appropriate operator, depending on how many values are present when generating the SQL query. You should check out the SQL inspector to see this in action.

QUESTION: *We are using Oracle E-Business Suite and have recently attended one of your Discoverer 10.1.2 end-user courses. When I got back to the office, the DBA told me that we cannot use Discoverer 10.1.2 because it not certified with Apps running on Solaris. Is this true?*

ANSWER: This is not true. Discoverer 10.1.2 is certified for use with Oracle E-Business Suite. You need to log in to Oracle MetaLink and do a search for document 313418.1. This is a white paper called Using Discoverer 10.1.2 with Oracle E-Business Suite 11*i*. As of December 2005, the only platform that has not been certified for 10.1.2.0.0 is IBM AIX. All of the others—Sun Solaris, Microsoft Windows, HP UX, and Linux—are fully certified. However, if you install the 10.1.2.0.2 version, even AIX is certified.

NOTE
As of January 2006, there are still some outstanding patches that need to be written in order to fully certify HP HP/UX 11.0 and IBM AIX for use with Single Sign-On. However, if you are not using Single Sign-On, then all platforms are supported. If you intend using Single Sign-On against Apps, you must use the latest Discoverer version 10.1.2.1. For the latest information regarding Discoverer certification against Apps, please refer to Oracle MetaLink document 313418.1.

QUESTION: *When we choose a connection or enter the connection details at the Discoverer 10.1.2 Plus login page, the screen flickers and then the connections page is displayed again. After this the Applet starts but in a different window. Is there a way to make Plus start in the same window?*

ANSWER: By default, Discoverer Plus is designed to launch in a separate window from the connection screen. However, to answer your question, yes, you can make Discoverer Plus use the same connection. To do this, you append the following to the end of the URL:

?_plus_popup=false&framedisplaystyle=embedded

If your standard URL is

http://server.my.com:7778/discoverer/plus

you change this to:

http://server.my.com:7778/discoverer/plus?_plus_popup=false&framedisplaystyle=embedded

This time you will see the Discoverer connections page, applet loading, and Plus interface all appear in the same window. You will also see loading messages and an hourglass display as the session starts, loads, and renders.

QUESTION: *I cannot see an option to add the total number of pages to the footer section of my Discoverer Plus worksheet. Has this been removed?*

ANSWER: Yes, this feature was removed when Plus 10.1.2 was introduced. According to Oracle, the token that used to generate this code (&Pages) has been phased out and is no longer supported within Discoverer. This is because it is computationally intensive to determine the number of pages and doing so would lead to unacceptable performance degradation.

If you still want to do this, you need to use Desktop to add the &Pages token. You must also print from within Desktop. If you set this up in Desktop and then try to print from within Plus, Discoverer will print the page numbers incorrectly. For example, if the print command was submitted when viewing page 4 of 12, all of the printed pages would show Page 4 of 12. If your printing started on page 1, all the printed pages would show Page 1 of 12.

QUESTION: *I noticed that Oracle recently published a revised version of the 10.1.2 Application Server called 10.1.2.0.2. I have also seen references to releases such as 10.1.2.1 and 10.1.2.0.0. Can you tell me the difference and whether I am missing anything, and can I upgrade from my older version of 10.1.2.0.0?*

ANSWER: You are right; Oracle did release an upgraded version of the Application Server in September 2005, and no, even though there are some bug fixes and updates to functionality in the newer 10.1.2.0.2, there is no upgrade path from the 10.1.2.0.0 that you have. Let me explain.

When Oracle first released 10.1.2 in January 2005 (10.1.2.0.0), that version did not come with Forms or Reports. The Business Intelligence components were also only available on their own CDs, although you could easily link them to an Infrastructure. With the 10.1.2.0.2 release, Oracle has included a BI & Forms option to the Application Server, which will install Forms, Reports, and BI Discoverer. According to Oracle, all of the components present in 10.1.2.0.0 are included in 10.1.2.0.2, and most are also providing updated versions that are primarily bug fixes.

With the 10.1.2.0.2 release, there are now two ways to install Discoverer. You can still install it stand-alone using the OBI (Oracle Business Intelligence) CDs, or as a component of the new Application Server.

Something that may interest you when you install Discoverer using the new 10.1.2.0.2 installer is that the version of Discoverer that gets installed is not 10.1.2.0.2 as you might expect, but 10.1.2.1.0. This is because the Discoverer Plus/Viewer version itself has slightly changed! Basically, any component that was present in 10.1.2.0.0 but has been changed because of bug fixes or enhancements has become 10.1.2.1.0. Any components that are totally new to phase 2 are named 10.1.2.0.2, while unchanged components still carry the 10.1.2.0.0 version number. For more information regarding these release numbers, please refer to document number 332925.1 on Oracle MetaLink.

NOTE

As of going to press, we heard that a patch set to Discoverer 10.1.2.0.0 is available. The version of Discoverer in this patch set is called 10.1.2.1.0. This means that the Discoverer versions in the 10.1.2.0.0 patched set and in the 10.1.2.0.2 referred to here will be the same. Therefore, if you are using Discoverer 10.1.2.0.0 and want to have the latest bug fixes, performance improvements, and minor UI changes but do not want to install 10.1.2.0.2 afresh, you will have to install this patch. The component version number can be found in the Help | About dialog box.

QUESTION: *I cannot control the paper size inside Discoverer Plus. Do you know of a way to do this?*

ANSWER: Up until the recent Application Server 10.1.2.0.2 release, this has not been possible. However, the version of Discoverer that ships with the 10.1.2.0.2 Application Server, 10.1.2.1, has a new drop-down on the Page Setup screen for managing the page size. The older version simply displays the page size but does not allow you to change it.

There is one proviso: You must have already saved the workbook before you can alter the page size. This is because Discoverer will store your page size preference. As a bonus, if you open the same worksheet in Viewer, Discoverer will remember the paper size that you set in Plus. This works the other way, too, in that if you set up a page size in Viewer and resave the workbook, the same setting will be available the next time you open Plus.

To help you know whether you have saved a worksheet in Viewer, Discoverer will display an asterisk alongside the sheet name in the Worksheets area.

QUESTION: *Blogging became really popular during 2005. Can you recommend any good web sites that I can go to for information concerning Discoverer?*

ANSWER: We know of two excellent blogs that are dedicated to business intelligence, and both are run by very good friends of ours.

The first is run by Abhinav Agarwal, our technical editor, and can be found at: http:/oraclebi. blogspot.com.

The second is run by Mark Rittman, who wrote most of the OLAP chapter, and can be found at: http://www.rittman.net. Incidentally, Mark is also authoring an Oracle Reporting Tools Forum at: http://www.rittman.net/forum.

We also recommend our own web site as a good source of additional information: http:// www.learndiscoverer.com. Keep your eyes glued to our website, because we will be adding our own dedicated Discoverer forum during late 2006. Our own blog, http://learn.discoverer. blogspot.com/, will be on line in the summer of 2006.

QUESTION: *One of our users created a crosstab worksheet. When she exported it to Excel, the headings were wrong and the side axis items moved up one row. Do you know why?*

ANSWER: Actually, this is a bug, but there is a work-around. You need to turn on your Axis labels, simple as that. Without these being enabled, Discoverer exports nothing in those cells, which causes Excel to push everything up.

Incidentally, you will probably also have noticed that your column widths are not retained when you export to Excel. In fact they all get set to the width of the heading. Unfortunately, there is no work-around for this one. Our only recommendation is to keep your headings to an absolute minimum and probably use a set of standard abbreviations such as Avg for Average, Std for Standard, Dlvd for Delivered, and so on.

QUESTION: *Do you know if I can pick up the "session variable" in Discoverer (Apps mode) that tells me the responsibility I am logged on as? The variable USER simply returns Apps, which is what I would expect. However, Discoverer must know the values because if I write a query, I can see that it is storing the value in the EUL5_EUL_USERS table, e.g., #10152#183. We are using Discoverer against E-Business Suite 11.5.9 on a 9i database.*

ANSWER: I use the following code in a custom folder created in Discoverer Administrator to get the responsibility plus other user information. You will, of course, need to replace the term *your_server* with your own server information.

```
SELECT
apps.fnd_global.resp_id@your-server,
apps.fnd_global.resp_name@your-server,
```

```
apps.fnd_global.user_id@your-server,
apps.fnd_global.user_name@your-server,
apps.fnd_global.employee_id@your-server,
apps.fnd_global.per_security_profile_id@your-server,
apps.fnd_global.org_id@your-server
FROM DUAL;
```

QUESTION: *We are using Discoverer Plus 10.1.2 and are using a 10g database. However, we are noticing severe performance issues when running the query predictor in that the prediction takes up most of the time. When we used a 9i database, everything was fine. Do you know what we are doing wrong?*

ANSWER: Because of a bug in the Oracle 10g database (4024370) as recorded in a posting on MetaLink on 15-JAN-2005, if you need to use the query predictor, you need to use a work-around for Discoverer that will force Discoverer to use explain plan instead of dynamic views. When I made these settings to the Registry and the mid-tier of the production system for a client of mine, then Discoverer ran as fast as it ever did.

First of all, I will discuss the Registry entries. There are two entries that need to be set for every developer machine. Both of these entries need to be created in the HKEY_USERS\Software\ ORACLE\Discoverer 10\Database folder.

- **DWORD**   Create an entry called QPPObtainCostMethod with a setting of 0.

- **DWORD**   Create an entry called QPPEnable with a setting of 0.

Turning our attention to the Application Server, to make these settings on the server, use the following workflow:

1. Edit PREF.TXT in the middle tier.

2. Create or edit the same settings just outlined, placing them in the [Database] section.

3. Save the PREF.TXT file.

4. Stop the Discoverer middle tier.

5. Apply the preferences using applypreferences.sh on UNIX or applypreferences.bat on Windows.

6. Restart the Discoverer middle tier.

By the way, if you want to turn off the query predictor, this is also controlled in two places. In the Registry, it is called QPPEnable and can be found here: HKEY_USERS\Software\ORACLE\ Discoverer 10\Database.

In the Application Server, use the preceding workflow to edit the PREF.TXT file, locate the entry for QPPEnable, and change it to 0. Don't forget to stop the middle tier before you apply the preferences.

Setting QPPEnable to 0 turns off query prediction, while setting it to 1 enables query prediction.

QUESTION: *I have a table that contains some columns of type NUMBER. I have created a business area that contains this table, but the columns that are NUMBER(8) in Discoverer appear with the icon of the varchar type. Then in the Discoverer Desktop Edition I cannot, for example, create a table report with a percentage. Do you know if I need a patch?*

ANSWER: It sounds like you have not defined the items to be Data Points. Only those items that are Data Points can be treated as numbers and thus be used in calculations and percentages.

Items that are not defined as Data Points will be treated as characters and can have a List of Values assigned to them. By the way, you cannot assign a List of Values to an item that is defined as a data point.

To check your current settings, please follow this workflow:

1. Log in to Discoverer Administrator as the EUL owner.
2. Open up the Business Area and Folder that has the problem.
3. Locate an item that has a problem.
4. Right-click the item.
5. From the pop-up box select Properties—the Item Properties dialog box will be displayed.
6. In the Item Properties dialog box make sure the General tab is the active tab and now look for the property called Default Position. In Default Position the valid options are

   ■ Data Point

   ■ Page

   ■ Side

   ■ Top

   ■ Top or Side

7. If your item is not defined as Data Point, left-click the current setting and from the drop-down list provided select Data Point.
8. Click Apply and, if you have more items that need to be fixed, go back to Step 3; otherwise, continue with Step 9.
9. When you have finished redefining the settings for all of the items that you wanted to fix, click OK.
10. Exit the Administrator Edition and launch one of the End-User Editions to verify that all is now working as you desire.

QUESTION: *I have been trying to create some materialized views in the database so that I can use external summary management. However, I am having trouble specifying the refresh interval. How can I refresh a materialized view at an interval of 2 hours on the exact even hours through the SQL prompt?*

ANSWER: I am surmising but guess that you specified the materialized view using something like this:

```
CREATE MATERIALIZED VIEW test
REFRESH COMPLETE
START WITH TRUNC(SYSDATE + 1) + 4/24
NEXT SYSDATE + 2/24
AS SELECT * FROM xxx
```

This will correctly do the first refresh at 4:00 A.M. tomorrow morning, but it will set up the following refresh to take place two hours after the previous refresh has completed. So if the previous refresh completes at 4.10 A.M., the next refresh will happen at 6.10 A.M. and not at 6:00 A.M. as you might think.

What you need to do is to provide a parameter to the TRUNC command. Look at this modified script:

```
CREATE MATERIALIZED VIEW test
REFRESH COMPLETE
START WITH TRUNC(SYSDATE + 1) + 4/24
NEXT TRUNC(SYSDATE,'HH') + 2/24
AS SELECT * FROM xxx
```

This code will set up the materialized view to do its first refresh at 4:00 A.M. tomorrow and then refresh every two hours on the hour, no matter when the last refresh completed (provided of course that it took less than one hour to run).

> **NOTE**
> *If you have a materialized view that is scheduled to refresh every two hours and it takes longer than one hour to complete each refresh, perhaps it needs to be tuned.*

Now look at this code:

```
CREATE MATERIALIZED VIEW test
REFRESH COMPLETE
START WITH TRUNC(SYSDATE + 1) + 11/24
NEXT NEXT_DAY(TRUNC(SYSDATE), 'MONDAY') + 15/24
AS SELECT * FROM xxx
```

This code creates a materialized view called test and runs it for the first time tomorrow at 11:00 A.M. The following refreshes will then be each Monday at 3:00 P.M.

QUESTION: *I have just installed a new EUL, but the option to install Oracle's sample data is grayed out. Do you know how I can install this?*

ANSWER: The option is grayed out because you do not have a user called VIDEO5 in the database, and the user you have connected to Discoverer Administrator as does not have the privilege to create a database user either.

To get the sample to install, use the following workflow:

1. Create a new user called VIDEO5, granting these privileges.

   ■ CONNECT

   ■ RESOURCE

   ■ ALTER ANY MATERIALIZED VIEW

   ■ ANALYZE ANY

   ■ CREATE ANY MATERIALIZED VIEW

   ■ CREATE PROCEDURE

   ■ CREATE TABLE

   ■ CREATE VIEW

   ■ DROP ANY MATERIALIZED VIEW

- EXECUTE ANY PROCEDURE

- GLOBAL QUERY REWRITE

- SELECT ANY TABLE

- UNLIMITED TABLESPACE

2. Launch the Administrator edition and connect as the owner of the EUL.

3. Navigate to Tools | EUL Manager.

4. The "Install the sample data option" will now be active and you should click it.

5. Give the password for the VIDEO5 user.

6. The sample database, along with its data, business area, and workbooks will now be created. Access will be granted to PUBLIC.

QUESTION: *Can you tell me how to add five minutes to SYSDATE? I want to set up a job and I want the job to fire off every five minutes until I stop it.*

ANSWER: The answer you want is SYSDATE + (1/288) or SYSDATE + 0.0034722.

Adding something to SYSDATE, or any other date for that matter, is a simple case of working out the decimal that needs to be added.

- **Example 1**   Add one hour (1/24 of a day) : SYSDATE + (1/24) or SYSDATE + 0.0416666.

- **Example 2**   Subtract 30 minutes (1/48 of a day): SYSDATE − (1/48) or SYSDATE − 0.0208333.

- **Example 3**   Add 1.5 days: SYSDATE + 1.5.

Therefore, to add five minutes you have to work out that there are 288 five-minute periods in a 24-hour period, so the answer is SYSDATE + (1/288) or SYSDATE + 0.0034722.

NOTE
*Do not forget the parentheses if you are mixing + or − with * or /.*

QUESTION: *What does it mean when an attribute in a folder is in bold letters or when it is italicized?*

ANSWER: This formatting is applied inside the Administrator edition to help you identify which items have been used in joins. The bold text signifies that the item is being used as the master item in a join; in other words, you have defined a 1:N join going from this item. Items that are formatted in italics are items that are being used as the detail item in a join; in other words, there is a join to this item from an item in another folder.

QUESTION: *I have heard talk of there being primary and secondary elements within Discoverer. Can you tell me what these are and how this affects my EUL?*

ANSWER: The primary elements in an EUL are as follows:

- Business areas

- Folders

- Items

The secondary elements are as follows:

■ Joins

■ Complex folder items

■ Item hierarchies

■ Item hierarchy nodes

■ Date hierarchy templates

■ Date hierarchy items

■ Item classes—lists of values

Primary elements must be uniquely named within the EUL. These names are assigned by the administrator, and you should take great care naming them. In fact, we recommend that you use meaningful names and identifiers for all primary elements.

Secondary elements must be uniquely named within the folder or business area, but the names can be assigned by Discoverer using the value of the Auto-Generate name property of the secondary elements.

QUESTION: *What does the Auto-Generate name property do?*

ANSWER: The Auto-Generate name property enables the names of secondary elements to be automatically updated whenever a primary element name is changed. The Auto-Generate name property is applied to secondary elements using Discoverer Administrator (its value can be set to 'Yes' or 'No'). When the value of the Auto-Generate name property is set to 'Yes' for a secondary element, Discoverer generates its name using the names of its primary elements (i.e., the folder and item names used in the secondary element).

NOTE
The Auto-Generate name property value is set to 'No' by default.

QUESTION: *Is there a way to set up Discoverer such that, when I import new objects from the database, the secondary elements are automatically named for me?*

ANSWER: Yes, you do this by setting the AutogenNameOnCreate Registry setting to 1. By default, this setting is not present and you will need to create it. The AutogenNameOnCreate Registry setting is a DWORD and should be located here: HKEY_CURRENT_USER\Software\Oracle\Discoverer 10\Database.

If the AutogenNameOnCreate Registry setting is present in the Registry and its value is set to 1, Discoverer will do the following:

■ If you install the sample data, Discoverer will set the Auto-Generate name property for all secondary elements to Yes.

■ When you create new secondary elements, Discoverer will set the Auto-Generate name property to Yes.

■ When an item has its Auto-Generate name property value set to Yes, it will display in the EUL in a different color from the other items; e.g., it will display in blue if you are using the Windows default color scheme.

If you export EUL objects and then import the EUL objects using the /auto_gen_name command modifier in the EUL Command Line for Java (or the Discoverer Command Line interface), Discoverer will set the Auto-Generate name property to 'Yes' for all the secondary elements contained in the EUL objects that you exported and imported.

QUESTION: *I have deleted a folder from the Business Area but not the EUL. Now that it's not appearing, is there any way to remove it from the EUL?*

ANSWER: Oracle calls these orphaned folders, and yes, you will be pleased to know that Discoverer has a mechanism to delete them.

To delete an orphaned folder, use the following workflow:

1. Launch the Discoverer Administrator edition.

2. From the toolbar, select Tools | Manage Folders.

3. In the Manage Folders dialog box, click the Orphaned Folders tab.

4. Locate the folder that you do not want and click Delete.

NOTE
Previous versions of Discoverer do not have this feature; you will need to reassign the folder to a business area before you can delete it.

QUESTION: *I have the following condition in Discoverer: WHERE NAME IN :pNAME. The parameter :pNAME can accept multiple values like john, joe. How can I convert the multiple values to uppercase? Adding the function UPPER(:pNAME) to the condition will only return JOHN. I have also used my own function to convert the string and return an uppercase string to Discoverer, but Discoverer still uses only the first value. Is there a way to do this?*

ANSWER: You can do what you want by substituting another character for the comma and then using the REPLACE command to convert that character back into a commAnswer: You need to do this because the UPPER function converts a single string into its uppercase values. If you include a comma inside a parameter, such as "john, joe", Discoverer will treat this as two strings.

You will notice that the parameter itself gets transformed into 'john','joe'. Applying UPPER to this parameter will return just 'JOHN'.

However, if you key in multiple values using some character other than a comma as the delimiter, then it will work. Try using / so that the user keys in "john / joe". The answer will be JOHN / JOE.

Now you just use the REPLACE command, and voilà, the comma gets reinstated:

REPLACE(UPPER(":pNAME"),'/',',') will now return JOHN, JOE.

QUESTION: *I have a folder that is based on a view. I changed the folder to remove a column, yet when I launch Discoverer Admin and use File | Refresh, Discoverer says that there are no changes. Do you have any idea why?*

ANSWER: You probably forgot to drop the column name from the list of aliases as well. If you edit a view definition that uses aliases, you must remember to remove the column from both places. If you edit the view and only drop a column without altering the alias list, the view will compile incorrectly. However, if you don't realize this and you go to the Discoverer Administrator and do a File | Refresh, Discoverer will say nothing has changed. This is not an error because nothing really has changed yet—not until you alter the view correctly.

Let me explain with the following example:

```
CREATE OR REPLACE VIEW TEST_VIEW
(PRODUCT, DESCRIPTION, REASON)
AS
SELECT
TABLE1.PRODUCT_CODE,
TABLE2.PRODUCT_DESCRIPTION,
TABLE2.PRODUCT_RSN_CD
FROM
TABLE1, TABLE2
WHERE
TABLE1.ID = TABLE2.ID
```

Let's say we want to drop the REASON and edit the view like this:

```
CREATE OR REPLACE VIEW TEST_VIEW
(PRODUCT, DESCRIPTION, REASON)
AS
SELECT
TABLE1.PRODUCT_CODE,
TABLE2.PRODUCT_DESCRIPTION
FROM
TABLE1, TABLE2
WHERE
TABLE1.ID = TABLE2.ID
```

The view will not compile and will be invalid. However, if you don't spot this and try to refresh, Discoverer will think that there are no changes. Here is the correct alteration:

```
CREATE OR REPLACE VIEW TEST_VIEW
(PRODUCT, DESCRIPTION)
AS
SELECT
```

```
TABLE1.PRODUCT_CODE,
TABLE2.PRODUCT_DESCRIPTION
FROM
TABLE1, TABLE2
WHERE
TABLE1.ID = TABLE2.ID
```

QUESTION: *I want to trim a field that has this character in common : '|' For example, 17x75|WIDGET, 17.00 X .175 should display as just 17x75. Can you please help me or direct me to the right place?*

ANSWER: RTRIM will not do the job for you. It only eliminates spaces to the right of your field. You will need to use a combination of the INSTR and SUBSTR functions:

- **INSTR**   Finds the position of the character that you are seeking (for example, INSTR('17x 75|WIDGET','|') will return position 6).

- **SUBSTR**   Outputs part of a string. It takes two additional parameters, a start point and a length. It then returns a new string starting at the position you have nominated of the length you stated, e.g., SUBSTR('STRING', starting Position, Length).

As an example,

```
SELECT SUBSTR('17x75|TIRE', 1, INSTR('17x75|TIRE','|')-1) FROM DUAL;
```

will output '17x75' as required.

QUESTION: *I am using Desktop and my company has introduced a new database for me to connect to. Our DBA told me to update my TNS Names file, but I don't know where it is located. Can you help?*

ANSWER: The TNS Names file (tnsnames.ora) can be found here: $ORACLE_HOME/network/admin.

If you used an out-of-the-box installation of Desktop, your Oracle home will probably be: c:\oracle\BIToolsHome_1.

A typical TNS Names entry looks like this:

```
VIS =
  (DESCRIPTION =
    (ADDRESS = (PROTOCOL = TCP) (HOST = 192.168.2.116) (PORT = 1521))
    (CONNECT_DATA =
      (SID    = VIS)
  ))
```

Here, there are three important sections that you need to fill in:

- **HOST =**   You type in the IP address or the server name for the connection you want to make. If you are using a server name, you may also need to have an entry in your HOSTS file linking the server with its IP address.

- **PORT =**   You type in the number of the port for the database that you will be connecting to. The default port for all Oracle databases is 1521, but many DBAs will change this.

- **SID =**   You type in the database identifier provided by your DBA.

I usually copy and paste a good TNS entry inside my tnsnames.ora file, replacing the relevant entries with the items specified here. You also need to make sure that you assign a unique name to the entry. In the example shown, I have named this VIS. Inside Discoverer Desktop, I will use this name in the Connect box.

QUESTION: *I will be traveling around the country for my job and need to connect to various client systems in order to run Discoverer Plus. Someone told me that I should update my HOSTS file. Can you tell me a) where I can find this file, and b) what I must do to edit it?*

ANSWER: Every Discoverer server that is running Plus or Viewer, no matter whether this is Linux, UNIX or Windows, needs to have a fully qualified domain name (FQDN). This FQDN is then associated with a unique IP address. On the server, this is set inside the HOSTS file.

In Linux and UNIX you will find this file here: /etc.

In Windows you will find this file here: c:\windows\system32\drivers\etc.

In order for your laptop to connect to a client's Discoverer server, either the client needs to let you connect to their domain or you need to update your local HOSTS file. If the client has a DNS server and allows you to connect to their domain, you should have no issues.

However, in some situations where you cannot connect to the client's domain you will need to manually add a new entry to your HOSTS file. In Windows, as mentioned, you will find this in c:\windows\system32\drivers\etc. The good news is that this file can be edited with a standard text editor such as Notepad.

When you edit this file for the first time, it will have a single entry that looks like this:

```
127.0.0.1  localhost
```

Do not change this entry. To add a new entry to this file, you need to find out from the client the name of the server that they want you to use and the IP address that the server is using. Having obtained this information, you add the new entry to your HOSTS file using this syntax:

"IP address" "FQDN" "short name"

For example, if the client says that the server you should connect to is oraias.learndiscoverer.com and that it is using IP address 192.168.2.102, you should add the following entry and then save and close the file:

```
192.168.2.102 oraias.learndiscoverer.com oraias
```

When you save and close the HOSTS file, any changes that you made will take effect immediately. There is no need to reboot your laptop.

QUESTION: *We have an Oracle Apps EUL, and I have created a report which links the supplier header and sites with the invoices table. What I want is a list of the vendors who have never had a transaction. It sounded simple at the time, but I do not know how to create this report. Do you have any ideas?*

ANSWER: Presumably, what you have done is to join the vendor folder to your vendor sites and subsequently to your invoice folder. When you do this, you will get data for vendors who have transactions. If the vendor has no transactions, then the vendor record will not be available to your report.

There are two ways to overcome this within Discoverer. You can use either a subquery or a custom folder.

To use a subquery, use the following workflow:

1. Launch Discoverer Desktop—you cannot create subqueries using Plus.

2. Create a workbook that selects all vendors who have an invoice.

3.   Create a new worksheet in the same workbook and make this just a listing of vendors.

4.   Create a condition such that the vendor is not in the first worksheet.

NOTE

You cannot create a subquery in Plus. However, if you create the report in Desktop, you will be able to run it in both Plus and Viewer.

To use a custom folder, use the following workflow:

1.   Launch the Discoverer Administrator edition.

2.   Open the business area and folder that you want to work in.

3.   Right-click the business area, and from the pop-up menu select New Custom Folder.

4.   Type in some SQL that would bring up a list of vendors who do not have a transaction, such as

```
SELECT VENDOR_NAME
FROM VENDORS
WHERE VENDOR_NAME NOT IN
(SELECT VENDOR_NAME
FROM VENDORS VEND, TRANSACTIONS TRX
WHERE VEND.VENDOR_ID = TRX. VENDOR_ID)
```

5.   Give the folder a suitable name.

6.   Click the Validate SQL button and keep refining the SQL until it is valid.

7.   Close the Administrator edition.

8.   Open Plus and create a workbook against this new folder.

If you are comfortable with a custom folder, I recommend this approach because you have control over the SQL, performance will be better, and your users can create this report in Plus.

QUESTION: *We have a lot of SQL views that we would like to concert to run as custom folders in Discoverer. Do you know of a method for converting SQL to custom folders?*

ANSWER: Here are the basic rules for converting SQL code into code that is suitable for use within Discoverer:

■   There should be no hard-coded filters or constraints unless absolutely necessary, e.g., when constraining for a certain set of books.

■   There should be no optional parameters.

■   There should be no hard-coded formatting.

■   There should be no embedded formatting.

■   All columns should use aliases.

■   You should replace all parameters that are based on ID columns with meaningful descriptor columns that Discoverer users can build parameters against.

■   You should remove all Order By clauses.

- You should remove all subqueries, if at all possible.

- You should check the new code in SQL using a tool such as TOAD before you import it into Discoverer. This will allow you to work on the explain plan to optimize the code. Don't forget that when you test the code, you need to add additional where clauses equivalent to what a Discoverer user would do, e.g., AND RAC.CUST_NAME = 'SMITH'.

QUESTION: *We are using Oracle E-Business Suite and would like to know if you have a script that returns the party information.*

ANSWER: You should find the following script to be of use:

```
CREATE OR REPLACE VIEW DISCO_PARTIES_V
AS
SELECT
PRT.PARTY_NUMBER   ACCOUNT,
PRT.PARTY_NAME     ACCT_NAME,
PRT.PARTY_TYPE     PARTY_TYPE,
PRT.STATUS         STATUS,
PRT.CATEGORY_CODE  CATEGORY_CODE,
LOC.ADDRESS1       ADDRESS1,
LOC.ADDRESS2       ADDRESS2,
LOC.ADDRESS3       ADDRESS3,
LOC.ADDRESS4       ADDRESS4,
LOC.CITY           CITY,
LOC.POSTAL_CODE    POSTAL_CODE,
LOC.STATE          STATE,
LOC.COUNTRY        COUNTRY
FROM
APPS.HZ_PARTIES       PRT,
APPS.HZ_LOCATIONS     LOC,
APPS.HZ_PARTY_SITES   STE
WHERE
PRT.PARTY_TYPE   = 'ORGANIZATION'
AND STE.PARTY_ID    =  PRT.PARTY_ID      -- Party to Party Sites
AND STE.LOCATION_ID =  LOC.LOCATION_ID   -- Party Sites to Locations
```

QUESTION: *We are using Oracle E-Business Suite and would like to know if you have a script that returns the customer information.*

ANSWER: You should find the following script to be of use:

```
CREATE OR REPLACE VIEW DISCO_CUSTOMERS_V
AS
SELECT ALL
CUST.CUSTOMER_ID      CUST_ID,
CUST.CUSTOMER_NAME    CUST_NAME,
NVL(CUST.CUSTOMER_CLASS_CODE,'{Unknown}') CUST_CLASS_CODE,
CUST.CUSTOMER_NUMBER CUST_NUMBER,
DECODE(CUST.STATUS, 'A', 'Active',
   'I', 'Inactive', CUST.STATUS) CUST_STATUS
FROM
APPS.RA_CUSTOMERS CUST
```

QUESTION: *We have both the 10.1.2 and 4i versions of Discoverer. When I save a workbook to the database in 4i, I am unable to see the workbook in 10g. Am I doing something wrong?*

ANSWER: You are not doing anything wrong. The problem is that the 4*i* workbooks are stored in a table called EUL4_DOCUMENTS, whereas the 10*g* workbooks are stored in a table called EUL5_DOCUMENTS. The 10*g* version of Discoverer does not have access to the EUL4 tables, and conversely the 4*i* version does not have access to the EUL5 tables.

The reason for the difference is that the two end-user layers are different. They have different data structures and operate using different algorithms.

If you want to know which version of the EUL you are connected to, when you are logged in to Discoverer use Help | About from the menu bar. The 10*g* screen looks like this.

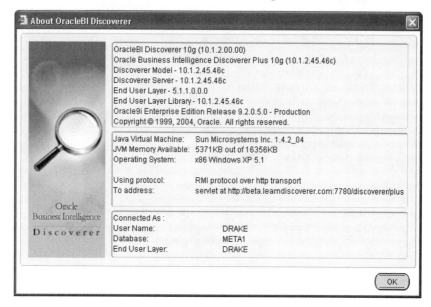

QUESTION: *Our working week always ends on a Friday. Can you tell me the code to use inside a Discoverer calculation that will return the date for Friday?*

ANSWER: When the end of the week is a Friday, use this code to get the date:

```
trunc(sysdate, 'ww')+6
```

Here are some more algorithms that you may find useful:

- **Yesterday**   trunc(sysdate)-1

- **Beginning of the current month**   trunc(sysdate, 'mm')

- **Beginning of the previous month**   add_months(trunc(sysdate, 'mm'),–1)

- **Monday of the current week**   trunc(sysdate, 'ww')+2

- **Beginning of the current quarter**   trunc(sysdate, 'Q')

- **End of the current month**   last_day(trunc(sysdate, 'mm'))

- **Beginning of last week** trunc(sysdate, 'ww')–5

- **Beginning of quarter 1** to_date('1/1/'||to_char(sysdate,'yy'), 'mm/dd/rr')

- **End of last year's quarter 1** to_date('3/31/'||to_char(sysdate-365,'yy'), 'mm/dd/rr')

Extending this example, why not create a function that allows a user to key a token, returning one of the preceding values. For instance, look at this function:

```
CREATE OR REPLACE function
disco_date(p_date in varchar2) return date is
the_results date;
Bad_Date_Submitted exception;
PRAGMA EXCEPTION_INIT(Bad_Date_Submitted, -20001);
BEGIN
if upper(p_date) = 'YESTERDAY' then
    the_results := trunc(sysdate)-1;
elsif upper(p_date) = 'BOM' then
    the_results := trunc(sysdate, 'mm');
elsif upper(p_date) = 'BOW' then
    the_results := trunc(sysdate, 'ww')+2;
elsif upper(p_date) = 'BOQ' then
    the_results := trunc(sysdate, 'Q');
end if;
return the_results;
EXCEPTION
when others then
    raise_application_error(-20001,'Use dd/mm/yy, dd-mm-yy or dd-mon-yy
    or yesterday, '|| 'bow, bom, boq', FALSE);
END;
```

If you execute this function as follows:

```
select disco_date('BOM') from dual
```

it will return the date corresponding to the beginning of the current month.

The next step would be to import this function into Discoverer and make it available to your end users inside a condition.

QUESTION: *Oracle tells me that Discoverer is not certified for use on a Citrix terminal server. We have no choice but to use a terminal server. Do you have any recommendations for optimizing Discoverer against a terminal server?*

ANSWER: Traditional terminal server environments place a single copy of Discoverer Desktop on the server and then allow Citrix to manage the multi-user access. First of all, you need to make sure that you purchase the relevant number of licenses for the number of users who will be accessing Discoverer. Desktop is licensed on a named user basis, not on a concurrent user basis, which means that you must own one license for every user who will be using Discoverer.

So with licensing taken care of, there are (aren't there always) some things to think about when setting up Citrix to work with Discoverer. These are the main ones:

- You need to determine whether you will be using anonymous connections or local connections. I recommend using an anonymous connection for standard users and a local connection for both administrators and users who need to have secure connections to areas such as finance and HR.

■ You need to think about whether users will be able to access their local drives and printers from within Citrix or whether you are going to set up and maintain these centrally.

■ I recommend the creation of a large, centrally located, shared folder either on the terminal server or on a dedicated server nearby for users to store workbooks and results of workbooks. You should have a predefined storage hierarchy such as a folder for each department or region in your company, and make users save into only the designated areas. If you don't do this, you will find that your terminal server(s) get clogged with user queries and output and you will have no idea who did it.

■ You need to discourage users from exporting within Discoverer directly to their desktops. Discoverer does not handle this sort of long-distance exporting very well. I recommend users save to a file on the central server first and then use Windows Explorer to copy the file to their local drive. Don't forget to tell users to delete the file on the central server to avoid wasting space; otherwise, well, you can guess what will happen next!

■ I recommend purging stored workbooks and output after a period of time. You need to determine what period of time is suitable for you, but somewhere in the range of 12 to 18 months should be considered a maximum.

■ You need to make sure that when users exit their session, no matter how they do it, their session is disconnected. This will prevent rogue sessions from staying open, consuming memory and terminal server sessions.

■ You need to make sure that user sessions are automatically disconnected after a reasonable period of inactivity. Most user sessions can safely be disconnected after 30 minutes, but you may need to increase this timeout to 120 minutes for some power users.

NOTE
Even though Discoverer may be running a query, if a user has done nothing on the terminal server screen for a while, Citrix thinks nothing is going on and will terminate the session. This is why you need to allow power users more time than ad hoc users. Training a user to occasionally visit the terminal server screen and move the mouse is sufficient to make Citrix think that there is some ongoing activity.

■ You need to make sure that you clean up your user profiles and temporary files on a weekly basis. You will find that the TEMP folder gets clogged with old sessions and profiles. These should be deleted. Citrix will not let you delete an active session. You will also find hundreds of files ending in .TMP in the Discoverer home folder. These should be removed too.

■ Discoverer does not scale well on a Citrix server, and unless you have plenty of processing power and memory available to the users, you will quickly find yourself out of resources. I have seen Citrix handle 16 Discoverer sessions with ease yet max out on CPU with 17 sessions.

QUESTION: *Can I upgrade from 4i to 10.1.2 directly, or must I go though some other version first?*

ANSWER: I am pleased to tell you that you can upgrade from 4*i* to 10.1.2 without upgrading via any intermediate release. The upgrade is very straightforward and should be painless. You basically install and launch the 10.1.2 Administrator Edition and connect as the owner of the 4*i* EUL. When you do this, Discoverer will display the following:

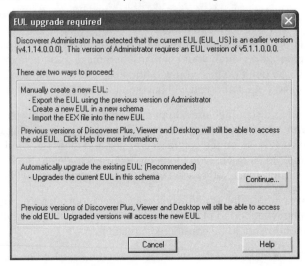

As you can see in this illustration, Discoverer has recognized that there is a 4.1 version of the EUL. The message tells you that you have two ways to continue:

■ Manually create a new EUL and then export / import the old one.

■ Automatically upgrade the existing EUL by clicking Continue.

Because the upgrade is easy, we recommend you take the automatic route. When you click Continue, Discoverer displays the following:

On this screen you are being advised that you should take a database export of your original EUL schema before starting the upgrade. As you can see, the button called Proceed with Upgrade is grayed out and will continue to be grayed out until you check the radio button confirming that you have completed a database export of your original EUL schema.

NOTE
Discoverer has no way of knowing whether you have or have not taken a database export. Even though most of the time this upgrade is 100 percent effective, because you are working with a database, any failure to create the upgrade, such as being out of tablespace, will require you to restore the schema to its original state. If you click the Confirm radio button without having taken an export, you proceed at your own risk!

Having taken the required export, check the Confirm button and then click Proceed with Upgrade.

As the upgrade continues, you will see all of your existing objects being upgraded. Toward the end of the upgrade you will see this message, saying that your workbook dependencies are being transferred.

Not long after this screen has been displayed, the EUL upgrade will finish and you will see the following screen.

At this point you have successfully upgraded your 4.1 EUL to 10.1.2. You will now need to install the Discoverer 10.1.2 end-user versions, Desktop, Plus, and Viewer, before your users can connect.

NOTE
The upgrade from version 4 to version 10.1.2 is nondestructive. This means that your original EUL will be unaffected by the upgrade and your users will be able to connect to both versions at the same time. After you have tested your upgrade, you should remove the old version 4 by running the script eul4del.sql in SQL*Plus when connected as the owner of the end-user layer.

QUESTION: *Two of our folders have data items that have a data type of LONG. We would like our users to be able to query these inside Discoverer reports. Do you know if there is a way to do this?*

ANSWER: Yes, this can be done. To make the data in a LONG variable available inside Discoverer, use the following workflow:

1. Launch the Discoverer Administrator tool.

2. Navigate to the business area and folder that contains the item.

3. Right-click the LONG item and from the pop-up menu, select Properties.

4. Set the Default Width to something like 50.

5. Set Max Char Fetched to the length that you want to see, e.g., 512.

6. Set Word Wrap to Yes.

7. Close the Item Properties dialog box.

This will allow your users to query the LONG item inside Discoverer. With these settings, Discoverer will wrap the first 512 bytes of the LONG item into a field that is 50 characters wide.

NOTE
Your users must never try to include a LONG item in the same query as the SUM of anything. A SUM causes SQL to add a GROUP BY clause, and you cannot use GROUP BY with a LONG item. Therefore, you must ensure that all data items are brought in using Detail.

QUESTION: *When I create a parameter I want to be able to give the users some form of context-sensitive help that will let them know how to fill in the parameter correctly. Is there a way to do this in Discoverer?*

ANSWER: When you are creating the parameter, you should use the box called Description as the placeholder for your context-sensitive help. This is a free-form box, and you can type anything you like. Here are some tips that might help:

■ In Plus, if you uncheck the box called "Require users to enter a value," you should tell users that if they leave the parameter blank, they will see all values. This parameter cannot be created in Desktop. However, your Desktop users will be able to run a query that users an optional parameter.

■ In both Desktop and Plus, there is a drop-down button to the right of the Default box. If this button is active, not grayed out, this means that a list of values exists for the parameter. You should let your users know that a list of values exist and advise them to select from the drop-down.

■ If you are aware that the value you are expecting from the user must be in any special form of casing, use the Description box to tell the users. For example, if the values in your Status are all in uppercase, you should tell the users this.

NOTE
If uppercase input is required, you might be better advised to alter the condition that is associated with the parameter to automatically uppercase the value returned from the keyboard. Supposing that the parameter name is Status, the use of UPPER(:Status) will do this.

QUESTION: *I have seen the term UIX referred to many times in conjunction with Discoverer Plus. Can you tell me what this stands for?*

ANSWER: The UIX (User Interface XML) is a set of Oracle technologies that constitute a framework for building web applications. The main focus of this UIX is the user interface layer of an application. There is also some added functionality that manage events and manage the state of the application flow.

In 10.1.2 the Oracle Discoverer Portlets and Discoverer Viewer pages are rendered using UIX rather than XSL, as was the case in previous versions. Therefore, if you want to make changes to the look and feel or layout, over and above what is possible with the Application Server Control, you now have the ability to change the appropriate UIX files—that is, if you feel confident about making such changes.

For more information concerning UIX, please take a look at the Oracle 10*g* XML Developer's Kits Guide, which you can find on OTN. The Oracle XML Developer Kit itself is a component of the Application Server.

The UIX files themselves are all located here:

$ORACLE_HOME/j2ee/OC4J_BI_Forms/applications/discoverer/discoverer

$ORACLE_HOME/j2ee/OC4J_BI_Forms/applications/discoverer/discoverer/UIX

NOTE
Before you start modifying these files, we cannot overly stress the importance of backing up the original files to a safe location before you start. The motto better safe than sorry has added significance here because you could easily stop your user interface from working if you make changes to a UIX file that you should not have changed.

QUESTION: *I have created a crosstab, and I created a calculation to take one of my data items and split it into two so that both values appear side by side, rather than use a grand total at the right. When I try to do this, I get an ORA-00979, not a GROUP BY expression. Can you help?*

ANSWER: Presumably you are seeing this message.

This is caused when you create a calculation wrong and you do not aggregate at the right level. Let me explain using my own database. I have created the following query:

			Order Qty SUM		
		▶ Channel	▶ EXTERNAL	▶ INTERNET	Sum
▶ Status	▶ Product Size				
▶ SHIPPED	▶ LARGE		2123507	2589045	4712552
	▶ MEDIUM		2898499	3225603	6124102
	▶ MINI		806964	1099803	1906767
	▶ SMALL		887777	1399649	2287426

As you can see, we have a grand total on the right. However, I think what you are asking for is to be able to see the data displayed like this:

Status	Product Size	Order Qty	External	Internet
▶ SHIPPED	▶ LARGE	4712552	2123507	2589045
	▶ MEDIUM	6124102	2898499	3225603
	▶ MINI	1906767	806964	1099803
	▶ SMALL	2287426	887777	1399649

This illustration shows a significant saving in real estate from the original. However, it is not so easy to create as you might think, not until you know the trick, anyway!

The trick is in the calculations used to define the two new items, External and Internet. I used the following CASE statement, with an outer SUM:

```
SUM(CASE WHEN Channel = 'EXTERNAL'
THEN "Order Qty" ELSE 0 END)
And
SUM(CASE WHEN Channel = 'INTERNET'
THEN "Order Qty" ELSE 0 END)
```

The GROUP BY error that you are seeing is caused when you create the calculations like this:

```
CASE WHEN Channel = 'EXTERNAL'
THEN "Order Qty SUM" ELSE 0 END)
```

Do you see the difference? Look carefully and you will see that the aggregation is being done outside of the CASE statement, rather than being an integral part of it. You might think that using a CASE of the Order Qty SUM would be correct, and it would be if it were not for the implied Group Sort that is being done on the Status.

By the way, if I convert this to a Table and rename the Order Qty heading to Total, I can create a tabular worksheet that has a row-wise total. Try doing this with standard totals and you will fail miserably because you can only create totals on columns in a table!

	Status	Product Size	Total	External	Internet
1	SHIPPED	LARGE	4712552	2123507	2589045
2		MEDIUM	6124102	2898499	3225603
3		MINI	1906767	806964	1099803
4		SMALL	2287426	887777	1399649

QUESTION: *Is there any way to filter the records for the last date of the month using Discoverer?*

ANSWER: You should create a calculated item using the function LAST_DAY() and then create a condition on this item. Assuming that the dates have already been truncated, the condition should look like this:

```
date_item = LAST_DAY(date_item)
```

Otherwise, you will need to use

```
TRUNC(date_item) = LAST_DAY(TRUNC(date_item))
```

This will return only rows where the date is the last day of the month.

QUESTION: *Do you know where the expressions or calculations that are used to create an item in a folder are stored? I can find the names of the items in the EUL5_Expressions table but not the calculation used to create them.*

ANSWER: You are actually looking in the right place because the table EUL5_EXPRESSIONS, or EUL4_EXPRESSIONS if working in 4*i*, contains the calculation. Mind you, at first glance you would never know it.

First of all, create a filter on this table to show only calculated items. You do this by setting EXP_TYPE = 'CI'. That's C for calculated and I for item. By the way, the other values are: JP for joins, CO for columns, and FIL for admin conditions.

Now that you have done that, look at the column called EXP_FORMULA1. This is the actual calculation. However, it is encrypted, which is why you would not at first glance spot that this is the column containing the calculation.

Taking a closer look at this column, you will see that it contains entries like the following:

```
[1,96]([6,101300],[6,101294])
    [1,102]([6,111099],[5,2,"1"],[5,1,"Yes"],[5,1,"No"])
    [1,61]([6,110527])
```

Each set of characters within square brackets is a code, and the important sets are those that begin with 1, 5, or 6. These are

- **1** Functions

- **5** Literal values

- **6** Pointers to other items in the EUL_EXPRESSIONS table

The sets that begin with 1 are functions and take two arguments like [1,96]. In fact, this one is the ninety-sixth function in the master list of functions. By the way, the master list of functions can be decoded by looking at the table called EUL5_FUNCTIONS. Search on the column called FUN_ID using the number of the function obtained from the second argument in the set, and then read the column called FUN_NAME. So, for example, when I search FUN_ID using 96, the FUN_NAME is *, which is the code for multiply. Incidentally, the database functions are in the range 1–99999, while user-defined PL/SQL functions have numbers greater than 99999. The database functions are numbered sequentially, while the user-defined ones come from the master EUL sequence number generator. You will therefore see gaps in the numbers above 99999. This is normal; you don't have missing functions.

The sets that begin with 5 have three arguments like [5,1,"Yes"] and [5,2,"1"]. These are literal values. The second argument in the set is the data type, where 1 is a String, 2 is a Number, and 4 is a Date, while the third argument is the actual literal itself.

The sets that begin with 6 have two values like [6,111099]. These are pointers to other items in the EUL5_EXPRESSIONS table. Use the second number in the EXP_ID column and then read off the EXP_NAME.

So, now that I have given you a lesson on EUL metadata, let me explain what the three earlier examples do.

In the case of [1,96]([6,101300],[6,101294]), because 1 means function and 96 means *, this simply means multiply the item 101300 by the item 101294.

In the case of [1,102]([6,111099],[5,2,"1"],[5,1,"Yes"],[5,1,"No"]), as 1,102 is the decode function, 5,2,"1" means take the numeric literal 1, while 5,1,"Yes" means use the string literal Yes and 5,1,"No" means use the string literal No. Putting all this together, we get: DECODE(item 111099,1,"Yes","No").

This is easy stuff, isn't it?

For [1,61]([6,110527]), because 1,61 is the TO_NUMBER function, this means TO_NUMBER(the item 110527).

QUESTION: *When I look inside the EUL5 tables, I see a column called NOTM. Do you know what this is used for?*

ANSWER: This stands for Number of Times Modified.

QUESTION: *When I create a simple OracleBI Discoverer worksheet, the default behavior includes the drill icon as part of the column heading. My users can click that drill icon and then "drill to related" items. Is there a way to stop this, i.e., disable or remove the drill icon?*

ANSWER: That setting is controlled in the Administrator edition on the Privileges page. Use the following workflow to turn off that privilege:

1. Launch Discoverer Administrator.

2. From the menu bar, select Tools | Privileges.

3. Select the user you want to work with.

4. On the Privileges tab, uncheck Item Drill.

5. Click OK. The drill icon will no longer appear.

If you want to adjust this for all users, and you have set up your EUL as a public EUL, you need to edit the privileges for the PUBLIC role.

QUESTION: *We are having a problem with the sessions in Discoverer, and I have a couple of questions. How can I increase the sessions in Discoverer and how can I prevent this from happening again? Here is the error message we are receiving:*

Attempt 1. CORBA protocol : Hard limit on number of sessions reached. Please contact your administrator or retry after some time. Hint: An administrator can further diagnose connection problems by running the "checkdiscoverer" script under <ORACLE_HOME>/discoverer/util.

ANSWER: It sounds like a memory issue, or that you have a large number of hanging sessions. Stopping and restarting the Discoverer services will probably have little impact because this won't cause the operating system to free up memory. I would reboot the server.

QUESTION: *We are running Discoverer Plus. How much memory do you suggest individual PCs should have? We are strictly using Discoverer Plus and Viewer and find the performance to be really slow.*

ANSWER: Your question concerning memory on the client is most interesting. Even though Plus and Viewer are web-based applications, the amount of memory available on the client does make a significant difference. I used to say that 512Mb was needed, but I have personally come across performance issues at a client whose machines have that amount of memory. My own laptop, which has 2Gb of RAM, has no such issues. I will therefore be recommending a minimum of 1Gb from now on with an optimum of 2Gb. If you can possibly afford it, your new Plus machines should have at least 1Gb and be capable of expanding to 2Gb should the need arise. Of course, if you can get 2Gb to begin with you will have far fewer issues.

QUESTION: *We are running Desktop across a T1 line from our branch office to our data center, which is located about 1000 miles away. Our queries run fine for the selection part of the query, but then take what seems like forever to sort. I have a worksheet that takes only 10 seconds to* *select the data, but then takes almost 5 minutes to complete the sorting. Do you have any idea of what could be wrong?*

ANSWER: I do indeed. After connecting to your system and examining the query you refer to, I noticed that the worksheet in question has a large number of complex calculations, using primarily the CASE function. I also noticed that it is using five sorts, three of which are based on these complex calculations. Upon further investigation, I spotted that you are using complex calculated items in your page items.

When you sort using a complex calculation based on a CASE statement every time two data elements are interchanged, their new positions are determined only after the re-execution of the complex functions for both data elements. Even though your final result only contains 400 rows of data, the three sorts based on complex calculated elements are generating thousands and thousands of function comparisons. Therefore, even though you may think your functions are being run once per row, they aren't. In addition, the placement of complex calculated items in the page items is tantamount to running yet more sorts!

Where possible you should not sort on complex calculated items. If these calculations use complex functions such as CASE and DECODE, I would go further and say that you should never sort by these items. You should also not place these items in your page items. If you really need to use these complex calculations, you ought to consider using a materialized view that precomputes the values in advance. Then you can pull in the data you need and sort it in one go. If you also supply a composite index that matches your conditions, the entire query will execute in no time at all.

I took the liberty of altering your worksheet, removing the page items and as many complex calculations as I could from the sorts. I was able to get the report to run in about 30 seconds. You need to edit your remaining workbooks and do likewise.

QUESTION: *I heard that I should disable automatic updates for the Sun Java Plug-In. Is this true and how do I do it?*

ANSWER: Yes, this is true. By default, the Sun JRE comes with an automatic update feature that will periodically update the JRE as newer versions become available. This update should be disabled to prevent future problems with Discoverer Plus. To disable the Sun JRE automatic updates, use the following workflow:

1. From the Windows Start menu, select Settings | Control Panel.
2. Double-click the icon for the Java ™ Control Page. It is usually named Java.
3. When the Java Control Panel opens, click the Update tab.
4. Uncheck the box labeled "Check for updates automatically."
5. Click OK to save and exit.

QUESTION: *My organization has a very strict policy when it comes to installing software on my PC. For example, I am not allowed to be a local administrator on my machine. When I launch the connection to Plus, it tries to install the Sun JRE but because I do not have administrative rights, the install fails. Is there a way for my IT department to install the Sun JRE software independently?*

ANSWER: Yes, your IT department can install the Sun JRE in advance by following this workflow:

1. Download the Sun JRE 1.4.2_4 software from the Sun website. It can be found at: http://java.sun.com/products/archive/j2se/1.4.2_04/index.html.

2. On this page, look for the 32-bit/64-bit for Windows entry.

3. Alongside this entry are two download links, one for JRE and one for SDK. Click on the download link under the heading JRE.

4. On the next page, you will need to read and accept the license agreement.

5. After checking the box labeled "Accept License Agreement," download the software labeled "Windows Offline Installation, Multi-Language." This file is about 15Mb in size.

6. Your IT staff should now connect to your machine as a local administrator and install the software. The Application Server will recognize that the software has already been installed and will not try to install it again, thus allowing Plus to run.

NOTE
The file that is downloaded is an executable, and at the time of going to press was called: jr2e-1_4_2_04-windows-i586-p.exe.

QUESTION: *I have created two worksheets and they are located in different workbooks. One of the worksheets uses a parameter that allows multiple values. However, when I created a hyper-drill from the other worksheet and tried to pass two parameters, the commas were removed, and the destination workbook reported that no data could be found. Are you aware of this and is there a workaround?*

ANSWER: Yes, I am aware of this and it is very inconvenient. As things stand right now, if I pass two parameters, as 1,2, across a hyper-drill, the parameter in the destination worksheet receives this as 12. For the time being, you will have to make sure that you pass single parameters across hyper-drills.

A workaround is to create multiple parameter entries in the destination worksheet and pass a single parameter value to each parameter in turn from the calling worksheet. I recommend you not get carried away, though, and suggest you limit the number of such parameters to three. In the destination worksheet you will need to allow for the passing of one, two or three parameter values by creating an appropriate complex Boolean condition.

NOTE
Boolean complex conditions are explained in detail in Chapter 12.

QUESTION: *I am a big user of Discoverer Plus and I am wondering if there is a way to disable the <All> from displaying as the last item in the page items in a tabular report? I seem to remember that our previous version of Discoverer did not do this.*

ANSWER: You are correct in your understanding that earlier versions of Discoverer did not add <All> to the dynamic list of values in page items for a table. You will be delighted to hear that if you follow this workflow you will be able to suppress this:

1. Edit the pref.txt file located on your mid-tier at this location: $ORACLE_HOME/ Discoverer/Util.

2. Locate the section called Database.

3. Locate the property called EnhancedAggregationStrategy.

4. Set this to 0.

5. Save the pref.txt and apply the preferences.

6. Launch Plus and run the tabular worksheet that contains the page items you would like to suppress.

7. From the menu bar, select Edit | Worksheet Properties.

8. Click the Aggregation tab.

9. Uncheck the recommended behavior and check either "Show values that cannot be aggregated as" or "Show the sum of the values in the contributing cells."

10. Look at the drop-down list of values alongside your page items. You should notice that the <All> value no longer displays.

NOTE
This only works in a tabular report and only in Plus. However, because this setting is stored with the worksheet, you can apply these on an individual worksheet basis.

QUESTION: *I have some calculations in my worksheet that result in integers. When I have a zero value in these calculations, they display as 00 instead of 0. Do you know why?*

ANSWER: Yes, this is caused by your default format, which is probably set to something like 99999990. You need to change this so that there is no zero at the end of the format mask. To correct this, use the following workflow:

1. Right-click in the column that is displaying as 00.

2. From the pop-up list select Format Data.

3. Click the Number tab.

4. Select Custom and from the list select 99999999.

5. Save this setting and your zero values will display correctly.

NOTE
If this is happening on data items that are pulled directly in from the EUL, your administrator has assigned the wrong default format for that item. Please bring this to his or her attention and ask them to remove the zero from the end of the format mask.

QUESTION: *When I customize a report in Portal and customize the same report in Viewer it seems as though I can customize different things. Do you have a list of the things that can be customized from within the two environments?*

ANSWER: I do indeed. I am glad you asked because this is a common area of confusion to users of all levels.

As you know, you can customize a Discoverer portlet within Portal. You can format data cells in a table or crosstab, add stoplight formats on cells or items, and even change the display formatting of numbers. For graphs you can choose to change the graph type (change a pie graph to a dual-y bar graph, for example), add or remove 3-D effects, or even add or remove gradients. You can also choose to display the worksheet as a table or crosstab, or graph, or both. You can make all of these changes without having to leave Portal.

This is very similar to the customizations you can do with Discoverer worksheets in Portal. If the portlet has the Analyze link enabled, you can launch the worksheet in Viewer. In there, you can make changes such as drilling, pivoting, slicing, and so on. Just as within Portal, you can also apply stoplight or conditional formats in Viewer, format the data, change the graph types, and so on, and then save these back to Portal as your own customizations.

Summary

Well, there you have it. You asked and I have answered. I hope you have as much fun reading through these answers as I had in putting them together for you.

APPENDIX
B

SQL Functions

his appendix contains an alphabetic listing of all of the SQL functions available within Discoverer. Each function is listed with its correct syntax, an explanation of its purpose or use, and the Discoverer folder in which you will find the function. For most functions, we will give you examples. We also explain in depth how to use the wildcard characters within Discoverer and give you an overview of how to use analytic functions.

We will give you a complete listing of all the format masks that can be applied to functions. Finally, we will give you a listing of the standard American Standard Code for Information Interchange (ASCII) character set.

We were complimented many times on this appendix following the publication of the first book. The intention was and still is to provide as comprehensive as possible an overview of the functions that are used within Discoverer. One of the amazing discoveries that we uncovered is the fact that not all of the functions perform exactly the same way that they do in standard SQL. This is because Oracle has tried to remove the possibility of crashes by trapping more error situations than you will find in normal SQL.

We are extremely pleased with the way that Oracle has implemented functions in Discoverer. If you know SQL, you will know that it can be very unforgiving—demanding that you get the syntax right. With Discoverer, most of the errors that you could make have been allowed for and will not cause your query to crash. Instead, the worst that can happen is that the function returns a null value.

This appendix is not designed to teach you all about SQL functions, only to explain in simple terms what each function does. If you want a complete understanding of Oracle's functions, we recommend you look at *Oracle Database 10*g*: The Complete Reference*, an Oracle Press book by Kevin Loney (McGraw-Hill/Osborne, 2004).

Standards Used in the Listing

Within the listing of the functions, we refer to data types. Functions usually operate on one data type at a time, although some may be able to use more. The following are the data types referred to in this appendix:

- **Date**   This data type represents a date, a date and time combination, or a data item that can be used like a date in an expression or calculation. Format masks can be applied to dates. A full listing of the date and time format masks can be found later in this appendix. Dates are entered within single quotes, for example 'JUL-24-2006'.

- **Character**   This data type consists of a single character. Examples of this data type are 'A', 'b', and '1'. Characters are entered into Discoverer surrounded by single quotes, as shown here, and can be in uppercase or lowercase.

- **Integer**   This data type represents whole numbers. These numbers can be positive or negative. Examples of this data type are –5, 0, and 50.

- **Number**   This data type represents numbers with decimal places. These numbers can be positive or negative. Examples of this data type are –5.15, 0, and 47.775. Format masks can be applied to numbers. A full listing of the numeric format masks can be found in the section "Number Format Masks" later in this appendix.

- **String** This data type represents combinations of characters and is entered into Discoverer surrounded by single quotes. Strings can use any combination of uppercase and lowercase characters. Examples of strings are 'Hello', 'ZIP 55555', and 'CAP'.

Wildcards

Many of the Discoverer functions will allow you to enter wildcard characters into strings. The wildcard characters used within Discoverer are as follows:

- **%** The percent symbol is a wildcard character used to represent any number of characters in a string. It can be used in any position and any number of times within the string.

- **_** The underscore character is a wildcard character used to represent a single character in a string. It can be used in any position and any number of times within the string.

Wildcard Examples

The following examples show how to use both of the wildcards in strings:

- **'AB%'** This would constrain the string to values beginning with the uppercase characters 'AB'. Valid examples of this are 'AB' and 'ABRACADABRA'.

- **'_b%'** This would constrain the string to values of any length, but where the second character is lowercase 'b'. Valid examples of this are 'Abbey' and 'Ebony'.

- **'%m%'** This would constrain the string to values that contain the lowercase character 'm' anywhere within the string. Valid examples of this would be 'mountain' and 'America'.

- **'941%'** When used in a condition against U.S. ZIP codes, this will constrain a worksheet to only return data for customers in San Francisco, California.

NOTE
When using the % wildcard character, there do not need to be any characters in the position indicated by the % character. Hence, in the preceding examples, 'AB' is a valid match for the constraint 'AB%' and 'mountain' is a valid match for '%m%'.

Folders in Discoverer

When you open a calculation in Discoverer and click the Functions radio button, Discoverer displays a list of folders. If the Discoverer Administrator has registered custom PL/SQL functions, you will see nine folders, including one called Database. If no custom PL/SQL functions are registered, then you will not see a folder called Database. As you can see in Figure B-1, our system has displayed nine folders.

FIGURE B-1 *The folders containing functions*

Alphabetical Listing of Functions

This section lists all of Discoverer's functions in alphabetical order.

NOTE
For completeness, we have included the syntax and basic description of each of the analytic functions in this appendix. For a more · complete description and overview of some of Discoverer's most useful analytic functions, please see the end of this appendix.

+ (Addition)

Syntax: value1 + value2
Description: value1 + value2 means add together the two values to produce a new value of the same type. This function can be used with data types of date, integer, and number, and generally you can mix the data types, although you cannot add numbers to dates.
Folder: Addition can be found in the Numeric folder, as seen in Figure B-2.
Examples:

- **Date**   SYSDATE + 1 returns tomorrow's date.

- **Integer**   177 + 192 + 6 returns the answer 375.

- **Number**   10.55 + 8.00 returns the answer 18.55.

- **Mixed**   177 + 10.55 returns the number 187.55.

NOTE
Multiple additions can be applied at the same time. In the second example, we added three integers to get the answer we were looking for. Generally, you can mix the data types, although you cannot add numbers to dates.

− (Subtraction)

Syntax: value1 − value2
Description: value1 − value2 means subtract the second value from the first value to produce a new value. This function can be only used with data types of date, integer, and number.
Folder: Subtraction can be found in the Numeric folder, as seen in Figure B-2.
Examples:

- **Date** '5-JUL-2006' – '25-JUN-2006' returns 10.

- **Mixed Date** SYSDATE – 1 returns yesterday's date.

- **Integer** 200 – 192 – 8 returns the answer 0.

- **Number** 10.55 – 8.00 returns the answer 1.45.

- **Mixed** 200 – 10.55 returns the number 189.45.

NOTE
Multiple subtractions can be applied at the same time. In the second example, we subtracted three integers to get the answer we were looking for. Generally, you can mix the data types, although you cannot subtract numbers from dates.

* (Multiplication)

Syntax: value1 * value2
Description: value1 * value2 means multiply the first value by the second value to produce a new value. This function can be only used with data types of integer and number.
Folder: Multiplication can be found in the Numeric folder, as seen in Figure B-2.

/ (Division)

Syntax: value1 / value2
Description: value1 / value2 means divide the first value by the second value to produce a new value. This function can be only used with data types of integer and number. You need to be very careful when using division that you do not finish up dividing by zero; otherwise, Discoverer will return an error. Please see Chapter 13 for tips on how to avoid division by zero errors.
Folder: Division can be found in the Numeric folder, as seen in Figure B-2.

|| (Concatenation)

Syntax: value1 || value2
Description: value1 || value2 means append or concatenate the character or string with the value of value2 to the end of the character or string in value1. The result is always a string. This function is identical to the CONCAT function described later.
Folder: Concatenation can be found in the String folder, as seen in Figure B-4.
Examples:

- **Character** 'A' || 'B' returns the string 'AB'.

- **String** 'Apple' || ' ' || 'Pie' returns 'Apple Pie'.

- **String** 'Moms' || ' ' || 'Apple' || ' ' || 'Pie' returns 'Moms Apple Pie'

NOTE
As you can see in the preceding example, you can combine multiple concatenation functions together in order to derive more complex strings.

- SUBSTR(SSN,1,3)||'-'||SUBSTR(SSN,4,2)||'-'||SUBSTR(SSN,6.4) takes a social security number (SSN) and converts it into the more typical format used in the United States. For example, if the SSN is 123456789, this example converts this to 123-45-6789.

- '('||SUBSTR(TEL,1,3)||')'||SUBSTR(TEL,4,3)||'-'||SUBSTR(TEL,7,4) takes a typical 10-digit telephone number and converts it into a more readable format. For example, if the number is 1234567890, this example converts it to (123) 345-7890.

NOTE
The two preceding examples combine multiple concatenation functions with the SUBSTR function.

ABS (Absolute Value)

Syntax: ABS(value)
Description: This function returns the absolute value of the item in parentheses, as a positive number, whether the original item is positive or negative. The item must be a number, whether this is a literal number, a string containing only numbers, the name of a column containing a number, or the name of a string column containing only numbers.
Folder: ABS can be found in the Numeric folder, as seen in Figure B-2.
Examples:

- ABS(-55) returns the value 55.

- ABS('18') returns the value 18.

- ABS(968.51) returns the value 968.51.

ACOS

Syntax: ACOS(value)
Description: This function returns the arc cosine of a value. The number x must be between –1 and 1. The function returns a value in the range of 0 to *pi*. The result is expressed in radians.
Folder: ACOS can be found in the Numeric folder, as seen in Figure B-2.
Example: ACOS(.2) returns 1.37

ADD_MONTHS

Syntax: ADD_MONTHS(date, integer)
Description: This extremely powerful function adds the integer number of months to the date specified, returning a new date that is that number of months in the future or in the past. The date specified must be a valid date. If the date you want to check is not currently a valid date, you must convert it into a valid date first. The second parameter should be an integer. If you provide a negative value, the date returned will be in the past. If you provide a number with decimal places, Discoverer ignores the decimal part. If the date you provide is the null value, then the result will be null.

FIGURE B-2   *Discoverer's numeric functions*

Folder: ADD_MONTHS can be found in the Date folder, as seen in Figure B-3.
Examples:

- ADD_MONTHS(SYSDATE, 1) returns the date one month from today.

- ADD_MONTHS(ship date, 2) returns the ship date plus 2 months.

- ADD_MONTHS(TO_DATE('JULY 24, 2006', 'MONTH DD, YYYY'),2) returns the date 24-SEP-2006. This takes the given date as a string, adds 2 months, and produces a new date. You cannot supply a string directly to ADD_MONTHS, because the date supplied *must* be a valid date in its own right.

- TO_CHAR(ADD_MONTHS(SYSDATE,1),'Month') returns the next month.

- TO_CHAR(ADD_MONTHS(SYSDATE,-1),'Month') returns the previous month.

- ADD_MONTHS(TRUNC(SYSDATE, 'YY'),12)-1 returns the end of the current year.

- ADD_MONTHS(TRUNC(SYSDATE,'Q'),-3) returns the beginning of last quarter.

ASCII

Syntax: ASCII(string)
Description: This function takes a string and returns the ASCII (American Standard Code for Information Interchange) value of the first character. The code is based on a series of numbers

from 0 to 254, with 65 representing the character 'A', 66 representing 'B', and so on. The numbers 0 through 9 are represented by the ASCII values 48 through 57. For the table of standard ASCII values, see the "ASCII Character Set" section later in this appendix.

See the function CHR for the opposite function that converts a number to a character.

Folder: ASCII can be found in the String folder, as seen in Figure B-4.

Examples:

- ASCII('A') returns the value 65.

- ASCII('BANANA') returns the value 66. Only the letter 'B' is used in the function.

- ASCII('-15') returns the value 45, because the minus sign is number 45 in the ASCII list.

ASCIISTR

Syntax: ASCIISTR(string)

Description: You may pass a string from any character set to ASCIISTR and it will return the string in ASCII. Non-ASCII characters will be converted to the form \xxxx. The xxxx represents a UTF-16 code. For the table of ASCII values, see the "ASCII Character Set" section later in this appendix.

Folder: ASCIISTR can be found in the Conversion folder, as seen in Figure B-6.

Example: ASCIISTR('ABÄCDE') returns AB\00C4CDE

ASIN

Syntax: ASIN(value)

Description: This function returns the arc sin of x. The number x must be between –1 and 1. The function returns a value in the range of 0 to *pi*. The result is expressed in radians.

Folder: ASIN can be found in the Numeric folder, as seen in Figure B-2.

Example: ASIN(.5) returns 0.5236

ATAN

Syntax: ATAN(x)

Description: This function returns the arc tangent of x. The value x can be in an unbounded range and returns a value in the range of -*pi*/2 to *pi*/2. The result in expressed in radians.

Folder: ATAN can be found in the Numeric folder, as seen in Figure B-2.

Example: ATAN(.4) returns 0.3805

ATAN2

Syntax: ATAN2(x , y)

Description: This function returns the arc tangent of x and y. The value x can be in an unbounded range and returns a value in the range of –*pi* to *pi*. The result depends on the signs of x and y, which are expressed in radians. ATAN2(x,y) is the same as ATAN(n/m).

Folder: ATAN2 can be found in the Numeric folder, as seen in Figure B-2.

Example: ATAN2(.3, .2) returns 0.9827

AVG (Average)

Syntax: AVG(value)

Description: This function returns the average. The value parameter can be any value, database item, or calculation. Discoverer has this function associated with every datapoint item, so a user

using Discoverer Desktop or Discoverer Plus usually does not need to use the AVG function from the New Calculation dialog box. A user creating a new item through Discoverer Administrator, or a user interested in using the Analytic features may find AVG quite useful. For details about the analytic clauses, please refer to the section called "Analytic Functions" later in this appendix.
Folder: AVG can be found in the Group and Analytic folders, as seen in Figures B-5 and B-7.
Example: AVG(Profit SUM) OVER(PARTITION BY Product Name ORDER BY Year)

AVG_DISTINCT

Syntax: AVG_DISTINCT(value)
Description: This function returns the distinct average of all the unique items in the list. Please note that null values are ignored by this function, a fact that may affect your results.
Folder: AVG_DISTINCT can be found in the Group and Analytic folders, as seen in Figures B-5 and B-7.
Example:

- AVG_DISTINCT(list)   When the list contains "null, 1, 1, 3, 5, 5, 5, 5, 7, 7, 7", the answer is 4. This is because Discoverer computes the average of the values 1, 3, 5, and 7. If we had used AVG on this same list, the answer would have been 4.6. Which one is correct depends upon your viewpoint and how you want to display the result.

CASE

Syntax: CASE WHEN x THEN y ELSE z END equates to the following:
  IF value = x THEN y ELSE z
Description: This expression, like DECODE, is extremely powerful and flexible. After the WHEN clause you may include any Boolean logic. If the logic after WHEN evaluates to TRUE, the result will be y. If the logic after the WHEN is FALSE, the result will be z. You can also embed CASE statements one within another. If you do this, do not forget that each statement ends with the word END; otherwise, Discoverer will generate an error. The y and z components must be the same data type.
Folder: CASE can be found in the Others folder, as seen in Figure B-8.
Examples:

- CASE WHEN 1=2 THEN 'Hello' ELSE 'Goodbye' END returns Goodbye because 1=2 always evaluates to false.

- CASE WHEN ship_date > order_date + 14 THEN 'Delivery Late' ELSE 'Delivery on Time' END returns the phrase Delivery on Time if the order was shipped within two weeks of the order date. However, if it took more than two weeks to ship the order then the phrase Delivery Late will be returned.

- CASE WHEN test_value < 0 THEN 'CR' || test_value ELSE test_value END returns a number prefixed by the CR characters if the test value is less than zero. This is useful for reports in the banking industry.

- CASE WHEN status = 'SHIPPED' THEN 'Customer has the Goods' ELSE CASE WHEN status = 'CANCELED' THEN 'Customer Canceled' ELSE 'Order is Open' END END returns the string 'Customer has the Goods' if the status of the customer's order is SHIPPED, the string 'Customer Canceled' if the status of the order is CANCELED, or 'Order is Open' in all other cases.

CEIL

Syntax: CEIL(value)
Description: This function takes the value given and returns the smallest integer larger than or equal to that value. Refer to FLOOR for the function that returns the highest integer. You cannot use the null value in this function. If you use the null value the result will be an error.
Folder: CEIL can be found in the Number folder, as seen in Figure B-2.
Examples:

- CEIL(7) returns the value 7.

- CEIL(-6.75) returns the value –6.

- CEIL(100.55) returns the value 101.

CHARTOROWID

Syntax: CHARTOROWID(string)
Description: This function takes a string and makes it act like an internal Oracle row identifier. This function should never be needed for reporting. It apparently is used as a debugging tool yet somehow has made its way into Discoverer.
Folder: CHARTOROWID can be found in the Conversion folder, as seen in Figure B-6.

CHR (Character)

Syntax: CHR(integer)
Description: This function takes an integer and returns the ASCII (American Standard Code for Information Interchange) character that corresponds to the integer. The code is based on a series of numbers from 0 to 254, with 65 representing the character 'A', 66 representing 'B', and so on. The numbers 0 through 9 are represented by the ASCII values 48 through 57. For the table of ASCII values see the "ASCII Character Set" section later in this appendix.

See the function ASCII for the opposite function that converts a character into a number.
Folder: CHR can be found in the String folder, as seen in Figure B-4.
Examples:

- CHR(45) returns the character that is the minus sign.

- CHR(65) returns the character 'A'.

- CHR(66) returns the character 'B'.

NOTE
Discoverer will only convert numbers to ASCII if the number is less than 128. If you try to use numbers greater than 127, Discoverer returns #NUM!

COALESCE

Syntax: COALESCE(value1, value2, value3)
Description: This function takes a list of values, scans the list, and then returns the first non-null value in the list. The list is scanned in the order in which you supply the values.
Folder: COALESCE can be found in the Others folder, as seen in Figure B-8.

Examples:

- COALESCE(NULL, NULL, NULL, NULL, 4004, NULL, NULL) returns 4004.

- COALESCE(manufacturers_suggested_retail_price, wholesale_price * 2, 3000) will return 3000 if both the manufacturer's suggested retail price and the wholesale price are null; otherwise, it returns whichever non-null price is found first.

CONCAT

Syntax: CONCAT(value1, value2)
Description: CONCAT(value1, value2) means append or concatenate the character or string with the value of value2 to the end of the character or string in value1. The result is always a string. This function is identical to the || function described earlier, except that when you want to concatenate multiple items, you must use multiple sets of parentheses.
Folder: CONCAT can be found in the String folder, as seen in Figure B-4.
Examples:

- **Character**   CONCAT('A', 'B') returns the string 'AB'.

- **String**   CONCAT('Apple ', 'Pie') returns 'Apple Pie'.

- **String**   CONCAT('Apple', CONCAT('Pie ', CONCAT('is ', 'excellent'))) is an example of using multiple CONCAT statements together. This returns the single string 'Apple Pie is excellent'.

CONVERT

Syntax: CONVERT(string, destination_set [, source_set]])
Description: This function takes a string and converts all the characters from one standard bit representation, or set, to another set. You would normally do this when the characters cannot be properly displayed on your screen or printed. To find out what character set is currently in use on your system, use the USERENV function.
Folder: CONVERT can be found in the Conversion folder, as seen in Figure B-6.
Example sets:

- **F7DEX**   Digital's 7-bit ASCII for France

- **US7ASCII**   The standard 7-bit ASCII set

- **WE8DEC**   Digital's 8-bit ASCII set for Western Europe

- **WE8HP**   Hewlett Packard's 8-bit ASCII set for Western Europe

- **WE8ISO8859P1**   International Standards Organization's 8859-1 8-bit character set for Western Europe. See the last section of this appendix for more about this character set.

CORR (Correlation)

Syntax: CORR(value1, value2)
Description: This statistical function returns the coefficient of correlation of value1 and value2. It is known as Pearson's Product Moment (PPM) correlation coefficient, r. Simply, the sample correlation coefficient is a measure of extent to which two values are linearly related. Pearson's

r-values can range between –1.00 to +1.00. A correlation coefficient of +1.00 signifies a perfect positive relationship, while –1.00 shows a perfect negative relationship. The smallest correlation is zero.

Smallest correlation also means no correlation; therefore, a correlation of zero signifies that there is no correlation between the two values.

Folder: CORR can be found in the Group and Analytic folders, as seen in Figures B-5 and B-7.

Examples:

- CORR(list_price, min_price) calculates the coefficient of correlation between the list price and the minimum price.

- CORR (SUM(ship_price), SUM(quantity_shipped)) OVER (ORDER BY ship_month) calculates the cumulative coefficient of monthly sales revenue and monthly units sold.

COS (Cosine)

Syntax: COS(value)

Description: This function takes the value given and returns the trigonometric cosine of that value. The function returns an angle expressed in radians.

Folder: COS can be found in the Numeric folder, as seen in Figure B-2.

Examples:

- COS(-60) returns the value 0.5

- COS(0) returns the value 1.0

- COS(180) returns the value –1.0

COSH (Hyperbolic Cosine)

Syntax: COSH(value)

Description: This function returns the hyperbolic cosine of the given value. The function returns an angle expressed in radians.

If you are mathematically oriented, the hyperbolic cosine is defined as $\cosh(x) = (e^x + e^{-x})/2$.

Folder: COSH can be found in the Numeric folder, as seen in Figure B-2.

Examples:

- COSH(0) returns the value 1.0.

- COSH(0.3) returns the value 1.04534.

- COSH(0.9) returns the value 1.43309.

COUNT

Syntax: COUNT(expression)

Description: This function returns a count of the number of non-null items in the given expression.

Folder: COUNT can be found in the Group and the Analytic folders, as seen in Figures B-5 and B-7.

Examples:

- COUNT(Order_Number) returns a count of the number of orders. If you include a condition such as Order Month = 'JULY 2006' and then use the COUNT(Order Number), this will return the number of orders placed in July 2006.

■ COUNT(DECODE(age_count, 'over 12', 1, NULL)) ensures that the result of the DECODE can be aggregated. If you try adding a total to a calculation such as DECODE(age_count, 'over 12',1, NULL) and any of the rows evaluate to NULL, you will not get a total. However, if you place the COUNT function around the calculation, Discoverer will now be able to compute the total.

COUNT_DISTINCT

Syntax: COUNT_DISTINCT(expression)
Description: This function returns a count of the number of non-null, unique items in the given expression. Please note that null values are ignored by this function, which may affect your results.
Folder: COUNT_DISTINCT can be found in the Group and the Analytic folders, as seen in Figures B-5 and B-7.
Example:

■ **COUNT_DISTINCT(list)**   When the list contains "null, 1, 1, 3 ,5, 5, 5, 5, 7, 7, 7", the answer is 4. This is because Discoverer only counts the items 1, 3, 5, and 7. If we had used COUNT on this same list, the answer would have been 10. Which one is correct depends upon your viewpoint and how you want to display the result.

COVAR_POP

Syntax: COVAR_POP(value1, value2)
Description: This statistical function returns the population covariance of two values. The population covariance of two values is the product of their deviations from their population mean.
Folder: COVAR_POP can be found in the Group and Analytic folders, as seen in Figures B-5 and B-7.

COVAR_SAMP

Syntax: COVAR_SAMP(value1, value2)
Description: This statistical function returns the sample covariance of two values.
Folder: COVAR_SAMP can be found in the Group and the Analytic folders, as seen in Figures B-5 and B-7.

CUME_DIST

Syntax: CUME_DIST(value1, value2)
Description: This statistical function calculates the cumulative distribution of a single value among a group of values. CUME_DIST will return values that are greater than 0 and less than or equal to 1. When the values are the same, they always evaluate to the same cumulative distribution value.
Folder: CUME_DIST can be found in the Group and the Analytic folders, as seen in Figures B-5 and B-7.

CURRENT_DATE

Syntax: CURRENT_DATE
Description: This function returns the current date of the user's database session. A traditional alternative is SYSDATE. It is important to understand that SYSDATE is the date of the database server whereas CURRENT_DATE is sensitive to the location of the user submitting the query. For

this function to be useful, the user must submit an ALTER SESSION SET TIME_ZONE = 'number' command upon connecting to the database.

Folder: CURRENT_DATE can be found in the Date folder, as seen in Figure B-3.

DBTIMEZONE

Syntax: DBTIMEZONE

Description: This function returns the time zone of the database server.

Folder: DBTIMEZONE can be found in the Date folder, as seen in Figure B-3.

Examples:

- DBTIMEZONE will returns +08:00 if the user is eight hours ahead of GMT.

- DBTIMEZONE will return America/Denver if the DBA has altered the database and set this zone as the server time zone.

> **NOTE**
> *The following SQL: select tzname, tzabbrev from V$TIMEZONE_ NAMES where zabbrev = 'MST' lists all of the time zone names within the Mountain Standard Time zone.*

DECODE

Syntax 1: DECODE(value, x, y, z) equates to the following:

IF value = x THEN y ELSE z

Syntax 2: DECODE(value, x1, y1, x2, y2, z) equates to the following:

IF value = x1 THEN y1 ELSE IF value = x2 THEN y2 ELSE z

> **NOTE**
> *The x and y values in the preceding function are grouped together as a parameter set and can be repeated as many times as are required.*

Description: This function is, in our opinion, one of the most powerful and useful of all of Discoverer's functions. Mastery of this function lies at the heart of unlocking the true power of Discoverer.

As stated in the syntax, the basic structure of this function is:

IF value = x (where value can be any expression, algorithm, data value, or literal)

THEN y

ELSE z – the default value

The DECODE statement can, and frequently does, check multiple values, culminating eventually with an ELSE, the default expression to be used when all else fails. You can also embed DECODE statements inside one another, which when mixed with other functions, makes for very powerful algorithms. If no default expression is specified, the result of DECODE will be the null value.

When using the DECODE statement, you might think that you always have to find a value that equates to equality. However, this is not the case, and Discoverer can be made to work with values greater than, equal to, and less than. To do this though, you will have to create special calculations using the SIGN function. The final example shows this construct. You may use the CASE expression as an alternative to DECODE.

Folder: DECODE can be found in the Others folder, as seen in Figure B-8.

Examples:

■ **DECODE(requested date, SYSDATE, 'Y', 'N')**   In this example, if the requested date equals the current date, then the function returns the value 'Y'; otherwise, the value 'N' is returned. This algorithm can be used to work out which orders are due for shipment.

NOTE
You will need to use the TRUNC function in conjunction with the preceding code in cases where your system stores the time as well as the date in the requested date column. The preceding example would then become: DECODE(TRUNC(requested date), TRUNC(SYSDATE), 'Y', 'N').

■ **DECODE(code value, 123, 'Classic', 456, 'Old Style', 'New Style')**   In this example, if the code value is 123 the function returns the value 'Classic', and if the code value is 456, the function returns the value 'Old Style'. If the code value is neither 123 nor 456, the function returns the value 'New Style'.

■ **DECODE(SOB_ID,1,'NON-REGULATED',2,'REGULATED', 'UNKNOWN')**   This example looks at the parameter called SOB_ID (which presumably stands for the Sets of Books ID), and if this is 1, it returns the value NON-REGULATED. If the parameter contains 2, the function returns the value REGULATED. Any value other than 1 or 2 will cause the function to return UNKNOWN.

■ **DECODE(customer, 'ABC', DECODE(SUM(owed), 0, 5000, 5000 – (SUM(owed) / 2)), 10000)**   This more complicated example calculates customer credit limits. If the customer is 'ABC' and the total amount owed is zero, then the credit limit is set to 5000. However, if the total amount owed by 'ABC' is not zero, then we set their credit limit to be 5000 minus half the amount owed. Finally, for all other customers, the credit limit is set to 10000.

■ **DECODE(SIGN(SUM(owed) / 15000), -1, 20000, 20000 – SUM(owed))**   This is a clever combination of the SIGN and DECODE functions. Because SIGN returns a value of –1 for all numbers less than 1, if the amount owed by the customer is less than 15000, we will allow them to have a credit limit of 20000; otherwise, the credit limit is reduced by the amount owed.

■ **DECODE(ITEM,LEAST(ITEM,26),'0-25',DECODE(ITEM,LEAST(ITEM,51),'26-50',DECODE(ITEM,LEAST(ITEM,76),'51-75','Over 75')))**   This example is explained as follows:

IF ITEM equals the lesser of the ITEM or 26

THEN include the item in the set called '0-25'

ELSE IF the ITEM equals the lesser of the ITEM or 51

THEN include the item in the set called '26-50' and so on, which means that we are categorizing ITEM into buckets of (0 to 25, 26 to 50, 51 to 75, over 75).

NOTE
The preceding example is a clever way to overcome the fact that DECODE(a,b,c,d) requires a and b to be equal, thus allowing constructs such as these:
IF a < b
THEN c
ELSE d

DENSE_RANK

Syntax: DENSE_RANK() OVER (PARTITION BY value1 ORDER BY value2)
Description: This function computes rank. If it is given a row within an ordered group of rows, it will returns the numerical rank starting with the number 1. When a tie occurs, all numbers within the tie will be given the same ranking. It is dense, as no ranking numbers are skipped. This function is useful to find the top or bottom *n* values. For example, if I wanted to find the ten best sales representatives and half of the sales representatives sold exactly $10000 and the other half sold exactly $20000, the first half would all be ranked with 1 and the second half would all be ranked with 2.
Folder: DENSE_RANK can be found in the Group and Analytic folders, as seen in Figures B-5 and B-7.
Example:

- DENSE_RANK() OVER (ORDER BY salary DESC) could be used alongside a grade to return values like this:

Grade	Student	Salary
1	abc0	5000
2	abc1	4000
2	abc2	4000
3	abc3	3500
4	abc4	3000

If you are using page items or group sorts, make sure you include a PARTITION BY clause. See the section on analytic functions later in this appendix.

DUMP

Syntax: DUMP(string [, format [, start [, number_to_dump]]])
Description: This function takes a string and displays it in a new format. The function optionally takes a start position and length. If these are provided, Discoverer dumps the string from the start position for the number of characters specified. The format can be 8 for octal, 10 for decimal, 16 for hex, and 17 for character.
Folder: DUMP can be found in the Others folder, as seen in Figure B-8.
Example:

- DUMP('michael', 16) returns 'Type=96 Len=7: 6d,69,63,68,61,65,6c' where each character of the string was dumped into hex.

FIGURE B-3 *Discoverer's date functions*

EUL_DATE_TRUNC

Syntax: EUL_DATE_TRUNC(date, format)

Description: This function takes a date and a format mask and truncates the date based on the format mask. The date specified must be a valid date. If the date you want to check is not currently a valid date, you must convert it into a valid date first. This function is automatically used by Discoverer when the administrator creates a date hierarchy.

Folder: EUL_DATE_TRUNC can be found in the Date folder, as seen in Figure B-3.

Examples: In the following examples, suppose that the current date is 24-JUL-06.

- EUL_DATE_TRUNC(SYSDATE,'YY') returns '01-JAN-06'.   Because we only specified the year within our format, Discoverer truncated the current date to the earliest date of the year.

- EUL_DATE_TRUNC(SYSDATE, 'MM') returns '01-JUL-06'.   Because we specified just the month within our format, Discoverer truncated the current date to the earliest date of the current month.

- EUL_DATE_TRUNC(SYSDATE, 'DD') returns '24-JAN-06'.   Because we specified just the day within our format, Discoverer truncated the current date to the earliest day of the year equal to the current day.

EXP (Exponential)

Syntax: EXP(*n*)

Description: This function returns *e* to the *n*th power, where *e* is the universal constant 2.718281828. It goes on forever repeating the numbers 1828, but for Discoverer usage, the number given here will suffice.

The opposite of EXP(*x*) is the natural logarithm LN(*x*), so that if you compute the exponential of the natural logarithm LN(*x*), you get *x* back. This works either way, as seen in the examples that follow.

Folder: EXP can be found in the Numeric folder, as seen in Figure B-2.

Examples:

- EXP(1) returns the universal constant, 2.718281828.

- EXP(4) returns the value 54.589150—that is, 2.718281828 to the power 4.

- EXP(LN(8)) returns the number 8.

FIRST_VALUE

Syntax: FIRST_VALUE(expr [IGNORE NULLS]) OVER (PARTITION BY expr1 ORDER BY expr2 RANGE BETWEEN expr3 AND expr4)

Description: This function returns the first value in an ordered set of values. If the first value is null, then the function returns null. If you specify IGNORE NULLS, then the function will return the first non-null value within the ordered list, somewhat similar to the COALESCE function.

Folder: FIRST_VALUE can be found in the Analytic folder, as seen in Figure B-7.

FLOOR

Syntax: FLOOR(value)

Description: This function takes the value given and returns the highest integer smaller than or equal to that value. Refer to CEIL for the function that returns the largest integer.

Folder: FLOOR can be found in the Numeric folder, as seen in Figure B-2.

Examples:

- FLOOR(7) returns the value 7.

- FLOOR(-6.75) returns the value –7.

- FLOOR(100.55) returns the value 100.

- TO_CHAR(DECODE(Cost,FLOOR(Cost),FLOOR(Cost),ROUND(Cost,1))) will return an integer if cost has no decimal places, and will round the original value to one decimal place if the cost has decimal places. For example, if Cost = 1000.00, this function returns 1000, but if the cost is 675.55, it will return 675.6. If the Cost is 5.99, it will return 6.

NOTE
The preceding example shows a practical use for combining the TO_CHAR, FLOOR and ROUND functions.

GLB

Syntax: GLB(label)

Description: This function is an operating system function and would not normally be used within Discoverer. It returns the greatest lower bound of a secure operating system label.

Folder: GLB can be found in the Group folder, as seen in Figure B-5.

GREATEST

Syntax: GREATEST(value1, value2, ...)
Description: This function returns the value that is the greatest of the given list of values. If one of the arguments in the list is the null value, the result will be null. You can use all of the data types with this function, although some unexpected results may occur if you are not careful. The number 27 is obviously greater than the number 7, but the string '7' is greater than the string '27'. Strings are compared using their ASCII number. You therefore must be careful when comparing strings, especially if those strings contain dates or numbers. If you want to compare dates that are stored as strings, you must use the TO_DATE function. If you want to compare numbers that are stored as strings, you must use the TO_NUMBER function.
Folder: GREATEST can be found in the Others folder, as seen in Figure B-8.
Examples:

- GREATEST(9, 18, 5, 60) returns the value 60.

- GREATEST('23-JUN-06','14-OCT-06') returns the string '23-JUN-06'.

- GREATEST(TO_DATE('23-JUN-06'), TO_DATE('14-OCT-06')) returns the date 14-OCT-06.

- GREATEST(TO_NUMBER('2'), TO_NUMBER('14')) returns the number 14.

GREATEST_LB

This function has been dropped from the current version of Discoverer. If you have any workbooks that use this function, you will need to use an alternative function.

HEXTORAW

Syntax: HEXTORAW(hex_string)
Description: This function changes a character string of hex numbers into binary.
Folder: HEXTORAW can be found in the Conversion folder, as seen in Figure B-6.

INITCAP (Initial Capitals)

Syntax: INITCAP(string)
Description: This function takes a string and returns a new string with the first letter of each word capitalized. The function also recognizes the presence of punctuation and uppercases the first letter following any punctuation. The punctuation symbols include the comma, period, colon, semicolon, hyphen, and so on.
Folder: INITCAP can be found in the String folder, as seen in Figure B-4.
Examples:

- INITCAP('armstrong-smith') returns 'Armstrong-Smith'.

- INITCAP('the cat is on the mat') returns 'The Cat Is On The Mat'.

INSTR

Syntax: INSTR(string1, string2 [, start [, n]])
Description: This function takes a string and finds the position of a second string in that string. The function will optionally begin the search at a given start position and return the position of the nth set. If you omit the start position, Discoverer will search from the beginning. If you use a

negative number for the start, Discoverer begins the search at the end of the string and searches backward. If you use zero for the start position, the answer will be zero.

Folder: INSTR can be found in the String folder, as seen in Figure B-4.

Examples:

- INSTR('San Francisco', 'an') returns 2.

- INSTR('San Francisco', 'an', 1, 2) returns 7.

- INSTR('San Francisco', 'an', -1, 2) returns 2.

This function is quite useful when used nested inside of the SUBSTR function.

Further Examples:

- SUBSTR('Jackson, Arnold', 1 ,INSTR('Jackson, Arnold', ',')-1) returns Jackson.

- SUBSTR('McFly, Marty', 1 ,INSTR('McFly, Marty', ',')-1) returns McFly.

NOTE
As you get used to working with the INSTR function, you will find that you will also be using the SUBSTR function more times than not.

INSTRB

Syntax: INSTRB(string, set [, start [, occurrence]])

Description: This function, like INSTR, takes a string and locates the position of a set of characters in that string. However, INSTRB locates the string you are looking for at the byte position. Within Discoverer, we recommend you use INSTR instead of this function.

Folder: INSTRB can be found in the String folder, as seen in Figure B-4.

LAG

Syntax: LAG(expr, n) OVER (PARTITION BY expr1 ORDER BY expr2)

Description: This function allows you to compare one row in set of rows to another row in the same set. You may now say good-bye to your slow friend the self-join. In the OVER clause you specify how to group and sort a set of rows. In the LAG clause you specify what column's values you want returned, and how many rows to lag behind to determine what value to return.

Folder: LAG can be found in the Analytic folder, as seen in Figure B-7.

LAST_DAY

Syntax: LAST_DAY(date)

Description: This function returns the date that is the last day of the month for a given date. The date specified must be a valid date. If the date you want to check is not currently a valid date, you must convert it into a valid date first. If you supply a null date, then the result will also be null.

Folder: LAST_DAY can be found in the Date folder, as seen in Figure B-3.

Examples:

- LAST_DAY(TO_DATE('16-OCT-06')) returns 31-OCT-06.

- LAST_DAY(ship date) returns the last day of the month in which the item shipped. Setting a condition such that ship_date = LAST_DAY(ship_date) will produce a report showing only the shipments that were sent on the last day of the month. You could use this to analyze last minute shipments.

- LAST_DAY(TO_DATE('')) returns null.

LAST_VALUE

Syntax: LAST_VALUE(expr [IGNORE NULLS]) OVER (PARTITION BY expr1 ORDER BY expr2 RANGE BETWEEN expr3 AND expr4)
Description: This function returns the last value in an ordered set of values. If the last value is null, then the function returns null. If you specify IGNORE NULLS, then the function will return the last non-null value within the ordered list.
Folder: LAST_VALUE can be found in the Analytic folder, as seen in Figure B-7.

LEAD

Syntax: LEAD(expr, n) OVER (PARTITION BY expr1 ORDER BY expr2)
Description: This function allows you to compare one row in set of rows to another row in the same set. Like LAG, this function may be used as an alternative to performing a self-join. In the OVER clause you specify how to group and sort a set of rows. In the LEAD clause you first specify what column you want returned. The second argument specifies how many rows ahead you want to receive the value from.
Folder: LEAD can be found in the Analytic folder, as seen in Figure B-7.

LEAST

Syntax: LEAST(value1, value2, …)
Description: This function returns the value that is the least of the given list of values. If one of the arguments in the list is the null value, the result will be null. You can use all of the data types with this function, although some unexpected results may occur if you are not careful. The number 7 is obviously less than the number 27, but the string '7' is greater than the string '27'. The date 24-JUL-06 is prior to 14-OCT-06, but the string '24-JUL-06' is greater than the string '14-OCT-06'. Strings are compared using their ASCII number. You therefore must be careful when comparing strings. If you want to compare dates that are stored as strings, you must use the TO_DATE function. If you want to compare numbers that are stored as strings, you must use the TO_NUMBER function.
Folder: LEAST can be found in the Others folder, as seen in Figure B-8.
Examples:

- LEAST(9, 18, 5, 60) returns the value 5.

- LEAST('24-JUL-06','14-OCT-06') returns the string14-OCT-06'.

- LEAST(TO_DATE('24-JUL-06'), TO_DATE('14-OCT-06')) returns the date 24-JUL-06.

- LEAST(TO_NUMBER('2'), TO_NUMBER('14')) returns the number 2.

NOTE
The LEAST function works very well inside the DECODE statement to handle calculations such as IF a< b. Please look back at the DECODE function in this section for an example.

LEAST_UB

This function has been dropped from the current version of Discoverer. If you have any workbooks that use this function, you will need to use an alternative function.

LENGTH

Syntax: LENGTH(string)
Description: This function returns the length of a string, number, date, or expression.
Folder: LENGTH can be found in the String folder, as seen in Figure B-4.
Example: LENGTH('Hien Nguyen') returns 11.

LENGTHB

Syntax: LENGTHB(string)
Description: This function takes a string and returns the length as a number of bytes, as opposed to a number of characters. Within Discoverer, we recommend you use LENGTH instead of this function.
Folder: LENGTHB can be found in the String folder, as seen in Figure B-4.

LN (Logarithm)

Syntax: LN(number)
Description: This function returns the natural, or base e, logarithm of a number, where e is the universal constant (see EXP for an explanation of e). If the number specified is the null value, the result will be null. The number or expression you provide must be positive; otherwise, you will encounter an error.

The opposite of LN(x) is EXP(x), so that if you compute the natural logarithm of EXP(x), you get x back. This works either way, as seen in the examples that follow.
Folder: LN can be found in the Numeric folder, as seen in Figure B-2.
Examples:

- LN(1) returns the value 0.

- LN(8) returns the value 2.079.

- LN(EXP(8)) returns the number 8.

- x / LN(x-1) returns the approximate number of prime numbers not exceeding the value x. This is included just for fun and is something you can experiment with yourself to show the usage of LN.

LOG

Syntax: LOG(base, number)
Description: This function returns the power to which a number, called the base, must be raised in order to obtain a given positive number. Common logarithms use 10 as the base. Napierian logarithms (named after John Napier, the Scottish inventor of logarithms and, incidentally, the decimal point) use the number e (the universal constant) as the base.
Folder: LOG can be found in the Numeric folder, as seen in Figure B-2.
Examples:

- LOG(10,10) returns the number 1.

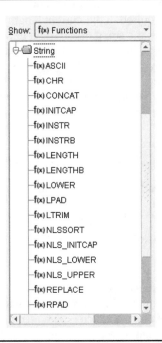

FIGURE B-4 *Discoverer's string functions*

- LOG(10, 100) returns the number 2.

- LOG(EXP(1), 3) returns 1.0986, because $e^{1.0986}$ is 3. See the section on EXP for more details on the universal constant *e*.

LOWER
Syntax: LOWER(string)
Description: This function takes a string and returns a new string with every letter in lowercase.
Folder: LOWER can be found in the String folder, as seen in Figure B-4.
Examples:

- LOWER('Armstrong-Smith') returns the string 'armstrong-smith'.

- DECODE(LOWER(state), 'california', 'CA', 'texas', 'TX', 'US')

NOTE
By using the LOWER function within a DECODE function, you assure that your search will match upper- and lowercase data.

LPAD (Left Pad)
Syntax: LPAD(string, number [, characters])
Description: This function takes a string, a number, and optionally a set of characters, and pads the string to the length specified by the number. If the current length of the string is less than the

number specified, Discoverer inserts as many sets of characters into the beginning of the string as it can, until the length is as required. If the current length of the string is greater than the number specified, Discoverer truncates the string, returning a new string with only that number of characters remaining—counting from the left. When padding, if no character set is specified, Discoverer pads out the string with spaces. If either the specified string or the character set is the null value, or the number is not positive, the overall result will be the null value. If the number specified is a decimal, Discoverer ignores the decimal portion, acting on the number before the decimal point.

Folder: LPAD can be found in the String folder, as seen in Figure B-4.

Examples:

- LPAD('Armstrong', 5) returns 'Armst', containing only the first five characters.

- LPAD('Smith', 15, 'Darlene') returns 'DarleneDarSmith'.

- LPAD(' ',5,'M') returns a null string because the initial string is empty, but

- LPAD(' ',LENGTH('Luke')+1, '*') returns '****'.

LTRIM (Left Trim)

Syntax: LTRIM(string [, characters])

Description: This function takes a string, and optionally a set of characters, and returns a new string with all occurrences of those characters removed from the beginning of the original string. If no characters are specified, Discoverer removes all leading spaces. If either the specified string or the set of characters is the null value, the result will be the null value.

Folder: LTRIM can be found in the String folder, as seen in Figure B-4.

Examples:

- LTRIM(' Armstrong') returns 'Armstrong' with all leading spaces removed.

- LTRIM('Armstrong-Smith', 'Armstrong-') returns 'Smith'.

- LTRIM('', 'Jones') returns null.

LUB

Syntax: LUB(label)

Description: This function is another of those operating system functions that would not normally be used within Discoverer. It returns the least upper bound of an operating system label.

Folder: LUB can be found in the Group folder, as seen in Figure B-5.

MAX (Maximum)

Syntax: MAX(argument)

Description: From the argument, column, or set of values specified, this function returns the item that has the largest value. MAX ignores null values.

Folder: MAX can be found in the Group and Analytic folders, as seen in Figures B-5 and B-7.

Examples:

- MAX(ship date) returns the most recent ship date held on the system.

- MAX(NVL(ship date,SYSDATE)) will overcome null values in the ship date, thus allowing further calculations and aggregations to be applied to this calculation.

MAX_DISTINCT

Syntax: MAX_DISTINCT(argument)
Description: From the argument, column, or set of values specified, this function returns the item that has the largest value. MAX ignores null values. This function is identical to the MAX function.
Folder: MAX_DISTINCT can be found in the Group and Analytic folders, as seen in Figures B-5 and B-7.

MIN (Minimum)

Syntax: MIN(argument)
Description: From the argument, column, or set of values specified, this function returns the item that has the lowest value. MIN ignores null values.
Folder: MIN can be found in the Group and Analytic folders, as seen in Figures B-5 and B-7.
Examples:

- MIN(ship date) returns the oldest ship date held on the system.

- MIN(NVL(ship date,SYSDATE)) will overcome null values in the ship date, thus allowing further calculations and aggregations to be applied to this calculation.

MIN_DISTINCT

Syntax: MIN_DISTINCT(argument)
Description: From the argument, column, or set of values specified, this function returns the item that has the lowest value. MIN_DISTINCT ignores null values. This function is identical to the MIN function.
Folder: MIN_DISTINCT can be found in the Group and Analytic folders, as seen in Figures B-5 and B-7.

MOD (Modulus)

Syntax: MOD(value, divisor)
Description: This function divides the given value by the divisor, and returns the remainder. Both the value and the divisor can be any real number. If the divisor is zero, Discoverer returns the original value in the result.
Folder: MOD can be found in the Numeric folder, as seen in the Figure B-2.
Examples:

- MOD(7, 8) returns 7.

- MOD(8, 7) returns 1.

- MOD(-8,7) returns –1.

- MOD(8,0) returns 8.

MONTHS_BETWEEN

Syntax: MONTHS_BETWEEN(first_date, second_date)
Description: This function returns the number of months between the first_date and the second_date. Both dates specified must be valid dates. If either date you want to check is not currently a valid date, you must convert it into a valid date. If the first_date precedes the second_date, the

result will be negative. In most Oracle databases, the result of this function will be a number with decimal places; however, if you are using Oracle Lite, the result will be an integer. If you want to compare a date prior to 01-JAN-2000 with a date after this, you must give the complete four-digit year.

Folder: MONTHS_BETWEEN can be found in the Date folder, as seen in Figure B-3.

Examples:

- MONTHS_BETWEEN(TO_DATE('01-DEC-1999'), TO_DATE('26-MAY-2000')) returns the value 5.80645.

- MONTHS_BETWEEN(TO_DATE('01-DEC-99'), TO_DATE('26-MAY-00')) returns the value −1194.19355.

NEW_TIME

Syntax: NEW_TIME(date, this_zone, destination_zone)

Description: This function returns the date and time for the destination_zone based on the specified date and time in this_zone. This is a very useful and clever function that can be used to work out the current time in different parts of the world. Both this_zone and destination_zone must be supplied as three-letter abbreviations. A list of the valid time zones used within Discoverer can be found in the section "Time Zones" later in this appendix.

By the clever use of the TO_CHAR function, and knowing how many hours ahead or behind you are to other countries, you can work out the time anywhere in the world. To calculate the time in China, for example, we know that China is 15 hours ahead of California. Therefore, we need to add 15/24 to the current time.

Folder: NEW_TIME can be found in the Date folder, as seen in the Figure B-3.

Examples: In the following examples, suppose that the current time zone is PST (Pacific Standard Time).

- NEW_TIME(SYSDATE, 'PST', 'GMT') returns the date in London.

- TO_CHAR(NEW_TIME(SYSDATE, 'PST', 'GMT'),'HH24:MI') returns the time, based on the 24-hour clock, in London.

- TO_CHAR(NEW_TIME(SYSDATE + (15 / 24), 'PST', 'PST'),'DD-MON-YY HH24:MI') returns the date and time in China.

If you are in a part of the world that does not have a supported time zone, do not despair. The solution is very simple. You calculate the time difference between your offices, insert that instead of the word "diff" in the function that follows, and then run the function. Make sure both of the quoted time zones are the same. We inserted 'GMT', but this works with all supported zones.

- TO_CHAR(NEW_TIME(SYSDATE + (diff / 24), 'GMT', 'GMT'),'DD-MON-YY HH24:MI') returns the date and time of your office.

NEXT_DAY

Syntax: NEXT_DAY(date, string)

Description: This function returns the date of the first weekday, named by string, which is later than the date given. The string must contain at least the first three letters of a day of the week.

Folder: NEXT_DAY can be found in the Date folder, as seen in Figure B-3.

Examples:

- NEXT_DAY(SYSDATE, 'Wednesday') returns the date for next Wednesday.

- NEXT_DAY(ship_date, 'FRI') returns the date for the Friday following the ship date.

- NEXT_DAY(SYSDATE-7, 'Wednesday') returns the preceding Wednesday, or the present day if the function was run on a Wednesday.

NLSSORT

Syntax: NLSSORT(string [, nls_parameters])
Description: This function gives the string of bytes used to sort a string.
Folder: NLSSORT can be found in the String folder, as seen in Figure B-4.
Examples:

- NLSSORT('DARLENE', 'NLS_SORT = Xdutch') returns the code 2314644B28552800.

- NLSSORT('mike', NLS_SORT = Xswiss) returns the code 503C46280.

NOTE
As you can see, if you look at these two examples, the single quotes around the NLS_SORT = parameter are optional.

NLS_INITCAP

Syntax: NLS_INITCAP(string [, nls_parameters])
Description: This function is identical to INITCAP, except that it takes an optional NLS (National Language Support) string of parameters. If provided, this string must take the form 'NLS_SORT = option', where option is a linguistic sort sequence. These sequences should be used whenever your Oracle database is not based on the English language. These rules are required in order for Discoverer to work out exactly how to initialize the given string.
Folder: NLS_INITCAP can be found in the String folder, as seen in Figure B-4.
Example: NLS_INITCAP('ijsland', NLS_SORT = Xdutch) returns 'IJsland'.

NLS_LOWER

Syntax: NLS_LOWER(string [, nls_parameters])
Description: This function is identical to LOWER, except that it takes an optional NLS (National Language Support) string of parameters. For an explanation of NLS, see the function NLS_INITCAP.
Folder: NLS_LOWER can be found in the String folder, as seen in Figure B-4.

NLS_UPPER

Syntax: NLS_UPPER(string [, nls_parameters])
Description: This function is identical to UPPER, except that it takes an optional NLS (National Language Support) string of parameters. For an explanation of NLS, see the function NLS_INITCAP.
Folder: NLS_UPPER can be found in the String folder, as seen in Figure B-4.

NTILE

Syntax: NTILE(n) OVER (PARTITION BY expr1 ORDER BY expr2)

Description: This function evenly distributes sorted values into different buckets. Based upon the ORDER BY, it gives all rows in the bucket that is first the number 1. The rows at the top are given the number *n*. All rows in between are given an evenly distributed number between 1 and *n*.
Folder: NTILE can be found in the Analytic folder, as seen in Figure B-7.
Example: NTILE(10) OVER(ORDER BY SUM(Selling Price)) computes ten equal-sized buckets for the Selling Price.

NULLIF
Syntax: NULLIF(value1, value2)
Description: This function compares value1 to value2. If the values are equal, it returns NULL. If they are not equal, it returns value1.
Folder: NULLIF can be found in the Others folder, as seen in Figure B-8.
Examples:

- NULLIF (10,10) returns NULL.

- NULLIF (10,5) returns 10.

NOTE
The two values must be of the same data type. NULLIF(10,'A') will produce an error, as will NULLIF(NULL,7).

NUMTODSINTERVAL
Syntax: NUMTODSINTERVAL(value1, [second|minute|hour|day])
Description: This function converts the number given as value1 to the INTERVAL DAY TO SECOND data type. The second parameter determines whether value1 is a second, a minute, an hour, or a day.

NOTE
Oracle requires that, when using the RANGE clause in analytic functions, you submit the RANGE in an INTERVAL data type.

Folder: NUMTODSINTERVAL can be found in the Date folder, as seen in Figure B-3.

NUMTOYMINTERVAL
Syntax: NUMTOYMINTERVAL(value1, [year|month])
Description: This function converts the number given as value1 to the INTERVAL YEAR TO MONTH data type. The second parameter determines whether value1 is a year or a month.
Folder: NUMTOYMINTERVAL can be found in the Date folder, as seen in Figure B-3.

NVL
Syntax: NVL(expr1, expr2)
Description: If the first expression is null, Discoverer returns the second expression. If the first expression is not null, Discoverer returns that expression.
Folder: NVL can be found in the Others folder, as seen in Figure B-8.
Examples:

- NVL(code, 'Y') returns the code if it is not null; otherwise, it returns the value 'Y'.

- NVL(ship quantity, 0) returns the ship quantity if there is one; otherwise, it returns zero.

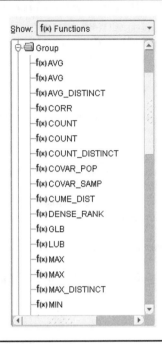

FIGURE B-5 *Discoverer's group functions*

NVL2

Syntax: NVL2(value1, value2, value3)
Description: When using the function, if value1 is not null, then it will return value2. If value1 is null, then it will return value3.
Folder: NVL2 can be found in the Others folder, as seen in Figure B-8.
Examples:

- NVL2(NULL, 1, 0) returns 0.

- NVL2('X', 'Y', 'Z') returns Y.

PERCENTILE_CONT (Percentile Continuous)

Syntax: PERCENTILE_CONT(value1) WITHIN GROUP (ORDER BY value2 ASC|DESC)
Description: This function is an inverse distribution function that depends upon a continuous distribution of values. It receives a percentile, value1, and a sort specification, value2, and returns an interpolated result that would fit into that percentile with attention to the sort specification. To help understand this function, consider that MEDIAN is a specific example of the function where value1 defaults to 0.5.
Folder: PERCENTILE_CONT can be found in the Group and Analytic folders, as seen in Figures B-5 and B-7.
Example: PERCENTILE_CONT(0.4) WITHIN GROUP (ORDER BY Profit DESC)

PERCENTILE_DISC (Percentile Discrete)

Syntax: PERCENTILE_DISC(value1) WITHIN GROUP (ORDER BY value2 ASC|DESC)
Description: This function is an inverse distribution function that depends upon a discrete distribution of values. It receives a percentile, value1, and a sort specification, value2, and returns a specific value from the set.
Folder: PERCENTILE_DISC can be found in the Group and Analytic folders, as seen in Figures B-5 and B-7.
Example: PERCENTILE_DISC (0.4) WITHIN GROUP (ORDER BY Profit DESC)

PERCENT_RANK

Syntax: PERCENT_RANK([value1, value2]) WITHIN GROUP (ORDER BY value3, value4)
Description: This function determines a ranking and returns the result as a percentage. Value1 and value2 are optional and would be used to determine the answer to a what-if question. For example, what if an employee's salary was 25000 and commission was 0.2, then what would the percentage rank be?
Folder: PERCENTILE_RANK can be found in the Group and Analytic folders, as seen in Figures B-5 and B-7.
Example: PERCENT_RANK(25000, .2) WITHIN GROUP(ORDER BY salary, commission)

POWER

Syntax: POWER(base number, *n*)
Description: This function raises the base number given to the *n*th power. The base and the exponent can be any numbers; however, if the base number is negative, the exponent must be an integer. A negative exponent means divide the answer into 1.
Folder: POWER can be found in the Numeric folder, as seen in Figure B-2.
Examples:

- POWER(2.5, 2) returns 6.25, which is 2.5 squared.

- POWER(2.5, -2) returns 0.16, which is 1 divided by 6.25.

- POWER(-3,-3) returns –0.37037037 and so on, which is 1 divided by –27.

RANK

Syntax: RANK([number, number]) [WITHIN GROUP|OVER] ([PARTITION BY value] ORDER BY value)
Description: This function determines a value's rank among a group of numbers. When multiple rows have equal values, they receive the same rank. Ranks might not be consecutive, as Oracle adds the number of rows that have a tie to the ranking of the tied values to compute the next rank.
Folder: RANK can be found in the Group and Analytic folders, as seen in Figures B-5 and B-7.
Examples:

- RANK() OVER(ORDER BY Ship Qty SUM DESC)

- RANK(5)WITHIN GROUP(ORDER BY Selling Price)

- RANK() OVER (ORDER BY salary DESC) could be used alongside a grade to return values like this:

Grade	ename	Salary
1	abc0	5000
2	abc1	4000
2	abc2	4000
4	abc3	3500
5	abc4	3000

RATIO_TO_REPORT

Syntax: RATIO_TO_REPORT(value) OVER(PARTITION BY value)
Description: This function computes the ratio of a number to the total of a group of numbers.
Folder: RATIO_TO_REPORT can be found in the Group and Analytic folders, as seen in Figures B-5 and B-7.
Example: RATIO_TO_REPORT(Profit SUM) OVER(PARTITION BY "Year")

RAWTOHEX

Syntax: RAWTOHEX(raw)
Description: This function takes a raw string of decimal numbers and converts it into a string of hexadecimal numbers.
Folder: RAWTOHEX can be found in the Conversion folder, as seen in Figure B-6.

REGR_xxx (Linear Regression)

Syntax: REGR_xxx (value1, value2)
Description: Oracle provides a set of linear regression functions. Linear regression is used to make predictions about a single value. Simple linear regression involves discovering the equation for a line that most nearly fits the given data. That linear equation is then used to predict values for the data. For example, if a university wants to predict a student's grade on a freshman college calculus midterm based on his/her SAT score, then it may apply *linear regression.*
Folder: The REGR_xxx functions can be found in the Group and Analytic folders, as seen in Figures B-5 and B-7.

REGR_AVGX

Description: This function computes the average of the independent variable of the regression line.

REGR_AVGY

Description: This function computes the average of the dependent variable of the regression line.

REGR_COUNT

Description: This function returns the quantity of number pairs used to fit the regression line.

REGR_INTERCEPT

Description: This function returns the y-intercept of the regression line.

REGR_R2
Description: This function returns the coefficient of determination.

REGR_SLOPE
Description: This function returns the slope of a line.

REPLACE
Syntax: REPLACE(string, search_string [, replace_string])
Description: This function takes a string and returns a new string that has had every occurrence of the search_string replaced with the replace_string. If the replace_string is omitted or it is null, all occurrences of the search_string are removed. If the search_string is null, the original string is returned.
Folder: REPLACE can be found in the String folder, as seen in Figure B-4.
Examples:

- REPLACE('JACK and 'JUE', J', 'BL') returns 'BLACK and BLUE'.

- REPLACE('The Cat is at the Mat', 'at') returns 'The C is the M'.

- REPLACE('GEORGE', 'GE') returns 'OR'.

ROUND (for Dates)
Syntax: ROUND(date, format)
Description: This function rounds a date according to the format specified. When no format is specified, the date is rounded to noon tomorrow if the time is later than midday, or to noon today if the time is before midday. In either case, the resulting time is set to noon. For a full list of the formats allowed, see the section "Date Format Masks" later in this appendix.
Folder: ROUND can be found in the Date folder, as seen in Figure B-3.
Examples: All examples for this function can be found in the section "Date Format Masks" later in this appendix.

ROUND (for Numbers)
Syntax: ROUND(number, places)
Description: This function rounds a number to the number of decimal places specified. If the number of places is omitted, Discoverer rounds to zero decimal places. If a negative value is supplied for the number of places, Discoverer rounds the digits to the left of the decimal point. If any decimals are supplied in the number of places, these are ignored. This function is not the same as TRUNC. We have used the same examples in both functions to show you the difference.
Folder: ROUND can be found in the Numeric folder, as seen in Figure B-2.
Examples:

- ROUND(578.666, 2) returns 578.67.

- ROUND(578.666, 0) returns 579.00.

- ROUND(578.667, -1) returns 580.00.

- ROUND(578.667, -2) returns 600.00.

FIGURE B-6   *Discoverer's conversion functions*

ROWCOUNT
Syntax: ROWCOUNT
Description: This function returns the total number of rows returned by the query. This total includes duplicates and null values.
Folder: ROWCOUNT can be found in the Group folder, as seen in Figure B-5.

ROWIDTOCHAR
Syntax: ROWIDTOCHAR(rowid)
Description: This function takes an internal row identifier, or rowid, and converts it into a string. According to the information that we have gathered together, this function should never be needed. It apparently is used as a debugging tool yet somehow has made its way into Discoverer. Your Discoverer administrator will be the one who uses this. There does not seem to be a great use for this function in normal queries, and we advise you not to use it.
Folder: ROWIDTOCHAR can be found in the Conversion folder, as seen in Figure B-6.

ROWNUM
Syntax: ROWNUM
Description: This function returns a number indicating the order in which the row was selected by the query. The number is assigned before any sorting is done and gives you the true order in which the row was selected.
Folder: ROWNUM can be found in the Others folder, as seen in Figure B-8.

ROW_NUMBER

Syntax: ROW_NUMBER(value) OVER (PARTITION BY value1 ORDER BY value2)
Description: This highly versatile analytic function assigns a unique consecutive number to each row in a set of rows. The OVER clause allows you to specify the grouping and sorting of the rows you would like numbered. This function is quite useful when used within a from clause query.
Folder: ROW_NUMBER can be found in the Analytic folder, as seen in Figure B-7.

RPAD (Right Pad)

Syntax: RPAD(string, number [, character])
Description: This function takes a string, a number, and optionally a character and appends the character defined as the third parameter as often as is needed to give the string the length specified in the second parameter. If no character set is specified, Discoverer pads out the string with spaces. If the specified string is the null value, the result will be the null value. If the specified number or character, if supplied, is the null value, Discoverer will report an error. If the length of the original string is already equal to or bigger than the number specified, Discoverer returns the original string.
Folder: RPAD can be found in the String folder, as seen in Figure B-4.
Examples:

- RPAD('Armstrong', 14) returns a new string 'Armstrong   ', now with a length of 14, with five space characters having been appended to the end.

- RPAD('Jones', 7, '-') returns 'Jones—'.

RTRIM (Right Trim)

Syntax: RTRIM(string [, characters])
Description: This function takes a string, and optionally a set of characters, and returns a new string with all occurrences of those characters removed from the end of the original string. If no second string is specified, Discoverer removes all trailing spaces. If either the specified string or the set of characters is the null value, the result will be the null value.
Folder: RTRIM can be found in the String folder, as seen in Figure B-4.
Examples:

- RTRIM('Armstrong ') returns 'Armstrong' with all trailing spaces removed.

- RTRIM('Armstrong-Smith', '-Smith') returns 'Armstrong'.

- RTRIM('Michael','') returns the null value because the character set is null.

SESSIONTIMEZONE

Syntax: SESSIONTIMEZONE
Description: This function returns the number of hours difference between the time zone of the Discoverer user's session and Greenwich Mean Time (GMT). Discoverer accesses the time zone from the operating system and submits it to the Oracle database upon connecting.
Folder: SESSIONTIMEZONE can be found in the Date folder, as seen in Figure B-3.
Example: If you are in Mountain Time, SESSIONTIMEZONE will return –06:00.

SIGN

Syntax: SIGN(numeric expression)

Description: This function returns three possible vales; –1, 0, and 1. These values are assigned depending upon whether the numeric expression evaluates to less than zero (–1), zero (0), or greater than zero (1). Using SIGN in conjunction with DECODE produces very effective "if, then" type expressions.

Folder: SIGN can be found in the Numeric folder, as seen in Figure B-2.

Examples:

- SIGN(133) returns 1.

- SIGN(-15) returns –1.

- SIGN(0) returns 0.

SIN (Sine)

Syntax: SIN(value)

Description: This function takes the value given and returns the sine of that angle. The function returns a result expressed in radians.

Folder: SIN can be found in the Numeric folder, as seen in Figure B-2.

Examples:

- SIN(30) returns a value of 0.5.

- SIN(90) returns a value of 1.

SINH (Hyperbolic Sine)

Syntax: SINH(value)

Description: This function takes the value given and returns the hyperbolic sine of that value. The function returns an angle expressed in radians.

Folder: SINH can be found in the Numeric folder, as seen in Figure B-2.

SOUNDEX

Syntax: SOUNDEX(string)

Description: This function takes a string and returns the soundex code for that string. Using SOUNDEX in a parameterized condition can help you or your user find data phonetically. This function is great for bad spellers who want to search for words with similar sounds.

Folder: SOUNDEX can be found in the String folder, as seen in Figure B-4.

Examples:

- SOUNDEX('m') returns the value M000.

- SOUNDEX('michael') returns the value M240.

SQRT (Square Root)

Syntax: SQRT(number)

Description: This function takes a number and returns the square root of that number. You must take care to ensure that the number does not evaluate to a negative number; otherwise,

Discoverer will return an error. The square roots of negative numbers are imaginary numbers and cannot be displayed in Discoverer.
Folder: SQRT can be found in the Numeric folder, as seen in Figure B-2.
Examples:

- SQRT(169) returns the value 13.

- SQRT(-7) returns the value '#NUM!'.

STDDEV (Standard Deviation)

Syntax: STDDEV(value)
Description: This function gives the standard deviation from the norm of values in a group of rows. The function is applied to the set of values derived from the argument values by the elimination of null values.
Folder: STDDEV can be found in the Group folder, as seen in Figure B-5.

STDDEV_DISTINCT (Distinct Standard Deviation)

Syntax: STDDEV_DISTINCT(value)
Description: This function gives the standard deviation from the norm of values in a distinct group of rows. The function is applied to the set of values derived from the argument values by the elimination of null values and duplicates.
Folder: STDDEV_DISTINCT can be found in the Group and Analytic folders, as seen in Figures B-5 and B-7.

STDDEV_POP

Syntax: STDDEV_POP(value1)
Description: This function computes the population standard deviation and delivers the square root of the population variance.
Folder: STDDEV_POP can be found in the Group and Analytic folders, as seen in Figures B-5 and B-7.

STDDEV_SAMP

Syntax: STDDEV_SAMP
Description: This function computes the cumulative sample standard deviation and delivers the square root of the sample variance.
Folder: STDDEV_SAMP can be found in the Group and Analytic folders, as seen in Figures B-5 and B-7.

SUBSTR (Substring)

Syntax: SUBSTR(string, start [' count])
Description: This function takes a string and returns a portion of that string, beginning at the start position, making the portion count characters long. If you omit the count or provide a count that is bigger than the length of the original string, Discoverer returns a new string with the start number of characters removed. If you provide a start number that is bigger than the length of the original string, the result will be an empty string.
Folder: SUBSTR can be found in the String folder, as seen in Figure B-4.

Examples:

- SUBSTR('Michael', 5) returns 'ael', with the first 5 characters of 'Michael' removed.

- SUBSTR('Michael', 2, 3) returns 'ich'.

- SUBSTR(SSN,1,3)||'-'||SUBSTR(SSN,4,2)||'-'||SUBSTR(SSN,6.4) takes a social security number (SSN) and converts it into the more typical format used in the United States. For example, if the SSN is 123456789, this example converts this to 123-45-6789.

- '('||SUBSTR(TEL,1,3)||')'||SUBSTR(TEL,4,3)||'-'||SUBSTR(TEL,7,4) takes a typical ten-digit telephone number and converts it into a more readable format. For example, if the number is 1234567890, this example converts it to (123) 345-7890.

NOTE
The two preceding examples make excellent use of the concatenate function.

SUBSTRB

Syntax: SUBSTRB(string, start [count])
Description: This function takes a string and returns a substring of that string, beginning at the start byte position and going on for count number bytes.
Folder: SUBSTRB can be found in the String folder, as seen in Figure B-4.

SUM

Syntax: SUM(values)
Description: This function returns the sum of all the values in the expression or row.
Folder: SUM can be found in the Group and Analytic folders, as seen in Figures B-5 and B-7.
Example: SUM(ship quantity) returns the total quantity shipped.

SUM_DISTINCT

Syntax: SUM_DISTINCT(values)
Description: This function is similar to the SUM function, except that it returns the sum of all the unique values in the expression or row.
Folder: SUM_DISTINCT can be found in the Group and Analytic folders, as seen in Figures B-5 and B-7.

SUM_SQUARES

Syntax: SUM_SQUARES(number)
Description: This function returns the total of the square of the number given. If you select this function and then edit the calculation, you will notice that Discoverer changes the function to SUM(POWER(number, 2)).
Folder: SUM_SQUARES can be found in the Group folder, as seen in Figure B-5.
Example: SUM_SQUARES(3) returns 9, and Discoverer writes this as SUM(POWER(3,2)).

SYSDATE (System Date)

Syntax: SYSDATE

Description: This function returns the current date and time. You can use this date inside many other functions, because it acts exactly like a DATE data type.
Folder: SYSDATE can be found in the Date folder, as seen in Figure B-3.
Examples:

■ TRUNC(SYSDATE -1) returns yesterday's date, minus the time. Most data warehouses store dates in this format, so if you want to look for all shipments that occurred yesterday, you would create this condition: ship_date = TRUNC(SYSDATE-1).

■ SYSDATE + (1/288) or SYSDATE + 0.0034722 will add five minutes to the current time.

> **NOTE**
> *Adding something to SYSDATE, or any other date for that matter, is a simple case of working out the decimal or fraction that needs to be added. Therefore, to add five minutes, once you have worked out that there are 288 five-minute periods in a 24-hour period, the calculation is simple.*

TAN (Tangent)

Syntax: TAN(value)
Description: This function takes the value given and returns the trigonometric tangent of that value. The function returns an angle expressed in radians.

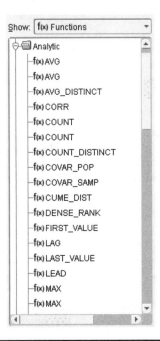

FIGURE B-7   *Discoverer's analytic functions*

Folder: TAN can be found in the Numeric folder, as seen in Figure B-2.
Examples:

- TAN(-60) returns a value of –1.73205.

- TAN(0) returns a value of 0.

- TAN(30) returns a value of 0.577350.

TANH (Hyperbolic Tangent)

Syntax: TANH(value)
Description: This function takes the value given and returns the hyperbolic tangent of that value. The function returns an angle expressed in radians. For those of you who are mathematically oriented, the hyperbolic tangent is defined as $\tan(x) = (e^x - e^{-x}) / (e^x + e^{-x})$.
Folder: TANH can be found in the Numeric folder, as seen in Figure B-2.
Examples:

- TANH(0) returns a value of 0.

- TANH(0.3) returns a value of 0.291313.

- TANH(0.5) returns a value of 0.462117.

TO_CHAR (Dates)

Syntax: TO_CHAR(date, format [,nls_parameters])
Description: This function converts a date into a string by applying the specified format. The date provided must be a valid date. The function also takes an optional NLS (National Language Support) string of parameters. For an explanation of NLS, see the function NLS_INITCAP. For a list of all of the date format masks, please refer to the section "Date Format Masks" later in this appendix.
Folder: TO_CHAR can be found in the Conversion folder, as seen in Figure B-6.
Examples: In the examples that follow, suppose the current date is 24-JUL-06 at 3:52 P.M.

- TO_CHAR(SYSDATE, 'fmDay, Month DD, YYYY HH:MI:AM') returns 'Monday, July 24, 2006 3:52 PM'.

- TO_CHAR(SYSDATE, 'MM/DD/YY') returns '07/24/06'.

- TO_CHAR(TO_DATE('24-JUL-06'), 'Month-YYYY') returns the string 'July -2006'. You need to be very careful when supplying strings directly to the TO_CHAR because the date supplied *must* be a valid date in its own right.

TO_CHAR (Labels)

Syntax: TO_CHAR(label, format [,nls_parameters])
Description: This function converts a label into a string by applying the specified format. The function also takes an optional NLS (National Language Support) string of parameters. For an explanation of NLS, see the function NLS_INITCAP. This function is for use by administrators only.
Folder: TO_CHAR can be found in the Conversion folder, as seen in Figure B-6.

TO_CHAR (Numbers)

Syntax: TO_CHAR(number, [format [,nls_parameters]])
Description: This function converts a number into a string by applying the specified optional format. The function also takes an optional NLS (National Language Support) string of parameters. For an explanation of NLS, see the function NLS_INITCAP. For a list of all of the number format masks, please refer to the section "Number Format Masks" later in this appendix.
Folder: TO_CHAR can be found in the Conversion folder, as seen in Figure B-6.
Examples:

- TO_CHAR(678) returns the string '678'.

- TO_CHAR(678.7,'999D99') returns the string '678.70'.

- TO_CHAR(678, 'RN') returns the string 'DCLXXVIII'—that is, 678 in roman numerals.

TO_DATE

Syntax: TO_DATE(string, format)
Description: This function converts a string in the given format into a standard Oracle date. Only if the string is already in the standard Oracle format of 'DD-MON-YY' can the format option be omitted. For a full listing of the valid format options, please see the section "Date Format Masks" later in this appendix.
Folder: TO_DATE can be found in the Conversion folder, as seen in Figure B-6.
Examples:

- TO_DATE('14/10/58', 'DD/MM/YY') returns the Oracle date 14-OCT-58.

- TO_DATE('09-09-51', 'MM-DD-YY') returns the Oracle date 09-SEP-51.

TO_LABEL

This function has been dropped from the current version of Discoverer. If you have any workbooks that use this function, you will need to use an alternative function.

TO_MULTI_BYTE

Syntax: TO_MULTI_BYTE(string)
Description: This function converts each of the single-byte characters in the string into their multibyte equivalents. If the character has no multibyte equivalent, the function leaves the character unchanged.
Folder: TO_MULTI_BYTE can be found in the Conversion folder, as seen in Figure B-6.

TO_NUMBER

Syntax: TO_NUMBER(string, format [,nls_parameters])
Description: This function converts a string into a number by applying the specified optional format. The function also takes an optional NLS (National Language Support) string of parameters. For an explanation of NLS, see the function NLS_INITCAP. For a list of all of the number format masks, please refer to the section "Number Format Masks" later in this appendix. Discoverer is very good at converting strings into numbers, and we recommend you avoid supplying a format mask.
Folder: TO_NUMBER can be found in the Conversion folder, as seen in Figure B-6.

Examples:

- See the functions GREATEST and LEAST.

- TO_NUMBER('765.43') returns the number 765.43.

- TO_NUMBER(order_number) will convert the database field called order_number into a number. Care should be taken when doing this that all of the strings being converted are indeed numbers.

- TO_NUMBER('0.5555','990D9999') returns 0.56, 0.556 or 0.5555, depending upon the format you have applied to the column.

NOTE
Be careful when specifying the optional format mask. If you supply a mask, you must ensure that the mask corresponds exactly to the number within the string. Supplying an incorrect format mask causes Discoverer to error out with an ORA-01722 error. The following function will fail: TO_NUMBER('0.5555','990D99') returns an error because the format mask being applied does not match the actual number of decimal places in the string.

TO_SINGLE_BYTE

Syntax: TO_SINGLE_BYTE(string)
Description: This function converts each of the multibyte characters in the string into their single-byte equivalents. If the character has no single-byte equivalent, the function leaves the character unchanged.
Folder: TO_SINGLE_BYTE can be found in the Conversion folder, as seen in Figure B-6.

TRANSLATE

Syntax: TRANSLATE(string, search, replace)
Description: This function takes the string and looks at each character in the string. It then looks to see if any of the characters in the search string are in the original string. If any of the search characters are there, Discoverer replaces them with the character in the replace string that is in the same position as the character in the search string.
Folder: TRANSLATE can be found in the String folder, as seen in Figure B-4.
Example:

- TRANSLATE('MICHAEL SMITH', 'AEI', '123') returns 'M3CH12L SM3TH'. As you can see, Discoverer has replaced each occurrence of 'A' with a '1', each 'E' with a '2', and each 'I' with a '3'.

TRUNC (Dates)

Syntax: TRUNC(date, format)
Description: This function takes a date and truncates the time component from it, leaving just the date. Refer to the section entitled "Using Formats When Rounding Dates" later in this appendix.
Folder: TRUNC can be found in the Date folder, as seen in Figure B-3.

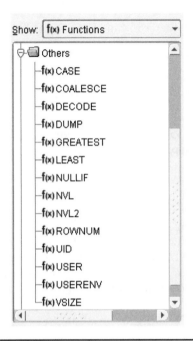

FIGURE B-8   *Discoverer's other functions*

Examples:

■   TRUNC(SYSDATE) returns the current date minus the time.

■   TRUNC(ship date) returns the ship date minus the time. If you have shipped many items in the same day, truncating the date allows you to group all of the items together.

TRUNC (Numbers)

Syntax: TRUNC(number, precision)

Description: This function truncates a number according to the precision specified. If the precision is omitted or is zero, Discoverer truncates all of the decimal places. If a negative value is supplied for the precision, Discoverer truncates (makes zero) that number of digits to the left of the decimal point. If any decimals are supplied in the precision, these are ignored. This function is not the same as ROUND. We have used the same examples in both functions to show you the difference.

Folder: TRUNC can be found in the Numeric folder, as seen in Figure B-2.

Examples:

■   TRUNC(578.666, 2) returns 578.66.

■   ROUND(578.666, 0) returns 578.00.

■   ROUND(578.667, -1) returns 570.00.

■   ROUND(578.667, -2) returns 500.00.

UID

Syntax: UID
Description: This function returns the user ID of the current user as assigned by Oracle. The number is unique on the current database.
Folder: UID can be found in the Others folder, as seen in Figure B-8.

UPPER

Syntax: UPPER(string)
Description: This function uppercases every character in the string.
Folder: UPPER can be found in the String folder, as seen in Figure B-4.
Example:

- UPPER('Darlene') returns 'DARLENE'.

USER

Syntax: USER
Description: This function returns the user name by which the user is known to the system. Users running Discoverer in Apps mode need to understand that this function will not return the user name they have logged in as, but rather the database username the application is using to log them in to the database.
Folder: USER can be found in the Others folder, as seen in Figure B-8.

USERENV

Syntax: USERENV(option)
Description: This function returns information in a string about the current user session. The valid options are 'CLIENT_INFO', 'ENTRYID', 'INSTANCE', 'ISDBA', 'LANG', 'LANGUAGE', 'SESSIONID', and 'TERMINAL'.
Folder: USERENV can be found in the Others folder, as seen in Figure B-8.
Examples:

- USERENV(TERMINAL) returns the terminal ID you are connected to. If you are using a terminal server, this returns the server name.

- USERENV(ISDBA) returns TRUE if the logged-in user is a DBA; otherwise, it returns FALSE.

- USERENV(LANG) returns the ISO language for the system you are working on. In our system this returns US.

- USERENV(LANGUAGE) returns the language and territory currently used by your session along with the database character set in use. In our system, this function returns AMERICAN_AMERICA WE8ISO8859P1. This tells me that the language I am using is American, the territory I am in is America, and the character set I am using is the ISO 8859-1 Western European 8-bit character set.

VARIANCE

Syntax: VARIANCE(number)
Description: This function returns the variance for all values, except null values, of a group of rows. The variance is the authorized deviation.
Folder: VARIANCE can be found in the Group and Analytic folders, as seen in Figures B-5 and B-7.

VARIANCE_DISTINCT

Syntax: VARIANCE_DISTINCT(number)
Description: This function returns the variance for all unique values, except null values, of a group of rows. The variance is the authorized deviation.
Folder: VARIANCE_DISTINCT can be found in the Group and Analytic folders, as seen in Figure B-5 and B-7.

VAR_POP (Population Variance)

Syntax: VAR_POP(value)
Description: This function returns the population variance, except null values, of a group of rows.
Folder: VAR_POP can be found in the Group and Analytic folders, as seen in Figures B-5 and B-7.

VAR_SAMP (Sample Variance)

Syntax: VAR_SAMP(value)
Description: This function returns the sample variance, except null values, of a group of rows.
Folder: VAR_SAMP can be found in the Group and Analytic folders, as seen in Figures B-5 and B-7.

VSIZE

Syntax: VSIZE(value)
Description: This function tells you how much storage space is being taken up by the item concerned. For strings, the size is the same as the length of the string. For numbers, it is usually smaller because less space is needed to store numbers.
Folder: VSIZE can be found in the Others folder, as seen in Figure B-8.
Examples:

- VSIZE('Michael') returns 7.

- VSIZE(16.8765) returns 4.

WIDTH_BUCKET

Syntax: WIDTH_BUCKET(value1, min_value, max_value, n)
Description: This very useful function will evenly distribute a range between your min_value and your max_value. It will then break this range into $n+2$ buckets and place all the values from value1 into one of these buckets. You always receive two more buckets than you request, as it creates an overflow bucket and an underflow bucket. This is used to create equiwidth histograms.
Folder: WIDTH_BUCKET can be found in the Group and Analytic folders, as seen in Figures B-5 and B-7.
Example:

- WIDTH_BUCKET(Order Qty SUM,0,800000,10) generates ten evenly distributed buckets for the Order Quantity between zero and 800,000.

Time Zones

The following is a list of the valid time zones that can be used within the Discoverer NEW_TIME date function:

- **'AST', 'ADT'** Atlantic standard or daylight saving time

- **BST', 'BDT'** Bering standard or daylight saving time

- **'CST', 'CDT'**   Central standard or daylight saving time

- **'EST', 'EDT'**   Eastern standard or daylight saving time

- **'GMT'**   Greenwich mean time

- **'HST',' HDT'**   Alaska-Hawaii standard or daylight saving time

- **'MST', 'MDT'**   Mountain standard or daylight saving time

- **'NST'**   Newfoundland standard time

- **'PST', 'PDT'**   Pacific standard or daylight saving time

- **'YST', 'YDT'**   Yukon standard or daylight saving time

Using Formats When Rounding Dates

When using the ROUND function on a date, the following is a list of formats available, along with an example of each. All of the examples given assume that the current date is Monday, 24-JUL-2006, and that the time is 12:35:40 A.M.

- CC, SCC rounds to the first January 1st of the century. It rounds at midnight on the morning of January 1st of 1951, 2001, 2051, and so on.

- ROUND(SYSDATE, 'CC') rounds to noon on 01-JAN-2001.

- SYEAR, SYYY, Y, YY, YYY, YYYY, YEAR rounds to January 1st of the year. It rounds at midnight on the morning of July 1st.

- ROUND(SYSDATE, 'YEAR') rounds to noon on 01-JAN-2007.

- Q rounds to the first day of a quarter. Based on quarters beginning January, April, July, and October, it rounds on the sixteenth day of the second month of the quarter, regardless of how many days there are in the month.

- ROUND(SYSDATE, 'Q') rounds to noon on 01-JUL-2006.

- MONTH, MON, MM rounds to the first date of a month. It rounds on the sixteenth day of the month, regardless of how many days there are in that month.

- ROUND(SYSDATE, 'MONTH') rounds to noon on 01-AUG-2006.

- WW rounds to the nearest date that has the same day of the week as the beginning of the year.

- ROUND(SYSDATE, 'WW') rounds to noon on 23-JUL-2006.

- W rounds to the nearest date that has the same day of the week as the beginning of the current month.

- ROUND(SYSDATE, 'W') rounds to noon on 22-JUL-2006.

- DDD, DD, J rounds to the next day. This is the same as applying ROUND with no format.

- ROUND(SYSDATE, 'DD') rounds to noon on 24-JUL-2006.

- DAY, DY, D rounds to the following Sunday, the first day of the week. It rounds at noon on Wednesday.

- ROUND(SYSDATE, 'D') rounds to noon on 23-JUL-2006.

- HH, HH12, HH24 rounds to the next whole hour. It rounds at 30 minutes and 30 seconds past the hour.

- ROUND(SYSDATE, 'HH') rounds to 01:00 A.M. on 24-JUL-2006.

- MI Rounds to the next whole minute. It rounds at 30 seconds past the minute.

- ROUND(SYSDATE, 'MI') rounds to 12:36 A.M. on 24-JUL-2006.

Date Format Masks

The following sections contain a full list of the format masks that can be used within the TO_CHAR and TO_DATE functions in Discoverer, along with an example value based on Monday, July 24, 2006.

Day Format Masks

Mask	Description	Example
D	Number of the day of the week	2
DD	Number of the day of the month	24
DDD	Number of the day in the year, since January 1st	205
DY	Three-letter uppercase abbreviation of the day	MON
Dy	Three-letter INITCAP abbreviation of the day	Mon
dy	Three-letter lowercase abbreviation of the day	mon
DAY	The uppercase full name of the day	MONDAY
Day	The INITCAP full name of the day	Monday
day	The lowercase full name of the day	monday

Month Format Masks

Mask	Description	Example
MM	Number of the month	07
RM	Roman numeral for the month	VII
MON	Three-letter uppercase abbreviation of the month	JUL
Mon	Three-letter INITCAP abbreviation of the month	Jul
mon	Three-letter lowercase abbreviation of the month	Jul
MONTH	The uppercase full name of the month	JULY
Month	The INITCAP full name of the month	July
month	The lowercase full name of the month	july

Year Format Masks

Mask	Description	Example
Y	Last digit of the year	6
YY	Last two digits of the year	06
YYY	Last three digits of the year	006
YYYY	Full four-digit year	2006
SYYYY	A signed year if the year is BC, for example 255 BC	–255
I	Last digit of the ISO (International Organization for Standardization) year	6
IY	Last two digits of the ISO year	06
IYY	Last three digits of the ISO year	006
IYYY	Full four-digit ISO year	2006
YEAR	Uppercase year spelled out in full	TWO THOUSAND SIX
Year	The INITCAP year spelled out on full	Two Thousand Six
year	Lowercase year spelled out in full	two thousand six
RR	Last two digits of the year, possibly in another century	06

Other Date Masks

Mask	Description	Example
Q	Number of the current quarter of the year	3
WW	Number of the week in the year	30
W	Number of the week in the month	4
IW	Week of the year, based on the ISO standard	29
J	Number of "Julian" days since December 31, 4713 BC	2453941
AD or BC	Displays AD or BC without periods	AD
ad or bc	Displays AD or BC in lowercase without periods	Ad
A.D. or B.C.	Displays AD or BC with periods	A.D.
a.d. or b.c.	Displays AD or BC in lowercase with periods	a.d.
CC	Displays the current century	21
SCC	Displays the current century and prefixes BC dates with '-' and AD dates with a space	21

Time Format Masks

In this section, suppose the current time is 7:02:22 P.M. This is how Discoverer can format that time:

Mask	Description	Example
HH or hh	The hour of the day with leading zeros	07
HH12 or hh12	The hour of the day with leading zeros	07
HH24	The hour of the day in the 24-hour clock	18
MI or mi	The number of minutes in the hour	02
SS or ss	The number of seconds in the minute	22
SSSSS	The number of seconds since midnight	68542

Special Format Masks

Discoverer allows you to insert special punctuation characters into the TO_CHAR function so that the result is easy to understand. Within the TO_DATE function, you can use the same punctuation to inform Discoverer of the characters that are to be ignored.

Mask	Description	Example
/	Inserts or ignores a forward slash character	23/07/2006
,	Inserts or ignores a comma	23, July, 2006
-	Inserts or ignores a hyphen	23-JUL-06
:	Inserts or ignores a colon	7:02:22
.	Inserts or ignores a period	19.02.22

Prefixes and Suffixes

Within the TO_CHAR function only, Discoverer allows you to add prefixes and suffixes to some of the standard format masks. These prefixes and suffixes further enhance the functionality of the function. The prefixes and suffixes allowed are as follows:

- **fm** This can be prefixed to both Day and Month, such that the format mask looks like fmDay or fmMonth. Using this mask forces Discoverer to suppress padding of the month or day. Without this prefix, the days of the week and months of the year are padded to make them all display as the same length.

- **TH or th** This can be suffixed to dd and DD to force Discoverer to display the date as 24th or 24TH. The capitalization is applied according to whether you choose dd or DD, or a combination like Dd or dD.

- **SP or sp** This can be suffixed to most date numbers and forces Discoverer to spell out the number in full. Using this suffix, you can spell out the date—thus, twenty fourth. Again, the capitalization is applied in accordance with the case of the number to be spelled in full.

- **SPTH or THSP** This suffix is a combination of SP and TH. Using this suffix, you can force Discoverer to apply both of the preceding two masks.

Number Format Masks

The following is a full list of the format masks that can be used within the TO_CHAR function when working with numbers in Discoverer:

- **9999990**   The number of nines or zeros determines the maximum number of digits that can be displayed.

- **999,999,999.99**   Discoverer inserts commas and the decimal point at the places specified in the pattern. If the value is zero, the result will be blank.

- **999990**   This causes Discoverer to display zero if the value is zero.

- **099999**   This causes Discoverer to display numbers with leading zeros, such that 678 will display as 000678.

- **$99999**   This causes Discoverer to insert the dollar symbol in front of every number.

- **B99999**   This causes Discoverer to display a blank field when the value is zero.

- **99999MI**   For negative numbers, this causes Discoverer to place the minus sign to the right of the number. Normally, Discoverer places the minus sign to the left.

- **99999S**   Same as 99999MI.

- **S99999**   For negative numbers, this causes Discoverer to place the minus sign to the left of the number.

- **99D99**   This causes Discoverer to insert a decimal point in the position specified.

- **C99999**   This causes Discoverer to display the ISO currency character in this position, such that 678 will display as USD678.

- **L99999**   This causes Discoverer to display the local currency character in this position, such that if your local currency is the US dollar, 678 will display as $678.

- **RN**   This causes Discoverer to display the number in Roman numerals.

- **99999PR**   For negative numbers, this causes Discoverer to display the number surrounded by the < and > symbols.

- **9.999EEEE**   This causes Discoverer to display the number in scientific notation.

- **999V99**   This causes Discoverer to multiply by $10 \times n$, where n is the number of digits to the right of the V character. For example, 9753 displays as 975300.

ASCII Character Set

As some of Discoverer's string functions make use of the American Standard Code for Information Interchange (ASCII, pronounced *ask-ee*) character set, we thought it would be a good idea to give you more background information concerning this well-used character set. The standard ASCII character set uses seven bits for each character, which means that there are 128 characters in the set. There are many larger character sets that use eight bits, which gives them an additional 128 characters, making 256 characters altogether. These extra characters are used to represent non-English characters, graphics symbols, and mathematical symbols. Several companies and organizations have proposed extensions for these 128 characters. The DOS operating system uses a superset of ASCII called extended ASCII or *high ASCII*.

A more universal standard is the ISO Latin 1 set of characters, which is used by many operating systems, as well as Web browsers. Officially named ISO-8859-1, this character set was devised by the Geneva-based International Organization for Standardization (ISO). One of the authors has the pleasure of having a good friend inside ISO; the name, by the way, is not an acronym but is derived from the Greek word *iso*, which means equal.

Table B-1 contains the standard ASCII character set.

In Table B-1, the first 32 characters (0–31) are considered to nonprinting characters. ASCII was originally designed for use with teletype machines, and so today the descriptions, as shown in Table B-2, are somewhat obscure.

You may think that these characters have no use in Discoverer, and generally, you would be correct. However, the character associated with number 13 is very useful. This is the carriage return character and as such can be concatenated with other strings. To format an address, for printing on labels for example, so that each line of the address is on a separate line, use a calculation like this:

ADDRESS1 || CHR(13) || ADDRESS2 || CHR(13) || CITY || CHR(13) || STATE || CHR(13) || ZIP

0	NUL	16	DLE	32	SPC	48	0	64	@	80	P	96		112	p
1	SOH	17	DC1	33	!	49	1	65	A	81	Q	97	a	113	q
2	STX	18	DC2	34	"	50	2	66	B	82	R	98	b	114	r
3	ETX	19	DC3	35	#	51	3	67	C	83	S	99	c	115	s
4	EOT	20	DC4	36	$	52	4	68	D	84	T	100	d	116	t
5	ENQ	21	NAK	37	%	53	5	69	E	85	U	101	e	117	u
6	ACK	22	SYN	38	&	54	6	70	F	86	V	102	f	118	v
7	BEL	23	ETB	39	'	55	7	71	G	87	W	103	g	119	w
8	BS	24	CAN	40	(	56	8	72	H	88	X	104	h	120	x
9	TAB	25	EM	41	)	57	9	73	I	89	Y	105	i	121	y
10	LF	26	SUB	42	*	58	:	74	J	90	X	106	j	122	z
11	VT	27	ESC	43	+	59	;	75	K	91	[	107	k	123	{
12	FF	28	FS	44	,	60	<	76	L	92	\	108	l	124		
13	CR	29	GS	45	-	61	=	77	M	93	]	109	m	125	}
14	SO	30	RS	46	.	62	>	78	N	94	^	110	n	126	~
15	SI	31	US	47	/	63	?	79	O	95	_	111	o	127	DEL

TABLE B-1   *Standard ASCII Character Set*

0	Null	8	Backspace	16	Data link escape	24	Cancel
1	Start of heading	9	Horizontal tab	17	Device control 1	25	End of medium
2	Start of text	10	New line	18	Device control 2	26	Substitute
3	End of text	11	Vertical tab	19	Device control 3	27	Escape
4	End of transmission	12	Form feed	20	Device control 4	28	File separator
5	Enquiry	13	Carriage return	21	Negative acknowledge	29	Group separator
6	Acknowledge	14	Shift out	22	Synchronous idle	30	Record separator
7	Bell	15	Shift in	23	End of trans block	31	Unit separator

TABLE B-2 *Descriptions of First 32 Characters*

which will print out as:

> 7531 Smith Road
> Suite 17a
> Any Town
> My State
> 12345-6789

If you turn on text wrapping, Discoverer will even display your addresses like this in your report.

Analytic Functions

In this section we will show you how to use some of the most useful of Discoverer's analytic functions.

What Are Analytic Functions?

Analytic functions are functions that run against the data in a query *after* the query has computed its normal results. Whereas standard functions such as margin and profit execute on a row-by-row basis as the query runs, analytic functions run against the results. They support basic business intelligence calculations such as moving averages, rankings, and running totals. Prior to Oracle's introduction of analytic functions in their 8*i* database, queries that required the use of this analytical horsepower were extremely difficult to build. In Discoverer, they were almost impossible. The authors understand that, although these functions are not part of the ANSI standard, there is a review underway to have them included within the standard set.

Essential Concepts

Before we get into explaining how they are used, we need to give you an explanation of the four basic concepts of analytical design. If you understand these concepts, you will have a much better chance of understanding how to use analytic functions.

The four basic concepts of analytical design are:

- Processing order

- Partitions

- Windows

- Current row

Discoverer Processing Order

In order to build a Discoverer worksheet that makes use of analytical functions, you need to build some worksheets in the following order:

1. Build the base query.

2. Add Page Items and Group Sorts.

3. Define the analytic function.

4. Create the remaining sorts.

Partitions

Do not confuse this term with database partitions. In analytic terms, and as it relates to Discoverer, the partition is simply the set of Page Items and Group Sorts that you are using. Thus you would define the PARTITION BY clause of the analytic function to use the Page Items and Group Sorts.

Windows

For each row within the partition that you have defined, you can define a sliding window of data. This window determines the number of rows that will be used by the calculation. You might think that the rows would simply be the number of rows within the partition, and in most cases you would be right. However, Discoverer allows you to take a subset of the rows such that you can tell Discoverer to give you a running total, using the first row of the partition as the start point and the current row as the end point, adding up everything between those two rows.

Using windowed analytic functions such as SUM, AVG, Standard Deviation, and Variance allows you to compute cumulative, moving, and centered averages.

Current Row

Every analytic function is executed in relation to the current row of the partition. It is used as the reference point to determine the start and end of the current window.

> **NOTE**
> *When we refer to the current row of a partition, we are referring to a row of the results, not the base rows of data as they are pulled from the database.*

Using Analytic Functions

In older releases of Discoverer, even though they supported analytic functions, you had to manually type the function yourself. In recent editions of Plus, Oracle has inserted a new button on the New Calculation dialog box called Insert Formula from Template.

FIGURE B-9 *List of analytic templates*

As you can see in Figure B-9, clicking the Insert Formula from Template button allows you to access many of the most common analytic functions, as shown here.

f(x) Rank
f(x) Percent Rank
f(x) Difference
f(x) Percent Difference
f(x) Preceding Value
f(x) Following Value
f(x) Running Total
f(x) Percent Running Contribution
f(x) Moving Total
f(x) Group Total
f(x) Percent Contribution
f(x) Band by Value
f(x) Band by Rank

In the following sections, we will walk you through two analytic functions, one for Rank and one for a Running Total. We will also discuss the concept of the partition and the window.

Figure B-10 shows the results of the base query that we will use for our analytic function examples.

		Profit	Revenue
▸ Product Size	▸ Product Name		
▸ LARGE	▸ AVR-800	$5,778,222	$10,899,194
	▸ AVR-900	$10,693,810	$20,193,326
	▸ CD-500	$6,490,672	$12,297,448
	▸ CD-550	$5,121,106	$9,522,374
	▸ CD-625	$19,945,287	$39,064,838
	▸ QB-1000	$4,523,600	$9,437,698
	▸ QB-2000	$5,284,350	$10,866,016
	▸ QB-3000	$5,853,476	$12,038,326
▸ MEDIUM	▸ AVR-500	$20,288,355	$35,776,325
	▸ AVR-550	$12,324,148	$21,681,081
	▸ CD-100	$11,440,747	$20,015,292
	▸ CD-200	$10,383,272	$18,181,974
	▸ QB-5000	$9,570,416	$18,195,109
	▸ QB-5500	$9,039,564	$17,172,184
	▸ QB-6000	$9,828,920	$18,897,604
▸ MINI	▸ DS-1200	$739,513	$2,760,838
	▸ DS-1300	$973,487	$3,028,431
	▸ MS-1200	$1,241,307	$4,307,810
	▸ MS-1300	$612,993	$1,935,768
▸ SMALL	▸ AB-2000	$5,842,489	$12,685,076
	▸ AB-2500	$5,907,660	$11,517,753
	▸ AB-3000	$9,981,105	$19,101,428

FIGURE B-10   *Base query used for analytic examples*

Creating a Ranking

Starting from our base query, as shown in Figure B-10, we launched the New Calculation dialog box and clicked the Insert Formula from Template button. From the list of available templates, as shown in Figure B-9, we selected Rank. This caused Discoverer to open the Rank dialog box shown in Figure B-11.

In the Rank dialog box, you will notice the following four areas:

■ **Rank based on**   Use this area to define the item(s) on which the ranking should be based. Discoverer will always try to populate this area for you. By default, it will use the first data point that it finds. If this is not the one that you want to rank by, change it. You can also change whether the highest value or the lowest value should be used to start the ranking.

■ **Restart ranking at each change on**   This is the partition area. Discoverer will automatically populate this area using the Page Items and Group Sorts that you are using. As you can see in Figure B-10, we have a Group Sort based on the Product Size. Discoverer has automatically brought this into the formula. Discoverer will restart the ranking according to the items that you place in here, inserting these items into the PARTITION BY clause of the SQL.

FIGURE B-11 *Rank dialog box*

■ **Rank Ties**   This area is used to tell Discoverer whether to use standard ranking or dense ranking. A standard ranking, as you can see in the example given in Figure B-11, will omit a number when there is a tie for the preceding number, whereas in the dense ranking all possible values are used.

■ **Calculation**   This area is used by Discoverer to display the SQL code that will be generated when you click OK. You cannot manually change this code. To change the code, you need to use the template.

Once you have completed the template, clicking OK causes Discoverer to create the function. Discoverer places a copy of the SQL into the New Calculation dialog box. Assuming you have defined the function correctly, all that remains now is for you to give the function a name and click OK. After completing the function, you should check the format for both the heading and the data. We typically center all of our rank functions. Here is the result.

▶ Product Size	▶ Product Name	Profit	Revenue	Rank
▶ MINI	▶ DS-1200	$739,513	$2,760,838	3
	▶ DS-1300	$973,487	$3,028,431	2
	▶ MS-1200	$1,241,307	$4,307,810	1
	▶ MS-1300	$612,993	$1,935,768	4
▶ SMALL	▶ AB-2000	$5,842,489	$12,685,076	3
	▶ AB-2500	$5,907,660	$11,517,753	2
	▶ AB-3000	$9,981,105	$19,101,428	1
▶ LARGE	▶ AVR-800	$5,778,222	$10,899,194	5
	▶ AVR-900	$10,693,810	$20,193,326	2
	▶ CD-500	$6,490,672	$12,297,448	3
	▶ CD-550	$5,121,106	$9,522,374	7
	▶ CD-625	$19,945,287	$39,064,838	1
	▶ QB-1000	$4,523,600	$9,437,698	8
	▶ QB-2000	$5,284,350	$10,866,016	6
	▶ QB-3000	$5,853,476	$12,038,326	4
▶ MEDIUM	▶ AVR-500	$20,288,355	$35,776,325	1
	▶ AVR-550	$12,324,148	$21,681,081	2
	▶ CD-100	$11,440,747	$20,015,292	3
	▶ CD-200	$10,383,272	$18,181,974	4
	▶ QB-5000	$9,570,416	$18,195,109	6
	▶ QB-5500	$9,039,564	$17,172,184	7
	▶ QB-6000	$9,828,920	$18,897,604	5

In order to complete the query, we need to add a sort on the Profit, the item that is being used to generate the rank. However, because we used a crosstab for the base query, we are unable to complete this sort. Ideally we want to be able to sort by the Profit within the Product Size, but because of the presence of the Product Number in the left axis, we are unable to do so. We therefore switched our worksheet to being a table. Once we created a group sort on the partition item, the Product Size, and a standard high-to-low sort on the ranking item, the Profit, everything worked fine as you can see here.

	▶ Product Size	▶ Product Name	▶ Profit	▶ Revenue	▶ Rank
1	LARGE	CD-625	$19,945,287	$39,064,838	1
2		AVR-900	$10,693,810	$20,193,326	2
3		CD-500	$6,490,672	$12,297,448	3
4		QB-3000	$5,853,476	$12,038,326	4
5		AVR-800	$5,778,222	$10,899,194	5
6		QB-2000	$5,284,350	$10,866,016	6
7		CD-550	$5,121,106	$9,522,374	7
8		QB-1000	$4,523,600	$9,437,698	8
9	MEDIUM	AVR-500	$20,288,355	$35,776,325	1
10		AVR-550	$12,324,148	$21,681,081	2
11		CD-100	$11,440,747	$20,015,292	3
12		CD-200	$10,383,272	$18,181,974	4
13		QB-6000	$9,828,920	$18,897,604	5
14		QB-5000	$9,570,416	$18,195,109	6
15		QB-5500	$9,039,564	$17,172,184	7
16	MINI	MS-1200	$1,241,307	$4,307,810	1
17		DS-1300	$973,487	$3,028,431	2
18		DS-1200	$739,513	$2,760,838	3
19		MS-1300	$612,993	$1,935,768	4
20	SMALL	AB-3000	$9,981,105	$19,101,428	1
21		AB-2500	$5,907,660	$11,517,753	2
22		AB-2000	$5,842,489	$12,685,076	3

You therefore need to be careful using Rank within a crosstab.

SQL Used in Rank   Here is the SQL that Discoverer generated:

```
RANK() OVER(PARTITION BY Product Size ORDER BY Profit SUM DESC)
```

Creating a Running Total

Having altered our query to work off a table rather than a crosstab, we find it a very simple task to add a running total to the query. Once again you launch the New Calculation dialog box and then click the Insert Formula from Template. As one of the options on the template list is Running Total, selecting this opens the dialog box shown in Figure B-12.

In the Running Total dialog box, you will notice the following four areas:

- **Running total on**   Use this area to define the item upon which you want the running total. Discoverer will automatically choose the first named data point.

- **Order rows by**   Use this area to define the item(s) that you want to order the query by. This will typically be the same item that is being used for the running total calculation itself.

- **Restart running total at each change in**   Once again, this is the partition area. Discoverer will automatically populate this area using the Page Items and Group Sorts that you are using. As you can see in Figure B-10, we have a Group Sort based on the Product Size. Discoverer has automatically brought this into the formula. Discoverer will restart the ranking according to the items that you place in here, inserting these items into the PARTITION BY clause of the SQL.

FIGURE B-12   *Running Total dialog box*

■ **Calculation** This area is used by Discoverer to display the SQL code that will be generated when you click OK. You cannot manually change this code. To change the code, you need to use the template.

Having completed the template, click OK for Discoverer to create the function. Discoverer places a copy of the SQL into the New Calculation dialog box. Assuming you have defined the function correctly, all that remains now is for you to give the function a name and click OK. After completing the function, you should adjust the format to make sure that it is displayed in the same way as the column upon which it is based. Here is the result.

	▸ Product Size	▸ Product Name	▸ Profit	▸ Revenue	▸ Rank	▸ Running Total
1	LARGE	CD-625	$19,945,287	$39,064,838	1	$19,945,287
2		AVR-900	$10,693,810	$20,193,326	2	$30,639,097
3		CD-500	$6,490,672	$12,297,448	3	$37,129,769
4		QB-3000	$5,853,476	$12,038,326	4	$42,983,245
5		AVR-800	$5,778,222	$10,899,194	5	$48,761,467
6		QB-2000	$5,284,350	$10,866,016	6	$54,045,817
7		CD-550	$5,121,106	$9,522,374	7	$59,166,923
8		QB-1000	$4,523,600	$9,437,698	8	$63,690,523
9	MEDIUM	AVR-500	$20,288,355	$35,776,325	1	$20,288,355
10		AVR-550	$12,324,148	$21,681,081	2	$32,612,503
11		CD-100	$11,440,747	$20,015,292	3	$44,053,250
12		CD-200	$10,383,272	$18,181,974	4	$54,436,522
13		QB-6000	$9,828,920	$18,897,604	5	$64,265,442
14		QB-5000	$9,570,416	$18,195,109	6	$73,835,858
15		QB-5500	$9,039,564	$17,172,184	7	$82,875,422
16	MINI	MS-1200	$1,241,307	$4,307,810	1	$1,241,307
17		DS-1300	$973,487	$3,028,431	2	$2,214,794
18		DS-1200	$739,513	$2,760,838	3	$2,954,307
19		MS-1300	$612,993	$1,935,768	4	$3,567,300
20	SMALL	AB-3000	$9,981,105	$19,101,428	1	$9,981,105
21		AB-2500	$5,907,660	$11,517,753	2	$15,888,765
22		AB-2000	$5,842,489	$12,685,076	3	$21,731,254

SQL Used in Running Total Here is the SQL that Discoverer generated:

```
SUM(Profit SUM) OVER(PARTITION BY Product Size ORDER BY Profit SUM DESC
ROWS UNBOUNDED PRECEDING)
```

Do you see how this SQL has been put together and how it differs from the SQL that was generated for the Rank function?

First of all, you should notice that the name of the function being used is not RUNNING TOTAL but SUM. This is because a running total is a specialized type of SUM. You should also notice that we are using some windowing commands for the first time. Unless stated otherwise, the base row for all analytical functions is the current row.

We could easily have written the SQL to explicitly reference the current row, as follows:

```
SUM(Profit SUM) OVER(PARTITION BY Product Size ORDER BY Profit SUM DESC RANGE
BETWEEN
UNBOUNDED PRECEDING AND CURRENT ROW)
```

The end results of running these two sets of SQL are identical. This is because an implied CURRENT ROW is being used in the first example, whereas an explicit CURRENT ROW command is being used in the latter case.

Editing Analytical Functions

Unfortunately, the templates that we have shown you in the Rank and Running Total examples are available only at the creation stage. If you want to edit an existing analytic function, you have to do this manually, altering the SQL yourself.

At first, this can seem daunting, especially if you are not very good at SQL or have not had much exposure to it. The authors hope that in a future release of Discoverer Oracle will be able to bring back the template for editing purposes, not just for creation purposes.

We will now show you how to edit both the Rank and Running Total examples. We have added another component to our query, by inserting the Product Line as a Page Item. This gave us the initial result shown in Figure B-13.

As you can see in Figure B-13, the inclusion of an additional Page Item has upset both of our calculations. This is because both calculations use a PARTITION and, as mentioned previously, the partition consists of both Page Items and Group Sorted items.

Editing the Rank

If we edit the Rank function and change the SQL as follows, the function will be correct:

```
RANK() OVER(PARTITION BY Line Name, Product Size ORDER BY Profit SUM DESC)
```

The intermediate result is as follows:

Page Items: Line Name: MEGA-WIDGET ▾

	▶ Product Size	▶ Product Name	▶ Profit	▶ Revenue	▶ Rank	▶ Running Total
1	LARGE	CD-625	$19,945,287	$39,064,838	1	$19,945,287
2		CD-500	$6,490,672	$12,297,448	2	$37,129,769
3		CD-550	$5,121,106	$9,522,374	3	$59,166,923
4	MEDIUM	CD-100	$11,440,747	$20,015,292	1	$44,053,250
5		CD-200	$10,383,272	$18,181,974	2	$54,436,522
6	SMALL	AB-2500	$5,907,660	$11,517,753	1	$15,888,765

Editing the Running Total

If we next edit the Running Total function and change the SQL using one of the following extracts, this function will also be correct:

```
SUM(Profit SUM) OVER(PARTITION BY Line Name, Product Size ORDER BY
Profit SUM DESC ROWS UNBOUNDED PRECEDING)
```

or

```
SUM(Profit SUM) OVER(PARTITION BY Line Name, Product Size ORDER BY
Profit SUM DESC RANGE BETWEEN UNBOUNDED PRECEDING AND CURRENT ROW)
```

The final result is shown here.

Page Items: Line Name: MEGA-WIDGET ▾

	▶ Product Size	▶ Product Name	▶ Profit	▶ Revenue	▶ Rank	▶ Running Total
1	LARGE	CD-625	$19,945,287	$39,064,838	1	$19,945,287
2		CD-500	$6,490,672	$12,297,448	2	$26,435,959
3		CD-550	$5,121,106	$9,522,374	3	$31,557,065
4	MEDIUM	CD-100	$11,440,747	$20,015,292	1	$11,440,747
5		CD-200	$10,383,272	$18,181,974	2	$21,824,019
6	SMALL	AB-2500	$5,907,660	$11,517,753	1	$5,907,660

	Product Size	Product Name	Profit	Revenue	Rank	Running Total
1	LARGE	CD-625	$19,945,287	$39,064,838	1	$19,945,287
2		CD-500	$6,490,672	$12,297,448	3	$37,129,769
3		CD-550	$5,121,106	$9,522,374	7	$59,166,923
4	MEDIUM	CD-100	$11,440,747	$20,015,292	3	$44,053,250
5		CD-200	$10,383,272	$18,181,974	4	$54,436,522
6	SMALL	AB-2500	$5,907,660	$11,517,753	2	$15,888,765

Page Items: Line Name: MEGA-WIDGET

FIGURE B-13 *Query modified to include Product Line*

Windowing Options

In the SQL examples that we have given you for a Running Total, you can see that we have used some windowing code to define exactly the range of rows that the function should use.

When working with analytic windows, you can either explicitly or dynamically tell Discoverer which rows should be used within the window.

Explicit Windows

An *explicit* window uses fixed points to define the start and end rows. As previously mentioned, unless you state otherwise, Discoverer uses the current row as the end point. When using ranges for windows, you can use one of the following three fixed windows:

- **CURRENT ROW**   Explicitly use the current row as one of the end points.

- **UNBOUNDED PRECEDING**   Explicitly use the first row of the window as one of the end points.

- **UNBOUNDED FOLLOWING**   Explicitly use the last row of the window as the end point.

Explicit Example   Using both UNBOUNDED PRECEDING and UNBOUNDED FOLLOWING at the same time effectively includes the whole window. You can take advantage of this to use the SUM function over the whole range. Try altering the Running Total calculation as follows:

```
SUM(Profit SUM) OVER(PARTITION BY Line Name, Product Size ORDER BY
Profit SUM DESC RANGE BETWEEN UNBOUNDED PRECEDING AND UNBOUNDED FOLLOWING)
```

Without looking at the illustration that follows, can you work out what this does?

The revised calculation that we have given is no longer a Running Total but a grand total for the whole window. In the following illustration, we have altered and renamed the calculation.

Page Items: Line Name: MEGA-WIDGET

	Product Size	Product Name	Profit	Revenue	Rank	Grand Total
1	LARGE	CD-625	$19,945,287	$39,064,838	1	$31,557,065
2		CD-500	$6,490,672	$12,297,448	2	$31,557,065
3		CD-550	$5,121,106	$9,522,374	3	$31,557,065
4	MEDIUM	CD-100	$11,440,747	$20,015,292	1	$21,824,019
5		CD-200	$10,383,272	$18,181,974	2	$21,824,019
6	SMALL	AB-2500	$5,907,660	$11,517,753	1	$5,907,660

Using this calculation, you could now create other calculations that use the grand total. For example, one such calculation could divide the profit by the grand total to give you the percentage.

Dynamic Windows

A *dynamic* window, as its name implies, uses variable pointers or offsets to define the window. You can take advantage of this feature to use the AVG or SUM functions over that range, effectively doing a running total over a moving range. For this next example, we will use the following new query:

	Channel	Year	Quarter	Revenue
1	EXTERNAL	FY2003	2003-Q1	$4,992,798
2			2003-Q2	$4,623,845
3			2003-Q3	$6,017,527
4			2003-Q4	$4,661,013
5		FY2004	2004-Q1	$5,967,519
6			2004-Q2	$5,132,998
7			2004-Q3	$6,133,925
8			2004-Q4	$5,733,493
9		FY2005	2005-Q1	$4,931,790
10			2005-Q2	$6,375,212
11			2005-Q3	$3,851,334
12	INTERNET	FY2003	2003-Q1	$5,283,613
13			2003-Q2	$7,866,356
14			2003-Q3	$7,530,882
15			2003-Q4	$10,484,868
16		FY2004	2004-Q1	$10,162,536
17			2004-Q2	$7,551,283
18			2004-Q3	$13,478,211
19			2004-Q4	$11,286,725
20		FY2005	2005-Q1	$14,599,099
21			2005-Q2	$15,771,478
22			2005-Q3	$11,486,008
23			2005-Q4	$11,305

By adding the following new calculation, we can generate a moving average.

```
AVG(Selling Price SUM) OVER(PARTITION BY Channel ORDER BY Ship
Date."Quarter End Date" ROWS 2 PRECEDING)
```

As you can see in this illustration, we have generated a three-month moving average:

To change the moving average, you simply alter the value for the number of rows in the PRECEDING command; e.g., with the query reporting by quarter, if you change the number of rows to be 3 PRECEDING, you are effectively creating a yearly moving average.

A very interesting possibility arises when moving analytic functions to the Page Items. If you move the moving average calculation out from the body of the table and into Page Items, you get a list of all the moving average amounts in low-to-high order. Using the list of values that Discoverer automatically creates on a Page Item allows you to take in the highest or lowest moving average at a glance.

	Channel	Year	Quarter	Revenue	Moving Avg
1	EXTERNAL	FY2003	2003-Q1	$4,992,798	$4,992,798
2			2003-Q2	$4,623,845	$4,808,321
3			2003-Q3	$6,017,527	$5,211,390
4			2003-Q4	$4,661,013	$5,100,795
5		FY2004	2004-Q1	$5,967,519	$5,548,686
6			2004-Q2	$5,132,998	$5,253,843
7			2004-Q3	$6,133,925	$5,744,814
8			2004-Q4	$5,733,493	$5,666,805
9		FY2005	2005-Q1	$4,931,790	$5,599,736
10			2005-Q2	$6,375,212	$5,680,165
11			2005-Q3	$3,851,334	$5,052,779
12	INTERNET	FY2003	2003-Q1	$5,283,613	$5,283,613
13			2003-Q2	$7,866,356	$6,574,984
14			2003-Q3	$7,530,882	$6,893,617
15			2003-Q4	$10,484,868	$8,627,369
16		FY2004	2004-Q1	$10,162,536	$9,392,762
17			2004-Q2	$7,551,283	$9,399,562
18			2004-Q3	$13,478,211	$10,397,343
19			2004-Q4	$11,286,725	$10,772,073
20		FY2005	2005-Q1	$14,599,099	$13,121,345
21			2005-Q2	$15,771,478	$13,885,767
22			2005-Q3	$11,486,008	$13,952,195
23			2005-Q4	$11,305	$9,089,597

The Power of Analytics

As we hope you have learned from the preceding discussion, the use of analytic functions opens up another dimension in Discoverer reporting. As a bit of fun, and as an example of the power of analytics, we will give you one final example.

Take a look at the following example:

	Products that generate at least 10% of revenue per product line			

Page Items: ▮ Year: FY2005 ▾ ▮ Region: NORTH AMERICA ▾

	▸ Line Name	▸ Total Sales per Line	▸ Product Name	▸ Product Revenue
1	MEGA-WIDGET	$8,599,045	CD-625	$2,909,683
2			AB-2500	$1,042,950
3			CD-500	$1,021,611
4			CD-200	$1,166,076
5			CD-100	$1,707,710
6	MINI-WIDGET	$1,181,684	MS-1200	$344,994
7			DS-1300	$341,399
8			MS-1300	$178,140
9			DS-1200	$317,151
10	SUPER-WIDGET	$10,191,395	AVR-550	$2,421,727
11			AVR-900	$1,963,997
12			AVR-800	$1,038,807
13			AB-3000	$1,653,654
14			AVR-500	$3,113,210
15	WONDER-WIDGET	$8,032,178	QB-5500	$1,489,939
16			QB-5000	$907,724
17			QB-3000	$1,187,508
18			QB-1000	$1,292,330
19			AB-2000	$1,289,534
20			QB-6000	$1,202,823

What this does is show only those products that have generated more than 10 percent of the total revenue for the product line. It uses one calculation and one condition.

The first calculation shows the total revenue for a line using this analytic function:

```
SUM(Selling Price SUM) OVER(PARTITION BY Ship Date."Year",
Customer.Region, Products.Line Name ORDER BY Selling Price SUM DESC RANGE BETWEEN
UNBOUNDED PRECEDING AND UNBOUNDED FOLLOWING)
```

This generates the same grand total for all rows. However, in order to show the result only once, we added a GROUP SORT to this item.

Next we created a new condition such that we include only those products that have generated revenue greater than 10 percent of the analytic calculation, and that's it. Discoverer handled the rest!

This section on analytic functions is not intended to be a manual that teaches you how to use analytics but to give you a flavor of the power of analytics. Please use this appendix as a reference to the analytics, using the earlier part of the chapter as a cross-reference for the syntax of all of the analytic functions.

Summary

In this appendix, we listed all of the functions that are used within Discoverer, along with their syntax and many examples. After this, we included a comprehensive listing of the format masks that can be used, along with a table listing the ASCII character set. Finally, we introduced you to analytic functions and showed you how to use a template to help you create these powerful functions.

APPENDIX C

Databases and Views

his appendix explains several database concepts. We begin by explaining the difference between traditional schemas, relational schemas, and star schemas. During the discussion on relational schemas, we give you an introduction to the techniques known as normalization and denormalization. Following this, we will take a look at the use of Discoverer with the Oracle E-Business Suite. We explain why views are used and introduce you to Oracle's Business Views and Oracle Daily Business Intelligence. We then look in depth at Noetix Corporation's NoetixViews.

Database Schemas

There are two basic schemas or types of database structures that you will encounter when working with Discoverer. These are as follows:

- Relational schemas

- Star schemas

Relational Schemas

A *relational* schema is the traditional type of structure that is used by most databases today. These schemas depend on parent-child relationships, with primary keys and foreign keys. There is also no redundancy in the tables. These schemas are not designed for reporting and can become very complex.

For example, in a typical database of this type, there will be a table of addresses, a table of cities, and a table of countries, with each one appearing in the database once. Therefore, to print a full address, you would have to open up several Discoverer folders.

Relational schemas are based on the relational model for database management, put forward by Edgar F. Codd, a British computer scientist who devised the model while working for IBM during the 1960s and 1970s. Much to his disappointment, IBM did not fully embrace this new database model until after rivals such as Oracle started to embrace them. You may not be aware of this fact, but Edgar Codd also devised the term OLAP and wrote the laws for online analytical processing.

The Relational Concept

As defined by Codd in 1985, there are a number of rules that concisely define what constitutes a relational database. In actual fact there are 13 rules, because the rules are numbered Rule 0 to Rule 12; however, they are commonly known as the 12 rules.

These 12 rules have become the guideline for the design of all relational databases ever since. However, we must be careful using the term "guideline" because, to date, no commercial relational database system conforms to all 12 of the rules. We will not discuss all of the 12 rules here. However, we will mention that, in its simplest form, to be classified as relational, a database must have tables that have primary keys, interlinked to other tables using foreign-key relationships and constraints. The system must also support the concept of having null data and be able to support the use of views to present the data to users in different logical combinations. You will notice that Discoverer obeys all of these rules.

For a full understanding of the 12 rules, we recommend you take a look at the following link: http://en.wikipedia.org/wiki/Codd's_12_rules.

Normalization and Denormalization

You may have heard of the terms normalization and denormalization. *Normalization* is where the data is stored within the database once and once only. This is the pure relational schema and allows for the quickest method of inserting and updating data in the database. Because the data is stored only once, there is no redundancy of data, but this could make for poor performance when reporting.

The most common level of normalization is called third normal form, otherwise known as 3NF. To be classified as third normal form, all of the data in a row of data must be dependent upon the primary key, the whole of the primary key, and nothing but the primary key. In other words, if you have any data in the row that does not have a strict 1:1 relationship with the primary key, you are not strictly adhering to 3NF. Also, if you have calculated items such as totals that can be derived using other items within the row, you are not using a fully normalized structure.

Denormalization allows for the data to be stored multiple times when and where required. This allows for faster reporting but slower insertion and updating. A data warehouse uses mainly denormalized data structures. In Discoverer terms, you would use a complex folder to denormalize a schema to make it easier for your users to query from.

Using a classroom setting as an example, the following illustration shows a typical normalized, relational schema:

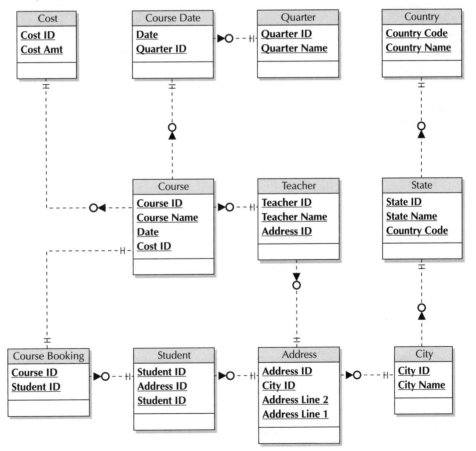

As you can see in the preceding illustration, we have eleven normalized tables. Each table has a unique numeric ID or code, and no data is being duplicated. In order to find all of the students who graduated in a particular quarter and then mail them their certificates, you would need to join nine tables together.

Star Schemas

Otherwise known as a dimensional model, a denormalized *star* schema is traditionally used in a data warehouse. There is no attempt to reduce redundant data; instead, data is copied as many times as is needed in order to make querying as efficient and easy as possible. In a star schema, you normally have a central fact table, surrounded by many dimension tables. A pure fact table contains nothing except a foreign key for each of the dimension tables, and facts or metrics such as costs, quantities, and so on. Using a star schema with Discoverer, if you select an item from the fact table, all of the other tables are available. If you begin selecting from a dimension table, your next selection must come from the fact table.

Using the same classroom setting from our previous example, the following illustration shows the database as a star schema:

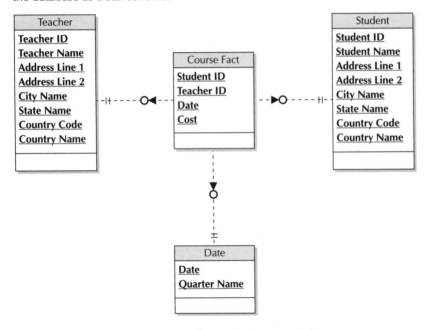

This schema differs from the relational schema as follows:

- The course table has been dropped and has been replaced by a fact table. This fact table contains the foreign-key ID of each of the dimension tables.

- The cost table has been dropped, with the cost of the course added to the fact table.

- The ID of the fact table is made up by concatenating all of the foreign keys together.

- All of the address information has been denormalized and is now stored in the Student and Teacher tables.

- All of the time information has been denormalized and is in the Date table.

Not all databases have data in a denormalized state, and few databases, other than data warehouses, have anything remotely resembling a star schema. During the section of this book that covers Discoverer administration, we showed the administrator how to create a pseudo star schema using complex folders. Users seem to be able to relate to star schemas better than traditional relational schemas. Discoverer itself works best against a star schema model. Thus, if you can take the time to either build a star schema within the database, perhaps using materialized views and lookup tables, or a star model within Discoverer, your users will thank you for it. Most failed Discoverer implementations are not the fault of the product but the fault of either poor database design or a poor business area design.

Accessing Oracle Applications Using Discoverer

Oracle Applications E-Business Suite provides world-class functionality through transactional power and the ability to support complex business processes. The data stored within its tables is a valuable information asset. Using Discoverer, this data can be leveraged to provide information used across the entire spectrum of decision making. This section deals with and explains various mechanisms for how your company could use Discoverer to access Oracle Applications.

Trying to query from Oracle Applications can be daunting. In order to enjoy the benefit, you have to know the database structures, the field names, and how the tables are joined together. Added to this is the fact that Oracle has made its applications flexible. By flexible, we mean that they have provided flexfields, fields that you can use to customize your database. The use of these fields causes Oracle Applications to dynamically change the screens that you use for order entry. This is perfect for your data entry staff, but just how do you query these fields? You don't know which flexfield is being used, and you certainly won't know the rules or list of values.

In an Oracle Application, a flexfield is made up of a number of segments. Each segment has an assigned name and a set of valid values. Oracle Applications uses flexfields to capture information about your organization. There are two kinds of flexfields:

■ **Key flexfields** These are required within Oracle applications to record key data elements. They are predefined, with each key flexfield being owned by a specific Oracle Application but being shared across all the applications. The most well-known is the Accounting flexfield, which is owned by the General Ledger (GL) application and is used to represent an organization's chart of accounts. Even though it is owned by GL, it is used across nearly all of the applications. During setup your organization will choose how to define the key flexfields by deciding how many segments each field uses. For example, one organization may decide to customize the Accounting flexfield to have three segments called Company, Department, and Account, while another organization may need to use five segments called Company, Cost Center, Account, Sub–Account, and Product. Examples of other key flexfields are the Grade flexfield in Human Resources (HR), the Item Categories flexfield in Oracle Inventory, and the Bank Details Key flexfield in Oracle Payroll.

■ **Descriptive flexfields** These are user-defined and are used to store additional, required data elements that are not provided by the standard Oracle Applications functionality. Just about every major table in Oracle Applications has these descriptive flexfields. Using them, you can customize the system to capture additional information without the need for additional programming.

When using query and reporting tools against Oracle Applications, issues arise with concern to flexfields and lookup codes. Out of the box, these tools have no way of knowing the techniques that Oracle has used to add this flexibility. For example, if you have used the Vendor tables in the Purchasing module, you will know that SEGMENT1 is used to store your Vendor Number. However, your query tool does not know this, and so when you query the PO_VENDORS table, you have to remember to alias it every time, like this:

```
select vend.segment1 vendor_no,
vend.vendor_name
from po_vendors vend
```

In Appendix A we have provided some further simple SQL scripts you can use against Oracle applications.

Given that this situation makes for difficult querying, Oracle provides the ability to create views of the data. A *view* is simply a way to pull together data from related tables into one place, in a very efficient manner. A view knows how to join the tables together and can change the Oracle field names to make them more meaningful to you. Views do not contain any data, though; they are only pointers to the data, but you can access them in Discoverer just as if they were tables.

Most companies use views of the database. They simplify querying and they also ensure that the same joins are being made each time, thereby releasing you from having to worry about linking the Oracle tables together. Using a combination of views and an end-user query tool like Discoverer takes away all of the pain and hardship that writing your own queries creates.

Until the late 1990s there was really only one company, Noetix Corporation, that provided a total set of views against the Oracle E-Business Suite. Their product, NoetixViews, is well known and works very well with Discoverer. More recently, Oracle developed its own views, called Business Views. A third option is for your company to build your own views.

We will give you an overview of all three approaches in the next section.

Oracle Applications Business Views

Oracle released its Business Views at the same time that the original Oracle Discoverer Handbook was being submitted for publication. Until the most recent releases, these views have been incorporated in every release of the 11*i* Oracle Applications. We believe that the last major release of Oracle Applications to come with the Oracle Business Intelligence Suite was 11.5.8.

If you have Apps 11.5.8 or earlier, there are nearly 800 views in the Oracle Business Intelligence System (BIS), covering virtually all modules. Using these views, you can perform ad hoc and custom reporting using Discoverer. Oracle even provides you with prewritten Discoverer business areas and workbooks for use within the business areas. We think this is a wonderful feature.

Oracle Business Views and Discoverer are two of the essential components of Oracle's BIS. Business Views is a layer of database views relating business entity descriptions for use in ad hoc queries against Oracle Applications data. These views deliver the following three important features:

- The ability to present information at a level that is of interest to business users

- The ability to present information in user-friendly terminology

- The ability to present information with consistency across the various Applications products

Oracle Business Views comes in two flavors: base views and full views. The base views are typically created on a single underlying table or view, perhaps joining two at most. Full views, on the other hand, may point to several underlying tables or views. These full views will, therefore, contain several joins and take slightly longer to query from—as opposed to the base views.

Security

Another really wonderful feature of Business Views is that it provides out-of-the-box support for Oracle Applications security—incidentally, enabling Discoverer to be the only ad hoc query solution on the market with this capability. Oracle Applications has a very sophisticated security mechanism, and anyone implementing Discoverer against Oracle Applications using Business Views can leverage the same security structures. This ensures consistent access control across both the main database and business intelligence systems. All of the user accounts and responsibilities that have been set up in your main E-Business suite application are available in Discoverer immediately, without any extra setup by your Discoverer administrator.

In particular, you gain the ability to use existing Oracle Applications usernames, passwords, and responsibilities through Discoverer. Oracle Discoverer is fully cognizant of the Oracle Applications security model, and it is capable of returning data that is dependent on the user's userid and Application responsibility combination.

Cross-Organization Support

Discoverer also provides the same level of multi-organization access control that is available through Oracle Applications. Cross-organization reporting is also supported. With cross-organization reporting support, end users have access to a list of organizations within Oracle Applications, as opposed to a single organization. Discoverer's users access the data pertaining to the organizations to which the Applications administrator has granted them access.

Oracle Applications is designed to allow the ability to run reports across multiple organizations captured within your enterprise resource planning (ERP) system. These are distinct operating entities and are implemented via row-level security within most Applications tables and views. These tables and views are tagged with an org_id column. This column specifies which row in a given table is logically grouped into which organization. Whenever an application user logs in with a given Applications userid and responsibility combination, the system sets up a security mechanism that contains that user's org_id key. Thus, any queries run against a given Application table or view will return only a subset of the data in that table, depending on that user's org_id. This enables Oracle Applications to efficiently store multiple reporting organizations within one set of tables and views.

Oracle Business Intelligence System

Oracle's Business Intelligence System (BIS) is a performance management system for Oracle Applications, built with the proven technology of Oracle Discoverer, Alert, and Workflow. Oracle Discoverer is integrated with BIS to provide powerful analysis solutions for Oracle Applications. BIS is an integrated set of intelligence modules for Financials, Purchasing, Operations, Human Resources, and Process Manufacturing. Each intelligence module comes with prebuilt Discoverer workbooks that provide ad hoc and detailed analysis of critical day-to-day performance measures, calculated from Oracle Applications. BIS also includes the Oracle Applications EUL for Discoverer.

The Oracle Applications EUL is a complete set of easy-to-understand business definitions that represent Oracle Applications data. The EUL simplifies the entire Oracle Applications database and enables users to quickly create and modify analysis reports in any business area. BIS is ideal for customers looking for a prepackaged out-of-the-box solution that has comprehensive coverage of almost all Applications modules. One big advantage of the BIS solution was that it offered a dramatic time reduction over a "do it yourself" approach. Another advantage is that as new releases of Oracle Applications were introduced, the shipped BIS EUL was updated to accommodate these changes, which meant less maintenance for you. Now that BIS is no longer being developed and is not part of 11.5.9 onward, the picture is less clear than it was. We believe that Oracle has designated Daily Business Intelligence (DBI) as the replacement for BIS. However, this is very new, and we have not been able to get our hands on a copy to try this out for you.

Daily Business Intelligence

As mentioned, DBI has been designated as the replacement for BIS. The base DBI comes with its own reporting layer and has nothing to do with Discoverer. However, DBI is not customizable. In order to customize DBI, you will need to use NoetixViews.

In a press release issued on July 25, 2005, Noetix Corporation and Oracle announced that "they are working together to enhance the integration of Noetix software with Oracle® Daily Business Intelligence, the embedded management reporting system of the Oracle E-Business Suite. This arrangement will demonstrate the combined value of Noetix's market-leading NoetixViews® products for Oracle E-Business Suite with the recently released Oracle Daily Business Intelligence Designer tool, enabling Oracle Daily Business Intelligence customers to extend the value of the reporting system's pre-built dashboards, key performance indicators (KPIs), and reports with custom-built content based upon NoetixViews."

The press release continues, "Oracle Daily Business Intelligence provides hundreds of pre-built KPIs, dashboards, and reports that deliver accurate, timely, and actionable information to decision makers across the enterprise. Noetix technology enables users of Oracle Daily Business Intelligence to rapidly create additional KPIs and reports directly within its framework to provide a more flexible and extensible solution."

According to Oracle, they are "experiencing unprecedented adoption of DBI among their E-Business Suite customers. Oracle Daily Business Intelligence helps customers maximize their investment in our applications by delivering better, more timely information out of the box. In conjunction with NoetixViews, Oracle Daily Business Intelligence offers robust extensibility features that provide a highly productive and efficient solution for creating custom content."

Flexfield Management

Companies differ from each other in organizational structure and operational procedures. This is obvious through the differences in information systems. To accommodate these different business processes, Oracle Applications is highly customizable and enables customers to set up and configure their OLTP systems in a flexible manner. Descriptive and key flexfields are one of the features of Oracle Applications that provide this type of flexibility. You can set up these flexfields to suit your particular business practices. The architecture of Discoverer supports flexfields. At each customer site, the flexfield customizations are displayed as EUL items within appropriate folders.

Flexfield configuration information is determined once the Discoverer EUL and Applications Business Views are installed on your site. Each Business View contains placeholders, or tokens, that represent site-specific variable information. These tokens represent the key and descriptive flexfields that you have set up in your system. During the installation and setup process on your site, the Business Views Generator (a new component of the Applications Object Library that is part of Oracle Applications 11*i*) program runs, taking as input the "tokenized" views that have been shipped and your specific flexfield configuration.

This program replaces the tokens with columns, derived from the flexfield configuration information, and produces a modified set of views as the output. Discoverer's built-in "refresh" functionality adds the same new columns to the appropriate folders in the EUL. The end result is a complete EUL based on your flexfield customizations, an environment that provides a complete end-user ad hoc query and analysis solution.

Oracle Help and Guides

Oracle has provided comprehensive information and procedures that are of use to both end users and administrators of Oracle Applications. The guides that are of use to Discoverer users are as follows:

- **BIS 11*i* User Guide Online Help**   This guide, in HTML format, is provided as an online help from the BIS application and includes information about the various Discoverer workbooks that are available.

- **Oracle Discoverer Administration Guide**   This guide provides reference information for your Discoverer administrator. It contains information on how to define security, manage the EUL, create and customize business areas, and manage summary information.

- **Oracle BIS Implementation Guide**   This guide contains all information necessary to implement the Oracle Business Intelligence System in your company. It contains an overview of the Discoverer workbooks and worksheets that are provided by the system.

NoetixViews

NoetixViews converts Oracle Applications data tables into a user-friendly set of business views. Used with Discoverer, NoetixViews delivers a total solution for end-user reporting and ad hoc queries. We have seen NoetixViews in use for several years and can recommend it to anyone considering purchasing a suite of views to use against Oracle Applications 10.7, 11.0, and 11*i*.

Quoting further from the press release referred to earlier, when you install NoetixViews, Noetix MetaBuilder "uses a unique auto-discovery process to 'crawl' your specific Oracle E-Business Suite database, generating a set of business views that transforms complex data structures into business intelligence content. Using this innovative technology, Noetix is able to accelerate greatly the deployment of a wide range of BI tools, from custom and ad hoc report development to analytical and dashboard solutions technology."

Noetix MetaBuilder automatically analyzes your applications database looking for customizations that you have made, and flexfields that you have set up, creating what Noetix calls a "comprehensive library of metadata." This metadata is presented to you as a series of database views. In these views, Noetix makes data available to you using your business terminology—the terms that you used to set up the system.

For example, let's say that you have decided that ATTRIBUTE1 is being used to store the Airport Name, and that ATTRIBUTE2 is being used to store the three-character Airport Code. NoetixViews will display these fields as Airport_Name and Airport_Code, making it much easier for you to create queries. Another thing that NoetixViews does for you is to remove the complexity of the underlying data structures by making the necessary joins between the base tables for you. Thus, you end up with one view.

The following Oracle E-Business Suite Applications are supported: Financials, Manufacturing, Benefits, Supply Chain, Projects, Human Resources, and Payroll. To identify the business areas or roles, Noetix prefixes the views with a two- or three-letter code indicating which module is being used. For example, BOM indicates Bills of Materials, INV for Inventory, OE for Order Entry, and so on. During the install, NoetixViews examines each set of books, business group, operating unit, or organization and creates a separate role for each. It then appends one or two letters to indicate which organization the view belongs to. Let's say you have three organizations: US for

America, EU for Europe, and AF for Africa. Using these codes, BOMUS would be used as the prefix for the Bills of Materials business area for America, while OEAF would be used as the prefix for the Order Entry business area for Africa.

When you open Discoverer, these are the areas that you would look for. Opening one of these business areas displays the folders within. Each folder corresponds to a single view. When you open up a folder, you can see the items that you need. Noetix uses codes to indicate which items are indexes and which are flexfields. NoetixViews also includes an extensive online help system that is available from both the client and the server. The help system, described later in this section, assists you in finding the right data and how to understand its usefulness.

Codes Used Within NoetixViews

When you open a folder based on a view that is part of NoetixViews, you will notice the following codes being used:

- **A$** This code is added as a prefix to all columns that are indexed. NoetixViews classifies these columns as Search By columns. You should always select indexed columns when you can, and always try to create conditions based on indexed values. Your query will return data much quicker when you do this. For example,

    - A$CUSTOMER is an index based on the customer name.

    - A$SHIP_DATE is an index based on the ship date.

NOTE
Whenever possible, you should always use Search By columns to locate your data. If you do not use these columns, the data will still be located; however, it will take Discoverer much longer. This is because Discoverer has to scan all of the rows in the Oracle table.

- **$** When you see the dollar symbol embedded inside a column name, this indicates that the column is a flexfield. The flexfield can be either an Oracle key flexfield or a descriptive flexfield.

For example, POLIN$Ship_Date is the column associated with the flexfield that you have defined as being the ship date. The word POLIN preceding the dollar symbol is a code for the Oracle table that the field is coming from. The word Ship_Date following the dollar symbol is the name that you have given to one of the flexfields on the purchase order line.

Noetix also provides an excellent help file. The preceding terminology is repeated in the help file so that you can see at a glance the fields in the system.

NoetixHelp File

When you install NoetixViews, it builds a context-sensitive help file for you to use. Opening this help file gives you a list of all of the business areas that NoetixViews has created. Clicking a business area allows you to drill down to see a list of the folders that make up that business area. NoetixViews then gives a brief description of each folder and classifies each as being basic, value added, or cross-functional.

These folder types are described as follows:

- **Basic** The folders that are classified as basic draw their information from a single Oracle form or data entry screen. These folders pull their data from a maximum of four tables. Querying from a basic folder is fast.

- **Value added**   The folders that are classified as value added draw their information from several forms or data entry screens, but all within the same Oracle module. These folders pull their data from four to eight tables and are slower to query from than basic folders.

- **Cross-functional**   The folders that are classified as cross-functional draw their information from forms or entry screens across two or more Oracle modules. These folders pull their data from eight to fourteen tables and are by far the slowest to query from.

Each view contains hints to give you the quickest and most efficient access to your data. These hints tell you how to choose the best columns upon which to apply conditions. Using these hints to build a query is a very fast way of getting up and running.

The list of column names uses the same dollar codes outlined earlier in this section. In addition, you may also see columns prefixed by Z$. These are joins to other views and give you an indication as to what Discoverer folders will be active should you decide to select a column from this view.

Tips for Using NoetixViews with Discoverer

There are a number of ways that you can help yourself write efficient Discoverer queries when using NoetixViews. The following is a list of tips we recommend you follow:

- Have the NoetixViews help file open on your desktop.

- Look at the hints given in the help file for clues on how to build queries. When a hint states that you need to apply a certain condition on an item, you should always do so.

- Try to query from basic folders whenever possible.

- Try to use Search By columns whenever possible.

- Always try to apply conditions on the Search By columns.

- Try not to join to more than four other folders in the same query, and even then try to use only basic folders.

NoetixViews Customization Certification

To meet the need of custom reporting requirements, it is possible to customize the views. Modifying aspects of a view—for example, by adding columns, tables, and where clauses—requires proper training and certification from Noetix. NoetixViews Customization Certification (NVCC) is an instructor-led training course offered by Noetix. This course provides students with the knowledge and skills necessary to efficiently create customizations. Further, if you are certified to customize the NoetixViews, your customizations will be supported by Noetix. However, if you are not certified, any changes you make to the views will be unsupported, and you could easily make a mess of your whole reporting system. Our recommendation, therefore, is to take the course.

EUL Generator from Noetix Corporation

The Noetix EUL Generator is a companion tool that can be used to populate the End User Layer of Discoverer, allowing minimal administration of NoetixViews Business Areas.

The following is a list of the tasks that the EUL Generator takes care of:

- Business Area creation

- Security

- Item classes

- Sorts

- Hierarchies

Why Use NoetixViews?

During the course of our consultations, we are frequently asked why companies should use NoetixViews. First of all we reply "apart from the fact that they are superbly coded and work out of the box you mean?" We sometimes hear "we cannot afford to buy NoetixViews, what should we do?" To this we answer "if you have Oracle E-Business Suite, you cannot afford not to use NoetixViews!"

When you install NoetixViews, each Oracle E-Business Suite module comes with between 30 and 50 views. Even if you can replicate the code inside each view, and that you could do this in one day, it will take you between 30 and 50 man days to write your own views. This excludes the amount of time and effort required to build a Discoverer business area of these 30 to 50 interlinked views. So let's allow another two weeks of development effort for each business area, bringing the effort to between 8 and 12 weeks.

What happens if you have ten modules? This will take you 80 to 120 man-weeks of effort. Would you really want to make your users wait between one and two years to get at the data? Of course not, which is why we say that, for the moment, NoetixViews is the only game in town.

Here are a few more points for you to consider:

- The authors are not on commission from Noetix. Our recommendation is based purely upon experience.

- If you are using multiple organizations and multiple currencies, you can double or triple the time estimates just given.

- If you write your own views, you need to retain the services of at least one developer.

Company-Built Views

Probably the easiest way to get a quick view of the database is to get someone from your IT department to build a SQL script. Most companies use SQL. If you are lucky enough to have experienced IT staff, fluent in the complexities of writing SQL scripts, you probably already have a number of existing queries that you use today.

In order to use these scripts, you either have your IT department run them for you or you log in to the database and run them yourself. The big disadvantage of this approach is that you cannot quickly modify the script, nor can you use it for ad hoc reporting.

However, it only takes a small step further to turn these scripts into views. Then you have your Discoverer administrator create a new folder based on the view and, voilà, there you have converted a SQL script into a Discoverer folder. Now you, and everyone else who has access to the folder, can create ad hoc queries.

Another thing to consider when it comes to creating your own custom views is database optimization. Even though your Discoverer administrator has the ability to add a database hint to any of the folders that are based on a database object, we have rarely seen this used to good effect. If you are having difficulty with the performance of a complex folder within Discoverer, you ought to give serious consideration to converting these complex folders into database views. You can then insert powerful optimization hints into the view to force the database to pull the data in the most efficient way. The optimization hints that you can provide within a view are far more potent than you could ever provide from within Discoverer. We have seen occurrences of non-optimized views and Discoverer complex folders taking ten or more minutes to pull the data, with a modified view containing database hints running in only a matter of seconds.

Summary

This appendix explained several database concepts. We began by explaining the difference between traditional schemas, relational schemas, and star schemas. Following this, we took an in-depth look at normalization and denormalization. We explained why views are used and introduced you to Oracle's Business Views and Oracle Daily Business Intelligence. We then took an in-depth look at Noetix Corporation's NoetixViews.

APPENDIX
D

Tutorial Database

his appendix contains an entity-relationship diagram (ERD) of the tutorial database used in this book. It also contains all table names, including primary keys, foreign keys, and the majority of the data items. For small tables, we show you all of the values. For the larger tables, such as Sales and Day, we can show you only an extract because of space limitations.

Entity-Relationship Diagram for the Global Widgets Sales Database

The following is the ERD for the Global Widgets tutorial database:

NOTE

If you are familiar with data modeling, you will notice that this is almost a star schema. To convert this model into a star schema, you could move the region, district, and city data into the Customer table, move the product lines into the Product table, and create a new fiscal timetable using the Day, Month, Quarter, and Year.

The Global Widgets Tables

The following twelve tables are the tables used in the Global Widgets tutorial database:

- **GS Sales**   The Sales Fact table
- **GS Channel**   Sales Channel
- **GS Products**   Products
- **GS Prodline**   Product Lines
- **GS Customer**   Customer Master
- **GS City**   City locations for our customers
- **GS District**   Sales Districts
- **GS Region**   Sales Regions
- **GS Day**   Used for Order Date, Requested Date, Cancelled Date, and Ship Date
- **GS Month**   Fiscal months
- **GS Quarter**   Fiscal quarters
- **GS Year**   Fiscal years

GS_SALES

This is a fact table and is the main table used in the Global Widgets database. All of the aggregations, costs, and quantities are pulled from this table. The Sales Fact table has the following primary key and foreign keys:

- **ORDID**   Primary key
- **CUSTID**   Foreign key, links to the Customer table
- **PRODID**   Foreign key, links to the Product table
- **CHANNELID**   Foreign key, links to the Sales Channel table
- **ORDERDATE**   Foreign key, links to the Date table
- **REQDATE**   Foreign key, links to the Date table
- **CANCELDATE**   Foreign key, links to the Date table
- **SHIPDATE**   Foreign key, links to the Date table

The following table shows an extract from the Sales table for some orders that were received in June 2005:

ORDID	CUSTID	PRODID	CHANNELID	ORDER DATE	SHIP DATE	STATUS
12460	13	22	2	6/11/2005	6/12/2005	SHIPPED
12461	14	23	2	6/11/2005	6/12/2005	SHIPPED
12462	4	42	2	6/11/2005	6/12/2005	SHIPPED
12463	7	45	1	6/11/2005	6/12/2005	SHIPPED
12464	31	62	2	6/11/2005	6/12/2005	SHIPPED
12465	1	67	2	6/11/2005	6/12/2005	SHIPPED
12466	12	21	2	6/11/2005	6/11/2005	SHIPPED
12467	13	14	1	6/12/2005	6/17/2005	SHIPPED
12468	17	12	1	6/12/2005	6/15/2005	SHIPPED
12469	11	22	2	6/12/2005		OPEN
12470	15	63	2	6/12/2005		OPEN
12471	8	46	2	6/12/2005		OPEN
12472	33	21	2	6/13/2005		OPEN
12473	38	41	2	6/13/2005		OPEN

GS_CHANNEL

This is the table for the sales channel. It has the following primary key:

- **ChannelID**   Primary key

CHANNELID	NAME
1	EXTERNAL
2	INTERNET

GS_PRODUCTS

This is the table for the products. It has the following primary and foreign keys:

- **PRODID**   Primary key

- **LINEID**   Foreign key, links to the Product Line folder

PRODID	NAME	PRODSIZE	COST	PRICE	LINEID
11	DS-1200	MINI	3.85	5.35	4
12	MS-1200	MINI	3.95	5.55	4
13	MS-1300	MINI	4.10	6.00	4
14	DS-1300	MINI	4.02	5.95	4

21	AB-2000	SMALL	7.22	13.5	1
22	AB-2500	SMALL	5.99	12.75	2
23	AB-3000	SMALL	9.88	21.25	3
41	QB-5000	MEDIUM	8.33	17.66	1
42	QB-5500	MEDIUM	8.33	17.66	1
43	QB-6000	MEDIUM	8.33	17.66	1
44	CD-100	MEDIUM	6.21	15.25	2
45	CD-200	MEDIUM	6.21	15.25	2
46	AVR-500	MEDIUM	11.48	26.95	3
47	AVR-550	MEDIUM	11.48	26.95	3
61	QB-1000	LARGE	12.42	23.45	1
62	QB-2000	LARGE	12.42	23.45	1
63	QB-3000	LARGE	12.42	23.45	1
64	CD-500	LARGE	10.62	22.18	2
65	CD-550	LARGE	10.62	22.18	2
66	CD-625	LARGE	10.62	22.18	2
67	AVR-800	LARGE	15.94	34.65	3
68	AVR-900	LARGE	15.94	34.65	3

GS_PRODLINE

This is the table for the product lines. It has the following primary key:

- **LineID**   Primary key

LINEID	NAME
1	WONDER-WIDGET
2	MEGA-WIDGET
3	SUPER-WIDGET
4	MINI-WIDGET

GS_CUSTOMER

This is the table for the customers. It has the following primary and foreign keys:

- **CUSTID**   Primary key
- **CITYID**   Foreign key, links to the City table

The following extract shows the first twelve customers and their associated CITYID:

CUSTID	NAME	CITYID
1	CEBU WIDGET CO	1
2	WONDER WIDGETS	2
3	WIDGETS ON THE WEB	8
4	WIDGETS DE MEXICO	13
5	MUM'S WIDGET CO	3
6	WIDGETS BY THE BAY	2
7	CASA DE WIDGETS	9
8	THING'S	14
9	WIDGETS R US	2
10	WIDGET O THE MERSEY	3
11	HONG KONG WIDGETS	16
12	WIDGETS MARKET	2

GS_CITY

This is the table for the cities. It has the following primary and foreign keys:

- **CITYID**   Primary key
- **DISTRICTID**   Foreign key, links to the District table

The following extract shows all of the cities and their associated DISTRICTID:

CITYID	NAME	DISTRICTID	COUNTRYCODE
1	MANILLA	6	PH
2	SAN FRANCISCO	1	US
3	LIVERPOOL	3	GB
4	LISBON	4	PT
5	RIO DE JANEIRO	5	BR
6	LONDON	3	GB
7	PARIS	3	FR
8	ROME	4	IT
9	MADRID	4	ES
10	DENVER	1	US
11	PHILADELPHIA	1	US
12	QUEBEC	1	CA
13	MEXICO CITY	2	MX
14	SAO PAULO	5	BR

15	TOKYO	6	JP
16	HONG KONG	6	HK
17	SEOUL	6	KR
18	GENEVA	3	CH
19	ATLANTA	2	US
20	DALLAS	2	US
21	NEW YORK	2	US
22	LIMA	5	PE
23	WARSAW	7	PL
24	KANSAS CITY	2	US
25	BOCA RATON	2	US
26	SANTIAGO	5	CL
27	COOKEVILLE	2	US

GS_DISTRICT

This is the table for the districts. It has the following primary and foreign keys:

- **DISTRICTID**   Primary key
- **REGIONID**   Foreign key, links to the Region table

DISTRICTID	NAME	REGIONID
1	NA-NORTH	1
2	NA-SOUTH	1
3	EU-NORTH	2
4	EU-SOUTH	2
5	SA-ALL	3
6	FE-ALL	4
7	EU-EAST	2

GS_REGION

This is the table for the regions. It has the following primary key:

- **REGIONID**   Primary key

REGIONID	NAME
1	NORTH AMERICA
2	EUROPE
3	SOUTH AMERICA
4	FAR EAST

Fiscal Time

The tutorial database uses a set of tables to define the fiscal time used by the system. There is one date table, but it is joined to the Sales folder four times, once each for the Order, Requested, Cancelled, and Ship Dates. The Day table is joined to the Month table, which in turn is joined to the Quarter table, which is finally joined to the Year table. Using these relationships, we are able to build time hierarchies for each of the dates in the Sales folder.

GS DAY

This is the table for the dates. It has the following primary and foreign keys:

- **DAYID**   Primary key

- **MONTHID**   Foreign key, links to the Month table

In the following extract from the GS Day table, we show the dates used in late August and early September 2005. You will see how the fiscal month changed:

DAYID	MONTHID
8/23/2005	AUG-05
8/24/2005	AUG-05
8/25/2005	AUG-05
8/26/2005	AUG-05
8/27/2005	SEP-05
8/28/2005	SEP-05
8/29/2005	SEP-05
8/30/2005	SEP-05
8/31/2005	SEP-05
9/1/2005	SEP-05
9/2/2005	SEP-05
9/3/2005	SEP-05

GS MONTH

This is the table for the months. It has the following primary and foreign keys:

- **MONTHID**   Primary key

- **QUARTERID**   Foreign key, links to the Quarter table

In the following extract from the GS Month table, we show the months used in 2004. You will see how the fiscal quarter and month end dates change:

MONTHID	ENDDATE	SEQUENCENO	QUARTERID
JAN-04	1/30/2004	76	2004-Q2
FEB-04	2/27/2004	77	2004-Q2
MAR-04	3/26/2004	78	2004-Q2
APR-04	4/30/2004	79	2004-Q3
MAY-04	5/28/2004	80	2004-Q3
JUN-04	6/25/2004	81	2004-Q3
JUL-04	7/30/21011004	82	2004-Q4
AUG-04	8/27/2004	83	2004-Q4
SEP-04	9/24/2004	84	2004-Q4
OCT-04	10/29/2004	85	2005-Q1
NOV-04	11/26/2004	86	2005-Q1
DEC-04	12/31/2004	87	2005-Q1

GS QUARTER

This is the table for the months. It has the following primary and foreign keys:

- **QUARTERID**   Primary key
- **YEARID**   Foreign key, links to the Year table

In the following extract from the GS Quarter table, we show the quarter used in fiscal years 2003, 2004, and 2005. You will see how the fiscal year and quarter end dates change:

QUARTERID	ENDDATE	YEARID
2003-Q1	12/27/2002	FY2003
2003-Q2	3/28/2003	FY2003
2003-Q3	6/27/2003	FY2003
2003-Q4	9/26/2003	FY2003
2004-Q1	12/26/2003	FY2004
2004-Q2	3/26/2004	FY2004
2004-Q3	6/25/2004	FY2004
2004-Q4	9/24/2004	FY2004
2005-Q1	12/31/2004	FY2005
2005-Q2	3/25/2005	FY2005
2005-Q3	6/24/2005	FY2005
2005-Q4	9/30/2005	FY2005

GS YEAR

This is the table for the years. It has the following primary key:

- **YEARID** Primary key

In the following extract from the GS Year table, we show the years 2000 to 2005. You will see how the start dates change:

YEARID	ENDDATE
FY1998	9/25/1998
FY1999	9/24/1999
FY2000	9/29/2000
FY2001	9/28/2001
FY2002	9/27/2002
FY2003	9/26/2003
FY2004	9/24/2004
FY2005	9/30/2005

Entity-Relationship Diagram for the Fan Trap

The following is the ERD for the Fan Trap tutorial database.

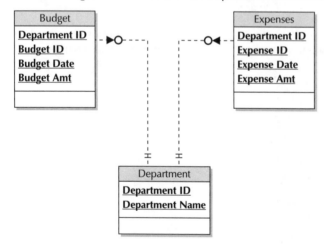

The Fan Trap Tables

The following three tables are used in the Fan Trap tutorial database:

- **FAN_Department** Department Master

- **FAN_Expenses** An example table of expense data
- **FAN_Budget** An example table of budget data

FAN_DEPARTMENT

This is the table for the departments. It has the following primary key:

- **DEPTNO** Primary key

DEPTNO	DEPTNAME
10	SALES
20	HR
30	MIS
40	MARKETING
50	TRAINING

FAN_BUDGET

This is the table for the budgets. It has the following primary and foreign keys:

- **BUDGETID** Primary key
- **DEPTNO** Foreign key, links to the Department table

BUDGETID	DEPTNO	AMOUNT	REASON	BGT_DATE
1	10	5000	EQUIPMENT	3/19/2005
2	20	2000	EQUIPMENT	3/21/2005
3	30	25500	EQUIPMENT	4/15/2005
4	40	4250	EQUIPMENT	2/24/2005
5	50	2090	EQUIPMENT	2/24/2005
6	10	40000	TRAVEL	3/20/2005
7	20	200	TRAVEL	3/21/2005
8	30	10000	TRAVEL	4/15/2005
9	40	25000	TRAVEL	2/24/2005
10	50	200	TRAVEL	2/24/2005

FAN_EXPENSES

This is the table for the expenses. It has the following primary and foreign keys:

- **EXPENSEID** Primary key

■   **DEPTNO**   Foreign key, links to the Department table

EXPENSEID	DEPTNO	EXPENSES	EXP_DATE
1	10	150	2/25/2005
2	10	250	4/16/2005
3	10	1000	4/28/2005
4	20	1025	4/12/2005
5	30	12000	4/28/2005
6	40	2750	4/26/2005

Summary

In this appendix, we showed you an entity-relationship diagram of the tutorial database covered in the book. We hope that, using this appendix, you will be able to fully understand our tutorial database and get a "look and feel" for the data. You can find a copy of this tutorial database available for download on the authors' website: http://learndiscoverer.com.

Index

D

E

F

GET YOUR FREE SUBSCRIPTION
TO ORACLE MAGAZINE

Oracle Magazine is essential gear for today's information technology professionals. Stay informed and increase your productivity with every issue of *Oracle Magazine*. Inside each free bimonthly issue you'll get:

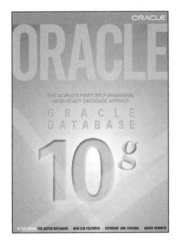

- Up-to-date information on Oracle Database, Oracle Application Server, Web development, enterprise grid computing, database technology, and business trends
- Third-party vendor news and announcements
- Technical articles on Oracle and partner products, technologies, and operating environments
- Development and administration tips
- Real-world customer stories

IF THERE ARE OTHER ORACLE USERS AT YOUR LOCATION WHO WOULD LIKE TO RECEIVE THEIR OWN SUB-SCRIPTION TO ORACLE MAGAZINE, PLEASE PHOTOCOPY THIS FORM AND PASS IT ALONG.

Three easy ways to subscribe:

① Web
Visit our Web site at otn.oracle.com/oraclemagazine. You'll find a subscription form there, plus much more!

② Fax
Complete the questionnaire on the back of this card and fax the questionnaire side only to +1.847.763.9638.

③ Mail
Complete the questionnaire on the back of this card and mail it to P.O. Box 1263, Skokie, IL 60076-8263

FREE SUBSCRIPTION

○ **Yes, please send me a FREE subscription to *Oracle Magazine*.**   ○ **NO**

To receive a free subscription to *Oracle Magazine*, you must fill out the entire card, sign it, and date it (incomplete cards cannot be processed or acknowledged). You can also fax your application to +1.847.763.9638.
Or subscribe at our Web site at otn.oracle.com/oraclemagazine

○ From time to time, Oracle Publishing allows our partners exclusive access to our e-mail addresses for special promotions and announcements. To be included in this program, please check this circle.

○ Oracle Publishing allows sharing of our mailing list with selected third parties. If you prefer your mailing address not to be included in this program, please check here. If at any time you would like to be removed from this mailing list, please contact Customer Service at +1.847.647.9630 or send an e-mail to oracle@halldata.com.

signature (required) _____ date _____

X _____

name _____   title _____

company _____   e-mail address _____

street/p.o. box _____

city/state/zip or postal code _____   telephone _____

country _____   fax _____

YOU MUST ANSWER ALL TEN QUESTIONS BELOW.

① WHAT IS THE PRIMARY BUSINESS ACTIVITY OF YOUR FIRM AT THIS LOCATION? (check one only)
- □ 01 Aerospace and Defense Manufacturing
- □ 02 Application Service Provider
- □ 03 Automotive Manufacturing
- □ 04 Chemicals, Oil and Gas
- □ 05 Communications and Media
- □ 06 Construction/Engineering
- □ 07 Consumer Sector/Consumer Packaged Goods
- □ 08 Education
- □ 09 Financial Services/Insurance
- □ 10 Government (civil)
- □ 11 Government (military)
- □ 12 Healthcare
- □ 13 High Technology Manufacturing, OEM
- □ 14 Integrated Software Vendor
- □ 15 Life Sciences (Biotech, Pharmaceuticals)
- □ 16 Mining
- □ 17 Retail/Wholesale/Distribution
- □ 18 Systems Integrator, VAR/VAD
- □ 19 Telecommunications
- □ 20 Travel and Transportation
- □ 21 Utilities (electric, gas, sanitation, water)
- □ 98 Other Business and Services

② WHICH OF THE FOLLOWING BEST DESCRIBES YOUR PRIMARY JOB FUNCTION? (check one only)
Corporate Management/Staff
- □ 01 Executive Management (President, Chair, CEO, CFO, Owner, Partner, Principal)
- □ 02 Finance/Administrative Management (VP/Director/ Manager/Controller, Purchasing, Administration)
- □ 03 Sales/Marketing Management (VP/Director/Manager)
- □ 04 Computer Systems/Operations Management (CIO/VP/Director/ Manager MIS, Operations)
IS/IT Staff
- □ 05 Systems Development/ Programming Management
- □ 06 Systems Development/ Programming Staff
- □ 07 Consulting
- □ 08 DBA/Systems Administrator
- □ 09 Education/Training
- □ 10 Technical Support Director/Manager
- □ 11 Other Technical Management/Staff
- □ 98 Other

③ WHAT IS YOUR CURRENT PRIMARY OPERATING PLATFORM? (select all that apply)
- □ 01 Digital Equipment UNIX
- □ 02 Digital Equipment VAX VMS
- □ 03 HP UNIX
- □ 04 IBM AIX
- □ 05 IBM UNIX
- □ 06 Java
- □ 07 Linux
- □ 08 Macintosh
- □ 09 MS-DOS
- □ 10 MVS
- □ 11 NetWare
- □ 12 Network Computing
- □ 13 OpenVMS
- □ 14 SCO UNIX
- □ 15 Sequent DYNIX/ptx
- □ 16 Sun Solaris/SunOS
- □ 17 SVR4
- □ 18 UnixWare
- □ 19 Windows
- □ 20 Windows NT
- □ 21 Other UNIX
- □ 98 Other
- □ 99 None of the above

④ DO YOU EVALUATE, SPECIFY, RECOMMEND, OR AUTHORIZE THE PURCHASE OF ANY OF THE FOLLOWING? (check all that apply)
- □ 01 Hardware
- □ 02 Software
- □ 03 Application Development Tools
- □ 04 Database Products
- □ 05 Internet or Intranet Products
- □ 99 None of the above

⑤ IN YOUR JOB, DO YOU USE OR PLAN TO PURCHASE ANY OF THE FOLLOWING PRODUCTS? (check all that apply)
Software
- □ 01 Business Graphics
- □ 02 CAD/CAE/CAM
- □ 03 CASE
- □ 04 Communications
- □ 05 Database Management
- □ 06 File Management
- □ 07 Finance
- □ 08 Java
- □ 09 Materials Resource Planning
- □ 10 Multimedia Authoring
- □ 11 Networking
- □ 12 Office Automation
- □ 13 Order Entry/Inventory Control
- □ 14 Programming
- □ 15 Project Management
- □ 16 Scientific and Engineering
- □ 17 Spreadsheets
- □ 18 Systems Management
- □ 19 Workflow
Hardware
- □ 20 Macintosh
- □ 21 Mainframe
- □ 22 Massively Parallel Processing
- □ 23 Minicomputer
- □ 24 PC
- □ 25 Network Computer
- □ 26 Symmetric Multiprocessing
- □ 27 Workstation
Peripherals
- □ 28 Bridges/Routers/Hubs/Gateways
- □ 29 CD-ROM Drives
- □ 30 Disk Drives/Subsystems
- □ 31 Modems
- □ 32 Tape Drives/Subsystems
- □ 33 Video Boards/Multimedia
Services
- □ 34 Application Service Provider
- □ 35 Consulting
- □ 36 Education/Training
- □ 37 Maintenance
- □ 38 Online Database Services
- □ 39 Support
- □ 40 Technology-Based Training
- □ 98 Other
- □ 99 None of the above

⑥ WHAT ORACLE PRODUCTS ARE IN USE AT YOUR SITE? (check all that apply)
Oracle E-Business Suite
- □ 01 Oracle Marketing
- □ 02 Oracle Sales
- □ 03 Oracle Order Fulfillment
- □ 04 Oracle Supply Chain Management
- □ 05 Oracle Procurement
- □ 06 Oracle Manufacturing
- □ 07 Oracle Maintenance Management
- □ 08 Oracle Service
- □ 09 Oracle Contracts
- □ 10 Oracle Projects
- □ 11 Oracle Financials
- □ 12 Oracle Human Resources
- □ 13 Oracle Interaction Center
- □ 14 Oracle Communications/Utilities (modules)
- □ 15 Oracle Public Sector/University (modules)
- □ 16 Oracle Financial Services (modules)
Server/Software
- □ 17 Oracle9i
- □ 18 Oracle9i Lite
- □ 19 Oracle8i
- □ 20 Other Oracle database
- □ 21 Oracle9i Application Server
- □ 22 Oracle9i Application Server Wireless
- □ 23 Oracle Small Business Suite

Tools
- □ 24 Oracle Developer Suite
- □ 25 Oracle Discoverer
- □ 26 Oracle JDeveloper
- □ 27 Oracle Migration Workbench
- □ 28 Oracle9i/AS Portal
- □ 29 Oracle Warehouse Builder
Oracle Services
- □ 30 Oracle Outsourcing
- □ 31 Oracle Consulting
- □ 32 Oracle Education
- □ 33 Oracle Support
- □ 98 Other
- □ 99 None of the above

⑦ WHAT OTHER DATABASE PRODUCTS ARE IN USE AT YOUR SITE? (check all that apply)
- □ 01 Access
- □ 02 Baan
- □ 03 dbase
- □ 04 Gupta
- □ 05 IBM DB2
- □ 06 Informix
- □ 07 Ingres
- □ 98 Other
- □ 99 None of the above
- □ 08 Microsoft Access
- □ 09 Microsoft SQL Server
- □ 10 PeopleSoft
- □ 11 Progress
- □ 12 SAP
- □ 13 Sybase
- □ 14 VSAM

⑧ WHAT OTHER APPLICATION SERVER PRODUCTS ARE IN USE AT YOUR SITE? (check all that apply)
- □ 01 BEA
- □ 02 IBM
- □ 03 Sybase
- □ 04 Sun
- □ 05 Other

⑨ DURING THE NEXT 12 MONTHS, HOW MUCH DO YOU ANTICIPATE YOUR ORGANIZATION WILL SPEND ON COMPUTER HARDWARE, SOFTWARE, PERIPHERALS, AND SERVICES FOR YOUR LOCATION? (check only one)
- □ 01 Less than $10,000
- □ 02 $10,000 to $49,999
- □ 03 $50,000 to $99,999
- □ 04 $100,000 to $499,999
- □ 05 $500,000 to $999,999
- □ 06 $1,000,000 and over

⑩ WHAT IS YOUR COMPANY'S YEARLY SALES REVENUE? (please choose one)
- □ 01 $500, 000, 000 and above
- □ 02 $100, 000, 000 to $500, 000, 000
- □ 03 $50, 000, 000 to $100, 000, 000
- □ 04 $5, 000, 000 to $50, 000, 000
- □ 05 $1, 000, 000 to $5, 000, 000

100103